A TRANSLATOR'S HANDBOOK

ON

THE GOSPEL OF JOHN

Helps For Translators Series

Technical Helps:

Old Testament Quotations in the New Testament
Section Headings for the New Testament
Short Bible Reference System
New Testament Index
Orthography Studies
Bible Translations for Popular Use
*The Theory and Practice of Translation
Bible Index
Fauna and Flora of the Bible
Short Index to the Bible
Manuscript Preparation
Marginal Notes for the Old Testament
Marginal Notes for the New Testament
The Practice of Translating

Handbooks:

A Translator's Handbook on Ruth
A Translator's Handbook on the Book of Amos
A Translator's Handbook on the Book of Jonah
A Translator's Handbook on the Gospel of Mark
*A Translator's Handbook on the Gospel of Luke
A Translator's Handbook on the Gospel of John
A Translator's Handbook on the Acts of the Apostles
A Translator's Handbook on Paul's Letter to the Romans
A Translator's Handbook on Paul's Letter to the Galatians
A Translator's Handbook on Paul's Letter to the Ephesians
A Translator's Handbook on Paul's Letter to the Philippians
A Translator's Handbook on Paul's Letters to the Colossians and to Philemon
A Translator's Handbook on Paul's Letters to the Thessalonians
A Translator's Handbook on the First Letter from Peter
A Translator's Handbook on the Letters of John

Guides:

A Translator's Guide to Selections from the First Five Books of the Old Testament
A Translator's Guide to Selected Psalms
A Translator's Guide to the Gospel of Matthew
A Translator's Guide to the Gospel of Mark
A Translator's Guide to the Gospel of Luke

A TRANSLATOR'S HANDBOOK
on
THE GOSPEL OF JOHN

by
BARCLAY M. NEWMAN
and
EUGENE A. NIDA

UNITED BIBLE SOCIETIES
London, New York,
Stuttgart

Books in the series of Helps for Translators that are marked with an
asterisk (*) may best be ordered from

United Bible Societies
Postfach 81 03 40
7000 Stuttgart 80
West Germany

All other books in the series may best be ordered from

American Bible Society
1865 Broadway
New York, N.Y. 10023
U.S.A.

ISBN 0-8267-0137-X
ABS-1982-2,000-3,500-CM-2-08620

PREFACE

This Translator's Handbook on the Gospel of John is a continuation of the series of Handbooks in the UBS Helps for Translators. The format and emphasis is similar to that of the recent Handbooks in the series. Special attention has been given to the structure of the discourse so that the translator will be able to understand the movement and development of the sections of this Gospel and how they contribute to the message of the whole.

The TEV and the RSV translations are shown at the beginning of each section. The TEV is then reproduced again at the beginning of the discussion of each verse. When the TEV is quoted in the discussion the words are underlined, while quotation marks are used when other translations are quoted.

As is true for all the Handbooks in the series, this volume concentrates on exegetical matters that are of prime importance for translators, and it attempts to indicate possible solutions for translational and linguistic problems that may occur. The authors do not attempt to provide the kind of help other scholars and theologians may be seeking, since much of that information is available elsewhere. A number of commentaries and other sources were consulted; however, the commentaries of Raymond E. Brown and C.K. Barrett were the most useful, and dependence upon them is acknowledged throughout the Handbook. A limited Bibliography is included for the benefit of those who are interested in further study. A Glossary is provided that explains certain technical terms, and an Index gives the location by page number of some of the important words and subjects discussed in the Handbook.

Special thanks are due to Dr. Birger Olsson, University of Uppsala, for his assistance in reviewing the content of the manuscript, and to Paul C. Clarke, Gloria Horowitz, and Lorraine Pellon for their valuable help in the editing and preparation of the text for offset reproduction.

CONTENTS

ABBREVIATIONS USED IN THIS VOLUME

Bible text and versions cited

BJ	Bible de Jerusalem (French)
Brc	Barclay
Gdsp	Goodspeed
GeCL	German Common language translation
JB	Jerusalem Bible
KJV	King James Version
Mft	Moffatt
NAB	New American Bible
NEB	New English Bible
Phps	Phillips
RSV	Revised Standard Version
Seg	Segond Revisé, Nouveau Testament
Syn	Synodale Version, La Sainte Bible
TEV	Today's English Version
Zür	Zürcher Bibel

Books of the Bible

Col	Colossians	Kgs	Kings
Cor	Corinthians	Lev	Leviticus
Deut	Deuteronomy	Mal	Malachi
Eph	Ephesians	Matt	Matthew
Exo	Exodus	Num	Numbers
Ezek	Ezekiel	Phil	Philemon
Gal	Galatians	Prov	Proverbs
Gen	Genesis	Psa	Psalms
Heb	Hebrews	Rev	Revelations
Hos	Hosea	Rom	Romans
Jer	Jeremiah	Sam	Samuel
Josh	Joshua	Tim	Timothy

Other Abbreviations

A.D.	in the year of our Lord
B.C.	before Christ
ff	and the following
UBS	United Bible Societies

INTRODUCTION

It is essential for the translator to have an overview of the structure of the Gospel of John, and also of some of its literary characteristics, before he begins to translate. But even prior to these considerations the translator should be conscious of the fact that he is translating a Gospel, and not simply a biography of Jesus of Nazareth. This is not to say that the events of the life of Jesus are unimportant. They are important in the translation of the Synoptic Gospels, and no less important in the translation of the Gospel of John. However, for the writer of this Gospel there is an inseparable relation between event and interpretation, and so he combines narrative and discourse in a way that may at times seem odd to the modern reader. For John it is the Spirit that gives life, and the mere presentation of the deeds of Jesus without the significance given to them by the Spirit would be regarded as meaningless.

Throughout this commentary it is assumed that the present arrangement of the text of the Gospel (with the exception of 7.53--8.11, which presents severe textual problems) stands as the author (or final editor) intended it, and the arrangement is intentional and intelligent. None of the suggested rearrangements of the text have any manuscript support, and it is doubtful that any of the theories behind such rearrangements make any better sense of the text than that of the present order.

At least one scholar has suggested that the manner in which John presents his material is closer to a symphonic masterpiece than to a logically ordered set of propositions. That is, a theme is introduced and then followed by a second or third theme, and so on; and these themes are interwoven into various patterns. A theme may even be dropped momentarily, only to appear later in combination with other themes (for example, the theme of "light"). But throughout the Gospel the person and work of Jesus Christ bring all these diverse themes into a closely knit unity, and in this way the author achieves his purpose.

I. The Prologue (1.1-18)

The prologue is inseparably linked with the Gospel, though scholarly opinion differs regarding its precise function. Is it an overture to the Gospel, a kind of hymn of praise of Christ to introduce him to the reader, or is it to be understood as the beginning of the Gospel itself? These and other questions remain unsolved, but it is important to recognize that the themes of light, witness, the world, glory, truth, revelation, if not that of judgment, are introduced. Everything that follows in the Gospel must be understood in light of verse 14: "The Word became a human being and, full of grace and truth, lived among us. We saw his glory, the glory which he received as the Father's only Son."

II. John the Baptist and the First Disciples (1.19-51)

Here the theme of "witness" is continued, first by John the Baptist (1.19-34) and then by the first disciples (1.35-51). Jesus is declared to be the unique bearer of the Spirit (1.32-33), the Son of God (1.34,49), the Lamb of God (1.29,36), the Messiah (1.41), the one Moses and the prophets wrote about (1.45), the King of Israel (1.49), and the one through whom God's revelation to the world comes (1.51).

III. The "Book of Signs" (2.1-12.50)

Although this section may loosely be referred to as "the Book of Signs," even a superficial glance at the distribution of the signs throughout these chapters will indicate that they alone do not offer an adequate basis for division. More than signs are involved, and in general one may say that this section both continues themes introduced earlier and introduces the motif of "fulfillment."

In a real sense the first sign, the changing of water to wine (2.1-11), sets the stage for what is to follow, for through this sign Jesus reveals his glory (2.11). The final revelation of Jesus' glory can only take place through his death and resurrection, but the first sign is at least a partial and preliminary revelation of it. At the same time the changing of water to wine clearly points to Jesus as the one in whom the Jewish religion finds its consummation and fulfillment.

The next scene takes place in the Temple at Jerusalem, the heart of the Jewish religion. Jesus cleanses the temple of its sacrificial animals and promises to replace it with the true temple, the temple of his body (2.21). The theme of the replacement of the Temple is picked up again in Jesus' dialogue with the Samaritan woman (4.21), but first John introduces the conversation between Jesus and Nicodemus.

Nicodemus, a leader of the Jews, a Pharisee (3.1), and a teacher of Israel (3.10), symbolizes the best that Pharisaic Judaism has to offer. But even he cannot understand the necessity of the new birth, the birth from above (3.4), Jesus reveals further mysteries to Nicodemus: this birth from above is made possible through the Son of Man who came from heaven, who in turn is identified as the Son whom God sent into the world. This conversation suddenly breaks off with the theme of judgment (3.18-21).

Some scholars would like to remove 3.22-30 from its present position and place it elsewhere, but it is not necessary to do this, for thematically the passage suits the context well. In his conversation with Nicodemus, Jesus has spoken of the necessity of birth through water and the Spirit, and this saying is perhaps the clue to the inclusion of this passage at this particular place. John intends that his readers see a contrast: John the Baptist offers a baptism of water, indicating repentance, but this baptism is not enough; one must also be born of the Spirit, and this birth comes only through faith in the One whom God has sent (3.31-36).

In his dialogue with the Samaritan woman, Jesus affirms that he is not only the fulfillment of orthodox Judaism (represented by the water jars, the Temple, and Nicodemus), but of heretical Judaism as well (represented by the Samaritan place of worship on Mount Gerizim). Both forms of worship, the Samaritan as well as the Jewish, will be replaced by Jesus, and through him the real worshipers will worship the Father in the way made possible through God's Spirit (4.23).

In the healing of the official's son (4.43-54) and of the lame man (5.1-18), the primary focus is on Jesus as the one who gives life (5.21).

[2]

This theme is developed in 5.19-29, which speaks of the origin of the Son's authority, and in 5.30-47, which introduces once again the motif of witness. But now another aspect is in focus, which is important for the unfolding of the events which follow. Jesus has done something on the Sabbath that only God has the authority to do, thus making himself equal with God, and at the same time claiming authority over the Jewish sacred day. So, then, John has presented Jesus as the fulfillment of the Sabbath, and he now proceeds to show how Jesus is the fulfillment of still other Jewish holy days.

The feeding of the five thousand took place at Passover (6.4), a detail not mentioned in the Synoptic accounts (Matt 14.13-21; Mark 6.30-44; Luke 9.10-17). This observation is significant for the meaning of the miracle in the Johannine account. The Passover motif is also obvious in 6.51-58; it is implied in the mention of the manna (6.31), which plays an important role in the Passover liturgy, and it is perhaps alluded to in the walking on the water (6.16-21), which may be taken as a counterpart to the crossing of the Sea on the departure from Egypt. Thus Jesus is the fulfillment of the Jewish Passover. It is admitted that, in themselves, the arguments presented to support this conclusion may seem a bit fanciful, but if this section is considered in the light of what precedes and what follows, that conclusion is considerably strengthened. That Jesus is the source of life has been a constant theme of the Gospel, and in the discourse on the meaning of the miracle (6.25-65) this theme becomes the major emphasis.

Tabernacles (or "Shelters") was the most popular of all the Jewish festivals, and the events of Chapters 7 and 8 are set against the background of this annual celebration. Of importance here is the fact that in New Testament times the celebration of this festival was associated with the themes of life-giving water and of light. If, then, in the course of this festival, Jesus declares himself to be the source of life-giving water (7.37-39) and of light for the world (8.12-20), he is declaring that he is the reality of what was symbolized by the Festival of Shelters.

The truth of Jesus' words is rejected by the Jewish leaders, and this rejection leads to a heated debate regarding Jesus' origin and destiny (8.13-30), and finally to a judgment against the Jewish leaders themselves, who have no valid claim to be the descendants of Abraham (8.31-41). They are in reality the children of the Devil, who from the beginning has opposed the truth, and consequently they are blind to the revelation of the truth in Jesus (8.42-47). The healing of the man born blind serves as a further testimony to Jesus as the light of the world and as a means of proving the spiritual blindness of the Jewish leaders who have rejected the light (9.1-41).

The Festival of Dedication (10.22) celebrated the restoration and rededication of the Jewish Temple by Judas Maccabeus in 165 B.C. It is against the background of this festival that the allegory of the Good Shepherd (10.1-21) must be understood. The Jews would be willing to follow someone who would lead them in rebellion against Rome in the hope of gaining national freedom, even as the Maccabean leaders led them against the Syrians, but they are not willing to follow the Good Shepherd, who is willing to die for his sheep.

It is not surprising that the chapter on the Good Shepherd is followed immediately by the account of the raising of Lazarus from death, because it is this event that leads to the plot against Jesus and ultimately to his death (11.53). The calling forth of Lazarus from the grave is a dynamic and undeniable proof that Jesus is in truth the resurrection and the life (11.25), a theme closely related to the earlier presentations of Jesus as the water of life and the bread of life.

Chapter 12 tells of the anointing at Bethany (12.1-8) and the triumphal entry into Jerusalem (12.12-19). Both these events are closely interwoven with the events which lead to the death of Jesus (see 12.9-11 and 12.19). The climax of the chapter is the coming of the Greeks to see Jesus (12.20-26), which the reader is to understand as a fore-shadowing of the time when Jesus would be lifted up and would draw all men to himself (12.32). Jesus now knows that the hour of his death is near, and he makes one final appeal to the Jews (12.27-36a); but they still refuse to believe in him (12.36b-43), so they remain under God's judgment (12.44-50). Jesus' public ministry is now closed. He has come to his own people, and they have rejected him, but to the few who do believe he has given the promise of eternal life.

IV. The "Book of Glory" (13.1-20.31)

The structure of the "Book of Glory" is not as complex as the structure of Chapters 1-12. In the following five chapters (13-17) Jesus instructs the Eleven in the meaning of discipleship, promises them the help of the Holy Spirit, and prays for them and for future disciples. Then, by the experience of his death (Chapters 18-19) and resurrection (20.1-29), he reveals to them his true glory. John originally closed his book with a statement of his purpose in writing it (20.30-31).

V. The Epilogue (21.1-25)

This chapter was probably added to the Gospel to clear up a mis-understanding (21.20-24) and to include important material that might otherwise have been lost. A second and final conclusion is given (21.25).

[4]

Today's English Version   (1.1-5)   Revised Standard Version

THE WORD OF LIFE

1 Before the world was created, the Word already existed; he was with God, and he was the same as God. 2 From the very beginning the Word was with God. 3 Through him God made all things; not one thing in all creation was made without him. 4 The Word was the source of life,^{a} and this life brought light to mankind. 5 The light shines in the darkness, and the darkness has never put it out.

^{a}The Word was the source of life; *or* What was made had life in union with the Word.

1 In the beginning was the Word, and the Word was with God, and the Word was God. 2 He was in the beginning with God; 3 all things were made through him, and without him was not anything made that was made. 4 In him was life,^{a} and the life was the light of men. 5 The light shines in the darkness, and the darkness has not overcome it.

^{a}Or *was not anything made. That which has been made was life in him*

Although it has long been realized that John incorporated hymnic material into his prologue, the commentators are not all agreed as to what part of this prologue reflects a hymn (and consequently has poetic structure) and how much is to be understood as prose. In fact, the question of the structure of the prologue is currently debated even more rigorously than its relation to the Gospel. Moffatt (Mft), Jerusalem Bible (JB), New American Bible (NAB), and the German common language translation (GeCL) all attempt to maintain the assumed poetic structure of some of the verses, but they are not agreed as to what part is poetry and what part is prose. For example, JB places all eighteen verses in poetry, while Mft has only 1-5 and 10-11 in poetry; NAB and GeCL attempt a poetic structure for 1-5, 9-12,14, and 16. Most modern translations prefer to render the entire prologue in prose, in the manner of Today's English Version (TEV).

Even if one decides to render the entire prologue as prose, there is still the problem of where the transitions take place. All that can be said with certainty is that verses 6-8 and verse 15 are distinct segments within the prologue, since they deal with the testimony of John the Baptist to Jesus. More attention will be given to these problems in the exegetical comments to follow.

Before treating the section heading The Word of Life, it may be useful to comment briefly upon some of the problems inherent in the title The Gospel of John. It is true that this title occurs frequently in English, but a literal translation can be misleading, for it might mean either "The Good News about John" or "The Good News that belonged to John." A more satisfactory title is usually "The Good News according to John." Even this expression may be misleading in some languages, since the phrase or term "Good News" normally requires some kind of grammatical goal; that is to say, "The Good News about Jesus Christ." In a number of languages, therefore, the title of this Gospel must be given as "The Good News about Jesus Christ as John wrote it" or "What John wrote about the Good News concerning Jesus Christ." It may even be useful to have two different titles of the Gospel: one longer, so that no one will misinterpret the relation between the Good News and the writer, and a shorter title which may be convenient as a reference. The longer title may be "The Good News about Jesus Christ as John wrote it," and the shorter title "The Good News according to John" or "The Good News written by John."

The manner in which the section heading The Word of Life is translated will depend in large measure upon the way in which Word is rendered in verses 1 and 2. If the rendering suggests "message," it would be appropriate to employ such a title as "The message that causes people to live" or "A message that produces life." It would be inadequate to employ a phrase meaning merely "A message about life," for the Word is described as the "source of life" (verse 4), and hence the relation between Word and Life must involve a causative element and not merely a statement about life.

1.1   Before the world was created, the Word already
           existed; he was with God, and he was the same as God.

Before the world was created, the Word already existed represents the Greek "in (the) beginning was the Word." As the commentaries point out, John obviously intends that his readers see a parallel between the opening words of his Gospel and the opening words of Genesis. "In (the) beginning" refers to the period before creation (creation is not mentioned until verse 3), and so TEV renders this phrase before the world was created [see New English Bible (NEB) "when all things began," NEB alternative rendering "the Word was at the creation," and GeCL "In the beginning, before the world was created"]. John wants his readers to understand that at whatever point the creation began, the Word already existed.

In a number of languages it is difficult to translate literally "in the beginning," since a word such as "beginning" requires some indication of what began. Some translators attempt to use the phrase "in the beginning of the world," but this phrase may not make sense, since in some languages only events begin, and not objects, such as the world. The problem is sometimes avoided by using another type of expression, for example, "before there was anything" or "when things first came into existence." Other translators prefer to transform the passive expression "the world was created" into an active one, for example, "before God created the world." However, to do so introduces a minor complication, for later in the same passage the creation is spoken of as being performed through the Word. Note, however, that in TEV the relation of the Word to creation is clearly indicated as secondary agency. God is the one who makes all things, but he does so through the Word (verse 3). Some of these problems are overcome in certain languages by an idiomatic expression which identifies creation as "in the beginning of life" or "when there was as yet nothing." Such expressions, however, depend entirely upon the idiomatic usage in the language into which the translation is being made. Otherwise such a rendering can be misleading.

The term the Word has a rich heritage, by way of both its Greek and Jewish backgrounds. For the Greeks who held to a theistic view of the universe, it could be understood as the means by which God reveals himself to the world, while among those who were pantheistic in outlook, the Word was the principle that held the world together and at the same time endowed men with the wisdom for living. In the Greek translation of the Old Testament, the Word could be used both of the means by which God had created the world (Psa 33.6) and through which he had revealed himself to the world (Jer 1.4; Ezek 1.3; Amos 3.1). Among certain of the Greek-speaking Jews of New Testament times, there was much speculation about the "wisdom" of God, which God "made in the very beginning, at the first, before the world began" (Prov 8.22-23). In the Wisdom of Solomon (written during the first century B.C.), "wisdom" is close to becoming a personal being, standing beside God when he made the world (9.9) and making holy souls to be God's friends (7.27). In philosophical Judaism of New Testament times, the Word largely assumes the functions assigned to "wisdom" in these writings. Thus, by the time that John writes his Gospel, the Word is close to being recognized as a personal being, and it has roles relating to the manner in which God created the world and to the way in which God reveals himself to the world that he brought into being. Mft, realizing the difficulty in finding a term equivalent in meaning to the one used by John, transliterates the Greek term: "the Logos existed in the very beginning"; while Phillips (Phps) at least makes an effort to give his translation meaning: "at the beginning God expressed himself." Some translations include Word as a glossary item (GeCL), or give a footnote to help the reader (JB, NAB).

Though the Greek term logos may be rendered "word," it would be wrong to think it indicates primarily a grammatical or lexical unit in a sentence. Greek has two other terms which primarily identify individual words, whether they occur in a list (as in a dictionary) or in a sentence. The term logos, though applicable to an individual word, is more accurately understood as an expression with meaning; that is, it is "a message," "a communication," and, as indicated, a type of "revelation." A literal translation, therefore, more or less equivalent to English "word," is frequently misleading.

In some languages there are additional complications. For example, in some languages the term "word" is feminine in gender, and therefore any reference to it must also be feminine. As a result, the possible use of pronouns in reference to Jesus Christ can be confusing. Furthermore, in many languages a term such as "word" must be possessed. One cannot speak about "the word" without indicating who spoke the word, since words do not exist apart from the persons who utter them.

Because of these and other difficulties, many translators treat the term "Word" or Logos as a title, and that is precisely what it is. The very fact that it is normally capitalized in English translations marks it as a title; but in many languages the fact of its being a title must be more clearly indicated by some explicit expression, for example, "the one who was called the Word" or "the one known as the Word." In this way the reader can understand from the beginning that

"Word" is to be understood as a designation for a person. Therefore, this first sentence in John 1.1 may be rendered "Before the world was created, the one who was known as the Word existed" or "...the person called the Word existed."

In languages which employ honorific forms it is particularly appropriate to use such an indication with the title "Word." Such a form immediately marks the designation as the title of deity or of a very important personage, depending, of course, upon the usage in the language in question.

In translating John it is particularly important to avoid suggesting that "word" indicates merely "a voice" or "one who speaks" or that in the creation there was merely a great deal of talk. Such translations gained acceptance simply because in the account in Genesis 1 the text says "God spoke...and it was so," but this is obviously not what John 1.1 means.

He was with God is literally "and the Word was with God." TEV renders the Greek word "and" by a semicolon, and "the Word" (logos) by he. In Greek "the Word" is masculine, and so to use a pronoun, as TEV does, makes the clause read more naturally in English.

It may be convenient in some languages to break this first verse into two completely separate sentences, even though the relation between the sentences is very close. The first sentence would be "Before the world was created, the Word already existed," and the second, "He was with God, and he was the same as God." It is important, however, that the reference to "he" be clear in the second sentence, especially if God as creator is introduced in the first sentence.

The meaning of the preposition with (Greek pros) has occasioned some difficulty, but most commentators and translators apparently favor the meaning "to be with" or "to be in the company of." This preposition often conveys the sense of reciprocity, that is, the Word was not merely in the presence of God, but there existed a mutual and reciprocal relationship between the Word and God. This relationship must be expressed in some languages as "God and the Word were together." In other languages, however, an indication of purely spatial relation seems to be sufficient, and therefore one may say "the Word was there where God was" or "...in company with God."

He was the same as God appears in most translations as "the Word was God" [Revised Standard Version (RSV), JB, NAB]. NEB renders by "what God was, the Word was" and Mft "the Logos was divine" [Goodspeed (Gdsp) "the Word was divine"]. Zürcher Bibel (Zür) has "the Word was God," with a footnote indicating that this means the Word possessed a divine nature.

These many differences in translation are due to the Greek sentence structure. In this type of equational sentence in Greek (A = B) the subject can be distinguished from the predicate by the fact that the subject has the article before it and the predicate does not. Since "God" does not have the article preceding it, "God" is clearly the predicate and "the Word" is the subject. This means that "God" is here the equivalent of an adjective, and this fact justifies the rendering he (the Word) was the same as God. John is not saying that "the Word" was God the Father, but he is affirming that the same divine predication can be made of "the Word" as can be made of God the Father, and so "the Word" can be spoken of as God in the same sense.

Many languages have two quite different types of equational sentences. One type indicates complete identity in such a sentence as "My husband is John Smith" or "John Smith is my husband," that is, the two parts of the sentence are completely equivalent. In the second type, however, one may say "John Smith is a teacher" but cannot say "A teacher is John Smith." "A teacher" merely qualifies "John Smith" and indicates the class of persons to which he belongs. The latter is precisely the type of equational sentence which occurs in this verse. "God" completely characterizes "the Word," and all that is true of God is true of the Word. This does not mean, however, that the two elements can be inverted, and that one can translate "God was the Word" any more than one can make "Love is God" an inversion of the biblical statement "God is love." It is difficult for some people to recognize that this equational sentence in Greek belongs to the second class because in the predicate the term "God" refers to a unique object. Since this type of equational sentence may be misleading with "God" in the predicate, it is better to translate it "The Word was the same as God" or "Just what God was that is what the Word also was."

In some languages there is an additional problem in this verse and some of the following verses, namely, the problem of tense. In some languages a past tense indicates something which existed in past time but no longer exists. Thus, if one translated "he was with God and he was the same as God," the statement would presumably apply to a past situation no longer true. This possible misunderstanding is avoided in some languages by the use of the so-called perfect tense, which carries the meaning "He has been with God, and he has been the same as God" or "He was and still is with God, and he is the same as God." In still other languages a so-called "timeless tense" must be used in order to avoid wrong implications with regard to the temporal relations.

1.2   From the very beginning the Word was with God.

This verse is not a mere repetition of the one preceding. In verse 1 John said that the Word was in the beginning and that the Word was with God; here he is careful to affirm that the two existed simultaneously, that is, from the very beginning, the Word was with God.

In rendering "from the very beginning," it may be necessary in some languages to repeat the first clause of verse 1, for example, "from the time before the world was created." However, in some languages reference to the time before creation may simply be indicated by a temporal substitute, for example, "from that very time."

Since, however, the relation of the Word to God has continued into the present time, in some languages a so-called perfect tense may be required, for example, "the Word has been with God." Otherwise, as already noted, a pure past tense may suggest a state which no longer exists.

1.3a   Through him God made all things;

This statement is literally "all things through him came into being." The Greek phrase <u>through him</u> indicates that <u>the Word</u> was the agent in creation, but at the same time the context clearly implies that God is the ultimate source of creation; TEV makes this explicit. Similar expressions are found in Paul's writings and in the Letter to the Hebrews. In 1 Corinthians 8.6 Paul distinguishes between "God, the Father, who is the creator of all things" and "Jesus Christ, through whom all things were created." Again, in Colossians 1.15-16 Paul refers to "the first-born Son," by whom "God created everything in heaven and on earth." In Hebrews 1.2 the writer speaks of the Son as "the one through whom God created the universe."

The Greek text indicates clearly that the Word was the instrument or agency employed by God in the creation. Accordingly, in some languages one must distinguish clearly between the primary agent or initiator, which would be God, and the secondary agent or immediate agent, which is the Word. Such a relation may be expressed in some languages as "God caused the Word to make all things" or "God made all things; the Word did it" or "God used the Word to make all things."

<u>1.3b-4</u>   not one thing in all creation was made without him. 4 The Word was the source of life,^{a} and this life brought light to mankind.

   ^{a}The Word was the source of life; *or* What was made had life in union with the Word.

The last half of verse 3 presents a punctuation difficulty. It is possible to make a full stop at the end of verse 3 (so TEV, RSV, JB, Mft, Phps, NAB) or to make a full stop before the end of the verse, and so connect the last half with verse 4 (see TEV and RSV alternative renderings and NEB). The oldest Greek manuscripts have no punctuation here, and even if there were some punctuation, it would merely reflect the exegesis current when the punctuation was introduced into the text. The UBS Committee on the Greek text favors the second of the two alternatives for two reasons: (1) it represents the consensus of opinion of the ante-Nicene writers, orthodox and heretical alike; (2) this punctuation is more in keeping with what is believed to be the rhythmical pattern of the prologue. However, the same UBS Committee also suggests several good arguments in favor of following the punctuation represented by the majority of modern English translations: (1) John often begins a sentence with the preposition "in" (<u>en</u>), as would be the case if a full stop were placed at the end of verse 3; (2) it would be more in keeping with John's repetitive style; (3) it reflects Johannine thought (see 5.26,39; 6.53).

If one follows the TEV text, the second part of verse 3 is an emphatic negative statement, essentially equivalent in meaning to the first part of the verse. Such an emphatic combination of positive and negative expressions may be found in certain languages in such forms as "by means of the Word God created all things. There was not anything that he did not create without the Word" or "...He did not create anything without the Word."

[10]

The Word was the source of life is literally "in him (the Word) was life." The intention of this statement is not to affirm that the Word was alive, as might be suggested by a literal translation. Rather, it is to declare, as TEV makes clear, that the Word was the source of life.

JB also makes it clear that this is the meaning "(All that came to be) had life in him," as does NEB "(All that came to be) was alive with his life," and the GeCL "he gave life to all living beings." Bible de Jerusalem (BJ) adds a footnote, "If the Word, the Son of the living God (6.57), is the source of eternal life for men (3.15, etc.), it is because he has life in himself (5.26) and because he himself is life (11.25; 14.6; see 1.1, etc.)."

If, however, the second part of verse 3 is combined with the beginning of verse 4, there is a logical relation between the two clauses essentially equivalent to "God did not create anything without the Word, since the Word was the source of life." This logical relation, however, is simply implied, not specifically indicated, in the Greek text.

What is the meaning of the word life in this context? Is it a reference to natural life or to eternal life? Since life is one of the basic themes of the Gospel of John (see 20.31, where the purpose of the Gospel is stated to be "that through your faith in him you may have life"), it is probable that life here is equivalent to "eternal life." Even though "everlastingness" is one quality of eternal life, it is not the primary emphasis in John's Gospel. For John life ("eternal life") describes a quality of existence, that is, the kind of life that man has when God rules in his life. The word life (Greek zoē) is used 36 times in John's Gospel, never in the sense of "natural life" or "biological life," but always with the meaning of "real life" or "true life."

The concept of light is also characteristic of John's Gospel. According to this Gospel, Jesus is not only the life (see 11.25; 14.6), but also the light of the world (8.12; 9.5). In the Old Testament the concept of light was something desirable and pleasant, as opposed to darkness. The world of the living was a world of light, while the world of the dead was a place of darkness. During the interval between the Old and New Testaments, however, the concept of light took on a new dimension. It became equated with the power of good, which was engaged in a struggle with darkness, the power of evil. This use is reflected, not only in Jewish sources of that period, but also in the religious and philosophical thought of other religions. In such contexts light becomes symbolic for the true revelation of God, and almost an equivalent term for God himself and for the salvation that he brings to men.

This life brought light to mankind is literally "this life was the light of men," but the meaning of this genitive construction is obviously "this life was the light for men" (Mft, Zür).

If one understands life in terms of a particular quality of life, and not mere existence, there seems to be no special shift of meaning in verse 4. Otherwise, the first occurrence of life would refer to physical life, while the second occurrence would certainly indicate a quality of life which enlightens men. The really serious difficulty in translating this verse occurs in languages which do not employ a noun for life, but which use only verbs, since with such verbal expressions there must be an indication of who is living. In such instances the first part of verse 4 may be rendered "The Word was the one who caused people to really live." The second clause may then be rendered "this way of living..." or "this way that people could truly live caused people to see" or "...to perceive." Frequently it is not possible to speak of "bringing light to men," since such an expression would refer only to carrying a torch. The focus here is not upon physical light but upon spiritual enlightenment, and therefore the passage may be translated "...caused people to truly perceive" or "caused people to perceive the truth," but note the important symbolic significance of "light" in verse 5.

1.5   The light shines in the darkness, and the darkness
             has never put it out.

In Johannine thought darkness is everything that light is not. It is evil and sin and death. The present tense of the verb shines is in direct contrast to the aorist tense in verse 11 (he came). The present tense refers to an eternal quality of the light (that is, it always shines), while the aorist tense in verse 11 (see also in verse 3) refers to a specific moment in time.

Has never put it out is difficult, in regard both to the meaning of the verb itself and the tense. The original meaning is "to grasp," and it may be used either in a hostile sense ("to overcome") or in an intellectual sense ("to grasp with the mind," that is, "to understand"). TEV (has never put it out; so also Gdsp and Phps), together with RSV ("has not overcome it") and JB ("could not overpower"; see also NAB), accepts the first of these two interpretations. Few translations, in fact, follow the second.

It is difficult to tell what Mft ("but the darkness did not master it") and NEB ("and the darkness has never mastered it") intend. Either they take the first of these possibilities, or they attempt to combine the two, trying to bring together both meanings in the one phrase "to master." The Zür rendering ("the darkness did not receive it") is possibly based on the assumption that the verb (katalambanō) is equivalent to the Greek paralambanō (TEV receive) in verse 11.

Not only is the meaning of the word difficult, but the significance of the tense is also disputed. A number of translators assume that the aorist tense here signifies a timeless truth (TEV the light shines in the darkness, and the darkness has never put it out; see also NEB, Gdsp, Phps, RSV). Others see in the aorist as used here a reference to a specific event in the past (Mft "amid the darkness the light shone, but the darkness did not master it"; see also NAB, JB).

In some languages the translation of verse 5 is particularly difficult because of clear distinctions in the use of words designating light. One term or set of terms refers to particular sources of light (fires, torches, lamps, and so forth), while another term or series of terms may refer to daylight, shining, brightness, and so forth, without indicating the particular instrument or the source of the light. Moreover, in some languages all terms for light are verbs rather than nouns. Therefore, "light shines" may be equivalent to "there is shining" or "it lights." The abstract term the darkness may be rendered in some languages only as a general term for space, plus a characterization of that space as being "dark," for example, "in places where it is dark." Accordingly, the first clause of verse 5 may be rendered "There is shining in places where it is dark." The second clause is even more difficult than the first, since in some languages one cannot take such an abstract term as the darkness and make it an instrument of "putting out the light." The relation, however, may often be expressed as a kind of negation of cause and effect, for example, "Just because it is dark does not mean that the light has been put out" or "...that the light has been caused to go out." Rather than being the direct agent of some activity, darkness only identifies a condition which has not succeeded in causing the light to go out.

TEV	(1.6-9)	RSV
God sent his messenger, a man named John, 7 who came to tell people about the light, so that all should hear the message and believe. 8 He himself was not the light; he came to tell about the light. 9 This was the real light-- the light that comes into the world and shines on all mankind.		There was a man sent from God, whose name was John. 7 He came for testimony, to bear witness to the light, that all might believe through him. 8 He was not the light, but came to bear witness to the light. 9 The true light that enlightens every man was coming into the world.

These verses introduce the second part of the prologue. Whereas the earlier verses referred to that which took place before history began, in these verses the stage of history is reached.

<u>1.6</u>   God sent his messenger, a man named John,

TEV transforms the Greek passive structure (NEB "there appeared a man named John, sent from God") into an active one, God sent his messenger, a man named John. The verb rendered "appeared" (NEB, RSV "there was"; JB "came") is aorist, and the participle translated sent is perfect, and so both are in contrast with the imperfect tense (was) of verses 1, 2, 4 and the present tense of verse 5 (shines). The significance in this change of tense is that the imperfect and the present point to something which exists outside the limits of time, while the aorist and perfect suggest an event which took place in history. The Greek participle ("sent") is rendered as a finite verb plus an object (sent his messenger).

A literal rendering of verse 6, such as "There was a man sent from God, whose name was John," presents so many complications in translation that it is better to employ a rendering which clearly indicates God as the agent of the sending.

An appositional phrase, a man named John, can then be placed after the expression his messenger. If one follows the Greek text literally, a reader in any one of several languages may seriously misunderstand the relation between the clause "whose name was John" and the immediately preceding referent, namely, "God." In fact, in some languages this is precisely what people understand--that God's name was John.

Though the Greek text does not have a noun meaning messenger, the verb translated sent really means "to send as a messenger" or "to send with a message." TEV simply restructures this expression, placing the meaning of "messenger" in a noun form, rather than inadequately translating it as a verb, such as "sent."

A man named John may be rendered in some languages "a man whom people called John" or "a man who had the name John."

1.7   who came to tell people about the light, so that all
           should hear the message and believe.

In Greek, verse 7 is a sentence complete in itself (literally, "This one came for witnessing, in order that he might give witness concerning the light, in order that all might believe through him"). Many modern translations (RSV, JB, Mft, NEB) render "this one" by the third person pronoun "he." TEV renders "this one" by who, and connects the first part of this verse as a relative clause continuing the sentence begun in verse 6.

The theme of "witness" or "witnessing" is basic to John's Gospel, and carries the meaning of "speak for the benefit of/in a person's favor," as well as "reveal who a person is." John the Baptist is a witness, 1.7; the Samaritan woman is a witness, 4.39; Jesus' works are a witness, 5.36; 10.25; the Old Testament is a witness, 5.39; the crowds are a witness, 12.17; God himself is a witness, 5.37; and the Holy Spirit, as well as those whom our Lord chooses, are witnesses to him, 15.26,27.

Though the Greek usually rendered "witness" or "testify" may frequently be rendered simply "speak" or "tell," there are two important components in the Greek term which may be made explicit in some languages. In the first place, there is an element of personal relation to the events mentioned, that is, one normally testifies or witnesses to something which one has personally experienced or seen. The second component involves an element of importance or significance in the content of what is said. Since the Greek term was frequently used in connection with witnessing in court, the associations of "important truths" are often significant in particular contexts. In this context it seems that the writer is emphasizing the importance of John's message concerning Jesus, and therefore chooses a term which carries more significance than merely some expression for "talking" or "speaking about."

It may be necessary to qualify the light as being "this light which comes to mankind," to make certain that the reference is to the same light mentioned in the second part of verse 4.

So that all should hear the message and believe is a clause of purpose, and is literally "so that all should believe through him." The phrase "through him" is recognized by all commentators as a reference to John the Baptist; and since the English sentence structure can carry this force implicitly, without the actual rendering of the phrase, TEV translates it in this way, and thus avoids the possibility of an ambiguous rendering.

It is important in most languages to indicate clearly the goal of "believing," that is, one must specify what is believed. A literal rendering, such as "that all might believe through him," can therefore be misleading. The rendering in English "so that all should hear the message and believe" implies clearly that they should "believe the message," but in some languages it may be necessary to say "so that all should hear what he had to say and believe his message." On the other hand, the object of the verb may be "the light" (= Jesus), and some few translations have made this meaning explicit (GeCL, Phps, Gdsp). But whatever exegesis is followed, the translation should be made explicit and clear.

1.8   He himself was not the light; he came to tell about
           the light.

This verse expresses in a negative form the thought of the previous verse; the negative statement following the positive statement is a form of emphasis. This same technique was followed in verse 3.

He himself (so also NEB, NAB; "he" of RSV, Mft, Gdsp, JB; "that man" of Phps) is literally "that one." The second clause of this verse contains no verb, but most translations supply the verb came (Phps "was sent"). The GeCL restructures completely: "his task was only to point to the Light."

In some languages it may not make sense to say He himself was not the light, since this could be interpreted as saying "John was not a torch"--an obvious truth. Therefore, it may be necessary to render this clause "He himself was not the one who brought light to mankind."

Because of the contrast between the negative and positive statements, it may be important to emphasize this distinction by translating the second clause of verse 8 "he came just to tell about that light."

1.9   This was the real light--the light that comes into
           the world and shines on all mankind.

Scholars are divided in their opinions of the relation between this verse and the previous and following verses. Some make it the conclusion of the paragraph begun in verse 6 (TEV, NEB, NAB, Mft), while others place it at the beginning of the following paragraph (Phps, Gdsp, JB, RSV, GeCL). On the other hand, the UBS Greek New Testament makes verses 6-13 into one paragraph. Two arguments favor placing verse 9 as a continuation of the paragraph begun in verse 6, rather than as the beginning of a new paragraph. First, verses 1-5 reflect a kind of poetic structure, which is picked up again in verse 10. From the viewpoint of the sentence structure, therefore, verse 9 fits more naturally with the prose of verses 6-8. Secondly, as the commentators point out, the pronominal reference in verse 10 (Greek "he"; TEV the Word) is the Word (see NEB alternative rendering), and not "the light." It would seem, therefore, that it is better to place verse 9 with verses 6-8.

Another problem of translation in this verse grows out of the

[15]

observation that the Greek text may be punctuated in two different ways. These alternatives are represented (1) in the TEV text (the light that comes into the world and shines on all mankind) and (2) in the alternative rendering given in certain editions of TEV (the light that shines on all men who come into the world). Most modern commentators and translators accept as their first choice the rendering represented in the TEV text. Although both renderings are grammatically possible, at least two reasons favor this interpretation: (1) In the context the focus is on light, and not on mankind. (2) John elsewhere speaks of Jesus as "coming into the world" (6.14; 9.39; 11.27; 16.28), and in 12.46 Jesus says "I have come into the world as light"; but nowhere in John's Gospel are men spoken of as "coming into the world."

The adjective translated real (Mft, Gdsp, NEB, NAB) refers to that which is real or genuine, as opposed to that which does not exist or is an imitation of that which is authentic. Elsewhere in John's Gospel this adjective appears in 4.23,37; 6.32; 7.28; 8.16; 15.1; 17.3; and 19.35.

The precise connotation of the verb rendered shines on is difficult to determine. A number of translations understand it in the sense of "to enlighten" (Mft, RSV, JB, NEB). It can have this meaning (see Eph 1.18; Heb 6.4; 10.32), but generally those who interpret the present passage in this fashion presuppose a Hellenistic background for the prologue of the Gospel. Two considerations oppose this interpretation. (1) Nowhere else in John's Gospel is it implied that all men are given a divine illumination; in fact, it is often explicitly stated that men do not recognize the truth when it comes to them, and it requires a special act of God's grace for them to become his children. (2) Elsewhere in this Gospel the function of light is "to show men up for what they are," that is, to bring men under God's judgment (see especially 3.19-21; see also Paul's use of this word in 1 Cor 4.5). Most translators prefer either to remain ambiguous (TEV, Phps; and, so it seems, Gdsp "sheds light upon"), or to render with the force of "to enlighten" (NAB "gives light to"; Anchor Bible also appears to go in this direction).

A number of translational problems are associated with verse 9. In the first place, there is a shift of tense between "this was the real light" and the explanation concerning the light, that it "comes into the world" and "shines on all mankind." The first clause must often be rendered "this light is the real light," in which the subject becomes a specific identification of the "light" just mentioned in verse 8. The rendering of "real" as a qualification of "light" is difficult, since a literal translation would suggest to many readers that it was a physical light: that is, a torch or lamp. In reality, John is using "light" in a spiritual sense, and therefore it may be necessary to translate "This light was surely true." On the other hand, some languages express genuineness by a negation, for example, "There is nothing at all false in this light."

Certain complications appear when one speaks about "the light coming into the world." It might be interpreted almost exclusively in the sense of "the dawning of the morning." In the present context, the "coming" is not so much the arrival of the light in the physical world as its coming to mankind. It may be appropriate, therefore, to translate the final qualifications of light as "the light that comes to the people in the world and shines on all of them."

It is essential to understand the expression all mankind in the sense of "all people." A translation of "men" which might be interpreted as not including women should certainly be avoided.

In some languages it is not sufficient to say shines on all mankind, which would imply merely the light of a lamp or a torch shining on people. The emphasis here is that people are caused to see the light, and so in some languages one may render the final expression in verse 9 as "causes all men to see the light."

TEV	(1.10-13)	RSV

10 The Word was in the world, and though God made the world through him, yet the world did not recognize him. 11 He came to his own country, but his own people did not receive him. 12 Some, however, did receive him and believed in him; so he gave them the right to become God's children. 13 They did not become God's children by natural means, that is, by being born as the children of a human father; God himself was their Father.

10 He was in the world, and the world was made through him, yet the world knew him not. 11 He came to his own home, and his own people received him not. 12 But to all who received him, who believed in his name, he gave power to become children of God; 13 who were born, not of blood nor of the will of the flesh nor of the will of man, but of God.

This section, which tells of the coming of God's Word (= "the light"), contains the author's reflection on the historical result of Jesus' coming into the world.

<u>1.10</u>   The Word was in the world, and though God made the world through him, yet the world did not recognize him.

World is used in John's Gospel in three senses. (1) It may indicate the created order (see 11.9; 17.5,24; 21.25). (2) More generally it is often used in the sense of "the world of mankind," and as such has a neutral meaning. (3) However, especially in the second half of the Gospel, the world is equated with those people who are aligned with the power of evil in opposition to God. While it is true that the major focus of attention in verse 10 is the world of men, it is necessary in some languages to distinguish between the two different emphases in this verse. The first clause refers to the Word being in the world, that is to say, in a particular place. It is further identified as the world which was made through the Word. This meaning includes the people who are in the world, but in the last clause the world obviously refers to the people in the world who did not recognize and acknowledge Christ as the Word of God. Accordingly, in some languages the first two instances of world may refer to the physical world, but the third instance of world must be translated "people in the world."

The word translated recognize, literally "know," especially in

[17]

light of its Jewish background, implies more than mere recognition. In
the Old Testament, "to know God" is not only to recognize who he is,
but more important, to respond to him in obedience and faith. In John's
Gospel both ideas are important, but "to respond in faith" is primary.
"To recognize" may thus be rendered "to recognize him for who he was"
or "to acknowledge him." The specific manner in which people did not
recognize him is explained in verses 11 and 12, but it is important in
verse 10 to anticipate this explanation by an adequate rendering of
"recognize."

<u>1.11</u>   He came to his own country, but his own people
             did not receive him.

His own country represents the Greek "his own," a neuter phrase in
Greek. Although translators differ as to the specific way in which they
render this phrase, most commentators indicate that the reference is
specifically to his own country, perhaps to the region of Judea in
particular, which, together with Jerusalem and the Temple, is placed
in focus in John's Gospel.

His own people is literally "his own," a masculine expression in
Greek. It is best taken as a reference to the Jewish people. It is
possible, of course, to take the first expression as a reference to the
world in general, and the second as a reference to the peoples of the
world in general, but the more restricted choice is preferable. However, Gdsp ("he came to his home, and his own family did not welcome
him"), though possible, seems too narrowly restricted. Perhaps Gdsp
bases this interpretation on the fact that the neuter phrase "his own"
is used in 19.27 as a reference to the disciple's "own home."

Should He came to his own country be interpreted as "the country
which he possessed" or "the country to which he belonged"? If it is a
reference to the land of the Jewish people and to his rejection by his
own Jewish people, then "country" should be understood in the sense of
the country to which he belonged. However, it is important to avoid any
implication that it was a country to which he belonged prior to his
coming to it.

Depending upon viewpoint, it may be necessary in some languages
to say "he went to his own country." In saying "he came," one might
have to assume that the writer of this Gospel was actually in Palestine
when he wrote the book.

His own people did not receive him may be rendered "the people of
which he was a part did not welcome him." It is often necessary to
render his own people "the people of which he was a part" or "the
people to which he belonged"; otherwise readers may think that these
people were his own possession, either "his own slaves" or "those over
whom he ruled."

In some languages "to receive a person" may be expressed idiomatically as "to greet him in one's home," "to say welcome to him," "to
accept him with happiness," or even "to greet him as a kinsman."

1.12   Some, however, did receive him and believed in him;
         so he gave them the right to become God's children.

The verb translated receive in this verse is the simple form of the verb (Greek lambanō), while the verb translated receive in the previous verse has a prepositional prefix (Greek paralambanō). However, it is agreed that the words are synonyms in this passage.

The verb translated believed is a participle in Greek, and it is in apposition with the indirect object of the verb gave. However, the restructuring of TEV carries through the meaning of the Greek and is more natural for the English reader.

It is important in rendering the verb "believe" to indicate more than merely accepting the truth about some statement. John's use of the expression believed in him refers certainly to confidence and trust placed in Christ as the Word. Therefore, it is not merely "believed what he said," but "trusted in him" or "put their confidence in him" or, as expressed idiomatically in some languages, "hung onto him with the heart" or "leaned their weight upon him."

The word translated right appears elsewhere in John's Gospel (5.27; 17.2; 19.10,11). It carries the idea of "authority" or "right," not the meaning of "power." It is difficult in some languages to find an appropriate equivalent for right as the term is used here. The closest equivalent may be an expression of possibility; for example, "he made it possible for them to become God's children." It may be expressed as direct discourse in some languages, for example, "now he said, 'You can become God's children.'" In other languages, it may be best simply to use a causative expression, for example, "so he caused them to be-come God's children." In still other instances it may be important to express some delegation of right or permission. It may be expressed in some languages as a kind of "position" or "status," for example, "he gave them the place of being God's children."

In him represents "in his name," but in biblical thought "the name" of a person is often equivalent to the person himself and to what he is (for example, in John, Jesus is the Messiah, Son of God, Savior of the world). See 14.13 for a more detailed discussion.

Although in many languages it is impossible to make the distinction, it is interesting to note that in John's Gospel believers are referred to as God's children and never as "God's sons." According to the Gospel of John, Jesus is the only Son of God.

1.13   They did not become God's children by natural
         means, that is, by being born as the children
         of a human father; God himself was their Father.

TEV, together with many modern translations, radically restructures this verse, which reads: "who were not born of bloods, neither of the will of the flesh, neither of the will of a man, but of God." "Of bloods" is taken by most modern translators to mean "of human origin" (NEB "of any human stock"; JB "of human stock"; Phps "the course of nature"), in light of the ancient belief that the embryo was created from the blood of the father and the mother. In TEV this phrase appears as by natural means.

The meaning of the next two phrases is debated. The word "flesh" is taken by some to have an evil connotation (so NAB "by carnal desire"; NEB "fleshly desire"; JB "urge of the flesh"). However, in John's Gospel "flesh" is not regarded as evil in itself (see in particular verse 14), but rather as standing for man over against God, as in the Old Testament. It seems best, therefore, to interpret "flesh" in a neutral sense in this passage. Moreover, the word "man" is the word used of an adult male, and most frequently of a husband. In the ancient world, the man was looked upon as the primary agent in procreation; the woman was merely the vessel in which procreation took place. So it is best to take the phrase "through the will of a man" in a general sense, without any evil connotation attached to it.

TEV understands the entire verse to be a contrast between birth by natural means and birth by God's Spirit. Moreover, it takes the last two phrases ("through the will of the flesh" and "through the will of a man") as equivalent, the one qualifying the other. This interpretation is the basis for the rendering by being born as the children of a human father. GeCL translates the entire verse "They did not become this (that is, God's children of verse 12) by natural birth, but because God himself gave them new life."

Though it is possible to render verse 13 literally, such a rendering would almost always involve severe distortion in the meaning of the original text, carrying the implication that natural birth is in some way related to evil sexual desires. Furthermore, "who were born not of blood" has been understood in some languages to mean that the children of God had no blood in them when they were born. In still other languages, this clause would be interpreted as meaning that there was no afterbirth when the children of God were born.

The expression "of the will of the flesh" may be either misunderstood or meaningless, especially in a language in which the flesh itself (simply as the softer body tissues in contrast with the bones) cannot be spoken of as having any desires or will.

However, to translate They did not become God's children by natural means may also produce difficulties. "By natural means" is a generic expression, though it is explained by the following clause, by being born as the children of a human father. It is possible in some languages to express this passage as "They did not become God's children just by being born as human beings, that is, by being born as the children of a human father." In other languages, however, this meaning may be expressed more fully as "They did not become God's children in the same way that people become the children of their parents, that is, by being born as children of a human father."

God himself was their Father accomplishes at least two things translationally. First, in the Greek clause structure "God" is in focus, which accounts for the rendering God himself. Secondly, such an expression as "were begotten" is difficult in English; the nearest equivalent is was their Father.

Rather than saying God himself was their Father, it may be more satisfactory to translate "God himself caused them to be his children." God himself was their Father might suggest that the children of God were to be virgin born or that God himself would in some way influence their conception. The use of "caused them to be his children" will remove the possibility of misunderstanding in most cases.

[20]

TEV   (1.14-18)   RSV

14 The Word became a human being and, full of grace and truth,
lived among us. We saw his glory,
the glory which he received as the
Father's only Son.

15 John spoke about him. He
cried out, "This is the one I was
talking about when I said, 'He
comes after me, but he is greater
than I am, because he existed before I was born.'"

16 Out of the fullness of his
grace he has blessed us all, giving us one blessing after another.
17 God gave the Law through Moses,
but grace and truth came through
Jesus Christ. 18 No one has ever
seen God. The only Son, who is
the same as God and is at the
Father's side, he has made him
known.

14 And the Word became flesh
and dwelt among us, full of grace
and truth; we have beheld his glory,
glory as of the only Son from the
Father. 15 (John bore witness to
him, and cried, "This was he of
whom I said, 'He who comes after
me ranks before me, for he was before me.'") 16 And from his fulness have we all received, grace
upon grace. 17 For the law was
given through Moses; grace and
truth came through Jesus Christ.
18 No one has ever seen God; the
only Son,*b* who is in the bosom of
the Father, he has made him known.

*b*Other ancient authorities read
God

In a sense, verse 14 constitutes a climax in the introductory summary to the Gospel of John which begins at verse 1. The writer has purposely spoken of the eternal Christ simply as the Word, referring to him
by means of this title in order to emphasize the crucial fact of the incarnation, that is to say, the Word's becoming a human being.

1.14   The Word became a human being and, full of grace
              and truth, lived among us. We saw his glory, the glory
              which he received as the Father's only Son.

At this point it may be particularly important to render the Word
as constituting a title, for example, "He who was called the Word became a human being" or "...a person," or "...came to be really a person."
Most translators render the Word became a human being "the Word
became flesh." Phps, however, is close to TEV ("so the Word of God became a human being"), and commentators generally realize that the meaning of "flesh" in this context is "a human being." Gdsp tries to
capture this meaning by translating "so the Word became flesh and
blood," and JB indicates it by a note, "the 'flesh' is man considered
as a frail and mortal being." It is better to bring out the meaning in
the text of a translation than to relegate it to a footnote, because
in many languages "flesh" is understood merely as "meat," like that
sold in the marketplace.
For a discussion of the phrase grace and truth, see Appendix II,
"Translating 'In Spirit and Truth' and 'the Spirit of Truth' in the
Gospel of John," section III.
The rendering of grace and truth is made even more difficult by the

fact that these words are referred to as qualities of which the Word is full. In many languages it is simply impossible to speak of a person being "full of grace and truth." Under such circumstances, the meaning of grace must be expressed in terms of the abundance of this feature of personality. For this particular context, the term grace is probably best understood as reflecting two important features of meaning: "love" and "kindness." In fact, a very useful equivalent in some languages is "kind love" or "love which is kind." The use of such a term as "kind" helps to suggest love which actively seeks to help the object of love, and emphasizes the fact that this kind of love depends upon the personality of the individual who loves, rather than upon any merit in the object of his love.

If one translates truth in the manner in which some persons have traditionally understood this passage, it would be possible to say "one who very much reveals the truth," but this rendering does not do justice to the real meaning of truth and does not seem to fit satisfactorily the context in combination with grace. It is also possible to understand "truth" in the sense of "faithfulness." Therefore, the Word may be described as "one who showed his kind love abundantly and who could be completely trusted." This last expression is one of the most common ways in which "faithfulness" can be satisfactorily rendered.

In rendering the expression full of grace and truth, there is, as noted, a problem involved in the phrase full of. In most languages one simply cannot be full of such qualities as "grace and truth." Furthermore, if grace is rendered as "steadfast love" or "kind love" (in order to emphasize something of the undeserved character of such love), it is impossible to speak about a person being "full of this." However, one can indicate the abundance of such love by saying "he showed kind love abundantly" or "he very much loved us," or "he showed us his goodness."

In rendering the meaning of full of...truth, one can say in some languages "he showed us the complete truth about God" or "he caused us to know completely the truth about God." However, abundance may also be expressed in such a phrase as "he very much showed us the truth about God." On the other hand, rather than translating full of...truth as being merely something which Jesus revealed about God, it seems preferable to indicate that Jesus himself was this true revelation of God. Therefore, one may translate "he himself was the true (or complete) revelation of God" or "what he was shows completely what God is." This interpretation seems to be closer to the meaning and to the way in which truth is employed generally in the Gospel of John.

The word translated lived is literally "to live in a tent," and it is taken by many to indicate temporary living (Gdsp "lived for a while"; Mft "tarried"). Elsewhere this verb is used only in Revelation 7.15; 12.12; 13.6; and 21.3, and it is difficult to see in any of these passages the idea of "to live temporarily." In light of the Old Testament usage of this word and of its usage in Revelation, the idea of "living temporarily" does not seem to be in focus. In Exodus 25.8-9 the people of Israel are commanded to make a tent, so that God can live among them. Thus "a tent" was looked upon as the dwelling place of God among men, and God's presence could be spoken of as "setting up its tent." If, in the present passage, John says that the Word "set up his tent" among men, then the meaning is that in the Word God has come to dwell among men. It is likewise the focus of the verb as used in Revelation 7.15 and 21.3: in the eternal Word, who became a human being, God came to dwell among men. Verse 14 is the very heart of John's Gospel; everything else that John says must be understood in light of this verse.

The focus of "lived" is not upon "being alive" but upon "dwelling." Lived among us is rendered in some languages as "he dwelt with us" or "he lived where we lived." In some other languages it is literally "he had his house where we were" or even "his house was in our village."

Though the pronoun us in the first sentence of verse 14 refers essentially to mankind in general, it is also a specific historical reference to the incarnation and the fact that Jesus lived on earth at a particular time. Even though us is, in a sense, a reference to mankind in general, in this particular context the pronoun must be in the exclusive first person plural in languages which make a distinction between inclusive and exclusive first person plural forms. This usage makes the pronominal reference agree with the following use of we, which must apply to those who actually saw the glory of the Father's only Son.

Perhaps it should be pointed out that even though TEV begins a new sentence with We saw his glory, in Greek all of verse 14 is one sentence. Not only does TEV make two sentences of what is a single sentence in Greek, but it reorders some of the elements in the last part, in order to make the concepts fit more naturally into English discourse structure.

Throughout his Gospel, John uses five different words meaning "to see." Some commentators attempt to see in these words a varying scale of meaning, proceeding from mere physical sight to deep spiritual insight. However, the supposed differences in meaning are not maintained consistently. It is best to decide on the meaning of each verb in its particular context, rather than to insist that each verb has a fixed meaning, regardless of the context in which it appears. This means that the verb translated saw in this passage (Greek theaomai) does not necessarily have the meaning of "to look on with contemplation," a meaning it clearly has in some other contexts. In fact, in the present context the meaning seems to be simply "to see," in the widest sense of the word.

The concept of glory is likewise difficult. In the Old Testament the word glory is often used concerning the visible manifestation of the invisible God, especially as he made himself known through the mighty things that he did for his people. This Old Testament usage seems to be the clue for understanding John's use of the term in his Gospel. For John, Jesus bears the glory of God, because he has the very nature of God and performs the works of God. From this basic use of the word other meanings are derived. These meanings will be discussed as they appear in their respective contexts.

In many languages it is extremely difficult to find a satisfactory word for glory, especially in a context like the present one, which has no specific reference to a "shining" or an "appearance." A literal translation of "brightness" or "shining" (translations which have been recommended and used in some languages) gives rise to a notion of a halo or aura of light surrounding Jesus. This meaning is obviously not what is intended by the author. A more satisfactory rendering in some languages is "we saw how wonderful he is." In other instances glory combines the

[23]

components of prestige and importance, almost equivalent to "we saw how great he is."

It may be difficult to translate in some languages the glory which he received, since this quality of "being wonderful" is not something which one can "receive" as one receives some particular object. However, it may be possible to speak of "causing a person to be wonderful," and in some languages the second part of verse 14 must be translated precisely in this manner, for example, "This is how the Father caused him to be wonderful" or "...him who was his only Son to be so wonderful." It is possible to see in the last phrase, as the Father's only Son, a causal relation. Therefore, one may render the final part of verse 14 "The Father caused him to be so wonderful because he was his only Son."

Only Son is the rendering of all modern translations. There is no doubt regarding the meaning of the Greek word used here (monogenēs); it means "only" and not "only begotten." The meaning "only begotten," which appears in the Vulgate, has influenced KJV and many other early translations. This same Greek word is used elsewhere in the New Testament in Luke 7.12; 8.42; 9.38; and Hebrews 11.17.

John spoke about him. He cried out, "This is the one I was talking about when I said, 'He comes after me, but he is greater than I am, because he existed before I was born.'"

Once again (see verses 6-9) the testimony of John the Baptist interrupts the prologue. This interruption shows how important the author of the Gospel understood the testimony of John the Baptist to be, especially since cried out denotes a solemn proclamation and is used of prophetic activity (see 7.28,37 and 12.44). For the meaning of the verb spoke about, see verse 7. Spoke about is in the present tense, and cried out is in the perfect tense in Greek. In this context, these tenses have essentially the same significance, that is, they point to the present significance of John's testimony.

It may be necessary in some languages to indicate to whom John spoke or cried out, for example, "John spoke to the people about him. He cried out to them." The important components of meaning in the expression cried out are the loudness of voice and the urgency of the message, equivalent in some languages to "shout with insistence" or "shout strongly" or "shout urgently." It is important to avoid terms which may seem contradictory, for in some languages a translation of spoke and of cried out may appear to be contradictory; in the one instance one would simply say "he spoke," but in the other, "he shouted."

He comes after me (see 1.27,30) is, of course, a reference to the historical appearance of Jesus, while he existed before I was born is a reference to the eternal pre-existence of the Word (see verse 1). He comes after me must be rendered as a temporal expression and not one of position, that is to say, Jesus followed John in time. However, since Jesus' manifestation of himself was later than that of John, it may be necessary in some languages to use the future tense, for example, "he will come later." However, such a translation must not suggest any special interval of time between the ministry of John the Baptist and that of Jesus.

He is greater than I am must be interpreted as expressing greater
importance, for example, "he is more important than I am." It may be
expressed in some languages as "he is stronger than I am" (though in
such instances the term "strong" has nothing to do with physical
strength). In other languages the concept of importance may be related
to leadership in the sense of "he is more of a chief than I am."
     It is important to avoid a translation of he existed before I was
born which would suggest merely that Jesus was older than John, a meaning often conveyed by translations which render "existed" as "lived."

1.16   Out of the fullness of his grace he has blessed
             us all, giving us one blessing after another.

     Most translators and commentators agree that verses 16-18 once
again introduce the statement of the author of the Gospel and do not
continue the words of John the Baptist.
     Out of the fullness of his grace he has blessed us all represents
the Greek "because from his fullness we all received." The word fullness was a frequent term among the heretical gnostic religions of the
first century A.D. It referred to the full nature of the true deity as
opposed to that which did not possess the divine nature. Paul took this
term and applied it to God's Son (see Col 1.19; 2.9; Eph 1.23; and
4.13). However, in John's Gospel this word is used in a nontechnical
sense and refers back to the phrase grace and truth in verse 14. Among
the translations, only TEV and Mft ("for we have all been receiving
grace after grace from his fulness") appear to make this connection explicit, though a number of commentators call attention to it. In the
last part of this clause, the Greek "we all received" is restructured
by TEV to read he has blessed us all.
     It is dangerous to attempt a literal translation of the clause
"from his fullness have we all received." In one language the people
understood it to mean "we got what he stuffed himself on"! In some
languages a far better rendering would be "because he was so gracious,
he has blessed us all" or "because of his great love for us, he has been
so good to us all."
     In this context the use of the pronoun "us" is probably best inter-
preted as inclusive. Undoubtedly John wrote his Gospel to Christians to
whom he wished to explain more fully the significance of the incarnation
and ministry of Christ.
     Giving us one blessing after another is literally "grace for grace."
The phrase is ambiguous, and some translations (for example, NEB "grace
upon grace") prefer to remain ambiguous. The majority of modern commentators take this phrase in the same sense that TEV takes it, that is,
that the Christian life consists of one expression of God's grace after
another. Mft ("for we have all been receiving grace after grace from
his fulness") and Gdsp ("received blessing after blessing") follow this
interpretation, and NAB ("love following upon love") seems also to accept this viewpoint. At least two other interpretations are possible,
and these are both represented by JB, one in the text, "grace in return
for grace," and the other in a note, which points out that this phrase
may mean that the grace of God revealed in the new covenant in Christ

[25]

Jesus has now replaced God's grace as expressed in the old covenant at
Mt. Sinai. A third possible interpretation is that the grace of God in
the Christian's life is a result of and grows out of the grace of God
in Jesus Christ (see JB note, "a grace answering to the grace that is
in Christ"). This interpretation seems to be the basis for Phps ("there
is a grace in our lives because of his grace"). Of the three interpretations, the first is most widely received, but there is no absolute
argument in favor of any of them.

In some languages one cannot speak of giving us one blessing after
another, but may use "blessing" as a verb in the sense of "to show goodness to" or "to cause goodness to happen to someone." If "blessing" is
rendered as a verb, it is possible to say "God has blessed us time after
time" or "God has caused goodness to happen to us time after time." In
some languages the expression of one blessing after another is rendered
"we received good things and still more good things." In others the
rendering is quite idiomatic, for example, "he was big-hearted to us
time after time." In one language this passage has been rendered idiomatically "all of us have received what his heart was full of. This happened many times." In still another, the rendering is "we received what
he has so abundantly; he has looked upon us for good and looked upon us
for good more and more."

1.17   God gave the Law through Moses, but grace and truth
            came through Jesus Christ.

The Greek passive ("the Law was given") is rendered by an active
in TEV, with God as the explicit subject: God gave the Law. In some
languages God gave the Law through Moses must be rendered as a causative
with secondary agency, for example, "God caused Moses to give the Law."

Since this verse contains a specific reference to the Jewish Law,
TEV and most modern translations spell Law with a capital "L." In some
languages, however, it is not possible to speak of the numerous laws of
the Pentateuch as "the Law." Rather than a singular collective expression, it is necessary to use a plural, for example, "God caused Moses
to give the laws to the people."

Grace and truth must be understood in the light of the observations
made in verse 14. John is reminding his readers that God's ultimate expression of love and his absolute faithfulness to his covenant are both
seen in Jesus Christ.

Though in English it is appropriate to say grace and truth came
through Jesus Christ, this is impossible in many languages, since one
cannot speak of grace and truth "coming." One may avoid the direct reference to God as the initiating agent by saying "It is by means of Jesus
Christ that we experience grace and truth." It is also possible to make
this second clause of verse 17 parallel with the first, for example,
"God showed grace and truth through Jesus Christ" or "God showed his
love and revealed the truth about himself through Jesus Christ." This
type of rendering makes the phrase grace and truth parallel with what
has been said in verse 14. This focus upon truth as the revelation of
God fits well with the following verse.

No one has ever seen God. The only Son, who is
the same as God and is at the Father's side, he
has made him known.

The first sentence in this verse occasions no exegetical problem,
but the second sentence does present a serious textual difficulty. There
are several possible readings: (1) The strongest Greek manuscript evidence supports the reading "only God," while one of the best single
Greek manuscripts reads "the only God." The inclusion of the definite
article "the" (see 1.1) appears to have been an early attempt to im-
prove on the text. There is no way to explain how the article was later
omitted, if it was in the text originally. (2) Other Greek manuscripts
read the only Son. This reading is judged to be the easier, and, as such,
perhaps a scribal assimilation to John 3.16,18; 1 John 4.9. It is difficult to understand why this reading was changed, if it was the original reading. (3) "God's only Son" (so NEB) represents an attempt to
make a composite text from the alternative possibilities. (4) Another
possibility is "the only one." This solution, while attractive, has very
weak manuscript evidence in its support.

If one follows the recommendation of the UBS Committee on the Greek
text and accepts the first textual possibility, literally, "the only God,"
the expression can be divided into two parts: (1) "the only one"; and
(2) "one who is the same as the Father." TEV accepts this choice of text
and makes explicit "the only one" as the only Son, to avoid a misleading
reference to Jesus Christ (of the preceding verse) as the only one who
was with the Father before all time began. This reading is important,
since Jesus Christ is a historical figure, the incarnation of the eternal Son (or Word).

At the Father's side (Anchor "ever at the Father's side"; NEB, JB
"nearest to the Father's heart") is literally "in the bosom of the
Father" (Gdsp "who leans upon his Father's breast"), and is simply a
way of expressing the closest possible relationship between the Father
and the Son. The precise force of the present tense (is) is disputed.
Some assume that it has a past connotation, but it is best in English
to render the verb in the present tense.

Expressions for close association often depend upon close spatial
relations, for example, "is beside the Father," "remains near the
Father," or "is constantly with the Father." However, one may express
this association in other ways, for example, "closely associates with
the Father," "always speak together," or "there is never any difference
between them." Sometimes the relationship is expressed idiomatically,
for example, "who lives in the heart of the Father" or "whom the
Father embraces."

The verb has made him known (so most translations; NAB "has revealed him") etymologically means "to lead," but that meaning is absent
in New Testament usage. The Greek term in this context is related to
the English derivative term exegesis, and the focus of meaning here is
upon "clear revelation" or "clear explanation." It is possible to translate it in some languages "he has clearly made God known" or "he has
clearly shown to people who God is." In other instances it may be necessary to say "he has caused people to know just what God is like."

TEV   (1.19-28)   RSV

JOHN THE BAPTIST'S MESSAGE

19 The Jewish authorities in Jerusalem sent some priests and Levites to John to ask him, "Who are you?"

20 John did not refuse to answer, but spoke out openly and clearly, saying: "I am not the Messiah."

21 "Who are you, then?" they asked. "Are you Elijah?"

"No, I am not," John answered.

"Are you the Prophet?"[b] they asked.

"No," he replied.

22 "Then tell us who you are," they said. "We have to take an answer back to those who sent us. What do you say about yourself?"

23 John answered by quoting the prophet Isaiah:

"I am 'the voice of someone
　　shouting in the desert:
Make a straight path for the
　　Lord to travel!'"

24 The messengers, who had been sent by the Pharisees, 25 then[c] asked John, "If you are not the Messiah nor Elijah nor the Prophet, why do you baptize?"

26 John answered, "I baptize with water, but among you stands the one you do not know. 27 He is coming after me, but I am not good enough even to untie his sandals."

28 All this happened in Bethany on the east side of the Jordan River, where John was baptizing.

[b]THE PROPHET: *The one who was expected to appear and announce the coming of the Messiah.*

[c]The messengers, who had been sent by the Pharisees, then; *or* Those who had been sent were Pharisees; they

19 And this is the testimony of John, when the Jews sent priests and Levites from Jerusalem to ask him, "Who are you?" 20 He confessed, he did not deny, but confessed, "I am not the Christ." 21 And they asked him, "What then? Are you Elijah?" He said, "I am not." "Are you the prophet?" And he answered, "No." 22 They said to him then, "Who are you? Let us have an answer for those who sent us. What do you say about yourself?" 23 He said, "I am the voice of one crying in the wilderness, 'Make straight the way of the Lord,' as the prophet Isaiah said."

24 Now they had been sent from the Pharisees. 25 They asked him, "Then why are you baptizing, if you are neither the Christ, nor Elijah, nor the prophet?" 26 John answered them, "I baptize with water; but among you stands one whom you do not know, 27 even he who comes after me, the thong of whose sandal I am not worthy to untie." 28 This took place in Bethany beyond the Jordan, where John was baptizing.

The Gospel proper, following the prologue, begins with the testimony

of John, given on three days (verses 19-28, 29-34, 35-42). This first
section (the first day) may be divided into three parts: (1) John's
denial that he is any of the figures expected in Jewish eschatological
thought and his affirmation that he is merely the voice of one who
shouts in the desert (19-23). (2) In light of the fact that he is not
one of the expected eschatological figures, John explains why he baptizes (24-27). (3) Finally, verse 28 is a purely geographical statement,
identifying the place where John was baptizing. In this section, as
elsewhere in the Gospel, one should notice the dramatic character of
his presentation, especially his use of dialogue, as well as his own
comments scattered throughout the text.

The section heading, John the Baptist's Message, is in a sense
appropriate to more than this first section (verses 19-28). Accordingly,
some might wish to use here such a heading as "The Jewish authorities
question John the Baptist" or "John the Baptist describes his role" or
"...his work" or "...his purpose." One could even use a question, "Who
is John the Baptist?"

This introductory section, describing the ministry of John the
Baptist, contains a number of translational problems because of the
rapid give and take in the questions and answers between the Jewish
authorities and John the Baptist. To make matters more complicated,
there is the parenthetical explanation about the direct quotation coming from the prophet Isaiah (end of verse 23) and an additional explanation of who the messengers were (verse 24).

1.19   The Jewish authorities in Jerusalem sent some
              priests and Levites to John to ask him, "Who are
              you?"

For a formal translation of this verse, see RSV.

The fact that this section begins with "and" indicates that we have
here a form of Semitic Greek. In the Old Testament the "and" was a natural way of connecting one section with another. TEV indicates this
transition by beginning a new paragraph and including a section heading.

The clause "this is the testimony of John" is shifted in TEV to
verse 20 (saying), where it serves to introduce John's words. But it is
also preserved in the section heading of TEV: John the Baptist's Message.

The Jewish authorities translates "the Jews," the phrase regularly
used by John to refer to the official leaders of Judaism who opposed
Jesus and his disciples. Here, of course, they stand in opposition to
John the Baptist. See Appendix I, "The Jews in the Gospel of John," by
Robert G. Bratcher, which discusses each occurrence of the word in
the Gospel.

In many languages authorities are spoken of as "leaders" or "chiefs,"
in others they may be simply "important men," while in certain instances
the closest equivalent may be "government officials." Despite the fact
that in New Testament times ultimate authority rested with the Romans,
the Jewish authorities did have certain administrative functions and
therefore can be regarded as "officials."

The Levites were a lesser grade of priests whose primary function

[29]

was to help in the temple services, especially as musicians. According
to rabbinical sources, they sometimes served as temple police. In the
New Testament Levites are mentioned elsewhere only in Luke 10.32 and
Acts 4.36. In some languages one may speak of Levites as "helper
priests" or even "second grade priests," provided that "second grade"
does not carry a wrong connotation of inferiority.

The TEV rendering to John is supplied translationally, not on the
basis of manuscript evidence. However, some manuscripts do have "to
him" (that is, to John).

The question Who are you? must be understood in terms of the following verses. This same question is directed to Jesus in 8.25. In each
instance the force of the question is to ask John or Jesus Who are you?
in light of the Jewish eschatological expectation. In translating this
question, it is important to avoid the impression that the Jewish
authorities had no information about John the Baptist's name. What they
were interested in was his role or ministry. In many languages the
closest equivalent is "What sort of a person are you?"

1.20   John did not refuse to answer, but spoke out
             openly and clearly, saying: "I am not the Messiah."

In Greek, this verse begins with the words "and he confessed and
he did not deny and he confessed." TEV places the negative statement
first and interprets the twice-used "he confessed" as indicating emphasis. Moreover, by the introduction of the name John, the pronominal
reference "he" is made explicit: John did not refuse to answer, but
spoke out openly and clearly. In NEB this entire clause appears as "he
confessed without reserve and avowed," and in Mft as "he frankly con-
fessed--he did not deny it, he frankly confessed."

In some languages did not refuse to answer may be appropriately
translated "did not hesitate to answer" or "answered immediately." In
order to reflect as accurately as possible the emphasis in the Greek
text (indicated by the repetition of "he confessed"), one can translate
"he told them so clearly that everyone could understand" or "he said
to all there and made it clear" or "he spoke out so as not to leave
anyone in doubt." In some languages one can simply say "he didn't hide
anything; he just told them all the truth" or "he did not mumble his
words; he spoke right out."

In John's statement, I am not the Messiah, the pronoun I is emphatic. Accordingly, the force of John's answer would probably be "I
am not the Messiah, but there is one who is." The Messiah (so also NEB,
NAB) is literally "the Christ" (so most translations). "The Christ" is
the Greek translation of the Hebrew term the Messiah (literally "the
anointed one"); it refers to the future Davidic King who was expected
to free the Jews from foreign oppression. In New Testament times most
Jews believed that the Messiah would be a political-military figure,
and we find this view expressed in the New Testament itself (Luke 1.71).
To translate the Messiah as a proper name (Phps "I am not Christ") fails
to convey the fact that this term is a title (see comments at 1.41).
However, to translate as the Messiah requires a footnote or a glossary
entry for most readers. Instead of "the Messiah," GeCL has "the promised

Savior," both here and in most other places. (In Matt 2.4 it has "the promised King," but see Matt 2.2 for the reason for the shift.) Either "the promised King," "the promised Savior," or even "the promised Savior King" expresses accurately the meaning that the original readers would have received.

Most translations prefer to transliterate the term the Messiah, since they believe that a close connection exists between this statement and the prophetic utterances of the Old Testament. This usage is more satisfactory than merely borrowing a form of the Greek term "Christ," a term almost inevitably interpreted merely as a proper name. There is much to be said, however, for such a translation as "the promised Rescuer" or "the Savior whom God has promised." A footnote can be employed to indicate that in the Bible this term referred to "the Messiah" (as in Hebrew), or "the Christ" (as in the Greek text).

1.21   "Who are you, then?" they asked. "Are you Elijah?"
"No, I am not," John answered.
"Are you the Prophet?"[b] they asked.
"No," he replied.

[b]THE PROPHET: *The one who was expected to appear and announce the coming of the Messiah.*

On the basis of Malachi 4.5 (in the Hebrew text, Mal 3.23), many Jews also believed that Elijah would appear before the end of time to prepare the way for the day of the Lord. When asked, Are you Elijah? John replied emphatically, No, I am not.

In translating the sentence Are you Elijah? it is important not to suggest merely "Is your name Elijah?" In languages which require some specification as to whether a person is dead or still living, the introduction of such a marker would indicate clearly that the Jewish authorities were asking John the Baptist whether he was a kind of reincarnation of Elijah. Most languages, however, have no such convenient device, and simply to ask one person whether he is someone else may not make sense. Therefore, in some languages the rendering is "Is your work the work of Elijah?" or even "Are you the same as Elijah?"

According to Deuteronomy 18.15,18, Moses promised that God would continue to send Israel prophets like himself. But by New Testament times the Prophet was a particular figure of Jewish eschatological expectation. In 7.40-41 also, the Prophet is distinguished from the Messiah. Evidently the author of the Gospel intends to make it clear to his readers that John the Baptist did not understand himself to be any of those persons expected in Jewish religious thought.

In some languages it may not be sufficient to use a definite article such as "the" in the question Are you the Prophet? Such a use of the article would be misleading in some languages, since "the Prophet" has not been previously identified in this particular context. Accordingly, in some languages such a phrase as "that special prophet" is justified, and it may be desirable to introduce a marginal note to indicate the relation of this question to Old Testament prophecies and to the views of Jewish religious leaders in New Testament times.

1.22   "Then tell us who you are," they said. "We have to
       take an answer back to those who sent us. What do you
       say about yourself?"

Although there are no difficult exegetical problems in this verse,
there are some translational problems, particularly in the command
Then tell us who you are. As we have noted, this is not a demand for
John the Baptist's name, but rather an insistence that he explain his
role or function. It is almost equivalent to the colloquial expression
in English "Then tell us who you think you are." The focus in such a
statement is not upon the name of the individual but upon his role and
the justification for his activities.
We have to take an answer back may be rendered in some languages
"We must give an answer to" or "We must reply to."
The final question, What do you say about yourself?, indicates
clearly that the questions posed by these representatives of the Jewish
authorities were designed to find out how John viewed his ministry,
equivalent to "Who do you really claim to be?"

1.23   John answered by quoting the prophet
       Isaiah:
           "I am 'the voice of someone shouting
               in the desert:
           Make a straight path for the Lord to
               travel!'"

This verse begins literally, "he said, I (am)," which is followed
by the quotation from Isaiah, and then the statement "as Isaiah the
prophet said." Most translations render "he said" literally, but Phps
omits it altogether and depends upon the English punctuation to carry
its force. Many translations mistakenly include John the Baptist's
"I am" as part of the quotation from Isaiah. The TEV distinguishes between John's own words and the included quotation from Isaiah by setting off the second in single quotes.
The statement following the quotation ("as Isaiah the prophet
said") is probably not part of the words of John the Baptist (as in
RSV, Mft, Gdsp, JB), but rather those of the writer of this Gospel (as
in TEV, NEB, NAB, Zür, GeCL), to identify the source of the quotation
for its readers. John's hearers, of course, would immediately recognize
the source. The fourth edition of TEV places this information at the
beginning of the verse: John answered by quoting the prophet Isaiah,
and NEB does likewise (see also NAB). Placing this statement at the
beginning of the verse may indicate more clearly that the response of
John the Baptist consists of a quotation from the prophet Isaiah. One
can say "John answered by quoting what the prophet Isaiah said: I am
'the voice...'" or "John spoke the words of the prophet Isaiah when he
answered: I am 'the voice...'"
The quotation is from the Septuagint of Isaiah 40.3, where it differs slightly from the Hebrew text. Whereas the Septuagint connects
the phrase "in the desert" with "the one who shouts" (that is, "Someone
shouts in the desert, 'Prepare a way...'"), the Hebrew text connects

"in the desert" with the verb phrase "make a straight path" (that is, "Someone shouts, 'Prepare a way in the desert...'").

In some languages it is difficult to translate "I am the voice of someone shouting in the desert," for it may be impossible to speak of a person being merely a voice. But one can say "My voice is like the voice of one who shouts in the desert." In languages which have no noun for "voice" verbs must be used. An equivalent may be "When I shout, it is like one who shouts in the desert."

The literal Greek expression "the way of the Lord" is explicit in TEV: path for the Lord to travel.

1.24   The messengers, who had been sent by the Pharisees,

The messengers, who had been sent by the Pharisees is the meaning given this verse in TEV, RSV, JB, NAB, GeCL, and the Anchor Bible. Others (NEB, Gdsp, TEV margin) take this with a meaning similar to Mft: "Now some Pharisees had been sent to him." Both translations are possible on the basis of the Greek, but the translation represented by TEV has in its favor that it represents the more difficult translation in the context. The difficulty is that priests and Levites would normally not have belonged to the Pharisaic group, but would have been Sadducees. However, by the time this Gospel was written, these distinctions were no longer important, because the Pharisees were then the only representatives of Judaism. In fact, for John the Pharisees have become synonymous with the religious leaders of the Jewish people, who have the right to pass judgment. Generally they are connected with Jerusalem as here (see 3.1; 7.32,47f; 9.13,15f,40; 11.46f,57; 18.3).

The passive expression had been sent can, of course, be made active by inversion, for example, "The Pharisees were the ones who had sent the messengers." It is important, moreover, that a glossary note identify the Pharisees as a strict religious sect of Judaism. In publications containing other books of the New Testament, cross references can be given to other places where the Pharisees and their beliefs are mentioned.

1.25   then^c asked John, "If you are not the Messiah nor
              Elijah nor the Prophet, why do you baptize?"

              ^{c}The messengers, who had been sent by the Pharisees, then;
              or Those who had been sent were Pharisees; they

This verse presents no exegetical problems. However, in rendering the question why do you baptize? one should try to avoid the impression that the Messiah or Elijah or the Prophet was thought of in terms of a person who was coming to baptize.

As can be noted in discussions of the term "baptism" in other Translators Handbooks, a number of difficulties are involved in finding a completely appropriate term. The basic principle of the Bible Society is that one should not employ an expression which will specifically rule out the mode of baptism employed by any Christian constituency within the respective language area. For this reason preference is usually given to some form of transliteration of the term "baptism" or "baptize," since such a form is obviously neutral in meaning. In essence, of course, it is a "zero term," since it has a significant absence of meaning. However, in most languages the term has been borrowed by missionaries and others and is already widely used by the time a translation is made.

In some languages there are indigenous terms for baptism. For example, in Maya the term means literally "to enter the water." This form of expression was first employed by Roman Catholics and later by Presbyterians, and it is fully acceptable to Baptists as well. When all groups accept the indigenous term, there is certainly no need to revert to a borrowed form. The decision on a term for "baptism" should not be based primarily upon etymology. What counts is the meaning of a term in ordinary usage. For example, in some languages "to put water on" has become a standard term, widely used by various churches practicing different modes of baptism, and even employed by churches which do not practice baptism in any form. What is important in the meaning of a term for baptism is not the quantity of water indicated, but the fact that it serves to identify the initiation ceremony by which a person affirms his faith in Jesus Christ and becomes a part of the Christian community. It should be a term which can be combined with such phrases as "with water" and "with the Spirit."

1.26   John answered, "I baptize with water, but among
        you stands the one you do not know.

Although the phrase with water (instrument) may be rendered "in water" (location), the former meaning seems intended in light of the parallel in verse 33 (with the Holy Spirit). All modern translations have with water.

I baptize with water must be rendered in some languages "I baptize people with water." In other languages a special habitual form of the verb is required, for example, "I habitually baptize people with water" or "It is my custom to baptize people with water."

In the clause you do not know, the pronoun you is emphatic. This statement must not necessarily be taken to imply that none of the people there knew Jesus, but rather that they did not recognize him for who he was. In some languages it may be useful to translate know as "recognize," and even in a somewhat expanded form, "you do not recognize him for who he is."

1.27   He is coming after me, but I am not good enough
        even to untie his sandals."

He is coming after me (see 1.15,30) must be taken in a temporal sense. In rendering this clause it may be necessary to make a significant shift in the tense, since Jesus' ministry was to take place after this statement by John the Baptist. Therefore, one may translate "He will be coming after me." In many languages, however, just to employ a verb "to come" is not enough, for it is a matter not of movement but of coming into prominence. Therefore it may be necessary to say "He will become conspicuous after I am no longer conspicuous" or "He will come into prominence when I am no longer prominent."

It was the task of the slave to untie his master's sandals; John indicates that he is <u>not good enough</u> to perform even this humble task for the one who is <u>coming after him</u>. In most languages it is quite clear that untying another person's sandals is a menial task, and the significance of this statement of John the Baptist is readily understood. However, if this is not so in the language concerned, one can either introduce a marginal note or specify the humble character of such an act by saying "I am not even important enough to do such a humble thing as to untie his sandals for him," or "...to be his servant."

<u>1.28</u>   All this happened in Bethany on the east side
        of the Jordan River, where John was baptizing.

<u>All this</u> may need to be made more specific in some languages, for example, "this conversation" or "these questions and answers between the messengers and John" or even "the messengers and John said these things in Bethany."

The exact site of the <u>Bethany</u> mentioned in this verse is not known. It was a town east of the <u>Jordan</u> River, not to be confused with the Bethany near Jerusalem.

<u>The east side of the Jordan River</u> is literally "on the other side of the Jordan," but it is written from the viewpoint of one who is on the west side, and so the equivalent is <u>the east side</u>. On the east side of the Jordan River may be rendered in some languages "on the sun rising side of the Jordan River." In most languages "east" is most conveniently described in terms of the rising sun.

      TEV   (1.29-34)   RSV

THE LAMB OF GOD

29 The next day John saw Jesus coming to him, and said, "There is the Lamb of God, who takes away the sin of the world! 30 This is the one I was talking about when I said, 'A man is coming after me, but he is greater than I am, because he existed before I was born.' 31 I did not know who he would be, but I came baptizing with water in order to make him known to the people of Israel."

32 And John gave this testimony: "I saw the Spirit come down like a dove from heaven and stay on him. 33 I still did not know that he was the one, but God, who sent me to baptize with water, had said to me, 'You will see the Spirit come down

29 The next day he saw Jesus coming toward him, and said, "Behold, the Lamb of God, who takes away the sin of the world! 30 This is he of whom I said, 'After me comes a man who ranks before me, for he was before me.' 31 I myself did not know him; but for this I came baptizing with water, that he might be revealed to Israel." 32 And John bore witness, "I saw the Spirit descend as a dove from heaven, and it remained on him. 33 I myself did not know him; but he who sent me to baptize with water said to me, 'He on whom you see the Spirit descend and remain, this is he who baptizes with the Holy Spirit.' 34 And I have seen and have

[35]

and stay on a man; he is the one   borne witness that this is the
who baptizes with the Holy Spirit.' Son of God."
34 I have seen it," said John,
"and I tell you that he is the Son
of God."

The Lamb of God may not carry much meaning in some languages, and
therefore such a section heading as "The one who takes away the sin of
the world" may be preferable.
    Nearly all translations make this section into two paragraphs. The
first (29-31) draws attention to Jesus as the Lamb of God and the one
who existed before John was born. The second (32-34) is John's testimony to Jesus as the one on whom the Holy Spirit comes and remains.

1.29   The next day John saw Jesus coming to him, and
          said, "There is the Lamb of God, who takes away the
          sin of the world!

    There is (Mft, NEB, JB "look, there is"; Gdsp "there is") represents
a formula (Greek ide) used several times in the Gospel of John in this
same sense (1.36,47; 19.26,27). The force of this expression is to focus attention on the person referred to and to follow with some description of that person.
    Both the background and the precise meaning of the phrase the Lamb
of God are difficult. These difficulties are compounded by the fact
that scholars disagree as to whether the statement is intended to reflect the theology of John the Baptist or of John, the author of the
Gospel. If this phrase is to be taken purely in the light of the thought
of John the Baptist, then the best background seems to be the victorious
lamb of Jewish apocalyptic, who would come and destroy the evil powers
on the earth (see, for example, Rev 17.14). This picture is in harmony
with the preaching of John the Baptist, as it is reflected in the other
Gospels. Accordingly, the verb rendered takes away (so also NEB, RSV,
NAB, JB, Phps "will take away"; Mft, Gdsp "remove") must be understood
in the sense of "to do away with" (the meaning which this same verb
appears to have in 1 John 3.5).
    On the other hand, if one sees in this passage the reflection of
Johannine theology, then the reference may be to the Passover lamb. According to John's Gospel, Jesus was crucified at the same time that the
Passover lambs were being put to death in the Temple (19.14). The fact
that the soldiers did not break Jesus' legs (19.33) is understood to be
the fulfillment of Exodus 12.46, which prescribes that no bones of the
Passover lamb should be broken (19.36). Originally, the Passover lamb
was not looked upon as a sacrifice, but since the priests had taken
over the responsibility of killing the lambs, it is probable that in
New Testament times many people would look on it as a kind of sacrifice.
Although the Passover lamb was not looked upon as a sin offering in
Judaism, it is easy to see why Christians would view it this way, on
the basis of their understanding of Christ's death. If one understands
the Lamb of God on the basis of Johannine theology, rather than on the
basis of what seems to have been the thought of John the Baptist, the

meaning would be something like "the lamb that God provides to forgive the sin of the world." The decision between these two possibilities is not an easy one to make, but most commentators lean toward the second view.

In the present passage, as in most places in the Gospel, John refers to sin in the singular, and so the focus is on the sinful condition of the world, rather than on particular sinful deeds. For the singular see 1.29; [8.3]; 8.21,34 (twice),46; 9.41 (twice); 15.22,24; 16.8,9; 19.11; the plural occurs only three times, twice in the same structure in 8.24 and once in 9.34.

As already indicated, one may interpret who takes away the sin of the world as a reference to the destruction of evil powers on the earth. Therefore an appropriate rendering might be "who destroys the evil in the world." However, it seems preferable to translate this expression in accordance with Johannine theology, for example, "who causes the sin of the world to be forgiven." In some languages one can use a singular for "sin" in the sense of "sinful condition" or "sin as a principle of behavior." In other languages it is not possible, and therefore a plural must be used. Otherwise the readers might think that the function of the Lamb of God was merely to remove one single misdeed. If it is necessary to use an active relation in the verb "to forgive," one can say "the Lamb by which God forgives the sin of the world" or "the Lamb by which God shows that he forgives the sins of the people in the world," or "the Lamb who forgives sinners."

1.30   This is the one I was talking about when I
          said, 'A man is coming after me, but he is
          greater than I am, because he existed before
          I was born.'

This verse repeats essentially the contents of verse 15; as in 1.15, 27, so here the phrase after me is temporal rather than spatial.

But he is greater than I am is literally "who has become before me." All translators and commentators recognize this clause as a reference to rank rather than to precedence in time (for example, NEB "who takes rank before me"; Mft "has taken precedence of me"). He is greater than I am may be readily rendered in some languages "he is more important than I am," but it may also be rendered idiomatically "he is more of a chief than I am," "he stands first ahead of me," or "he stands high above me."

He existed before I was born (NEB "before I was born, he already was") is also a reference to precedence in time. Note the problems of translation of this clause discussed under 1.15.

1.31   I did not know who he would be, but I came
          baptizing with water in order to make him
          known to the people of Israel."

Compare John's statement here that he did not know Jesus with the Lucan infancy narrative, according to which John and Jesus were related

(Luke 1.36; 39-45). But the point that the Gospel of John makes may be that John the Baptist did not know that Jesus was "the coming one."

I did not know who he would be may cause complications in certain languages, for in this particular context the immediate pronominal reference of "he" is somewhat obscure, referring merely to "a man coming after me." In some cases one may say "I did not know just what person would be that individual who would be greater than I am."

To make him known is actually a passive construction in Greek (literally "in order that he might be made known"). "To make known" (Greek phanerooō) is a favorite Johannine expression (2.11; 3.21; 7.4; 9.3; 17.6; 21.1 [twice],14), but it occurs only once in the Synoptic Gospels (Mark 4.22). In each of these instances the reference is either to Jesus' manifestation of himself, his glory, his works, or his name.

The passive expression to make him known to the people of Israel may be made active in the form "in order to cause people of Israel to know who he is." In this context "know" must be understood in the sense of "to recognize him for what he is."

In John's Gospel Israel always has a good connotation (in contrast to "the Jews"), and is equivalent to "God's people."

1.32   And John gave this testimony: "I saw the Spirit come down like a dove from heaven and stay on him.

And John gave this testimony renders the Greek "and John testified saying that" (see 1.7). As already noted under 1.7, the term "testimony" or "testify" indicates a clear pronouncement about what one has personally experienced. It would not be sufficient in this instance to translate merely "John said," but one could use such an expression as "John related clearly" or "John described just what had happened" or "...what he had seen."

I saw is the same verb discussed in 1.14. The Greek verb is in the perfect tense, which focuses attention on the continuing effect of a past action, that is, John saw the Spirit come on Jesus at his baptism, and the Spirit stayed on him.

As TEV makes clear, the verb stay on refers to the Spirit, and not to the dove. A translation such as NEB ("I saw the Spirit coming down from heaven like a dove and resting upon him") may be taken to imply that it was the dove that was remaining on Jesus. The translator should not try to force this account of Jesus' baptism to conform with the accounts in the Synoptic Gospels, which have differences among themselves.

Like a dove can be understood either "in the form of a dove" or "in the manner of a dove," that is, fluttering down as a dove would flutter down. In this context it is better to adopt the second of these interpretations, namely, the manner in which the Holy Spirit came down, rather than the form the Holy Spirit assumed.

There are certain problems implied in the expression "stay on him." It would suggest that the Holy Spirit perched on Jesus, which, of course, is not what is meant. Therefore, it may be necessary to adopt such an expression as "remained with him" or "continued to be with him."

One of the problems involved in translating verses 32-33 is the

temporal sequence of events. First, there is the statement that John
saw the Spirit coming down like a dove from heaven and staying on Jesus.
Then there is the statement from God saying that John the Baptist would
see the Spirit come down and stay on a particular person, as a sign that
this individual would baptize with the Holy Spirit. Finally, in verse 34,
John the Baptist states that he has seen this event and therefore can
declare that such a person is the Son of God. From this rather confusing
sequence, it is difficult to determine whether God spoke to John the
Baptist concerning the sign before or after he actually saw the Spirit
descend. Therefore, it may be necessary to restructure the order of
material in verses 32-33 to read as follows: "This is the way John described what happened: I did not know who this one would be, but God,
who sent me to baptize with water, said to me, 'You will see the Holy
Spirit come down and stay on a man; he is the one who baptizes with the
Spirit.' And I did see the Spirit come down like a dove from heaven and
stay on him"; or, to translate verse 32 as the TEV has done, and begin
verse 33 as "Previously I did not know who he would be, but God..." But
for a language such as English the sequence can be made clear by the use
of a pluperfect tense: "I did not know him, but God...had said to me..."

1.33   I still did not know that he was the one, but
       God, who sent me to baptize with water, had said
       to me, 'You will see the Spirit come down and
       stay on a man; he is the one who baptizes with
       the Holy Spirit.'

I still did not know that he was the one is the same phrase used in
verse 31 (I did not know who he would be; Greek "I did not know him").
John the Baptist is represented as repeating a statement and following
it the second time with a more complete explanation. This interpretation
is altogether in keeping with the style of the Fourth Gospel.
Although in Greek the article the does not appear before Holy Spirit,
most modern translators render the phrase here by the Holy Spirit.
Anchor Bible ("a holy Spirit") is the sole exception; Mft and Gdsp render by "the holy Spirit." By the use of a lower-case "h" in "holy,"
these three translations attempt to capture the original meaning of John
the Baptist's words, apart from the influence of Christian theology.
That is, they realize that John the Baptist would not be speaking of
"the Holy Spirit" in the same sense that a Christian would understand
the term. However, it is quite probable that John's words should be
understood in light of the theology of the Fourth Gospel, and so be
translated the Holy Spirit. In light of all these considerations, the
following conclusions seem valid: (1) To translate either "a holy Spirit"
or "the holy Spirit" is problematical in view of the theology of the
fourth evangelist. (2) The translation "the Holy Spirit" says more than
the historical Baptist probably intended. (3) The neutral solution seems
to be to render the expression as "God's Spirit" (GeCL). What John is
saying is that "the coming one" will inaugurate the age of God's salvation when God's Spirit will purify mankind. This meaning comes out
clearly in the Gospels of Matthew and Luke, where "the coming one"
baptizes not only with "God's Spirit" but "with fire" (Matt 3.11; Luke

3.16). In those Gospels "the coming one" is looked upon not only as inaugurating the age of salvation but also as bringing God's judgment on those who have rejected God's authority.

In some languages serious problems are involved in translating baptizes with the Holy Spirit, because the expression for "baptize" contains within itself a reference to "water." The meaning of this passage might then be understood as "initiates with water with the Holy Spirit." When the basic term for "baptism" means essentially "to initiate into the faith," it may be better to eliminate specific reference to water in this context and simply say "initiates by means of the Holy Spirit" or "purifies by giving God's Spirit." The function of the Holy Spirit may be spoken of as causative, and the final clause of verse 33 may be translated "he is the one who causes the Holy Spirit to initiate us into faith."

1.34   I have seen it," said John, "and I tell you that
            he is the Son of God."

Both verbs in this verse (I have seen...I tell) are in the perfect tense in Greek. The force of the perfect is the same here as in verse 32, that is, it focuses attention on the continuing effect of the past action. I have seen translates a different verb from the one rendered I saw in verse 32 and we saw in verse 14, but no distinction in meaning can be made between the two verb roots (see at 1.14).

I have seen it may require some expansion to ensure that the pronominal reference of it may refer to the entire event, for example, "I have seen what happened" or "I saw this happen."

For the meaning of I tell you, see 1.7.

Said John is not actually in the Greek text; it is included in TEV in order to identify the speaker.

TEV, Gdsp, RSV, Mft, Zür, and Phps all read the Son of God, but several other translations have the equivalent of "the Chosen One of God" (NEB, Anchor Bible, JB, NAB). The manuscript evidence favors the reading the Son of God, which is in keeping with the theological terminology of the Fourth Gospel. But the very fact that "Son of God" is so frequent in John tends to make the reading suspect. It is easy to see why a scribe would change "the Chosen One of God" to read the Son of God, but it is almost impossible to see why a scribe would change the text to read the other way around. Moreover, the Son of God may have been introduced in order to harmonize the Fourth Gospel with the Synoptic accounts of baptism, which have my own dear Son. Although the UBS Committee on the Greek text favors the reading the Son of God (rating their decision as "B"), "the Chosen One of God" may be the better choice. If so, one may translate "the One whom God has chosen and sent."

It is important that the pronoun he in verse 34 be understood as referring to the person on whom the Spirit has descended, rather than to the Holy Spirit or to God. It may be necessary, therefore, to say in some languages "I tell you that this man is the Son of God" or "I tell you that this person is the Son of God."

The phrase "the Son of God" rarely offers any difficulty, but in a few instances this expression may already have a definite meaning in a receptor language. For example, in one language "sons of God" is simply a way in which the people identify themselves, while all foreigners are called "sons of the Devil." Under such circumstances it is important to use a specific expression in translating this statement of John the Baptist, for example, "the unique Son of God" or "the special Son of God."

If, instead of the Son of God, one adopts as a text "the Chosen One of God," it may be necessary to use such a phrase as "that special One whom God has chosen" or "...has specially designated."

<table>
<tr><td>TEV</td><td>(1.35-42)</td><td>RSV</td></tr>
</table>

THE FIRST DISCIPLES OF JESUS

35 The next day John was standing there again with two of his disciples, 36 when he saw Jesus walking by. "There is the Lamb of God!" he said.	35 The next day again John was standing with two of his disciples; 36 and he looked at Jesus as he walked, and said, "Behold, the Lamb of God!" 37 The two disciples heard him say this, and they followed Jesus. 38 Jesus turned, and saw them following, and said to them, "What do you seek?" And they said to him, "Rabbi" (which means Teacher), "where are you staying?" 39 He said to them, "Come and see." They came and saw where he was staying; and they stayed with him that day, for it was about the tenth hour. 40 One of the two who heard John speak, and followed him, was Andrew, Simon Peter's brother. 41 He first found his brother Simon, and said to him, "We have found the Messiah" (which means Christ). 42 He brought him to Jesus. Jesus looked at him, and said, "So you are Simon the son of John? You shall be called Cephas" (which means Peter[c]).
37 The two disciples heard him say this and went with Jesus. 38 Jesus turned, saw them following him, and asked, "What are you looking for?"	
They answered, "Where do you live, Rabbi?" (This word means "Teacher.")	
39 "Come and see," he answered. (It was then about four o'clock in the afternoon.) So they went with him and saw where he lived, and spent the rest of that day with him.	
40 One of them was Andrew, Simon Peter's brother. 41 At once he found his brother Simon and told him, "We have found the Messiah." (This word means "Christ.") 42 Then he took Simon to Jesus.	
Jesus looked at him and said, "Your name is Simon son of John, but you will be called Cephas." (This is the same as Peter and means "a rock.")	[c]From the word for *rock* in Aramaic and Greek, respectively

The section heading The First Disciples of Jesus is deceptively simple. A literal translation in some languages can mean "the most important disciples of Jesus," which is obviously not what is intended. The term "first" must be shown to relate to the calling of the disciples, or the appointing of them, rather than to their rank or status. In some languages one may translate "How some men were first to become disciples of Jesus" or "How Jesus first finds some of his disciples."

On this, the third day of John the Baptist's witness, according to John's account (see 1.29), Jesus calls his first disciples. Verses 35-39 relate how two of John the Baptist's disciples become disciples of Jesus, while verses 40-42 begin with the calling of Andrew, Simon Peter's brother, and end with Simon's name being changed to Cephas, which means "Rock."

It is immediately recognized that the account of the calling of the disciples in John's Gospel is different from that in the Synoptics; indeed, the account in Luke differs significantly from the accounts in Matthew and Mark. The translator should not attempt to harmonize these traditions but should accept them as independent witnesses, each one having its own theological significance.

1.35   The next day John was standing there again with
    two of his disciples,

Was standing there (Anchor, NAB "was there"; JB "stood there") is rendered "was standing" in most translations. The verb means simply that John was present, but one commentator sees in it a picture of John the Baptist standing and waiting for Jesus. The reader is not told where John was, but the implication is that these events take place in the same locality as the previous events, that is, in Bethany, on the east side of the Jordan River (verse 28).

Two of John the Baptist's disciples were present with him; one of these was Andrew (verse 40), but the other is not definitely known. All four Gospels agree that John the Baptist had a group of close followers, called disciples. He taught them specific prayers (Luke 11.1; compare 5.33), and they had their own rules for fasting (Mark 2.18).

Terms for disciples are normally of two types: the first based on the meaning of "learning" or "being taught"; the second based on the concept of "following," "being associated with," or "being an adherent of." It is important in such a context to be able to use exactly the same term for the disciples of John as for those of Jesus, even though the Greek term often rendered "disciples" must be translated in some portions of Acts as "believers." Though an expression based upon the concept of "learning" or "being taught" is often useful, it may suggest a kind of classroom relationship between teacher and pupil. Jesus did teach his disciples, but they were more than just his pupils. They were chosen to be with him and to be sent out to preach (Mark 3.14). For that reason translators increasingly prefer to use some term which means "follower of" or "adherent to," rather than one which would suggest "pupils" in a classroom.

1.36   when he saw Jesus walking by. "There is the Lamb
    of God!" he said.

The verb rendered saw, though different from either of the verbs previously used (1.14,34), has the same force as those other verbs.

For the phrase There is the Lamb of God! see verse 29.

[42]

1.37   The two disciples heard him say this and went
         with Jesus.

The verb went with means literally "to follow." In several New Testament passages (including some in John's Gospel), it has the meaning of
"to become one's disciple." However, at least in verses 37 and 38, this
verb seems to be used in its literal sense.

1.38   Jesus turned, saw them following him, and asked,
         "What are you looking for?"
              They answered, "Where do you live, Rabbi?"
         (This word means "Teacher.")

By the question Jesus asked, What are you looking for? John indicates
that discipleship is based upon the initiative of Jesus.
   Rabbi is used of Jesus in 1.38,49; 3.2; 4.31; 6.25; 9.2; 11.8. This
title, which literally means "my great one," that is, "my master," was
used in Judaism of those qualified to expound and apply Jewish law. In
the Gospel of John it is used as the equivalent of Greek didaskalos,
"teacher," which occurs here, as well as in 11.28; 13.13f; 20.16.
   The parenthetical expression (This word means "Teacher ") may often
be rendered simply as "The word Rabbi means Teacher." However, in some
languages a more appropriate way of introducing the meaning of a borrowed term would be "This word in our language means Teacher" or "The
word Rabbi was used to speak about a teacher."

1.39   "Come and see," he answered. (It was then about
         four o'clock in the afternoon.) So they went with him
         and saw where he lived, and spent the rest of that day
         with him.

It was then about four o'clock in the afternoon is literally "It was
about the tenth hour." John seems to follow Roman custom in reckoning
the hours from daybreak, which would be about 6:00 a.m., and so "the
tenth hour" is equivalent to 4:00 p.m. It is a reference to the time
when Jesus invited the two men to come and see where he was staying.
In the Greek this parenthetical statement appears at the end of the
verse. However, it refers to the time when Jesus invited the two men
to visit him, and therefore it is appropriate to introduce it earlier
in the verse. Otherwise it could be misunderstood to refer to the time
when the two men left Jesus after their visit.
   The rest of that day represents the Greek "that day," but in English
it is more natural to add the rest of because the time involved is after
four in the afternoon.

1.40   One of them was Andrew, Simon Peter's brother.

The way in which Simon Peter is introduced suggests that he was well
known to John's readers.

[43]

The Greek text contains an expression in verse 40 which identifies Andrew as "one of the two who had heard about Jesus from John and who had accompanied Jesus." Since the reference is clear, it is enough to say "one of them was Andrew" or perhaps "one of John's two disciples was Andrew."

Some languages do not use a term for "brother" without indicating whether the person named is a younger or an older brother. Although Greek and Hebrew do not make such a distinction, Hebrew and Semitic Greek tend to name the older brother first. However, the fact that Simon Peter's name precedes that of his brother in the synoptic accounts of their vocation (Mark 1.16 and parallels) and in the lists of the Twelve (Matt 10.2 and parallels) probably indicates his prominence rather than his greater age. In John 1.44 Andrew's name appears before that of Peter.

1.41   At once he found his brother Simon and told him, "We have found the Messiah." (This word means "Christ.")

There is a textual problem in this verse, resulting in at least three choices: (1) The TEV rendering at once (NEB "the first thing he did") translates the Greek prōton, and is preferred by most translators because of its early and diverse manuscript support. (2) An alternate possibility is that the text should read prōtos, and so be rendered "Andrew was the first to find and tell." Although this reading has the support of some Greek manuscripts, it is not accepted by any modern translators. (3) JB reads "early next morning" (Mft "in the morning"; see NEB note "some witnesses read 'in the morning he found'"). This reading assumes that the Greek text should read prōi, but this reading is not found in any Greek manuscripts and is supported by only two or three Latin manuscripts. Apparently it was introduced to avoid the ambiguities of the two other readings and to make the narrative read smoothly from verse 39. The reading in TEV is to be preferred, on the basis of both the external manuscript evidence and the fact that it is the most difficult reading.

In some languages a clear distinction is made between two different meanings of "find." One implies that the individual or thing involved is lost; the other means that one goes and locates a person or thing. Obviously the second meaning is involved in this context.

On Messiah see comments at 1.20.

Since the term Messiah is here identified as meaning Christ, it is important to retain the borrowed form. The explanation may be given in some languages that "this word has the same meaning as Christ." In reality, both "Messiah" and "Christ" are borrowed terms: one from Hebrew, the other from Greek. The meaning of "Messiah" may be given as "the Chosen One" or "the Anointed One." In order to retain the borrowed terms and, at the same time to give a clear meaning in the context, one might translate, "We have found the Promised Savior, the one we call 'the Messiah.' (In Greek 'Messiah' is 'Christ')."

1.42   Then he took Simon to Jesus.
           Jesus looked at him and said, "Your name
       is Simon son of John, but you will be called
       Cephas." (This is the same as Peter and means
       "a rock.")

Then he took Simon to Jesus (NEB "he brought Simon to Jesus") is
literally "he brought him to Jesus."

Apparently all modern translations refer to Simon as the son of
John, based on the best manuscript evidence. The reading of KJV ("the
son of Jona") is based on manuscripts which seek to harmonize this passage with the reading of Matthew 16.17.

There is a potential ambiguity in the expression "Your name is
Simon son of John." Since the only other person identified as John in
this context is John the Baptist, some readers might conclude that John
the Baptist was the father of Simon Peter. In order to make clear that
this John is another person, not yet identified in the context, it may
be necessary to translate "You are Simon, your father's name is John."

The Greek word Petros renders the Aramaic kepa, the Greek form of
which, Kephas, appears in this verse. This information can be conveyed
by translating literally and providing a footnote, as in RSV. However,
it seems preferable to follow the technique of TEV or NEB, which make
this information explicit in the text: Your name will be Cephas. (This
is the same as Peter and means "a rock.") In JB this passage is translated "you are to be called Cephas--meaning Rock."

A term chosen to translate "Rock" should have a meaning which focuses
primarily on durability and permanence. The Greek work petros is a masculine form corresponding to the feminine form, petra, normally referring to bedrock (compare Matt 16.18). Since Peter is a man, the masculine form is required, even though it imperfectly renders the original
Aramaic. Of course, in this context "rock" does not mean simply a large
stone but rather a rock outcrop, on which a house could be built (compare Matt 7.24). One must be careful in the selection of a term for
"rock," since such terms may carry special connotations. In some languages, for example, a term for "rock" can suggest "incurably stubborn"
or "difficult to deal with." Although Simon's new name is not explained
in this verse, it clearly does not have these connotations.

Some persons have thought that the use of the name "Petros" (that is,
Peter) is a reference to the character of Simon, a person as dependable
as bedrock to be used as a foundation for a house. In Matthew 16.18,
however, the reference to Peter as "a rock" is generally interpreted
as being related to Peter's declaration (Matt 16.16) that Jesus was "the
Messiah, the Son of the living God."

TEV	(1.43-51)	RSV

JESUS CALLS PHILIP AND NATHANAEL

43 The next day Jesus decided to go to Galilee. He found Philip and said to him, "Come with me!"	43 The next day Jesus decided to go to Galilee. And he found Philip and said to him, "Follow me."

(44 Philip was from Bethsaida, the town where Andrew and Peter lived.) 45 Philip found Nathanael and told him, "We have found the one whom Moses wrote about in the book of the Law and whom the prophets also wrote about. He is Jesus son of Joseph, from Nazareth."

46 "Can anything good come from Nazareth?" Nathanael asked.

"Come and see," answered Philip.

47 When Jesus saw Nathanael coming to him, he said about him, "Here is a real Israelite; there is nothing false in him!"

48 Nathanael asked him, "How do you know me?"

Jesus answered, "I saw you when you were under the fig tree before Philip called you."

49 "Teacher," answered Nathanael, "you are the Son of God! You are the King of Israel!"

50 Jesus said, "Do you believe just because I told you I saw you when you were under the fig tree? You will see much greater things than this!" 51 And he said to them, "I am telling you the truth: you will see heaven open and God's angels going up and coming down on the Son of Man."

44 Now Philip was from Bethsaida, the city of Andrew and Peter. 45 Philip found Nathanael, and said to him, "We have found him of whom Moses in the law and also the prophets wrote, Jesus of Nazareth, the son of Joseph." 46 Nathanael said to him, "Can anything good come out of Nazareth?" Philip said to him, "Come and see." 47 Jesus saw Nathanael coming to him, and said of him, "Behold, an Israelite indeed, in whom is no guile!" 48 Nathanael said to him, "How do you know me?" Jesus answered him, "Before Philip called you, when you were under the fig tree, I saw you." 49 Nathanael answered him, "Rabbi, you are the Son of God! You are the King of Israel!" 50 Jesus answered him, "Because I said to you, I saw you under the fig tree, do you believe? You shall see greater things than these." 51 And he said to him, "Truly, truly, I say to you, you will see heaven opened, and the angels of God ascending and descending upon the Son of man."

In rendering calls in the section heading Jesus Calls Philip and Nathanael, it is important to avoid any suggestion of "shouting to." A more appropriate equivalent in some languages is "Jesus invites Philip and Nathanael to follow him."

Structurally this passage (especially verses 43-50) follows very closely that of verses 35-42. In the earlier account, Jesus meets two disciples of John the Baptist and invites them to follow him. Here he meets Philip, whom he likewise invites to follow him. In the first account Andrew goes and finds Simon and tells him, We have found the Messiah. In this account Philip finds Nathanael and tells him, We have found the one whom Moses wrote about in the book of the Law and whom the prophets also wrote about. Finally, in the earlier account Jesus looked at Simon and immediately changed his name to Cephas. In this account Jesus sees Nathanael coming to him and says about him, Here is a real Israelite; there is nothing false in him!

<u>1.43</u>   The next day Jesus decided to go to Galilee.
            He found Philip and said to him, "Come with me!"

In Greek, the subject of the verb <u>decided</u> is literally "he," but
all commentators understand it to be a reference to Jesus, and a number
of translations make this information explicit.

The text does not make clear where Jesus <u>found Philip</u>. Some believe
that Jesus found Philip before he set out for Galilee, while others
maintain that he did not find him until after his arrival there, that
is, west of the Jordan River. (The earlier incidents occurred on the
east side of the river, verse 28.) There is no certainty in this matter,
but 2.1 may hint that Jesus called Philip and Nathanael before going to
Galilee.

As suggested in connection with 1.41, it is necessary to select carefully an equivalent of the verb "find." It should not be suggested that
Philip was lost and that Jesus went looking for him and found him. The
context suggests "came across Philip." Again, a rendering suggesting
that what Jesus did was merely accidental and unintentional must be
avoided. One can say "he went to where Philip was."

<u>Come with me</u> translates the same verb discussed in 1.37. The command
addressed to Philip is an invitation to become a follower of Jesus. In
some languages the equivalent is "Join with me" or "Become one of my followers."

<u>1.44</u>   (Philip was from Bethsaida, the town where Andrew
            and Peter lived.)

<u>Bethsaida</u> was actually Bethsaida Julias, built at the northeastern-
most point of the Lake of Galilee by Philip, the ruler of the territory
of Iturea and Trachonitis. Technically, the city was not in the region
of Galilee, but it is possible that the whole region around the lake
was loosely called Galilee. This region had a large Gentile population,
and it is interesting that both <u>Philip</u> and <u>Andrew</u> are Greek, rather
than Jewish, names.

Though in connection with 1.40 it was suggested that Simon Peter
may have been the older brother of Andrew because Peter is usually
named first in the listing of the disciples, note that in verse 44 the
name of Andrew occurs before that of Peter. It is possible, therefore,
that Andrew was indeed the older brother and that in this particular
verse, rather than in the other instances, we have the normal way in
which two brothers would be listed in Hebrew or Semitic Greek. Nevertheless, on the basis of the more usual pattern, we are probably justified in regarding Peter as the older of the two.

<u>1.45</u>   Philip found Nathanael and told him, "We have
            found the one whom Moses wrote about in the
            book of the Law and whom the prophets also
            wrote about. He is Jesus son of Joseph, from
            Nazareth."

<u>Nathanael</u> (mentioned only here and in 21.2) means "God gives" or

"God has given." Nathanael does not appear in any list of the Twelve, and the arguments used to identify him with either Simon the Cananean, Bartholomew, or Matthew are either fallacious or farfetched. It is better to assume that he was not one of the Twelve.

In Philip's statement, the words the one whom are in the emphatic position. In biblical times the normal Jewish way of distinguishing one man from another with the same name was to mention the name of his father along with his name: Jesus son of Joseph. Philip thus identifies Jesus in the typically Jewish manner. In 6.42 the phrase Jesus son of Joseph is used by Jews who do not believe in him, but there is nothing derogatory about the phrase itself.

The book of the Law must be rendered in some languages as "the book which contains the laws" or "the book in which the laws are written down."

It is important to indicate that the phrase from Nazareth qualifies Jesus, and not Joseph. It must be expressed in some languages "he is Jesus from the town of Nazareth, he is son of Joseph," since in such languages the town from which a person comes is normally stated before the name of his father.

1.46   "Can anything good come from Nazareth?"
           Nathanael asked.
           "Come and see," answered Philip.

It is possible that the words Can anything good come from Nazareth? was a proverb used by the people of Cana in reference to the nearby town of Nazareth (note that Nathanael was from Cana, 21.2). On the other hand, it is thought by some scholars that the real focus of attention is Galilee, rather than Nazareth in particular (see 7.41,52). In either case the words reflect the form of a proverb and are best translated with this idea in mind.

In this type of context "good" refers not to moral behavior, but to "beneficial event." It is equivalent in some languages to "Can anything helpful come out of Nazareth?" or "Can anything which is of benefit to people happen because of anyone from Nazareth?"

1.47   When Jesus saw Nathanael coming to him, he said
           about him, "Here is a real Israelite; there is nothing
           false in him!"

Here is a real Israelite (Anchor "Here is a genuine Israelite"; NAB "This man is a true Israelite") is literally "Here is truly an Israelite," but it is possible to take the adverb "truly" in this type of sentence structure as the equivalent of an adjective. Some commentators understand "truly" to have here the force of "one worthy to have the name of Israel" (JB "There is an Israelite who deserves the name"; NEB "Here is an Israelite worthy of the name"). Israelite occurs only here in the Gospel of John, and it obviously has a positive connotation, whereas the expression "the Jews" in its many occurrences throughout the Gospel is generally derogatory in connotation.

There is nothing false in him (so also NEB) appears in RSV as "in whom is no guile" (Mft "There is no guile in him"). Perhaps a reference is intended to the deceitfulness of Jacob, who was later called "Israel." This possibility is strengthened by the observation that verse 51 quotes Genesis 28.12, though the word may have the more generic meaning of "sin" or "impurity," as some commentators suggest. On the other hand, it may be that this statement is simply an amplification of the meaning of the preceding statement, Here is a real Israelite.

It is not easy to translate literally there is nothing false in him. It would imply that falsehood could in a sense lie within a person, or that something not genuine could be inside one. A more appropriate equivalent in some languages is "this man would never lie" or "this man would never deceive anyone." In some other languages a positive expression is much more appropriate, for example, "he is a person who really tells the truth sincerely."

1.48   Nathanael asked him, "How do you know me?"
        Jesus answered, "I saw you when you were under
      the fig tree before Philip called you."

How do you know me? (so most translations) is literally "From where do you know me?" However, there are parallels both in Semitic and Classical Greek to indicate that the adverb "from where" may be used in the sense of "how." How do you know me? may, of course, be interpreted merely in the sense of "How do you know who I am?" But the focus in this context seems to be more upon Jesus' knowledge about Nathanael's character, and therefore a more appropriate equivalent may be "How do you know what sort of a person I am?"

A number of suggestions have been offered as to what Jesus meant by under the fig tree, but there is no consensus among scholars as to its meaning. It is best to take the phrase merely as a way of indicating the supernatural knowledge of Jesus, and not try to find a symbolic meaning in the expression. That is, these words are best taken as a specific instance of Jesus' ability to know all things, an emphasis brought out clearly in the Gospel of John.

Two translational problems are involved in the clause when you were under the fig tree. First, the use of the definite article the suggests a tree already mentioned in the context. The fig tree, however, can be regarded as definite only in the sense that it was the one already known to Nathanael, who was sitting under it. This type of meaning is difficult to communicate in some languages, and thus there is a tendency to employ such a rendering as "under a fig tree."

Secondly, there is a problem in identifying the tree as one that produces a particular kind of fruit named "figs." The tree can be identified by a borrowed term based on the sound of the word "fig." However, unless it is identified as a particular kind of fruit tree often grown in home gardens for shade, much of the meaning may be lost. A full identification may be reflected in such a translation as "under a fruit tree producing fruit called figs," but this type of rendering is over-elaborate and sounds like a legal language. Accordingly, the tendency is to use a generic expression, for example, "under a fruit tree" or "under a tree called fig." In some languages there is an additional complication in speaking about being "under a tree," for this may imply "in the ground under a tree," in the sense of being buried. In such languages it is necessary to say "in the shade of a tree."

In some languages it may be important to alter the order of the clauses in the statement made by Jesus so that they will seem to approximate more closely the chronological order of events. Since Nathanael's being in the shade of the fig tree was presumably for a longer period of time than Jesus' actual "seeing" him, and since both these events took place before Philip called Nathanael, it may be useful to translate as follows: "While you were still under the fig tree, I saw you there; then later Philip called you."

1.49   "Teacher," answered Nathanael, "you are the
      Son of God! You are the King of Israel!"

Teacher is transliterated as "Rabbi" in most translations. "Rabbi" is, of course, the title given to the Jewish teachers of the Law (see 1.38).

In some languages it is impossible to address a person by a title which identifies his function or profession. For example, one cannot directly address a person as "Teacher." However, one can introduce this term into the structure of verse 49 by saying "Nathanael replied to Jesus as to a teacher" or "Nathanael addressed Jesus as a teacher and said."

King of Israel is definitely used as a Messianic title. In 2 Samuel 7.14 and Psalm 2.7 God addresses the Messianic king as "my son." Since both these terms are equally Messianic titles, there is no anticlimax in the present passage which places King of Israel after Son of God. The order is perfectly logical and reflects a definite temporal sequence, for it is only as Jesus is designated the Son of God that he can become the King of Israel in this Messianic sense.

Jesus is once again designated King of Israel in 12.13. In 6.15 the Jews want to make Jesus their king, but he refuses. In Chapters 18-19 Jesus is several times referred to as the king of the Jews. However, there is no indication that Jesus encouraged the use of this title. All the evidence points to the contrary.

1.50   Jesus said, "Do you believe just because I told
      you I saw you when you were under the fig tree? You
      will see much greater things than this!"

Jesus said is literally "Jesus answered and said to him." The literal form of these words is a Semitism, and most translations handle this expression as TEV does.

Jesus' words Do you believe...under the fig tree? appear as a question in most translations, though some take them to be a statement (JB "You believe that just because I said: I saw you under the fig tree ").

In some languages sentences expressing cause and effect must preserve a particular order. Normally the cause is stated first, the effect second. In such languages the order of the clauses in the sentence Do

you believe just because I told you I saw you when you were under the
fig tree? must be altered, for example, "Because I told you I saw you
when you were under the fig tree, do you believe?" or "I told you I
saw you when you were under the fig tree. Is it just because of that
that you believe?"

You will see much greater things than this must be translated with
care to avoid the impression that Nathanael was going to see great objects. The term things refers not to objects but to events, that is,
to "happenings." Therefore, greater things must be understood in terms
of "more spectacular happenings." GeCL renders "You will experience
much greater things!"

1.51   And he said to them, "I am telling you the truth:
you will see heaven open and God's angels going
up and coming down on the Son of Man."

And he said to them is literally "And he says to him." There is no
problem in taking the present tense ("he says") as the equivalent of a
past tense (he said); the present is often used with this force in a
narrative context. TEV translates "to him" as to them to indicate to
the English reader that the pronoun you (in I am telling you the truth)
is plural in Greek, a fact which otherwise may be missed by the English
reader. Some translations even omit "to him" so that the reader will
not be led to think that Jesus was speaking only to Nathanael (JB "and
then he added"; NEB "then he added"). NAB handles this clause precisely
as TEV does ("he went on to tell them").

I am telling you the truth is literally "Amen, amen, I say to you."
In traditional English translations this statement is generally rendered "Truly, truly, I say to you" (RSV, for example). Only in the Gospel
of John is the double "Amen" used, and here it occurs some twenty-five
times. The Synoptic Gospels generally have either the simple statement
"I say to you" or "Amen, I say to you." In the Gospel of John this expression seems to serve a two-fold purpose: (1) it emphasizes the words
of Jesus which follow; (2) it confirms the truth of what Jesus says.
Needless to say, this expression appears in a variety of ways in modern
translations (NEB "in truth, in very truth I tell you"; NAB "I solemnly
assure you"; JB "I tell you most solemnly").

In some languages traditional renderings of "Truly, truly, I say to
you" are misleading, since they can be interpreted as meaning merely
"I am really talking to you." Even a literal translation of I am telling
you the truth can be misleading, since it is not always evident that the
expression the truth refers to what is to follow. Therefore, in some
languages one must say "What I am going to tell you is the truth." But
this kind of expression may be awkward, and it may be better to connect
the phrase with the statement whose truth it is intended to emphasize,
for example, "you will certainly see the heaven open..." In other languages a declaration of the truth of some statement is more likely to
follow than to precede. In this case one may translate "You will see
heaven open and God's angels going up and down on the Son of Man. This
will certainly come true."

Before the words you will see heaven open some ancient manuscripts have "from now on." This is apparently a scribal error introduced from Matthew 26.64.

The words of Jesus in this verse are an obvious allusion to Genesis 28.12, the account of Jacob's dream, but in this verse <u>the Son of Man</u> takes the place of Jacob's ladder.

"Son of Man" is one of the most problematic of all New Testament phrases both to interpret and to translate. Except for its use in Acts 7.56, it is confined solely to the Gospels, where it is used only by Jesus himself as a self-designation, never by another person in reference to him, except, perhaps in Mark 2.10. In the Synoptic Gospels the title is used by our Lord in three ways: (1) as a reference to his earthly life, (2) to his suffering and death, and (3) to his exaltation and glorification. These meanings are closely related, and the first two are essentially synonymous. All three have in common the basic emphasis that "the Son of Man" is the one whom God has appointed to speak and act with divine authority. It is true that "the Son of Man" has accepted the limitations of human existence, and that he is misunderstood and rejected by men, but he is nevertheless the one who speaks and acts with God's own authority. This meaning also is the basic understanding of "the Son of Man" in John's Gospel: He has his origin in heaven (6.27,33), and he will return again to his place of glory (6.62) by way of the cross (3.14; 8.28; 12.23,34; 13.31). Accordingly, when this title is translated, some phrase should be selected that suggests at once the divine origin and authority of "the Son of Man."

For the reader of English who does not have theological training, "Son of Man" is generally either a zero term, or else it is misunderstood as a reference to Jesus' human nature. It is unfortunate that English translations have not contributed something more dynamic toward the understanding of this most important term.

It is perhaps the parallelism between the two phrases "Son of God" and "Son of Man" which has tended to preserve the form "Son of Man," even though it has relatively little significance for many readers. It is possible to insist that the focus upon Jesus' acquired humanity is indirectly an emphasis upon his divine origin, but for most readers of the Gospels this fact is hardly recognizable. Therefore, in any translation of the Scriptures which preserves a more or less literal rendering of "Son of Man," it is important to supply a note which will explain some of the historical and cultural background of this title.

The rendering of the phrase <u>Son of Man</u> into other languages poses a number of problems. First, the choice of such a phrase as "the Son of a man" causes complications, since it seems to deny the virgin birth. In order to avoid this complication, translators often use for <u>Man</u> a term which more or less designates "mankind"; but it is almost impossible to conceive of how Jesus could be called "the Son of mankind." As a result, some translators use a phrase which renders <u>Son of Man</u> "one who is (or "has become") truly man." This focus upon Jesus' humanity is not a denial of his deity, but simply an indirect emphasis on his divine origin. Because it is often difficult to see how such an expression can also suggest deity, some translators use the expression "he who has become truly man." This type of expression is particularly important in languages which have two words for "son," one designating the son of a male, and the other, the son of a female. That is to say, when one speaks of a son as the son of his father, one term is used, but when one speaks of him as the son of his mother, the other term is employed. Obviously, to translate the expression Son of Man by a term which would specify Jesus as the son of a male would be a complete denial of the virgin birth. It is therefore essential that some other type of expression be employed.

Going up and coming down on the Son of Man (an allusion to the dream of Jacob in which he sees the ladder extended between heaven and earth) can present a number of difficulties. It might seem to some readers that the Son of Man is merely some giant on which angels climb up and down. In order to show clearly that the meaning here is symbolic, some translations add the phrase "as it were." Even in the use of the terms going up and coming down, one must be careful to avoid making the Son of Man into a sort of elevator. If one chooses terms which are too specific, the whole figure becomes absurd.

TEV   (2.1-12)   RSV

THE WEDDING IN CANA

2 Two days later there was a wedding in the town of Cana in Galilee. Jesus' mother was there, 2 and Jesus and his disciples had also been invited to the wedding. 3 When the wine had given out, Jesus' mother said to him, "They are out of wine."

4 "You must not tell me what to do," Jesus replied. "My time has not yet come."

5 Jesus' mother then told the servants, "Do whatever he tells you."

6 The Jews have rules about ritual washing, and for this purpose six stone water jars were there, each one large enough to hold between twenty and thirty gallons. 7 Jesus said to the servants, "Fill these jars with water." They filled them to the brim, 8 and then he told them, "Now draw some water out and take it to the man in charge of the feast." They took him the water, 9 which now had turned into wine, and he tasted it. He did not know where this wine had come from (but, of course, the servants who had drawn out the water knew); so he called the bridegroom 10 and said to him, "Everyone else serves the best wine first, and after the guests have drunk a lot, he serves the ordinary wine. But you have kept the best wine until now!"

11 Jesus performed this first miracle in Cana in Galilee; there he revealed his glory, and his disciples believed in him.

12 After this, Jesus and his mother, brothers, and disciples went to Capernaum and stayed there a few days.

2 On the third day there was a marriage at Cana in Galilee, and the mother of Jesus was there; 2 Jesus also was invited to the marriage, with his disciples. 3 When the wine gave out, the mother of Jesus said to him, "They have no wine." 4 And Jesus said to her, "O woman, what have you to do with me? My hour has not yet come." 5 His mother said to the servants, "Do whatever he tells you." 6 Now six stone jars were standing there, for the Jewish rites of purification, each holding twenty or thirty gallons. 7 Jesus said to them, "Fill the jars with water." And they filled them up to the brim. 8 He said to them, "Now draw some out, and take it to the steward of the feast." So they took it. 9 When the steward of the feast tasted the water now become wine, and did not know where it came from (though the servants who had drawn the water knew), the steward of the feast called the bridegroom 10 and said to him, "Every man serves the good wine first; and when men have drunk freely, then the poor wine; but you have kept the good wine until now." 11 This, the first of his signs, Jesus did at Cana in Galilee, and manifested his glory; and his disciples believed in him.

12 After this he went down to Capernaum, with his mother and his brothers and his disciples; and there they stayed for a few days.

Chapters 2-12 relate a series of seven "signs" (TEV <u>miracles</u>) that Jesus performed during the course of his public ministry--a ministry brought to a close in Chapter 12. This section of John's Gospel is therefore often referred to as "the book of signs."

The account of the wedding at Cana, which forms the occasion for Jesus' first <u>miracle</u>, is a self-contained unit. It is connected with the preceding events by the temporal marker <u>two days later</u> (verse 1). Transitional verse 12, <u>After this, Jesus and his mother, brothers, and disciples went to Capernaum, and stayed there a few days</u>, loosely joins it to the account of the cleansing of the temple.

The account can be analyzed as follows. Verses 1-2 indicate the setting: Jesus and his disciples have been invited to a wedding, and Jesus' mother is also there. Verse 3 provides the immediate occasion for the miracle: all the wine has been drunk. Verses 4-5 indicate that Jesus acts independently of all human authority, even that of his mother, and so even his mother is obedient to him in matters relating to the revelation of his true glory.

Verse 6 explains the presence and purpose of the water jars at the feast, while verses 7-8 relate the words of Jesus that produce the miracle, though the miracle is not actually indicated until verse 9. Verse 10 gives the response of the man in charge of the feast to the water that has now become wine, and the concluding verse (11) indicates the true nature of the miracle (<u>there he revealed his glory</u>) and its effect on his disciples (<u>his disciples believed in him</u>).

The section heading, <u>The Wedding in Cana</u>, may require some minor expansion in some languages, since it is possible to confuse the word <u>wedding</u> with "marriage." What is important is the emphasis upon a kind of "wedding feast" or "a feast accompanying marriage" or "a feast to celebrate a marriage." It may also be useful to identify Cana as a place name, and therefore the title may read in some languages "A marriage feast at a town called Cana" or "...at Cana town."

2.1   Two days later there was a wedding in the town of
        Cana in Galilee. Jesus' mother was there,

<u>Two days later</u> is literally "and on the third day" (JB "three days later"). Most translations omit "and" from their text, since it is merely a reflection of Semitic style. In Greek the phrase "on the third day" would normally be taken to mean "the day after tomorrow," since it was generally the practice to count both the first and the last day in any sequence. Other solutions are possible, but it seems best to understand that the wedding occurred two days after the call of Philip and Nathanael, the last day mentioned in the narrative up to this point (1.43). If one sees symbolic significance in the mention of three days, which is quite possible in this particular narrative, it would be best to maintain the explicit mention in the translation.

<u>In the town of Cana in Galilee</u> translates "in Cana of Galilee." It was known to John's original readers that Cana was a town, but this information may be missed by present readers unless it is made explicit. It may also be useful in some languages to identify <u>Galilee</u> as a province or region. If so, one may translate "in the town of Cana, which was in the region of Galilee."

In the New Testament Cana is mentioned only in the Gospel of John (2.1,11; 4.46; 21.2). John may have more than a geographic interest in mind when he mentions Galilee. This was not merely to distinguish Cana in Galilee from other Canas, but to indicate that Jesus' first miracle took place in Galilee, rather than in Judea, where the hostility against Jesus originated.

As already mentioned, it may be important to indicate that the wedding consists of a "wedding feast" or "a feast to celebrate a marriage." It is not sufficient to translate merely "marriage," since the focus is upon the feast celebrating the marriage.

Jesus' mother is mentioned several times in John's Gospel, though never by name (2.12; 6.42; 19.25).

2.2   and Jesus and his disciples had also been invited
           to the wedding.

A literal translation of this verse might read "and Jesus was invited to the wedding and his disciples." In Semitic Greek it was not uncommon to have a singular subject followed by a singular verb to which a plural subject would be linked by "and." The nearest natural equivalent in English is to join the singular and plural subjects by "and" and to use a plural verb. It is awkward to maintain the form of the Greek, as some translations do; the restructuring of NEB and JB (but not of BJ) is similar to that of TEV.

A literal translation of Jesus and his disciples had also been invited to the wedding may actually be misleading. It may suggest that Jesus and his disciples were invited but did not go to the wedding, if one translates more or less literally the pluperfect tense "had been invited." In some languages such a translation suggests an action which had taken place but may not have had a positive result. Therefore, it may be necessary to say "Jesus and his disciples had also been invited to the wedding, and they were there," or "Jesus and his disciples had also accepted the invitation to the wedding."

Jesus' followers are called disciples (see 1.35) in all the Gospels. In Matthew the term is used to refer strictly to the Twelve, but the other Gospel writers use the term in a wider sense to include other followers of Jesus. Acts extends it even further, so that it designates all Christian believers. In John the Twelve are mentioned only in Chapter 6 (verses 67, 70, 71).

In this particular context the term used to render disciples should probably suggest a relatively small group. In fact, there is no evidence from the Gospel of John or elsewhere that all the twelve apostles had been chosen by this time. It is possible to use a phrase such as "those whom Jesus was teaching" or "those who were learning from Jesus." In some translations "close followers," an expression which would designate a relatively small group of associates, may be used, but one should not use such an expression as "those who believed in him"--a phrase which can often be used for "disciples" in Acts.

2.3   When the wine had given out, Jesus' mother said
       to him, "They are out of wine."

When the wine had given out must be rendered in an active form in
many languages, and in that case those who drank the wine must be specified, for example, "When the guests at the wedding had run out of
wine."
    There may be certain complications in identifying the referent of
they in the expression they are out of wine. They could, of course,
refer to the guests at the wedding, who had no more wine, or it could
be the host and his family, who were responsible for providing the
wine. The problem may be resolved in some languages by simply translating "There is no more wine."

2.4   "You must not tell me what to do," Jesus replied. "My
       time has not yet come."

Jesus' use of "woman" (RSV) in direct address was normal and polite
(compare Matt 15.28). It showed neither disrespect nor lack of love, as
can be clearly seen by the parallel use in 19.26. TEV has omitted mention
of "woman" as a noun of address, because it is not necessary in English
and tends to convey the impression that Jesus was disrespectful.
    A number of serious problems are involved in translating "woman"
literally. In some languages a man would address his own wife this way,
and so this rendering cannot be employed here. In other languages, to
address one's mother as "woman" would be insulting; it could even be
interpreted to mean that Jesus was denying that Mary was his mother. The
closest equivalent in many languages is simply "my mother" or "mother,"
but in others an equivalent expression showing proper respect would require the omission of any expression of direct address, as in TEV.
    You must not tell me what to do translates a Semitism (literally
"what to me and to you?") It appears in the Septuagint with at least
two different meanings. In Judges 11.12, Jephthah's reply to the
Ammonite king is best taken to mean "What is your quarrel with us?"
In 2 Samuel 16.10, David's response to Abishai and Joab may be translated, "This is none of your business." In the New Testament the same
expression is used by demons when confronted by Jesus (Mark 1.24; 5.7)
and is rendered in TEV as "What do you want with us?" In the present
passage the force of the expression seems to be to deny the authority
of Mary over Jesus in the revelation of his true glory. That is, the
time and the manner in which the Son would reveal his glory to the
world was determined by God the Father and not by any earthly person,
not even Jesus' mother. This judgment is validated by what Jesus says
immediately afterward, "My time has not yet come." The time (literally
"hour") of Jesus is his death on the cross and his resulting exaltation
in glory. In 7.30 and in 8.20, John indicates that Jesus' opponents were
not able to arrest him, because his hour had not yet come. Elsewhere
Jesus' time is spoken of as being imminent (12.27; 13.1; 17.1).
    In order to avoid what seems to be Jesus' rebuke of his mother, a
number of translators render this Semitic idiom "Why is this our
concern?" but the fact that Jesus speaks of "my hour" suggests that he
is denying only his own involvement. Furthermore, this is not the

correct meaning of the Semitic idiom. On the other hand, it is not necessary to say "You must not tell me what to do." Other possibilities are "Why are you bothering me about this?" or "Do not try to direct me."

My time has not yet come may require some slight modification, since in many languages no abstract term for "time" exists to identify a particular occasion. Rather, the tendency is to use such words as "day" or even "hour." In some languages such expressions as "The day for me to act has not yet come" or "This is not yet the day for me to do something about it" may be useful.

2.5   Jesus' mother then told the servants, "Do whatever
             he tells you."

Although Mary cannot determine the time for the complete and full revelation of Jesus' glory, she does not take his answer as a denial of her specific request. So she tells the servants, "Do whatever he tells you."

There may be some complication in rendering the servants, since no servants have as yet been mentioned in the context. It may be more natural, therefore, to say "the servants in that household" or "the persons who were serving the wine" or "...had been serving the wine."

In some instances the use of the pronoun he (in an expression such as do whatever he tells you) could be interpreted as somewhat standoffish or even disrespectful, since a mother might be expected to speak to servants about her own son by some such an expression as "Do whatever my son tells you to do." As is so often the case, one must be very sensitive to the use of pronominal forms, since they frequently carry rather subtle connotations.

2.6   The Jews have rules about ritual washing, and
             for this purpose six stone water jars were there, each
             one large enough to hold between twenty and thirty
             gallons.

Most translations continue the paragraph begun in verse 1 through verse 10. But Gdsp and TEV, in keeping with contemporary English style, begin a new paragraph whenever a new speaker is introduced (1-3,4,5). Moreover, a new topic is introduced at verse 6. A paragraph break is therefore logical from the viewpoint of discourse structure, especially since this verse is a remark by the author of the Gospel.

The Greek word order of this verse can be seen by consulting RSV: "Now six stone jars were standing there, for the Jewish rites of purification, each holding twenty or thirty gallons." In introducing new information in English, it is more natural to go from the general to the specific, and so TEV reorders this sentence: The Jews have rules about ritual washing, and for this six stone water jars were there, each one large enough to hold between twenty and thirty gallons. That is, TEV mentions the general information about the Jewish religious rules, and then on the basis of this, it explains the purpose of the six stone water jars.

A number of complications may be involved in rendering the Jews
have rules about ritual washing. In the first place, a phrase such as
ritual washing may be equivalent to "being acceptable to God by washing,"
but such an expression may be difficult to combine readily with the
meaning of "rules." One way of expressing these relations is "In the
way in which the Jews worship God, they have many rules about how to
wash themselves" or "In order for Jews to make themselves acceptable to
God they must obey many rules about how to wash" or "The Jews must wash
themselves and things very carefully, if they are to worship God in the
way they think is right." GeCL renders "They (=the water jars) are used
for the purification required by Jewish Law."

Some scholars see a symbolic meaning in the number six (that is,
the imperfection of Judaism), but such symbolic significance is not at
all clear and for purposes of translation is unimportant.

The fact that the jars are stone, rather than earthenware, is
important. According to Jewish law, earthenware jars, if contaminated,
had to be broken, but contaminated stone jars could simply be washed.

The relation between the parts of the phrase six stone water jars
must be made more explicit in some languages, for example, "six large
jars made of stone and used for holding water."

Between twenty and thirty gallons (see RSV, NEB, JB, Gdsp) is literally "two or three measures." Most scholars take a "measure" to be
equal to about nine or ten gallons, but some understand it to be equal
to about eight or nine gallons (NAB "fifteen to twenty-five gallons";
Mft "about twenty gallons"). It is entirely appropriate in some languages to adapt the measure of between twenty and thirty gallons to a
rough equivalent in "liters," for example, "between 80 and 120 liters."
It is important not to use an expression which would narrowly restrict
the measure to twenty-five gallons. What is intended here is simply an
approximate measure; therefore one may say in some languages "approximately twenty to thirty gallons" or "about twenty or thirty gallons."
In languages which do not use gallons or liters, one may translate by
an appropriate measure, such as, "about (so-and-so) number of bamboos,"
an expression occurring in a number of languages in Southeast Asia.

2.7   Jesus said to the servants, "Fill these jars with
           water." They filled them to the brim,

To the servants renders "to them" of the Greek text, but several
translations take this pronominal phrase to be an explicit reference
to the servants (TEV, JB, NEB, BJ).

In choosing a word to translate fill, it is important not to suggest that the servants carried these huge jars out to fill them with
water; rather it should be suggested that the jars remained in place
while water was brought to fill them.

To the brim (so most translations) is mentioned to show that there
was no room left to add anything to the water in the jars. In some
languages to the brim is equivalent to "until there was water flowing
down the outside" or "until water reached the brim" or "until they were
completely full."

2.8   and then he told them, "Now draw some water out and
           take it to the man in charge of the feast." They took
           him the water,

There is much controversy regarding the exact meaning of the verb
rendered draw some water out, since technically this word means "to
draw water from a well," and the question is whether John uses it here
with its technical meaning or in a more general sense. If it has the
sense of "to draw water from a well," then there is no indication that
the water in the jars was changed into wine. That is, those who adopt
this view say that Jesus left the six water jars filled with water
(symbolic of the imperfection of Judaism), while he had the servants
draw fresh water from a well, and that this latter water was changed
into wine. Most modern commentators, however, believe the verb "draw
out" is used loosely in this instance; they understand that Jesus told
the servants to draw water from the jars. The same verb is used in 4.7
of drawing water from a well, but that meaning does not determine its
usage here. Accordingly, if the translator must be explicit, it is best
to say that the water was drawn from the jars. Draw some water out may
probably be best translated as "Dip some water out" or "Put in a small
jar and take some water out of the stone jars" or "Put in a pitcher and
..."
    The Greek word rendered the man in charge of the feast (NAB "the
waiter in charge") is rendered "steward" by most translators. The Greek
word probably refers to a slave appointed to be in charge of a banquet,
though some commentators understand it to refer to one of the guests who
was appointed "toastmaster" in charge of the banquet, chosen for this
function because of his close relation with the bridegroom.
    If one wishes to translate the man in charge of the feast as "the
waiter in charge," then one can say "the servant who directed the other
servants at the feast" or "the servant who told the other servants what
they should do in serving the guests." If, however, one chooses to follow
the interpretation of "toastmaster" or "master of ceremonies," then one
can employ the phrase "the guest who directed the feast" or "the guest
who said what should happen at the feast" or "...what the guests should
do during the feast."
    They took him the water is simply "and they took" in Greek. Very
few translators render this clause literally; most seek to bring out the
information implicit in the Greek (for example, NAB "they did as he instructed them"; NEB "and they did so"; JB "they did this").

2.9   which now had turned into wine, and he tasted it.
           He did not know where this wine had come from (but,
           of course, the servants who had drawn out the water
           knew); so he called the bridegroom

Most translations have a full stop at the end of verse 8, in keeping with the structure of the Greek. However, it is important that a
translation should indicate the meaning of the original in whatever
form is most natural for the receptor language. TEV continues the first
part of this verse as the last part of the sentence begun in the previous

verse. It translates the Greek noun "steward" (verse 9) by the pronoun "he," since it is more natural in English to have a pronoun, and not a noun, referring back to a pronoun. In this way, the repetition of a long descriptive phrase (the man in charge of the feast) is avoided. The same thing is true of the clause he called the bridegroom, where the pronoun he again translates the Greek noun "steward."

John does not indicate the amount of the water which now had turned into wine. He may mean either the one jar from which the water was drawn or all six jars. Those who believe that the water was drawn from the well assume that only the water taken to the man in charge of the feast was turned to wine. It is best not to be explicit unless the receptor language demands it, in which case it is suggested that the meaning be "the water from the jar containing the water that had turned into wine."

The parenthetical explanation in this verse seems almost overly obvious, and hence it may be useful, in fact even necessary, to qualify it by such an introductory expression as "naturally," for example, "but naturally the servants knew."

The water which now had turned into wine may require some modification in certain languages, since it may be necessary to specify the agent, for example, "the water which Jesus had caused to become wine." If the agent is not specified, it might be suggested that the water had become wine in some yet unexplained manner.

It is not possible in some languages to translate literally where this wine had come from, since one cannot speak of "wine coming." It is necessary in such instances to say "where the servants had gotten this wine" or "from where they had dipped out this wine."

Because the sentence beginning in the middle of verse 9 continues until almost the end of verse 10, it may be useful to break the sentence after the parenthesis (but, of course, the servants who had drawn out the water knew). Therefore, one may begin the next sentence as "Because of this, he called the bridegroom...."

2.10　　　　and said to him, "Everyone else serves the best wine
　　　　　　first, and after the guests have drunk a lot, he serves
　　　　　　the ordinary wine. But you have kept the best wine until
　　　　　　now!"

The first part of this verse is in the form of a parable: "The host serves the best wine first, and after the guests have drunk a lot, he serves the ordinary wine."

Everyone else (NEB "everyone"; JB "people generally") is literally "every man," while the guests (so also JB, NEB, BJ; Gdps, Mft "people") is "they" in Greek.

The best wine (so also NEB, JB; NAB "the choice wine") is rendered literally by most translators as "the good wine." However, the context indicates that the contrast is not between good wine and poor wine, but between the best wine (that one has) and ordinary wine or cheaper wine (JB "the cheaper sort"; Gdsp "his poorer wine"; Mft "the poorer wine"; NAB "a lesser vintage").

The verb rendered "drunk a lot" literally means "to become drunk"

(see Zür, Luther Revised, Segond; note BJ <u>sont gais</u>), but most translations seem to prefer the meaning TEV has (NEB, Mft, Gdsp; RSV "have
drunk freely"; JB "have had plenty to drink"; NAB "have been drinking
awhile"). It is not necessary to press the meaning "to become drunk" in
this context, because the degree of intoxication is irrelevant. The
important element is the contrast between the new wine and the old. Commentators generally agree that the point of the story is to mark the
contrast between the new way of Jesus and the old way of Judaism, symbolized by the new wine and the old.

<u>2.11</u>   Jesus performed this first miracle in Cana in
        Galilee; there he revealed his glory, and his
        disciples believed in him.

The word translated <u>first</u> may mean more than the initial one in a
series. It may mean that <u>this</u> is a "basic sign," in that it is symbolic
of the creative power of Jesus. This word reflects again one of the
problems in translating this Gospel; John often appears to use words
in more than one sense.

The Greek word rendered <u>miracle</u> in TEV is translated "sign" in
most translations. This word has a rich religious heritage, especially
through its use in the Septuagint, the Greek translation of the Hebrew
Old Testament. It may denote something miraculous--though not always--
but it always has a religious significance beyond the event itself. That
is, a "sign" is a means of revealing a greater reality to which the
"sign" itself merely points. The Gospel of John speaks of seven "signs"
of Jesus, and these are "signs," not necessarily because the are miracles, but because they point to a truth beyond themselves, to a truth
regarding God's salvation. Therefore, it is important that if possible
the translator find a term which means not merely a miracle--but one
which can carry the force of pointing beyond itself to a greater truth.

There are two types of expressions in receptor languages which
frequently translate <u>miracle</u>. These focus either upon the greatness or
magnitude of an event (for example, "mighty work" or "great deed") or
upon the reactions of those who witness such an event, for example,
"a mouth-opening event" or "a long-necked thing" (implying that people
stretched their necks in order to see). However, rather than employ a
term which simply means "an unusual event," it is better, as indicated
in the above paragraph, to use an expression which will show that such
an event has special significance or meaning. It is rendered in some
languages "a great deed which reveals" or "a powerful work which teaches"
or even "a miracle which tells something."

On the word <u>glory</u> see 1.14. John interprets the incident in Cana
as a revelation of Jesus' glory in the sense that a certain aspect of
his true nature is revealed in what he does here. The final and absolute revelation of Jesus' glory comes only through his death and
exaltation, but in some ways this miracle at Cana also is a revelation
of his true nature. An immediate result of Jesus' revelation of his
glory is that his disciples believe in him. They believe because of the
mighty work which they see Jesus perform.

<u>There he revealed his glory</u> may be rendered "there he showed how

wonderful he was." The final clause <u>and his disciples believed in him</u> may be rendered "and therefore his disciples believed in him" or "... came to trust him." In many languages it is not enough to use a coordinate conjunction such as <u>and</u>; one must make the logical connection explicit. Otherwise, the text might seem to be denying such a meaningful relation.

<u>2.12</u>　　　　　　After this, Jesus and his mother, brothers, and disciples went to Capernaum and stayed there a few days.

<u>After this</u> and the similar phrase "after these things" are simple formulas denoting an indefinite but brief time sequence. These formulas are used synonymously throughout the Gospel and are translated in various ways in TEV: <u>after this</u>, <u>afterwards,</u> and <u>then</u>. It is not possible to determine the precise length of time indicated by these phrases. In a number of languages <u>after this</u> is rendered "the next thing that happened" or "after that had happened."

<u>Jesus</u> (so also Gdsp, Phps) is literally "he" in Greek, but in introducing a new paragraph it is better in English to use the noun. In this verse John uses a structure similar to the one discussed in verse 2, where a singular verb is used with a singular subject, with a plural subject appended. In English it is natural to make these into a compound subject, as TEV and many other translations do.

In languages which make a distinction between older and younger brothers, one must in this context say "his younger brothers." Some scholars insist (largely for theological reasons) that these "brothers" must be interpreted as "cousins" or "male relatives," but there is no direct biblical evidence for this interpretation.

For <u>disciples</u> see note at 1.35 and 2.2.

<u>Went to</u> is literally "went down to." This verb expresses a geographical situation: Cana is in the hill country, while Capernaum is below sea level, on the shore of Lake Galilee. The same phrase is again used in 4.47 for the journey from Cana to Capernaum. For languages which employ specific indications of direction and level of movement, it may be entirely appropriate to say "went down to Capernaum." However, the term chosen must clearly indicate that the meaning is not like that of "going down into a mine," but simply going down from hill country toward the shore of a lake.

<u>A few days</u> is literally "not many days," a frequently used Semitic Greek expression: JB has "only a few days"; Gdsp and Mft "for a few days." In some languages it is difficult to be indefinite about temporal relations or periods of time, for example, one must often choose between terms which would specify about one week's duration, one month's duration, or a considerably longer period of time. Possibly the most satisfactory solution in this instance would be an expression equivalent to "a week or so," for the Gospel of John seems to emphasize a rapid pace of developments. Note, for example, the expressions of temporal setting in 1.29,35,43 and 2.1. This same emphasis on temporal sequence is to be found in 2.13.

[63]

TEV   (2.13-22)   RSV

JESUS GOES TO THE TEMPLE

13 It was almost time for the Passover Festival, so Jesus went to Jerusalem. 14 There in the Temple he found men selling cattle, sheep, and pigeons, and also the moneychangers sitting at their tables. 15 So he made a whip from cords and drove all the animals out of the Temple, both the sheep and the cattle; he overturned the tables of the moneychangers and scattered their coins; 16 and he ordered the men who sold the pigeons, "Take them out of here! Stop making my Father's house a marketplace!" 17 His disciples remembered that the scripture says, "My devotion to your house, O God, burns in me like a fire."

18 The Jewish authorities came back at him with a question, "What miracle can you perform to show us that you have the right to do this?"

19 Jesus answered, "Tear down this Temple, and in three days I will build it again."

20 "Are you going to build it again in three days?" they asked him. "It has taken forty-six years to build this Temple!"

21 But the temple Jesus was speaking about was his body. 22 So when he was raised from death, his disciples remembered that he had said this, and they believed the scripture and what Jesus had said.

13 The Passover of the Jews was at hand, and Jesus went up to Jerusalem. 14 In the temple he found those who were selling oxen and sheep and pigeons, and the money-changers at their business. 15 And making a whip of cords he drove them all, with the sheep and oxen, out of the temple; and he poured out the coins of the money-changers and overturned their tables. 16 And he told those who sold the pigeons, "Take these things away; you shall not make my Father's house a house of trade." 17 His disciples remembered that it was written, "Zeal for thy house will consume me." 18 The Jews then said to him, "What sign have you to show us for doing this?" 19 Jesus answered them, "Destroy this temple, and in three days I will raise it up." 20 The Jews then said, "It has taken forty-six years to build this temple, and will you raise it up in three days?" 21 But he spoke of the temple of his body. 22 When therefore he was raised from the dead, his disciples remembered that he had said this; and they believed the scripture and the word which Jesus had spoken.

The account of Jesus' cleansing of the Temple occurs in all four Gospels. It is in a notably different position in the Gospel of John from where it occurs in the other three. In the Synoptic Gospels this incident occurs during the last week of Jesus' ministry (Matt 21.12-13; Mark 11.15-17; Luke 19.45-46), while in John it is placed at the beginning of his ministry. Since most scholars believe that it is not something which Jesus is likely to have done twice during the course of his ministry, commentators attempt to explain the difference in chronology in various ways. It is possible that John had a different chronological outline of Jesus' ministry. However, verses 21 and 22 suggest that the cleansing of the Temple was placed here for theological rather than chronological reasons. In the Synoptics Jesus' cleansing of the Temple is in the direction of Temple reform, whereas in John it points to the destruction of the Temple. That is, John interprets this event as referring to the destruction of the Jewish cult and the raising of a new temple, Jesus' body, in which God and man meet. In fact, this entire section (2.13--4.54) shows that Jesus is the true fulfillment of all that the Temple was intended to accomplish.

The section heading, Jesus Goes to the Temple, may seem inadequate, since it was not Jesus' arrival in the Temple but what he did there which is important. One may, for example, translate "Jesus drives out of the Temple the merchants and the moneychangers" or "Jesus drives out of the Temple those who were ruining it."

2.13   It was almost time for the Passover Festival, so Jesus went to Jerusalem.

It was almost time for the Passover Festival is literally "and the Passover of the Jews was near." TEV qualifies the Passover as a Festival in order to make this information immediately explicit for its readers, who otherwise might not have a background for understanding the term. It was customary for Jews to go to Jerusalem to celebrate Passover. John mentions this festival in two other places in his Gospel (6.4; 11.55; and possibly it is intended in 5.1). It is interesting to note that in 6.4 John himself qualifies the Passover as "the feast of the Jews." The Passover Festival took place on Nisan 14 (around April 1). It celebrated the deliverance of the Israelites from slavery in Egypt (see especially Exo 12.1-27; Deut 16.1-8).

It is difficult to find an appropriate term to translate Passover or Passover Festival. A literal translation of Passover may be misleading, since it may appear to mean that some people passed over a river or some kind of barrier. It may be important, especially at the first mention of the Passover Festival, to indicate that it was "a festival to celebrate the passing over of the angel in ancient times." In any translation of a Gospel or New Testament, a glossary should be provided, giving a description of major factors in the event of the ancient Passover in Egypt, just preceding the exodus of the Jews from that land.

Traditionally the Passover has been spoken of as the "feast of Passover," but the term "feast" hardly seems appropriate in a present-day English version. For that reason the term "festival" is used, since it implies more than mere eating. The Passover was a joyous occasion which took a considerable period of time (especially in view of the need for people to go to and from Jerusalem), and a number of events were connected with it in addition to the ceremonial meal. Since festivals are common in most societies, an appropriate equivalent term can usually be found. The difficulty is that the terms associated with such festivals are often highly specific. If the fact that a term is specific prevents it from being used, it may be necessary to employ such a phrase as "a time of celebrating" or "days when the Jews celebrated the passing over of the angel," or "...their deliverance from Egypt."

It was almost time for may be rendered in some languages "a few
days later would be the time for" or "soon it would be time for" or "in
only a few days it would be the day for."

Jesus went to Jerusalem is literally "Jesus went up to Jerusalem."
The verb "to go up" is the usual verb for describing a journey to Jerusalem, which was situated in the Judean hill country (compare 5.1; 7.8;
11.55; 12.20). Note the similar use of the verb "to go down to" in
verse 12.

Both clauses in 2.13 begin with "and," a common connective in
Jewish Greek. Most translators into English use more natural transitional formulas.

2.14   There in the Temple he found men selling cattle,
        sheep, and pigeons, and also the moneychangers sitting
        at their tables.

The word for Temple (Greek hieron) in this and the following verses
refers to the court of the Gentiles (that is, the outer court) of the
Temple. The sanctuary (Greek naos), the Temple proper, is mentioned in
verses 19 and 20. It may be useful to translate Temple in this context
as "the temple area," to avoid giving the impression that the merchants
and moneychangers were actually inside the sanctuary itself.

The Greek merely has "the moneychangers sitting," while TEV has
the moneychangers sitting at their tables. The meaning is that the
moneychangers were sitting there while carrying on their business. Most
translations make this information explicit in one way or another. For
example, RSV has "the money-changers at their business"; NEB "the moneychangers seated at their tables"; JB "the changers sitting at their
counters." The animals and birds were there to be sold to persons who
came to offer sacrifices, while the moneychangers were there to change
Roman coins into Jewish coins, since no coins bearing imperial or Roman
portraits were permitted to be used to pay the temple tax. For the amount
of this tax see Matthew 17.27.

2.15   So he made a whip from cords and drove all the animals
        out of the Temple, both the sheep and the cattle; he
        overturned the tables of the moneychangers and scattered
        their coins;

There is a minor textual problem in this verse, which is reflected
in the translation of NAB, "He made a (kind of) whip of cords." The
additional Greek word hōs ("kind of") has been attributed to a scribe
who could not imagine a whip made out of cords. However, this reading
has the support of two ancient papyri. The Greek word used to translate
whip in this passage comes from a Latin word, which sometimes describes
a whip used for driving cattle, and that may be the meaning in this context. No weapons of any sort (not even sticks) were permitted within the
Temple precincts, and this rule may account for the fact that Jesus had
to make a whip from cords.

The order of the Greek text of the last part of this verse reads "he scattered the coins of the moneychangers and overturned their tables." TEV rearranges this clause (he overturned the tables of the moneychangers and scattered their coins), as NEB and NAB also do. Thus the turning over of the tables is made the cause of the scattering of the coins, which would seem to be the more logical sequence.

The term moneychangers may need recasting as "those who were exchanging one kind of money for another" or "those who were exchanging Roman money for money acceptable in the Temple" (which was their specific function).

Rather than say specifically overturned the tables, one may say simply "he knocked over the tables" or "pushed the tables over."

And scattered their coins may be best translated as "and thus caused their coins to scatter" or "in this way made the coins go in all directions." Unless one shows the relation between overturning the tables and scattering the coins, the implication may be that Jesus stooped down, picked up the coins, and purposely threw them in various directions. Since such an act is not implied by the story, it is better to make specific the relation between overturning the tables and scattering the coins.

2.16   and he ordered the men who sold the pigeons, "Take them out of here! Stop making my Father's house a marketplace!"

He ordered represents "he said," but the Greek word "to say" covers a large semantic domain, and the present context indicates that something stronger than merely "said" is intended.

Stop making translates a present imperative in Greek, referring to action already in progress. In order to emphasize this particular aspect of the present tense in Greek, one may say "Do not any longer cause my Father's house to be a marketplace" or "You must stop causing my Father's house to be a marketplace."

The second part of this verse has a play on the word "house" (literally something like "Do not make my Father's house a house of commerce"), which cannot be seen from TEV. Most modern English translators render the phrase "house of commerce" either by "market" or "marketplace." But RSV has "house of trade" and in this way reflects the play on words. It is possible in some languages to reflect the play on words by using a rather general term for "house," for example, "Do not make this place that belongs to my Father into a place where you do business" or "Do not take my Father's place and make it into a marketplace."

2.17   His disciples remembered that the scripture says, "My devotion to your house, O God, burns in me like a fire."

My devotion to your house appears in many translations as "zeal for your house." The "zeal" spoken of is that of devotion to God's house. Burns in me like a fire is literally "will destroy me," and in the Johannine context may be intended as an allusion to the moment of Jesus'

[67]

death. TEV takes it in a metaphorical, rather than a literal sense, which explains the basis for its rendering; the destruction referred to is not necessarily that of a fire, though it may be. GeCL combines both fire and destruction "My love for your house is like a fire which will consume." The passage of scripture referred to is Psalm 69.9.

My devotion to your house is best translated in some languages as "My love for your house," as in GeCL. In others it may be expressed idiomatically as "My hunger for your house has grabbed me." Rather than render "will destroy me" or burns in me like a fire, some languages express this concept by such an idiom as "will eat me up" or even "will cause my death."

2.18   The Jewish authorities came back at him with
     a question, "What miracle can you perform to show
     us that you have the right to do this?"

This verse begins in Greek with "So then the Jews answered and said to him." The words "so then" represent the Greek particle oun, sometimes referred to as "John's favorite particle," because it is found in this Gospel much more frequently than in any other part of the New Testament. John uses oun over 200 times, whereas the three Gospels together use it only 111 times. Furthermore, John's use of this particle is confined to the narrative portions of his Gospel; it is seldom found in discourse material.

A particle is a small word with a rather limited grammatical force and often does not need to be translated. John sometimes uses oun to indicate either a transition or a climax in a narrative, but often it carries no real grammatical force; it merely represents a trait of John's style. TEV and many other modern translations vary in their treatment of this peculiarity of style. Sometimes oun is rendered by actual words in the translation, for example, so then. At other times the introduction of a new paragraph represents sufficiently John's use of this particle. Occasionally it is passed over and not represented at all in the translation. A translator should not assume that oun must always be represented in translation.

To show the relationship between Jesus' action and the question posed by Jewish authorities, verse 18 may begin with such a phrase as "As a result of what Jesus had done" or "Because of what Jesus did in the Temple."

Jewish authorities translates "the Jews." See the discussion at 1.19 and Appendix I, "The Jews in the Gospel of John."

"Answered and said" is again an example of Semitic Greek style, which frequently uses two verbs to introduce direct discourse where English uses only one. TEV translates came back at him with a question, and NEB has "challenged Jesus."

The word translated miracle is literally "sign," (see the comments at 2.11). In the present passage it refers to the Jewish leaders' demand that Jesus perform a miracle as proof to them of who he is. The Greek term here translated "miracle" is not used precisely as in contexts in which Jesus' deeds are spoken of as signs of his power and glory. Nevertheless, the Jewish authorities are concerned with a

miracle which would not merely demonstrate his supernatural power, but
would indicate as well a corresponding right to act in a way which
seemed a gross violation of the existing tradition. In a sense, therefore, the use of the special Greek term meaning "sign" is appropriate
in this context.

To show us that you have the right to do this? is literally "do
you show us, that (or "because") you do these things?" The question
clearly concerns the right or authority Jesus has for his actions in
the Temple. A number of translations make this information explicit.
Note, for example, NEB "What sign...can you show as authority for your
action?"; NAB "What sign can you show us authorizing you to do these
things?"; JB "What sign can you show us to justify what you have done?"
A literal rendering, by failing to make the question of authority explicit, may fail to convey the significance of the question.

It may not be easy to find precisely the correct wording for the
expression to show us that you have the right to do this. In some
languages an equivalent may be "to prove to us that your doing this was
all right." Since, in a sense, the right to cleanse the Temple could
come only from God himself, it may be appropriate in some languages to
say "to show that God has given you the right to do what you have done"
or "to show that God has said that you may do this."

2.19   Jesus answered, "Tear down this Temple, and
              in three days I will build it again."

This verse also begins with a Semitic expression that sounds odd to
the English reader: "Jesus answered and said to them." TEV has simply
Jesus answered.

As mentioned under verse 14, the word for Temple in this and the
following verse refers to the sanctuary itself. Mft, Gdsp, and JB
render the word in this verse by "sanctuary" and the word in verse 14
by "temple," in order to make the distinction.

Some commentators understand the imperative "tear down" in the
sense of a conditional clause, "if you tear down." It is true that this
could be a Semitic expression in which an imperative is used with the
force of a conditional. However, in the present context it is best to
take this imperative with its full force, rather than as a conditional
clause. All translations seem to go in this direction, and it is quite
typical of the Old Testament prophets to use an imperative in an ironical sense. This seems to be the case in this instance with Jesus. However, in some languages it would be wrong to employ an imperative,
since it could be interpreted as a command by Jesus for the people to
destroy the Temple. Therefore, one must use a conditional; for example,
"If you tear down this Temple, then in three days I will build it
again."

In choosing terms for tear down and build, it is important to
employ expressions which can appropriately be applied to a building,
despite the fact that in verses 21 and 22 it is made clear that Jesus
is referring to his own body, and therefore to his death. However, one
cannot anticipate this meaning in verse 19, since this would make non-
sense of the response of the Jewish authorities recorded in verse 20.

"Are you going to build it again in three days?"
          they asked him. "It has taken forty-six years to
          build this Temple!"

     TEV reorders the response of the Jewish authorities to Jesus. In
Greek the mention of the forty-six years that it took to build the
Temple comes before the question, Are you going to build it again in
three days? But for purposes of English style the present order is more
forceful, since, in responding to a shocking statement or command, it
is more natural in conversational English to use a question first, and
then to expand its implication by a statement.
     In some languages it is appropriate to introduce the question in
verse 20 as being the idea of someone; for example, "Do you think that
you are going to build it again in three days?" or "How do you imagine
that you are going to build it again in three days?" In this way some
of the irony and surprise can be brought out.
     It has taken forty-six years to build this Temple may be more
literally rendered "this Temple was built in forty-six years." The
verb "was built" is aorist, and so focuses attention on the completion
of the act of building, rather than on the process. Actually, the
Temple was not completed until A. D. 63. Some scholars believe that
John made a chronological error here, assuming that the Temple was completed at the time of Jesus' ministry, when actually it was not. However, it is natural to take "was built" as a summary of the whole
process of building, without necessarily implying that the building was
completed at the time the statement was made. It is interesting that in
the Septuagint of Ezra 5.16 the same aorist form of the verb is used of
the building of the Temple, and there also the Temple was not yet completed.
     It is possible to transform the passive expression It has taken
forty-six years to build this Temple into an active one by introducing
an indefinite subject, such as "men" or a more definite subject such as
"builders," for example, "Men worked forty-six years to build this
Temple" or "Builders have worked forty-six years to complete this
Temple."
     As in many other contexts, the term Temple must be translated as
simply "the house of God," as it is called in many Old Testament contexts. This same type of expression occurs also in the New Testament.
Such a phrase, however, must not be confused with a term for heaven,
which in some languages is "the place where God dwells" or "the place
where God is."

2.21   But the temple Jesus was speaking about was his body.

     Jesus is literally "that one," rendered "he" in most translations.
TEV uses the noun Jesus, since a new paragraph is introduced. Elsewhere
in John's Gospel "that one" also refers to Jesus (see 5.11; 7.11;
9.12,28,37; 19.21).
     Jesus' body may truly be spoken of as the temple of God, because
it was through the person of Jesus that God fully revealed himself, and
it is through encounter with Jesus that men meet and worship God.

The sentence But the temple Jesus was speaking about was his body is syntactically compressed. It may therefore be necessary to expand the statement, for example, "But when Jesus was speaking about the temple, he was talking about his body" or "But when Jesus said the temple, he really meant his body."

2.22　　　　So when he was raised from death, his disciples re-
　　　　　　membered that he had said this, and they believed the
　　　　　　scripture and what Jesus had said.

TEV and a number of others (RSV, Mft, Phps, Zür, Segond, NAB, Luther Revised) take the first verb of this verse to be transitive passive when he was raised, with God as the implied agent (for example, "when God raised him from the dead"). Others take the verb to be in-transitive, "when Jesus rose from the dead" (JB, BJ, Gdsp). NEB is neutral and translates "after his resurrection." The verb may be in-transitive (compare John 10.17-18), since John's Gospel emphasizes Jesus' identity with the Father and consequently his unique power more than any other Gospel. In verse 19 Jesus said that he would raise the Temple up in three days. On the other hand, a number of passages in the New Testament state explicitly that God raised Jesus from the dead and that could well be the meaning here. No decision can be absolute, though most modern translators evidently accept the choice of rendering that TEV has.

In some languages a neutral position between intransitive and transitive passive may be rendered "when Jesus came back from death." The intransitive meaning would be rendered in some languages "when Jesus caused himself to live again." However, translators generally employ either a passive form or an active form with God as the agent; for ex-ample, "when God caused Jesus to rise from death" or "when God caused Jesus to live again."

He had said this is in the imperfect tense and so may imply that Jesus said it on more than one occasion. To reflect fully the possible implications of the imperfect tense, one may translate "he said this from time to time" or "he said this on different occasions." In in-direct discourse Greek retains the original tense of the verb, whereas English requires a change in tense, if the controlling verb is in the past tense, as here ("they remembered"). This explains the use of the English pluperfect by RSV and TEV.

To point out the logical relation between the second and third clauses of verse 22, one may begin the final section "and as a result of this, they believed the Scripture and what Jesus had said" or, as in some languages, "and therefore they believed what was written in the Scriptures..."

　　　　　　　TEV　　　　　　(2.23-25)　　　　　　RSV

JESUS' KNOWLEDGE OF HUMAN NATURE

23 While Jesus was in Jerusalem　　23 Now when he was in Jerusalem
during the Passover Festival, many　at the Passover feast, many believed

believed in him as they saw the miracles he performed. 24 But Jesus did not trust himself to them, because he knew them all. 25 There was no need for anyone to tell him about them, because he himself knew what was in their hearts.	in his name when they saw the signs which he did; 24 but Jesus did not trust himself to them, 25 because he knew all men and needed no one to bear witness of man; for he himself knew what was in man.

This brief section of three verses continues the account of what happened when Jesus went up to Jerusalem during the Passover Festival.

The section heading, Jesus' Knowledge of Human Nature, may be expressed more effectively in many languages "Jesus knows the hearts of all people" or "Jesus knew just how all people think."

2.23   While Jesus was in Jerusalem during the Passover Festival, many believed in him as they saw the miracles he performed.

Although the Greek of this sentence merely has "he," TEV introduces the name Jesus, since a new section begins here.

In him is literally "in his name"; see comments at 14.13.

As in most contexts in the Gospel of John, believed in him must be understood in the sense of "trusted him" or "put their faith in him." It means more than merely believing what he said or giving assent to his message. There is always the implication of confidence, loyalty, and trust.

Miracles is the same word discussed in 2.11. In speaking of "performing miracles" one must use an expression which is natural in the receptor language. This may differ from language to language, for example, "the miracles which he caused to happen," "the wonderful deeds which he did" or "the revealing great things which he made."

2.24-25   But Jesus did not trust himself to them, because he knew them all. 25 There was no need for anyone to tell him about them, because he himself knew what was in their hearts.

In Greek verses 24 and 25 are one sentence. The verb rendered trust...to is the same verb translated believe in in the previous verse. Verse 24 serves as an excellent commentary on the meaning of the word. To believe in Jesus is not merely to agree to certain facts about him; it is rather a commitment or trust of one's life to him and to his way of life.

Because he knew them all is literally "because he knew all (men)." In earlier editions of TEV the text was "all men," since in Greek "all" is masculine. However, in this context the meaning is generic, "all people," and this explains the change in the fourth edition. NEB renders this clause "he knew men so well, all of them," and Gdsp "for he knew them all."

Because he himself knew what was in their hearts (NAB "he was well

[72]

aware of what was in man's heart") is rendered more literally by NEB ("he himself could tell what was in a man") and RSV ("he himself knew what was in man"). These two expressions, <u>because he knew them all</u> and <u>because he knew what was in their hearts,</u> carry essentially the same meaning. They are different ways of expressing Jesus' insight into the human heart. For similar instances of Jesus' insight into men's characters see 1.48; 5.42; 6.61,64; 13.11. In 13.11 the Greek verb <u>oida</u> is used for "to know"; this is different from the verb used in the present verse and in 1.48 and 5.42 (<u>ginōskō</u>), but these verbs are essentially synonymous in John's Gospel.

<u>He knew them all</u> may be rendered "He knew very well what all people were like." In some languages this sentence may be more appropriately rendered "He knew just how all people thought" or "He knew exactly why people did what they did."

<u>There was no need for anyone to tell him about them</u> may be better rendered in some instances "He did not need anyone to tell him about people" or "No one could add to what Jesus already knew about people."

<u>What was in their hearts</u> may be better expressed in some languages as "what was in their minds" or "how people thought." However, some other part of the human anatomy is used in some languages as the seat of mental activity and will. Accordingly, one may speak of "what was in people's liver" or "how they think in their abdomen."

C H A P T E R 3

JESUS AND NICODEMUS

3 There was a Jewish leader named Nicodemus, who belonged to the party of the Pharisees. 2 One night he went to Jesus and said to him, "Rabbi, we know that you are a teacher sent by God. No one could perform the miracles you are doing unless God were with him."

3 Jesus answered, "I am telling you the truth: no one can see the Kingdom of God unless he is born again."*d*

4 "How can a grown man be born again?" Nicodemus asked. "He certainly cannot enter his mother's womb and be born a second time!"

5 "I am telling you the truth," replied Jesus, "that no one can enter the Kingdom of God unless he is born of water and the Spirit. 6 A person is born physically of human parents, but he is born spiritually of the Spirit. 7 Do not be surprised because I tell you that you must all be born again.*e* 8 The wind blows wherever it wishes; you hear the sound it makes, but you do not know where it comes from or where it is going. It is like that with everyone who is born of the Spirit."

9 "How can this be?" asked Nicodemus.

10 Jesus answered, "You are a great teacher in Israel, and you don't know this? 11 I am telling you the truth: we speak of what we know and report what we have seen, yet none of you is willing to accept our message. 12 You do not believe me when I tell you about the things of this world; how will you ever believe me, then, when I tell you about the things of heaven? 13 And no one has ever gone

3 Now there was a man of the Pharisees, named Nicodemus, a ruler of the Jews. 2 This man came to Jesus*d* by night and said to him, "Rabbi, we know that you are a teacher come from God; for no one can do these signs that you do, unless God is with him." 3 Jesus answered him, "Truly, truly, I say to you, unless one is born anew,*e* he cannot see the kingdom of God." 4 Nicodemus said to him, "How can a man be born when he is old? Can he enter a second time into his mother's womb and be born?" 5 Jesus answered, "Truly, truly, I say to you, unless one is born of water and the Spirit, he cannot enter the kingdom of God. 6 That which is born of the flesh is flesh, and that which is born of the Spirit is spirit.*f* Do not marvel that I said to you, 'You must be born anew.'*e* 8 The wind*f* blows where it wills, and you hear the sound of it, but you do not know whence it comes or whither it goes; so it is with every one who is born of the Spirit." 9 Nicodemus said to him, "How can this be?" 10 Jesus answered him, "Are you a teacher of Israel, and yet you do not understand this? 11 Truly, truly, I say to you, we speak of what we know, and bear witness to what we have seen; but you do not receive our testimony. 12 If I have told you earthly things and you do not believe, how can you believe if I tell you heavenly things? 13 No one has ascended into heaven but he who descended from heaven, the Son of man.*g*

up to heaven except the Son of
Man, who came down from heaven."

*d*again; *or* from above.

*e*again; *or* from above.

*d*Greek *him*

*e*Or *from above*

*f*The same Greek word means both
wind and *spirit*

*g*Other ancient authorities add *who
is in heaven*

The account of the dialogue between Jesus and Nicodemus is an artistically organized unit, tied to what precedes it by the we in 3.2
(see there). Three times Nicodemus addresses Jesus (verses 2,4,9), and
each instance provides an occasion for Jesus to move on to a deeper
spiritual truth. Each reply Jesus makes is introduced and emphasized by
the words I am telling you the truth.
Verses 1-8 are controlled by the truth that birth from above is
necessary before one can see or enter the Kingdom. But Nicodemus fails
to understand what Jesus is talking about, and his inability to grasp
what Jesus means serves as a transition in the dialogue (verse 9). Jesus
then indicates that his own authority (and that of his followers--note
the plural we in verse 11) and the authority of his message have come
from heaven. Verse 13 then serves as a climax to what Jesus has said
and as a transition to verses 14-17: the Christian message has indeed
come from heaven, for it came through the Son of Man, whose origin is
in heaven.
But the Son of Man is not merely the one who brings down God's message from heaven; he himself is God's only Son and secures man's salvation by his death on the cross, which is made analogous to the lifting
of the bronze serpent on a pole by Moses in the desert (14-17). Verses
18-20 continue this theme of salvation: God's salvation is available
to all who believe, but his judgment falls on all who reject the Son.
One of the problems in verses 13-21 is that of identifying the
speaker--another example of the difficulty of the Johannine discourse.
John so interweaves his own theological statements with the words of
Jesus that it is difficult to tell where Jesus finishes speaking and
where the Gospel writer himself begins. As far as the truth of what is
said is concerned, there is no problem, because the Spirit of God has
led John to say what he says. But there is a problem in translating,
especially where it is necessary to identify speakers. This problem will
be dealt with in the course of the exegesis.
The section heading, Jesus and Nicodemus, is entirely appropriate
in a publication where the readers are likely to be aware of Nicodemus
and the fact that he had this extended conversation with Jesus. However,
in some languages, simply to say "Jesus and Nicodemus" would imply that
the two were associated in some kind of activity. Therefore it may be
better to say "Jesus talks with Nicodemus" or "Jesus and Nicodemus converse."

3.1   There was a Jewish leader named Nicodemus, who belonged
           to the party of the Pharisees.

[75]

This verse serves to introduce a new participant into the Gospel of John. Nicodemus is identified by name, by his relationship to his nation, and by his affiliations within the religious structure of his nation. In Greek, the introduction of these last two elements is in reverse order from the order in English, but in English it is easier to go from the more general (Jewish leader) to the particular (who belonged to the party of the Pharisees). The fact that Nicodemus was a Jewish leader probably means that he was a member of the Sanhedrin, the highest governing body of the Jewish people. This body was presided over by the High Priest, and most of its 70 members were Sadducees, but there were some Pharisees among its members.

In this context, a Jewish leader would not refer to a government official; it is best translated "an important man among the Jews." The local equivalent in some receptor languages is "an elder among the Jews" or "a Jewish counselor," referring to the position of the leading men in a society, who give their advice to a chief or king. Nicodemus is mentioned only in the Gospel of John; he appears again in 7.50 and 19.39. Nicodemus is actually a Greek name, but it was not an unusual name among Jews.

In some languages it may be important to identify the nature of the party of the Pharisees by calling it "a religious group called Pharisees." In any publication of a Gospel or New Testament, it is essential that such a term as Pharisees be properly identified in a glossary, so that some of the distinctive views and types of behavior characteristic of the Pharisees of biblical times may be understood.

3.2   One night he went to Jesus and said to him, "Rabbi,
        we know that you are a teacher sent by God. No one
        could perform the miracles you are doing unless God
        were with him."

This verse gives the setting for the dialogue; it took place one night. A number of reasons have been suggested as to why Nicodemus came to Jesus at night, but all are based on speculation, and none are important as far as translation is concerned.

In some languages it may be important to identify the place as well as the time of this conversation. Though it is impossible to be specific about the place, however, it does seem natural to say, "One night he went to where Jesus was" or "...to where Jesus was staying." To do so will provide a setting for the conversation and avoid the implication that Nicodemus met Jesus unexpectedly.

Nicodemus speaks not only for himself but for others as well. This is indicated by the use of the first person plural: We know. Commentators are not agreed as to whom the we includes. Elsewhere collective speech is used by the Pharisees (9.24; see Mark 12.14), so Nicodemus may be referring to the Pharisees as a group. It is also possible that he refers to the leaders as a group or even to the leaders and the Pharisees together. Most likely, however, the we refers back to the many of 2.23, that is, to those people who believed on the basis of Jesus' miracles. In languages which distinguish between inclusive and exclusive first person plural, the form of we in this context is exclusive; it would not include Jesus.

[76]

In Greek he is literally "this man" (RSV), and Jesus is literally "him."

The word here translated Rabbi was used in 1.49 where it is rendered teacher by TEV. Here TEV transliterates this Greek word as a means of address, and so avoids the use of teacher twice in this verse. In the TEV glossary Rabbi is defined as "a Hebrew word which means 'my teacher.'" In languages in which one cannot address a person with a title which designates his function, it may be possible to incorporate the meaning of Rabbi in the introductory statement, for example, "and addressed Jesus as a teacher, saying to him..."

Sent by God (so also NEB) translates "you have come from God." TEV and NEB change the active construction to a passive, making God the explicit agent. The words by God (literally "from God") are in the emphatic position in the sentence, thus indicating that Jesus is not simply any teacher but a teacher who has divine authority.

Miracles is the same term (literally "signs") used in 2.11.

You are doing is in the present tense in Greek, signifying the continuous activity of Jesus in performing mighty works.

In some languages the conditional sentence with two negatives, No one could perform the miracles you are doing unless God were with him, presents a number of difficulties in translation. Accordingly, it may be more satisfactory to change the double negative into a positive statement, for example, "A person could only do the miracles you are doing if God were with him." The inversion of the conditional clause, as required by some receptor languages, may result in such a sentence as "Only if God is with a person, can he then perform the miracles that you are performing." However, the shift between third person and second person is rather complex in some languages. An equivalent expression in some instances may be "Only if God is with you, could you possibly perform the miracles that you are doing."

3.3   Jesus answered, "I am telling you the truth: no one can see the Kingdom of God unless he is born again."[d]

[d]again; *or* from above.

Jesus answered is literally "Jesus answered and said to him." Again this phrasing represents the stylistic redundancy of Semitic Greek (see 1.50 and 2.18,19).

I am telling you the truth is the same expression discussed in 1.51.

In his reply to Nicodemus, Jesus picks up the same words Nicodemus has used: no one. However, in the Greek the wording of the two verses is not so close as in TEV.

TEV inverts the order of Jesus' words. In the Greek the dependent clause (unless he is born again) precedes the independent clause (no one can see the Kingdom of God). This inversion is merely a matter of style; the same inversion occurs in NAB ("no one can see the reign of God unless he is begotten from above").

In this verse as in the double negative conditional clause of verse 3.2, it may be necessary to modify the conditional expression, for example, "only if a person is born again can he see the Kingdom of God."

The verb see in this passage has the meaning of "to experience" or "to share in," as its parallel expression in verse 5 indicates (no one can enter the Kingdom of God). "To see" is used elsewhere in the Gospel of John with a similar meaning (see 3.36 and 8.51). In many languages it is not possible to use such a verb as "see" with the meaning of "to experience," and therefore one must translate see the Kingdom of God "experience God's rule" or "be a part of God's Kingdom" or "have a share in God's ruling."

The Kingdom of God is mentioned only twice in the Gospel of John, here and in verse 5; but it is a familiar theme throughout the Synoptic Gospels. It has the significance of God's rule in the lives of men, rather than of a territory over which God rules. The expression see the Kingdom of God is therefore often translated "experience God's ruling over one" or "have God as one's ruler" or "enjoy the ruling of God over one."

The verb rendered by most translations born can refer to being born of a mother or to being begotten of a father. Most commentators and apparently most modern English translations prefer the meaning of "to be born." However, the Johannine parallels (1.13; 1 John 3.9) refer to being begotten rather than being born.

The word translated again may also carry the meaning "from above," as the alternative rendering of TEV indicates. The use of a word with a possible double meaning is characteristic of John's Gospel. It often serves as a means of transition in thought, on the basis of the misunderstanding of the person or persons with whom Jesus is speaking (see 3.4; 4.11; 8.22; 11.13; 13.36-38). Gdsp attempts to incorporate both areas of meaning "born over again from above." On the problem of such a translation see the comments on verse 4.

Expressions meaning "to be born" are often idiomatic, for example, "to see the light," "to come into the light," "to come from between," or "to be dropped." Because of the extraordinary implications involved in an expression meaning "to be born again," it may be necessary to emphasize the meaning of "again," for example, "to be born all over again" or even "to be born again, that is, twice." Without such special emphasis, the implications of the statement may be missed.

3.4   "How can a grown man be born again?" Nicodemus
        asked. "He certainly cannot enter his mother's womb
        and be born a second time!"

In Greek this verse consists of an introductory statement ("Nicodemus said to him") followed by two questions, which TEV makes into one question followed by an exclamation. For reasons of style, the phrase Nicodemus asked is placed between the question and the exclamation.

Grown man (so also JB) is literally "old man," but in the present context the emphasis is not that on age, but rather on maturity; the contrast is between a baby and a full-grown man. Born again (Phps "born a second time") is literally "born," but here the reference is clearly to that of being born a second time.

Obviously, Nicodemus took the word rendered again in TEV to mean again rather than "from above" (its other possible meaning). How Nicodemus understood the word does not necessarily imply what Jesus meant by it or how John intended it to be understood when used by Jesus in the preceding verse. It is impossible to find in English a word or phrase which would carry the possible double meaning that the word again has in verse 3. Since the reply of Nicodemus would sound foolish if Jesus' words were translated "from above" in verse 3, it seems necessary to employ again in that verse. Similarly, although the verb used in verse 3 can have the meaning "to be born" or "to be begotten," on the basis of Nicodemus' reply to Jesus, it is in keeping with the overall context to translate it "to be born."

Since it is almost impossible in most receptor languages (even as in English) to find a single word which will mean both "again" and "from above," it may be desirable to have a marginal note here, indicating that the same Greek word can have both senses. Such a note will help the reader understand how the reply of Jesus can shift to an emphasis on the spiritual birth. An alternative translation would be inadequate, since it would not explain to the reader the original ambiguity in the Greek text.

There is often an advantage in shifting the second question posed by Nicodemus to an emphatic statement, especially in languages in which rhetorical questions are rare. It is evident that Nicodemus is not asking whether a man can enter his mother's womb and be born a second time; rather, he is emphasizing the impossibility of such a thing happening. Therefore, "He certainly cannot enter...!"

3.5   "I am telling you the truth," replied Jesus, "that
           no one can enter the Kingdom of God unless he is born
           of water and the Spirit.

I am telling you the truth is the same phrase discussed in 1.51.

As in verse 3, so here, TEV inverts the sentence order of the Greek, placing the independent clause before the dependent clause.

Though the expression enter the Kingdom of God appears to have a spatial significance which is not present in see the Kingdom of God (verse 3), there is no essential difference in meaning. Therefore, the same type of expression can be employed in verses 3 and 5. It may be particularly advantageous to use such an expression as "God's rule" for the Kingdom of God.

The phrase of water and the Spirit (literally "water and spirit" in Greek) offers many difficulties. First, this phrase is substituted for the word again in verse 3, and it may be assumed that John is still speaking of the same topic. However, the mention of "water and spirit" opens an opportunity for a further development of Jesus' thought. Second, it is not clear just what "water" refers to; and several possibilities have been suggested, of which two are the most widely accepted. Some persons, for example, have suggested that in this context "water" refers to the baptism of John the Baptist or to Jewish purification as a whole, inclusive of the baptism of John, which would be understood as being insufficient, in contrast with that which the Spirit accomplishes.

On the other hand, other scholars have seen in this occurrence of "water"
a reference to Christian baptism: "water" being the reference to the outward symbol and "Spirit" a reference to the transforming power of God
in the life of the believer. Since the phrase is "water and Spirit," it
is important that the two be joined in such a way as not to suggest any
contrast.

As indicated above, the phrase is literally "water and spirit,"
without a definite article before "spirit." However, on the basis of
verses 6 and 8 (literally "the spirit") it seems most likely that the
Spirit is referred to in this verse. A number of translations make this
clear. In fact, the entire context indicates that God's Spirit is meant.
Thus to translate "water and spirit" (Phps, NEB) would be to fail to
bring out the real force of the meaning.

Certain serious complications may arise from a literal translation
of born of water. In some languages this expression is a specific reference to "afterbirth." In the present context born clearly refers to the
rebirth. Therefore it may be appropriate in some languages to translate
"if he is not born again by means of water and by means of the Spirit."
This rendering would be taken to refer to some kind of baptism by water
and the transformation produced by the Spirit of God, spoken of as "the
baptism of the Spirit."

It may be important to indicate specifically that the Spirit is
"the Holy Spirit." Otherwise a reader could interpret "not born of water
and of spirit" as meaning simply "a person born without any lymph fluid
in his body and without any human spirit."

3.6   A person is born physically of human parents, but
        he is born spiritually of the Spirit.

This verse is in the form of a general statement, similar to a
parable. A self-evident truth from everyday life is used to explain what
Jesus has just said.

In Greek verse 6 is literally "that which is born of the flesh is
flesh, and that which is born of the spirit is spirit." John is not contrasting two aspects of human nature. Rather, he is speaking of two
orders of existence, that of the physical world and that of the world
of the Spirit. So "the flesh" is best taken as a reference to human
parents, and "the spirit" as a reference to God's Spirit, who brings
about spiritual birth. Gdsp makes this explicit: "Whatever owes its
birth to the physical is physical, and whatever owes its birth to the
Spirit is spiritual." The entire verse is a kind of parable in which
Jesus makes an analogy between a familiar experience in this world and
that which happens in the realm where God's Spirit works: human parents
give life to their children, but only the Spirit can give spiritual life.

It is difficult in some languages to speak of something being
"born physically" or "born spiritually," because such abstracts as
"physically" or "spiritually" do not exist as adjectives or adverbs.
However, much the same type of meaning may be communicated in a different
form, for example, "Our human parents give birth to our bodies" or "A
man gets his body from his human parents" or "A man receives his body
from his father and mother." In a parallel manner one may say "the Spirit

of God gives birth to the spirit in us" or "...causes us to have spirit."
Or it may be possible to say "Our parents cause our body to have life,
but the Spirit of God causes our spirit to have life." Care must be taken
in the use of singular or plural in referring to "spirit" or "spirits" in
order not to suggest that each person has a number of different spirits.
Rather, there should be simply one spirit for each individual. This passage refers, of course, to man's spiritual nature or capacity.

3.7   Do not be surprised because I tell you that you
        must all be born again.[e]

    [e]again; *or* from above.

    Do not be surprised was an expression frequently used in everyday
Jewish life and by the rabbis. In John it expresses a negative attitude,
indicating lack of insight by the person addressed.
    The first you in this verse is singular, while the second you is
plural; for this reason TEV translates the second as you...all (note
also Phps, NEB, Mft). In Greek the clause is in direct discourse (I tell
you, "You..."), but the 4th edition TEV has shifted to indirect.
    Again is the same word used in verse 3, and it may also have the
meaning of "from above," as the alternative rendering in TEV suggests.
For the reasons mentioned earlier (see verse 4), it seems better to
translate again in the text and to use "from above" as an alternative
rendering. It may be advisable to include a note here, indicating the
ambiguity of meaning or explaining what may be thought of as a "play on
the meaning." The similarity of problems in meaning may be mentioned in
relation to both verses 4 and 7.

3.8   The wind blows wherever it wishes; you hear the
        sound it makes, but you do not know where it comes
        from or where it is going. It is like that with
        everyone who is born of the Spirit."

    In this verse there is a play on words which comes through in
Greek or in Hebrew but is difficult to bring out in English. In Greek,
as in Hebrew, the same word may mean either wind or "spirit." In this
context wind is the primary comparison, and so TEV and most other translations render it in that way. Some translations add a footnote, indicating that the word for wind may also mean "spirit" (BJ, JB, NEB, NAB,
Zür).
    Here, as in verse 6, Jesus is speaking in parables. He is drawing
an analogy between something that happens in this world (the freedom
of the wind to blow where it will), and what happens in the realm where
God's Spirit operates (the freedom of the Spirit to give spiritual birth
to whomever he will).
    In some languages it may be impossible to speak of an inanimate
force ("wind") as "wishing." The closest equivalent may be "The wind
blows in any and all directions" or "The wind blows now in one direction and then in another direction." In some receptor languages an

equivalent phrase would be "You never know from what direction the wind will be blowing."

Some languages have no noun for "wind" but only a verb "to blow," which refers to the movement of air through the atmosphere. The equivalent expression in such instances would be "There is blowing in any and all directions."

It is not even possible in some languages to speak of "the wind making a sound." The wind moves objects or comes in contact with objects and the objects make a noise. Note also that it is the wind that "comes" and "blows" and not the sound; but it may not be possible to speak of a wind coming or going, if such verbs are restricted to the movement of animate objects. An equivalent may be "You do not know from where it is blowing or to where it is blowing."

It is like that with everyone who is born of the Spirit may be rendered "This is just what happens with everyone to whom the Spirit gives birth," but it may be important to use a verb meaning "rebirth" or "gives new life to." Otherwise, the reference might be understood to be to some malevolent spirit giving supernatural birth to a person. The use of the fuller phrase "Holy Spirit" may remove this possible misinterpretation.

3.9   "How can this be?" asked Nicodemus.

Once again the technique of misunderstanding on the part of one to whom Jesus is speaking serves as a means of transition in the dialogue.

The question posed by Nicodemus How can this be? must refer not to all that Jesus says in verses 5-8 or even to all of verse 8, but to the final statement concerning the way in which one is born of the Spirit. In English, the demonstrative pronoun this does not specify how much of the preceding statement is questioned. In some languages it is important to indicate precisely what is involved, and therefore it may be necessary to indicate that it is "this last statement" which Nicodemus finds so difficult to understand.

3.10   Jesus answered, "You are a great teacher in Israel,
            and you don't know this?

Jesus answered (see 1.50; 2.18,19; 3.3).

You are a great teacher in Israel is literally "You are the teacher of Israel" (see Gdsp); the Greek text does not read "you are a teacher of Israel" (See RSV, Phps) or "you, a teacher in Israel" (Mft, JB). Commentators agree that the use of the definite article "the" before "teacher" is to emphasize the status and position of Nicodemus as a teacher in Israel (NEB "this famous teacher of Israel"; NAB "You hold the office of teacher of Israel"). A great teacher in Israel may be in some languages "an important teacher among the people of Israel" or "a teacher to whom many people of Israel look for teaching." The grammatical construction in Israel does not mean necessarily that Nicodemus was one who "taught Israel." The more probable meaning is that "among the people of Israel, Nicodemus was a famous teacher."

You don't know this? may be rendered in some languages "you do not understand this?" but in order to make it an exclamatory question, one may translate "and how is it possible that you do not understand this?" This is literally "these things," but the use of the singular or of the plural in the receptor language is purely a matter of style, so long as the antecedent is made clear.

3.11   I am telling you the truth: we speak of what we
        know and report what we have seen, yet none of you
        is willing to accept our message.

The shift from singular to plural should be carefully noted. The verse begins with the first person singular (I) addressing the second person singular (you). The shift is then made to the first person plural (we...our) addressing the second person plural (none of you). A number of theories exist as to why this shift is made, but the most probable solution is that John has shifted the time perspective from Jesus' day to the time in which he writes his Gospel. If so, then "we" represents the Christian believers of John's own day who are in dialogue with the Jews represented by "you (plural)." It is important for the translator to maintain the singular and plural contrast, and when using the first person plural to make it exclusive rather than inclusive. That is, in using the terms we and our, Jesus does not include Nicodemus.

As elsewhere, the expression I am telling you the truth may be rendered "What I am going to say to you now is certainly true."

The two expressions, we speak of what we know and report what we have seen, amount to essentially the same thing; in other words, each attests to what one has personally experienced and therefore knows. It may be necessary in some languages to indicate to whom "we" are speaking, for example, "We are speaking to you all about what we know, and we are telling you all what we ourselves have seen."

To accept our message is equivalent in a number of languages to "to believe what we say" or "to put confidence in what we declare."

3.12   You do not believe me when I tell you about
        the things of this world; how will you ever
        believe me, then, when I tell you about the
        things of heaven?

The things of this world (JB "things in this world"; NEB "things on earth") is literally "earthly things," and the things of heaven (so also NEB) is literally "heavenly things." The problem is to determine precisely what is intended by these expressions. The least complicated solution is to assume that the things of this world refers to the things that Jesus has already spoken to Nicodemus about, while the things of heaven points forward to what Jesus will now say to him. Jesus has drawn analogies between things that happen on earth and things that happen in the realm where God's Spirit operates, but Nicodemus has failed to perceive the spiritual truths of which Jesus is speaking. Now, without the use of earthly analogies, Jesus will speak directly to Nicodemus about

the things of heaven (perhaps verses 13-15). If the use of earthly analogies could not make Nicodemus understand and believe, how can he be
expected to believe when Jesus speaks directly about the things of
heaven?

It may be misleading to translate literally the things of this
world, which would be understood in many languages to refer merely to
particular physical objects. A more satisfactory equivalent may be "You
do not believe me when I tell you about happenings here in this world"
or "...what takes place here in this world" or "...what happens here on
earth." What follows must then be so translated as to provide the maxi-
mum of contrast; for example, "about happenings in heaven" or "about
what takes place in heaven."

You throughout this verse is plural, that is, "you all" and not
simply Nicodemus alone.

3.13   And no one has ever gone up to heaven except
                the Son of Man, who came down from heaven.

The purpose of this verse is to emphasize the heavenly origin of
the Son of Man. John is the only one of the Gospel writers to emphasize
this truth; it is basic to his theology. What gives the Son of Man his
authority is his heavenly origin. The Son of Man...came down from heaven
to tell men on earth about the things of heaven (verse 12). That is, the
coming of the Son of Man is an act of divine revelation. But more than
revelation is involved, as can be seen from the following verses--it is
also an act of self-giving which leads to the death of the Son of Man.

Some scholars maintain that the verb has gone up refers to the
Son of Man, and so implies that he had already ascended to heaven at
the time these words were written. That is, they assume that this verse
contains John's comments about the Son of Man and that it reflects the
post-resurrection theology of John, rather than the words of Jesus. It
is thus one way of explaining the use of the perfect tense (has gone
up).

However, the statement no one has ever gone up to heaven is possibly intended merely to deny that up to that time anyone had gone up
to heaven to learn about the things of heaven. If this is the meaning,
no reference to the ascension of the Son of Man is intended. Moreover,
just as the first half of the verse denies that anyone else knows about
the things of heaven, so the second half affirms that only the Son of
Man has knowledge about those things, because his origin is in heaven.
It is possible that the verse is intended to carry this meaning. However, in John's Gospel the verb tenses are not always those one would
expect, and it may be that the perfect tense here does not imply that
the Son of Man has already ascended to heaven. For example, in 4.38 the
past tense is used (TEV have sent) of an action which Jesus has not yet
done, according to the time sequence of the Gospel. For translation it
is suggested that the equivalent of a perfect tense (or even of a simple
past tense) be used for has gone up, without the implication of "has
gone up and is now there."

Verse 13 involves a number of subtle problems for the translator.
The use of the perfect tense "has gone up" would almost inevitably

indicate this was a reference to the resurrection, and therefore would tend to be interpreted as a prophecy or an interpolation by the Gospel writer. To avoid such an implication the phrase except the Son of Man can be translated "except for the Son of Man, who will go up to heaven." However, the focus of verse 13 is not on a future resurrection, but on the fact that the Son of Man has come down from heaven and is therefore in a position to reveal truth about God and his purposes for man's salvation. In order to indicate this contrast vividly and in order to avoid the implication of an anachronism, it is possible to translate "but the Son of Man has come down from heaven." Such a rendering avoids one difficulty by eliminating a possible interpretation. It seems best, however, simply to translate this verse, along with certain of its exegetical obscurities and ambiguities, and to leave the interpretation to commentators. Even though this solution might allow some slight confusion for the average reader, there is at least no serious distortion of the truth through a more or less "close translation."

There is also a textual problem in this verse. Some ancient manuscripts read "and no one has ever gone up to heaven except the one who came down from heaven, the Son of Man, who is in heaven." JB, NEB, Mft, and Zür all accept the words "who is in heaven" as a part of the original text. NAB, however, places them in brackets, and Zür and NEB both have a footnote, indicating the absence of these words from some manuscripts. The other translations which include them give no note (except Segond). This phrase occurs in a few Greek manuscripts, in the Latin, and in a few Syriac versions. The textual evidence in its favor is weak and diverse. Yet the phrase is so difficult that it is hard to see why any manuscript would include it if it were not an original part of the text. The UBS Committee on the Greek text supports the shorter reading because of the strong manuscript evidence. They believe that the words "who is in heaven" were added later as a further Christological interpretation of this verse.

| | TEV | (3.14-21) | RSV |

14 As Moses lifted up the bronze snake on a pole in the desert, in the same way the Son of Man must be lifted up, 15 so that everyone who believes in him may have eternal life. 16 For God loved the world so much that he gave his only Son, so that everyone who believes in him may not die but have eternal life. 17 For God did not send his Son into the world to be its judge, but to be its savior.

18 Whoever believes in the Son is not judged; but whoever does not believe has already been judged, because he has not believed in God's only Son. 19 This is how the judg-

14 And as Moses lifted up the serpent in the wilderness, so must the Son of man be lifted up, 15 that whoever believes in him may have eternal life."[h]

16 For God so loved the world that he gave his only Son, that whoever believes in him should not perish but have eternal life. 17 For God sent the Son into the world, not to condemn the world, but that the world might be saved through him. 18 He who believes in him is not condemned; he who does not believe is condemned already, because he has not believed in the name of the only Son of God. 19

ment works: the light has come into the world, but people love the darkness rather than the light, because their deeds are evil. 20 Anyone who does evil things hates the light and will not come to the light, because he does not want his evil deeds to be shown up. 21 But whoever does what is true comes to the light in order that the light may show that what he did was in obedience to God.	And this is the judgment, that the light has come into the world, and men loved darkness rather than light, because their deeds were evil. 20 For every one who does evil hates the light, and does not come to the light, lest his deeds should be exposed. 21 But he who does what is true comes to the light, that it may be clearly seen that his deeds have been wrought in God.

[h]Some interpreters hold that the quotation continues through verse 21

In Greek the speaker in these verses is not explicitly identified. Some scholars assume that the words are a continuation of Jesus' comments to Nicodemus, while others believe that at least part of this section is John's commentary on Jesus' words. Mft, Phps, JB, NEB, and NAB all attribute these words to Jesus, while RSV and Gdsp end Jesus' words with verse 15. Since Segond and the Luther Revised do not use quotation marks, it is difficult to tell precisely how they interpret this passage. Segond does indicate a break after verse 13, since he introduces 14-21 with a new section heading. Zür does not use quotation marks either, but it obviously takes the entire passage through verse 21 as the words of Jesus, since no paragraph break is introduced. TEV understands 14-21 to be the comments of the author of the Gospel.

3.14   As Moses lifted up the bronze snake on a pole in the desert, in the same way the Son of Man must be lifted up,

Lifted up the bronze snake on a pole translates "lifted up the snake." This verse refers to the actions of Moses described in Numbers 21.9. To translate "the snake" literally may leave a wrong impression with readers who have a limited knowledge of its biblical background. TEV, intended for persons less familiar with the Old Testament account than were John's readers, builds into its text information which makes explicit what Moses did. This solution is not adding to the text; it is merely an attempt to give present-day readers the same meaning that the original readers would have derived from the simple statement in John's text. This information was made clearly implicit for John's readers by use of the definite article "the" before "snake," referring to a known entity. The point of comparison is the lifting up; the Son of Man is not being compared to a snake. In John's Gospel the verb "to lift up" is used only of the Son of Man, and it always has a double point of reference--his being lifted up on the cross and his being lifted up to glory. Although the double reference is always present, each particular context has its specific emphasis, and the translator should attempt to see which aspect is in focus in any given verse. Here the lifting up on the cross is more nearly in focus than his being lifted up to glory.

Verse 14 involves a number of subtle problems in translation. For example, in translating lifted up it is necessary in some languages to distinguish between whether the bronze snake was lifted up and put on a pole, or whether it was attached to a pole and the pole lifted up. Ultimately, of course, the difference is not great, but if one wishes to maintain closely the analogy with the crucifixion, the second meaning will probably be preferred.

It may be difficult or awkward to translate precisely the meaning of bronze snake. It should be made clear that bronze was not simply the color of the snake or its name; the reference is to an "image of a snake made of bronze" or "...made of metal." It may be necessary to indicate that this metal snake was attached rigidly to a pole, either "nailed to a pole" or "tied to a pole."

It may be important to indicate as well the relationship of in the desert to on a pole. Was this a pole already existing in the desert, or did Moses lift up the bronze snake in a place which was desert? The second meaning is the correct one. Therefore in some languages the locative expression may better occur at the beginning of the clause; for example, "as in the desert Moses lifted up the bronze snake on a pole."

Must be lifted up does not mean that an obligation is imposed to lift up the Son of Man in a similar fashion. It is a statement of emphatic prophecy, and therefore the equivalent expression may be "the Son of Man will be lifted up in precisely that same way" or "it is certain that the Son of Man will be lifted up in just this same way."

3.15   so that everyone who believes in him may have eternal
            life.

This verse tells why the Son of Man must be lifted up; it is so that everyone who believes in him may have eternal life. TEV and most other modern translations take the phrase in him (Greek en autō) with the verb "to believe" and so render believes in him. A number of commentators point out that the preposition in (Greek en) is never elsewhere used in John's Gospel with the verb "to believe." The usual expression is literally "into him" (Greek eis auton). For this reason a few translations connect the phrase in him with eternal life rather than with believes. For example, JB reads "so that everyone who believes may have eternal life in him" (see also NAB, Zür). But in New Testament Greek the preposition eis ("into") is frequently used as an equivalent to the preposition en ("in"); and the construction "believes in (eis) him" is no more strange than "eternal life in (eis) him." NEB makes the object of faith explicit, while connecting the phrase in him with the idea of eternal life: "so that everyone who has faith in him may in him possess eternal life." If one is convinced that the phrase "in him" must be connected with the idea of eternal life, rather than that of believing, it may be necessary to render as NEB does, since some languages require that the object of faith be made explicit. NEB does not add to the text; it simply makes the object of faith explicit, while connecting "in him" with the concept of eternal life. For the one who believes,

eternal life is a present experience; he shares now in the life that
God gives. This idea, of course, does not exhaust the concept of eternal
life. Eternal life continues to be the possession of the believer, but
one strong emphasis in the Gospel of John is the present experience of
eternal life for those who believe.

The point has been made (see the comments on 1.4) that eternal life
is primarily qualitative; it describes the quality of life a man has
when God rules in his life. The phrase eternal life comes from a Hebrew
phrase, literally "life in the (coming) age." For the Hebrews "the
coming age" was the age in which God would destroy the power of sin and
evil in the world and set up his own rule of love and peace. In the
earliest notions of this coming age, it was probably not looked upon as
something that would never end; it was not "eternal" in our sense of the
word. However, there is no doubt that by New Testament times "life in the
age" was looked upon by many Jews as an everlasting experience. In the
New Testament it definitely has this meaning, even though the main emphasis is always on the quality of life one experiences when God rules his
life. That is, in the Gospel of John eternal life is basically qualitative, but it is also conceived of as life that never ends, because it
comes from God.

The indefinite relative clause everyone who believes in him may be
rendered in many languages as a conditional clause; for example, "if
anyone believes in him." It is also possible to express the meaning of
the indefinite relative clause by "all"; for example, "all who believe
in him." As noted in other contexts, believes in him involves far more
than mere intellectual assent. It is equivalent in most languages to
"puts his trust in him" or "shows complete loyalty to him" or, expressed
figuratively, "leans on him" or "hangs on him."

In many languages eternal is expressed as a negative, "that which
never ends," but it may be expressed positively as "that which goes on
and on." However, since the meaning of eternal life certainly involves
a qualitative distinction, and thus is not a matter of mere continued
existence, some translations employ such qualifiers as "real" or "new";
for example, "will have real life that never ends." Such a phrase tends
to focus upon the distinctive features of this new life in Christ, and
so helps to avoid the idea that those who believe in Jesus will simply
never die.

In some languages, however, there is no noun for "life." One must
employ some verbal expression, since life really does refer to an event
or state, and is not an object. In such languages one may be able to say
"really live unendingly" or "never come to the end of real living."

If one adopts the interpretation of "eternal life in him," it is
necessary to indicate that Jesus is the instrumentality or agent by which
this eternal life is possible. This meaning is expressed in many languages as a causative, for example, "will have unending life because of
him" or "he will cause such people to have unending life."

3.16   For God loved the world so much that he gave his only
                 Son, so that everyone who believes in him may not die
                 but have eternal life.

The purpose of this verse is to indicate that the work of Christ and the salvation he offers have their origin in the will and action of God himself.

In Greek, the tense of the verb loved points to a specific action in the past; that is, to God's giving of his Son.

Many languages have various words which may be translated "loved." They generally refer to different types of interpersonal relations: parents to children, children to parents, chiefs to people, people to chiefs, affection between spouses, sexual love, love of possessions, etc. It is convenient to have a term for "love" which may be applicable to many different interpersonal relations. When it is not possible, the usual practice is to refer to God's love as like that between parents and children. The equivalent meaning, therefore, is "God loved the people of the world just as a father loves his children." In some languages, the more appropriate term for this kind of affection would imply the love of a mother for her children, and this meaning likewise can often be adapted.

In this verse the world must be understood in the sense of "the world of men" (see 1.10).

The adverb translated so much in TEV refers more to the manner than the degree of love. That is, it would explain the way in which God showed his love for the world rather than the intensity or extent of his love, for example, "Here is the way that God loved the world: he gave his only Son..." However, almost all translations render this adverb as TEV does.

All modern translations read only Son rather than "only begotten Son" (KJV). This same word is discussed in 1.16.

The verb translated die (so also NEB, NAB) is a characteristic Johannine word. It is used in contrast to eternal life both here and in 10.28. In the theology of John's Gospel there is no third alternative; The final destiny of a man is either eternal life or eternal death. TEV translates this same verb was lost and be lost in 17.12.

It is important to indicate clearly that everyone who believes in him refers to the Son, not to God. It may be necessary in some languages to say specifically "everyone who believes in God's Son" or "if anyone puts his trust in God's Son."

There is probably no way of avoiding the difficulty in the expression may not die but have eternal life. It has been misinterpreted to imply that if people simply believed in Jesus they would never experience physical death. This meaning is not that intended by the Gospel of John. He does use here a bold rhetorical figure as a means of contrasting spiritual death with spiritual life. Any explanation of this contrast should be left to teaching or to a marginal note; it should not be introduced directly into the text.

3.17   For God did not send his Son into the world to be
      its judge, but to be its savior.

In form this verse is a typical Johannine structure: a remark introduced by the Greek conjunction gar ("for").

The verb send is parallel to the verb gave in the previous verse; these same two words are used of the Helper in 14.16,26.

TEV transforms the verb expression, "in order that he might judge the world," to a noun expression, to be its judge. In the following clause as well, a passive verb with an agent ("in order that the world might be saved through him") is changed to a noun expression: to be its savior. The basis for these changes is primarily stylistic: the nouns judge and savior are much easier for the ordinary reader to understand than is a long descriptive phrase. The Greek verb phrase that TEV renders by judge may have either the fairly neutral meaning "to judge" or the more severe meaning "to condemn" (JB, NAB). The same verb occurs several other times in John's Gospel, and on each occasion one must depend on the context to determine which meaning is in focus. In the present passage the idea of condemnation seems to be primary, as suggested by the contrast between savior and judge.

Though in English the use of the nouns judge and savior is stylistically preferable, in many receptor languages such nouns cannot be used. Thus it may be necessary to specify more clearly what "judge" really means--in this context "to condemn." The contrast may then be worded, "For God did not send his Son to earth in order to condemn people, but rather he sent him so that he could save people.

In some receptor languages it is difficult to find precisely the right term for savior or for "one who saves." Generally, the terms translated "to save" reflect two different kinds of situations or experiences. The first involves "rescuing from danger"; the second "restoring to health" or "re-establishing one's original state." In some languages a term for savior is roughly equivalent to "deliverer," that is, "one who frees from bondage." However, usually it is better to retain this type of term for use in contexts where deliverance is emphasized. Often a term is employed for savior which suggests one who rescues from danger, but there is a distinct advantage in using an expression which suggests "restoration" or "causing one to return to a state of complete wholeness." The focus then shifts from merely eliminating danger to the more positive aspect of restoring the full expression of potentialities.

3.18   Whoever believes in the Son is not judged; but
        whoever does not believe has already been judged,
        because he has not believed in God's only Son.

In the Son is literally "in him," but the pronominal reference is made explicit in order not to confuse "him" with God, also mentioned in the previous verse.

It is important to note the verb tenses used in this verse. The verb believes and the verb phrase is not judged are both in the present tense and so indicate that the believer is no longer under God's judgment. The expression does not believe is also in the present tense, but it is followed by two verbs in the perfect tense (already been judged... has not believed). The force of this construction is to emphasize the continuing effect of God's judgment on those who have refused to believe. That is, according to John's Gospel, eternal life is not only a hope of the future, but also a present reality; and so also God's judgment on a man's life begins here and now, whenever a man refuses to be obedient to God.

In God's only Son translates "in the name of God's only Son." See
the discussions at 1.14 and 14.13 for "only" and "name." JB has a note:
"Semitism: the 'name' is the person."

In some languages it is necessary to introduce the agent of judging.
It may also be necessary to change the indefinite relative clause whoever
believes in the Son into a conditional; for example, "If anyone believes
in the Son, God does not condemn him." This sentence may also be restructured: "God does not condemn those who believe in his Son." The
following clause may then be made parallel; for example, "but God has
already condemned those who do not believe in his Son." Such a translation tends to make superfluous the final clause because he has not
believed in God's only Son, but this clause may be made emphatic by
rendering "he condemns him precisely because he has not believed in his
only Son."

3.19   This is how the judgment works; the light has come
              into the world, but people love the darkness rather
              than the light, because their deeds are evil.

This verse continues the theme of judgment introduced in the two
preceding verses. If God sent his Son into the world to save the world,
why then are some men still under God's judgment? Verses 19 and 20 answer this question.

This is how the judgment works is literally "this is the judgment,"
which TEV takes to mean "This is how God judges the world," and so it
refers to the way in which God's judgment is accomplished. That is, God
sends his light...into the world, and the judgment is a natural outcome
of man's rejection of the light. NEB also takes this expression as a
reference to the way God brings about his judgment, and so translates
"Here lies the test." Although condemnation is an inevitable outcome of
the coming of the light into the world, the focus seems to be on the way
God judges the world, rather than on the resulting condemnation. However, NAB makes the aspect of condemnation explicit: "The judgment of
condemnation is this." JB reads "On these grounds is sentence pronounced," laying stress on the manner in which the judgment is accomplished and suggesting the nature of the sentence.

The meaning of this is how the judgment works may be expressed in
some languages as: "This is the basis on which God judges the world";
"This is how God decides whether people are guilty or innocent"; "This
is how God counts things up when he judges people" or "This is just how
God says you are innocent or you are condemned." In some languages it
may be necessary to be clear about distinctions in judging, and therefore a fuller expression may be required, for example, "This is how God
says to some people, You are innocent, and how he says to other people,
You are guilty."

The light has come into the world refers to a past action that has
a continuing effect in the present: the light has come and remains in
the world. It may be meaningless to say the light has come into the
world, for to some people it may mean merely that daybreak has come, or
that the sun is shining. Since, as noted in 1.5, light refers to the
truth about God, one can possibly say, "the light, as truth about God,

has come into the world," which would specify what is meant by light. When it is not possible to say "light as truth has come," one may say that people themselves are aware of such truth, for example, "People in the world have become acquainted with the light from God" or "...the light about God."

Love translates a Greek tense that would normally refer to an act in past time. This meaning is suggested by the past tense rendering of "loved" (RSV, NAB) and "preferred" (NEB). Or this same Greek tense can be used to describe events which habitually take place when people confront the light. This sense is conveyed by TEV and by JB "have shown they prefer" (see also Mft). Phps has "have preferred," and Gdsp, "have loved."

In some languages it is possible to preserve the figurative meaning of the clause but people love the darkness rather than the light by translating "but people love night rather than daylight." However, only rarely can the contrast between night and day also suggest the difference between evil and righteousness. Light is more than mere truth about God; it is the kind of truth which leads to moral or righteous behavior. Similarly, darkness is not merely the absence of knowledge, but the sin which proceeds from the rejection of truth. The figurative meanings in this sentence may therefore be expressed in some languages as "but people love the darkness of their sins rather than the light of truth about God" or "...the light which comes from God."

On the meaning of light and darkness, see 1.5. It is obvious that light here refers to God's revelation of himself, while darkness suggests the opposite.

The Greek expression that TEV renders rather than can also have the meaning "more than." In the present context it is obvious that the meaning is rather than, and nearly all modern translators render the expression in this way. The fact is not that men love darkness "more than" light, but rather that they love darkness rather than light. According to John's thinking, light and darkness are absolute categories, as are life and death.

Because their deeds are evil is similar in thought to 7.7. It may be both appropriate and necessary to introduce into the clause because their deeds are evil an expression indicating habitual action, roughly equivalent to "because they constantly do what is evil" or "since they habitually engage in evil actions."

3.20   Anyone who does evil things hates the light and
        will not come to the light, because he does not
        want his evil deeds to be shown up.

Anyone who does evil things is a Semitism, as is the contrasting expression in the following verse, whoever does what is true.

His evil deeds is literally "his deeds." Several Greek manuscripts do include "evil," but TEV includes this information on translational, rather than on textual grounds. That is, either TEV makes explicit the meaning of "deeds" in the context, or, more likely, the meaning of evil is derived from the verb (see below).

Having already suggested in the preceding verses that light

involves the revelation of truth, it may be possible in this verse to eliminate any specific identification or qualification for light; one may, for example, say "anyone who customarily does evil always hates the light of truth" or "...the light which reveals the truth." The following expression may then be translated "and he will not come to where there is this light."

The verb to be shown up (evil) is translated "to be shown up" by NEB also. Mft, Gdsp, Phps, RSV, JB, and NAB all have "to be exposed." The Greek verb itself (elencho) means, first, "to bring to light" or "to expose," and then "to convince/convict (someone) of something." Depending on the context, the meaning may be specifically either "to expose (something to be evil/wrong)" or "to convince/convict (someone) of something (evil/wrong). In 8.46 (see the comments there) the meaning is "to convict (of sin)," and so TEV renders prove...guilty of sin. In 16.8 (see the comments there), a very difficult passage, the same verb is used of the Holy Spirit who will "convict the world about sin," that is, will prove to the people of the world that they are wrong about sin. In the present passage no personal object is used; it is as in the other two passages where this verb occurs, and so the meaning is simply "to expose (as evil)." This meaning is apparently the basis for the rendering evil (deeds) to be shown up; though this rendering may also be supported by the observation that in the present context "deeds" are implicitly evil deeds.

The passive expression to be shown up may possibly be transformed into an active phrase by saying "because such a person does not want the light to reveal to others his evil deeds" or "...does not want the light to shine on his evil actions."

3.21   But whoever does what is true comes to the light in order that the light may show that what he did was in obedience to God.

As indicated under 1.14, "truth" is not an abstract idea in biblical thought. When the statement is made that God is true, it means basically that God is faithful. Accordingly, when the writer here speaks of persons who do what is true, he refers to those who continue in faithful obedience to God. Specifically, in the context of this verse, the idea is that of responding faithfully to the revelation of light that God has given concerning himself.

In some languages it makes little sense to say "to do what is true," for "truth" would relate only to some verbal formulation or statement and would not be applicable to a particular kind of deed. In such instances it is better to base a translation upon the meaning of this expression, for example, "whoever does what God says is right" or, better, "whoever obeys the truth, that is, God himself" or simply "whoever obeys God, who is true."

In some instances comes to the light may be more appropriately interpreted as "exposes himself to the light" or "lets the light shine on him." This meaning is more adequately expressed in some languages as "lets everyone see what he is doing." In this context, "light" is not to be interpreted abstractly, but as providing the means by which a

[93]

man's deeds may be seen. This meaning is made particularly clear in the second half of this verse.

In order that the light may show that what he did was in obedience to God is literally "in order that it might be shown that his works have been worked in God." TEV makes explicit the agent of the passive verb "that it might be shown" and changes to an active construction, that the light may show. The idea of "doing work in God" sounds to the English reader like a spatial relationship. TEV avoids this idea by the rendering that what he did was in obedience to God. NEB has "that God is in all he does." The idea either of obedience to God or "union with God" is a legitimate interpretation of this verse, but such pitfalls as the rendering found in JB, "what he does is done in God" or RSV, "his deeds have been wrought in God," should be avoided, since the phrase "in God" is at best a zero meaning for the average reader of English.

What he did was in obedience to God must undergo a certain amount of restructuring in some languages, for example, "he did what he did because he was obedient to God" or "what he did showed that he was obeying God."

| | TEV | (3.25-30) | RSV |

JESUS AND JOHN

22 After this, Jesus and his disciples went to the province of Judea, where he spent some time with them and baptized. 23 John also was baptizing in Aenon, not far from Salim, because there was plenty of water in that place. People were going to him, and he was baptizing them. (24 This was before John had been put in prison.)

25 Some of John's disciples began arguing with a Jew^f about the matter of ritual washing. 26 So they went to John and told him, "Teacher, you remember the man who was with you on the east side of the Jordan, the one you spoke about? Well, he is baptizing now, and everyone is going to him!"

27 John answered, "No one can have anything unless God gives it to him. 28 You yourselves are my witnesses that I said, 'I am not the Messiah, but I have been sent ahead of him.' 29 The bridegroom is the one to whom the bride be-

22 After this Jesus and his disciples went into the land of Judea; there he remained with them and baptized. 23 John also was baptizing at Aenon near Salim, because there was much water there; and people came and were baptized. 24 For John had not yet been put in prison.

25 Now a discussion arose between John's disciples and a Jew over purifying. 25 And they came to John, and said to him, "Rabbi, he who was with you beyond the Jordan, to whom you bore witness, here he is, baptizing, and all are going to him." 27 John answered, "No one can receive anything except what is given him from heaven. 28 You yourselves bear me witness, that I said, I am not the Christ, but I have been sent before him. 29 He who has the bride is the bridegroom; the friend of the bridegroom, who stands and hears him, rejoices greatly at the bridegroom's voice; therefore this joy of mine is now full. 30 He must increase but I

longs; but the bridegroom's friend, who stands by and listens, is glad when he hears the bridegroom's voice. This is how my own happiness is made complete. 30 He must become more important while I become less important."

must decrease."[i]

[i]Some interpreters hold that the quotation continues through verse 36.

[f]a Jew; *some manuscripts have* some Jews.

This section has only a loose chronological connection with the preceding passages. (After this is equivalent to the expression used in 2.12). Though perhaps not immediately apparent, the theme of this section is how people flock to Jesus and become his disciples. The working out of this theme is accomplished by showing the superiority of Jesus over John the Baptist. When this Gospel was written, there were persons who called themselves disciples of John the Baptist and claimed that he was superior to Jesus. This fact perhaps accounts for the concern in the Fourth Gospel to point out clearly the unique role of John the Baptist, and at the same time to emphasize that it is Jesus, not John, who is the Messiah.

The section heading, Jesus and John, may suggest in some languages a joint activity of Jesus and John. Such an idea would provide a wrong basis for identifying the content of this section, and therefore some modifications may be made, for example, "John speaks about Jesus," "John tells about how Jesus is more important" or "Jesus is compared with John."

3.22   After this, Jesus and his disciples went to the province of Judea, where he spent some time with them and baptized.

The precise meaning of the Greek phrase "the land of Judea" (TEV the province of Judea) is not clear. Some believe that this phrase implies that Jesus left the city of Jerusalem to go into the country regions of Judea (so JB "into the Judean countryside"). But it seems more probable that the phrase refers to the Judean territory in general (NAB "into Judean territory"; Gdsp, Phps, "the country of Judea"), and not specifically to the Judean countryside; this interpretation is given in TEV. Because of the chronological problems occasioned by this verse, Mft places 22-25 after 2.12, but there is no textual evidence to support this alteration.

The verb translated spent some time (Greek diatribō) is not the usual verb that John uses when speaking of Jesus in this way (Greek menō). In fact only in this verse in this Gospel is this particular verb used. However, the two verbs have the same meaning. It is difficult, of course, to estimate the amount of time involved in such an expression as some time. Since, however, in some languages, one must clearly distinguish whether it means a few days, a few weeks, or several months, it is better to select the expression roughly equivalent to "several weeks."

The tense of the Greek verb translated baptized suggests repeated or habitual action. This verse states explicitly that Jesus himself baptized; it does not imply that Jesus' disciples baptized on his authority, while Jesus himself did not baptize. Any attempt to harmonize this verse with 4.2 would be unwarranted, for here John states explicitly that Jesus himself did baptize. It may be necessary to indicate clearly some goal to the action baptized, and therefore one may say "baptized people." It may likewise be necessary to introduce a goal to the verb baptizing in the following verse (verse 23). See comments at 1.25 for a further discussion of baptism.

3.23   John also was baptizing in Aenon, not far from Salim, because there was plenty of water in that place. People were going to him, and he was baptizing them.

Aenon, not far from Salim cannot be identified with certainty. One ancient tradition locates these places on the west bank of the Jordan River, about eight miles south of the town of Scythopolis. It is thought by others that if this were the location intended, it would be unnecessary to mention that there was plenty of water in that place. Some scholars even take these names to be symbolic, and such an interpretation is possible, but it seems more probable that the Fourth Gospel intends actual places.

People were going to him, and he was baptizing them is literally "and they were going and they were being baptized." All commentators understand "they" in both occurrences to refer to the people of that region, and to him (that is, "to John") is implied in the sentence construction. TEV makes this information explicit and further transforms the second of these verbs from a passive to an active construction: he was baptizing them.

3.24   (This was before John had been put in prison.)

This verse is best taken as a parenthetical statement by the author of the Gospel. A number of translations, including TEV, place the verse in curved brackets. The verse seems intended to give a background for verse 30.

There may be problems of tense sequence in the parenthetical expression This was before John had been put in prison. An equivalent may be "John was only later put in prison" or "Up to this time John was still not in prison."

3.25   Some of John's disciples began arguing with a Jew[f] about the matter of ritual washing.

[f]a Jew; *some manuscripts have* some Jews.

A strong term such as "argument" (NEB, Mft "dispute"; NAB "controversy") should be chosen to describe what happened between John's disciples and this man; "discussion" (Gdsp, JB) or "question" (Phps) is too weak.

For a Jew some manuscripts read plural, "Jews," as TEV footnote indicates. Both readings are supported by strong ancient manuscript evidence, but the singular is the more difficult reading. Since John regularly uses the plural and since the singular causes a problem in the present context, it is easy to see why a scribe would change from the singular to the plural, but not the other way around. For this reason, most modern translators consider "a Jew" to be the original reading.

About the matter of ritual washing is literally "concerning purification." Although commentators are divided in their opinions as to the precise reference involved, it seems best to take this expression as referring to the matter of Jewish purification in general (it is used in this sense in 2.6), rather than as reflecting a controversy about the relative value of the baptisms performed by Jesus and John the Baptist. TEV takes it as a reference to Jewish purification in general, and at the same time makes clear to its readers that a kind of ritual washing is meant.

In some instances ritual washing may be translated as "religious washing" or "the kind of washing one does in his religion" or "...because of his religion." However, this phrase may also be expanded in some languages as "washing to make one religiously pure" or "washing to eliminate taboo." However, it is possible to avoid specific reference to "washing" by saying "how one becomes clean from taboo" or "how one removes taboo." Note, however, that in these instances "taboo" must be understood in terms of "negative taboo," that is, defilement from contact with unclean objects or events. In some instances, one may actually translate "how one may remove uncleanness." However, this expression is likely to be understood only in the sense of "washing away dirt."

3.26   So they went to John and told him, "Teacher, you
          remember the man who was with you on the east
          side of the Jordan, the one you spoke about? Well,
          he is baptizing now, and everyone is going to him!"

In Greek the subject of the verbs went and told is not clear. It could be taken in an impersonal sense, "people went to John and told him." However, it seems better to take it as referring back to some of John's disciples.

Teacher (literally "Rabbi") is the same word of address used of Jesus in 1.38.

You remember the man who was with you on the east side of the Jordan is literally "he who was with you on the other side of the Jordan." In Greek this expression represents a stylistic way of calling attention to a person already known by both the speaker and the person addressed. TEV tries to reflect the conversational style of this verse. In English one way of accomplishing it is to introduce the statement by "You remember..." NEB handles this matter on a more formal basis by rendering "Rabbi, there was a man with you on the other side of the Jordan..."

[97]

The one you spoke about is literally "to whom you have given witness." As indicated earlier (1.7), the theme of "witness" is basic to John's Gospel. It should be noted that the verb spoke about is in the perfect tense, indicating the continuing effect of John's witness to Jesus. NAB attempts to capture this aspect of the Greek tense by rendering "the one about whom you have been testifying." NEB and several other translations reproduce a pure biblicism, "to whom you bore your witness." This expression may be rendered idiomatically in some languages as "That man who was with you on the other side of the Jordan, that one you spoke about, well, he is baptizing people now..."

Well, he (NEB "here he is") is an attempt to bring out the force of the emphatic Semitic expression "behold this one." The adverb now is introduced by TEV to bring out the emphatic nature of the present tense in this verse. The force of what these people are saying to John the Baptist is that the one about whom John spoke so highly is now baptizing, and so he is in competition with John. Not that Jesus was really working in competition with John the Baptist or that John was competing with Jesus, but evidently John's disciples felt this way about it. JB translates in a similar way, "the man...is baptizing now."

If the receptor language has a tendency to understand "everyone" in an absolute sense, it would be wrong to say "everyone is going to him." Obviously, there were still people who were going to John and whom he was baptizing. An equivalent expression for the last clause in verse 26 would be "people are now flocking to him" or "many, many people are now going to him."

3.27   John answered, "No one can have anything unless
        God gives it to him.

John answered translates a Hebraism which is redundant for the English reader (literally "John answered and said").

Unless God gives it to him is literally "unless it has been given to him from heaven." But "from heaven" is merely a Semitic way of speaking of God, and so TEV makes the information explicit, at the same time transforming the passive expression into an active one. NEB does likewise ("a man can have only what God gives him"), while Phps attempts to reproduce the meaning by spelling "Heaven" with a capital H. In 19.11 the adverb "from above" is used in the same sense, and in TEV this phrase appears as by God.

Some difficulties may be involved in a literal translation of verse 27, since anything seems to refer specifically to objects, while the reference in this particular context may be to events, that is, the popularity of Jesus as demonstrated by throngs of people who went to be baptized by him. To indicate specifically that the reference here is to an event, one may say, "Nothing can happen to anyone like this unless God causes it."

3.28   You yourselves are my witnesses that I said, 'I
        am not the Messiah, but I have been sent ahead
        of him.'

You yourselves is emphatic in the Greek sentence. The reference is perhaps to the disciples of John the Baptist, though others may also be included.

You yourselves are my witnesses may be rendered "you yourself heard me say" or "you yourself can declare what I said." For further comments on the meaning of "witness," see the discussion on 1.7.

For the statement I am not the Messiah, see 1.20.

The agent of the passive expression I have been sent is God; that is, "God has sent me."

The phrase ahead of him may be understood in purely spatial terms, but the significance here is essentially temporal, that is, "God sent me before he came along" or "God sent me earlier than Jesus."

3.29   The bridegroom is the one to whom the bride belongs; but
          the bridegroom's friend, who stands by and listens, is
          glad when he hears the bridegroom's voice. This is how
          my own happiness is made complete.

The bridegroom's friend is the nearest equivalent to the "best man" (NAB) of our day. This expression is not a technical term in Greek, but represents the "shoshben" of Jewish life. The "shoshben" was the groom's closest friend and he took care of arranging the particulars of the wedding. In the context the primary focus is on John the Baptist, rather than on the bridegroom in the parable-like saying.

The bridegroom is the one to whom the bride belongs may be inverted ("the bride belongs to the bridegroom"). This clause may then form a contrast to the following clause, and one may translate "but the bridegroom's friend stands by and listens, and he is glad..."

The exact picture portrayed by the words stands by and listens is not known. It is possible that the best man is standing guard at the brides's house, waiting for the groom's procession to arrive. On the other hand, it is possible that this expression describes the experience of the best man after the bride has been brought to the groom's home. That is, he is happy to hear the bride and groom speaking joyfully with each other. In any case, the translator must be careful not to suggest any deed of impropriety on the part of the bridegroom's friend when translating stands by and listens.

Is glad when he hears the bridegroom's voice translates a Semitism, "with joy he rejoices because of the voice of the bridegroom." This sentence may be rendered "He is happy when he hears what the bridegroom says" or "...hears the bridegroom speak."

This is how my own happiness is made complete is literally "This, therefore, my happiness has been made full." Most modern English translations render "full" by complete. Elsewhere in the Gospel this same verb is used to describe happiness (15.11; 16.24; 17.13). This is how refers back to the previous statement, not to the following one. In some languages it is impossible to speak about "happiness made complete." One can, however, say "Because of this I am extremely happy" or "...completely happy" or "Because of this there is nothing lacking in my happiness."

3.30   He must become more important while I become less
        important."

NAB and certain other translations render this verse literally:
"he must increase, while I must decrease." In the present context the
meaning of "increase" is taken to mean become more important, while the
meaning of "decrease" is become less important. NEB reads "As he grows
greater I must grow less," which can be ambiguous. However, the meaning
may be "to increase the number of disciples." If so, one could translate:
"He must win more and more followers, while the number of my followers
will decrease."

A literal translation of "He must increase and I must decrease" can
be misunderstood, since it may be taken to refer to differences of physical size. As noted in 1.30, greatness must be considered in terms of
importance--an interpretation which often leads to metaphorical exten-
sions of meaning.

In this context the auxiliary must may be rendered in some languages
as equivalent to "it is inevitable that," but in other languages the
closest equivalent may be "it will surely be." Must renders a verb
commonly used in the New Testament to indicate divine necessity; the
same verb is used in verse 14.

                TEV   (3.31-36)   RSV

    HE WHO COMES FROM HEAVEN

    31 He who comes from above is   31 He who comes from above is
greater than all.\He who is from   above all; he who is of the earth
the earth belongs to the earth and   belongs to the earth, and of the
speaks about earthly matters, but   earth he speaks; he who comes from
he who comes from heaven is above   heaven is above all. 32 He bears
all. 32 He tells what he has seen   witness to what he has seen and
and heard, yet no one accepts his   heard, yet no one receives his
message. 33 But whoever accepts   testimony; 33 he who receives his
his message confirms by this that   testimony sets his seal to this,
God is truthful. 34 The one whom   that God is true. 34 For he whom
God has sent speaks God's words,   God has sent utters the words of
because God gives him the fullness   God, for it is not by measure that
of his Spirit. 35 The Father loves   he gives the Spirit; 35 the Father
his Son and has put everything in   loves the Son, and has given all
his power. 36 Whoever believes in   things into his hand. 36 He who
the Son has eternal life; whoever   believes in the Son has eternal
disobeys the Son will not have   life; he who does not obey the Son
life, but will remain under God's   shall not see life, but the wrath
punishment.   of God rests upon him.

Once again the translator is faced with the problem of identifying
the speaker (see comments at 3.14-21), and there are three possible
choices. (1) It may be John the Baptist, since he was the last speaker
clearly identified (verses 27-30). If this is the case, then John the
Baptist is continuing the contrast between himself and Jesus begun in

verse 30. Phps, JB, and Luther Revised (Lu) all attribute these words to John the Baptist as the speaker, but a footnote cites the problem involved and concludes "Perhaps an originally independent discourse of Jesus has been brought here by way of comment on the two preceding scenes of chapter 3."

(2) Some scholars assume that Jesus is the intended speaker, basing their conclusions on the observation that the style of this passage closely resembles the language of Jesus elsewhere in this Gospel, especially in the dialogue with Nicodemus. Attention has been called to the NAB footnote which points in this direction; Anchor Bible (Anc) accepts the same conclusion. Mft also assumes this to be the case, but he inserts verses 31-36 immediately after verse 21; making them a part of the same discourse.

(3) Finally, it is possible that these words are the comments of the author of the Gospel. This is the opinion held by TEV, NEB, RSV, and Gdsp. If this is the case, there is a parallel between verses 14-21 (or 16-21) and the present passage. That is, the earlier section represents the author's commentary on Jesus' dialogue with Nicodemus, while this passage serves as a commentary on the relationship between Jesus and John the Baptist. It is impossible to tell what Zür intends, since it uses no quotation marks, but it does introduce a new paragraph at verse 31.

If it is assumed that Jesus is the speaker in this section, certain complications are involved in languages in which a third person reference cannot be used when an idividual speaks about himself. Such receptor languages require the shift from "he" to "I," but such a shift would produce a number of difficulties in this paragraph. It is probably more satisfactory, therefore, to assume that either John the Baptist or the writer of the Gospel is the source of this statement.

The section heading, He Who Comes from Heaven, may make an awkward statement in some receptor languages, especially if section headings normally require complete statements. One can, of course, use "The One from heaven is above all" or "The One from heaven speaks God's words."

3.31 He who comes from above is greater than all.
    He who is from the earth belongs to the earth and
    speaks about earthly matters, but he who comes from
    heaven is above all.

From above translates the same word rendered again in verse 3 (see the comments there). In the present context it obviously means from above and refers to heaven, as the contrast between heaven and earth indicates. In many receptor languages it is better to be specific in rendering the phrase from above, that is, "he who comes from heaven."

Greater than all and above all translate exactly the Greek phrases. In both the meaning is the same, that is, above all in the sense of greater than all. The Greek word translated all can be either neuter or masculine, but in the present passage it is probably better taken as masculine, contrasting Jesus with all other people. In translating greater than all and above all it is probably best to indicate precisely what the reference is, that is, "greater than all people" or "above all other persons." In some languages it is probably better to use the same expression each time, rather than to shift between "greater than all" and "above all."

A literal translation of the second half of verse 31 gives rise to serious complications. It may suggest, as it actually does in some languages, that the one who is "from the earth" really comes from demonic powers. This difficulty occurs in some of the languages of Latin America, where an expression rendered literally "from the earth" suggests association with the devil. An equivalent expression in some languages is "he who is from this world below." Belongs to the earth may be rendered "is typical of those who are in this world" and speaks about earthly matters may be rendered "speaks about things which happen here in this earth."

Although in John's Gospel the term world often signifies opposition to God, the word earth is neutral, and merely contrasts the created order with the Creator. Jesus is the one who comes from above, while John the Baptist is the one who is from the earth. To signify that John the Baptist is from the earth is not to intimate that he is evil, but rather to stress the contrast between one who belongs to the natural order and one who comes from above.

Note that the final sentence, He who comes from heaven is above all, is identical with the first clause of the verse. The repetition is essentially for emphasis. In order to avoid repetition and to indicate clearly the emphatic character of this second sentence, it may be possible to combine the two statements and translate "The one who comes from heaven is indeed above everyone else."

Toward the end of this verse there is a textual problem. In the Greek text followed by TEV, the words above all are included as a part of the text, and a full stop is placed at the end of the verse. However, it is possible that above all was not an original part of the text. If it was not, the last part of verse 31 and the first part of verse 32 must read "He who comes from heaven tells what he has seen and heard." The manuscript evidence is about equally balanced, and good arguments can be made for either the inclusion or the omission of above all. Accordingly, the UBS Committee on the Greek text decided to retain the words, but to enclose them within square brackets. TEV, RSV, Zür, Gdsp, and Mft include these words as part of the text and make a full stop after verse 31. Lu, Phps, and Segond also include them, but do not place a full stop at the end of the verse (Lu "He who comes from heaven is above all and testifies to what he has seen and heard"). NAB includes the words in brackets. JB and NEB omit them, but have a footnote indicating that some manuscripts include them.

3.32   He tells what he has seen and heard, yet no one
        accepts his message.

Has seen translates a Greek perfect tense; heard translates an aorist tense. On the basis of this difference of tenses, some scholars maintain that the emphasis is on "seeing" rather than on "hearing." However, not all scholars take this position. It is quite likely that no distinction in emphasis should be made here. In 1 John 1.3 both verbs are used in the perfect tense, and the two passages are probably parallel in meaning.

The implication of he tells what he has seen and heard is that "he tells what he has seen and heard in heaven." Compare 3.11-13.

He tells is literally "he gives witness concerning"; message is literally "witness." On the meaning of these terms, see 1.7. No one accepts his message may be rendered "no one believes what he has said" or "no one puts confidence in what he has to say."

3.33   But whoever accepts his message confirms by this
       that God is truthful.

Message is again literally "witness" (see 1.7).

Confirms by this is more literally rendered in RSV "sets his seal to this." This same verb is used of God in 6.27, where TEV translates it has put his mark of approval on. The metaphor used is that of placing a seal on a legal document, thus indicating approval. In NEB this entire phrase is translated "to attest that God speaks the truth." JB has "attesting the truthfulness of God." NAB translates "certifies that God is truthful." Gdsp has "acknowledged that God is true," and Phps, "acknowledging the fact that God is true." Mft translates "certifies to the truth of God."

In the present passage it is difficult to determine precisely what is meant by the statement God is truthful. In the context of the Old Testament, such a statement would normally mean that "God is faithful (to what he has said he would do)." On the other hand, in this context the meaning may be "that what God has said is true" (see, for example, NEB), and so one may translate "Whoever accepts his message has shown by this that he has accepted the message of God as true." This translation suits the context well, especially the verse following. This meaning may also be expressed as follows: "If anyone trusts his message, he shows that he has believed that what God has said is true."

3.34   The one whom God has sent speaks God's words,
       because God gives him the fullness of his Spirit.

This verse gives the basis for Jesus' authority: he is the one whom God has sent. Has sent (so also JB and NAB) is: "sent" in many translations. The Greek verb tense is aorist, and therefore may focus attention on the initial act of sending; if so, then the better rendering may be "sent" rather than has sent.

In saying the one whom God has sent speaks God's words, it is important to avoid the impression that Jesus is simply "mimicking God." The focus here is not on the particular manner of pronunciation, but on the content of the message. It is therefore appropriate to translate "The one whom God has sent speaks the message that comes from God" or "...delivers God's message."

Because God gives him the fullness of his Spirit is literally "for he gives the spirit not by measure." The phrase "not by measure" is often used in Rabbinic writings, where it has the meaning of "completely" or "fully." TEV transforms this adverbial expression into a noun and renders it the fullness; NEB makes it into an adjective, "so measureless is God's gift of the Spirit," and Phps into a verb, "there can be no measuring of the Spirit given to him."

In Greek the subject of the verb gives is ambiguous, and no indirect object (one to whom the Spirit is given) is indicated. Some scholars hold that Jesus is the subject of the verb gives, which would mean that the indirect object would be "those who believe in Jesus." In support of this view is the argument that 6.63 forms a good parallel to this verse. In 6.63 it is Jesus who speaks words that bring God's lifegiving Spirit. Moreover, in 15.26 Jesus says that he will send the Spirit. On the other hand, God is elsewhere spoken of as the one who sends the Spirit (14.26), and several ancient scribes have added either "God," "the Father," or "God the Father" as the subject of the verb gives in 3.34. On the basis of the verse following it seems that this conclusion is correct and several translations make this meaning explicit (Gdsp, NEB, JB). It is God who gives the Spirit, and in the context he gives it to the one whom he has sent, that is, to the Son. This interpretation makes good sense of the passage, and adds strength to the argument regarding the source of Jesus' authority.

In many languages it is meaningless to speak about "the fullness of the Spirit." The concept of fullness can be expressed only in terms of "completeness," that is, "because God gives his Spirit to him completely." However, in some languages "completeness" is expressed as a negation of "lack," that is, "There is no lack in the manner in which God gives his Spirit to him." In some languages it is impossible to speak about "giving the Spirit," since the Spirit does not belong to the class of objects which can be given, in the sense of passing from one person to another. However, one may say "he causes his Spirit to come upon" or "he makes his Spirit live in."

3.35   The Father loves his Son and has put everything
          in his power.

The first part of this verse and the first part of 5.20 are almost identical, the Father loves the Son, but a different verb is used for "love" in each of the two passages. The Greek verb used in 3.35 is agapaō, and in 5.20 it is phileō. At one time it was customary for scholars to differentiate between the use of these two verbs in John's Gospel, but most scholars now agree that there is no distinction in meaning between them. There is certainly no distinction in these two verses. When translating either of the verbs for "love," one should remember that the primary focus in the biblical concept of love is always that of giving rather than of receiving. One loves another for the sake of benefiting the one he loves, rather than for the sake of receiving benefit from the object of his love. See the discussion of "love" at 3.16.

The verb loves is in the present tense and indicates that the Father constantly and always loves his Son.

It is impossible in many languages to translate "the Father," for such kinship terms as "father," "son," "mother," etc., must occur with some kind of possessive and imply a relation, for example, "his father," "my father," "our father," etc.--not "the father." Since in this context

"the Father" is a substitute for "God," some translators simply say
"God loves his Son." This solution is, of course, the easiest one, but
it does not adequately reflect the meaning of verse 35. In some languages
the expression "our Father" (using "our" in the inclusive first person
plural form) is frequently used as a substitute for "God," and in such
languages an appropriate equivalent would be "our Father loves his Son."
To make this meaning more explicit, some languages require "our Father
God loves his Son."

Has put (perfect tense in Greek) suggests that what has been put in
the Son's power remains within his power. The phrase in his power translates a Semitic expression (literally "in his hand"); JB has simply "to
him" and NAB "over to him."

Has put everything in his power may be rendered in some languages
"has given him control over everything" or, in the causative sense,
"has caused him to have power over everything" or "...to control everything" or "has caused that he may command everything."

3.36   Whoever believes in the Son has eternal life;
            whoever disobeys the Son will not have life,
            but will remain under God's punishment.

The meaning of the verb believes (see 2.24-25) and the concept of
eternal life (see 1.4 and 3.15) have been discussed. It is important to
notice in the present verse that the possession of eternal life is looked
upon as a present experience of the believer (has eternal life).

Disobeys occurs only here in John's Gospel; it is obviously the opposite of believes, and so JB and Phps translate "refuses to believe."
It is possible to argue that the meaning of disobeys throws some light
on the meaning of believes, that is, this kind of belief is the belief
which leads to obedience. Therefore one may translate "Whoever obeys
the Son has eternal life, and whoever disobeys the Son will never have
life." However, it is better to retain the terms "believes" and "disobeys," since the very lack of clear opposition tends to reinforce the
meaning of the respective terms.

Will not have is literally "will not see." However, the verb
"to see" is used here in the sense of "to experience" (Gdsp "will not
experience life"), as it is used in 3.3. The second time that life
occurs in 3.36 it means eternal life. Will not have life may be so
translated as to refer to the distinctive quality of life implied in
"eternal life," for example, "will not have real life" or "will not
really live."

But will remain under God's punishment is literally "but the wrath
of God remains on him." The force of the present tense, "remains," indicates not only that God's wrath is presently upon the person who disobeys the Son, but also that the punishment will continue. This fact is
emphasized in the TEV rendering will remain under.

The traditional rendering, "God's wrath," does not refer primarily
to God's feelings (as might be suggested by such a translation as "God's
anger"). Rather, it refers to God's action in judging and punishing men
for their sins. A literal translation of "wrath" too often suggests that
God is attempting to get even with those who oppose him. The shift from

[105]

the traditional term "wrath" to "God's punishment" is not intended to eliminate reference to God's stern opposition to sin but rather to focus upon the primary component in the meaning of "wrath," namely, the fact of judgment. However, it is extremely difficult to translate such a phrase as will remain under God's punishment. This expression is commonly rendered "will continue to be punished by God" or "God will continue to punish him." The use of such an auxiliary as "continue" suggests both a present activity and a future continuation of an event.

CHAPTER 4

JESUS AND THE SAMARITAN WOMAN

4 The Pharisees heard that Jesus was winning and baptizing more disciples than John. (2 Actually, Jesus himself did not baptize anyone; only his disciples did.) 3 So when Jesus heard what was being said, he left Judea and went back to Galilee; 4 on his way there he had to go through Samaria.

5 In Samaria he came to a town named Sychar, which was not far from the field that Jacob had given to his son Joseph. 6 Jacob's well was there, and Jesus, tired out by the trip, sat down by the well. It was about noon.

4 Now when the Lord knew that the Pharisees had heard that Jesus was making and baptizing more disciples than John 2(although Jesus himself did not baptize, but only his disciples), 3 he left Judea and departed again to Galilee. 4 He had to pass through Samaria, 5 So he came to a city of Samaria, called Sychar, near the field that Jacob gave to his son Joseph. 6 Jacob's well was there, and so Jesus, wearied as he was with his journey, sat down beside the well. It was about the sixth hour.

In the preceding two chapters (2 and 3) John has shown that Jesus is not only superior to the orthodox Jewish faith but is its fulfillment. Now John indicates that Jesus is also the true fulfillment of heretical Judaism, represented by the Samaritan faith (1-42). Thematically this section is related to both what precedes and what follows. Chapters 2 and 3 mention water (2.6-9; 3.5); here Jesus is portrayed as the source of life-giving water. Moreover, the mention of food in verses 32 and 34 points forward to a further mention of food in 6.27, 55. In each of these passages spiritual food is contrasted with the food of this world.

Verses 1-4 serve as a transition from Chapter 3, and verses 5-6 provide the setting for the narrative. The main body of this section consists of two scenes, a dialogue between Jesus and the Samaritan woman (7-26) and a dialogue between Jesus and his disciples (27-38). Verses 39-42 conclude both scenes and tie them together. In this conclusion the Samaritan woman is again mentioned, but it is shown that the faith of the Samaritans is based, not on her testimony, but on their own discovery that Jesus really is the Savior of the world.

The theme of verses 7-15 is living water. Jesus initiates the discussion by asking the woman to give him a drink of water (7). She remarks that by doing so he has defied the customs which prohibited association between Jews and Samaritans. Jesus replies that she does not recognize the one who is speaking to her, for if she did, she would ask him for the living water. Verses 11 and 12 are an indication that the woman has misunderstood, for she assumes both that Jesus is speaking of physical water and that Jacob is greater than Jesus. Jesus then explains that he is speaking of the water of eternal life (13-14), to which the woman responds by asking him to give her this water (15).

In verses 16-26 the theme shifts to that of true worship. Jesus again takes the initiative by giving the woman a command related to her own personal life (16). She gives a deceptive answer (17), which gives Jesus an opportunity to uncover further her sinful condition (18). In 19-20 the woman tries to draw attention away from herself by bringing up the matter of the proper place of worship, by indicating the true nature of worship (21-24). From his words, the woman begins to recognize who Jesus really is (25-26).

Verses 27-30 set the stage for the next section (31-38), a dialogue between Jesus and his disciples. Their misunderstanding about food (31-34) parallels the woman's misunderstanding about water in the previous scene. From the discussion about food the topic is enlarged to that of the harvest, and a parallel is drawn between the earthly and the spiritual harvests (35-38).

Though in many languages the title Jesus and the Samaritan Woman is entirely clear and acceptable, it may be misleading in some other languages. It may suggest, for example, that Jesus was somehow related to the woman of Samaria or that he and she together were joint agents in some activity. In such circumstances it is better to make explicit the relation between Jesus and the woman of Samaria by saying "Jesus meets with..." or "Jesus talks with a woman from Samaria."

4.1   The Pharisees heard that Jesus was winning and
           baptizing more disciples than John.

In Greek, verses 1-3 are one sentence, which begins with the clause that TEV introduces as the first part of verse 3 (When Jesus heard what was being said). TEV does so for the sake of natural English discourse structure, as does NEB. This technique avoids the complication of breaking into the major statement with the parenthetical statement of verse 2, as many translations do.

This clause, which TEV includes in verse 3, presents a textual problem. Instead of when Jesus heard, some manuscripts have "when the Lord heard." Jesus may be the more difficult reading, since it seems unlikely that a scribe would have replaced "the Lord" by Jesus if the text had originally been "the Lord." However, some scholars argue in the other direction and mention that "the Lord" represents the more difficult reading in a narrative passage. It is also possible that originally neither of these terms was included in the text, and that the subject of the verb was left unclear. If so, then some scribes inserted Jesus while others inserted "the Lord." It is important that the translation of this verse be explicit, so that the reader will understand who the subject is, whether translated as "the Lord" or as Jesus.

As already indicated (see 3.1), it is possible to identify the Pharisees by a type of classifier, for example, "a religious sect called Pharisees" or "a religious group called Pharisees." Such an identification should be made only once or twice, at the beginning of the Gospel. Further information can and should be included in a glossary.

In this context the word disciples refers to more than the twelve immediate disciples of Jesus. Therefore, disciples is best translated here by some term identifying them as "followers" or "adherents." Parti-

cular care must be taken in rendering such a term as winning. In many
languages it is rendered as a causative, for example, "causing people to
follow" or "causing people to join with him."

The seeming contradiction in the use of baptizing in verse 1 and
the explanation which occurs in verse 2 (compare John 3.22) could be resolved by translating baptizing here as "causing disciples to be baptized."
Verse 2 may be translated "Jesus himself did not actually baptize anyone,
but his disciples did the baptizing."

All languages have some way of indicating a comparative, though
they frequently do not use such a conjunction as than. In some languages
of Africa, for example, one may say, "Jesus was surpassing John in
gaining and baptizing disciples." In other languages a positive-negative
contrast is employed, for example, "Jesus was gaining and baptizing many
disciples; John was not." What counts is not the particular form used to
indicate comparison, but the meaning communicated.

4.2   (Actually, Jesus himself did not baptize anyone;
       only his disciples did.)

The form of the Greek text seems to indicate a direct contradiction
between Jesus was baptizing (1) and Jesus did not baptize anyone (2),
but obviously the writer of this Gospel intended no such contradiction.
We have already discussed this problem under verse 1 (5th paragraph).
For languages which make no clear distinction between a causative and a
noncausative, one can often translate in a form similar to that in both
the Greek and the English of verse 2. Some further explanation may be
given in a marginal note.

4.3-4   So when Jesus heard what was being said, he left
        Judea and went back to Galilee; 4 on his way there
        he had to go through Samaria.

The passive expression contained in the clause what was being said
may be rendered as active in such a form as "When Jesus heard what people
were saying about him." In Greek this clause appears in verse 1; see
there.

Actually the geography of the country did not require that Jesus
had to go through Samaria in order to get to Galilee from Judea. The verb
had to translates the same verb that appears in 3.14, 30, where it denotes
a divine necessity. The intimation is that it was God's will or purpose
that Jesus should pass through Samaria.

The name Samaria goes back to the 9th century B.C., when King Omri
gave this name to his capital city (1 Kgs 16.24). Later the use of the
name was extended to the entire northern kingdom. In 721 B.C. the
Assyrians captured Samaria and deported the Israelites, bringing in
foreigners to take their place. When the Jews returned from exile, a
definite break occurred between them and the Samaritans. This breach
continued, and the people of Samaria developed their own distinctive
religious customs. In New Testament times Samaria was part of the same
political unit as Judea and was ruled by a Roman governor.

It is possible to introduce classifiers with Judea, Galilee, and

Samaria, for example, "the province of Judea," "the province of Galilee," and "the province of Samaria." Or instead of "province" one may use a more general designation, such as "region" or "territory." However, after such classifiers have been used once or twice at the beginning of the book, it is better not to continue their use, unless demanded by the receptor language. Further information about these regions may be included in a glossary.

4.5   In Samaria he came to a town named Sychar which
             was not far from the field that Jacob had given to
             his son Joseph.

Although there are problems involved, Sychar is usually identified with the modern town of Askar, which is near the traditional site of Jacob's well. This town is not mentioned in the Old Testament, but some ancient and modern scholars identify Sychar with Shechem. In fact, "Shechem" appears instead of Sychar in one Syriac manuscript, and this reading is followed by NAB. However, no Greek manuscripts have "Shechem."
   For the reference to the field that Jacob had given to his son Joseph see Genesis 33.19; 48.22; and also Joshua 24.32.
   The adverbial phrase not far from translates one word in Greek, which means "near."
   There is a considerable time gap between the two events mentioned in verse 5, namely, Jacob's giving the field to Joseph and the arrival of Jesus at this place. It may be important to mark this difference in time more specifically than is implied by the pluperfect tense had given, for example, "which was not far from the field that Jacob many generations before gave to his son Joseph" or "...that Jacob gave to his son Joseph in ancient times." In some languages it is also important to distinguish between various kinds of giving. For example, the giving of some object which may be handed from one person to another may require a different verb from the one used in the giving of land. For the latter type of giving, a more specific statement, such as "bequeath to," or "hand the title over to," or "name him as the new owner" may be required.

4.6   Jacob's well was there, and Jesus, tired out by the
             trip, sat down by the well. It was about noon.

Jacob's well is not mentioned in the Old Testament. Archaeologists place its location at the foot of Mount Gerizim. In this type of context the phrase may best be translated as "the well that belonged to Jacob" or "the well that used to belong to Jacob." By employing the expression "used to," the lapse in time between the coming of Jesus to Sychar and the historical background involved is emphasized.
   In Greek the verb sat down is followed by an adverb which means "thus" or "so." It is best to connect this adverb with the adjective phrase tired out by the trip, and so give it the meaning "just as he was" (Gdsp "So Jesus, tired with his journey, sat down just as he was"; Mft "Jesus exhausted by the journey, sat down at the spring, just as he was"; see also Phps), though JB apparently takes it with the verb sat down ("Jesus, tired by the journey, sat straight down by the well"). TEV and

some other modern translations do not render this adverb explicitly, though by implication it is linked with the phrase tired out by the trip.

Although the Greek word translated well sometimes means "spring" (Mft, Gdsp, for example), most scholars agree that in the present context the meaning is well. The Greek word could evidently be used of a deep well with a spring at the bottom--that is, a source of water which flowed in readily--in contrast with the kind of well in which water would seep in slowly. The fact that this spring at Sychar was at the bottom of an extensive excavation from which water had to be drawn by jars or buckets on a rope could justify its being called a well, even though it could also be designated technically as a "spring."

It was about noon (see NEB, NAB, Mft, and JB note) is literally "it was about the sixth hour." It is assumed that John reckons the time of day from about six o'clock in the morning (see 1.39, where TEV translates "the tenth hour" as four o'clock in the afternoon), and so "the sixth hour" was about noon. Normally, water would be drawn from a well either in the morning or in the evening, and for that reason some assume that John must be reckoning time from midnight, rather than from six in the morning. If so, the time indicated would be about 6:00 a.m. Although that method of reckoning time may suit the present verse, it would not apply at all to "the sixth hour" mentioned in 19.14, where the reference is obviously to noon.

Various languages employ many different types of expressions to indicate time, and many relatively idiomatic phrases to speak of noon, for example, "when the sun is falling straight upon us," "when the sun is above our heads," "when the sun stops" (implying that the sun is just beginning to start down), or "when the sun crosses over."

| TEV | (4.7-15) | RSV |

7 A Samaritan woman came to draw some water, and Jesus said to her, "Give me a drink of water." (8 His disciples had gone into town to buy food.)

9 The woman answered, "You are a Jew, and I am a Samaritan--so how can you ask me for a drink?" (Jews will not use the same cups and bowls that Samaritans use.)*g*

10 Jesus answered, "If you only knew what God gives and who it is that is asking you for a drink, you would ask him, and he would give you life-giving water."

11 "Sir," the woman said, "you don't have a bucket, and the well is deep. Where would you get that life-giving water? 12 It was our ancestor Jacob who gave us this well; he and his sons and his

7 There came a woman of Samaria to draw water. Jesus said to her, "Give me a drink." 8 For his disciples had gone away into the city to buy food. 9 The Samaritan woman said to him, "How is it that you, a Jew, ask a drink of me, a woman of Samaria?" For Jews have no dealings with Samaritans. 10 Jesus answered her, "If you knew the gift of God and who it is that is saying to you, 'Give me a drink,' you would have asked him, and he would have given you living water." 11 The woman said to him, "Sir, you have nothing to draw with, and the well is deep; where do you get that living water? 12 Are you greater than our father Jacob, who gave us the well, and drank from it himself, and his sons, and his cattle?" 13

flocks all drank from it. You don't claim to be greater than Jacob, do you?"

13 Jesus answered, "Whoever drinks this water will get thirsty again, 14 but whoever drinks the water that I will give him will never be thirsty again. The water that I will give him will become in him a spring which will provide him with life-giving water and give him eternal life."

15 "Sir," the woman said, "give me that water! Then I will never be thirsty again, nor will I have to come here to draw water."

Jesus said to her, "Every one who drinks of this water will thirst again, 14 but whoever drinks of the water that I shall give him will never thirst; the water that I shall give him will become in him a spring of water welling up to eternal life." 15 The woman said to him, "Sir, give me this water, that I may not thirst, nor come here to draw."

g Jews will not use the same cups and bowls that Samaritans use; *or* Jews will have nothing to do with Samaritans.

4.7   A Samaritan woman came to draw some water, and
         Jesus said to her, "Give me a drink of water."

In this verse a Samaritan woman (so also JB, Gdsp, Mft, NEB) is literally "a woman of Samaria," while in verse 9 the woman is literally "the Samaritan woman." In English, however, it is more natural to say a Samaritan woman than to say "a woman of Samaria." And since the woman has already been identified, it is not necessary to identify her again as a Samaritan in verse 9.

Different languages may employ quite distinct means of indicating the relation of a person to his "home region," for example, "a woman born in Samaria," or "a woman who calls Samaria her home," or "a woman from Samaria region." Sometimes the region from which a person comes is identified as related to the dialect spoken there, for example, "a woman speaking the Samaria speech."

To draw some water may be rendered "to get water from the well." In some instances it may be necessary to be specific, for example, "to let her jar down into the well and to pull up water."

Give me a drink of water is literally "give me to drink," but the context makes it clear that water is requested, and TEV makes this information explicit. Most translations have "give me a drink."

At this point a marginal note may be needed to explain "give me a drink of water," for in some receptor languages this type of request may have misleading implications. For example, in some societies this type of request is a subtle form of requesting sexual relations. It is, of course, impossible to change the nature of Jesus' request, but a footnote may be introduced to indicate that there are no improper connotations.

In translating give me a drink of water, it is important to avoid suggesting a demand or impolite request. A form equivalent to "Please give me a drink of water" may be desirable.

<u>4.8</u>   (His disciples had gone into town to buy food.)

By including this bit of background information, John is able to
set the stage for the dialogue between Jesus and the Samaritan woman.
TEV, Mft, and NAB take this verse as a parenthetical statement. Phps
connects it with the last part of verse 7, and translates "'Please give
me a drink,' Jesus said to her, for his disciples had gone away to the
town to buy food." NEB handles the problem by introducing this verse
before verse 7: "(8) The disciples had gone away to the town to buy
food. (7) Meanwhile a Samaritan woman..." This solution represents the
elements as they would naturally appear in English narrative. That is,
it is more natural to introduce the information that the disciples were
gone before bringing a new character on the scene. If the order of the
two verses is not reversed, it is better to set off verse 8 as a parenthetical explanation, setting the background for the narrative.

<u>4.9</u>   The woman answered, "You are a Jew and I am a
          Samaritan--so how can you ask me for a drink?"
          (Jews will not use the same dishes that Samaritans
          use.)^g

^{g} <i>or</i> Jews will have nothing to do with Samaritans.

<u>The woman answered</u> is literally "therefore the Samaritan woman says
to him." Here again John uses his favorite particle (<u>oun</u>--see the comments
on <u>oun</u> on page 68   ), represented in the literal rendering by "there-
<u>fore</u>."
RSV represents a fairly literal translation of the next part of
this verse, "How is it that you, a Jew, ask a drink of me, a woman of
Samaria?" For the sake of emphasizing the contrast between Jews and
Samaritans, TEV introduces this information first in the woman's statement, <u>you are a Jew and I am a Samaritan</u>. The reader thus knows immediately that there is some significant difference between Jews and Samaritans, and so the woman's question is readily understood.
If translated literally, <u>how can you ask me for a drink?</u> may suggest
the wrong meaning in some receptor languages; for the source of the
woman's surprise is not the ability of Jesus to ask her for a drink, but
the high improbability that he would do so. In some languages this
question may be translated "How is it possible that you would ask me for
a drink?" or "I cannot imagine your asking me for a drink" or "Isn't
it very strange indeed that you ask me to give you water to drink?"
<u>Will not use the same dishes</u> (NEB "do not use vessels in common")
is taken by most translators in the sense of "do not associate with" or
"have nothing to do with" (NAB). The more recent commentaries on the
Gospel of John seem to prefer the meaning TEV gives this verb. If this
is the true meaning, the account reflects a Jewish religious regulation
in force around A.D. 65. According to this regulation, Samaritan women
were in a state of perpetual ritual impurity from the time of their birth,
and anyone who had contact with them would share this ritual impurity.
The regulation adds that for this reason "the Jews do not use dishes in
common with the Samaritans." The more recent commentaries favor this

[113]

interpretation, while the majority of translations follow the other one. No dogmatic conclusion is possible. Whether the reference was to using dishes in common with Samaritans or merely associating with them, Jesus ignored the custom.

Since there are two distinct interpretations of the Greek text, translators should indicate this fact by putting one interpretation in the text and the other in a marginal note. The interpretation followed by TEV may be rendered "Jews do not eat or drink from the same dishes or cups that the Samaritans do" or "When Jews eat and drink, they do not use the same dishes that Samaritans use." If, however, an interpretation relating to complete avoidance is employed, it is always possible to say, "The Jews will have no dealings whatsoever with the Samaritans." It may be expressed idiomatically in some languages as "The Jews never join with the Samaritans" or "The Jews and the Samaritans never use anything together" or "There is nothing which Samaritans use which Jews would also use."

4.10   Jesus answered, "If you only knew what God gives,
           and who it is that is asking you for a drink, you
           would ask him and he would give you life-giving water."

Once again the person with whom Jesus is speaking misunderstands (compare 3.4) and thus gives Jesus an opportunity to explain further what he means.

Here also the verse begins with a Semitic formula for introducing discourse which is redundant in English: "Jesus answered and said to her" (TEV Jesus answered).

What God gives is a noun phrase in Greek (literally "the gift of God"). It is rendered as a verb phrase in some translations (Phps "what God can give"; NEB "what God gives"; JB "what God is offering"). Some commentators understand "God's gift" to be Jesus, and it is possible that NAB takes it in this way ("If only you recognized God's gift, and who it is that is asking you for a drink"). However, in the context the gift of God seems to be other than Jesus himself, perhaps God's Spirit or the life-giving water to which Jesus refers. Of course in the theology of the Gospel of John, there is no final distinction to be made.

The verb knew must be rendered in some languages as essentially equivalent to "recognized" or "were aware of" and the clause "what God gives" must be slightly modified to suggest "what God offers to give," for the meaning is not what God was in the process of giving to the woman but rather what he would like to give her. However, it is possible to interpret what God gives as a general reference to God providing spiritual gifts to people who respond to him. This clause can therefore be translated "what God gives to people."

Since Jesus refers to himself in who it is that is asking you for a drink, it may be necessary in some languages to use a first person rather than a third person singular, that is, "who I am who am asking you for water to drink."

For readers of English and most other languages, such a phrase as "living water" has zero meaning. The meaning is, of course, "water that gives life" and so the 4th edition of TEV translates life-giving water.

[114]

This concept of life-giving water appears in several places in John's Gospel (3.5; 4.10-15; 7.38; 19.34). A literal translation of "living water" can be misleading in some languages. It may be taken to mean water that is alive with tadpoles, minnows, and other forms of life. Or it may suggest in some languages a kind of magic water. It is better, therefore, to translate "living water" as "water which causes life" or "water which causes people to live."

4.11   "Sir," the woman said, "you don't have a bucket, and the well is deep. Where would get that life-giving water?

The word translated Sir in TEV (as in most modern English translations) may simply indicate polite address, or it may have the specialized Christian meaning of "Lord." It is used again by the woman to address Jesus in verses 15 and 19. Though it is possible that the term translated in TEV as Sir could have the meaning of "Lord," this meaning would seem to be particularly inappropriate in verse 19, where the Samaritan woman acknowledges Jesus to be a prophet; it would be strange for her to acknowledge him as a prophet if she had already recognized him as "Lord." The context would certainly seem to indicate that such a meaning as "Sir" is required. However, in some languages this type of formal address is not employed and the terms should simply be omitted in translation.

The reply of the woman to Jesus in this verse and in verse 12 reflects her misunderstanding--a technique John uses to further the discourse. In this verse the Greek word for well is different from the one used in verse 6. The word used in verse 6 (pēgē) technically means "spring" or "fountain," and it is used again in verse 14 (TEV spring). The Greek word used in verse 11 (phrear) comes closer to the meaning of "cistern" or "well." On the basis of this distinction, some scholars conclude that in the discussion of natural water Jacob's well is spoken of as a "spring" (verse 6), while in this verse, where the reference is to spiritual water, Jacob's well is referred to as merely a "cistern" or a "well." However, most translators and commentators do not make this distinction. Mft is one of the few who consistently maintain the etymological distinction; in verse 6 he has "spring" and here he has "well." NEB refers in verse 6 to "the spring called Jacob's well," and then states that Jesus "sat down on the well." Most other translations render both words as well, here and in verse 6, while giving the meaning of spring in verse 14.

In some languages the reference to a bucket implies "a bucket and a rope," that is, a bucket typically used at the end of a rope to draw water from a deep well. It is also possible to use a general descriptive statement, for example, "You do not have anything with which you can draw water from the well."

4.12   It was our ancestor Jacob who gave us this well; he and his sons and his flocks all drank from it. You don't claim to be greater than Jacob, do you?"

In Greek this verse is one long interrogative sentence. TEV makes it a statement followed by a question. Moreover, the question whether Jesus

is greater than Jacob is retained in TEV until the last part of the verse,
since it is the climactic element in what the woman has to say. The
other information conveyed in the verse (that Jacob gave the well, and
that he, his sons, and his flocks all drank from it) is background information, forming the basis for the question concerning the relation
between Jesus and Jacob.

Our ancestor Jacob is literally "our father Jacob," but in such a
context the reference is clearly to an ancestor rather than to a "father."
The statement that Jacob and his family drank from the well indicates
that the water was good, and the observation that his flocks also drank
from it indicates that the supply of water was plentiful.

There is an interesting problem of inclusive and exclusive first
person plural in the phrase our ancestor. If an inclusive form of "our"
is used, it means that the woman acknowledged that she, a Samaritan, and
Jesus, a Jew, had a common ancestor in Jacob. If an exclusive form is
used, it indicates that the woman emphasized that Jacob was the ancestor
of the Samaritans and not of the Jews. The translator is thus forced to
interpret the woman's intentions. From a purely historical point of view
it would be important to use the inclusive first person plural, but in
terms of this particular context and the way the Samaritan woman sets
her own tradition against the Jewish tradition, one could argue for the
exclusive first person plural. It would appear that translators are
divided as to which form to use in this context. This division does not
involve any serious theological problem, but it does highlight matters
of emphasis.

It may be important to make a distinction between "drank from it"
and "drank water that came from it." In some languages such a statement
as "drank from it" would mean that the water was at surface level and
that cattle could drink directly from the well, as from a spring or pool.
However, it seems clear that in this context the translation should be
"drank water that came from the well," to indicate that even in ancient
times the well was deep (verse 11).

You don't claim to be greater than Jacob, do you? may more literally
be rendered "You are not greater than Jacob, are you?" However, it is
clear that the woman is implying that Jesus is claiming to be greater
than Jacob, and TEV makes this claim explicit (see also NAB "Surely you
do not pretend to be greater than our ancestor Jacob...?"). In order to
indicate clearly that such a claim is possibly being made by Jesus, one
may translate "You do not say that you are greater than Jacob, do you?"
or "Is it possible that you think you are greater than Jacob was?"

4.13   Jesus answered, "Whoever drinks this water will
        get thirsty again,

Jesus answered is literally "Jesus answered and said to her" (see
verse 10).

Jesus now begins to clear up the woman's misunderstanding; he explains that he is referring to the water of eternal life (13-14).

4.14   but whoever drinks the water that I will give him will
        never be thirsty again. The water that I will give him

will become in him a spring which will provide
him with the life-giving water and give him
eternal life.

A contrast is evident between the tense of the verb drinks in this
verse and in the preceding verse. The verb in verse 13 is in the present
tense, suggesting habitual action; in verse 14 the word drinks is in the
aorist tense, suggesting a single action. Thus the water from Jacob's
well supplies only the physical needs of men, and only temporarily, so
that people must return for more. One drink of the water that Jesus gives
for the spiritual needs of people provides eternal life. The contrast
between the present and aorist forms of the verb drink may be indicated
in some languages by translating the first part of verse 14 "If anyone
ever drinks the water that I give him, he will never be thirsty again"
or "But if he once drinks the water..."

Will never be thirsty again (so JB; Mft "will never thirst any more";
see NEB, Gdsp) is literally "will not be thirsty into the age." In this
context "the age" (see comments at 3.15) is equivalent to "eternity" or
"forever," and when joined with a negative ("not...into the age"), the
meaning is never...again.

In the Greek the next sentence reads literally "but the water which
I will give to him will become in him a spring of water leaping up into
eternal life." To make explicit the meaning of "spring of water leaping
into eternal life," TEV has a spring which will provide him with life-
giving water and give him eternal life, which is clearly the meaning.
Most translations are rather formal in their rendering. NAB attempts to
make a dynamic equivalent by translating "the water I give shall become
a fountain within him, leaping up to provide eternal life." In certain
languages will become in him a spring may require some indication that
this statement of Jesus is to be understood figuratively, for example,
"will become in him just like a spring" or "will be in him something
resembling a spring."

The verb "leaping up" (see Acts 3.8, where TEV translates "jumped
up...jumping" in its double occurrence) denotes lively action. In the
Septuagint it is used of the coming of God's "spirit" on Samson, Saul,
and David, and some commentators believe it to be the background of its
use in the present passage.

If life-giving water is translated "water that gives life," it may
be important to unite this expression with the phrase give him eternal
life, that is, one may translate "provide him with water which gives him
eternal life" or, in some languages, "...real life which never ends"--to
emphasize the qualitative significance of eternal life, rather than
merely its duration.

4.15   "Sir," the woman said, "give me that water! Then
         I will never be thirsty again, nor will I have to
         come here to draw water."

The word Sir is the same word used in verse 11 (see there).
Said is literally "said to him," but in English "to him" is unnecessary in the context.

TEV	RSV
16 "Go and call your husband," Jesus told her, "and come back."	16 Jesus said to her, "Go, call your husband, and come here." 17
17 "I don't have a husband," she answered.	The woman answered him, "I have no husband." Jesus said to her, "You
Jesus replied, "You are right when you say you don't have a husband. 18 You have been married to five men, and the man you live with now is not really your husband. You have told me the truth."	are right in saying 'I have no husband'; 18 for you have had five husbands, and he whom you now have is not your husband; this you said truly." 19 The woman said to him,
19 "I see you are a prophet, sir," the woman said. 20 "My Samaritan ancestors worshipped God on this mountain, but you Jews say that Jerusalem is the place where we should worship God."	"Sir, I perceive that you are a prophet. 20 Our fathers worshiped on this mountain; and you say that in Jerusalem is the place where men ought to worship." 21 Jesus
21 Jesus said to her, "Believe me, woman, the time will come when people will not worship the Father either on this mountain or in Jerusalem. 22 You Samaritans do not really know whom you worship; but we Jews know whom we worship, because it is from the Jews that salvation comes. 23 But the time is coming and is already here, when by the power of God's Spirit people will worship the Father as he really is, offering him the true worship that he wants. 24 God is Spirit, and only by the power of his Spirit can people worship him as he really is."	said to her, "Woman, believe me, the hour is coming when neither on this mountain nor in Jerusalem will you worship the Father. 22 You worship what you do not know; we worship what we know, for salvation is from the Jews. 23 But the hour is coming, and now is, when the true worshipers will worship the Father in spirit and truth, for such the Father seeks to worship him. 24 God is spirit, and those who worship him must worship in spirit and truth."

4.16   "Go and call your husband," Jesus told her, "and
         come back."

This verse introduces a new aspect into the dialogue between Jesus and the Samaritan woman. Verse 15 indicates that the woman still does not understand what Jesus is talking about, and so, beginning in this verse, Jesus takes a different approach.

And come back must be made more specific in some receptor languages, for example, "and come back with him" or "bring him back with you." It is obviously implied that the woman should get her husband and return with him to talk further with Jesus.

The term husband is sometimes translated by such a phrase as "your man," but usually there is a more specific expression to designate the male partner in the marital relation. It can, of course, be expressed as "the man to whom you are married."

4.17   "I don't have a husband," she answered.
         Jesus replied, "You are right when you say
     you don't have a husband.

     She answered is literally "The woman answered and said to him."
(See verses 10 and 15.)
     I don't have a husband may be rendered in some languages "there is
no man to whom I am married" or "I am not now married to a man."
     In the second part of this verse the Greek employs direct discourse
embedded in direct discourse: 'You are right when you say, 'I don't have
a husband.'" TEV restructures it as indirect within direct discourse:
"...you say you don't have a husband..." In this manner TEV avoids the
use of "quotes within quotes" and provides a conversational style more
natural in English. Other translations which employ indirect discourse
here are NEB, NAB, and Gdsp.
     The relation between you are right and you say you don't have a
husband may be indicated in some languages not as a temporal relation,
translated in TEV as when, but as an expression of means, for example,
"By saying you don't have a husband you are telling the truth." It may
also be expressed as cause, for example, "Because you say you don't have
a husband you are saying what is right."

4.18   You have been married to five men, and the
         man you live with now is not really your
     husband. You told me the truth."

     Some scholars see a symbolic meaning in the mention of five men, but
as far as translation is concerned it must be taken as a simple statement of fact. Although any number of marriages were legally possible, the
Jewish rabbis did not approve of more than three.
     You told me the truth is literally "This truth you have said."
NEB is similar: "You told me the truth there." In some languages it is
difficult to employ such a noun as truth, but some type of qualifying
adjective is frequently used as an attributive, for example, "What you
have just told me is true" or "The words that you have just spoken to me
are true."

4.19   "I see you are a prophet, sir," the woman said.

     On the basis of Jesus' insight into her situation, the woman judges
that he is a prophet. She does not refer to him as "the prophet," as
though she had a specific reference in mind (as in Deut 18.15, 18), but
simply as a prophet. It does seem, however, that she assumes that a prophet might have authority to settle legal questions, as implied in the
next verse.
     The term prophet must be expressed in several different ways, de-
pending on the context in the Scriptures. In some instances the meaning
certainly is "one who foretells the future," in others the emphasis is
upon "one who makes inspired utterances." In some languages the tendency
has been to translate prophet by a term meaning "diviner" or "one who
foretells the future," but it is increasingly common to render prophet

as "one who speaks for God" or "a messenger from God." This type of expression fits well in the present context.

The woman addresses Jesus by the same word that she used in verses 11 and 15. Most translators and commentators understand sir here as a simple address; a few see a transition to the meaning of "Lord." For a discussion of the translational difficulties involved in rendering sir, see under verse 11.

4.20   "My Samaritan ancestors worshiped God on this mountain,
        but you Jews say that Jerusalem is the place where we
        should worship God."

My Samaritan ancestors is literally "our ancestors," but in translation "our" may be ambiguous, unless explicitly marked as exclusive. And you Jews (so also NEB; NAB "you people") is literally "you" (plural). The woman is, of course, contrasting the viewpoint of her Samaritan people with that of the Jewish people concerning the place of worship.

In contrast with the ambiguous use of our in verse 12, in which it is impossible to decide between the inclusive and exclusive implications, here it is clear that "our ancestors" must be understood as exclusive. In many languages "our ancestors" is rendered "our grandfathers" or "our fathers from ancient times." To make clear that these are "our Samaritan ancestors," one may say "our grandfathers from this Samaria region."

In Greek there is no stated object of the verb worshiped, but TEV makes the object explicit (worshiped God).

This mountain is a reference to Mount Gerizim. Even after their temple was destroyed by John Hyrcanus in 128 B.C., the Samaritans continued to use that mountain as their place of worship. The Samaritans were as firm in their worship on Mount Gerizim as were the Jews in their worship in Jerusalem; they interpreted the one sanctuary law of Deuteronomy to refer to Mount Gerizim rather than Jerusalem.

Where we should worship God is literally "where it is necessary to worship." As in other passages where the verb "it is necessary" is used, the reference here is to the necessity imposed by the divine will. (See at 3.14 and 4.4.) Where we should worship God may be rendered in some languages "where we ought to worship God." The divinely imposed necessity may even be expressed by saying "where God says that we should worship him."

4.21   Jesus said to her, "Believe me, woman, the time
        will come when people will not worship the Father
        either on this mountain or in Jerusalem.

In this context, believe should not be understood in the sense of "to trust in" or "to be loyal to," but simply "to accept as true what one says." This meaning may be made explicit in some languages as "believe what I am going to tell you."

The verb phrase people will...worship is literally "you (plural)... will worship." The use of "you" in such a context is generic; it refers to all people, not merely to the person or persons addressed. Thus Jesus is not referring merely to the woman herself or to her Samaritan countrymen; rather, he is making an all-inclusive statement.

Woman is the same form of address used in 2.4 and 19.26. It is a
polite form of address (see notes at 2.4) and in this context seems to
fit well. In some languages, however, it would be inappropriate, as de-
preciatory or derogatory. However, in some languages the word "woman,"
when used in direct address, is equivalent to "wife." In such instances
a different expression must be employed, or the term must be omitted.

4.22   You Samaritans do not really know whom you worship;
        but we Jews know whom we worship, because it is
        from the Jews that salvation comes.

You Samaritans is literally "you" (plural), while we Jews is literally "we." TEV and several other translations identify thus the persons
referred to.
Whom you worship is literally "what you worship." Most other translations render this phrase literally, using the neuter "what" rather
than the masculine whom. Although the term used in the Greek text is
neuter, the reference is obviously to God, and TEV accordingly uses the
masculine rather than the neuter. (GeCL makes the reference to God explicit: "you Samaritans do not know God.") In John 10.29 the neuter is
used of the believers whom the Father has given to the Son, and in 1
John 1.1 a neuter pronoun is used in reference to the Word. Phillips
certainly misses the point in rendering "You are worshiping with your
eyes shut. We Jews are worshiping with our eyes open."
Though some form of worship is universal, in various parts of the
world, the ways in which worship is designated may differ radically. In
some instances one may use simply an expression for "prayer," for example, "to speak to God." In others the attitude of the worshiper is in
focus, for example, "to be reverent before God" or "to be silent before
God." Sometimes the emphasis is upon the position of the worshiper, for
example, "to kneel down before God" or "to bow low before God." Sometimes
some activity associated with worship may be mentioned, for example, "to
bring gifts to God" or even "to sacrifice to God."
Because it is from the Jews that salvation comes affirms the reality
of the historical situation, in which God had revealed himself in a
unique way to the Jewish people. This verse both indicates that the
Gospel is not anti-Semitic in the modern sense of the word, and it affirms
the historical reality of the situation. A literal translation of because
it is from the Jews that salvation comes may be misleading in some languages and may even suggest that the Jews are the ones who will save
people. God, of course, is the agent of salvation, but the knowledge
about how God saves people comes from the Jews. This truth may be expressed in some languages as "because the Jews are the ones who can tell
how God saves people," or "...through whom God promised salvation." This
ability of the Jews to point the way to salvation reflects the historical
reality of God's special dealings with the Jewish nation.

4.23-24 But the time is coming and is already here,
         when by the power of God's Spirit people will
         worship the Father as he really is, offering
         him the true worship that he wants. 24 God is

[121]

> Spirit, and only by the power of his Spirit can
> people worship him as he really is."

The statement But the time is coming and is already here indicates
to some degree the historical-theological tension that exists in John's
Gospel. It reflects the same viewpoint the Synoptic Gospels present regarding the Kingdom of God: although it is present, it is yet to come.

In a number of languages such an abstract expression as time does
not exist. One must use a more specific reference to an occasion by
saying, "But the day is coming." However, in some languages one cannot
speak of a "day coming," since only animate objects may "come," but one
may say "The day is happening" or "It will soon be the day, and in fact
it is already the day."

Really is discussed under 1.9.

For a detailed discussion of "spirit," "truth," and the phrases "in
spirit and in truth" and "the spirit of truth," see Appendix II, "Translating 'In Spirit and Truth' and 'the Spirit of Truth' in the Gospel
of John."

It is obvious that not all the concepts treated in this appendix
can be included in a translation of the phrase "in spirit and in truth,"
but it is helpful to be conscious of the background of these terms before
trying to translate them. Translation has its limitations, and there
are points at which the full implications of certain theological terms
must depend upon the teaching ministry of the church. However, it is the
responsibility of the translator to render these terms in a way that
will provide the clearest possible understanding of their meaning by the
reader.

The TEV rendering, by the power of God's Spirit, may be expressed
in some languages "by means of God's Spirit," since by the power of
specifies primarily means or instrumentality. Since the Greek phrase
"in Spirit" is best interpreted as a reference to the Holy Spirit, its
relation to worship evidently refers to the way in which people are to
worship God.

As he really is translates a phrase which in Greek is literally "in
truth." Since it seems to refer to the "true revelation about God," it
is possible to translate it "will worship the Father as he truly is" or
"will worship the Father as the one who he truly is."

Offering him the true worship that he wants may require restructuring,
since it may not be possible to speak of "offering worship" or even of
"true worship." The closest equivalent may be "worshiping him in the
true way, the way that he wants" or "worshiping him genuinely, just as
he wants to be worshiped." In some languages true worship is equivalent
to "worship in the way in which one should." In other words, it is
equivalent to "right worship."

The content of verse 24 is essentially the same as the last part of
verse 23. The repetition, primarily for emphasis, serves to elaborate
the implications of the statement God is Spirit.

Perhaps the most difficult expression in verses 23 and 24 is the
clause God is Spirit. It is relatively easy to speak about "the spirit
of God" or "his Spirit," but to say that God is Spirit may cause difficulty, for to use "spirit" essentially as a designation of quality and

character is unusual. Even the meaning of Spirit offers certain complications, for though people may be accustomed to speaking about the
spirit of a person, they may be reluctant to think of the Spirit of God.

Many languages have several distinct words for "spirit." One of
them normally designates the spirit of a person, which leaves at death
and may even temporarily depart in dreams or during unconsciousness
(for example, as the result of an accident). The other term for "spirit"
designates some kind of supernatural, demonic personality, which has
never been a part of the person, but may for various purposes enter and
take control of him. Such spirits are regarded normally as having their
abode in the mountains, springs, streams, and forests. They are not
creators and are not in control of natural phenomena (if they were, they
would probably be called "gods"), but they do exert supernatural power,
usually with mischievous or malevolent purpose.

One difficulty in using the first type of word for "spirit" in
speaking of God is that the term may suggest that God himself had died,
and that consequently his spirit is active somewhere else in the universe.
The second word for spirit would degrade God to the level of the demons,
or suggest that God himself was inhabited by a kind of demonic force.
To avoid these wrong implications, translators sometimes borrow a foreign
term (from Greek, Latin, Hebrew, etc.), but this practice rarely proves
satisfactory, since an explanation of such a term must depend upon local
equivalences.

The usual practice is to adopt the "least unsatisfactory" term and
then use it consistently, with sufficient contextual conditioning to indicate clearly that the Spirit of God is referred to. Such a phrase as
"of God" or such a qualifier as "Holy" is then added. However, in this
particular context, God is Spirit, there is the additional complication
of trying to qualify the nature of God without declaring that he is a
particular spirit, like the demonic spirits. The closest equivalent in
some languages may be "God is like a spirit" or "to know what God is
like, one must know what a spirit is like."

For further discussion of some of the problems related to the translation of the term "spirit," see Bible Translating, page 210 and the
following pages.

TEV	(4.25-30)	RSV

25 The woman said to him, "I know
that the Messiah will come, and
when he comes, he will tell us
everything."

26 Jesus answered, "I am he, I
who am talking with you."

27 At that moment Jesus' disciples returned, and they were
greatly surprised to find him
talking with a woman. But none of
them said to her, "What do you
want?" or asked him, "Why are you
talking with her?"

25 The woman said to him, "I know
that Messiah is coming (he who is
called Christ); when he comes, he
will show us all things." 26 Jesus
said to her, "I who speak to you
am he."

27 Just then his disciples came.
They marveled that he was talking
with a woman, but none said, "What
do you wish?" or "Why are you talking with her?" 28 So the woman left
her water jar, and went away into
the city, and said to the people,

[123]

28 Then the woman left her water jar, went back to the town, and said to the people there, 29 "Come and see the man who told me everything I have ever done. Could he be the Messiah?" 30 So they left the town and went to Jesus.

29 "Come, see a man who told me all that I ever did. Can this be the Christ?" 30 They went out of the city and were coming to him.

4.25   The woman said to him, "I know that the Messiah will come, and when he comes, he will tell us every-thing."

On the meaning of the terms Messiah and Christ, see 1.20, 41. The Samaritans looked for a "messiah," and they referred to him as "Taheb," which means simply "he who returns."

4.26   Jesus answered, "I am he, I who am talking with you."

I am he, I who am talking with you appears in NEB as "I am he, I who am speaking to you now," and in JB as "'I who am speaking to you,' said Jesus, 'I am he.'" Most other translations are similar, though Mft has "'I am messiah,' said Jesus, 'I who am talking to you.'"; and Phps has "'I am Christ speaking to you,' said Jesus."

In the Gospel of John "I am" is used by Jesus in three different ways. (1) It appears as a simple statement of identity here and in 6.20; 18.5. (2) Most often it is followed by a predicate nominative (6.35, 51; 8.12; 10.7, 9, 11, 14; 11.25; 14.6; 15.1, 5). (3) In several places it is used absolutely (8.24, 28, 58; 13.19). It is necessary to look closely at the absolute use of the "I am" phrase. Although there is evidence of a similar use of this term in religious literature outside of the Old Testament, the Old Testament itself offers the best background for un-derstanding its use in this Gospel. In Exodus 3.14, the passage in which God reveals his name to Moses, the Greek Septuagint translates the Hebrew phrase as "I am the Existing One." This rendition of the divine name in Greek is paralleled elsewhere in the Old Testament. In several places "I am" (literally Hebrew "I [am] he") is used as a divine name. Isaiah 43.25 is a striking example. There the Hebrew reads "I, I am he, who wipes out sin." The Septuagint translates the first part of this state-ment by using the Greek expression "I am" twice. The Septuagint actually reads "I am I am who wipes out sin" and the second "I am" becomes the equivalent of the divine name. The Greek translators of Isaiah 51.12 followed the same procedure. In later Judaism the expression "I am" is definitely used as a name for God. Thus in those passages in John's Gospel where Jesus uses "I am" in an absolute sense, he is identifying himself with God. TEV attempts to indicate this divine title by the use of capitals (in 8.24, 28; 13.19 TEV has 'I AM WHO I AM'; in 8.58 'I AM').

In some languages the closest equivalent to the response of Jesus is "I am that very person, I the one who am talking with you" or "I, as the person talking to you, am that very individual" or "I am just that person, the same one who is talking to you."

4.27　　　　At that moment Jesus' disciples returned, and
　　　　they were greatly surprised to find him talking
　　　　with a woman. But none of them said to her, "What
　　　　do you want?" or asked him, "Why are you talking
　　　　with her?"

Jesus' disciples is literally "his disciples," another pronominal
reference which TEV makes explicit.

At that moment may be rendered "just then" or "just as he said that."
In some languages, the connection between sentences may be indicated by
repeating a brief part of the preceding sentence, or briefly referring
to its contents.

In some cases the return of the disciples should be made more explicit, for example, "returned to where they had left Jesus" or "returned from where they had been in town."

Greatly surprised (NEB "astonished"; Anchor Bible "shocked"; Phps
"very surprised") translates a verb tense in Greek which, in this context, stresses the intensity of the disciples' amazement. The surprise
of the disciples may have been merely that Jesus was talking with a
Samaritan woman, unusual for a Jew. Or their shock may have reflected
the rabbinic tradition which specified that no rabbi should speak with
a woman. However, since Jesus displayed no such standoffish attitude
toward women in general, their attitude was evidently occasioned by the
fact that the woman was a Samaritan.

The Greek text of this verse does not make explicit whether the
first question of the disciples was addressed to Jesus or to the woman.
TEV and NAB ("What do you want of him?") make this a question directed
to the woman, but most translations imply that the question was directed
to Jesus. In the Greek text the second question is explicitly directed
to Jesus, and on the basis of this observation it may seem natural to
have both questions directed to him (JB "What do you want from her?").
However, it is not possible to be positive on this point.

4.28　　　　Then the woman left her water jar, went back
　　　　to the town, and said to the people there,

To the people is literally "to the men," but all translations agree
that "men" is here used in a generic sense.

4.29　　　"Come and see the man who told me everything I
　　　have ever done. Could he be the Messiah?"

Come and see translates a Greek expression different from the one
used in 1.39, but the force is the same.

The woman's question Could he be the Messiah? implies a degree of
doubt on her part, though perhaps mixed with hope. The same type of
question is used in 7.26. In 18.35 and 21.5 it is also used, but with
the implication that the assumed answer is "No." Could he be the Messiah?
may be rendered "Is it possible that he may be the Messiah?" or "Do you
think that he is the Messiah?" Here the question does not concern the
potentiality of Jesus to be the Messiah, but rather the matter of prob-

ability. In this context a question implying doubt would be more effective in getting people to come and listen to Jesus than would an expression suggesting complete assurance. A statement of assurance would merely have stimulated controversy, rather than serious inquiry.

4.30   So they left the town and went to Jesus.

Once again TEV makes the pronominal reference (Greek "him") explicit as a reference to Jesus.

TEV	(4.31-34)	RSV

31 In the meantime the disciples were begging Jesus, "Teacher, have something to eat!"

32 But he answered, "I have food to eat that you know nothing about."

33 So the disciples started asking among themselves, "Could somebody have brought him food?"

34 "My food," Jesus said to them, "is to obey the will of the one who sent me and to finish the work he gave me to do.

31 Meanwhile the disciples besought him, saying, "Rabbi, eat." 32 But he said to them, "I have food to eat of which you do not know." 33 So the disciples said to one another, "Has any one brought him food?" 34 Jesus said to them, "My food is to do the will of him who sent me, and to accomplish his work.

4.31   In the meantime the disciples were begging Jesus,
         "Teacher, have something to eat!"

The focus of the narrative, in the form of a revelation discourse, now shifts from the woman and the people in the city back to Jesus and his disciples. Were begging (so also Phps; NEB, JB, NAB "were urging") translates a Greek verb tense which stresses the continuing action of the disciples.
     Teacher. On the meaning of this word, see 1.38.
     Have something to eat (see NEB; JB "do have something to eat"; NAB "eat something") translates one word in Greek, an imperative, which RSV renders "eat." Although the verb is an imperative, in the present context it is used in the sense of encouragement rather than of command. Thus an equivalent translation may often have essentially the meaning of "please eat something" or "we urge you to eat something." For languages in which the expression Teacher cannot be used as a form of direct address, one may translate "and the disciples begged Jesus as their teacher, 'Please eat something.'"

4.32   But he answered, "I have food to eat that you
         know nothing about."

The pronouns I and you are emphatic in Greek.
     The Greek word for food in the verse (brōsis) is different from the word used in verse 34 (Greek brōma), but the two words are used synonymously here.

In some languages it is essential to be more specific about the
relation of "eating" and "food," that is, one must distinguish between
"I have food which I will eat" and "I have food which I have eaten."
Since the disciples immediately began to ask among themselves whether
someone had brought him food, it may be necessary to use an expression
in verse 32 meaning "I have eaten food that you know nothing about."

4.33   So the disciples started asking among them-
        selves, "Could somebody have brought him food?"

Started asking translates a Greek verb tense which suggests that
the disciples were discussing this question among themselves rather than
that they merely asked it once.
    The question involves a matter of possibility. It may be translated
in some languages "Is it possible that someone has brought food to him?"
It is not the ability of someone to do it, as suggested by could, but
rather, the possibility, or even the probability, of its having happened.
The response is typical of the way this Gospel describes the initial
misunderstanding of Jesus' statements, and then the receiving of a fuller
and more spiritual explanation.

4.34   "My food," Jesus said to them, "is to obey the
        will of the one who sent me and to finish the work
        he gave me to do.

To obey the will is literally "to do the will," but in biblical
language "do" in such a context is equivalent to obey. In many languages,
though one can readily say "to obey a person," it is difficult to say
"to obey the will of him who sent me." However, to obey the will of the
one who sent me can be translated "to do what the one who sent me told me
to do" or "...wanted me to do." While it may be difficult to relate this
kind of expression to my food, this relation can sometimes be expressed
by saying "When I do what the one who sent me wanted me to do, then it
is just as though I had eaten food."
    Throughout the Gospel of John, God is frequently referred to as the
one who sent Jesus (see 3.17, 34; 5.36, 38; 6.29, 57; 7.28-29; 8.42;
10.36; 11.42; 17.8, 18, 21, 23, 25; 20.21).
    TEV makes explicit the meaning of the Greek phrase "his work" by
translating the work he gave me to do; otherwise it would sound as though
Jesus had been sent to finish some work that God had left undone. And
to finish the work he gave me to do is essentially an amplification of
to obey the will of the one who sent me. It may be made clear in some
languages by translating "to do what the one who sent me wanted me to do,
that is, to finish the work which he gave me to do." The translation
must not imply a contradiction between "obeying the will" and "finishing
the work." They are two aspects of essentially the same act of obedience.

           TEV   (4.35-38)   RSV

35 You have a saying, 'Four more   35 Do you not say, 'There are yet
months and then the harvest.' But   four months, then come the harvest'?
I tell you, take a good look at   I tell you, lift up your eyes, and

the fields; the crops are now ripe and ready to be harvested! 36 The man who reaps the harvest is being paid and gathers the crops for eternal life; so the man who plants and the man who reaps will be glad together. 37 For the saying is true, 'One man plants, another man reaps.' 38 I have sent you to reap a harvest in a field where you did not work; others worked there, and you profit from their work."	see how the fields are already white for harvest. 36 He who reaps receives wages, and gathers fruit for eternal life, so that sower and reaper may rejoice together. 37 For here the saying holds true, 'One sows and another reaps.' 38 I sent you to reap that for which you did not labor; others have labored, and you have entered into their labor."

4.35   You have a saying, 'Four more months and then the harvest.' But I tell you, take a good look at the fields; the crops are now ripe and ready to be harvested!

You have a saying is in Greek a question expecting an affirmative answer. Have a saying translates the same verb used in Matthew 16.2 (literally "you say"), where also a popular saying or proverb is introduced. That Jesus is quoting a proverb is indicated both by the form and by the brevity of the Greek expression. JB translates "Have you not got a saying?" and NAB "Do you not have a saying?"

When the language has an equivalent word for saying or adage, this word can be employed. If such a term is not available, the saying can be introduced by such an expression as "people often say" or "you often hear people say" or "the following words are often heard."

This saying may be taken from the viewpoint of Jesus' own time, and so indicate that there were four months from then until harvest time, or it may reflect popular reckoning, which thought of four month period between sowing and harvest. Both the famous Gezer agriculture calendar (10th century B.C.) and certain later rabbinic sayings speak of a four-month period between the time of sowing and the time of harvest.

In translating Four more months and then the harvest, it is appropriate to employ the same kind of succinct structure. However, in many languages two such phrases cannot be put together so as to make sense. It may be necessary to translate "In four more months we will harvest" or "After four months people gather in the harvest" or "From planting to harvest is four months."

Take a good look at is literally "lift up your eyes, and see," which Phps translates "open your eyes and look." JB has "Look around you, look..." and NAB "Open your eyes and see!"

The reference to the fields must indicate fields which have a cultivated crop, that is, "planted fields." The most specific reference would probably be to "fields of barley" or "fields of wheat."

The crops to which Jesus refers in this verse are clearly the people who are coming out from the city to see him. Nonetheless, the term for crops must be appropriate to harvested grain. It may be necessary in some languages to say "The grain is now ripe and ready to be harvested."

The term ripe as applied to grain may mean literally "hard" or "yellow," or "dry." It is important to use the correct designation to avoid any inconsistency in referring to fields of grain. Similarly, a receptor language term for harvested may mean literally "cut" or "brought in" or even "beat out," a specific reference to threshing, but with the more general meaning of harvesting.

The last word of the Greek text in verse 35 is now or "already." Translators are divided as to whether this word should go with the last part of verse 35 (NEB, Zür) or with the first part of verse 36 (Mft, Segond, Gdsp, Luther Revised, NAB with a note indicating the alternative possibility). Phps and JB apparently take it with both verses (JB "already they are white, ready for harvest! Already the reaper is being paid his wages..."). TEV takes this adverb with verse 35 (now...ready). The observation that both verses refer to present events may justify the translations of Phps and JB. That is, both verses are in the present tense (are ripe...being paid...gathers), and the fact that "already" occurs at the juncture of the two verses may be a way of tying together the aspects of the present tense in the two verses and giving emphasis to both.

4.36   The man who reaps the harvest is being paid and
        gathers the crops for eternal life; so the man
        who plants and the man who reaps will be glad
        together.

This verse contrasts the natural crops and the "spiritual crops." There is an interval of four months between sowing and harvesting natural crops, but it may be that this passage suggests that with the "spiritual crops" the results are immediate. What is emphasized is the joy which both the one who plants and the one who reaps have in common.

TEV makes explicit the object of the verb reaps (that is, the harvest), which is unexpressed in Greek. Gathers the crops for eternal life is literally "gathers fruit for eternal life," but the use of the plural crops is more natural in English than the singular "fruit." In this context the crops are people who believe, while the phrase for eternal life means "that these people who believe may have eternal life." However, though the sense of the imagery that Jesus uses may be explained in this way, it is usually unwise to remove the metaphor ("demetaphorize") when translating. Here, as in other passages of John, the imagery is so closely tied to the event to which it refers that to "demetaphorize" in translation may require so much reworking as to go beyond the legitimate limits of translation.

The phrase the man who reaps the harvest may be translated as more or less equivalent to "the man who harvests" or "the man who cuts the grain" or even "the man who brings the grain in from the field." The choice of a term or phrase will depend upon the most natural way of speaking about harvesting in the language concerned.

The passive expression is being paid may be made active by indicating the agent, who would be God, that is, "God pays the man who harvests." However, the introduction of God as the agent of the paying may be misunderstood. It may be better to use a so-called pseudo-passive, for example, "receive pay," since the pay the harvester receives is essentially eternal life. Here reaping the harvest and gathering the crops refer to the same process.

4.37   For the saying is true, 'One man plants, another man
        reaps.'

This verse begins with three Greek words which may be translated literally "for in this." The purpose of this expression is to tie the proverb to its application, and it is probable that the application of the proverb is found in verse 38, not in verse 36. TEV does not render these words explicitly, though some translations have "for here..." (JB "For here the proverb holds good:").

In some languages it is important to make a distinction in verbs for "planting." In one instance it may be the process of setting plants into the ground; in another, a matter of scattering seed. In this context a verb for scattering (or planting) seed is appropriate.

In some languages the saying is true may be translated "what people so often say is true" or "what people are in the habit of repeating is true." The connection between this saying and verse 38 may be indicated by an introductory expression, for example, "it is like this" or "that is how it is."

4.38   I have sent you to reap a harvest in a field where
        you did not work; others worked there, and you pro-
        fit from their work."

In the Greek sentence the pronoun I comes first in the sentence, indicating strong emphasis.

A harvest in a field where translates a Greek relative pronoun rendered by Mft and NEB as "a crop for which." In the second clause the adverb there is supplied by TEV because of the manner of translating the first half of the verse (in a field where).

A difficulty is presented by the expression where you did not work, since to reap a harvest certainly constitutes work. However, the reference is to the earlier work involved in preparing the ground and planting the seed. This difference in time or activity must be made explicit in some languages, for example, "I have sent you to harvest in a field where you did not previously work" or "...where you did not yourselves prepare the ground" or "...where you did not at an earlier time plow the ground."

You profit from their work is the meaning of the Greek expression rendered literally in RSV: "you have entered into their labor." Mft has "you reap the profit of their toil"; NAB "you have come into their gain"; JB "you have come into the rewards of their trouble"; and NEB "come in for the harvest of their toil." In some languages "profiting from someone else's work" may be expressed as "you have an advantage because of what others have already worked hard to do" or "you are better off because of what they did" or "you have gained because they worked hard."

TEV (4.39-42) RSV

39 Many of the Samaritans in that town believed in Jesus because the woman had said, "He told me everything I have ever done." 40 So when the Samaritans came to him, they begged him to stay with them, and Jesus stayed there two days.

41 Many more believed because of his message, 42 and they told the woman, "We believe now, not because of what you said, but because we ourselves have heard him, and we know that he really is the Savior of the world."

39 Many Samaritans from that city believed in him because of the woman's testimony, "He told me all that I ever did." 40 So when the Samaritans came to him, they asked him to stay with them; and he stayed there two days. 41 And many more believed because of his word. 42 They said to the woman, "It is no longer because of your words that we believe, for we have heard for ourselves, and we know that this is indeed the Savior of the world."

The focus now shifts back to the Samaritans and to the woman who told them about Jesus. (Compare verse 31, where the focus shifted from the woman and the people in the city to Jesus and his disciples.)

In some languages a serious problem is posed by the lack of a marked transition between verses 38 and 39. Merely marking the shift by beginning a new paragraph may be inadequate, especially since so many people hear the scriptures read, rather than reading them for themselves. Unless there is a more overt transition than exists in a literal rendering, those who hear the message may imagine that the words about planting and harvesting were directed to the Samaritans, and that it was because of this statement of Jesus that they believed. To avoid such a misunderstanding, it may be necessary to introduce verse 39 by a transitional expression, such as "But as for the Samaritans, many in that town believed..."

4.39   Many of the Samaritans in that town believed in Jesus because the woman had said, "He told me everything I have ever done."

Many of the Samaritans in that town believed in Jesus is literally "But from that town many believed in him of the Samaritans." Very few translations are literal here; most of them, like TEV, attempt a clearer way to convey the meaning. Note JB "Many Samaritans of that town had believed in him" and NEB "Many Samaritans of that town came to believe in him."

Believed in Jesus ("him") is a favorite Johannine expression (7.31; 8.30; 10.42; 11.45; 12.42). Initially the faith of the Samaritans was based on the woman's testimony, rather than on any mighty work they had seen Jesus do (compare 2.11, 23; 7.31; 11.45). But others came to believe because of their own immediate encounter with Jesus (see verse 42, and note also 8.30). Some translators are reluctant to use here the same expression for "believed in" employed in many other contexts in the

Gospel of John. To them it seems impossible that the Samaritans could have really "believed in Jesus" solely on the basis of what the woman had said. This tendency to "dilute" the meaning of the phrase "believe in" may reflect a wrong concept of the biblical meaning of "trust." At any rate, it is not legitimate to shift the evident intent of the writer simply because the context appears to be somewhat unusual.

Had said is literally "had witnessed." (On the meaning of the verb "to witness," see 1.7.)

It is true that the statement He told me everything I have ever done is a rhetorical exaggeration, technically called hyperbole. Obviously during the short conversation Jesus had with this woman, he did not relate to her everything she had done throughout her life. However, it is not justifiable to modify the statement of the writer on this basis. In all languages there are degrees of rhetorical exaggeration, and in this particular setting the statement of the woman can be readily understood and evaluated.

4.40   So when the Samaritans came to him, they begged
        him to stay with them, and Jesus stayed there
        two days.

The verb begged translates a verb tense in Greek which seems to focus attention on the action in progress and so may be rendered "kept begging."Gdsp's "they asked him" is certainly too weak.

As some commentators point out, there are theological overtones in the words rendered to stay and stayed (see especially John's use of the verb in 14.10 and 15.4). It is almost impossible to bring out this kind of overtone in translation, and such matters should be left to the teaching ministry of the church.

Jesus is not explicitly rendered in the Greek text, which has the pronoun "he."

4.41   Many more believed because of his message,

In Greek this verse actually begins with "and," but the conjunction marks the continuation of the discourse, and it is unnecessary to translate it.

It may be necessary in some languages to state specifically the nature of the contrast expressed in the comparative more. It may be made explicit by saying "Many believed because of what the woman had said, but many more believed because of what Jesus said" or "In comparison with the many who believed because of what the woman said, many more believed because of what Jesus said."

4.42   and they told the woman, "We believe now, not be-
        cause of what you said, but because we ourselves
        have heard him, and we know that he really is the
        Savior of the world."

We believe now, not because of what you said is literally "no longer because of what you said do we believe," in which the focus is obviously on not because of what you said.

Two problems are involved in translating this statement of the Samaritans. In such construction some languages require that the positive clause precede the negative clause. If so, one may translate "We believe now because we ourselves have heard him, and it is not because of what you said." A second problem is that some languages may require a shift of the negative from the clause of cause to the verb "to believe," for example, "We do not believe because of what you said, but we do believe because we ourselves have heard him speak" or "...have heard what he has said."

It should be noted that John focuses attention upon the Samaritans throughout verses 28-42. Although only implicitly referred to in verse 28 (they hear the woman's testimony about Jesus), they are mentioned in verse 30 (they left and went), verse 39 (many of the Samaritans...believed), verse 40 (the Samaritans came to him...begged him), verse 41 (many more believed), and verse 42 (they told...we believe...we have heard...we know).

Except for Luke 2.11 this verse is the only mention in the Gospels of the title Savior as applied to Jesus during the course of his earthly life, though it is used in that sense twice in Acts and several times in Paul's writings. In the Old Testament, God is the one who saves his people, and sometimes he is referred to as their Savior; in Luke 1.47 Mary says, "My soul is glad because of God my Savior," a statement based on an Old Testament passage (1 Sam 2.1-10). However, in the light of the fact that Samaria was largely under the influence of Greek culture, it may be better to look for the background of this term in the Greek world, where it was applied to gods, emperors, and various heroes.

Terms for Savior generally reflect two kinds of contexts. One refers to "the one who rescues" or "the one who delivers" (implying "from danger" or "from bondage"). The other involves the concept of restoration, and may be rendered "the one who restores" or "the one who makes us able again." For the phrase the Savior of the world it may be necessary to use a clause, for example, "the one who rescues the people of the world" or "the one who restores again all people."

TEV   (4.43-45)   RSV

JESUS HEALS AN OFFICIAL'S SON

43 After spending two days there, Jesus left and went to Galilee. 44 For he himself had said, "A prophet is not respected in his own country." 45 When he arrived in Galilee, the people there welcomed him, because they had gone to the Passover Festival in Jerusalem and had seen everything that he had done during the festival.	43 After the two days he departed to Galilee. 44 For Jesus himself testified that a prophet has no honor in his own country. 45 So when he came to Galilee, the Galileans welcomed him, having seen all that he had done in Jerusalem at the feast, for they too had gone to the feast.

In translating the section heading Jesus Heals an Official's Son,

[133]

it is important to choose a term for "heals" which will fit this context. A technical term in a receptor language may imply that Jesus used certain kinds of medicine, but this miracle was obviously performed at some distance, since Jesus simply spoke the word and told the official to go home and that his son would recover. In many languages it will be more appropriate to use a causative expression, for example, "Jesus Causes an Official's Son to Get Well." As elsewhere, it is important to use a verb tense appropriate for a heading. The tendency in English is to use the present tense, but in many languages a narrative tense form should be used in a section heading.

4.43   After spending two days there, Jesus left and
        went to Galilee.

Verses 43-46 are transitional, referring again to the journey interrupted in verse 3. After spending two days there, Jesus left and went to Galilee is literally "But after the two days, he went from there into Galilee."
In some languages it is essential that verbs of movement indicate clearly whether one is going to a new place or returning to where he was before. In such languages Jesus...went to Galilee must be translated "and he went back to Galilee."

4.44   For he himself had said, "A prophet is not re-
        spected in his own country."

Parallels to this proverb are found in Matthew 13.57; Mark 6.4; and Luke 4.24, but John uses it with a distinct focus. In the Synoptic Gospels it is used in connection with the rejection of Jesus in Galilee; John uses it to explain the reception of Jesus by the Galileans after he was rejected in Jerusalem. This use of the proverb is in keeping with the Johannine theology, whereby it is necessary for Jesus to suffer and to die at the hands of the Jewish leaders in Jerusalem. Commentators have a difficult time explaining the inclusion of this verse at this place. Some translators attempt to handle the difficulty by making it a parenthetical statement (for example, Mft, Phps, NAB). John does not indicate to whom Jesus had said these words, and the text gives no clue. This statement of Jesus may be introduced here to explain why the people of Samaria had received him more warmly than the Jews did; or it may refer to the way people from his own country apparently received him enthusiastically in Jerusalem, while they would not have been so likely to do so in Galilee, that is, in Jesus' own home territory. However, the reference is obscure, and it is best for the translator not to make a specific connection.
If it is necessary, as in some languages, to indicate to whom Jesus uttered this saying, one can say "for Jesus himself had said to his disciples" or "...to his followers." The passive expression, A prophet is not respected in his own country, may be changed to an active form, for example, "The people of a prophet's own country do not respect him" or "The people of a man's own country do not accept him as a prophet."

4.45   When he arrived in Galilee, the people there
         welcomed him, because they had gone to the
         Passover Festival in Jerusalem and had seen
         everything that he had done during the festival.

The people there (Phps "the people") is literally "the Galileans";
but the people there is more natural within the TEV restructuring of the
verse, since these words immediately follow when he arrived in Galilee.
    TEV restructures the last part of this verse, which appears in RSV
as "having seen all that he had done in Jerusalem at the feast, for they
too had gone to the feast." TEV first introduces the information that
the people had gone to the Passover Festival, thus providing the background for the explanation that they had seen everything that he had
done during the festival. In keeping with the consensus of New Testament
scholarship, "the feast" is identified as the Passover Festival.
    There are certain problems in the sequence of tenses in verse 45.
Note that the time of arrived precedes welcomed, but had gone precedes
both arrived and welcomed but is followed by had seen. It may be
necessary in some receptor languages to restructure this verse, for example, "The people in Galilee had gone to the Passover festival in
Jerusalem and they saw everything that Jesus did during the festival;
hence, when Jesus arrived in Galilee, the people there welcomed him."

| TEV | (4.46-54) | RSV |

46 Then Jesus went back to
Cana in Galilee, where he had
turned the water into wine. A
government official was there
whose son was sick in Capernaum.
47 When he heard that Jesus had
come from Judea to Galilee, he
went to him and asked him to go
to Capernaum and heal his son,
who was about to die. 48 Jesus
said to him, "None of you will
ever believe unless you see
miracles and wonders."
    49 "Sir," replied the offi-
cial, "come with me before my
child dies."
    50 Jesus said to him, "Go;
your son will live!"
    The man believed Jesus' words
and went. 51 On his way home his
servants met him with the news,
"Your boy is going to live!"
    52 He asked them what time it
was when his son got better, and
they answered, "It was one o'-
clock yesterday afternoon when

46 So he came again to Cana in
Galilee, where he had made the
water wine. And at Capernaum there
was an official whose son was ill.
47 When he heard that Jesus had
come from Judea to Galilee, he
went and begged him to come down
and heal his son, for he was at
the point of death. 48 Jesus therefore said to him, "Unless you see
signs and wonders you will not believe." 49 The official said to
him, "Sir, come down before my child
dies." 50 Jesus said to him, "Go;
your son will live." The man believed the word that Jesus spoke
to him and went his way. 51 As he
was going down, his servants met
him and told him that his son was
living. 52 So he asked them the
hour when he began to mend, and
they said to him, "Yesterday at
the seventh hour the fever left
him." 53 The father knew that
was the hour when Jesus had said
to him, "Your son will live"; and

the fever left him." 53 Then the
father remembered that it was at
that very hour when Jesus had
told him, "Your son will live."
So he and all his family believed.
   54 This was the second miracle that Jesus performed after
coming from Judea to Galilee.

he himself believed, and all his
household. 54 This was now the
second sign that Jesus did when
he had come from Judea to Galilee.

This story is the climax of section 1.19-4.54, which describes
various reactions of persons toward Jesus in terms of faith. The structure of the narrative itself is simple. First, the dilemma is described:
a man's son is about to die (46-47). Then Jesus heals the child, using
the healing as an opportunity to rebuke a faith that is based merely on
seeing miracles performed (48-50). Finally, the reaction of the persons
involved in the miracle is given (51-53), culminating in belief on the
part of the father and his family.

4.46   Then Jesus went back to Cana in Galilee, where
            he had turned the water into wine. A government
            official was there whose son was sick in Capernaum.

The clause where he had turned the water into wine may cause difficulty in some languages because it reflects an activity prior to the
time of the verb in the main clause. Since this clause is primarily explanatory or identificational, it may be translated as a parenthetical
statement in some languages, for example, "(That is where Jesus earlier
turned the water into wine)" or "(...caused the water to become wine)."
   The word TEV here translates government official is rendered in
other translations in various ways. RSV and Phps render "an official";
Mft and NAB "a royal official"; JB "a court official"; NEB "an officer
in the royal service." The word itself may denote either a person of
royal blood or one in the service of a king. Most translations take it
in the latter sense, which appears to be the meaning intended here. The
man may have been a Gentile, and possibly a soldier, though doubtless
there were many kinds of administrative officials in Capernaum. However,
what is important for John is the fact that he is from Galilee, as
opposed to Judea (or Jerusalem), the center of hostility against Jesus.
Since TEV identifies this person as a government official in the present
verse, when the word is used again in verse 49, it is simply translated
as the official.
   In this account John uses three different Greek words to describe
the son, and TEV attempts to maintain the distinction between them in
translation: son (huios, verses 46, 47, 50), child (paidion, verse 49),
and boy (pais, verse 51). In other contexts the last word (pais) may
mean "servant," but here the meaning of boy is evidently intended.
   Some receptor languages may present problems because of the locations
in verses 46 and 47. The spatial adverb there can be misleading, since
it may suggest that the government official was already in Cana. However,
the demonstrative there should refer to Galilee. As indicated clearly in
47, the official went to Cana, presumably from Capernaum.

4.47   When he heard that Jesus had come from Judea
           to Galilee, he went to him and asked him to
           go to Capernaum and heal his son, who was about
           to die.

The Greek verb translated asked is the same verb and tense rendered
begged in verse 40, and it may best be taken with that meaning here (see
the NEB).

To go to Capernaum is literally "that he might come down." The verb
"to come down" is the same one used in 2.12. In 2.13 the special term
for a journey to Jerusalem is used (literally "to go up"). TEV makes explicit the place to which Jesus was asked to come, namely, Capernaum.

In some languages the request the government official makes to
Jesus is best put into direct discourse, for example, "begged him, 'Come
to Capernaum and heal my son, who is about to die.'"

Who was about to die is translated by JB "as he was at the point of
death." In some languages the more appropriate way of saying about to
die may be "is now dying" or "is in the process of dying." In some languages one may even say "is half dead" or "is now leaving life."

4.48   Jesus said to him, "None of you will ever be-
           lieve unless you see miracles and wonders."

The Greek text begins this verse with John's favorite particle (see
comments on oun under 2.18). The clause unless you see miracles and
wonders comes first in the Greek order and is emphatic. The Greek text
has literally "signs and wonders," a construction (called "hendiadys")
often found in the Old Testament, in which two nouns joined by "and"
are used as the equivalent of a noun modified by an adjective. "Wonders"
is taken here as a way of modifying and intensifying the noun "signs."
Throughout the Gospel of John TEV renders "sign" as miracles, and wonders
is understood as the equivalent of an adjective, for example, "wonderful signs" or "wonderful miracles." NEB and JB have "signs and portents,"
but "portents" connotes a forewarning of evil, which is not intended
here. For languages in which it is difficult to use two terms such as
"miracles and wonders," or even "signs and wonders," it may be useful
to follow TEV's example and use one term as a qualification of the other,
for example, "wonderful miracles" or "remarkable signs."

Although Jesus addressed the man directly, he used the plural form
of "you." TEV makes this clear by translating None of you. It is important that the plural form of the verb be indicated in translation to
show that Jesus' words apply to others as well as to the official. Most
English translations give the impression that Jesus is directing his
remark solely to the official, without reference to others who undoubtedly were present on this occasion. In some languages it may be useful to
shift the order of the conditional elements in the statement to read,
"If you people do not see wonderful miracles, you will never believe." For
languages which require a grammatical object for a verb meaning "believe,"
it may be possible to translate "If you people do not see me perform
miracles, you will not trust me" or "...you will not have any confidence
in me."

4.49   "Sir," replied the official, "come with me before my child dies."

The word translated Sir may also have the full Christian meaning
of "Lord" (see verse 11). Most translations take the term here in the
sense of Sir.
    Because of the evident urgency of the situation and the nature of
the official's response to Jesus, it may be appropriate to use a strong
expression to render Come with me, for example, "Do come with me" or
"Come right now with me."
    In some languages it is difficult to express the temporal relation
suggested by the clause before my child dies. The closest equivalent
may be a conditional, for example, "if not, then my child will die."
Or the contrast may be made between such an expression as "now" and a
future tense, for example, "Come with me now or my child will die."

4.50   Jesus said to him, "Go; your son will live!"
The man believed Jesus' words and went.

Will live in this verse, is going to live in verse 51, and will
live in verse 53 are all in the present tense in Greek (literally "is
living"). Although the present tense is used, it is obvious that in each
instance the focus is on the fact that the child will continue to live.
The use of "to live" in the sense of "to recover" or "to regain one's
health" reflects a Hebraism; in the Old Testament the Hebrew verb "to
live" is frequently used in this sense. In some languages it may be
essential to reflect this Hebraism by translating "will get well again."
To say "will live" may suggest merely continuing in the same state of
ill health.
    The expression Jesus' words (TEV) reaches the English reader with
greater impact than the literal Greek, "the word which Jesus said to
him." JB has "The man believed what Jesus had said." NAB "The man put
his trust in the word Jesus spoke to him" may not sound natural to most
readers.

4.51   On his way home his servants met him with the
news, "Your boy is going to live!"

On his way home represents the Greek "as he was going down." The
use of "to go down" shows that the author had an accurate knowledge of
the geographical situation. To get from Cana to Capernaum, it is necessary to go eastward across the hills of Galilee and then down to the
Sea of Galilee. NEB translates the last part of verse 50 "and started
for home" and then begins verse 51 "He was on his way down," thus
making the meaning clear.
    Met him with the news (so also NEB and JB; see Mft) is literally
"met him saying to him." The natural equivalent in many languages is
"met him and said to him."
    While TEV and NEB use direct discourse ("Your boy is going to live!"),
the best Greek manuscripts use indirect discourse, "that his boy was
going to live." Some Greek manuscripts do have direct discourse, but TEV
and NEB use direct discourse mainly for stylistic reasons.

To be consistent with the will live in verse 50, it may be important to translate verse 51 "is going to get well again" or "is going
to recover" or "is recovering."

4.52   He asked them what time it was when his son
         got better, and they answered, "It was one o'
         clock yesterday afternoon when the fever left
         him."

The tense of the verb translated got better suggests a definite
change in the boy's condition. When his son got better may be rendered
"when his son began to recover" or "when his son began to get well again."
The question asked by the official is often best expressed as
direct discourse; for example, "He asked them, 'When did my son begin
to recover?'"
It was one o'clock yesterday afternoon is literally "it was the
seventh hour yesterday." As indicated earlier (4.6), John calculated the
hours of the day from about 6:00 a.m., and so "the seventh hour" would
be about one o'clock in the afternoon. Most modern English translations
are essentially the same.
The fever left him is the same expression used in Matthew 8.15 and
Mark 1.31. It is impossible in some languages to say that the fever left
him, for a fever cannot be spoken of as "coming" or "going." However,
in many instances one can say "he had no more fever" or "he grew cool
again" or "he was no longer hot."

4.53   Then the father remembered that it was at that
         very hour when Jesus had told him, "Your son
         will live." So he and all his family believed.

Remembered is literally "knew" (RSV), but the force of "to remember"
or "to realize" (Mft, NAB, JB) is more appropriate to the context. It
is important not to use a term for "remember" which would suggest that
the official had forgotten what Jesus had said. The appropriate meaning
in some languages is "realized," "became aware of," or "recognized."
So he and all his family believed is literally "so he believed and
all his family." This construction is the same type discussed earlier
(see 2.2). The word TEV translates family may have the wider meaning of
"household" (so many translations). In the present context the word believed means that the man and his family "became believers" (see Mft,
NEB, NAB); Phps translates this word "believed in Jesus." Such a translation is necessary if the object of faith must be expressed in the
receptor language.

4.54   This was the second miracle that Jesus per-
         formed after coming from Judea to Galilee.

The Greek text of this verse is redundant, since there are two
words that may mean "second." Acknowledging this redundance, most translations handle the text as TEV does. RSV seems to render each word
separately, the first by "now" and the second by "second" ("this was now

[139]

the second sign"). This same construction appears in 21.16. Second
miracle refers the reader back to Jesus' first miracle in Cana (2.11).
Miracle (literally "sign") translates the same word used in verse
48. (See the discussion at 2.11.)

A literal translation of verse 54 can be misleading in some languages, since it would imply that on this particular occasion, when
Jesus had come from Judea to Galilee, he performed two miracles. In reality,
the reference is to the second of two miracles, performed when Jesus returned to Galilee from Judea on two different occasions. The first relates the turning of water into wine (Chapter 2), and the second, in
the present context, is the healing of the official's son. Both are associated with Cana and both occurred upon a return of Jesus from Judea.
In translating this verse it may be necessary to say in some languages
"This was the second time that Jesus came from Judea to Galilee and
performed a miracle."

Chronologically Chapter 5 is connected with Chapter 4 by the words After this. Although only this loose chronological connection exists between the two chapters, there is a definite thematic relation. In his dialogue with the Samaritan woman Jesus declared that he had the power to give life-giving water; now, by healing the lame man, Jesus reveals his life-giving power (1-9a). This healing takes place on a Sabbath day and so leads to a conflict between Jesus and the Jewish authorities (9b-15). As a result, Jesus affirms his identity with the Father (17-18), and this claim leads to a controversy regarding the Son's authority (19-29). The Jewish authorities will not accept Jesus' own testimony regarding who he is (30-31), so Jesus appeals to other witnesses: to John the Baptist (32-35), to his own mighty works (36), to the Father (37-38), to the Jews' own sacred Scriptures (39), and finally to Moses, who will accuse the Jews before the Father because of their rejection of the Son (45-47). Jesus further indicates that he is not looking for praise from men, but that the Jewish authorities are looking for such praise, and therefore they reject him and his message (41-44). Viewed in its entirety, Chapter 5 revolves around the theme of the life-giving power of the Son, a power which he derives from the Father.

| TEV | (5.1-9a) | RSV |

THE HEALING AT THE POOL

5 After this, Jesus went to Jerusalem for a religious festival. 2 Near the Sheep Gate in Jerusalem there is a pool^h with five porches; in Hebrew it is called Bethzatha.^{i} 3 A large crowd of sick people were lying on the porches--the blind, the lame, and the paralyzed.^{j} 5 A man was there who had been sick for thirty-eight years. 6 Jesus saw him lying there, and he knew that the man had been sick for such a long time; so he asked him, "Do you want to get well?"

7 The sick man answered, "Sir, I don't have anyone here to put me in the pool when the water is stirred up; while I am trying to get in, somebody else gets there first."

8 Jesus said to him, "Get up, pick up your mat, and walk." 9 Immediately the man got well; he

5 After this there was a feast of the Jews, and Jesus went up to Jerusalem. 2 Now there is in Jerusalem by the Sheep Gate a pool, in Hebrew called Bethzatha,^{j} which has five porticoes. 3 In these lay a multitude of invalids, blind, lame, paralyzed.^{k} 5 One man was there, who had been ill for thirty-eight years. 6 When Jesus saw him and knew that he had been lying there a long time, he said to him, "Do you want to be healed?" 7 The sick man answered him, "Sir, I have no man to put me into the pool when the water is troubled, and while I am going another steps down before me." 8 Jesus said to him, "Rise, take up your pallet, and walk." 9 And at once the man was healed, and he took up his pallet and walked.

^{j}Other ancient authorities read

picked up his mat and started walking.

*h*Near the Sheep Gate...a pool; *or* Near the Sheep Pool...a place.

*i*Bethzatha; *some manuscripts have* Bethesda

*j*Some manuscripts add verses 3b-4: They were waiting for the water to move, 4 because every now and then an angel of the Lord went down into the pool and stirred up the water. The first sick person to go into the pool after the water was stirred up was healed from whatever disease he had.

Bethesda, others *Bethsaida*

*k*Other ancient authorities read wholly or in part, *waiting for the moving of the water; 4 for an angel of the Lord went down at certain seasons into the pool, and troubled the water: whoever stepped in first after the troubling of the water was healed of whatever disease he had*

The title, The Healing at the Pool, may be inadequate if translated literally. A more satisfactory section heading may be "Jesus Heals a Lame Man."

5.1   After this, Jesus went to Jerusalem for a religious festival.

After this is the same expression used in 3.22; it has the same meaning as the phrase used in 2.12, and it appears again in 6.1. An appropriate equivalent in some languages is "and then," "and later," or "after that." Since there is no way of knowing precisely what the lapse of time was, it is better to use an indefinite phrase that implies subsequent activity.

For a religious festival is literally "there was a feast of the Jews," and in the Greek sentence structure it is followed by the clause "and Jesus went up to Jerusalem." A few ancient manuscripts have "there was the (note the definite article "the") feast of the Jews," probably a reference either to the feast of Tabernacles or to the Passover. The textual evidence for this reading is weak, but the feast referred to was perhaps one of these two or possibly Pentecost, since on these three occasions the Jews were required to go to Jerusalem.

In some languages it is difficult to speak about a festival as merely "happening." Many receptor languages require participants to be identified in such an expression. Therefore it may be necessary to say "the people were celebrating a religious festival" or "the Jewish people were celebrating a special religious event."

Went is literally "went up" (so most translations); see 2.13.

Connecting Jesus' activity with the religious festival by a literal rendering of the Greek conjunction ("and") may not be adequate in some languages. Since there is a causal relation, TEV has Jesus went... for a religious festival.

Near the Sheep Gate in Jerusalem there is
a pool[h] with five porches; in Hebrew it is
called Bethzatha.[i]

[h]Near the Sheep Gate...a pool; *or* Near the
Sheep Pool...a place.

[i]Bethzatha; *some manuscripts have* Bethesda.

There are problems connected with the Greek text in this verse.
Even though the UBS Greek Committee rates the reading in its Greek New
Testament text as "B" (indicating that it is fairly certain but not
"virtually certain," as an "A" reading is), the problems should still
be pointed out. The first problem is that a word must be supplied to
complete the meaning of the text; the second textual problem is that the
word pool may be either the nominative or the dative case, with an at-
tendant difference in grammatical relations.

If pool is in the nominative case (as in the UBS Greek text), it
is modified by the participle it is called, but it cannot be modified by
the adjective Sheep. This requires the addition of a noun to complete
the meaning of Sheep. In Nehemiah 3.1 and 12.39 reference is made to "the
Sheep Gate," and on the basis of this reference the UBS Greek Committee
supplies the word Gate. This textual choice is followed in translation
by TEV, RSV, Phps, Zür, Luther Revised, GeCL, and Segond.

However, it is possible that the word pool is in the dative case
in Greek, and if so it relates to the word Sheep, and the translator
must supply a noun to be modified by the participle it is called. NEB
supplies "place" ("Now at the Sheep-Pool in Jerusalem there is a place");
JB "building" ("...there is a building"); and Mft "bath" ("Now in
Jerusalem there is a bath beside the sheep-pool"). Moffatt's rendering
assumes that in the original text the word "pool" appeared twice, first
as dative and then as nominative, and that by an oversight some early
scribe omitted the word in one instance as he was copying the manuscript.

No absolute decision can be made, but it is clear that the UBS
Committee on the Greek text has the support of most modern translations.
The Committee's judgment is based on the belief that the other readings
have arisen as attempts to remove the difficulties occasioned by the
original reading (represented by the translation in TEV, RSV, etc.).

There is also a textual problem related to the name Bethzatha. A
number of modern translations accept the same reading that TEV has (JB,
BJ, Mft, Phps, Gdsp, RSV), but others follow the reading "Bethesda" (NEB,
NAB, Segond, Zür, Luther Revised). It is possible also to follow a
third reading, "Bethsaida," which has strong textual support. However,
since the town of Bethsaida on the sea of Galilee is mentioned in 1.44
and elsewhere in this Gospel, it is possible that "Bethsaida" found its
way into the text through a scribe who was not familiar with the other
names.

"Bethesda" also has strong textual support, as evidenced by the
number of translations that accept it. The strongest evidence against
it is the belief that it was originally introduced into the text by a
scribe who was not familiar with the name "Bethzatha" and so attempted

[143]

to give the pool a symbolic name. (In Aramaic, Bethesda means "house of [divine] mercy.") But some modern scholars feel inclined to accept this reading because it seems to have been used in the copper scroll found at Qumran (the Dead Sea Community) in reference to a pool or a region in this general area. If "Bethesda" is accepted, it should be on its merits as a genuine place name, not because John saw any symbolic significance in the Hebrew name. Elsewhere John always gives the Greek equivalent of the Hebrew or Aramaic name of a person or place (see 1.38, 41,42; 4.25; 5.2; 9.7; 11.16; 19.13,17; 20.16).

On the whole, the least problematic reading is Bethzatha, which seems to have been the basis for the other readings. But as the "D" qualification in the UBS text indicates, there is a strong degree of doubt about the original reading.

In English the so-called expletive there is a convenient device for providing a "zero subject element" in sentences in which new information is placed in the predicate portion, that is, after the verb is. Many languages treat this type of sentence in a different way to indicate the existence of a particular object (in this case the pool) in a place (Jerusalem). For example, one may translate "a pool with five porches exists in Jerusalem near the Sheep Gate" or "in Jerusalem near the Sheep Gate a pool with five porches exists." Sometimes the existence of an object may be described in terms of what can be seen, for example, "in Jerusalem near the Sheep Gate one can see a pool with five porches" or "...a pool with five porches can be seen."

The equivalent of Sheep Gate may be "a gate by which sheep enter the city" or "a gate by which sheep are led into the city" or "...driven into the city."

There may be a problem in translating a pool with five porches. It would not be accurate to say "a pool with five porches around it," since this pool did not have the shape of a pentagon. It should be noted that the pool referred to has been discovered and excavated. It is quite large (95 meters [315 feet] long) and has a central partition, dividing it into two sections. On the partition and on the four sides there are colonnades, the five porches spoken of in the Gospel. It is impossible to convey all this information in translation, but the translation should not give the reader a wrong impression. Perhaps one can say "...a pool; there were five porches there." Information concerning the size and shape of the pool and the location of the five porches may be given in a marginal note.

In some languages even an expression for porches is difficult, but such a construction may be described as "covered areas" or "roofed-over open area."

The clause in Hebrew it is called Bethzatha may be rendered "people who speak the Hebrew language call the pool Bethzatha" or "the Hebrew name for the place is Bethzatha."

5.3   A large crowd of sick people were lying on the
       porches--the blind, the lame, and the paralyzed.*j*

       *j*Some manuscripts add verses 3b-4: They were
       waiting for the water to move, 4 because every

now and then an angel of the Lord went down
into the pool and stirred up the water. The
first sick person to go into the pool after
the water was stirred up was healed from
whatever disease he had.

In Greek this verse begins with the pronominal phrase "in these,"
which TEV makes explicit as on the porches and NEB as "in these colonnades."

TEV takes sick people as a generic term, qualified by the specific
terms the blind, the lame, and the paralyzed. The same exegesis is
apparently followed by NEB, JB, NAB, and Phps. It is possible to follow
RSV and others and take sick people as a specific category ("a multitude of invalids, blind, lame, paralyzed"). However, in Greek this term
is very general (literally "those who were weak"), and it is better taken
as a generic term followed by the specific types of illness.

A large crowd of sick people may be rendered "many, many sick
people."

Some languages may require an indication of the precise relation
between the generic expression sick people and a more specific description of them as blind, lame, and paralyzed. One may say, for example,
"These sick people included those who were blind, lame, and paralyzed."
Terms for these conditions may be rendered as negatives, for example,
"they could not see, they could not walk, and they could not move."

In TEV the last half of verse 3 and all of verse 4 are included
in a footnote, indicating that these verses do not appear in the earliest
and best Greek manuscripts. It seems likely that this part of the text
was added by some ancient scribe as a kind of marginal note, explaining
why the sick people gathered about the pool and how they reacted when
the water was stirred up (perhaps by an underground stream that flowed
in from time to time). This explanation probably represents a popular
belief held by the people of that day, that is, that the stirring up of
the water was caused by an angel of the Lord, and that whoever should
be the first sick person to go down into the pool after the water was
stirred up was healed from whatever disease he had.

In addition to the fact that they are omitted from the best Greek
manuscripts, verses 3b-4 offer serious textual problems.

In selecting a term for "moved" it is important to avoid the impression that the entire body of water moved. One may say "part of the water
moved." In some languages the term employed suggests "some water flowed
in." In others the meaning is essentially equivalent to "some water."

The temporal expression every now and then is indefinite in meaning,
and in the receptor language an expression should be selected which is
also indefinite. To do so is difficult in some languages, which demand
a choice among expressions meaning "every few hours," "every few days,"
or "every few months." If a choice is necessary, a translation suggesting
"every few days" would probably be the most appropriate.

It may be difficult to say in some languages was healed from whatever disease he had. An equivalent may be "would get well, no matter
what disease he had" or "got well, even if he had any kind of disease."

5.5   A man was there who had been sick for
             thirty-eight years.

That the man had been sick for thirty-eight years indicates at
once the completeness and the wonder of the healing. His lameness was
not something of a temporary nature; he had probably been lame all his
life--in other words, he was thirty-eight years old.
       Though the Greek term identifying the man as being sick merely
means "weak," it seems clear that this weakness was lameness, because
he is told to get up and take up his bed and walk. It may be necessary
in some languages to use a term for sick which means essentially "lame."
Otherwise, a term for "sick" might suggest some kind of debilitating
fever or infectious disease, which probably would not have lasted for
38 years.

5.6   Jesus saw him lying there, and he knew that
             the man had been sick for such a long time;
             so he asked him, "Do you want to get well?"

Saw and knew in the Greek text are participles dependent on the
main verb said. It is more natural in English to use a finite verb for
each of these participles (see most translations).
       In the question Do you want to get well? there is no need to
press the force of the verb want, as though to imply that the man's own
will had some force in effecting the cure. The question merely means
"Would you like to get well?"

5.7   The sick man answered, "Sir, I don't have
             anyone here to put me in the pool when the
             water is stirred up; while I am trying to get
             in, somebody else gets there first."

The sick man answered is literally "the sick man answered him,"
but it is unnecessary to express the indirect object in English.
       The word rendered Sir may also mean "Lord," but here, as in some
other passages, the meaning is simply "sir" (see 4.11,15,19,49). As used
here, the word is merely a polite form of address, not a confession of
the lordship of Jesus Christ.
       The temporal expression when the water is stirred up must often be
expressed as the first part of the sick man's statement, since it provides the temporal setting for his predicament.
       It also may be necessary to indicate more specifically the role of
a person who might potentially help the sick man, for example, "I have
no helper here to put me in the pool" or "there is no one here to help
me, that is, to put me in the pool."
       While I am trying to get in is literally "while I am coming" (NEB
"but while I am moving"; JB "while I am still on the way"). Phps is
closer to TEV, "While I'm trying to get there."

5.8   Jesus said to him, "Get up, pick up your
             mat, and walk."

The Greek word used for mat in this verse (krabbatos) is a colloquial term for the pallet or mattress that the poor had for bedding. It is used elsewhere in the New Testament only in Mark 2.4,9,11,12; 6.55; Acts 5.15; 9.33. It always refers to the bed of a sick person.

In some languages it may be important to distinguish between "walking around," as a kind of demonstration of one's ability to walk, and "walking away" or "going someplace." It is true that the ability to walk was to be demonstrated by the lame man, but the import of what Jesus has to say would refer to his ability to walk away healed, carrying his own mat.

5.9a   Immediately the man got well; he picked up his mat and started walking.

Immediately is omitted by the original scribe of one important Greek manuscript. It is possible that this word was added later in an attempt to heighten the effect of the miracle. The UBS Committee on the Greek text believes its omission was accidental, and most translations apparently accept the word as an original part of the text.

The ability of the man to pick up his mat and walk emphasizes the completeness of the cure. This verse forms the counterpart to the mention of the thirty-eight years in verse 5.

TEV	(5.9b-13)	RSV

TEV	RSV
9b The day this happened was a Sabbath, 10 so the Jewish authorities told the man who had been healed, "This is a Sabbath, and it is against our Law for you to carry your mat."	9b Now that day was the sabbath. 10 So the Jews said to the man who was cured, "It is the sabbath, it is not lawful for you to carry your pallet." 11 But he answered them, "The man who healed me said to me, 'Take up your pallet, and walk.'" 12 They asked him, "Who is the man who said to you, 'Take up your pallet, and walk'?" 13 Now the man who had been healed did not know who it was, for Jesus had withdrawn, as there was a crowd in the place.
11 He answered, "The man who made me well told me to pick up my mat and walk."	
12 They asked him, "Who is the man who told you to do this?"	
13 But the man who had been healed did not know who Jesus was, for there was a crowd in that place, and Jesus had slipped away.	

5.9b   The day this happened was a Sabbath,

In very few words John states the basis for the controversy that is to follow. Moffatt is literal in his rendering: "Now it was the sabbath on that day." Though some languages employ a transliteration of Sabbath, it is most frequently translated as "rest day" or "day on which people rested." Sometimes the matter of "resting" may be qualified by such an expression as "prescribed rest" or "ordered rest."

5.10   so the Jewish authorities told the man who
had been healed, "This is a Sabbath, and it
is against our Law for you to carry your mat."

On the Greek phrase "the Jews" translated Jewish authorities see
Appendix I. In many languages the closest equivalent is "the officials
among the Jews." In some, however, the best translation is "the leaders
among the Jews."

The use of the Greek imperfect tense for told (literally "were
telling") may be either a reflection of John's narrative style or an
attempt to emphasize the fact that the Jewish authorities kept repeating
this statement to the man who had been healed. The force of the imperfect tense may be indicated in some languages by translating "insistently
told the man."

The Jews had very strict laws concerning what could or could not
be done on the Sabbath, and it was a breach of their law for a man to
carry his sleeping mat on that day. It may be helpful to note the logic
(or lack of it) in the present situation. According to Jewish teaching,
certain situations demanded that the Sabbath law be overridden. For
example, a male child was to be circumcised on the eighth day after
birth, even if the eighth day fell on a Sabbath. If a person's life were
in immediate danger, measures to save it could be taken on the Sabbath.
However, here was a man who had been sick for 38 years and whose life
was obviously not in immediate danger. Therefore, to heal him on the
Sabbath was considered to be a breach of the Sabbath law. But from
Jesus' point of view the making of a sick man whole had priority over
the law of the Sabbath, even though the man's life was not in immediate
danger. Still another factor is involved. It is mentioned later by Jesus
in his controversy with the Jews: God does his works of goodness even
on the Sabbath, and for that reason the Son must also heal people on
that day.

It is against our Law is literally "it is not lawful." The reference is not to the Mosaic Law as such but to the rabbinic interpretation
of the Mosaic law. It is against our Law for you to carry your mat may
be rendered in some languages "our laws say that you must not carry your
mat" or "our laws contain these words, 'You must not carry your mat on
the rest day.'"

5.11   He answered, "The man who made me well
told me to pick up my mat and walk."

There is a notable contrast between the attitude of this man and
that of the blind man in Chapter 9. The man here will not even assume
responsibility for his own deeds, whereas the man who was healed of his
blindness is bold enough to stand up against his parents and the Jewish
authorities.

He answered is literally "but he answered them." Here again the
indirect object is redundant for the English reader (see verse 7).

5.12   They asked him, "Who is the man who told
you to do this?"

In Greek the text reads "Who is the man who said to you, 'Take up your mat, and walk'?" But the expression "pick up your mat and walk" has already occurred in verse 11; hence a substitute phrase, do this, may be employed here, as a matter of English style. Also this construction avoids the difficulty of "quotations within quotations."

The term man is perhaps used contemptuously by the Jewish authorities. Something of the meaning of contempt may be expressed in English by using the term "fellow," for example, "Who is this fellow who told you to pick up your mat and walk?"

5.13   But the man who had been healed did not
            know who Jesus was, for there was a crowd
            in that place, and Jesus had slipped away.

A literal translation of the last part of this verse may be misunderstood. Note, for example, RSV "...for Jesus had withdrawn, as there was a crowd in the place." This could intimate that Jesus left because of the crowd. TEV avoids this ambiguity by translating for there was a crowd in that place, and Jesus had slipped away, making it clear that the presence of the crowd made it possible for Jesus to slip away. NEB has "for the place was crowded and Jesus had slipped away." JB is even clearer: "since Jesus had disappeared into the crowd that filled the place."

In rendering the man who had been healed did not know who Jesus was, it is important not to employ forms which would be misleading, that is, which would suggest that the man did not know who he himself was. It may be necessary to say "the man who was healed did not know who Jesus was" or "...who it was who had healed him."

            TEV   (5.14-16)   RSV

14 Afterward, Jesus found him in the Temple and said, "Listen, you are well now; so stop sinning or something worse may happen to you."

15 Then the man left and told the Jewish authorities that it was Jesus who had healed him. 16 So they began to persecute Jesus, because he had done this healing on a Sabbath.

14 Afterward, Jesus found him in the temple, and said to him, "See, you are well! Sin no more, that nothing worse befall you." 15 The man went away and told the Jews that it was Jesus who had healed him. 16 And this was why the Jews persecuted Jesus, because he did this on the sabbath.

5.14   Afterward, Jesus found him in the Temple
            and said, "Listen, you are well now; so
            stop sinning or something worse may happen
            to you."

Afterward translates the same expression of time that is rendered after this in 5.1. It does not imply "immediately afterward." For languages which require a more specific indication of the lapse of time, an expression designating "later that day" or "within the next day or so" may be used. It would certainly be wrong to suggest that a much longer period of time had elapsed.

And said is literally "and said to him," but see verses 7 and 11. The context makes it apparent that Jesus is addressing the man.

In the Temple is the translation favored by most, but NAB has "in the Temple precincts." Temple is the same word used in 2.14 (see the comments there).

Listen is merely an English idiomatic way of expressing the Greek idiom (ide, literally "behold"), used for the purpose of drawing attention to something (see 1.29). Moffatt renders Listen, you are well now by "See, you are well and strong." A more satisfactory equivalent of Listen is "Pay attention" or "Hear what I am telling you."

Jesus' command and warning, so stop sinning or something worse may happen to you, should not be taken to imply that Jesus was saying that the man's illness was caused by his sins. Evidently the man had been lame since birth. Stop sinning may be rendered "cease your sinning" or "no longer sin."

It is difficult in some languages to translate literally something worse may happen to you. This expression may require complete recasting, for example, "or you may suffer even worse" or "or your suffering may be even more."

5.15   Then the man left and told the Jewish
              authorities that it was Jesus who had
              healed him.

On Jewish authorities see Appendix I.

In many languages the man's statement to the Jewish authorities must be given as direct discourse, for example, "told the Jewish authorities, 'It was Jesus who healed me'" or "...'Jesus was the person who healed me.'"

5.16   So they began to persecute Jesus, because
              he had done this healing on a Sabbath.

Since in many languages a cause or reason must precede a result, it may be necessary to invert the clauses in verse 16, for example, "Because Jesus had healed the man on a Sabbath, the Jewish authorities began to persecute him."

Began to persecute is literally "were persecuting," but several commentators and translators take this verb as TEV does, that is, with the focus on the initiation of the action.

In various languages there are several ways to express the idea of persecute, for example, "made it hard for him" or "caused him harm" or "caused him to suffer." Sometimes a general expression may suggest various forms of persecution, for example, "took action against him" or "declared him their enemy."

He had done this healing is literally "he was doing these things." Several translations take it in the sense of "did such things" (Phps; so also NEB, NAB, Mft, JB). That is, this action is taken as an illustration of the things that Jesus was in the habit of doing on the Sabbath day, and so it stirred up the Jewish authorities against him.

TEV	(5.17-18)	RSV

17 Jesus answered them, "My Father is always working, and I too must work."

18 This saying made the Jewish authorities all the more determined to kill him; not only had he broken the Sabbath law, but he had said that God was his own Father and in this way had made himself equal with God.

17 But Jesus answered them, "My Father is working still, and I am working." 18 This was why the Jews sought all the more to kill him, because he not only broke the sabbath but also called God his Father, making himself equal with God.

<u>5.17</u>   Jesus answered them, "My Father is always
            working, and I too must work."

Verses 17 and 18 are transitional. They serve as the climax to the story of healing the man on the Sabbath and as a transition to the discussion of the authority of the Son and of his relationship to the Father.

In a number of manuscripts Jesus is simply "he." However, whether one translates Jesus or "he" is also a matter of style. As far as the textual problem is concerned, it could be that Jesus was omitted from some manuscripts for stylistic reasons; on the other hand, it is just as possible that Jesus was added in some manuscripts to make explicit the subject of the verb answered.

Since Jesus is not responding here to specific denunciations by the Jewish authorities stated in direct discourse in the biblical text, it may be necessary to use some other expression than "answered," for example, "defended himself by saying." If persecute in the previous verse is translated "accuse," the beginning of verse 17 may read "Jesus answered their accusations by saying."

Always is literally "until now." The meaning is clearly as TEV gives it. The first part of this statement of Jesus is rendered by NEB "My Father has never yet ceased his work"; Gdsp and Phps read "My Father has always been at work." There is, however, a serious difficulty in the choice of a word for work. The meaning is obviously not physical labor. In some languages one may translate "My Father has always been doing such things." In others it may be necessary to be more specific, for example, "My Father has always been helping people" or "...doing things to help people." The statement made by Jesus concerning his own activities should then be parallel, for example, "and I also must do this" or "and I also must help people." The avoidance of the specific term work ("work" in the sense of "labor" was specifically forbidden on the Sabbath) does involve certain liabilities. However, it is even more misleading to use a term for "work" which suggests merely "manual labor."

Although must (in I too must work) is not an explicit part of the Greek text, it is implicit in Jesus' reply, and TEV accordingly makes this information clear. That is, since the Father always works, it is obligatory for the Son also to work.

[151]

    This saying made the Jewish authorities
all the more determined to kill him; not
only had he broken the Sabbath law, but he
had said that God was his own Father and in
this way had made himself equal with God.

This verse begins in Greek with the same words rendered so in
verse 16; as the clause beginning because in verse 16 explains these
words, so the clause beginning not only in this verse explains why the
Jews were determined to kill Jesus.

In some languages the motive which made the Jewish authorities
more determined to kill Jesus must be expressed as a cause, for example,
"because Jesus had said this, the Jewish authorities were all the more
determined to kill him" or "...decided definitely to kill him" or "...
to cause him to die."

The final two causes for the decision of the Jewish authorities
may be made even more explicit by saying "They not only decided to do so
because he had broken the Sabbath law, but also because he had said that
God was his own Father."

The Sabbath law may be rendered "the law about what people could
do on the rest day" or "the law about what was permitted on the rest
day."

But he had said that God was his own Father may be translated
"but also he said, 'God is my own Father'" or "but he also called God
his own Father" or "...spoke of God as his own Father."

The Jews were quick to see the implications of Jesus' argument
and concluded immediately that he had made himself equal with God. The
remainder of the chapter explains the sense in which Jesus claimed
equality with God.

Some translators endeavor to render made himself equal with God
as "said that there was no difference between himself and God." This
translation introduces theological difficulties, because Jesus does
speak of his Father as being different from himself. The concept of
equality may be expressed in some languages: "he measured himself with
God" or "he ranked himself with God" or "he put himself right alongside
of God."

TEV   (5.19-23)   RSV

THE AUTHORITY OF THE SON

19 So Jesus answered them, "I
tell you the truth: the Son can
do nothing on his own; he does
only what he sees his Father doing. What the Father does, the
Son also does. 20 For the Father
loves the Son and shows him all
that he himself is doing. He will
show him even greater things to
do than this, and you will all
be amazed. 21 Just as the Father

19 Jesus said to them, "Truly,
truly, I say to you, the Son can
do nothing of his own accord, but
only what he sees the Father doing;
for whatever he does, that the Son
does likewise. 20 For the Father
loves the Son, and shows him all
that he himself is doing; and greater
works than these will he show him,
that you may marvel. 21 For as the
Father raises the dead and gives

raises the dead and gives them
life, in the same way the Son
gives life to those he wants to.
22 Nor does the Father himself
judge anyone. He has given his
Son the full right to judge, 23
so that all will honor the Son
in the same way as they honor
the Father. Whoever does not
honor the Son does not honor the
Father who sent him.

them life, so also the Son gives
life to whom he will. 22 The Father
judges no one, but has given all
judgment to the Son, 23 that all
may honor the Son, even as they
honor the Father. He who does not
honor the Son does not honor the
Father who sent him.

Jesus' argument in verses 19-29 grows out of his claim of unity
with God the Father. The Son is able to do nothing on his own; he does
only what he sees his Father doing, and what he and his Father do is
essentially to give life (19-21). Moreover, not only has the Father
given the Son the power to give life, but he has also given him the
full right to judge (22-23). In verses 24-29 the themes of the Son's
power to give life and of his right to judge all people are woven together and placed in an eschatological context.

In some languages it may be necessary to modify the section heading, The Authority of the Son. In the first place, a section heading
may more appropriately be in the form of a complete sentence. Secondly,
it may be difficult to speak of "the Son" without specifying whose son
is meant. Therefore such a section heading as "God gives authority to
his Son" or "God causes his Son to have authority" may be needed. In
some languages the more appropriate equivalent is "God gives power to
his Son."

5.19   So Jesus answered them, "I tell you the
              truth: the Son can do nothing on his own;
              he does only what he sees his Father doing.
              What the Father does, the Son also does.

So Jesus answered them is literally "so Jesus answered and said
to them." Most translations do exactly as TEV does and eliminate this,
recognizing the use of two verbs as another instance of Semitic redundancy in introducing discourse. If the accusations of the Jewish authorities recorded in verse 18 are in the form of direct address, the inclusion of "answered" is quite appropriate. However, if the accusations
are in indirect form, it may be necessary to use some other type of
introductory statement for verse 19, for example, "So Jesus responded
to their accusations" or "So Jesus defended himself against their accusations by saying."

I tell you the truth is the same expression used in 1.51.

The Son can do nothing on his own expresses the same truth as
verse 30. In each case can is explicit in the Greek text.

Serious problems are involved in rendering this paragraph, in view
of the many references to the Father and the Son--expressions impossible
to render in languages in which such terms must always occur with a
possessor, that is, the terms used must indicate whose father or whose

son is intended. Moreover, in some languages it is impossible for a person to speak of himself in the third person. If this passage were to be translated literally into some receptor languages, the people would understand Jesus to be speaking about someone else, not about himself. In such languages, rather than saying the Son can do nothing on his own, one must say "I as God's Son can do nothing on my own" or "I as God's Son do nothing just by myself." The following statement, similarly, would read "I only do what I see my Father doing." The final sentence of verse 19 would then read "What my Father does, I as his Son also do."

On his own represents a favorite Johannine expression. See the similar expression in 7.18 (on his own), 11.51 (of his own accord), 15.4 (by itself), 16.13 (on his own), 18.34 (from you). In each instance TEV attempts to let the context determine the specific rendering of the idiomatic expression.

The next clause of this verse is literally "unless he sees the Father doing something." TEV has brought out the contrast indicated in the Greek text through the use of a semicolon, while "the Father" has been translated his Father. To translate "the Father" as his Father is legitimate, although most translations do not do so. In verse 17 Jesus refers to my Father; moreover, in a passage where "the" is used before a noun of kinship, it is usually possible to render it "my" or "our," according to the relation between the speaker and the audience. Here Jesus refers to himself in the third person (the Son) and obviously refers to God as his Father.

In the last sentence in this verse the Father is literally "that one." Again TEV makes a pronominal reference explicit by the use of a noun.

5.20   For the Father loves the Son and shows him all
        that he himself is doing. He will show him even
        greater things to do than this, and you will
        all be amazed.

The word for loves in this verse (Greek phileō) is not the same verb used in the similar statement in 3.35 (Greek agapaō). However, as indicated at 3.35, these two verbs are used interchangeably in the Gospel of John with apparently no difference in meaning or focus.

Since possessive pronouns must be used in some languages to identify the relation between kinship terms, the first sentence in verse 20 may be translated "For my Father loves me and shows me all that he himself is doing." It is possible to translate the Son as appositional, for example, "Since my Father loves me, his Son," but to do so may be unduly awkward and may not enhance the meaning.

In this context greater things has a double reference: the Son's power to raise people from the dead and his right to judge all men. This power is even greater than his power to heal men (1-9). Greater things may be understood in terms of "more important things," but since the focus of meaning here is upon the supernatural manifestations of the Son's power and authority, such an expression as "more marvelous things" may be used. Such a phrase would fit in very well with the meaning of "you will all be amazed."

Things to do is literally "works." In such a context "works" indicates the things that the Son himself is to do, which is the basis for the TEV rendering.

And translates a particle in Greek which indicates purpose. A number of translations use an infinitive here (Phps, NEB, "to fill you with wonder"), while others use a clause introduced by "that" (RSV "that you may marvel"). JB renders the whole statement by "and he will show him even greater things than these, works that will astonish you." In some languages the most effective way of indicating implied purpose is to suggest the result, for example, "and as a result you will all be amazed" or "and because of this you will all be greatly surprised." Amazement may often be expressed idiomatically: "You will have nothing to say," "You will stand there with your mouths open," or "You will stretch your necks to see."

You...all translates a plural form of the pronoun "you" in Greek. This pronoun, expressed in the Greek sentence, is intended to be emphatic.

5.21   Just as the Father raises the dead and
         gives them life, in the same way the
         Son gives life to those he wants to.

The phrases Just as...in the same way translate particles in Greek which help to convey the exact parallelism between the activity of the Father and the Son. The same particles occur again in verse 26.

Raises the dead and gives them life expresses a constant activity of the Father.

In languages requiring an identification of the relation between kinship terms, verse 21 may be rendered "In the same way that my Father raises the dead and causes them to live, in just that same way I, his Son, give life to those that I want to." It is also possible to translate "...in just that same way I give life to those I want to" or "...to those I choose to give life to."

5.22   Nor does the Father himself judge any-
         one. He has given his Son the full right
         to judge,

Nor does the Father himself judge anyone may be rendered "my Father does not judge anyone." There are, however, some difficulties in the selection of a term for judge. The tendency is to select a term which means "to condemn," but this specific function of God's Son is ruled out in the present passage. What is needed is a term for judge which will imply neutrality or unbiased judgment, resulting in spiritual life or death.

He has given his Son the full right to judge is literally "he has given all judgment to the Son." As in verse 19 (see there), so here TEV renders the definite article "the" as his.

It may be helpful to note the way in which He has given his Son the full right to judge is treated in various translations. NEB is essentially the same as TEV, but the level of language is different: "but has given full jurisdiction to the Son." JB "he has entrusted all judgment to the Son" and NAB "but has assigned all judgement to the Son" are rather close. Phps renders by "he has put judgment entirely into the Son's hands." Mft has "he has committed the judgment which determines life or death entirely to the Son," thus making explicit the meaning of the phrase "all judgment." Mft probably does not go too far, inasmuch as the judgment referred to in this verse includes both the power to give life and the power to condemn those who do evil. See further the comments on verse 23.

He has given his Son the full right to judge may be rendered idiomatically in some languages: "He has put in my hand the power to judge" or "He has said to me, 'You are the one to judge'" or "He has put me on the stool of judgment saying, 'Now you must be the judge.'"

5.23   so that all will honor the Son in the same
         way as they honor the Father. Whoever does
         not honor the Son does not honor the Father
         who sent him.

So that all will honor the Son in the same way as they honor the Father is connected by most translations with the idea of judgment in verse 22. This connection is legitimate, if it is realized that the full right to judge includes both the power to give life and to condemn. That is, the honor due the Son results not only from his right to condemn men to death but also from his right to raise them to life, as stated in verse 21. Hence, Mft does not go too far in making explicit the idea of a judgment which determines life or death as the basis for the honor due to the Son.

The purpose clause introduced by so that may be considered rather far removed from the specific action of the Father toward his Son in giving him the right to judge, and it may be useful to introduce verse 23 by a reference to this action. It can be done by saying, "My Father has done this so that all people will honor me in the same way that they honor my Father."

Does not honor certainly has the meaning of "refuses to honor" (see JB, NEB, NAB). This verse again states a truth that is at the heart of the Gospel. That is, that one cannot really know the Father except by means of the revelation that he has given through the Son, and to reject the Son is to reject the Father.

Honor may be expressed in a number of ways. One may speak of an attitude, for example, "to show respect to" or "to have valuable thoughts about." But honor may also be expressed in terms of verbal activities, for example, "to praise" or "to raise up the name of someone." Honor may also be described in terms of body motion or position, for example, "to bow down low before" or "to touch the ground before" or "to kneel in front of."

It is true that to translate the Son as "me" and the Father as "my Father" (for example, "If anyone does not honor me, he does not honor my Father who sent me") may give the impression, especially in the English form, of being an egotistical or self-centered statement on the part of Jesus. To avoid such an impression, some translators insist on rendering literally "the Father" and "the Son." The results,

[156]

however, are misleading in those languages which require the indication of kinship relations, especially if there is the added complication of avoidance of third person reference to the first person. Such translations are not only misleading but also awkward and ungrammatical. Accordingly, despite some connotative overtones which may seem unfortunate, it is essential to make these changes of pronominal reference, if sense is to be made of this passage in languages in which kinship terms must be possessed or in which third person reference to first person relations is impossible.

TEV	(5.24-29)	RSV

24 "I am telling you the truth: whoever hears my words and believes in him who sent me has eternal life. He will not be judged, but has already passed from death to life. 25 I am telling you the truth: the time is coming--the time has already come--when the dead will hear the voice of the Son of God, and those who hear it will come to life. 26 Just as the Father is himself the source of life, in the same way he has made his Son to be the source of life. 27 And he has given the Son the right to judge, because he is the Son of Man. 28 Do not be surprised at this; the time is coming when all the dead will hear his voice 29 and come out of their graves: those who have done good will rise and live, and those who have done evil will rise and be condemned.

24 Truly, truly, I say to you, he who hears my word and believes him who sent me, has eternal life; he does not come into judgment, but has passed from death to life. 25 "Truly, truly, I say to you, the hour is coming, and now is, when the dead will hear the voice of the Son of God, and those who hear will live. 26 For as the Father has life in himself, so he has granted the Son also to have life in himself, 27 and has given him authority to execute judgment, because he is the Son of man. 28 Do not marvel at this; for the hour is coming when all who are in tombs will hear his voice 29 and come forth, those who have done good, to the resurrection of life, and those who have done evil, to the resurrection of judgment.

5.24   I am telling you the truth: whoever hears my words and believes in him who sent me has eternal life. He will not be judged, but has already passed from death to life.

I am telling you the truth is the same expression discussed in 1.51.

My words is literally "my word" (RSV) and is equivalent to "my message." In the present passage the verb hears is probably used in the sense of "obeys"; Mft and JB have "listens to," while NEB has "gives heed to." In the Old Testament the verb "to hear" is frequently used in this sense, and the parallel to believes in the present passage would suggest the same meaning here. In some languages, whoever hears my words must be rendered "if anyone listens to and obeys my words" or "if anyone listens to and does what I say." As these renderings suggest, it may be useful to combine in the rendering of hears the two components of listening to and obeying.

It may be necessary in some languages to specify the referent of him in the phrase believes in him who sent me. One can, for example, translate "trusts in God, who sent me" or "puts his confidence in God, who sent me."

It is essential to keep the contrast between the verb tenses in this verse, as elsewhere in the Johannine dialogue: has eternal life... will not be judged...has already passed from death to life. Throughout John's Gospel there is always a tension between present and future. The believer already experiences in some degree the reality of eternal life which he will fully experience only at the end of time, and the one who refuses to believe is presently under God's judgment--a judgment which will be fully manifest only at the end of time. This means that just as eternal life is a present reality, so eternal death is also a present reality. This tension is clearly expressed in the following verse: the time is coming...the time has already come.

In some languages it is difficult to speak of "has eternal life," since eternal life would seem to refer to something in the future. However, it is essential to indicate that this kind of life has already begun. It may be necessary to translate "has already begun to live the life that will never end" or "has already started living in a way that will always continue."

Certain problems are involved in the passive expression he will not be judged. It can be made active, and the normal expression for judgment would suggest God as the agent, for example, "God will not judge him." Since, as indicated, judgment has been passed to the Son (verse 22), one may translate "I will not judge him." However, it is better, if possible, to employ a so-called pseudo-passive, for example, "he will not experience judging" or "he will not suffer the consequences of judging."

In some languages it is not easy to translate "has already passed from death to life." Often it is necessary to make it a type of simile, for example, "he is no longer, as it were, on the road that leads to dying, but has already begun to live." It may even be possible to say in some languages "he has already passed through dying and has begun to really live."

5.25   I am telling you the truth: the time is
                coming--the time has already come--when
                the dead will hear the voice of the Son
                of God, and those who hear it will come
                to life.

It is generally assumed that the dead in this verse refers to the spiritually dead, not to the physically dead. The latter are mentioned in verses 28 and 29. In the course of Jesus' ministry those who were spiritually dead did hear the voice of the Son of God, and those who obeyed it did live. This comes very close to the declaration in the Synoptic Gospels that the Kingdom of God has arrived. In Jesus Christ

not only God's rule, but God's life, have come into the world, and
those who are obedient to his message share in this life now.

For languages which have no general term for time or "occasion,"
it may be necessary to use such a term as "day," but in many languages
one cannot speak of "a day coming." The closest equivalent may be "there
will be a day." The time has already come must then be translated "but
that day is already here" or "it is already that day" or even "that
day has already been."

Since in this passage the dead refers to those who are spiritually
lifeless, it may be useful to introduce an expression which will mark
this term as a simile, for example, "when those persons who are just as
though they were dead will hear the voice of God's Son."

In some languages, however, to say "hear the voice of the Son of
God" might imply hearing the sound without understanding what is said.
It may be necessary to say "will hear what the Son of God has said."

As in verse 24 the verb hear involves more than listening to words.
It must suggest "hearing and believing." Thus one may translate "those
who hear and do what he says will live." For languages which do not
permit third person reference to the first person, it may be necessary
to say "those who hear and do what I say will live."

5.26   Just as the Father is himself the source
            of life, in the same way he has made his
            Son to be the source of life.

For the use of Just as...in the same way, see the note at verse
21.

Is himself the source of life is literally "has life in himself."
This statement is not a mere affirmation that "God is alive," but rather
an affirmation that God has the power to give life. TEV makes this meaning explicit. JB ("who is the source of life") and NEB ("has life-giving
power in himself") also make this meaning clear. (See also 1.4.)

In many languages the Father must be rendered "my Father" and the
source of life as a causative, for example, "in the same way as my
Father is the one who causes people to live." The same type of construction may be employed in the second half of verse 26, for example, "in
that same way my Father has made me to cause people to live" or "...has
given me the power to cause people to live."

5.27   And he has given the Son the right to
            judge, because he is the Son of Man.

Right, as used here, means "authority" (RSV), not "power." The
same noun is used in 1.12, and the thought of this verse is similar to
that in verse 22. In some languages it is difficult to speak about
"giving a right to," but the meaning may be expressed as "My Father
has said to me, 'You are now able to judge'" or "...'You may now judge.'"

In Greek the phrase the Son of Man is literally "Son of Man"
(Segond, Luther Revised). Only here in the New Testament is this term
used without the definite article ("the") before either noun. Because
of its absence some commentators conclude that the meaning in the

present passage is simply "man." However, it seems unlikely that, in a
passage where the theme of judgment is primary, the reference would be
to "man" in general and not to the Son of Man, especially since the
right to judge is an essential characteristic of the Son of Man. The
writer may even be reflecting the use in Daniel 7.13, where also the
phrase is used without the definite article before either noun.

For a discussion of some of the translational difficulties involved in the expression Son of Man, see 1.51. As elsewhere, it may be
necessary to indicate clearly that the title Son of Man refers to Jesus.
The final clause of verse 26 may thus be translated "because I am the
Son of Man." Otherwise, the reader in some languages will simply assume
that Jesus is speaking about someone else.

5.28   Do not be surprised at this; the time is
                  coming when all the dead will hear his
                  voice

Basically there are two problems of exegesis in the translation
of this verse. First, do the words at this refer to what precedes (that
is, that he is the Son of Man), or to what follows (the role of the Son
of Man in the resurrection of the dead)? Most scholars today take these
words as a reference to what follows. In most languages it is impossible
to be ambiguous about the reference of this. One must either say "Do
not be surprised at what I have just said to you" or "Do not be surprised at what I am going to say" or "...to these words which follow."

A second problem revolves around the meaning of the Greek word
hoti, the first word of the second clause in this verse. In TEV this
word is not translated. In some translations it is rendered "for" (RSV,
for example, "for the hour is coming..."). If taken in the sense of
"for" or "because," there is a causative connection between the two
clauses. Most modern translations appear to follow this exegesis, because it gives cumulative force to the argument and seems to make better
sense in the context. However, it is possible to take the Greek word
hoti in the sense of "that." The second clause would then explain the
content of this. If this exegesis is chosen, the following translation
may result: "Do not be surprised that the time is coming...." However,
the context better suits the first possibility.

All the dead is more literally rendered by NAB "all those in their
tombs," but the reference is clearly to the dead. NEB translates "all
who are in the grave." In earlier editions of TEV the phrase "in the
graves" was included in this verse. But in the 4th edition the phrase
is omitted, because of difficulties in translation. If "in the graves"
is translated as a restrictive phrase, it would imply that the dead who
are not in their graves (for example, persons who died accidental deaths
and therefore were not buried) would not hear the voice of the Son of
Man. Obviously, that is not intended, and therefore it is necessary in
many translations to omit "in the graves," as in the present edition of
TEV. The second part of verse 28 may then be translated "there will be
an hour when all who are dead will hear my voice." As in earlier verses,
it may be necessary to change his to "my," to avoid a misinterpretation
of a third person reference to the first person.

5.29   and come out ot their graves: those who
          have done good will rise and live, and
          those who have done evil will rise and
          be condemned.

Out of their graves is implicit in the Greek text, but it is made
explicit in TEV on the basis of the phrase "in their graves" in verse
28. If of their graves is likely to be understood restrictively, that
is, as implying that only the dead who are in graves will come out,
then it may be necessary to omit the phrase and to translate "the dead
will come forth" or "the dead will come from where they are."
Will rise and live is literally "to the resurrection of life"
(RSV). TEV transforms the nouns "resurrection" and "life" into verbs,
since they denote events rather than objects. At the same time it clari-
fies the meaning of the phrase "of life." Several other translations
use essentially the same technique (for example, JB and Phps "will rise
again to life"). The last phrase in this verse (literally "to the resurrection of judgment") is translated basically in the same way: will
rise and be condemned. It is evident that the judgment referred to is
a condemnatory judgment, and so TEV renders the noun "condemnation" as
be condemned. NAB translates this phrase "shall rise to be damned,"
while JB has "to condemnation." NEB is quite expressive, "will rise to
hear their doom."
Most translations take the noun "resurrection" in an active sense
("will rise"), but Mft takes it with a passive meaning, "to be raised."
According to Jewish and Christian teaching, it is God who raises the
dead, and so the passive voice may come closer to the meaning of this
passage.
In many languages the verb "to rise" or "to be raised" cannot be
used with the meaning of "coming back to life" or "to live again." One
may sometimes speak of "leaving death" or "throwing away death," but
more commonly it is necessary to use such an expression as "coming back
to life" or "living again." The second clause of verse 29 may be translated simply "those who have done good will live again," for in this
context will rise and live carry similar meanings. However, the final
clause of verse 29 may be rendered "those who have done evil will come
back to life and will be condemned."

          TEV   (5.30)   RSV

     WITNESSES TO JESUS

30 "I can do nothing on my own   30 "I can do nothing on my own
authority; I judge only as God   authority; as I hear, I judge; and
tells me, so my judgment is right,   my judgment is just, because I
because I am not trying to do   seek not my own will but the will
what I want, but only what he   of him who sent me.
who sent me wants.

It is often necessary to expand the section heading, Witnesses to
Jesus, for example, "Those who speak about Jesus" or "Those who reveal

the truth about Jesus" or "Those who tell who Jesus really is."

Some scholars see this verse as concluding the section begun with verse 19, while others see it as introducing a new section. It seems better to take it as beginning a new direction in Jesus' argument. In verses 19-29 the declaration that the Son can do nothing on his own is related to his power to give life and to his right to judge, while in verses 30-47 the affirmation that the Son can do nothing on his own is developed in a different direction. Here the emphasis is that the Son does nothing for his own glory but only what God tells him, and he does this to the glory of God (41-44). In support of this truth, Jesus appeals to several witnesses: John the Baptist, his own mighty works, the Scriptures, and the Father himself. Finally, he appeals to Moses as a witness to who he is and as the judge of those who reject him (45-47).

Here, as in verse 19, the word nothing is in the emphatic position.

On my own is the same expression used in verse 19. In this context it may require some restructuring, for example, "I am not able to do anything just on the basis of what I want to do" or "it is not my own power that I use in doing something."

I judge only as God tells me is literally "just as I hear, I judge." JB renders "I can only judge as I am told to judge." In the context it is clear that the one the Son "hears" is God, and this meaning is the basis for TEV rendering. Mft also makes this meaning explicit: "I pass judgment on men as I am taught by God." Throughout this section, with the exception of verses 42 and 44, God is referred to as "the Father," and that term may be used for God in this verse. That is, one could translate "I judge only as my Father tells me."

The Greek word rendered judgment (krisis) may be used either in the neutral sense of "judgment" or with the meaning of "condemnation." In the present verse the neutral idea of judgment seems to be indicated. So my judgment is right may be rendered in some languages as a conditional or temporal expression, for example, "So if I judge, I do so in a right way" or "Whenever I judge anyone, I judge correctly."

TEV renders the Greek noun expressions "my will" and "the will of the one who sent me" by verbal expressions: what I want...what he who sent me wants. He who sent me is clearly a reference to the Father.

Because of the internal complexities of verse 30 and the relations between the various clauses, it may be necessary in some languages to break up the sentence and to specify some of the relations more clearly, for example, "I am not able to do anything just on my own power. I judge people only as God tells me to judge them. As a result, when I do judge them, I do so in the right way. This is right, because I am not trying to do what I want to do. Rather, I do only what the one who sent me wants me to do."

TEV	(5.31-40)	RSV

TEV	RSV
31 "If I testify on my own behalf, what I say is not to be accepted as real proof. 32 But there is someone else who testifies on my behalf, and I know	31 If I bear witness to myself, my testimony is not true; 32 there is another who bears witness to me, and I know that the testimony which he bears to me it true. 33

that what he says about me is
true. 33 John is the one to whom
you sent your messengers, and he
spoke on behalf of the truth.
34 It is not that I must have
a man's witness; I say this only
in order that you may be saved.
35 John was like a lamp, burning and shining, and you were
willing for a while to enjoy his
light. 36 But I have a witness
on my behalf which is even greater than the witness that John
gave: what I do, that is, the
deeds my Father gave me to do,
these speak on my behalf and
show that the Father has sent
me. 37 And the Father, who sent
me, also testifies on my behalf.
You have never heard his voice
or seen his face, 38 and you do
not keep his message in your
hearts, for you do not believe
in the one whom he sent. 39
You study the Scriptures, because you think that in them you
will find eternal life. And
these very Scriptures speak
about me! 40 Yet you are not
willing to come to me in order
to have life.

You sent to John, and he has borne
witness to the truth. 34 Not that
the testimony which I receive is
from man; but I say this that you
may be saved. 35 He was a burning
and shining lamp, and you were
willing to rejoice for a while in
his light. 36 But the testimony
which I have is greater than that
of John; for the works which the
Father has granted me to accomplish,
these very works which I am doing,
bear me witness that the Father
has sent me. 37 And the Father who
sent me has himself borne witness
to me. His voice you have never
heard, his form you have never
seen; 38 and you do not have his
word abiding in you, for you do
not believe him whom he has sent.
39 You search the scriptures, because you think that in them you
have eternal life; and it is they
that bear witness to me; 40 yet
you refuse to come to me that you
may have life.

5.31   "If I testify on my own behalf, what
          I say is not to be accepted as real proof.

On the use of the word _testify_ or "witness" in the Gospel of John,
see comments on 1.8.

What I say is not to be accepted as real proof is literally "My
testimony is not true." NEB translates this clause "that testimony does
not hold good"; Phps "what I say about myself has no value"; NAB "you
cannot verify my testimony." JB has "my testimony would not be valid."
Mft translates "If I testify to myself, then my evidence is not valid."
As these translations all indicate, the point is not that Jesus is
saying that his testimony concerning himself is untrue but rather that
it could not be accepted as legal evidence in a court of law. The same
law mentioned here is appealed to in 8.17. According to Jewish law, a
man could not be convicted of a crime on the testimony of one witness
(Deut 19.15). The present context, of course, is different from a situation in which a person is accused of a crime and put on trial. Here the
witnesses are simply called in, as it were, to verify testimony.

As noted, it is often important to avoid a literal translation of

the second part of verse 31, since it would imply that Jesus' statements were untrue. In some languages an appropriate equivalent of verse
31 is "If I tell you about myself for my own sake, then you do not accept what I say as being true" or "...as evidence" or "If I merely
speak to you on my own behalf, then no one will believe my words."

5.32   But there is someone else who testifies
            on my behalf, and I know that what he
            says about me is true.

The someone else referred to in this verse is the Father, and in
translation it may be best to make this explicit, since the next person
mentioned in the passage is John, at the beginning of the next verse.
    In this context one may translate testifies as "says what he
knows about me" or "indicates who I am."

5.33   John is the one to whom you sent your
            messengers, and he spoke on behalf of
            the truth.

You is emphatic in the Greek sentence structure.
    In Greek there is no stated object of the verb sent. TEV and NEB
supply your messengers, since this information is implicit in the context. JB supplies "messengers."
    The verb spoke on behalf of is literally "has testified." It is
in the perfect tense in Greek, thus emphasizing the continuing validity
of John's testimony.
    The truth referred to is doubtless the truth concerning Jesus.
    In many languages it is difficult to translate literally he spoke
on behalf of the truth, since an abstract, such as truth, can be related only to specific kinds of utterances. It may be more satisfactory
to translate "he spoke what was true about me" or "he spoke about me
and that was true" or "...what he said was true."

5.34   It is not that I must have a man's
            witness; I say this only in order
            that you may be saved.

The first occurrence of I is emphatic, just as you is emphatic in
the preceding verse.
    It is not that I must have a man's witness is more literally "Not
that the testimony which I receive is from man" (RSV). This statement
is rendered by JB "not that I depend on human testimony"; NEB has "Not
that I rely on human testimony." The force of Jesus' words in this context is not to deny the truth of John's testimony, but rather to affirm
that he himself does not need the testimony of any human being. In some
languages one may render this clause "I really do not need other people's
words in order to prove who I am" or "It is really not necessary that
people say what they know about me."
    I say this only in order that you may be saved. This refers back
to verse 33, not to the first half of verse 34. Salvation comes through

believing in Jesus. Thus it is legitimate to appeal to John the Baptist, since his witness may teach people to believe. In order to make this clear it may be appropriate to say "I mention John's testimony only in order that you may be saved."

If the passive may be saved must be transformed into an active form, then "God" must be made the agent, for example, "in order that God may save you."

5.35   John was like a lamp, burning and shining,
        and you were willing for a while to enjoy
        his light.

The noun John translates a Greek demonstrative pronoun (literally "that one") which is translated "he" in RSV.

The Greek text says that John was a lamp, and TEV changes this equational statement to a simile: John was like a lamp. Since it was the activity of John, rather than his appearance, that was like a lamp, it may be important in some languages to translate "John shone, as it were, like a lamp" or "John gave light, as it were, just as a lamp would."

It may also be useful to incorporate one of the two participles, burning and shining, into the initial statement, for example, "John, as it were, was shining just like a burning lamp" or "..a lamp with a burning wick." The word burning must not be translated in such a way as to suggest that the lamp itself was burning. To do so might suggest that John himself was burning up!

Again the pronoun you is emphatic, and it is used in contrast with the pronoun I of the next verse, which is also emphatic.

The Greek term rendered in TEV as to enjoy is a strong word, as its use in 8.56 (TEV rejoiced) indicates.

The translation of You were willing for a while to enjoy his light is more complex than it may appear. A literal rendering of this sentence may give the impression that the Jews simply enjoyed the benefits from the lamp which John provided. An even more serious difficulty is involved in the expression enjoy his light, for light must be understood figuratively, as referring to what John said. Therefore one must say in some languages "What John said, which was like a light, caused you to be happy." The second part of verse 35 may then be translated "for a while you were willing to have his words, which were like a light, make you happy." Such translations make clear that John's words were the cause of the joy.

5.36   But I have a witness on my behalf which is
        even greater than the witness that John gave:
        what I do, that is, the deeds my Father gave
        me to do, these speak on my behalf and show
        that the Father has sent me.

But I have a witness on my behalf which is even greater than the witness that John gave is, more literally, "But I have the witness greater than John." Have a witness obviously refers to the testimony

[165]

that someone else gives on Jesus' behalf and not to the testimony which
Jesus himself gives. A literal rendering might be ambiguous, but the
inclusion of on my behalf makes the meaning clear. NEB removes the ambiguity by rendering "But I rely on a testimony higher than John's."
TEV makes the noun phrase "than that of John" into a verb clause with
the pronoun "that" made explicit: than the witness that John gave.

The first part of verse 36 is difficult to translate, because in
many languages it is not possible to speak of an activity as "a witness."
A person may act as a witness, but an event may not. It may therefore
be necessary to speak of Jesus' deeds as being the witness, in the sense
of "showing who he really is." Accordingly, the first part of verse 36
must be radically restructured, for example, "But what I do shows what
I really am in a way even more important than what was shown by what
John said about me." This initial part of verse 36 may then be followed
by "What I do is precisely what my Father told me to do." Note that in
this restructuring the term work is not rendered literally, because it
might refer only to physical labor.

The next two clauses in TEV (what I do, that is, the deeds my
Father gave me to do) are rendered in reverse order from that in the
Greek text, because in English it is more natural to give the general
clause first and the clause that qualifies it afterward. Here the first
clause introduces Jesus' deeds, and the second clause qualifies his
deeds as those the Father gave him to do. It is, of course, possible to
follow more closely the order of the Greek: "But I have a witness on my
behalf even greater than the witness that John gave: the deeds my Father
gave me to do. These deeds speak on my behalf..."

My Father is literally "the Father." Once again the article "the"
is used with the significance of a possessive pronoun (see verse 19).

Speak on my behalf and show translates one verb in Greek (literally "testifies"). It is not possible in some languages to talk about
deeds as able to "speak." One can, however, employ such an expression
as "what I do shows who I really am," which may be followed by the final
expression in verse 36, for example, "and what I do shows that my Father
has sent me."

It should be noted that the Greek text uses the plural deeds
rather than the singular "deed." This is to call attention to the
numerous "mighty deeds" that God has enabled Jesus to do.

5.37   And the Father, who sent me, also testifies
            on my behalf. You have never heard his voice
            or seen his face,

The verb testifies is in Greek a perfect tense (NAB "has...given
testimony"), which normally focuses attention on the continuing or present effects of a past action. However, the perfect tense in English
fails to bring out this emphasis, and often, as in the present verse,
the focus of the Greek perfect tense is better achieved by the use of
the present tense in English. In 8.18 this same saying of Jesus is repeated in the present tense in Greek.

In Greek the first sentence in this verse reads literally, "and
the Father, who sent me, that one testifies on my behalf." Several

translations attempt to render the force of "that one" by translating "and the Father himself." Testifies on my behalf may be rendered "speaks the truth about me."

You have never heard his voice or seen his face is more literally translated in RSV: "His voice you have never heard, his form you have never seen." The word translated face in TEV and "form" in RSV (so also NEB and NAB) is translated "shape" in JB and "what he is like" by Phps. The Greek word refers to the "visible form" or "outward appearance" of something or someone. In Exo 19.9 God told Moses that he would come down and speak to him so that the people also would be able to hear, and that he would come down in the sight of them all (19.11). On the basis of these statements, some Jewish rabbis taught that in Moses' day the people both heard God's voice and saw what he was like. It may be that this verse is arguing against this tradition.

5.38   and you do not keep his message in your
        hearts, for you do not believe in the one
        whom he sent.

Keep is literally "have remaining" (RSV "have...abiding"). The verb "to remain" is frequently used by John to describe the believers' relationship with Christ and Christ's relationship with the Father.

His message is literally "his word," but in the New Testament the singular "word" is often used in the sense of message. The phrase in your hearts (so also Phps, NAB) is literally "in you" (NEB, RSV, JB). The first half of verse 38 is rendered in NEB "But his word has found no home in you" and in JB "and his word finds no home in you." For many readers of English, the idea of a word finding a home in someone may be too figurative to be comprehended easily, because a translation of this nature shifts the focus of action away from the people to the word itself. Phps avoids this difficulty by translating "Nor do you really believe his word in your hearts."

Though a literal translation of the first part of verse 38 ("you do not have his word remaining in you") is relatively meaningless in many languages, it is also difficult to speak of "keeping his message in your hearts" or "his word finding no home in you." The closest equivalent in some languages may be "you do not accept his message" or "you do not welcome his message." The meaning may sometimes be expressed by a negation of permission, for example, "you do not let his message stay in your hearts" or "...in your minds."

Although TEV and JB translate the first verb in the next clause as believe in, there is some doubt as to its meaning in the present context. Many translators prefer the meaning of "believe the one." That is, in the present verse the focus is not on whether people have or do not have faith in Jesus, but whether they are willing to accept what he says as true. The meaning of "believe" therefore comes closer to fitting the context than believe in. The meaning of "believe," in contrast with believe in (usually translated as "trust" or "place confidence in"), may be rendered "you do not believe me that I am the one he sent."

5.39   You study the Scriptures, because you
              think that in them you will find eter-
              nal life. And these very Scriptures
              speak about me!

The you of this verse refers back to the Jews of verse 18. In
Greek the same verb form may be either an indicative (you study) or an
imperative ("study!"). Only the context can indicate the difference,
and most commentators and modern translators believe that the indicative
better suits the context. Jesus earlier made a statement concerning
the ways in which the Jews had accepted other witnesses; now he makes
a statement concerning the way in which they study the Scriptures: they
believe that in them they will find eternal life. He first makes the
statement and then makes a contrast, indicating that the Jews had missed
the true point of the Scriptures. They had missed the true point because they had sought to find eternal life in them, when the Scriptures
had actually testified about Jesus, the one who brings eternal life. In
Jewish thought the Law was the means by which God had ordained that
men should find eternal life, and this explains the importance of the
appeal that is made here to the Scriptures.
        Since in many languages eternal life must be expressed by a ver-
bal form, in them you will find eternal life may be translated "in them
you will find how to live forever" or "...to live without ceasing."
What is to be found in the Scriptures is not actually eternal life, but
rather the secret of eternal life, that is, the way in which this kind
of life may be obtained.
        The phrase these very Scriptures represents a demonstrative pro-
noun ("those") in the Greek text. In many languages it is not possible
to speak of "Scriptures speaking," since "writings" are not able to
"talk." One can, however, often say "these writings have words about me"
or "in these very writings there are statements about who I really am."

5.40   Yet you are not willing to come to me
              in order to have life.

Sometimes it may not be enough to say to come to me, since an expression of movement may be understood only in a literal sense. A more
satisfactory equivalent may be "to follow after me" or "to come and
learn from me."
        The preceding verse speaks of eternal life, and that is the mean-
ing of the word life in this verse. In order to emphasize the qualitative
distinction in the kind of life offered by Jesus, the final clause of
verse 40 may be translated "in order to really live."

              TEV   (5.41-47)   RSV

41 "I am not looking for human   41 I do not receive glory from men.
praise. 42 But I know what kind   42 But I know that you have not the
of people you are, and I know that   love of God within you. 43 I have
you have no love for God in your   come in my Father's name, and you
hearts. 43 I have come with my   do not receive me; if another comes

Father's authority, but you have not received me; when, however, someone comes with his own authority, you will receive him. 44 You like to receive praise from one another, but you do not try to win praise from the one who alone is God; how, then, can you believe me? 45 Do not think, however, that I am the one who will accuse you to my Father. Moses, in whom you have put your hope, is the very one who will accuse you. 46 If you had really believed Moses, you would have believed me, because he wrote about me. 47 But since you do not believe what he wrote, how can you believe what I say?"

in his own name, him you will receive. 44 How can you believe, who receive glory from one another and do not seek the glory that comes from God? 45 Do not think that I shall accuse you to the Father; it is Moses who accuses you, on whom you set your hope. 46 If you believed Moses, you would believe me, for he wrote of me. 47 But if you do not believe his writings, how will you believe my words?"

These verses are a strong denunciation of the position of the Jewish leaders. Jesus indicates that they actually have no love for God in their hearts, and that the very one whom they had trusted, Moses, will be their judge. In all their boasting that they were following God's will, these people actually rejected what Moses had said about God, and so Moses would condemn them.

5.41   "I am not looking for human praise.

In verse 34 Jesus said it was not necessary for him to have a man's witness, and in this verse he states that he is not looking for human praise. The word praise is the word usually translated "glory" in this Gospel. In Greek it appears first in this sentence, and so is emphatic. In 7.18 this word appears as glory, in 8.50 as honor, and in 12.43 as approval. "Praise," "glory," "honor," and "approval" all cover essentially the same area of meaning. In the present verse NEB renders it "honor"; JB and Phps "approval"; Mft "credit"; and NAB "praise."
     The verb looking for is literally "receive," but it appears in a variety of ways in the translations. NEB translates the whole verse "I do not look to men for honor"; Mft "I accept no credit from men"; JB "As for human approval, this means nothing to me."
     I am not looking for human praise involves certain subtle problems of translation: (1) looking must not be understood in the literal sense of "seeing"; (2) it is normal for an expression of praise to require men as a subject. It is possible to restructure the sentence in some languages as "I am not trying to get people to praise me" or "It is not my desire that people honor me."

5.42   But I know what kind of people you are, and
               I know that you have no love for God in your
               hearts.

But I know what kind of people you are, and I know that is literally
"but I know you that." TEV repeats the verb I know to fulfill the demands of English style and to make the sentence read smoothly. It explains
the meaning of "you" in the Greek by the phrase what kind of people
you are. JB translates "Besides, I know you too well: you have..."; NEB
has "But with you it is different, as I know well, for you have..."

It is useful in some languages to employ two different verbs for
know, one to indicate knowledge about a person, and the other to refer
to knowledge of a fact. One can say, for example, "But I am very well
acquainted with you indeed; I know that you have no love..."

Love for God is literally "love of God," an ambiguous phrase.
Elsewhere in the Gospel this phrase always means God's love for men,
but in the present context "one's love for God" seems to be the meaning.
NEB and Mft make this meaning explicit as "love for God." JB "you have
no love of God in you" also implies that this phrase means "love for
God." It is doubtful that John intentionally left the phrase ambiguous
in order to include both meanings, although some commentators suggest
this.

In your hearts is literally "in yourselves," a phrase which has
the same meaning as "in you" of verse 38, which TEV also translates in
your hearts.

In place of you have no love for God in your hearts, one normally
encounters a verb expression for love, for example, "you do not love
God in your hearts." However, in some languages the phrase "in your
hearts" would seem superfluous. A similar type of emphasis may be
achieved by rendering "I know that you really do not love God."

5.43   I have come with my Father's authority, but
     you have not received me; when, however,
     someone comes with his own authority, you
     will receive him.

With my Father's authority (NEB "accredited by my Father") is
literally "in the name of my Father." Here "the name" is taken as
equivalent to the authority, a use that "name" frequently has in biblical
thought. It is also found in the corresponding phrase in this verse
which TEV renders with his own authority (literally "in his own name";
NEB "self-accredited"). See comments at 14.13 for a discussion of "in
my name."

In some languages I have come with my Father's authority may be
rendered "I have come as one who represents my Father," but it is probably better to use such an expression as "I have come as one whom my
Father has sent to represent him." It may also be expressed as "I have
come as one whom my Father has specially sent."

Have not received is actually in the present tense in Greek. It
may be intended to focus attention on the present situation (note JB
"you refuse to accept me"). TEV translation (have not received me)
suggests that the Jews' rejection of Jesus had a wider reference. This
translation may be rendered in some cases "have refused to have anything
to do with me" or "have pushed me aside" or "have not been willing to
listen to me."

It seems preferable to take the someone of this verse as a
general axiom rather than as a specific reference to a particular person. It contrasts the Jews' unwillingness to accept Jesus and their
willingness to accept anyone who comes in his own authority and seeks
his own praise.

The clause when, however, someone comes with his own authority
may be rendered as conditional, for example, "if someone who speaks
only for himself comes." However, the condition may be divided into
two parts, for example, "if someone comes and speaks only for himself"
or "...has no authority other than his own."

5.44   You like to receive praise from one another,
          but you do not try to win praise from the
          one who alone is God; how, then, can you be-
          lieve me?

In Greek this verse is actually one sentence, a rhetorical question. TEV inverts the Greek order, making the first part of the sentence into a statement, followed by a question, how, then can you
believe me? The question is the first part of the Greek text.

The clause you like to receive praise from one another must
sometimes be restructured to indicate clearly the subject of the praise
and the effect it has upon the persons in question, for example, "When
the people praise you, you like it" or "...this makes you happy." On
the other hand, one may speak of praise as the goal of a desire, for
example, "You desire that people praise you." But such renderings omit
the concept of reciprocity in praise. Accordingly, one may prefer to
translate "When you are exchanging praises, you are happy."

In the one who alone is God (literally "the only God"), some
Greek manuscripts omit the word God. Most translations include it as
an original part of the text, though NAB places the word "God" in
brackets. Nowhere else in John's Gospel is God referred to as "the only
one," and therefore the word "God" seems to be required. In a Greek
manuscript, in which the letters were all capitals and there were no
spaces between words, a scribe could easily have omitted the two letters
which were the abbreviation for "God."

But you do not try to win praise from the one who alone is God
often involves difficulties in translation, since the one who alone is
God must be made the subject of the process of praise, and to win indicates a causal relation. One may sometimes translate "You do not try
to cause the one who alone is God to praise you," but this translation
is relatively unsatisfactory, since it suggests some kind of pressure
put on God to praise men. It seems better, therefore, to employ such an
expression as "You do not try to act in such a way that the one who
alone is God will praise you."

In this context it may be useful (and in some languages even
necessary) to introduce a grammatical goal for the verb believe, for
example, "How is it possible, then, for you to believe me?"

5.45   Do not think, however, that I am the one
          who will accuse you to my Father. Moses,

> in whom you have put your hope, is the
> very one who will accuse you.

I am the one who will accuse you to my Father may be rendered "I
will go to my Father and accuse you" or "I will accuse you in the
presence of my Father" or "I will speak to my Father and accuse you."
In some languages accuse is rendered simply "say that you have done
wrong."

Moses...is the very one who will accuse you is actually in the
present tense in Greek (RSV "it is Moses who accuses you"; Mft "Moses
is your accuser"). However, the present tense may be used in this
verse with a future significance, pointing to the day of final judgment,
since the preceding verb I am the one who will accuse you is in the
future tense. In fact, in the present context it seems the most probable meaning.

The verb have put your hope is in the perfect tense in Greek,
suggesting a hope which has a long, continuing history.

Moses, in whom you have put your hope may require some expansion
to make clear the manner in which Moses may be the object of hope. One
may, for example, say "Moses, who you hoped would help you" or "Moses,
who you expected would be on your side" or "...favor you." The term
hope is semantically complex, normally involving three closely related
components of meaning: (1) anticipation of, (2) something good, and
(3) a period of more or less patient waiting. It is not always possible
to introduce all these components, but in rendering hope "expect help
from," one represents at least two of them.

5.46   If you had really believed Moses, you
         would have believed me, because he
         wrote about me.

The if clause in this verse presupposes that the Jews did not
believe Moses. TEV translates it If you had really believed Moses. JB
has "If you really believed him."

There are difficulties involved in translating a condition contrary to fact in present or past time. The negation of such a condition
must sometimes be made explicit in a separate clause, for example, "If
you believed Moses--but you really have not believed him--then you
would believe me." It may even be necessary to indicate the negation of
the second part of the condition, for example, "you would believe me--
but you really do not." If the second part of the condition is set off
by a negative statement, it is necessary to treat the final clause in
a somewhat different manner, for example, "It is clear you do not believe Moses, because he wrote about me" or "it is clear you do not
believe what Moses wrote, because he wrote about me." The logical force
of this final clause, introduced by because, is made clearer in the
following verse.

5.47   But since you do not believe what he wrote,
         how can you believe what I say?

In Greek this statement also is conditional (beginning with "but if"). However, the condition is so stated as to assume that the Jews did not believe what Moses wrote, and so TEV renders But since you do not believe. Gdsp indicates it by "But if you refuse to believe...."

TEV   (6.1-15)   RSV

JESUS FEEDS FIVE THOUSAND MEN

6 After this, Jesus went across Lake Galilee (or, Lake Tiberias, as it is also called). 2 A large crowd followed him, because they had seen his miracles of healing the sick. 3 Jesus went up a hill and sat down with his disciples. 4 The time for the Passover Festival was near. 5 Jesus looked around and saw that a large crowd was coming to him, so he asked Philip, "Where can we buy enough food to feed all these people?" (6 He said this to test Philip; actually he already knew what he would do.)

7 Philip answered, "For everyone to have even a little, it would take more than two hundred silver coins^k to buy enough bread."

8 Another one of his disciples, Andrew, who was Simon Peter's brother, said, 9 "There is a boy here who has five loaves of barley bread and two fish. But they will certainly not be enough for all these people."

10 "Make the people sit down," Jesus told them. (There was a lot of grass there.) So all the people sat down; there were about five thousand men. 11 Jesus took the bread, gave thanks to God, and distributed it to the people who were sitting there. He did the same with the fish, and they all had as much as they wanted. 12 When they were all full, he said to his disciples, "Gather the pieces left over; let us not waste a bit." 13 So they gathered them all and filled twelve baskets with the pieces left over from the

6 After this Jesus went to the other side of the Sea of Galilee, which is the Sea of Tiberias. 2 And a multitude followed him, because they saw the signs which he did on those who were diseased. 3 Jesus went up into the hills, and there sat down with his disciples. 4 Now the Passover, the feast of the Jews, was at hand. 5 Lifting up his eyes, then, and seeing that a multitude was coming to him, Jesus said to Philip, "How are we to buy bread, so that these people may eat?" 6 This he said to test him, for he himself knew what he would do. 7 Philip answered him, "Two hundred denarii would not buy enough bread for each of them to get a little." 8 One of his disciples, Andrew, Simon Peter's brother, said to him, 9 "There is a lad here who has five barley loaves and two fish; but what are they among so many?" 10 Jesus said, "Make the people sit down." Now there was much grass in the place; so the men sat down, in number about five thousand. 11 Jesus then took the loaves, and when he had given thanks, he distributed them to those who were seated; so also the fish, as much as they wanted. 12 And when they had eaten their fill, he told his disciples, "Gather up the fragments left over, that nothing may be lost." 13 So they gathered them up and filled twelve baskets with fragments from the five barley loaves, left by those who had eaten. 14 When the people saw the sign which he had done, they said, "This is indeed the prophet who is to come into the world!"

five barley loaves which the
people had eaten.

14 Seeing this miracle that
Jesus had performed, the people
there said, "Surely this is the
Prophet who was to come into the
world!" 15 Jesus knew that they
were about to come and seize him
in order to make him king by
force; so he went off again to
the hills by himself.

15 Perceiving then that they
were about to come and take him
by force to make him king, Jesus
withdrew again to the hills by
himself.

^{k}Silver coins: *A silver coin was
the daily wage of a rural worker
(See Mt 20.2).*

The first four verses of this chapter give the spatial and temporal setting for the miracle of Jesus' feeding five thousand men. It took
place on a hill across Lake Galilee and near the time for the Passover
Festival of the Jews. These verses also include information about the
crowd which would witness the miracle. It was a large crowd, which had
seen Jesus' mighty works in healing the sick. Verses 5-6 make it clear
that the miracle was performed completely on the initiative of Jesus,
and that his question to Philip was not for information. In verses 7-10
the greatness of the miracle is emphasized by the mention of the large
number of people involved (five thousand men) and the small amount of
food available, five loaves of barley bread and two fish. The miracle
itself is narrated in verses 11-13, indicating that Jesus supplied not
only enough food for the needs of the people but that there was a good
deal left over. As a sequel to the miracle, verses 14-15 tell of its
effect on the people and of Jesus' response to their desire to make him
king.

The section heading, Jesus Feeds Five Thousand Men, reflects accurately the information given in verse 10. It does not mention the fact
that a number of women and children also participated in this miraculous
meal, as related in Matthew's account (Matt 14.21). It would be misleading if the title suggested that only five thousand men ate and that
women and children were excluded. While a title such as "Jesus Feeds the
Five Thousand" is traditional, it involves a certain difficulty: the
"Five Thousand" have not been identified, so the inclusion of the definite article ("the") can be misleading.

6.1   After this, Jesus went across Lake Galilee
            (or, Lake Tiberias, as it is also called).

After this is the same vague reference to time that we have seen
before in John's Gospel (see note on 2.12). The exact place where Jesus
crossed the lake is likewise vague. The place last mentioned in John's
Gospel is Jerusalem (5.1), which obviously is not intended to be the
point from which Jesus crossed the Lake of Galilee. To add to the problem,

the Greek text is rather clumsy (literally "Jesus went across the Lake of Galilee of Tiberias"), and some scribes attempted to clear up both the geographical ambiguity and the difficulty of the Greek text. One example of such "corrected" text is represented by NAB: "Jesus crossed the Sea of Galilee (to the shore) of Tiberias." According to this reading, Jesus performed the miracle near the city of Tiberias, on the southwest shore of Lake Galilee (see Luther Revised "across the Sea of Galilee where the city of Tiberias was located"). However, if this reading had been the original one, no scribe would have had reason to change it to the more difficult one. The same judgment must be made against other alterations of the Greek text, for example, the reading "Jesus went to the other shore of the Sea of Galilee" (Zür). Each of these readings represents an attempt to smooth out a difficult Greek text. TEV follows the UBS Greek text, as do most other modern translations. That is, Tiberias is simply a second name given to Lake Galilee. TEV, Mft, Phps, and NEB include the second name in parentheses, and others set it off by commas or dashes. Herod Antipas built the city of Tiberias in A.D. 26 and named it in honor of Emperor Tiberius. It must have been after that date that the name Tiberias was popularly applied to the lake. Lake Tiberias is next mentioned in 21.1.

The problem of transition at the beginning of Chapter 6 is a serious one in some languages. The phrase after this is indefinite, and there is no indication that Jesus had returned to Galilee. Some translators may wish to insert a clause saying "after Jesus had returned to Galilee," but to do so would be rewriting, not translating, the text. In a sense it would do violence to the type of literary structure the Gospel writer has employed. He is not really concerned with a biographical account, but rather with a series of vignettes, relating some of the important episodes in Jesus' life which reflect on aspects of his personality and power. Essentially for that reason, he employs indefinite transitional devices. The problem of transition can be assisted by using a phrase for after this which would suggest a considerable lapse of time, thus making possible an implied shift of location from Jerusalem to Galilee.

Each of the terms Galilee and Tiberias in combination with Lake should be considered simply as part of a proper name, and treated in receptor languages in the same way that such names as Lake Michigan or Lake Tanganyika would be treated. Thus in some languages such a phrase as "the lake called Galilee" or "the lake called Tiberias" would be used.

An additional problem results from the fact that there is no reference to Jesus' disciples until verse 3. The reader might assume erroneously that Jesus was alone when he crossed Lake Galilee, followed by the crowd, and went up a hill. Obviously the focus is on Jesus, but in some languages it may be awkward to introduce his disciples only in verse 3. The problem may be solved by translating "sat down with his disciples, who had been with him" or "...who had come with him." It may be necessary to indicate as early as verse 1 that Jesus' disciples went with him back across Lake Galilee; otherwise, the impression may be given that the disciples had been waiting for him on the other side of the lake, and that he had gone to meet them.

6.2   A large crowd followed him, because they had
           seen his miracles of healing the sick.

This verse actually begins with a particle, "but" (Anchor Bible),
rendered by "and" in some translations (RSV, JB, NEB). Since this
particle (Greek de) merely indicates the continuation of a narrative,
TEV, NAB, and Mft do not translate it.

NAB translates the verb followed as "kept following," to bring
out the progressive nature of the Greek imperfect tense. A literal translation of the reason given for the large crowd following Jesus can be
misleading. For example, RSV sounds as though Jesus was drawing pictures
on the sick people, "because they saw the signs which he did on those
who were diseased"; NAB reads as if Jesus was giving a public performance
for the sick, "because they saw the signs he was performing for the sick"
(see also Phps "they had seen the signs which he gave in his dealings
with the sick"). However, the meaning of this clause is perfectly understandable in Greek, and it is presented clearly by TEV, because they had
seen his miracles of healing the sick. This clause is similar to 2.23,
where John states that many believed in Jesus because they saw the
mighty works he did.

6.3   Jesus went up a hill and sat down with his
           disciples.

The same Greek particle (de) noted in verse 2 recurs in verses 3,
4, and 6. In these three verses also it is simply a device for continuing
the narrative. It reflects the Semitic background of John's Greek, but
it should not be preserved in translation.

A hill is literally "the hill" or "the mountain," but in this context hill is accurate. Although John uses the definite article "the"
before hill, it is impossible to know exactly what hill he had in mind.
RSV translates as "the hills" (plural).

It was customary for Jewish teachers to sit down while teaching,
and Jesus followed this custom (see Matt 26.55; Mark 4.1; 9.35; Luke
4.20; 5.3; John 8.2); but here John does not explicitly state that Jesus
sat down for the purpose of teaching.

Jesus' disciples were last mentioned in 4.33. On the basis of
verses 66-67 it would seem that his disciples included a larger group
than the twelve. Therefore one cannot be certain just which disciples
were involved in the scene that follows.

Since the disciples no doubt accompanied Jesus, it may be necessary
to say "Jesus and his disciples went up a hill, and they sat down together" or "...he sat down with them." Otherwise the impression may be
given that the disciples were already at the top of the hill and that
Jesus went up to meet them.

6.4   The time for the Passover Festival was near.

This is the second Passover mentioned in John's Gospel (the first
was mentioned in 2.13, 23). The Passover is doubtless mentioned primarily for its theological significance; John considers it important to

[177]

understand the words and actions of Jesus in light of their theological relation to the Jewish Passover. The Last Supper must likewise be understood in this same light (see 13.1). For a discussion of translational problems involved in the phrase Passover Festival, see the comments under 2.13 and 23.

6.5   Jesus looked around and saw that a large crowd was coming to him, so he asked Philip, "Where can we buy enough food to feed all these people?"

This verse begins with the Greek particle (oun), not rendered explicitly by TEV. (See under 2.18.)

Jesus looked around and saw translates the same verbs used in 4.35, more literally, "lifting up his eyes...and seeing" (RSV). "To lift up one's eyes" is a Hebraic idiom, which JB translates "looking up."

For the sake of natural English style TEV introduces the second clause with so.

Food is literally "breads," a reference to the small-sized loaves of bread (like large buns) that the Jews were accustomed to eat. Although most translations have "bread," the context suggests that the word is understood generically, as TEV takes it.

To feed all these people (NEB "to feed these people") is literally "in order that these might eat." TEV and NEB restructure the phrase; both make the subject, "these (people)," the object of the verb and change intransitive "eat" to transitive "feed."

6.6   (He said this to test Philip; actually he already knew what he would do.)

The verb translated to test is neutral in itself. When used of God or Jesus, it does not have the sense of "tempt," that is, lead to sin, which it has when "Satan" or "the devil" is the subject of the action (compare Matt 4.1; Luke 4.2). NAB renders the phrase "to test Philip's response."

Philip is "him" in the Greek text, but several translations (TEV, Mft, Phps, NAB, JB, and GeCL) make the pronominal reference explicit. TEV, NAB and Phps indicate that this verse is a parenthetical statement.

Though it is clear in English that the pronoun he refers to Jesus thoughout this verse (He said...he already knew...he would do), it may not be clear in other languages. In some the last two instances of the pronoun he could refer to Philip, since Philip is the last named person in the context. The translation must make the reference to Jesus clear in each case.

The adverb already must be expressed in some languages as a clause. Thus, for example, "Jesus knew even before he asked," and the adverb actually may sometimes be expressed as "the truth is." Thus the second part of verse 6 may be expressed as "the truth is that Jesus knew what he would do even before he asked Philip."

6.7   Philip answered, "For everyone to have even a little, it would take more than two hundred silver coins^k to buy enough bread."

^{k}Silver coins: *A silver coin was the daily
wage of a rural worker (See Mt 20.2).*

TEV reverses the order of the clauses in this verse; <u>for everyone
to have even a little</u> is the final clause in the Greek sentence.
<u>Two hundred silver coins</u> is literally "two hundred denarii" (RSV).
The problem is that the term "denarius" (plural "denarii") means nothing
to the average English reader, to whom this monetary unit is unknown.
The denarius was the average day's earnings for a laborer, and so NAB
and Anchor Bible render it "two hundred days' wages." Some translations
attempt a cultural equivalent by using a rather sizable sum of money.
Mft has "seven pounds," Phps "ten pounds," and NEB "twenty pounds."
Though earlier editions of the TEV New Testament employed "two hundred
dollars' worth of bread," the fourth edition reads, as noted above, <u>two
hundred silver coins to buy enough bread</u>. The new rendering seems to be
advisable in view of the frequent fluctuations in the purchasing power
of currencies all over the world. Any amount stated in terms of the
prices current at the time of translation may soon lose its significance
for the average reader. TEV's marginal note indicates that the silver
coin represented approximately a day's wage, and the total amount of
money would be equivalent to "two hundred days' wages worth." Such a
figure will remain significant for the reader regardless of any change
in prices.

The purpose expressed, <u>for everyone to have even a little</u> may in
some languages be rendered more effectively as a condition, for example,
"if everyone is to have even a little." The second part of this condition
may then be expressed as: "it would be necessary to buy more than two
hundred silver coins' worth of bread."

<u>Philip</u> was first mentioned in 1.43. Both in this passage and in
12.21-22 he is closely associated with Andrew.

6.8   Another one of his disciples, Andrew, who
       was Simon Peter's brother, said,

Some languages have distinct terms for older and younger brothers.
For the problem of whether Andrew was older or younger than Simon Peter
see 1.40, 44.

<u>Said</u> is literally "said to him," but TEV understands "to him" to
be implicit in the English text. In some languages it may be useful to
indicate clearly the one to whom Andrew spoke, that is, "said to Jesus."

6.9   "There is a boy here who has five loaves of
       barley bread and two fish. But they will cer-
       tainly not be enough for all these people."

The word translated <u>boy</u> in TEV and NEB appears only here in the
New Testament. It is a double diminutive, but this form does not necessarily mean "a small boy" (JB). In the Septuagint of Genesis 37.30 the
same word is used of Joseph, who was 17 years old at the time. The word

may also mean "servant" (Mft), a meaning well attested elsewhere. In the Greek translation of 2 Kgs 4.12, Gehazi, the servant of Elisha, is referred to by this word. Since this chapter contains the account of Elisha's miraculous feeding of one hundred men, in which he is assisted by his servant, some believe that John's choice of this word was influenced by the Old Testament account. However, it is not a necessary assumption, and most translators prefer the meaning boy rather than "servant."

Barley bread was the ordinary food of the poor, since it was cheaper than wheat bread. In the parts of the world where barley is not known, it may be possible to use such a phrase as "a wheat-like grain called barley." Or a classifying expression may be used, for example, "a grain called barley" or "barley grain," in which a term for "grain" would be applicable to any type of grain (rice, kafir corn, maize, etc.).

Originally the word translated fish (Greek opsarion) meant cooked food eaten with bread. However, it acquired the specific meaning, fish, especially dried or preserved fish, which seems to be the meaning here and in verse 11. In John 21.9, 10, 13 the word is used of freshly caught fish.

But they will certainly not be enough for all these people translates a rhetorical question in Greek, which in earlier editions of TEV appeared as a question ("But what good are they for all these people?") It was a valid question, especially since Luke 11.5 implies that three loaves were looked upon as the amount required for one meal for one person. This question may be rendered "But how will they help all these people?" or "How will they satisfy...?" or even "How will these be enough for all these people?"

6.10   "Make the people sit down," Jesus told them.
            (There was a lot of grass there.) So all the
            people sat down; there were about five thousand
            men.

In this verse people and men represent two different Greek words. The first word is generic, which explains TEV and RSV translations, but the second word refers specifically to male persons. Both RSV and NEB have "so the men sat down," which follows the Greek. TEV assumes that all the people whom Jesus told to sit down actually did so, although only the men, that is, male persons, were numbered (compare Matt 14.21). The word sit down technically means "to lie down" (Mft "get the people to lie down") or "recline" (NAB "get the people to recline"). However, it was the word normally used to describe the position taken in eating a meal. For English readers sit down sounds more natural than "lie down" or "recline," which suggest positions for rest or sleep.

Make the people sit down may be translated "cause the people to sit down." It may be expressed appropriately in some languages as "tell the people to sit down." It may be necessary to indicate clearly that Jesus was here speaking to his disciples and that they in turn were to communicate this information to the people. Therefore one may translate "Jesus said to his disciples, 'Tell the people to sit down.'"

In selecting a term for grass, it is important to distinguish between grass which has been cut (for example, hay) and grass which is

growing. Here, obviously, the reference is to grass growing on the hill-
side.

In order to indicate that five thousand men applied only to the
men and not to all the people, one may translate the last clause of
verse 10 "in the crowd there were about five thousand men."

6.11   Jesus took the bread, gave thanks to God,
            and distributed it to the people who were
            sitting there. He did the same with the
            fish, and they all had as much as they
            wanted.

Gave thanks is a participle in Greek which TEV translates as a
finite verb (so also Mft, NEB, Phps). To God (so also Mft) is not expressed explicitly in the Greek text, but it is clearly implied. Phps
has "gave thanks for them" (that is, for the loaves of bread), thus
supplying an object for the verb gave thanks.
    Gave thanks to God must be expressed in some languages as direct
discourse, for example, "said to God, 'We thank you for this.'" Other
languages may have "prayed to God saying, 'Thanks'" or "...'we are
grateful.'"
    A literal translation of distributed it to the people who were
sitting there may give the impression that Jesus himself distributed
the bread to all the people. This interpretation can be avoided by the
use of a causative, for example, "he caused it to be distributed to the
people who were sitting there."
    He did the same with the fish, and they all had as much as they
wanted translates only seven words in Greek. Here NEB has almost the
precise words of TEV, and JB is similar: "He then did the same thing
with the fish, giving out as much as was wanted."
    He did the same with the fish must be expressed in some languages
in a more specific manner, for example, "He thanked God for the fish
also and distributed the fish also" or "...caused the fish to be distributed to the people." In some languages the term distributed may be
readily translated "to give," sometimes with a special form indicating
a distributive plural, that is, the bread and the fish were given to
people not collectively but individually.

6.12   When they were all full, he said to his dis-
            ciples, "Gather the pieces left over; let us
            not waste a bit."

Were...full translates a verb which appears only here in the Gospel of John. Its intention is to indicate the completeness of the miracle.
Not only did the people eat until they were all full, but there were
enough pieces left over to be gathered up and fill twelve baskets.
    When they were all full may be rendered "When they had all had all
they wanted to eat" or "When they had all eaten sufficiently." It may
be expressed idiomatically in some languages as "When they all said,
'That is enough.'" or "When they could swallow no more" or "When their
stomachs were large."

Gather the pieces left over requires in some languages a careful choice of words. Were these pieces to be picked up from the ground after being dropped by those who were eating, or were they to be collected from the hands of those who had eaten sufficiently but still had food left over? The latter interpretation is more satisfactory, though there is no way of telling from the context precisely what happened.

Let us not waste a bit is, more literally, "that nothing may be lost" (NEB). Although the word "lost" is sometimes used to refer to the condition of persons estranged from God, in the present context the meaning is obviously that of being wasted (Mft "so that nothing may be wasted"; see also JB and NAB). TEV takes it with this meaning, and changes the passive structure into an active one with a direct object.

Let us not waste a bit may be rendered "we should not waste any of the food." The term waste may be rendered in some languages "cause to be ruined," but there are certain advantages in having it rendered "not be used," for example, "we should not cause this food not to be used" or, expressed positively, "we should cause all the food to be used."

6.13   So they gathered them all and filled twelve
        baskets with the pieces left over from the
        five barley loaves which the people had eaten.

So they gathered them all is literally "so they gathered," with no expressed object. Most modern translations attempt in one way or another to indicate that the object is the pieces left over (of verse 12). It may be useful to render this first clause of verse 13 "So they gathered up all the pieces that had been left over." It is also possible to translate "so they received back from the people all the pieces that were left over," if one assumes that the food was gathered up in this manner (see comments on verse 12).

The size of the baskets referred to cannot be precisely determined. Elsewhere in the New Testament this word is used in Matthew 14.20; 16.9; Mark 6.43; 8.19; Luke 9.17. In Matthew 15.37; 16.10 and Mark 8.8,20, a different word for basket is used--the same word used of the basket in which Paul was lowered from the wall (Acts 9.25). These baskets were evidently fairly large. It is possible that the term in John 6.13 had a general meaning and was used for baskets of various sizes and shapes. In many receptor languages there is a term for a special type of basket used for carrying agricultural produce, and this word would be the one to use in this context.

6.14   Seeing this miracle that Jesus had per-
        formed, the people there said, "Surely this
        is the Prophet who was to come into the
        world!"

This miracle is literally "sign," the same word used frequently throughout John's Gospel; its first occurrence is in 2.11. Some ancient manuscripts have the plural "signs" in this verse, but apparently no modern translator follows this text. The plural seems to have come in under the influence of 2.23 and 6.2.

Rather than a participial clause seeing this miracle that Jesus had performed, one may prefer a clause expressing cause, for example, "Because the people saw this miracle that Jesus had performed, they said." It may also indicate a temporal relation, for example, "after the people had seen this miracle that Jesus performed they said."

People translates the same Greek word translated people in verse 10. It means "men" in the generic sense, that is, it is not restricted to male persons.

The Prophet has already been mentioned as one of the expected messianic figures (1.21). Here he is further referred to as the one who was to come into the world, the prophet spoken of by Moses (Deut 18.15, 18).

It is not easy to render accurately the Prophet who was to come into the world. The past tense of the verb (was) suggests a prior event, while the infinitive to come suggests a coming event. It may be necessary to make specific the relation between these two events by saying "the Prophet who Moses said would come into the world" or "the Prophet about whom it says in the Scriptures, 'He will come into the world'" or "the Prophet who, the Scriptures said, will come into the world."

6.15   Jesus knew that they were about to come and
        seize him in order to make him king by force;
        so he went off again to the hills by himself.

Seize him in order to make him king by force may be literally rendered "take him by force and make him king" (JB). "Take by force" (one word in Greek) is a strong verb, often used with the connotation of physical force or violence (see Matt 11.12, TEV try to seize). To make him king by force may be rendered "to cause him to be king even if he didn't want to be."

Went off again is translated "withdrew" in RSV, NEB, and Mft, and it appears as "retired" in Phps. An alternative Greek text reads "fled" (NAB; JB "escaped"). If the reading of the original manuscript was "fled," it was changed to "went off again" by some scribe who perhaps felt that it was undignified for Jesus to flee. However, the UBS Committee on the Greek text believes that the verb "fled" was introduced by a certain scribal tradition in an attempt to enliven the narrative. They accept the reading went off again and rate it a "B" choice. Whichever text one follows the impact of the narrative is the same. Although Jesus is indeed king, his kingdom is not of this world (18.36), and so he would not let himself be forced into being made the kind of king these people were looking for. (See note at 1.49.)

It is not clear just what is meant by the statement that Jesus went off again to the hills. The scene began with the words Jesus went up a hill (verse 3), and there is no indication in the intervening verses of a change in location. Perhaps Jesus went further up the same hill, to get away from the crowd, or he may have gone off into other hills nearby. Both interpretations find support in modern translations. The term rendered "again" may simply suggest that such an action was typical of what Jesus often did.

TEV (6.16-21) RSV

JESUS WALKS ON THE WATER

16 When evening came, Jesus'
disciples went down to the lake,
17 got into a boat, and went
back across the lake toward
Capernaum. Night came on, and
Jesus still had not come to
them. 18 By then a strong wind
was blowing and stirring up the
water. 19 The disciples had
rowed about three or four miles
when they saw Jesus walking on
the water, coming near the boat,
and they were terrified. 20
"Don't be afraid," Jesus told
them, "it is I!" 21 Then they
willingly took him into the boat,
and immediately the boat reached
land at the place they were
heading for.

16 When evening came, his disciples went down to the sea, 17
got into a boat, and started across
the sea to Capernaum. It was now
dark, and Jesus had not yet come
to them. 18 The sea rose because
a strong wind was blowing. 19 When
they had rowed about three or four
miles,^{m} they saw Jesus walking on
the sea and drawing near to the
boat. They were frightened, 20 but
he said to them, "It is I; do not
be afraid." 21 Then they were glad
to take him into the boat, and
immediately the boat was at the
land to which they were going.

^{m} Greek *twenty-five or thirty stadia*

This brief narrative is found also in Matthew 14.22-27 and Mark 6.45-
52. Its main purpose in the Gospel of John seems to be to reveal the
true nature of Jesus, as opposed to the popular understanding of him,
either as the prophet who was to come or as the expected messianic king
(verses 14-15). Jesus is more than a miracle worker; he is to be identified with God himself, as suggested by the words "It is I!" Strictly
speaking, this passage is not one of those in John where "I am" is used
as an absolute title of Jesus (see note at 4.26). However, John no doubt
intends his readers to understand Jesus' words in this light. Moreover,
there also seems to be an intentional Passover symbolism in this account.
In the same way that God led his people across the Sea of Reeds after
the first Passover meal, so Jesus here guides his disciples safely across
the lake after having fed them miraculously.

The section heading Jesus Walks on the Water may be misleading,
particularly if the article the is translated literally, since no particular body of water has been referred to in the preceeding story. It is,
of course, possible to translate "Jesus walks on water." It would also
be possible to employ such a title as "Jesus walks on Lake Galilee."

6.16   When evening came, Jesus' disciples went down
        to the lake,

The Greek word translated evening may refer to any time in the
late afternoon (see 20.19; Matt 14.15, 23). As the following verse indicates, it was not yet dark when Jesus' disciples went down to the lake.

6.17   got into a boat, and went back across the lake
        toward Capernaum. Night came on, and Jesus
        still had not come to them.

In Greek the verb got (into) is actually a participle which TEV
and others render as a finite verb.
    Went back across is translated in a variety of ways. Some focus
attention on the completeness of the action (Phps "made their way
across"), while others stress the initiation of the action (NEB "pushed
off to cross"; see also RSV, JB, Mft). Commentators tend to see either
the action in progress ("were on their way across") or see the words as
representing an action the disciples were trying to do (NAB "intending
to cross the lake"). No final decision can be made, but the last two
possibilities seem to suit the context better than the first two. It is
clear, however, that went back across should not be so translated as to
indicate that the disciples had already reached their destination. Jesus
evidently met them while they were still on the lake, and it was only
after he was received into the boat that they immediately reached the
shore to which they were headed.
    The Greek word thalassa, which TEV translates here as lake, usually
means a body of salt water, rather than a freshwater lake. In Hebrew a
single term is used for both, and John's use of thalassa here reflects
his Semitic background. RSV has "sea," which in English can mean either
"ocean" or "lake." Although popular usage speaks of "the Sea of Galilee,"
TEV prefers lake here, in order to make clear what kind of body of water
is being referred to.

6.18   By then a strong wind was blowing and stirring
        up the water.

By then (RSV "now"; Mft "by this time"; NEB "already") is connected
in the Greek text with the statement night came on (verse 17). However,
TEV prefers to connect the adverbial expression with a strong wind was
blowing. Verses 17 and 18 are joined by the Greek conjunction te, which
is rare in John's Gospel. Some scholars understand it to be a strong
connective (NAB "moreover"). GeCL restructures as follows, making the
connective unnecessary: "17...It was night and Jesus still had not come
to them. 18 The weather was stormy and high waves were on the water."
    A strong wind was blowing and stirring up the water is literally
"the lake (sea) was being stirred up, there was blowing a strong wind."
TEV changes the passive construction of the Greek into a more natural
active expression in English. NEB translates "A strong wind was blowing
and the sea grew rough." This condition is expressed in some languages
as "there were many big waves" or "the waves had become large" or "the
water was foaming."

6.19   The disciples had rowed about three or four
        miles when they saw Jesus walking on the
        water, coming near the boat, and they were
        terrified.

The first clause of this sentence in Greek is actually a participial construction, and the second clause (when they saw Jesus walking on the water) is the main clause. A similar restructuring is found in JB: "they had rowed three or four miles when they saw Jesus walking on the lake..." In Greek this verse begins with the particle oun (see under 2.18).

In Greek the subject of this sentence is "they," which TEV makes explicit as the disciples.

Three or four miles (so also Mft, RSV, JB, NEB) is literally "twenty-five or thirty stadia." A "stadium" was about 607 feet. In languages where the metric system is better known, this distance may be expressed as "five or six kilometers."

Saw is literally "see." In Greek the present tense is often used to enliven a narrative, although the action is in the past.

The Greek phrase which is translated on the water is similar to the one in verse 16 which is rendered to the lake. Consequently, one commentator suggests that the phrase in verse 19 be translated "by the seashore." That is, the disciples saw Jesus walking along the shore of the lake. However, it is obvious that John intends a miracle here, and most translators have the equivalent of on the water. Moreover, as the last part of the verse indicates, Jesus was coming near the boat, something he could not have done had he been walking along the shore three or four miles away.

It is possible to punctuate this verse in various ways, but no real difference in meaning results. RSV and NEB put a full stop after "boat" and connect the verb that follows with verse 20: "They were frightened, but he said to them" (RSV); "They were frightened, but he called out" (NEB). TEV puts the full stop at the end of verse 19.

Some restructuring of verses 19 and 20 is necessary because there are so many embedded subject-predicate expressions. Note, for example, disciples had rowed, they saw, Jesus walking, Jesus...coming near, and they were terrified. The first subject-predicate expression may be the temporal setting for what immediately follows, for example, "After the disciples had rowed about three or four miles, they saw Jesus." It is possible to conclude these two clauses with a full stop and begin again with "Jesus was walking on the water; he was coming near the boat." The final subject-predicate expression may then be restructured: "therefore they were terrified." The translator must take care that the reader does not misunderstand the reason for the disciples' fear. They were not concerned for Jesus' safety but were awed by the miraculous character of the occurrence. The parallel account of this story in Mark makes explicit what was going through the disciples' minds: "'It's a ghost,' they thought, and screamed" (9.49).

6.20   "Don't be afraid," Jesus told them, "it is I!"

This verse may be more literally translated "But he said to them, 'It is I; do not be afraid'" (RSV). The restructuring of TEV is designed to bring the focus of the verse on the words of Jesus (Don't be afraid ...it is I!) rather than on the introductory statement Jesus told them. The tense of the verb rendered Don't be afraid implies that the disciples

were already frightened when Jesus spoke to them, and it may therefore
be translated "Stop being afraid" or "...being frightened."

It is I may be variously expressed in different languages, for
example, "I am the one who is speaking" or "I'm the one here" or "you
are looking at me" or "I am Jesus."

6.21   Then they willingly took him into the boat,
           and immediately the boat reached land at the
           place they were heading for.

It is difficult to tell whether the verb rendered willingly implies
an unfulfilled or a fulfilled wish. That is, did Jesus actually get into
the boat or not? Most English translations are ambiguous, as is the
Greek, though RSV ("they were glad to take him into the boat") and Phps
("so they gladly took him aboard") indicate a fulfilled wish. Mft sounds
as if the people in the boat took a formal vote ("so they agreed to take
him on board"). In TEV this same verb is translated wanted to in 7.44
and in 16.19 (both instances indicating unfulfilled wishes). In 1.43 it
is translated decided to, while in 5.35 it is rendered were willing. In
most languages it is not possible to be ambiguous here. One must indicate
either that the disciples took Jesus willingly into the boat, or that
they were willing to take him aboard, but he did not actually get into
the boat.

In translating took him into the boat, it is important not to suggest that they had to rescue him from the sea. One may simply say "they
received him into the boat" or "welcomed him aboard."

And immediately (so also NEB and RSV) is translated "suddenly" in
NAB, "instantly" in Mft, and "in no time" in JB. It seems probable that
the force of this adverb is to indicate a second miracle. That is, at
the very moment the disciples saw Jesus and he spoke to them, their
boat reached land. Since Lake Galilee at its greatest extent is about
seven miles wide and twelve miles long, it would seem that even if the
disciples were crossing the lake at one of its narrower points, a second
miracle is intended here, in addition to the one of Jesus' walking on
the water.

Reached land is the meaning that most translators give to the
Greek; "came aground" of NAB might imply that the boat had an unfavorable landing. A literal rendering of the boat reached land must suggest
in some receptor languages that the boat was self-propelled, that is,
had a motor. A more satisfactory equivalent would be "they reached land
in the boat."

The place they were heading for may be rendered "the place to which
they were going" or "the place where they wanted to land" or "the place
where they wanted to arrive."

              TEV   (6.22-24)   RSV

         THE PEOPLE SEEK JESUS

   22 Next day the crowd which   22 On the next day the people
had stayed on the other side of   who remained on the other side of

the lake realized that there had | the sea saw that there had been
been only one boat there. They | only one boat there, and that Jesus
knew that Jesus had not gone in | had not entered the boat with his
it with his disciples, but that | disciples, but that his disciples
they had left without him. 23 | had gone away alone. 23 However,
Other boats, which were from | boats from Tiberias came near the
Tiberias, came to shore near the | place where they ate the bread
place where the crowd had eaten | after the Lord had given thanks.
the bread after the Lord had | 24 So when the people saw that
given thanks. 24 When the crowd | Jesus was not there, nor his dis-
saw that Jesus was not there, | ciples, they themselves got into
nor his disciples, they got into | the boats and went to Capernaum,
those boats and went to Capernaum, | seeking Jesus.
looking for him.

The Greek of verses 22-24 seems somewhat confused. In addition, this passage has a number of textual variants. In a general sense, the meaning may be reconstructed as follows. When Jesus fed the five thousand, the people observed that there was only one boat at the scene of this miracle. The next day the crowd discovered that Jesus was gone, and they knew that he had not left with his disciples in that one boat. Meanwhile (next day), other boats had come from the town of Tiberias to the eastern shore of the lake. Not finding either Jesus or his disciples there, the crowd got into these boats and went to Capernaum looking for Jesus.

In the section heading, The People Seek Jesus, it may not be evident that The People are the crowds who have been fed (see verse 26). It may be better therefore to translate "The crowd seeks Jesus" or "the people who have been fed look for Jesus."

6.22   Next day the crowd which had stayed on the other side of the lake realized that there had been only one boat there. They knew that Jesus had not gone in it with his disciples, but that they had left without him.

In Greek this verse is a single sentence with only one main verb. RSV follows the Greek literally: "the people...saw that there had been only one boat there, and that Jesus had not entered the boat..." TEV restructures the Greek sentence into two English sentences and translates the main Greek verb twice, modifying the translation in accordance with the different context of the two English sentences: "the crowd realized ...They knew..." Compare NEB: "They had seen...and...they knew..."

John expresses the crowd's recollection of what they had seen the previous day in such a way as to suggest that they saw something which was actually already past. Compare RSV: "On the next day the people... saw that there had been only one boat there..." Other modern translations remove this illogicality in various ways. TEV does so by a contextual translation of the Greek verb: "Next day the crowd...realized" (compare NAB). NEB translates the Greek participle (TEV: had stayed) as "was standing" and makes the adverbial phrase modify it and not the main verb: "Next morning the crowd was standing..." NEB then translates the Greek aorist tense of the main verb as a pluperfect: "they had seen."

In some languages there is a complication in saying had stayed on the other side of the lake, since the question arises immediately: "other" in relation to what? To make the matter clear, it may be necessary to translate "the crowd which remained on the same side of the lake where they were" or "...remained on the side of the lake opposite from where Jesus and his disciples had arrived."

In the Greek text the word "boat" appears twice in verse 22 but in two different forms. The first occurrence (only one boat) is a diminutive (literally "a little boat"). TEV translates the second occurrence with a pronoun (had not gone in it). Here the Greek has the more common word for "boat," which also occurs in verses 17 and 21. The existence of these two terms is only one of the problems in the Greek text of this passage. According to our present understanding of the Greek text, despite this difficulty, both words must be taken to refer to the same object.

But that they had left without him is literally "but his disciples alone had left." TEV here translates a noun in the Greek text ("disciples") by a pronoun (they), to produce a more natural sentence structure in English. They had left without him may be rendered "they had left that side of the lake. Jesus was not with them."

6.23   Other boats, which were from Tiberias, came
        to shore near the place where the crowd had
        eaten the bread after the Lord had given
        thanks.

After the Lord had given thanks is omitted from some ancient manuscripts. NEB includes this clause in the text but has a footnote indicating that it is omitted by some manuscripts. JB omits the clause entirely. Most translations include the words without any hint of a textual problem. If these words were a part of the original Greek text, it is difficult to see how they were omitted from some ancient manuscripts. However, they are represented in most of the Greek texts, and for this reason the UBS Committee thought it best to include them, but as a "C" choice, indicating a considerable degree of doubt regarding their authenticity.

A problem is involved in the grammatical relation of the clause after the Lord had given thanks; it should go with the immediately preceeding verb had eaten. However, unless the precise relation of the events is made clear, it is possible to understand after the Lord had given thanks as related to the verb came. This problem may be resolved in two different ways. One may translate "to the place where the Lord had given thanks for the bread and then the crowd had eaten it" or "to the place where the crowd had eaten the bread; they ate it after the Lord had given thanks." Note that it is the existence of two prior activities in this clause which causes the complication.

6.24   When the crowd saw that Jesus was not there, nor
        his disciples, they got into those boats and went
        to Capernaum, looking for him.

It may be necessary in some languages to combine Jesus and his disciples as coordinate objects of the verb saw, for example, "when the crowd saw that neither Jesus nor his disciples were there." In some languages it is preferable to translate saw as "recognized" or "realized," since the experience was not merely visual.

Again in this brief passage TEV substitutes a pronoun for a noun in the Greek text because of the nature of English discourse structure. Looking for him is literally "looking for Jesus." This phrase may be expressed as purpose, for example, "in order to look for him" or "in order to try to find him."

It should be noted that once again John introduces a verse with the Greek conjunction oun (literally "therefore"). In RSV it is translated "so," but in TEV and some other translations it does not appear.

TEV   (6.25-35)   RSV

JESUS THE BREAD OF LIFE

25 When the people found Jesus on the other side of the lake, they said to him, "Teacher, when did you get here?"

26 Jesus answered, "I am telling you the truth: you are looking for me because you ate the bread and had all you wanted, not because you understood my miracles. 27 Do not work for food that spoils; instead, work for the food that lasts for eternal life. This is the food which the Son of Man will give you, because God, the Father, has put his mark of approval on him."

28 So they asked him, "What can we do in order to do what God wants us to do?"

29 Jesus answered, "What God wants you to do is to believe in the one he sent."

30 They replied, "What miracle will you perform so that we may see it and believe you? What will you do? 31 Our ancestors ate manna in the desert, just as the scripture says, 'He gave them bread from heaven to eat.'"

32 "I am telling you the truth," Jesus said. "What Moses gave you was not^m the bread from heaven; it is my Father who gives you the

25 When they found him on the other side of the sea, they said to him, "Rabbi, when did you come here?" 26 Jesus answered them, "Truly, truly, I say to you, you seek me, not because you saw signs but because you ate your fill of the loaves. 27 Do not labor for the food which perishes, but for the food which endures to eternal life, which the Son of man will give to you; for on him has God the Father set his seal." 28 Then they said to him, "What must we do, to be doing the works of God?" 29 Jesus answered them, "This is the work of God, that you believe in him whom he has sent." 30 So they said to him, "Then what sign do you do, that we may see, and believe you? What work do you perform? 31 Our fathers ate the manna in the wilderness; as it is written, 'He gave them bread from heaven to eat.'" 32 Jesus then said to them, "Truly, truly, I say to you, it was not Moses who gave you the bread from heaven; my Father gives you the true bread from heaven. 33 For the bread of God is that which comes down from heaven, and gives life to the world." 34 They said to him, "Lord, give us this bread always.

[190]

real bread from heaven. 33 For the bread that God gives is he who comes down from heaven and gives life to the world."

34 "Sir," they asked him, "give us this bread always."

35 "I am the bread of life," Jesus told them. "He who comes to me will never be hungry; he who believes in me will never be thirsty.

35 Jesus said to them, "I am the bread of life; he who comes to me shall not hunger, and he who believes in me shall never thirst.

m What Moses gave you was not;
or It was not Moses who gave you.

To analyze this discourse on the bread of life is difficult, and commentators are not agreed on where it should be divided and subdivided. The following analysis, based essentially on the divisions followed in TEV, will serve as a summary introduction.

Verses 22-24 may be taken as transitional, indicating how it was that the people who shared in the miracle came to be in Capernaum, where Jesus gave this discourse on the bread of life. Verses 25-27 may be taken as an introduction to the discourse. The people do not understand how Jesus came to Capernaum, nor do they understand the meaning of the miracle he performed on the eastern shore of the lake.

Verses 28-35 develop the discourse a step further. In verse 27 Jesus uses the word work, and the crowd misunderstands what he intends by this term. They understand it to mean the kind of work (religious duty) that God requires of men that they may be in a right relation with him. Jesus replies that the only work that God wants people to do is to believe in the one he sent. Obviously the crowd understands Jesus to be speaking of himself, and so they ask what mighty work he will perform so that they may see it and believe him. They further indicate that if Jesus really is the one whom God has sent, he should be able to perform the same kind of miracle that Moses performed in the desert. To this Jesus replies that they even misunderstand what Moses did. The bread that Moses gave was not really from heaven. Only God the Father gives the real bread from heaven, and this bread is the one who comes down from heaven and gives life to the world. The people then request that Jesus give them this bread always, and Jesus responds, "I am the bread of life."

In the next section (verses 36-40) Jesus indicates that though the people have seen him and heard him, they still refuse to believe him. He came down from heaven to do the will of the one who sent him, and his will is to give life to all who will believe.

Verses 41-46 form the next stage in the discourse. In response to Jesus' claims that he is the bread who came down from heaven, the Jews start grumbling. They know Jesus' father and mother; how, then, can he say he came down from heaven? Jesus tells them to stop grumbling and to realize that they have failed to respond to him because no one can come to him unless the Father draws that person to him. If they had really listened to the Father, they would come to him and would recognize that

he is the one who has come from God and is the only one who has seen
the Father.

In verses 47-51 Jesus again takes up the theme of the bread of
life and indicates how he is superior to the bread that their Jewish
ancestors ate in the desert. Those who ate manna in the desert died, but
those who eat the bread which he will give them will live forever.

A further misunderstanding on the part of the Jews (verse 52;
compare verses 25, 28, and 42) enables Jesus to bring the discourse to
a conclusion (verses 53-58). Jesus is the Son of Man, and whoever eats
his flesh and drinks his blood has eternal life. The living Father sent
him and he is the bread that came down from heaven, to give life to all
who eat this bread.

The last section of this chapter (verses 60-71) indicates the
response of Jesus' disciples to this teaching. The disciples of verses
60-65 include a larger group than the twelve, and their response is
similar to that of the Jews. Many of them cannot accept what he has said,
and so they turn from him. Simon Peter is the spokesman for the twelve,
and he realizes that Jesus has the words that give eternal life and that
he is the Holy One from God. However, even one of the twelve is a devil,
and with this observation Jesus concludes his discourse.

The section heading Jesus the Bread of Life must correspond to the
expression found in verse 48. There the translation may be "the bread
which gives life" or "the bread which causes people to live." In many
languages one should not use a term which identifies a loaf of bread
but a more generic expression meaning "food." The title would read
"Jesus as the food which causes life" or "...causes people to live."

6.25   When the people found Jesus on the other side
          of the lake, they said to him, "Teacher, when did
          you get here?"

The people is literally "they."
According to verse 24, the place on the other side of the lake is
Capernaum. It was located on the northern shore, slightly to the west.
However, in verse 22 the other side of the lake indicates the place
where the crowd had eaten bread blessed by Jesus and from which they
have just come. If translated literally in both verses, the phrase could
be misunderstood as designating one particular side of the lake, although
in fact two different places on the lake are meant. To make this clear,
it may be necessary to say in verse 25 "on the other side of the lake
from where they had just been" or "on the side of the lake to which they
had just come."

Teacher is literally "Rabbi," the term discussed in 1.38.
One might expect the question of the crowd to be: "how did you get
here?" However, if one considers that they did not see Jesus go across
the lake by boat, and did not know how he could have arrived in Capernaum
except by walking around the lake, their question becomes meaningful.

6.26   Jesus answered, "I am telling you the truth:
          you are looking for me because you ate the bread
          and had all you wanted, not because you under-
          stood my miracles.

Jesus answered is literally "Jesus answered and said to them."
I am telling you the truth is the expression first used in 1.51.
TEV inverts the order of the last two clauses in this verse; in
Greek the negative clause, not because you understood my miracles, comes
first. However, in English it is more natural to say "because...not because" rather than "not because...because." A similar translational
technique is used in verse 38.

In some languages a statement of cause must precede the result,
especially if there is a definite difference in the time sequence. For
example, one may need to translate "because you ate the bread and had
all you wanted to eat, you are now looking for me." The final negative
clause may then be translated "you are not looking for me because you
understood my miracles."

Had all you wanted is not the same verb as the one used in verse
11, but the meaning is essentially the same. You ate the bread and had
all you wanted is translated in JB "you had all the bread you wanted to
eat."

My miracles is literally "signs" (see 2.11). Most other English
translations render it literally; Phps has "my signs" and Mft has "Signs"
with a capital "S."

TEV takes the verb "saw" with the meaning of "understand," an
interpretation supported by the context. The expression understood my
miracles may require amplification, for example, "understood what my
miracles were trying to show." In this way one may reflect in part the
significance of the Greek term that literally means "signs."

6.27   Do not work for food that spoils; instead,
            work for the food that lasts for eternal
            life. This is the food which the Son of Man
            will give you, because God, the Father, has
            put his mark of approval on him."

Beginning with this verse and continuing through verse 30, the
Greek text has a play on the verb "to work (for something)" and the noun
"work." In this verse the meaning of the verb work for is "to strive
after."

Food that spoils is translated in JB as "food that cannot last"
and in NEB as "this perishable food." In Greek spoils is actually a
participle made from the same stem as the verb used in verse 12 (see
comments there on let us not waste a bit).

There is a problem in translating Do not work for food that spoils,
since the negative is attached to work rather than to food. It is not
an admonition "not to strive" but "to strive not for food that spoils."
In some languages it is necessary to place the negative directly before
"for the food that spoils." Thus it may be more satisfactory to introduce the positive statement first, for example, "Strive to obtain the
food that lasts for eternal life and not for the food that spoils."

Food that lasts for eternal life is translated in JB "food that
endures to eternal life" (see also RSV). The idea is that this food lasts
because it gives eternal life (see verses 33, 50, 54, 58). Mft translates
"that lasting food which means eternal life" and NEB "food that lasts,
the food of eternal life." (On the meaning of eternal life see comments
at 1.4 and 3.15.) It is important to indicate that it is not the food

that lasts forever, that is, "it is the food that causes people to live without end." Only in this sense is the food itself imperishable.

The Greek of this verse is one sentence, and this food is actually a relative pronoun ("which").

For the Son of Man see 1.51. As in many other instances where this phrase occurs, it may be necessary to introduce a first person pronoun, for example, "I, the Son of Man, will give you this food."

God, the Father, has put his mark of approval on him is more literally "it is on him that God the Father has set his seal" (NAB). In 3.33 the verb "to seal" is used with the believer as the subject and is rendered proves by this (see comments there). In the present passage God, the Father is the subject of the verb. A few commentators equate "the seal of God" with "the likeness of God" (see Col 1.15), which Christ possessed before time began. However, the verb tense more naturally suggests a point in time, such as the coming of Jesus into the world or the descent of the Spirit on Jesus. Other commentators take this sealing to mean either that God has validated the authority of Jesus (NEB "upon whom God the Father has set the seal of his authority") or that God has put his mark of approval on the Son, thus validating his work (Mft "has certified him"). TEV follows this last interpretation.

Elsewhere in the New Testament the idea of a "sealing" by God occurs only in 2 Corinthians 1.22; Ephesians 1.13; 4.30. In each of these passages God is spoken of as "sealing" the believer. TEV takes this term to mean that God has placed his mark of ownership on the believer. In the case of the Son of Man, God's action has a different significance.

The expression God...has put his mark of approval on him is likely to be understood only in too literal a sense if it is translated word for word, that is, "a mark which shows he approves of him." It may suggest that in some way God had branded Jesus or had provided him with some physical blemish or mark to show his approval. Accordingly, it may be better to drop this figure and translate the essential meaning, for example, "because God the Father has shown that he approves of him" or "...has said, 'I approve of him.'" If the first person singular pronoun has been introduced above in connection with the Son of Man title ("I, the Son of Man"), then a first person singular pronoun should replace the third person singular pronoun here (him). The translation would then read "because God my Father has shown that he approves of me."

6.28   So they asked him, "What can we do in order
          to do what God wants us to do?"

Asked is literally "said" (RSV), but it introduces a question and so is better rendered asked in English. What God wants us to do of this verse and what God wants you to do of the following verse are literally "the works of God" and "the work of God." The people raise the question in the plural ("works") and Jesus answers in the singular ("work"). (See verse 29.) Here the meaning of the question is "What are the things we must do in order to get God's approval?" NEB translates the question "Then what must we do if we are to work as God would have us work?" and JB as "What must we do if we are to do the works that God wants?"

6.29   Jesus answered, "What God wants you to do
          is to believe in the one he sent."

Jesus answered is literally "Jesus answered and said to them,"
again reflecting Semitic influence in John's writing.

As indicated in verse 28, what God wants you to do is singular.
The Jews are still thinking in terms of what they must do to obtain God's
approval. Jesus indicates, on the other hand, that God demands but one
thing of them: believe in the one he sent.

In pronominal reference it may be necessary to adjust the clause
believe in the one he sent to read "believe in me whom God sent."

6.30   They replied, "What miracle will you perform
          so that we may see it and believe you? What will
          you do?

The first part of this verse in Greek is literally "Therefore they
said to him, 'Therefore what sign are you doing...'" As noted earlier,
the word "therefore" (Greek oun) is used frequently in John's Gospel
without any particular grammatical force. For example, it appears again
at the beginning of verses 32 and 34 (see under 2.18).

Once again, miracle translates the word "sign," used so often in
John's Gospel. In the present passage it refers to some miraculous act
of power by which Jesus could prove to the crowd who he was. They have
already seen Jesus perform a sign of power, but they want a further sign.
If he claims to be greater than Moses, then he must perform some sign of
power greater than the signs that Moses did (see verses 31-32).

Will you perform. The pronoun you is emphatic in Greek.

It, as the object of the verb see, is supplied translationally in
TEV; it is implicit in the Greek text.

Believe you is taken by some translators in the sense of "believe
in you." The Greek construction is not the one normally used for believing in Jesus. Here the Jews are considering nothing more than
accepting Jesus' words as true.

It may be important to indicate clearly the relation between the
expressions we may see it and believe you. The relation is one of reason
and result; it may be made specific as "in order that we may see the
miracle and as a result believe you" or "...believe what you say."

6.31   Our ancestors ate manna in the desert, just
          as the scripture says, 'He gave them bread
          from heaven to eat.'"

Ancestors is literally "fathers," but in the present passage both
male and female ancestors are clearly meant.

For the story of manna see Exodus 16. The term manna is usually transliterated in texts of the Scripture, but it is possible to introduce a
description, for example, "food called manna" or "grain-sized food called
manna." A marginal note would be useful here, or this information may be
given in a glossary.

Just as the scripture says is literally "just as it has been written,"
a set formula for the introduction of a quotation from the Old Testament.
He gave them bread from heaven to eat is not an exact rendering of any
one passage in the Old Testament, though the UBS Greek New Testament
cites Psalms 78.24 and 105.40.

In some languages one cannot use the expression "the Scriptures say," for "writings" do not "speak." Sometimes one can say "in the Holy Writings there are words about" or "in the Holy Writings one may read how he gave them bread from heaven to eat."

The Scripture quotation He gave them bread from heaven to eat is interpreted by the crowd to mean that Moses gave them bread, and therefore the people desire a miracle greater than the one Moses performed. Jesus corrects that interpretation in verse 32. However, rather than introduce "Moses" as the subject of "gave them bread from heaven to eat," it is better to preserve the ambiguous pronominal reference "he."

6.32   "I am telling you the truth," Jesus said.
        "What Moses gave you was not*m* the bread from
        heaven; it is my Father who gives you the
        real bread from heaven.

      m What Moses gave you was not; *or* It was not
      Moses who gave you.

I am telling you the truth is the same formula discussed in 1.51.

This verse is typical of the Jewish method of Scripture interpretation. When someone has quoted a passage of Scripture, the interpreter says, "The text should not be read as X, it should be read as Y." Here the crowd has just quoted a passage of Scripture in which they have taken the pronoun he to refer to Moses ("He gave them bread from heaven to eat"), and Jesus corrects their presuppositions at several points: (1) My Father must be read in place of Moses; (2) the present tense gives must be substituted for the past tense gave; and (3) the real bread from heaven takes the place of what was not the bread from heaven.

In the Greek text the word real is in the emphatic position, indicating a strong contrast between the real bread from heaven and the manna, which was not true heavenly nourishment. Real (so also NEB, Mft, NAB) appears in some translations as "true." This same adjective is discussed in 1.9 (see comments there).

Since the Jews often referred to the Law as "bread," a further contrast between Moses and Jesus may be intended: Jesus is not only the source of the real bread from heaven but also of the authentic message which comes from God. This claim does not deny that Moses gave the people bread from heaven, or that he gave them God's Law, but it does indicate the temporary nature of what Moses gave, as compared to the eternal and absolute nature of what Jesus now gives. Moses indeed gave bread from heaven, but now the Son of Man gives the real bread from heaven, and this bread is able to give eternal life to the world (verse 33).

Note that TEV has two alternative renderings: What Moses gave you was not the bread from heaven or Moses did not give you the bread from heaven. As noted, there are three contrasts between the statement What Moses gave you was not the bread from heaven and it is my Father who gives you the real bread from heaven. The difficulty for the translator is that these contrasts cannot be marked easily by a single negative such as not. Theoretically one could say, "It was not Moses who gave

you the bread from heaven" or "It is not a matter of 'gave' but of
'gives,'" and "it is not a matter of the bread from heaven but of the
real bread from heaven." However, from a practical point of view, such
expansion is not recommended.

Throughout this section it may be necessary to use a word for
"food" rather than one that designates "bread." The basic concept is
the so-called "staff of life," that is, the particular kind of food
regarded as basic to life. In some societies a term for "bread" would
indicate a type of food associated only with foreigners. A more general
term, such as "food," would then be more appropriate.

6.33   For the bread that God gives is he who
        comes down from heaven and gives life
        to the world."

The literal Greek expression "the bread of God" is made explicit
in TEV and NEB as "the bread that God gives." The bread that God gives
is he who comes down may be translated "the bread that God gives comes
down." The problem is that in Greek the word "bread" is masculine, and
so the masculine Greek participle may refer either to the bread that
comes down or to the one who comes down. Most modern translators apparently prefer the exegesis which sees here "the bread coming down." NEB
follows this interpretation but adds a footnote indicating the alternative possibility of the TEV rendering. If the reference is intended
to be personal (he who), then it is obvious from the following verse
that the people failed to see this implication. The fact that beginning
in verse 35 Jesus interprets this bread of life as a personal reference
to himself, as the footnote in Zürich Bible indicates (see also verses
38 and 42), suggests that the personal interpretation of verse 33 is
the one that he intended.

The verb phrases comes down (33, 50), came down (41, 42, 51, 58),
and have come down (38) are used a total of seven times in this discourse on the bread of life. There is no real difference in meaning,
though the present comes down may place more emphasis upon Jesus as the
one who comes down, while the past tenses came down and have come down
lay more stress on the historical event of his having come down.

Life in this verse is obviously equivalent to "eternal life" (see
1.4).

The world is equivalent to "the world of mankind" (see 1.10).

In languages in which one cannot refer to the first person by a
third person reference, it will probably be necessary to introduce the
first person in this verse. To do so will anticipate the statement made
by Jesus in verse 35, but it is necessary in order to be consistent in
identifying the participants. It may be necessary to translate "I who
have come down from heaven and give life to the world am the bread that
God gives" or "the bread that God gives is I who have come down..." The
shift from the present comes to "have come" may be necessary to indicate
something that happened in the past, the implications of which continue.

Gives life to the world may be rendered "causes people of the
world to live" or "...to really live" in order to indicate the qualitative distinction involved in the term for life.

[197]

6.34   "Sir," they asked him, "give us this bread
    always."

   Sir is the meaning that most modern translators see in this verse,
though RSV and Phps render the Greek word as "Lord." It is doubtful
that these persons were calling Jesus "Lord" in the Christian sense of
the word; all that is indicated in this context is a polite form of
address.
  The failure of the crowd to understand what Jesus is saying is
typical of the way in which John provides a basis for a spiritual explanation.
  The adverb always is emphatic in the Greek sentence structure;
this adverb occurs again in 7.6; 8.29; 11.42; 12.8; 18.20.

6.35   "I am the bread of life," Jesus told
    them. "He who comes to me will never be
    hungry; he who believes in me will never
    be thirsty.

  The people think that Jesus possesses the bread of life and that
he can give it to them always. Jesus corrects both these errors. First,
he indicates that he himself is the bread of life (equals "bread which
gives life"), and that those who eat it will never again become hungry.
The thought of Jesus as the one who gives life is central to John's
Gospel.
  The metaphor in I am the bread of life is extremely difficult for
some people to comprehend. It may be useful to change this expression
into a simile, for example, "I am just like food that causes life."
  On the use of I am in the Gospel of John see the note at 4.26.
Here I am is not used absolutely but is followed by a predicate (the
bread of life).
  Comes to me and believes in me are placed together here and at
7.37-38; the phrases are parallel in meaning.
  In some languages the expression He who comes to me would not
convey the meaning of trust or confidence. It may be necessary to say
"he who becomes one of my followers." Or it may be better to combine
these two statements: "he who comes and believes in me will never hunger
and never be thirsty." This type of statement is equivalent in some
languages to a conditional, for example, "If anyone comes to me and believes in me, he will never be hungry or thirsty." It may even be
necessary to mark the expressions of hunger and thirst as similes, for
example, "If a man comes and believes in me, it will be as if he would
never be hungry or thirsty" or "...he will never be hungry and thirsty,
so to speak."

    TEV   (6.36-40)   RSV

36 Now, I told you that you have
seen me but will not believe. 37
Everyone whom my Father gives me
will come to me. I will never

36 But I said to you that you
have seen me and yet do not believe. 37 All that the Father
gives me will come to me; and

turn away anyone who comes to me,
38 because I have come down from
heaven to do not my own will but
the will of him who sent me. 39
And it is the will of him who
sent me that I should not lose
any of all those he has given
me, but that I should raise them
all to life on the last day. 40
For what my Father wants is that
all who see the Son and believe
in him should have eternal life.
And I will raise them to life on
the last day."

him who comes to me I will not
cast out. 38 For I have come
down from heaven, not to do my
own will, but the will of him
who sent me; 39 and this is the
will of him who sent me, that I
should lose nothing of all that
he has given me, but raise it up
at the last day. 40 For this is
the will of my Father, that every
one who sees the Son and believes
in him should have eternal life;
and I will raise him up at the
last day."

6.36   Now, I told you that you have see me but
            will not believe.

Some manuscripts do not have me in the text, but it is included
in most translations (NEB omits it but adds a note). If me is not an
original part of the text, then Jesus' words I told you that you have
seen clearly refer back to the signs of verse 26. The UBS Committee on
the Greek text rates its decision a "C" choice, preferring to retain
the word in the text on the basis of the antiquity and diversity of the
manuscript evidence in its favor.
    The adverbial transitional Now is equivalent in many languages to
an adversative, that is, such an expression as "but." The conjunction
but, which occurs later in this same verse, may be so restructured as
to introduce an expression of concession, for example, "But I told you
that even though you have seen me you will not believe." Believe is
used here in the sense of "trust," "put one's faith in." If the object
must be expressed, then the pronoun "me," referring to Jesus, may be
added.

6.37   Everyone whom my Father gives me will come
            to me. I will never turn away anyone who
            comes to me,

Everyone whom is a strange expression in Greek. It is actually a
neuter singular form, and it is rendered "all that" in a number of
translations (RSV, NEB, JB, NAB, Segond, Zür). The use of the neuter
singular where a masculine plural would be expected is a stylistic
feature of the Gospel of John (see verses 39; 17.2, 24; and note also
1 John 5.4). Agreement is not unanimous as to the exact force of this
unusual form, though the opinion of the best scholars is that it gives
greater collective force to the expression. Even though the neuter "all
that" represents more accurately the form of the Greek, it is clearer
in English to use a personal form, everyone whom (compare Mft "all
those").
    In Greek my Father is the absolute form, "the Father." In such
a context it carries the force of my Father or "our Father," depending
on the reference. Here the meaning my Father is obvious.

[199]

The first sentence in verse 37 combines two important concepts: (1) the initiative of God in giving certain persons to his Son and (2) the initiative of the individuals in coming to Jesus. In most languages a verb meaning "gives" is probably the most neutral expression which can be employed for the former concept. However, in some instances terms meaning, for example, "assigns to me" or "declares as belonging to me" may be more satisfactory. It may also be necessary to select a more specific expression than will come to me, for example, "will adhere to me" or "will become one of my followers" or "will join himself to me."

Although the expression everyone whom is a neuter singular form in Greek, anyone who (NEB "the man who"; JB "whoever") is in Greek a masculine singular form, indicating clearly that the reference is to persons.

Never translates a Greek construction which expresses strong negation. This same construction is used in Mark 14.25.

Turn away translates a very strong expression in Greek, literally "throw out." The same verb is used in Matthew 8.12; 22.13; 25.30. The Greek verb which is translated by turn away has two different meanings, depending on whether the person who is the object of the verb has or has not already been admitted to the company of the person who is the subject. In the former situation the verb means "refuse to accept" or "say 'no' to." In the latter it means "cause to go out" or "expel." In this verse it is the former situation: Jesus will not refuse to accept anyone who comes to him, seeking acceptance.

If possible to do so, the translation should maintain the contrast between the present tense gives of this verse and the perfect tense has given of verse 39.

6.38   because I have come down from heaven to do
        not my own will but the will of him who
        sent me.

To do not my own will but the will of him who sent me expresses the same truth as that stated in 5.30 (see also 4.34). In earlier editions of TEV the order was reversed: "to do the will of him who sent me, not my own will," and in some languages it would be more natural to place the positive clause first.

It may be useful to substitute "God" for him, for example, "to do what God who sent me wants me to do." Not my own will may then be rendered "I have not come just to do what I myself want to do."

6.39   And it is the will of him who sent me
        that I should not lose any of all those
        he has given me, but that I should raise
        them all to life on the last day.

And it is the will of him who sent me that is literally "but this is the will of the one who sent me, that...," which TEV has restructured to achieve a more natural English sentence.

Any of all those translates a neuter expression in Greek (note RSV "nothing of all that"), and them all is literally "it" in Greek. As in-

dicated in verse 36, the neuter singular gives a stronger collective
force, but in this context a neuter singular would sound odd in English.
It should be noted that NEB switches from the neuter singular to the
masculine plural in the last part of the verse ("them all"), even though
it retains the neuter form in the first part ("one of all that"), as it
does in verse 36 ("all that"). The persons referred to in this verse are,
of course, the same ones mentioned in verse 37.

By translating raise...to life TEV makes explicit the meaning of
the Greek word "raise." This same promise is made again in verses 40,
44, and 54.

The last day (see also verses 40,44,54; 11.24; 12.48) is a reference
to the day of judgment.

The obligation that God has placed upon Jesus, expressed in the
English translation as should not lose and should raise them, may be
expressed in some languages by an obligatory element more or less equivalent to "must." To do so may involve some shift in the structure, for
example, "The following is what God who sent me wants me to do: I must
not lose anyone of all those whom he has given to me; rather, on the last
day I must cause them all to come back to life."

6.40   For what my Father wants is that all who
        see the Son and believe in him should
        have eternal life. And I will raise them
        to life on the last day.

What my Father wants is that is literally "this is the will of my
Father, that," which represents a Greek clause structure similar to the
one in the preceding verse. TEV not only restructures the clause; it
also transforms the noun phrase "the will of my Father" into a verb
phrase, what my Father wants. Again, the reason for this restructuring
is to achieve a more natural expression in English.

Both verses 39 and 40 stipulate the will of God; verse 40 simply
amplifies what is already in verse 39.

To see the Son and to believe in him are parallel in meaning, as
are the phrases comes to me and believes in me of verse 35. In 12.45
Jesus says "Whoever sees me, also sees him who sent me."

The Greek verb which is translated see in this verse includes an
element of concentration. Here it is clear that understanding, and not
mere vision, is meant, since eternal life is promised to all who see the
Son. Earlier in the chapter, however, the same Greek verb was used of a
seeing which did not lead to understanding: The disciples...saw Jesus
walking on the water..., and they were terrified (6.19).

The switch from the third person reference to the Son to the first
person I should be noted; in the final sentence the I is emphatic. Though
in some languages it is possible to preserve the shift from third person
to first person, in others it cannot be done without considerable confusion. In fact, it may be necessary to use the first person reference
throughout this passage. Therefore, what my Father wants may be restructured as "he wants everyone who recognizes me as God's Son and believes
in me to have eternal life."

In Greek them is singular ("him"). TEV translates as plural, in
keeping with the first part of the verse, where the Greek "everyone who"
becomes all who.

The concept of eternal life has been discussed (see 1.4; 3.15).

	TEV	(6.41-46)	RSV

<table>
<tr><td>

41 The people started grumbling about him, because he said, "I am the bread that came down from heaven." 42 So they said, "This man is Jesus son of Joseph, isn't he? We know his father and mother. How, then, does he now say he came down from heaven?"

43 Jesus answered, "Stop grumbling among yourselves." 44 No one can come to me unless the Father who sent me draws him to me; and I will raise him to life on the last day.

45 The prophets wrote, 'Everyone will be taught by God.' Anyone who hears the Father and learns from him comes to me. 46 This does not mean that anyone has seen the Father; he who is from God is the only one who has seen the Father.

</td><td>

41 The Jews then murmured at him, because he said, "I am the bread which came down from heaven." 42 They said, "Is not this Jesus, the son of Joseph, whose father and mother we know? How does he now say, 'I have come down from heaven'?" 43 Jesus answered them, "Do not murmur among yourselves. 44 No one can come to me unless the Father who sent me draws him; and I will raise him up at the last day. 45 It is written in the prophets, 'And they shall all be taught by God.' Every one who has heard and learned from the Father comes to me. 46 Not that any one has seen the Father except him who is from God; he has seen the Father.

</td></tr>
</table>

6.41   The people started grumbling about him,
        because he said, "I am the bread that came
        down from heaven."

In Greek this sentence begins with the particle oun, which NEB and NAB translate "at this." (See under 2.18.) TEV introduces a new paragraph.

The people is literally "the Jews." See Appendix I.

Started grumbling (NEB "began to murmur"; NAB "started to murmur") renders the force of the Greek imperfect. RSV and Mft translate "murmured" and JB "were complaining." The verb grumbling is the simple form of the verb used in the Septuagint account of the grumbling of the Israelites during the Exodus (see Exo 16.2,7,8). The verb denotes more of complaint than of open hostility. Elsewhere in John it is used in 6.43,61; 7.32; and in the remainder of the New Testament only in Matthew 20.11; Luke 5.30; and 1 Corinthians 10.10 (twice). The noun form of the same stem occurs in 7.12. An equivalent of started grumbling may be "started speaking against" or "started complaining to one another about him."

6.42   So they said, "This man is Jesus son of Joseph,
        isn't he? We know his father and mother. How,
        then, does he now say he came down from heaven?"

NAB attempts to reproduce the force of the Greek imperfect (TEV said) by translating "kept saying."

In translating the Greek rhetorical question, TEV attempts to structure it so that the reader will understand the expected answer to be "Yes."

The adverb now (Greek nun) appears in some Greek manuscripts, while in others the particle oun appears. The adverb now does seem clumsy in the Greek sentence structure. Perhaps for this reason some ancient scribes omitted it and others changed it to oun. The UBS Committee on the Greek text concludes that nun (now) is an original part of the Greek text, though evaluating its decision as a "C" choice. Most modern translations include now; NAB omits it.

In Greek the last part of this sentence appears as direct discourse, "I have come down from heaven"; TEV renders it as indirect discourse, he came down from heaven, thus avoiding a quotation within a quotation and simplifying the English sentence structure.

How, then introduces an objection. Compare the objection of Nicodemus: How can this be? (3.9). In some languages a similar expression should be used here also, for example, "How then is he able now to say?" or "How is it possible that he can now say?"

The Greek word order is changed in translation. In Greek the phrase from heaven actually precedes the verb came down, placing the adverbial phrase in the emphatic position.

6.43   Jesus answered, "Stop grumbling among your-
     selves.

Jesus answered is literally "Jesus answered and said to them," another instance of Semitic style. TEV (Stop grumbling) and NEB ("Stop murmuring") both attempt to capture the force of the Greek present imperative, which indicates that the people are to stop an action they are already in the process of doing. A simple negative imperative, "Don't grumble," would not have this force.

6.44   No one can come to me unless the Father who
     sent me draws him to me; and I will raise
     him to life on the last day.

Jesus does not attempt to resolve the Jews' doubts about his true origin by means of human argumentation. Rather, he affirms that no one can come to him unless the Father draws that person to him (compare verse 65). Jesus is stating the basic biblical affirmation that salvation is always due to God's initiative. The words to me are not explicit in the Greek text, but they are implicit, as TEV makes clear. In 12.32 Jesus states that he will draw all men to himself. Draws him resembles the expression "to bring someone near the Law," which the Rabbis used to describe conversion to Judaism.

However, draws may suggest that God uses violent means to force a person against his will to come to Jesus. A more satisfactory expression, meaning "brings him to me" or "leads him to me," may be found in some languages.

6.45   The prophets wrote, 'Everyone will be taught
            by God.' Anyone who hears the Father and
            learns from him comes to me.

   The prophets wrote (literally "It is written in the prophets") may
suggest that John is referring to several prophetic books. Actually,
Everyone will be taught by God is a free rendering of Isaiah 54.13. Rather
than attempt to explain to the reader why prophets is the plural, it
may be better to translate "One of the prophets wrote" or "The following
words occur in one of the books written by the prophets."
   Anyone who hears the Father and learns from him comes to me is a
slight restructuring of the Greek "everyone who hears and learns from
the Father comes to me." Mft, NEB, and NAB all restructure in essentially
the same way. However, they differ from TEV in translating the two Greek
aorist participles in the past tense (NEB, for example, "has listened
to" and "learned"). The Greek aorist participles may have either the
force of a past tense or of a timeless tense, as in TEV. The same verb
tense is used of hearing the Father in 8.26, 40, and 15.15, where TEV
has either a past ("I heard") or a perfect ("I have heard"). In each
case it is Jesus who hears the Father.
   As in many other contexts, hears involves more than mere "listening
to." It is really equivalent to learns.

6.46   This does not mean that anyone has seen the
            Father; he who is from God is the only one
            who has seen the Father.

   This does not mean that (NEB "I do not mean that") is literally
"not that" (RSV, JB, NAB) and is merely a formula for introducing a
statement of contrast. An equivalent in some languages is "I am not
saying that..." or "do not understand my words to mean that...."
   He who is from God is the only one who has seen the Father is literally "except the one from God, this one has seen the Father." This
verse represents the same thought expressed in 1.18. Both passages apparently intend a contrast between Jesus and Moses. A shift from third
person to first person would result in the following restructuring: "I
who have come am the only one who has ever seen the Father" or "...my
Father."

            TEV   (6.47-51)   RSV

47 I am telling you the truth: he   47 Truly, truly, I say to you, he
who believes has eternal life. 48   who believes has eternal life. 48
I am the bread of life. 49 Your   I am the bread of life. 49 Your
ancestors ate manna in the desert,   fathers ate the manna in the wild-
but they died. 50 But the bread   erness, and they died. 50 This is
that comes down from heaven is of   the bread which comes down from
such a kind that whoever eats it   heaven, that a man may eat of it
will not die. 51 I am the living   and not die. 51 I am the living
bread that came down from heaven.   bread which came down from heaven;
If anyone eats this bread, he will   if any one eats of this bread, he

live forever. The bread that I will
give him is my flesh, which I give
so that the world may live."

will live for ever; and the bread
which I shall give for the life
of the world is my flesh."

6.47   I am telling you the truth: he who believes
           has eternal life.

On I am telling you the truth see 1.51. On eternal life see 1.4;
3.15.
It may be necessary in some languages to state the object of believes. If so, it would seem best to translate "he who believes in me."

6.48   I am the bread of life.

The bread of life is, of course, "the bread which gives life."

6.49-50   Your ancestors ate manna in the desert,
           but they died. 50 But the bread that
           comes down from heaven is of such a kind
           that whoever eats it will not die.

These verses repeat the arguments of 32-35. The death referred to
in verse 49 is physical death, while the death referred to in verse 50
is spiritual death.
A literal translation of verse 49 may lead to serious misunderstanding, for it may suggest that the ancestors died precisely because
they ate manna in the desert. The fact that eating manna did not contribute to their deaths must be expressed in some languages as a concessive relation, for example, "Even though your ancestors ate manna in
the desert, they died." This translation provides a useful basis for the
contrast which begins with verse 50.
TEV restructures verse 50, which in Greek reads literally "this is
the bread which comes down from heaven in order that one may eat of it
and not die." Since it is obvious that a contrast is intended between
verses 49 and 50, TEV introduces verse 50 with but. Moreover, in Greek
the demonstrative adjective "this" is used in this context to indicate
the qualitative significance of the bread, and so TEV translates "this"
by such a kind that. Finally, the Greek pronoun "one" is indefinite and
all inclusive, so TEV translates whoever, while most translations have
"a man."
To make the contrast between verses 49 and 50 clear and to point
out the conditional element involved in the clause whoever eats it, one
may restructure verse 50 as follows: "But in contrast with manna, the
bread which comes down from heaven is of such a kind that if anyone eats
it he will not die" or "...all who eat it will not die."

6.51   I am the living bread that came down from
           heaven. If anyone eats this bread, he will
           live forever. The bread that I will give
           him is my flesh, which I give so that the
           world may live."

The initial I of this verse is emphatic; Anchor Bible translates
it as "I myself." It is one of several instances in the Gospel of John
where "I am" is used with a predicate (see 4.26).

Living bread is synonymous with "bread of life," and both mean
"the bread which gives life." The last sentence of this verse introduces a new thought: the bread that I will give him is my flesh. The
shift from the present tense to the future (will give) points to the
time of Jesus' sacrificial death, when he will give himself for the needs
of his people, the event symbolized in part by the broken bread of the
Lord's Supper. TEV attempts to relate this last sentence to the preceding
one by introducing him as the object of the verb give, thus tying it to
anyone and he of the previous sentence.

In many languages my flesh can be translated as "my body." Some
translators suggest the use of "myself" here, but if this had been the
meaning intended, it would not have caused the argument which follows
in verse 52.

Which I give so that the world may live is literally "in behalf
of the life of the world." TEV transforms this series of noun phrases
into two verb phrases. Which I give so that picks up the meaning of "in
behalf of" (Greek huper), while "the life of the world" is taken to mean
the world may live. NEB retains the expression "for the life of the
world," though it reintroduces the verb "give" ("I give it for the life
of the world").

TEV   (6.52-59)   RSV

52 This started an angry argument among them. "How can this man
give us his flesh to eat?" they
asked.

53 Jesus said to them, "I am
telling you the truth: if you do
not eat the flesh of the Son of
Man and drink his blood, you will
not have the life in yourselves.
54 Whoever eats my flesh and drinks
my blood has eternal life, and I
will raise him to life on the last
day. 55 For my flesh is the real
food; my blood is the real drink.
56 Whoever eats my flesh and drinks
my blood lives in me, and I live
in him. 57 The living Father sent
me, and because of him I live also.
In the same way whoever eats me
will live because of me. 58 This,
then, is the bread that came down
from heaven; it is not like the
bread that your ancestors ate, but
then later died. The one who eats
this bread will live forever."

52 The Jews then disputed among
themselves, saying, "How can this
man give us his flesh to eat?" 53
So Jesus said to them, "Truly,
truly, I say to you, unless you
eat the flesh of the Son of man
and drink his blood, you have no
life in you; 54 he who eats my
flesh and drinks my blood has eternal life, and I will raise him up
at the last day. 55 For my flesh
is food indeed, and my blood is
drink indeed. 56 He who eats my
flesh and drinks my blood abides
in me, and I in him. 57 As the
living Father sent me, and I live
because of the Father, so he who
eats me will live because of me.
58 This is the bread which came
down from heaven, not such as the
fathers ate and died; he who eats
this bread will live for ever."
59 This he said in the synagogue,
as he taught at Capernaum.

59 Jesus said this as he taught
in the synagogue in Capernaum.

6.52   This started an angry argument among them.
            "How can this man give us his flesh to eat?"
            they asked.

This started an angry argument among them may be more literally
translated "So then the Jews were arguing angrily among themselves." In
this context the Greek particle (oun, "so then") is intended to show a
cause and effect relation between this verse and the preceding one. TEV
indicates this relation by translating this started, while NEB translates
"this led to." The verb rendered angry argument (NEB "fierce dispute")
literally means "to fight" and is a strong term, often used metaphor-
ically. In rendering angry argument it is important to indicate that the
people were angry not with one another but because of the statement
Jesus had made. It may be translated in some languages "The people got
angry at what Jesus had said and started an argument among themselves."
        This man is perhaps to be taken as an expression of contempt on
the part of the Jews.
        Some Greek manuscripts have "flesh" rather than his flesh, and the
evidence for the inclusion or omission of his is about equal. However,
the context makes it clear that Jesus' own flesh is referred to. Even
though the manuscript evidence may not absolutely support the inclusion
of this word, it is obligatory on translational grounds.
        No translation of this passage can completely eliminate the pro-
blems of readers or hearers in understanding it. In fact, in some
societies people will almost inevitably understand "eating his flesh"
as a reference to cannibalism. The total context makes it clear that
this meaning is not intended. But in no way can one be faithful to the
meaning John intends and at the same time avoid all problems of misunderstanding. If this discourse produced serious problems even for followers
of Jesus, it is inevitable that it will produce difficulties for the
present-day reader. However, the presence of serious difficulties does
not give the translator a warrant to rewrite the passage.

6.53   Jesus said to them, "I am telling you the
            truth: if you do not eat the flesh of the Son
            of Man and drink his blood, you will not have
            the life in yourselves.

This verse states negatively the same truths that were stated
positively in verse 51. Here, however, the Son of Man is mentioned, and
the necessity of drinking his blood. Commentators generally agree that
blood is introduced to call to mind the eucharist, and at the same time
to indicate that it is the total being of the Son of Man that gives
life--in Hebrew thought "flesh and blood" were equivalent to the total
person. Whatever the source of meaning of eat the flesh...drink his
blood, these terms cannot be demetaphorized. The picture of eating
flesh and of drinking blood may be offensive in some cultures (the Jews
themselves were forbidden to drink blood). However, meaning and symbol

[207]

are so closely related here that one cannot demetaphorize without destroying the meaning of the passage.

You will not have life in yourselves (JB "you will not have life in you") is actually in the present tense (RSV "you have no life in you"), but in the context it denotes a future possibility (NEB "you can have no life in you"). You will not have life in yourselves cannot be said in languages in which life cannot be possessed. Rather, it is necessary to speak of "living." The most appropriate equivalent may be "you will not really live." The explanation of this quality of life is contained in verse 54, which amplifies the meaning of verse 53 by introducing the theme of eternal life.

6.54   Whoever eats my flesh and drinks my blood has
        eternal life, and I will raise him to life on
        the last day.

The verb here translated eats was originally used only in reference to animals, and some commentators see here the meaning of "gnaw" or "munch," which would underscore the realism of this passage as a reference to the Lord's Supper. However, in New Testament times the verb was also used in reference to people, and so some commentators assume that John uses this verb for the present tense of "to eat." Most translations have the equivalent of eats in the present context, though NAB has "feeds on." The same verb is used four times in this paragraph (verses 54, 56, 57, 58) and in 13.18. It appears also in Matthew 24.38, where it is again used of people, not animals.

6.55   For my flesh is the real food; my blood is the
        real drink.

The word translated real is alēthēs, whereas in 1.9 and 6.32 real renders another Greek adjective, alēthinos. In the two earlier passages there is an element of contrast: real light, as opposed to natural light; real bread from heaven, as opposed to manna. Here, however, Jesus' flesh and blood are not contrasted with some other kind of food but are declared to be food in the proper sense. This food is often referred to in translation as "true food." Although one commentator gives a distinct meaning for alēthinos ("the only real"), the distinction between the two adjectives may be purely contextual, and in any case both can be translated by real. Differences of opinion exist with respect to the interpretation of real or "true." The most obvious meaning is that which equates the flesh and blood with physical food and drink. But real is understood by many persons as suggesting a higher level of reality than mere physical identification. Accordingly, real in this sense would be understood as pointing to the spiritual significance of the flesh and blood as being more real than the physical aspects. To justify this interpretation persons often refer to verse 63. TEV translates the adjective here as the real, while most translations have simply "real."

Instead of the adjective real, some ancient manuscripts have an adverb, "really." Apparently no modern translations follow that reading. The weight of the manuscript evidence is strongly in favor of the adjective real.

<u>6.56</u>   Whoever eats my flesh and drinks my blood
                    lives in me, and I live in him.

Verses 55 and 56 are not joined together by any connecting particle. The use of the present tense throughout should be noted: <u>eats...drinks ...lives...live</u>.

<u>Lives in me</u> and <u>I live in him</u> is literally "remains in me and I in him"; the thought is similar to 15.4. The verb "to remain" is one of John's most important terms, and he uses it of the relationship between the Father and the Son (14.10), as well as of the believer's relationship with the Son (6.56; 15.4). In 1.32-33 the Spirit descends and remains on Jesus. See also such key verses as 5.38; 8.31; 15.7, 9-10. Here the meaning is "lives in fellowship/union with me and I live in fellowship/union with him." This concept of fellowship or union with Christ is expressed in some languages as "share with," while in others one may speak of "being one together with."

<u>6.57</u>   The living Father sent me, and because of him
                    I live also. In the same way whoever eats me
                    will live because of me.

In Greek this verse reads "In the same way that the living Father sent me, and I live because of the Father, so he who eats me will live because of me." TEV restructures this complex sentence into two simpler sentences. Since the actual comparison is between the first two statements ("In the same way...because of the Father") and the final statement ("so he...because of me"), TEV does not introduce the comparison (<u>in the same way</u>) until the second sentence. Thus a more natural English structure is achieved, and at the same time a long, involved sentence is avoided. It should be noted that TEV substitutes the pronoun <u>him</u> for "the Father" in the phrase "because of the Father"--also in keeping with the desire to attain naturalness in English.

The expression <u>the living Father</u> does not occur elsewhere in the Scriptures, though the phrase "the living God" appears in both the Old and New Testaments. The phrase is probably used on the analogy of the <u>living bread</u> mentioned in verse 51, so that the meaning of <u>the living Father</u> would be "the Father who is the source of life" or "the Father who gives life."

Note that whereas the preceding verse reads <u>eats my flesh</u>, this verse reads <u>eats me</u>; the meaning is the same.

In 5.21 also the Father is said to have life-giving power; according to this passage the Son derives his power to give life from his union with the Father.

The agents expressed in the phrases <u>because of him</u> and <u>because of me</u> may be clearly marked by indicating a causal relation, for example, "the Father who causes people to live sent me, and he has caused me to live. In the same way if anyone eats me, I will cause him to live."

<u>6.58</u>   This, then, is the bread that came down from
                    heaven; it is not like the bread that your
                    ancestors ate, but then later died. The one
                    who eats this bread will live forever."

   This, then, is the bread that came down from heaven is verbally almost identical with the first part of verse 50 (but the bread that comes down from heaven is such that) except that in this verse the past tense came down is used. Note also the link with verse 31 and the dialogue that followed.

   It is not like the bread that your ancestors ate, but then later died is literally "not as the fathers ate and died." In NEB this passage is rendered "and it is not like the bread which our fathers ate: they are dead...." There is no problem in translating "fathers" as ancestors, since "fathers" is often used with this sense in the New Testament (see 6.31). The problem is whether to translate "our ancestors" (inclusive) or your ancestors (exclusive). There is some manuscript evidence in support of the reading your ancestors, but the best Greek manuscripts read simply "the ancestors." In many languages one simply cannot speak of "the fathers," since all kinship terms occur with so-called "obligatory possession." This means that one must have some pronominal or nominal reference to identify each kin relationship. But even in languages which do not have obligatory possession with kinship terms there is a tendency to specify kin relationships. Whether one chooses in English "your" or "our" in rendering "fathers" in this context depends primarily upon how one interprets the emotional tone of the discourse. The rendering "our fathers" suggests a more friendly atmosphere in the dispute which Jesus had with Jewish leaders, and the rendering "your ancestors" suggests a more hostile type of dialogue, in which Jesus separated himself from identification with the religious leaders of his own nation. That is, Jesus refers to your ancestors in a derogatory sense, in the same way that they referred to him as this man (verse 52). As has already been pointed out, in translating "the Father" one must often choose between "my Father" and "our Father," but in such contexts the decision as to which pronoun to use depends not on the emotional tone of the discourse but upon the probable relations of the heavenly Father, either exclusively with his Son (therefore, "my Father") or more inclusively with all the believers included in the particular context (therefore, "our Father").

   TEV translates "but then died" of the Greek text by but then later died, in order not to suggest that the persons who ate died immediately, perhaps as a result of eating the bread.

   While both TEV and NEB translate so that the comparison is between the bread that the ancestors ate and the bread that Jesus offers, NAB makes a comparison between the ancestors who ate and died ("unlike your ancestors who ate and died...") and those who eat the bread which Jesus will give. The Greek text itself can be understood to support either interpretation. However, the renderings of most translations are basically the same as that of TEV and NEB (see, for example, JB, Mft).

6.59   Jesus said this as he taught in the
            synagogue in Capernaum.

   Jesus said this is literally "these things he said"; the obvious antecedent of "he" is Jesus. Since Jesus has not been mentioned by name since verse 53, TEV mentions him explicitly in this concluding verse.

   In the synagogue is literally "in synagogue," but most translations have the definite article "the," as TEV does. NAB has the indefinite article "in a synagogue," while NEB translates literally "in synagogue," evidently attempting to construct a phrase that sounds like "in church." Translators frequently employ a transliteration of the term "synagogue." In some languages a descriptive equivalent is employed, for example, "in houses of worship used by Jews" or "in Jewish buildings for worship." It is true that synagogues were also used as places for civic gatherings and as schools, but the focus in most New Testament passages is on the synagogue as a place of Jewish worship.

	TEV	(6.60-65)		RSV

THE WORDS OF ETERNAL LIFE

60 Many of his followers heard this and said, "This teaching is too hard. Who can listen to it?"

61 Without being told, Jesus knew that they were grumbling about this, so he said to them, "Does this make you want to give up? 62 Suppose, then, that you should see the Son of Man go back up to the place where he was before? 63 What gives life is God's Spirit; man's power is of no use at all. The words I have spoken to you bring God's life-giving Spirit. 64 Yet some of you do not believe." (Jesus knew from the very beginning who were the ones that would not believe and which one would betray him.) 65 And he added, "This is the very reason I told you that no one can come to me unless the Father makes it possible for him to do so."

60 Many of his disciples, when they heard it, said, "This is a hard saying; who can listen to it?" 61 But Jesus, knowing in himself that his disciples murmured at it, said to them, "Do you take offense at this? 62 Then what if you were to see the Son of man ascending where he was before? 63 It is the spirit that gives life, the flesh is of no avail; the words that I have spoken to you are spirit and life. 64 But there are some of you that do not believe." For Jesus knew from the first who those were that did not believe, and who it was that should betray him. 65 And he said, "This is why I told you that no one can come to me unless it is granted him by the Father."

The verses reproduced above and the ones that follow (66-71) bring to a close Jesus' Galilean ministry. In summary, John indicates the results of that ministry. Many of Jesus' own disciples have turned back and will not go further with him, and even one who stays with him is going to betray him. However, Simon Peter speaks on behalf of the twelve and indicates that they believe and know that Jesus is the Holy One from God.

6.60   Many of his followers heard this and said, "This teaching is too hard. Who can listen to it?"

The same Greek verb appears twice in this verse; the first time
it is translated heard (so also most other translations), and the second
time listen to (so also RSV and NEB). Mft translates "hard to take in,"
NAB "hard to endure," and JB and Phps "accept." In the Greek text heard
is actually an aorist participle (RSV "when they heard"; NEB "on hearing"),
which TEV makes into a finite verb parallel with the verb said.

Verse 24 implies that Jesus' discourse was delivered to the crowd,
while verse 41 reveals that "the Jews" (TEV the people) were also present. Evidently John intends his readers to understand that Jesus' disciples were also present. Verses 66-67 indicate that his followers
include a much larger group than the twelve disciples. (See, for example,
Luke 10.1.)

The antecedent of this (in the construction heard this) is not
clearly marked, but it is perhaps best understood either as a reference
to the entire discourse concerning the bread of life (beginning with
verse 25) or to the closing words of the discourse (53-58).

This teaching is too hard is more literally rendered in RSV "This
is a hard saying." Mft ("This is hard to take in!") and NAB ("This sort
of talk is hard to endure!") are similar. JB, in a rather high level of
language, has "This is intolerable language," while NEB sounds colloquial,
"This is more than we can stomach!" The adjective too hard was originally
used of physical objects and meant "hard" or "rough." In the present
context it has the meaning "difficult to accept" rather than "difficult
to understand."

It (in the construction listen to it) may be either neuter (as in
TEV and most other translations) or masculine, "him." Most translators
have "it," while NEB has "such talk."

Who can listen to it does not mean that Jesus' words cannot be
heard but that it is impossible to comprehend what he is saying. One
may therefore translate this final question "Who is able to agree with
what he is trying to say?" Jesus' teaching is unacceptable (This teaching is too hard) precisely because it is not in accord with the people's
expectations.

6.61   Without being told, Jesus knew that they
              were grumbling about this, so he said to them,
              "Does this make you want to give up?"

Without being told, Jesus knew is more literally, "but Jesus knew
in himself." "To know in one's self" reflects Semitic Greek, and its
purpose is to indicate the supernatural knowledge Jesus had (see further
at 1.47-48 and 2.25). NEB and JB translate this expression "was aware,"
NAB "was fully aware," and Mft "inwardly conscious." This introductory
statement in verse 61 may be translated "No one told Jesus what the disciples were saying, but he knew anyway" or "...he knew that...."

Grumbling is the same verb used in verse 41.

Does this make you want to give up? may be translated more literally "Does this offend you?" This verb is used only here and in 16.1
in John's Gospel. In 16.1 the form is passive, but TEV focuses attention
on the subject and so renders the verb give up your faith. In the present passage JB translates "Does this upset you?" (see also Mft "So this
upsets you?"), NEB "Does this shock you?" and NAB "Does it shake your

faith?" In some languages the question may be translated "Does this make you want to turn away?" In other languages, "Does this cause you to lose your faith?" or "...to no longer want to believe?" or "Does this cause you to think differently?" may be appropriate translations.

6.62   Suppose, then, that you should see the Son of
         Man go back up to the place where he was be-
         fore?

In Greek this sentence is incomplete; it states a condition but does not give the conclusion. NAB reflects this incompleteness by translating "What, then, if you were to see the Son of Man ascend to where he was before...?" The fact that the sentence is grammatically incomplete has led commentators to suggest various ways of completing it. Some suggest that if the condition is fulfilled, the offense will be greater. Others suggest that if the condition is fulfilled, the offense will be lessened or removed altogether, because the Jews will then be led to believe. Still other scholars connect this question with the theme of the bread of life, saying in effect that if the condition is fulfilled, the Jews will understand the meaning of "the bread of life." Fortunately, the translator is not required to fill out the ellipsis in this sentence. In fact, he is obligated to indicate that a condition is given but no fulfillment is expressed.

The supposition posed by Jesus may be introduced in some languages in a variety of ways, for example, "Think about what would happen if you should see..." or "Imagine what it would be like if you should see ..." or "If you should see the Son of Man go back to the place where he was before, then what?" or "...then what would you think?"

To the place where he was before (so also NEB) is evidently to the Father (17.5), but it should not be stated explicitly in translation. Mft sounds unnecessarily theological: "to where he formerly existed."

6.63   What gives life is God's Spirit; man's power
         is of no use at all. The words I have spoken
         to you bring God's life-giving Spirit.

God's Spirit is literally "the spirit." However, where "spirit" is unmarked (that is, without attributive) in the New Testament, it normally refers to God's Spirit, as in the present context. It is strange that some translations spell Spirit with a lower case "s" (NEB, JB, NAB). God's Spirit frequently appears as the source of life in both the Old and New Testaments. This concept is given particular emphasis in the Gospel of John. For example, it is God's Spirit which brings about the new birth (3.5,8), and the Spirit is life-giving water (7.38-39). It may be necessary in some languages to invert the clause What gives life is God's Spirit and render it "God's Spirit is the one who causes people to live."

Man's power is literally "the flesh," as in most translations. In the Old Testament "flesh" is often used as a description of mortal man in contrast with God, who is life-giving Spirit. That is clearly the meaning in the present context, and TEV makes this meaning explicit.

[213]

Man's power is of no use at all may be rendered "people themselves cannot do this." It may be necessary to be even more explicit, for example,
"people themselves cannot cause people to live."

The pronoun I is emphatic in the second sentence of this verse.

Bring God's life-giving Spirit is literally "are Spirit and are
life." It is rendered "are Spirit and life" or similarly in most translations, though some have "spirit" with a lower case "s." Phps renders
Spirit as "spiritual," but is is difficult to see the reasoning behind
this rendering. But it is also difficult to see meaning in the literal
rendering "are Spirit and are life," since "and" normally indicates a
relation of balance between the things it connects. In this case, however, "and" may simply be used to indicate an unmarked relation between
"Spirit" and "life," and so the phrase may be rendered "Spirit that
gives life" or life-giving Spirit. Such an exegesis is in keeping with
John's theology and also with his Semitic Greek style, since in the Old
Testament terms which are not in a balanced relation are often joined
by the connective "and." This exegesis also fits the overall context of
the discourse on the bread of life, in which there is an implicit contrast between Jesus and Moses. Compare 2 Corinthians 3.6, "The written
law brings death, but the Spirit gives life."

A literal translation of bring God's life-giving Spirit could be
misleading, since it might imply that the words themselves carry the
Spirit. One may say in some languages "the words I have spoken to you
cause you to have God's Spirit, which gives life" or "...causes you to
live." However, it may be difficult to speak of "words causing the
Spirit to come." Therefore one may say "By means of the words which I
have spoken to you, I have caused God's life-giving Spirit to come to
you."

6.64   Yet some of you do not believe." (Jesus knew
        from the very beginning who were the ones
        that would not believe and which one would
        betray him.)

The second sentence of this verse is best taken as a parenthetical
statement, as in TEV and other translations (NAB and Mft, for example).

From the very beginning (JB "from the outset"; NEB "all along")
has reference either to the beginning of Jesus' ministry or to the time
of his calling the disciples; it does not refer to the beginning mentioned in 1.1. The same phrase is used in 16.4 and is translated at the
beginning. From the very beginning may be rendered "from the day that
he began to teach" or "all the time starting with the day he began to
teach."

If it is necessary to express the object of believe, then the
choice lies between (1) what Jesus said and (2) Jesus himself. The context supports either interpretation, and one may argue that to accept
Jesus' words as true is essentially equivalent to putting one's trust
in Jesus himself.

The ones that would not believe is literally "the ones who were
not believing." NAB ("the ones who refused to believe") has essentially
the same meaning as TEV.

The verb translated betray (so most translations) does not necessarily imply treachery. It may have the neutral sense of "to hand over" (NAB). It is used of God, who did not even keep back his own Son, but offered him for us all (Rom 8.32), and of Jesus himself, who, in Paul's words, loved me and gave his life for me (Gal 2.20). It is also used in quite a different sense for the passing on of tradition (1 Cor 11.2,23; 15.3). However, since Jesus was handed over (Mark 9.31; 10.33) to the authorities by one of the twelve, the word takes on a special meaning in relation to Judas Iscariot, who became the traitor (Luke 6.16). Since betrayal is a common experience in all societies, there is usually no difficulty in finding a satisfactory term. It may be equivalent to "turn him over to other people" or "cause him to be under the control of others" or "cause him to be arrested by others."

6.65   And he added, "This is the very reason I told you that no one can come to me unless the Father makes it possible for him to do so."

And he added is literally "and he was saying."
This is the very reason (literally "because of this") evidently refers back to some of you do not believe in verse 64. Jesus' words here, as in verse 44, affirm that salvation is due to God's initiative.
Unless the Father makes it possible for him to do so translates a passive construction in Greek, "unless it is granted him by the Father" (RSV). TEV makes the agent of the Greek passive verb ("the Father") the subject of an active verb in English and takes the verb "grant" to have the meaning of makes it possible. Both the meaning and the grammatical construction of this sentence are similar to 3.27. This final part of verse 65 may be rendered in some languages "unless my Father says, 'You may be a follower of Jesus'" or "...unless my Father says that he can be my follower."

TEV   (6.66-71)   RSV

66 Because of this, many of Jesus' followers turned back and would not go with him any more. 67 So he asked the twelve disciples, "And you--would you also like to leave?"

68 Simon Peter answered him, "Lord, to whom would we go? You have the words that give eternal life. 69 And now we believe and know that you are the Holy One who has come from God."

70 Jesus replied, "I chose the twelve of you, didn't I? Yet one of you is a devil!" 71 He was talking about Judas, the son of Simon Iscariot. For Judas, even

66 After this many of his disciples drew back and no longer went about with him. 67 Jesus said to the twelve, "Will you also go away?" 68 Simon Peter answered him, "Lord, to whom shall we go? You have the words of eternal life; 69 and we have believed, and have come to know, that you are the Holy One of God." 70 Jesus answered them, "Did I not choose you, the twelve, and one of you is a devil?" 71 He spoke of Judas the son of Simon Iscariot, for he, one of the twelve, was to betray him.

though he was one of the twelve
disciples, was going to betray
him.

6.66   Because of this, many of Jesus' followers
            turned back and would not go with him any more.

Because of this is ambiguous. It may be either consequential as
TEV has it (Phps "as a consequence of this") or temporal (most translations "after this"; NEB "from that time on").

Followers is literally "disciples." Here the larger group is contrasted with the twelve mentioned in the following verse. For this reason
TEV has followers in this verse and renders "the twelve" of the following verse as the twelve disciples, thus retaining the more specialized
term "disciples" as a reference to the twelve.

Turned back is translated in various ways. Mft and RSV translate
"drew back," while Phps and NEB have "withdrew." JB has "left him" and
NAB "broke away." It may be a Hebrew idiom, as is the expression (would
not) go with, which is translated "no longer went about with him" by
NEB and "stopped going with him" by JB. Phps translates "no longer followed him." Mft ("would not associate with him any longer") and NAB
("would not remain in his company any longer") seem to have a wrong
focus. The two expressions are essentially synonymous; one is used to
reinforce the other.

6.67   So he asked the twelve disciples, "And you--
            would you also like to leave?"

Here the twelve disciples is literally "the twelve." This is the
first time that the twelve are mentioned as such in John's Gospel. In
fact, the only time they are mentioned outside this section is in 20.24,
which suggests that John had little interest in focusing attention on
them as a group. A marginal note may be useful at this point.

In Jesus' question to the disciples, you is emphatic. TEV indicates
this emphasis by placing a dash after you. The question as stated in
Greek implies a negative answer.

6.68   Simon Peter answered him, "Lord, to whom
            would we go? You have the words that give
            eternal life.

The Greek expression "words of eternal life" means words that give
eternal life or "words that lead to eternal life."

6.69   And now we believe and know that you are
            the Holy One who has come from God."

And now is literally "and." TEV introduces now to indicate a
transition. It is not to be taken as a temporal marker.

The words believe and know are both in the perfect tense in the
Greek text (NAB "we have come to believe; we are convinced"). John often

uses two verbs in the perfect tense, and if this tense carries any particular force in the present context, it is to indicate that the disciples were continuing in their belief and in their knowledge that Jesus is the Holy One who has come from God. However, most translations attempt to bring this out by using the present tense.

The Holy One who has come from God is evidently intended as a messianic title; in Mark 1.24 and Luke 4.34 it is the confession made by a demon who has supernatural knowledge. The nearest parallel elsewhere in John's Gospel is in 10.36, where Jesus says that the Father chose him and sent him into the world. The verb translated chose in TEV at 10.36 is from the same root as the word Holy of this verse. Most modern translators prefer to render this phrase "the Holy One of God" (NAB "God's holy one"). GeCL avoids the difficulties related to the word "holy" and achieves the same effect by rendering "you are the sent one of God."

6.70   Jesus replied, "I chose the twelve of you,
      didn't I? Yet one of you is a devil!"

This verse may be punctuated in various ways, for example, "Didn't I choose the twelve of you, even though one of you is a devil?" or "I chose the twelve of you, didn't I? And yet one of you is a devil." or "...yet one of you is a devil!" The different ways of punctuating the reply of Jesus do not affect the meaning essentially.

One of you is a devil is what the Greek text has, and that is clearly what it means. Phps' translation "one of you has the devil in his heart" weakens the expression. Perhaps he is attempting to harmonize this statement with 13.2 and 13.27. The latter passage states that Satan entered into Judas. However, one should let this verse say what it says and not attempt to harmonize it with what is said later. Here the statement is simply that Judas is a devil.

Some languages present a difficulty in translating one of you is a devil, since they lack a definite term for "devil." However, they often have a term for "demon," and the devil is frequently spoken of as "the chief of the demons." In this context it may be satisfactory to say "one of you is a chief over demons" as the closest natural equivalent of "devil."

6.71   He was talking about Judas, the son of Simon
      Iscariot. For Judas, even though he was one
      of the twelve disciples, was going to betray
      him.

The manuscript evidence is strongly in support of connecting Iscariot with Simon rather than with Judas, and so most modern translations read Judas, the son of Simon Iscariot.

Judas in the second sentence is actually a pronoun in Greek (literally "this one"), which TEV renders by the noun Judas, in order to avoid suggesting that Simon Iscariot was one of the twelve and the one who would betray Jesus.

In Greek was going to betray him comes before even though he was

one of the twelve disciples. JB, Phps, and RSV have essentially the
same restructuring as TEV. Here, as in verse 67, the twelve disciples
is literally "the twelve."

TEV   (7.1-9)   RSV

JESUS AND HIS BROTHERS

7 After this, Jesus traveled in Galilee; he did not want to travel in Judea, because the Jewish authorities there were wanting to kill him. 2 The time for the Festival of Shelters was near, 3 so Jesus' brothers said to him, "Leave this place and go to Judea, so that your followers will see the things that you are doing. 4 No one hides what he is doing if he wants to be well known. Since you are doing these things, let the whole world know about you!" (5 Not even his brothers believed in him.)

6 Jesus said to them, "The right time for me has not yet come. Any time is right for you. 7 The world cannot hate you, but it hates me, because I keep telling it that its ways are bad. 8 You go on to the festival. I am not going^n to this festival, because the right time has not come for me." 9 He said this and then stayed on in Galilee.

^{n}I am not going; *some manuscripts have* I am not yet going.

7 After this Jesus went about in Galilee; he would not go about in Judea, because the Jews^n sought to kill him. 2 Now the Jews' feast of Tabernacles was at hand. 3 So his brothers said to him, "Leave here and go to Judea, that your disciples may see the works you are doing. 4 For no man works in secret if he seeks to be known openly. If you do these things, show yourself to the world." 5 For even his brothers did not believe in him. 6 Jesus said to them, "My time has not yet come, but your time is always here. 7 The world cannot hate you, but it hates me because I testify of it that its works are evil. 8 Go to the feast yourselves; I am not^o going up to this feast, for my time has not yet fully come." 9 So saying, he remained in Galilee.

^{n}Or *Judeans*

^{o}Other ancient authorities add *yet*

Some commentators believe that Chapter 7 originally followed Chapter 5, with Chapter 6 following Chapter 4. But if Jesus had just worked the miracle recorded in 5.1-15, the request of his brothers that he go to Judea and work some miracles there (7.3) seems pointless. In any case there is no textual evidence for the reordering of the chapters, and so the translator must retain the order in which they appear in the Greek text.

Verses 1-9 set the stage for the misunderstanding and hostility that Jesus will face in Jerusalem. Just as his own brothers misunderstand his intentions, so the Jewish authorities will misunderstand who Jesus is, and will want to kill him. Jesus' intention is not to make himself well known (verse 4) or to gain glory for himself (verse 18), but to make known the truth of God. Thus his actions are determined by divine decree (verses 6,8), and not by the urging of his brothers.

The section heading, Jesus and His Brothers, may be confusing in some languages, since the use of "and" may indicate some joint activity.

In reality the passage includes an account of the opposition of his
brothers to Jesus. In some translations a more satisfactory section
heading may be "Jesus' brothers challenge him to go to Judea" or "Even
Jesus' brothers do not believe in him."

7.1   After this, Jesus traveled in Galilee;
             he did not want to travel in Judea, because
             the Jewish authorities there were wanting
             to kill him.

After this translates the phrase first discussed in 2.12. See there.
Traveled (RSV, NEB "went about"; JB "stayed") translates a verb
tense denoting customary action. The same verb is used in 6.66 and 11.54
with essentially the same meaning that it has here. An appropriate
equivalent for traveled may be "went from place to place in Galilee" or
"visited one place after another in Galilee." In employing a verb for
traveled it is important to indicate that Jesus did not merely walk
from one place to another but that he visited the people in place after
place. The same expression for visiting town after town should be employed in the following clause, which refers to similar travel in Judea.
He did not want to travel in Judea represents the Greek text followed by most modern translations (see RSV, NEB, NAB, Phps, Mft, GeCL).
JB ("he could not stay in Judea") follows the reading of other manu-
cripts, and it is doubtless the more difficult reading. One can see
why a scribe would change from this reading to that followed in most
other translations, but it is difficult to see why the change would be
made in the other direction. However, the UBS Committee on the Greek
text feels that the manuscript evidence in support of the reading followed by TEV and most other translations outweighs any other considerations.
Jewish authorities is literally "Jews." See Appendix I for a full
discussion.
Were wanting to kill him is translated in different ways. NEB reads
"were looking for a chance to kill him" (so also NAB) while JB has "were
out to kill him." Phillips' level of language, "were planning to take
his life," is rather high.

7.2   The time for the Festival of Shelters was near,

The Festival of Shelters took place approximately six months after
the Passover Festival mentioned in 6.4. This fact indicates that the
temporal marker in verse 1 (after this) may have a wide distribution
of meaning.
The Festival of Shelters was the Jewish autumn harvest festival.
It was also known as the "feast of Booths" (NAB; see Mft), because
people celebrated it by living in the vineyards in temporary huts made
of tree branches. The original purpose for living in the vineyards
during this period was to guard the grape harvest against the ravages
of animals, but the practice later gained the significance of commem-
orating the time that the Israelites lived in tents during their

wanderings in the desert. Shelters, the most popular of all Jewish festivals, was often known simply as "the Festival." It lasted from the
15th to the 21st of Tishri (September-October), and the eighth day (the
22nd of Tishri) was a day for special celebrations. For basic information
regarding this festival, see Leviticus 23.33-36,39-43; Deuteronomy
16.13-15.

Festival of Shelters should be translated as to indicate that
during this festival people lived in shelters; for example, "a festival
in which people used shelters" or "...stayed in shelters" or even "a
festival in which people built shelters for themselves."

The time...was near may be rendered in some languages as "it was
almost the day for" or "only a few more days before."

7.3 so Jesus' brothers said to him, "Leave this place
    and go to Judea, so that your followers will see
    the things that you are doing.

Jesus' brothers were first mentioned at 2.12. Only here in John's
Gospel do they play a definite role. Nothing in this Gospel indicates
that they were other than the sons of Joseph and Mary. In 20.17 my
brothers is a reference to Jesus' followers. In Greek, Jesus' brothers
is literally "his brothers," but TEV makes the pronominal reference
explicit.

The suggestion made by Jesus' brothers indicates that they misunderstood the nature of his mission. His purpose was not to make a
public display of his power but to reveal the true nature of God.

On the basis of tradition and the usage of the corresponding term
in Hebrew, some exegetes would interpret brothers as being "relatives"
or "cousins," but there is no explicit evidence in the Gospel record
to indicate that they were other than his own brothers. In languages
which make a distinction between "older brothers" and "younger brothers,"
a term for "younger brothers" would obviously be required here.

The Greek verb translated leave is used figuratively in 5.24
(passed from death to life). In 13.1 it is used of Jesus' approaching
death by which he will leave this world. In 1 John 3.14 it is used in
a sense closely parallel to what it has in John 5.24. Leave this place
may be rendered in some languages "leave this region" or "...this
territory," since the brothers of Jesus were contrasting this place
with another province, Judea.

Chapter 6 clearly places Jesus' followers in Galilee, but this
verse seems to indicate that they were in Judea. In Greek the word is
"disciple," but John sometimes uses it of the twelve, and sometimes in
a wider sense. In the present context "disciples" should be understood
in its widest possible meaning, perhaps referring to the many followers
of Jesus who had recently turned back. The suggestion made by his
brothers must be understood in this light. They are urging him to go
to Judea and reveal his mighty power, so that those who have left him
will follow him again.

The term here translated "works" is not the same as the one rendered "miracles" or "signs" in certain other passages, but it is
certainly a reference to "miracles." One may therefore translate "will

[221]

see the miracles you are doing." Or a more general expression as "will see what you are doing" may be used.

No doubt the reference by Jesus' brothers to his "miracles" was ironic, involving a measure of sarcasm. This fact is made clear by verse 5, which states that his brothers did not believe in him.

7.4   No one hides what he is doing if he wants to
       be well known. Since you are doing these things,
       let the whole world know about you!"

Special care must be used in translating No one hides what he is doing. A literal translation may imply that Jesus was hiding away in some secret place things he had been making. The meaning of hides in this context is "to do something without letting people know what one is doing." An equivalent rendering may be "No one keeps people from knowing what he is doing, if he wants people to know who he really is."

To be well known is more literally rendered "to be known publicly" (NAB) or "to be known openly" (RSV). Mft translates this phrase "aims at public recognition" and NEB "to be in the public eye." It may be rendered simply "in order for many people to know about you" or "in order that everyone will know who you are."

Since (so also Mft and JB) is "if" in most translations. In Greek the "if" clause indicates that the condition stated is true. This meaning is more clearly indicated in English by since. NEB implies doubt ("If you really are doing such things as these"), which seems not to be in keeping with the force of the Greek.

Let the whole world know about you is literally "show yourself to the world." The whole world is equivalent to "the world of mankind" (see 1.10). The verb let may suggest mere permission in some languages, and a more appropriate rendering may be an expression of cause, for example, "cause everyone in the world to know about you."

7.5   (Not even his brothers believed in him.)

TEV places this verse in parentheses, indicating that it is an explanatory statement interrupting the flow of the narrative. So also Mft and NAB. NAB, however, misses the force of believed in, "not even his brothers had much confidence in him." The force of the verb here is definitely that of "to believe in" or "to place one's faith in," not a more general meaning as NAB suggests. NEB ("For even his brothers had no faith in him") likewise implies the more general idea of confidence, rather than faith.

It may be difficult to render the idea of Not even his brothers. It may even be necessary to say "his brothers didn't believe in him; and one would certainly have expected that they would" or "one wouldn't have thought so, but his brothers didn't believe in him." The emphasis here is upon a statement which though true, is contrary to expectation.

7.6   Jesus said to them, "The right time for me
        has not yet come. Any time is right for you.

The right time for me (so also JB, NEB, Phps, NAB) is more literally
"my time." The word translated right time by many (Greek kairos) refers
to a particular moment or period in time, not to time as a chronological
sequence. In John's Gospel it occurs only here and in verse 8. It is
used synonymously with the word translated time in 2.4 (Greek hora,
literally "hour"). In many languages The right time is literally "the
appropriate time" or, expressed in verbal form, "the time when I should
go."
        Has not yet come may be expressed as "the day is not here yet" or
"this is not yet the day."
        Any time is right for you is literally "your time is always ready."
Time is the same word translated right time in the first part of this
verse; NAB renders this part of the verse "the time is always right
for you"; NEB "any time is right for you." The impact of this verse is
to indicate that Jesus' mission is determined by divine decree, but
that his brothers can go to Jerusalem at any time, since it makes no
difference when they go or do not go.

7.7   The world cannot hate you, but it hates me,
        because I keep telling it that its ways are bad.

Jesus' words indicate how false was the presupposition of his
brothers stated in verse 4. He cannot "commend" himself to the world,
because the world of men stands in opposition to God and God's purpose.
        The world cannot hate you may be rendered "People in the world
cannot hate you." However, the possible implications in the rendering of
cannot may lead to misunderstanding. It is not that people in the world
are incapable of hating the brothers of Jesus, but that they have no
basis for hating them. One may say, for example, "People in the world
cannot find any reason for hating you" or "...have no reason for
hating you."
        I keep telling it that its ways are bad may more literally be
translated "I keep testifying concerning it that its deeds are bad."
In this sentence I is emphatic, while the verb tense denotes continuous
or progressive action. The verb "to testify" or "to witness" has already
been discussed (see 1.7). JB translates this clause "because I give
evidence that its ways are evil," while NEB has "for exposing the
wickedness of its ways."
        Though it is often possible to speak of the world in a collective
sense, in many languages it is necessary to speak about "people in the
world." Therefore one must say "because I keep telling them that their
ways are bad" or "...they behave badly" or "...what they do is evil."

7.8   You go on to the festival. I am not going[n] to this
        festival, because the right time has not come for me."

        [n]I am not going; *some manuscripts have* I am not yet
        going.

In the first sentence of this verse you is emphatic, and in the second sentence I is emphatic. Both sentences use the same main verb. In the first sentence TEV translates it go on and in the second sentence going. The verb literally means "to go up" and was normally used of the pilgrimage up to Jerusalem. However, some commentators see here a play on words, since Jesus uses this same verb to speak of his ascent to the Father (20.17 I have not yet gone back up to the Father).

As TEV points out in a footnote, some Greek manuscripts read "I am not yet going." Although many manuscripts have this reading, "not yet" was evidently introduced into the text to resolve the inconsistency between verses 8 and 10. The force of Jesus' words here is that he acts solely on the basis of God's will, not on the suggestions or commands of any human being. Parallels are to be found at 2.4 and 11.6, where Jesus also rejects human authority for what he does.

In because the right time has not come the verb not come is not the same verb, so translated in verse 6. However, the meaning is essentially the same.

7.9   He said this and then stayed on in Galilee.

There is a textual problem in this verse, but it makes no difference in translation, since in most languages it must be handled translationally. Some manuscripts include the pronoun "he" (Greek autos), which is actually redundant in the Greek text, since this information is contained in the verb ending. Some scribes therefore changed the reading "he" to "to them" (Greek autois). But the information that this was said "to them" (that is, to his brothers) is clearly implied in the Greek text. In some languages this information must be made explicit.

In translating stayed on in Galilee it may be necessary in some languages to suggest at least implicitly a period of time, for example, "stayed on for a few days." It is important to avoid a verb which would suggest permanently staying in Galilee.

| TEV | (7.10-13) | RSV |

JESUS AT THE FESTIVAL OF SHELTERS

10 After his brothers had gone to the festival, Jesus also went; however, he did not go openly, but secretly. 11 The Jewish authorities were looking for him at the festival. "Where is he?" they asked.	10 But after his brothers had gone up to the feast, then he also went up, not publicly but in private. 11 The Jews were looking for him at the feast, and saying, "Where is he?" 12 And there was
12 There was much whispering about him in the crowd. "He is a good man," some people said. "No," others said, "he fools the people." 13 But no one talked about him openly, because they were afraid of the Jewish authorities.	much muttering about him among the people. While some said, "He is a good man," others said, "No, he is leading the people astray." 13 Yet for fear of the Jews no one spoke openly of him.

These verses are transitional, indicating that Jesus did go to the Festival of Shelters, though he went secretly and on his own initiative. Moreover, they form the background for what Jesus would say at the festival, by intimating the attitude of the Jewish authorities and of the Jewish people in general.

Jesus' discourse may be divided into two parts, the first taking place when the festival was nearly half over (14-36) and the second on the last day of the festival (37-39). The last two sections of this chapter (40-44 and 45-52) indicate the response of the people and the Jewish authorities to what Jesus taught. The words of Jesus had brought a division among the people--such a division that even the guards who were sent to arrest him refused to do so. However, in spite of what he had done and taught, the Jewish authorities and the Pharisees remained firm in their opposition to him. Nicodemus is an exception. Although a Pharisee and one of the Jewish authorities, he is still receptive to Jesus.

It may be useful to include a verb in the section heading, for example, "Jesus attends the Festival of Shelters" or "Jesus goes to the Festival of Shelters."

7.10   After his brothers had gone to the festival,
              Jesus also went; however, he did not go openly,
              but secretly.

Jesus also went is literally "he also went up." The pronoun "he" of the Greek text obviously refers to Jesus.

But secretly follows the same Greek text that RSV translates "but in private." It is possible to follow other Greek manuscripts which read "but went--as it were in secret." For example, NAB reads "as if in secret," and Mft "as it were privately." Phps has "as though he did not want to be seen," and NEB "almost in secret." Actually, the best Greek manuscripts support the reading "as it were in secret." However, it seems likely that some ancient scribe changed the text to read in this way to soften the force of secretly. The UBS Committee on the Greek text rates their choice as "D," indicating that there is a high degree of doubt concerning the reading selected for the text.

He did not go openly, but secretly may be rendered "he did not go in such a way that people would recognize him, but he went in such a way that people wouldn't know who he was."

7.11   The Jewish authorities were looking for him
              at the festival. "Where is he?" they asked.

The fact that the Jewish authorities (Greek "the Jews") are contrasted with the crowd of the following verse indicates that, by his use of "the Jews," John means more than simply the Jewish people in general. This contrast is brought out even more clearly in verse 13.

Were looking for him at the festival can be understood to mean "were expecting him to come to the festival." However, it is better understood in the sense of "went around looking for him."

Where is he? is literally "Where is that one?" "That one" is possibly used in a derogatory sense, and so NAB translates "Where is that troublemaker?" Phps has "Where is that man?" But it is not necessary that "that one" be taken in a derogatory sense, and most translations employ an expression similar to that of TEV.

In many languages it is necessary to indicate clearly to whom such a question was asked. One may translate, therefore, "they asked the people there" or "they asked those attending the festival."

7.12   There was much whispering about him in the
              crowd. "He is a good man," some people said. "No,"
              others said, "he fools the people."

Much whispering is also the reading of NEB. NAB ("there was much guarded debate") and Phps ("there was an undercurrent of discussion") paint too formal a picture. Whispering comes from the same root as the verb used in 6.41 and 61. In the two earlier passages it was translated grumbling.

In some languages one cannot speak of much whispering. Rather, it is necessary to indicate that people were whispering about Jesus, for example, "Many people in the crowd were whispering with one another about Jesus" or "...talking in quiet ways" or "...speaking with one another so that others would not overhear them."

Some Greek manuscripts read "crowds" (NEB, Gdsp, Phps) in the place of crowd, and the plural is evidently the basis for JB, "People stood in groups whispering about him," but JB does give as an alternative rendering "there was whispering about him in the crowds." The singular crowd is more in keeping with the usage in John's Gospel (the plural "crowds" occurs nowhere else in this Gospel). However, the plural "crowds" has better textual support. Once again the UBS Committee on the Greek text evaluates their choice as "D," because of the high degree of doubt regarding the reading selected for the text.

To indicate the opposition or differences of opinion concerning Jesus, it may be necessary to say "some people contended...but others objected, saying..."

He fools the people may be rendered in some languages "he lies to the people" or "he is leading the people astray" or "he is leading the people off in the wrong way."

7.13   But no one talked about him openly, because
              they were afraid of the Jewish authorities.

No one talked about him openly may be rendered "no one spoke loudly about him" or "no one spoke up so that many could hear."

Because they were afraid of the Jewish authorities is literally "because of the fear of the Jews." It is obvious that "the Jews" is here an open reference to the Jewish authorities, because the crowds who feared "the Jews" were themselves certainly Jewish. They were afraid of the Jewish authorities may be expressed effectively in some languages as "they were afraid of what the Jewish officials would do to them" or "they were afraid the Jewish officials would punish them."

| TEV | (7.14-24) | RSV |

14 The festival was nearly half over when Jesus went to the Temple and began teaching. 15 The Jewish authorities were greatly surprised and said, "How does this man know so much when he has never been to school?"

16 Jesus answered, "What I teach is not my own teaching, but it comes from God, who sent me. 17 Whoever is willing to do what God wants will know whether what I teach comes from God or whether I speak on my own authority. 18 A person who speaks on his own authority is trying to gain glory for himself. But he who wants glory for the one who sent him is honest, and there is nothing false in him. 19 Moses gave you the Law, didn't he? But not one of you obeys the Law. Why are you trying to kill me?"

20 "You have a demon in you!" the crowd answered. "Who is trying to kill you?"

21 Jesus answered, "I performed one miracle, and you were all surprised. 22 Moses ordered you to circumcise your sons (although it was not Moses but your ancestors who started it), and so you circumcise a boy on the Sabbath. 23 If a boy is circumcised on the Sabbath so that Moses' Law is not broken, why are you angry with me because I made a man completely well on the Sabbath? 24 Stop judging by external standards, and judge by true standards."

14 About the middle of the feast Jesus went up into the temple and taught. 15 The Jews marveled at it, saying, "How is it that this man has learning,[p] when he has never studied?" 16 So Jesus answered them, "My teaching is not mine, but his who sent me; 17 if any man's will is to do his will, he shall know whether the teaching is from God or whether I am speaking on my own authority. 18 He who speaks on his own authority seeks his own glory; but he who seeks the glory of him who sent him is true, and in him there is no falsehood. 19 Did not Moses give you the law? Yet none of you keeps the law. Why do you seek to kill me?" 20 The people answered, "You have a demon! Who is seeking to kill you?" 21 Jesus answered them, "I did one deed, and you all marvel at it. 22 Moses gave you circumcision (not that it is from Moses, but from the fathers), and you circumcise a man upon the sabbath. 23 If on the sabbath a man receives circumcision, so that the law of Moses may not be broken, are you angry with me because on the sabbath I made a man's whole body well? 24 Do not judge by appearances, but judge with right judgment."

[p]Or *this man knows his letters*

In the structure of the Gospel this section (14-24) is closely related to the miracle of healing recorded in Chapter 5, though about fifteen months have elapsed since that time, assuming that the feast referred to there was Pentecost. The content of what Jesus taught on this occasion (verse 14) is not indicated. But the dialogue with the Jews begins once again at the point of their misunderstanding of Jesus and his origin. They begin by questioning how he can know so much when

[227]

he has not been trained by any of their rabbinical teachers (verse 15). Jesus replies that his teaching comes from God, and anyone open to the will of God will recognize the origin of his teaching (16-17). He indicates further that he does speak, not on his own, but for the purpose of bringing glory to God (verse 18).

Jesus then directs a polemic against the Jewish authorities, using the Law of Moses as a point of departure. They are attempting to kill Jesus, and so do not themselves actually obey their own Law. Moreover, according to Jewish teaching, the law of circumcision has priority over the law of the Sabbath day and so they are inconsistent. Here Jesus uses a typical Jewish argument, proceeding from the lesser to the greater. If the law of circumcision overrides the law of the Sabbath day, how much more then should the law of making a man completely well override the law of the Sabbath day. Jesus concludes the dialogue by tel'ing his opponents to stop judging by external standards, and to judge by true standards.

7.14   The festival was nearly half over when Jesus
                went to the Temple and began teaching.

This verse indicates that Jesus did not go up to the festival at the beginning, when his brothers indicated that he should, but he waited until the festival was nearly half over. In order to speak of the festival as being nearly half over, one may say in some languages "the people had completed half of the days of the festival" or "half of the days of the festival had passed."

Went is literally "went up" (see comments on verse 8).

Temple is the same word used in 2.14; it refers to the outer precincts, not to the Temple proper.

Began teaching is the force that a number of translations give to the verb tense used here. It may be necessary to indicate a goal for the verb of teaching, for example, "he began teaching the people there."

7.15   The Jewish authorities were greatly surprised and
                said, "How does this man know so much when he has
                never been to school?"

Once again John begins a verse with the Greek oun (see 2.18). Most translations omit it from explicit rendering.

Greatly surprised is translated "marveled" in RSV and "astonished" in NEB. Elsewhere in John's Gospel this verb is used in 3.7; 4.27; 5.20,28; and 7.21. It may be important to indicate the reason for the surprise of the Jewish authorities, for example, "The Jewish officials were very much surprised at the way in which he taught" or even "...at what he said."

How does this man know so much when he has never been to school? is translated in NEB "How is it...that this untrained man has such learning?" "Learning" is specifically knowledge about the Jewish Law, and school or "training" is a reference to studying under one of the noted Jewish teachers of the times. In another context the words would

more naturally mean "How did he learn to read? He has not been taught"
(JB) or "How can this uneducated fellow manage to read?" (Mft). However,
in the present context the reference is to Jesus' lack of formal rabbinical training, not to an inability to read, since every Jewish boy
was taught to read. Before a Jew became a rabbi, he normally studied with
another rabbi, who taught him what the former rabbis had said. Much of
the rabbinical training consisted in memorizing what former Jewish
teachers had taught concerning the Law. Phps comes close to expressing
the meaning, "How does this man know all this--he has never been taught?"
This passage may also be translated, "How does this man know so much,
since he has never been taught to be an expert in our Law?" The RSV rendering may give the impression that, while Jesus might have been an
intelligent student, he was a lazy one: "How is it that this man has
learning, when he has never studied?" A useful equivalent of the Greek
text is "This man has never had a teacher. How, then, can he know so
much?" In some languages one may say "How can he know so much when he
has never been trained?"

7.16   Jesus answered, "What I teach is not my own
              teaching, but it comes from God, who sent me.

Jesus answered is literally "therefore Jesus answered and said,"
again reflecting a Semitic style which is redundant in English.
What I teach is not my own teaching is literally "My teaching is
not mine." NEB translates "The teaching that I give is not my own." In
place of teaching NAB has "doctrine," but "doctrine" suggests a formal
body of collected teachings, which is certainly not the meaning here.
The idea that Jesus' teaching comes from God rather than from himself
is implied in 5.30 and stated explicitly in 8.28; 12.49; 14.10,24.
A literal rendering of What I teach is not my own teaching may
result in "What I teach is not what I teach," a complete contradiction.
It may be useful to introduce the real source of the teaching and then
explain Jesus' relation to it, for example, "What I teach comes from
God, who sent me. My teaching doesn't come just from me." In other languages the closest equivalent may be "God, who sent me, has told me
what I must teach. I have not decided this just by myself."
In the last part of this verse TEV makes explicit the reference to
the one who sent me, that is, God. John's Gospel constantly emphasizes
that both Jesus and his teachings come from God the Father.

7.17   Whoever is willing to do what God wants will know
              whether what I teach comes from God or whether I
              speak on my own authority.

Whoever (so also NEB; NAB "Any man who") is literally "if anyone,"
an expression equivalent to whoever in English.
Whoever is willing to do what God wants is more literally rendered
in RSV "if any man's will is to do his will." TEV transforms the noun
"will" into a verb phrase is willing to do. The ambiguous expression
"his will" is made explicit and translated as a verb phrase what God
wants. NEB clears up the ambiguity by translating "the will of God,"

substituting a noun phrase where TEV has a verb phrase. Phps ("If anyone wants to do God's will") is similar.

It is possible to render more or less literally the expression
Whoever is willing to do what God wants and still miss the point of
this passage, for in some languages "to be willing to do" may not suggest actually doing a thing, but merely having a favorable attitude
toward doing it. In such cases it may be necessary to say "If anyone
actually decides to do what God wants" or "If anyone is ready to obey
God."

Will know whether what I teach comes from God or whether I speak
on my own authority is literally "will know concerning the teaching,
whether it is from God or I am speaking from myself." In this sentence
"concerning the teaching" is obviously a reference to Jesus' own
teaching, and TEV translates this phrase what I teach. The phrase
"from myself" is taken by TEV (so also Mft) to mean on my own authority.
This meaning is obviously intended in other modern translations, though
they translate the phrase in different ways.

The grammatical structure of verse 17 is rather complex, for it
involves a number of embedded clauses. It may be useful to break the
contents of this verse into two or more sentences, for example, "If
anyone is ready to do what God wants him to do, then he will know about
what I teach. He will know whether God is the one who instructed me in
what I say or whether I speak just on my own" or "...whether these
things come just from my own head."

7.18   A person who speaks on his own authority is trying
        to gain glory for himself. But he who wants glory
        for the one who sent him is honest, and there is
        nothing false in him.

On his own authority is the same expression translated on my own
authority in the previous verse, except that here the third person
is used in place of the first. Sometimes it is difficult to render the
expression speaks on his own authority. It may be necessary to say
"speaks, claiming that his words are just his own" or "speaks, saying
that his words are his own thoughts alone" or "...saying that he himself
has thought up all that he says" or "speaks only from his own mind."
The meaning of is trying to gain glory for himself is clear, though
the Greek underlying this phrase is translated in a variety of ways. The
contrast is between a teacher who represents himself as the source of
knowledge and one who speaks as the representative of another from whom
he has received his knowledge. JB translates "is hoping to get honour
for himself," and NEB has "aims at honour for himself." Phps is rather
high level, "has an eye for his own reputation." Mft translates "aims
at his own credit." To gain glory for himself may be expressed idiomatically in some languages as "to raise up his own name," "to make
everyone shout his name" or "to make everyone say of him, Isn't he
wonderful?"
He who wants glory for the one who sent him may be rendered "he
who wants others to praise the one who sent him" or "he who wants the
person who sent him to be honored."

It is often necessary to place an adversative expression (English "but" or "however") at the beginning of the second sentence of verse 18, for example, "but he who wants people to honor the one who sent him." It is also possible to use a conditional expression, for example, "If anyone wants people to honor the one who sent him, then that one is honest." The difficulty with the conditional expression is that it makes the reference too broad; as a relative clause it is possible to make the reference more specifically applicable to Jesus.

The word translated honest (Greek alēthēs; RSV "true"; NAB "truthful"; JB, NEB "sincere") is used of God in 3.33 and in 8.26; in both cases it is translated true in TEV. In the present context honest is used of one who speaks what is true. The word translated false (so also NEB; RSV "falsehood"; Mft, NAB "dishonesty") is used only here in the Gospel of John. It is used many times in the Septuagint to translate the Hebrew word meaning "lie." In this verse it is obvious that honest and false are used in contrast to each other. This contrast may be expressed in some languages as "he tells the truth; he doesn't lie at all" or "he tells what is true; not at all does he tell what is not true" or "...false."

7.19 Moses gave you the Law, didn't he? But not
    one of you obeys the Law. Why are you trying
    to kill me?"

Moses gave you the Law, didn't he? is stated in such a way as to expect a positive answer. In languages in which a rhetorical question may be misleading (especially when there is no immediate answer), a strong declarative statement may be used, for example, 'Moses certainly gave you the Law" or "You will all agree, Moses gave you the Law."

Obeys the Law is literally "keeps the Law," a frequent Semitic expression. Mft translates "none of you honestly obeys the Law"; NEB "you all break it." Obeys the Law may be expressed as "does what the Law says" or "lives as the Law commands you" or "follows the laws in what you do."

7.20   "You have a demon in you!" the crowd answered.
    "Who is trying to kill you?"

In some languages it is not possible to say the crowd answered, for a crowd as such does not answer; rather "the people in the crowd answered."

You have a demon in you! is literally "You have a demon!" (RSV). TEV and RSV reflect the historical cultural situation. The people in Jesus' day believed in demons, and they believed that demons caused people to act in certain ways. Contemporary psychological terminology fails to convey this historical perspective, but some translators fail to recognize the importance of maintaining the biblical perspective. For example, Phps has "You must be mad!" while Mft, JB and the NAB have "You are mad!" "You are possessed!" (NEB) comes close to the meaning, but fails to make explicit the reference to demons. Although RSV renders this sentence correctly, its translation of the following sentence could be seriously misunderstood by a person hearing the Scripture read. If the Scripture is not read orally with the proper intonations, "You have a demon! Who is seeking to kill you?" may be understood by the hearers to mean "You have a demon who is seeking to kill you." To avoid this kind of ambiguity, it may be better to render the question as "What people are trying to kill you?" or "Who are the people who are trying to kill you?"

As noted elsewhere, one may speak of a person "having a demon" in different ways, for example, "being ridden by a demon," "being possessed by a demon," or "having a demon living inside of one." Demons are frequently spoken of as possessing people, rather than people possessing demons.

7.21   Jesus answered, "I performed one miracle, and
            you were all surprised.

Jesus answered is literally "Jesus answered and said to them." The redundancy once again reflects Semitic structure.

One miracle is literally "one work" JB (RSV "one deed"), evidently a reference to the miracle recorded in 5.1-9. John uses both "signs" and "works" to describe the miracles of Jesus; TEV makes it explicit that the reference is to a miracle. NEB suggests a wrong focus, "Once only have I done work on the Sabbath," intimating "one day of work" instead of one mighty miracle.

You were all surprised translates the same verb used in verse 15.

7.22   Moses ordered you to circumcise your sons
            (although it was not Moses but your ancestors
            who started it), and so you circumcise a boy
            on the Sabbath.

The first two words of verse 22 are literally "because of this." Most modern translations connect these words with the last part of this verse. TEV does so by implication, not by translating the words explicitly. In most translations these words appear as "at it" (note RSV, "I did one deed, and you all marvel at it."). "Marvel at it" or "are surprised at it" may be expressed in terms of cause for an emotional response, for example, "because of it you marveled" or "this miracle caused you to be very surprised."

Moses ordered you to circumcise your sons is literally "Moses gave you circumcision" (RSV, Phps, NAB). NEB translates "Moses gave you the law of circumcision"; Mft "Moses gave you the rite of circumcision"; and JB "Moses ordered you to practice circumcision." It is obvious that the expression "gave you circumcision" is equivalent to ordered you to circumcise. Since sons were the only ones who were circumcised, TEV makes this information explicit.

Although it was not Moses but your ancestors who started it is literally "not that it is from Moses but from the fathers." TEV makes the verb "is" transitive (started), thus shifting the subject of "is"

(it) into the objective place and making Moses and your ancestors subjects of the transitive verb. As indicated earlier, your ancestors is
literally "the fathers," rendered in a number of translations as "the
patriarchs." TEV attempts to avoid the more difficult term "patriarchs"
whenever possible. The patriarchs were a specialized group of ancestors,
that is, the noted founders of the Jewish nation. In the present context,
ancestors is sufficient to carry the force of Jesus' argument, and there
is no need to use the more technical term "patriarchs."

And so you circumcise a boy on the Sabbath is literally "on the
Sabbath you circumcise a man." The word "man" in the Greek text obviously means boy in the present context; it was customary for the Jews
to circumcise a baby boy on the eighth day after birth. To use the word
"man" in translation would suggest something untrue in the Jewish setting. Adult males (for example, proselytes) were circumcised, but probably not on the Sabbath day. Only for infants did the law indicate a
specific day for the rite. On the Sabbath is in the emphatic position
in this clause. According to Jewish teaching, the law of circumcision
had priority over the law of the Sabbath day. That is, if the eighth
day, the day of circumcision, fell on a Sabbath day, the child was
circumcised on that day.

Because of the complex relations among some of the clauses in
verse 22, it may be useful to change the order of presentation in some
languages. For example, one may begin with the final clause "you will
circumcise a boy on the Sabbath day" or "...rest day" and follow with
the statement concerning Moses' having ordered the circumcision. Finally, one may introduce the concessive clause in parentheses. This
order reduces what is called the "temporary memory" for the reader and
may make it easier for him to understand. The entire verse may then
read: "You circumcise a boy on the Sabbath, just as Moses ordered you
to do (although it was not Moses who initiated circumcision but it was
your ancestors who started the process of circumcising)."

There are also several lexical problems in this verse. First, the
term circumcise may present difficulties, especially in cultures where
circumcision is not practiced and the language does not have a specific
term for it. If one has to use some descriptive equivalent (for example,
"cutting off the foreskin of the penis"), such a phrase may appear too
vulgar to include in Scripture. Translators sometimes use such expressions as "to cut" or "to cut around" or "to cut off the skin," leaving
a precise explanation for a glossary. In some languages a borrowed term
is employed for circumcision, thus reducing the possibility of vulgar
connotations.

It is important to make certain that the term used for circumcision
is specifically applicable to the operation performed on boys and does
not include excision, an operation performed on girls. In order to make
clear what is involved, it may be necessary to add such expressions as
"boys" or "your sons."

The expression you circumcise a boy on the Sabbath indicates habitual action. It is therefore often translated "you have the custom" or
"it is your practice to do so."

Moses ordered you to circumcise your sons may be translated "Moses
gave you the Law saying, you must circumcise your sons." The clause
enclosed in parentheses in TEV may be expressed as an adversative, for

example, "but it was not Moses who started the process of circumcision" or "Moses was not the first who said you should circumcise." This clause may then be followed by a positive one, for example, "rather it was your ancestors who first began to circumcise" or "...who circumcised their sons."

7.23   If a boy is circumcised on the Sabbath so
        that Moses' Law is not broken, why are you
        angry with me because I made a man completely
        well on the Sabbath?

The agrument of this verse must be understood in the light of the preceding verse. Among the Jews, if two laws conflicted, it was necessary to decide which law had priority. The Jews had already decided that the law of circumcision had priority over the law of the Sabbath day. Jesus now argues that the law of mercy likewise overrides the law of the Sabbath day. From the Jewish point of view, however, this was not true. They would argue that if a person's life was in immediate danger, then the law of life would have priority over the Sabbath day. But in this situation the man's life was not in immediate danger. He had been lame for 38 years and Jesus could have waited one more day to heal him, so as not to break the law of the Sabbath day. Jesus argues once again from the lesser to the greater: the law of circumcision, which has priority over the law of the Sabbath, concerns only a part of a man's body. How much more, then, does the law of mercy have priority over the Sabbath day, since it concerns a man's whole body!

The passive verbs is circumcised and is not broken may be expressed as active, for example, "If you circumcise a boy on the Sabbath in order not to break Moses' Law" or "...in order that you may keep the law of Moses" or "...abide by the Law given by Moses."

Make a man completely well is literally "make a whole man well." It is translated by RSV "made a man's whole body well." NEB has the same meaning, though with a rather high level of language, "for giving health on the Sabbath to the whole of a man's body." Mft sees implicit here a contrast between the act of circumcision and Jesus' deed of healing a man, and so translates "for curing, not cutting, the entire body of a man"; but it is doubtful that one should attempt in this particular passage to bring out such a contrast.

7.24   Stop judging by external standards, and judge
        by true standards."

Stop judging (so also NAB) is the force of the Greek imperative here, and so JB translates "Do not keep judging" and Mft "give over judging." It may be necessary in some languages to express an object of the verb judging. If so, either Jesus himself, or what Jesus has done, may be understood as the object.

By external standards is rendered "by appearances" in some translations and "according to appearances" in JB ("superficially" in NEB). Judge by true standards is translated in JB as "let your judgment be according to what is right" and in NAB as "make an honest judgment." However this phrase and the preceding phrase are translated, they should indicate a contrast between an invalid judgment made on the basis of appearances and a valid judgment made on the basis of what is true.

It may be difficult to render verse 24 effectively because of the abstract terms external standards and true standards. In some languages one can say "Stop making up your minds on the basis of what things look like, but make them up on the basis of what is really true" or "Stop judging what people do just on the basis of what you see, but judge them on the basis of what has really happened" or "Do not form your opinions on the basis of what things seem to be, but upon the basis of what they really are."

| TEV | (7.25-31) | RSV |

IS HE THE MESSIAH?

25 Some of the people of Jerusalem said, "Isn't this the man the authorities are trying to kill? 26 Look! He is talking in public, and they say nothing against him! Can it be that they really know that he is the Messiah? 27 But when the Messiah comes, no one will know where he is from. And we all know where this man comes from."	25 Some of the people of Jerusalem therefore said, "Is not this the man whom they seek to kill? 26 And here he is, speaking openly, and they say nothing to him! Can it be that the authorities really know that this is the Christ? 27 Yet we know where this man comes from; and when the Christ appears, no one will know where he comes from." 28 So Jesus proclaimed, as
28 As Jesus taught in the Temple, he said in a loud voice, "Do you really know me and know where I am from? I have not come on my own authority. He who sent me, however, is truthful. You do not know him, 29 but I know him, because I come from him and he sent me."	he taught in the temple, "You know me, and you know where I come from? But I have not come of my own accord; he who sent me is true, and him you do not know. 29 I know him, for I come from him, and he sent me." 30 So they sought to arrest
30 Then they tried to seize him, but no one laid a hand on him, because his hour had not yet come. 31 But many in the crowd believed in him and said, "When the Messiah comes, will he perform more miracles than this man has?"	him; but no one laid hands on him, because his hour had not yet come. 31 Yet many of the people believed in him; they said, "When the Christ appears, will he do more signs than this man has done?"

This entire section (verses 25-31) concerns the questions some people of Jerusalem were asking themselves about Jesus. They thought that the Jerusalem authorities might have recognized that Jesus was the Messiah, because he was talking in public and nobody said anything against him (25-26). However, the people believed that he was not the Messiah, because no one would know where the Messiah comes from, but they all knew where Jesus came from (27). Verse 27 is a perfect illustration of the <u>judging by external standards</u> referred to in verse 24.

Jesus then takes up the theme introduced by the people, that they know where he comes from. He indicates that they do not know him or where he comes from. Not only that; they do not know the One who is true, the One who sent him (28-29). Verses 30-31 indicate the response of the people to Jesus' words. Some tried to arrest him, but they were unable to do so, because his hour had not yet come. However, many in the crowd believed in him.

Instead of using a question for a section heading, it may be preferable to employ a statement, for example, "Some people think Jesus is the Messiah" or "People question whether Jesus is the Messiah" or "People discuss whether Jesus is the one whom God sent."

<u>7.25</u>   Some of the people of Jerusalem said, "Isn't
            this the man the authorities are trying to kill?

This verse is introduced in Greek with a favorite Johannine particle (<u>oun</u>), already mentioned several times (see 2.18). Most translations, including TEV, indicate its function by the introduction of a new paragraph. In RSV, however, it is translated "therefore" and in JB "meanwhile" in this particular verse.

The question raised by the people of Jerusalem anticipates a "yes" answer. It is a rhetorical question and may be transformed into a strong declarative statement, for example, "This man is surely the one the authorities are trying to kill" or "...trying to cause to be killed."

The verb <u>said</u> is a Greek imperfect tense and so may have a progressive force, "were saying" (JB).

<u>Trying</u> (verse 30 <u>tried</u>) may also be translated "wanting." It is difficult to tell precisely what John intended by this verb. In English "try" implies action, and "want" has the force of intention. Perhaps John is indicating that the Jewish authorities had actually initiated action which they were unable to carry out because Jesus' <u>hour had not yet come</u> (verse 30). This interpretation is possible, in light of John's insistence that no one could lay a hand on Jesus until he permitted it (see 18.6-8). Although it is easy to read intention here rather than action, it seems more probable that John is indicating an action which the authorities were unable to carry out. That the Pharisees and the chief priests actually initiated action against Jesus is indicated in verse 32. It is likely that unofficial action by the people is indicated in verse 29, while official action by the Jewish authorities is indicated in verse 32. If so, then some action on the part of the Jewish leaders is perhaps referred to in verse 25. Accordingly, <u>trying to</u> suits the context better than "want to."

<u>7.26</u>   Look! He is talking in public, and they say
            nothing against him! Can it be that they really
            know that he is the Messiah?

<u>Look</u> is translated "and there he is" in several translations (for example, RSV, NEB, NAB, JB); it represents an attempt to render two

Greek particles (kai ide) which are used to indicate surprise and emphasis. Both Luther Revised and Segond have the equivalent of "and look," which is fairly close to a literal translation of the Greek. In public translates the same expression as well known in verse 4.

And they say nothing against him! is literally "and they are saying nothing to him." In such a context "to him" may easily have the force of against him, as in TEV. If the exegesis suggested in the previous verse is correct, they of this verse refers to the Jewish authorities of the preceding verse. The point is not that nobody said anything, but that the Jewish authorities did not say anything.

The question raised by the people, Can it be that they really know that he is the Messiah? expresses a degree of doubt or hesitation. Can it be...? may be expressed in some languages as "Is it possible...?" Such a possibility must often be expressed as someone's thought, for example, "Do you think that...?" or "Do you imagine that...?"

The Messiah is literally "the Christ." In the present context it is used as an equivalent of the technical Jewish term Messiah (see 1.41).

7.27   But when the Messiah comes, no one will know
        where he is from. And we all know where this
        man comes from."

TEV inverts the order of the Greek sentences in this verse. For the English reader it is more natural to introduce first the information that no one will know where the Messiah comes from, and then the people's claim that they all know where this man (=Jesus) comes from.

As this verse indicates, some Jews of Jesus' day apparently were of the opinion that no one would recognize the true origin of the Messiah when he did appear. Given that premise, they concluded that Jesus could not possibly have been the Messiah.

It was often customary to identify a person by the place of his origin, for example, "Jesus of Nazareth" and "Joseph of Arimathea." Evidently Jesus was known to have come from Nazareth; that is doubtless the implication here.

The clause when the Messiah comes must be rendered in most languages in the future "when the Messiah will come" rather than the present tense, since the assumption of the speakers is that the Messiah has not yet come. The second clause may be rendered "no one will know what town he is from" or "...what town he belongs to." It is Jesus' place of origin which is in question here, not the place from which he may have recently arrived.

7.28   As Jesus taught in the Temple, he said in a loud
        voice, "Do you really know me and know where I am
        from? I have not come on my own authority. He who
        sent me, however, is truthful. You do not know him,

TEV takes the verb "cried out" in conjunction with the participle "saying" to have the combined force of he said in a loud voice. Some commentators point out that the verb "to cry out" is used in John's

Gospel to introduce solemn proclamations (1.15; 7.28,37; 12.44): RSV therefore translates the Greek "cried out saying" as "Jesus proclaimed." JB ("He cried out") carries essentially the same impact as TEV, but NEB ("Jesus cried aloud as he taught in the temple") and Mft ("so Jesus cried aloud, as he was teaching in the temple") might imply to some readers that Jesus was actually crying while he taught in the Temple.

Do you really know me and know where I am from? is literally "And you know me and you know where I come from," which may be either a statement or a question (there is no punctuation in the early Greek manuscripts). Most translations that render these words as a statement imply that Jesus agreed that the people did in fact know where he came from. Since Jesus suggests in the following verse that the people do not really know where he comes from, it seems best to translate these words as a question with a hint of sarcasm.

There may be some complication involved in the translation of the rhetorical question Do you really know me and know where I am from? In some languages such a question demands an immediate answer, which in this case would probably be "No, indeed." If one transforms this question into a statement, it may be best introduced by such a phrase as "you think," for example, "You think you really know me and know where I am from."

On my own authority is the same expression used in 5.19,30; 7.17. I have not come on my own authority may be rendered in some languages "I did not send myself" or "I did not cause myself to come."

He who sent me is a frequent Johannine formula, and it always refers to God the Father. In 7.16 TEV makes explicit the reference to God in this formula.

Truthful translates the same adjective rendered real in 1.9. In this verse it is probably equivalent to the adjective translated honest (Greek alēthēs) in verse 18, and so has the force of "faithful," "reliable," or "true." Some take this adjective to have the force here that it normally has (see 1.9) and so translate "the One who truly is" (NEB) or "Him who is real" (Mft). Anchor ("there is truly One who sent me") and JB ("there is one who sent me and I really come from him") take this adjective with an adverbial force. NAB translates "One who has the right to send." As can be seen by the variety of translations, there are several options, and there is no unanimous agreement among commentators or translators as to the interpretation to be followed. It should be noted, however, that "reliable" or "truthful" (which also seems to be the basis for NAB rendering) at least makes some meaning in the context, whereas "real" is fairly meaningless. It is difficult to see why John would have used the adjective here with an adverbial force when he could easily have used an adverb. On the whole, the meaning suggested by TEV appears to be best in keeping with the thought of this passage. This same Greek adjective is used in 3.33 and 8.26 with the meaning "true."

In rendering He who sent me...is truthful, one may say "The one who sent me speaks the truth"; however, it is perhaps more satisfactory to emphasize the concept of faithfulness and reliability. Therefore, the statement may be rendered "You can fully trust the one who sent me" or "The one who sent me is one who can be trusted."

In the statement You do not know him, both pronouns are emphatic.

The inclusion of the separate form of the pronoun you, which is expressed in Greek by the verb suffix, makes it emphatic; and him is emphatic by reason of its position as the initial word in the clause. The force of know in this context is not merely "know about," but "have some experience of," for example, "You are not really acquainted with him" or even "You have no relation to him." In a similar way, the first part of verse 29 may be rendered "but I am well acquainted with him."

7.29   but I know him, because I come from him and
              he sent me."

The pronoun I in the statement but I know him is emphatic, as are the last two pronouns you and him in verse 28. The use of the pronoun I is optional in a Greek sentence, since the verb endings indicate person and number. The pronoun is sometimes added for the sake of emphasis, and I at the beginning of a sentence or clause (as here) is particularly emphatic. In this manner a strong contrast is made between you in the last clause of verse 28 and I in the first clause of verse 29. This emphasis and contrast are immediately evident, even though there is no conjunction, such as "but," connecting the two clauses. For the English reader, the emphatic contrast may be missed in a strictly literal translation, and so TEV adds the conjunction but at the beginning of verse 29 to indicate the contrast, as JB and Mft also do.
The Greek verbs translated sent in this verse and in verse 28 come from different verb stems, but there is no difference in meaning. Essentially the same formula (I know him) also appears in 8.55 and 17.25.
In some languages the rendering of come and sent may suggest a contradiction, since the first term would suggest the complete action of arriving, while a term for sent might suggest merely the process of sending someone forth. Therefore it may be more satisfactory to reverse the order, for example, "because he sent me and I have now come from him."

7.30   Then they tried to seize him, but no one
              laid a hand on him, because his hour had not
              yet come.

Then translates the Greek particle oun (see 2.18), which often is not represented in translation, as in verses 25 and 28 of this chapter.
They is best taken as a reference to some of the people of Jerusalem, as opposed to the Jewish authorities who initiate action against Jesus in verse 32. Because of the possible obscurity of the reference of the pronoun they, it may be best to translate "Then some of the people there tried to seize him."
John evidently implies a miraculous event by his statement that no one laid a hand on him, because his hour had not yet come (see Luke 4.30). No one laid a hand on him is a fairly literal translation of the Greek. Its meaning is clear, and most translations maintain the imagery. Phps has "no one laid a finger on him." But no one laid a hand on him may be rendered as "but no one succeeded in grabbing him."

[239]

On the expression his hour had not yet come, see 2.4 (note the similar expression in 7.6). Once again it should be emphasized that according to the Gospel of John, nothing does or can happen to Jesus apart from his own will, which is controlled by the will of his Father. There seems to be no indication in the Old Testament that miracles were expected of the Messiah, but evidently this expectation existed in the popular thinking of New Testament times.

To speak of his hour when referring to an occasion propitious for a particular person may be easy enough . However, to say that his hour had not yet come, when describing a difficulty or danger, may be misleading or confusing. One may say "for this to happen to him was not yet the time" or "the occasion for this to happen to him was not yet" or "this was not the hour when he was destined to be seized."

7.31   But many in the crowd believed in him and said,
        "When the Messiah comes, will he perform more
        miracles than this man has?"

Miracles is literally "signs" (see 2.11). The faith of these people was evidently based on the miraculous things that Jesus had done (see 2.23 and 4.48).

The comparison in will he perform more miracles than this man has? may be expressed in some languages as "will he surpass this man in doing more miracles?" or "will this man be at all inferior to the Messiah in performing miracles?"

TEV   (7.32-36)   RSV

GUARDS ARE SENT TO ARREST JESUS

32 The Pharisees heard the crowd whipering these things about Jesus, so they and the chief priests sent some guards to arrest him. 33 Jesus said, "I shall be with you a little while longer, and then I shall go away to him who sent me. 34 You will look for me, but you will not find me, because you cannot go where I will be."

35 The Jewish authorities said among themselves, "Where is he about to go so that we shall not find him? Will he go to the Greek cities where our people live, and teach the Greeks? 36 He says that we will look for him but will not find him, and that we cannot go where he will be. What does he mean?"

32 The Pharisees heard the crowd thus muttering about him, and the chief priests and Pharisees sent officers to arrest him, 33 Jesus then said, "I shall be with you a little longer, and then I go to him who sent me; 34 you will seek me and you will not find me; where I am you cannot come." 35 The Jews said to one another, "Where does this man intend to go that we shall not find him? Does he intend to go to the Dispersion among the Greeks and teach the Greeks? 36 What does he mean by saying, 'You will seek me and you will not find me,' and, 'Where I am you cannot come'?"

The previous section (25-31) describes the response of the people in Jerusalem to Jesus and his teaching during the feast; the present section describes the reaction of the Jewish authorities. They are unable to understand his teaching, and so they decide to arrest him, but their efforts end in failure.

This section actually ties in more closely with verses 10-13 than with the verses immediately preceding it. It looks forward to verse 45, when the guards report back to the chief priests and Pharisees. Its time relation is still determined by the statement in verse 14, the festival was nearly half over.

The passive of the section heading, Guards Are Sent to Arrest Jesus, may be changed to active and so read "The Authorities Send Guards..." Guards may be translated as "soldiers," but it is probably better to speak of them as "police in the temple," for they were not Roman soldiers.

7.32   The Pharisees heard the crowd whispering these
        things about Jesus, so they and the chief priests
        sent some guards to arrest him.

In Greek, whispering is a verb from the same stem as the noun used in verse 12.

Certain subtle complications are involved in rendering the clause The Pharisees heard the crowd whispering these things about Jesus. First of all, the phrase the Pharisees might be assumed to mean "all the Pharisees." Since this was clearly not the case, it may be necessary in certain receptor languages to employ an expression meaning "some Pharisees." It is also important to use a term for heard which means "overheard," in order not to give the impression that the crowd was whispering so loudly that the Pharisees could not help but hear. It may be necessary as well to say "people in the crowd were whispering," since in some languages one cannot speak of "a crowd whispering."

They and the chief priests is literally "the chief priests and the Pharisees." TEV restructures this phrase because the Pharisees are already mentioned in the first part of the verse. Most of the chief priests were Sadducees, and it was unusual to find them acting together with the Pharisees. But in John's Gospel the two groups appear together often (7.32,45; 11.47,57;and 18.3). John more often uses the general term "the Jews" (TEV generally the Jewish authorities) to describe the enemies of Jesus, but occasionally he refers to them as "the chief priests and the Pharisees" or "the authorities and the Pharisees."

As already noted, the word translated guards is best understood as a reference to "Temple police" (so NEB and several others). In 18.3 and 19.6 TEV translates the word temple guards, but elsewhere as guards (7.45,46; 18.18,22) or Jewish guards (18.12), except at 18.36, where it has a different meaning (TEV my followers). The persons referred to were certainly not Romans but Jews, perhaps Levites, and they were under the authority of the chief priests.

7.33   Jesus said, "I shall be with you a little while longer,
        and then I shall go away to him who sent me.

A little while is a frequent theme in John's Gospel (see 12.35;
13.33; 14.19; and 16.16). The time span suggested is probably one of
several months, though it is not possible to determine any precise
chronological order in the events highlighted in the Gospel of John.
In some languages one may translate "a few more moons" (or "months").
I shall go away is actually in the present tense (RSV "I go to
him"), but it has a future connotation and so is best translated as future. The verb go away (Greek hupagō) is used several times in this
Gospel in reference to Jesus' departure from the world (8.14,21-22;
13.3,33,36; 14.4-5,28; 16.5,10,17).
    As elsewhere in John's Gospel, him who sent me refers to God the
Father.

7.34   You will look for me, but you will not find me,
        because you cannot go where I will be."

You will look for me has reference to the time after Jesus has
returned to the Father. The implication is that there will be a time
when they will look for Jesus (to help them), but it will be too late.
It is, of course, in contrast to the present when they are looking for
him in order to kill him.
    Where I will be is literally "and where I am." Again the present
tense "I am" has a future reference and is better translated I will be.
It is possible, though not probable, that "I am" may really be "I go."
In Greek these two verbs are spelled alike except for the accent, but
very few commentators and apparently no translators understand the verb
here to mean "I go." The point is that Jesus will be with the Father
after his death, but these people cannot be with the Father even if
they die. In the clause you cannot go where I will be, the pronouns I
and you are emphatic, in strong contrast to each other.

7.35   The Jewish authorities said among themselves,
        "Where is he about to go so that we shall not find
        him? Will he go to the Greek cities where our people
        live, and teach the Greeks?

On Jewish authorities see Appendix I.
    In the question Where is he about to go so that we shall not find
him? the pronouns he and we are emphatic and contrasting, just as I
and you are in the preceeding verse.
    The Greek cities where our people live is more literally "the
Dispersion among the Greeks." In New Testament times "the Dispersion"
was a technical term used in reference to the Jews who lived outside
Palestine; accordingly, "of the Greeks" is taken in TEV to mean "among
the Greeks" (see RSV, JB, NEB). The technical term "Dispersion" is
avoided in this translation, since it is of zero meaning for most English
readers. However, it is possible to understand this phrase in a somewhat

[242]

different way. That is, "the Greeks" may be taken to refer to a group larger than those persons of Greek nationality; it may refer to all persons in the Roman world who were influenced by Greek culture and so could be loosely referred to as "Greeks." If so, the Jewish authorities are considering the possibility that Jesus will become one of the Jews of the Dispersion, living among the Gentiles and teaching them. The entire question may be translated to read "Will he go the cities outside our country where the Gentiles live and teach them?" The word "Greek" occurs in John's Gospel only here and in 12.20. In each case it is better not to limit the term to mean only persons of Greek nationality. In 12.20 the meaning is more nearly "non-Jews" or "Gentiles."

7.36   He says that we will look for him but will not
        find him, and that we cannot go where he will be.
        What does he mean?"

It should be noted that in the Greek text the question What does he mean? comes first, whereas in TEV it is placed last for purposes of English style. This question may be rendered as "What is he trying to say?" or "What is he trying to tell us?" or "What do his words mean?"

One Greek manuscript of the Gospels includes the story of the woman caught in adultery (7.53-8.11) after this verse. See the comments at 8.1.

	TEV	(7.37-39)	RSV

STREAMS OF LIFE-GIVING WATER

37 On the last and most important day of the festival Jesus stood up and said in a loud voice, "Whoever is thirsty should come to me and drink. 38 As the scripture says, 'Whoever believes in me, streams of life-giving water will pour out from his heart.'"[n] 39 Jesus said this about the Spirit, which those who believed in him were going to receive. At that time the Spirit had not yet been given, because Jesus had not been raised to glory.

[n] Jesus' words in verses 37-38 may be translated: "Whoever is thirsty should come to me, and whoever believes in me should drink. 38 As the scripture says, 'Streams of life-giving water will pour out from his heart.'"

37 On the last day of the feast, the great day, Jesus stood up and proclaimed, "If any one thirst, let him come to me and drink. 38 He who believes in me, as[q] the scripture has said, 'Out of his heart shall flow rivers of living water.'" 39 Now this he said about the Spirit, which those who believed in him were to receive; for as yet the Spirit had not been given, because Jesus was not yet glorified.

[q] Or let him come to me, and let him who believes in me drink. As

[243]

By New Testament times the Festival of Shelters had become the occasion for prayers for rain. The feast was celebrated at the end of September or in early October; if rain came at that time, it was taken as a guarantee that there would be sufficient rain for the crops. The prayer for rain was symbolized in dramatic fashion on each of the seven days of the festival. A procession would go down to the Gihon spring on the southeast side of the Temple hill. There a priest would fill a golden pitcher with water, and the choir would repeat the words of Isaiah 12.3, "With joy you will draw water from the well of salvation" (RSV). Then the procession would go up to the Temple through the water gate. When the crowd reached the altar in front of the Temple, they would go around waving the lulab with their right hands and the ethrog with their left hands. The lulab consisted of willow twigs and myrtle tied together with palm, and the ethrog could be either a lemon or a citron. As a climax, the priest would go up the ramp to the altar and pour the water into a silver funnel, through which it would flow to the ground.

In the light of this aspect of the Festival of Shelters, the words of Jesus have great significance. On the most important day of the festival, Jesus stands and exclaims, Whoever is thirsty should come to me and drink. The author of the Gospel points out for his readers that the living water to which Jesus referred was actually God's Spirit, which came after Jesus was glorified (7.39).

The section heading, Streams of Life-giving Water, may be rendered "Streams with water that gives life," but it may be equally appropriate to say "Water that gives life" or "Water that causes people to live."

7.37   On the last and most important day of the festival
       Jesus stood up and said in a loud voice, "Whoever is
       thirsty should come to me and drink.

Scholars differ as to what is meant by the last...day of the festival. Originally it was a seven-day celebration. Later an eighth day was added, but it was more a day of rest than of festive celebration. Did John mean the seventh day, the final day of the festival itself, or the added eighth day? Fortunately, the problem need not be resolved by the translator. It is even doubtful that John himself was aware that he would raise any problem by this phrase. The last...day of the festival may be rendered in some languages as "The last day on which people celebrated" or "The final day when the people were celebrating."

In Greek the first part of this verse reads "but on the last day, the great day of the feast, Jesus stood up and cried out saying." That the last day of the festival was the most important is new information; that is why TEV introduces it first, on the last and most important day of the festival. The observation that Jesus stood up perhaps indicates that he had been sitting and teaching, as was the custom with Jewish rabbis.

Most important may be expressed in some languages as "the great day of the celebration" or "the day when most important celebrations took place." Other languages may speak of such a day as "the high day," "the big day," or even "the most valuable day."

    <u>Said in a loud voice</u> translates essentially the same expression used in verse 28.

    <u>Whoever</u> is literally "if anyone" (see verse 17), equivalent in some languages to "all who."

    Some ancient manuscripts omit <u>to me</u>, but the UBS Committee on the Greek text judges this omission as accidental. In any case, the context makes it clear that Jesus intends that persons come to him. This information would have to be supplied translationally even if it had no support from the Greek manuscripts.

    In some languages <u>come to me and drink</u> may seem too abrupt, since with such a verb as "drink" it is necessary to indicate what is to be drunk. One may say, for example, "let him come to me and drink something" or "let him come to me, and I will give him something to drink."

7.38   As the scripture says, 'Whoever believes in me, streams of life-giving water will pour out from his heart.'"[n]

[n]*Jesus' words in verses 37-38 may be translated:* "Whoever is thirsty should come to me, and whoever believes in me should drink. 38 As the scripture says, 'Streams of life-giving water will pour out from his heart.'"

    The last part of verse 37 and all of verse 38 present translational problems growing out of alternative possibilities of exegesis and punctuation. A literal translation of this passage will show some of the problems: "If anyone thirsts let him come to me and let him drink (38) the one believing in me as the scripture says rivers will pour out from his stomach of living water." Basically, the possibilities are two, though these two alternatives offer various combinations within themselves.

    1. A major stop (a period or a semicolon) may be placed at the end of verse 37. It will give the meaning that the one who is thirsty and comes to Jesus to drink is the one to whom the scripture refers, that is, the one from whom <u>streams of life-giving water will pour out</u>. This exegesis is evidently preferred by most translators. In its support is the observation that the invitation to drink is more naturally offered to <u>whoever is thirsty</u> than to <u>whoever believes in me</u>. Moreover, after the thirsty man has come and drunk, he can then be spoken of as the believer from whom <u>streams of life-giving water will pour out</u>.

    2. Alternative translations are possible if one places either a comma, or no punctuation at all, at the end of verse 37, and puts a major stop after "the one believing in me." This exegesis is followed by JB:

         "If any man is thirsty, let him come to me!
         Let the man come and drink who believes in me!"
NAB also followed this exegesis:
         "If anyone thirsts, let him come to me;
         let him drink (38) who believes in me."
Those who argue in support of this exegesis see here a chiastic

arrangement, in which the first half of the first line is equivalent to the second half of the second line, while the first half of the second line is parallel to the second half of the first line. That is, "if any man is thirsty" is taken to be parallel to "who believes in me," while "let him come to me" is considered parallel to "let the man come and drink." However, this parallelism is not perfect; in fact, the first alternative makes a much simpler and more easily recognized parallelism. That is, whoever is thirsty should come to me and drink is parallel with whoever believes in me, streams of living water will pour out from his heart. According to this interpretation, the one who is thirsty and drinks becomes the source of living water for others, so that the second line takes up the first and expands it.

The problem of translation is further complicated by the phrase as the scripture says, since no precise quotation from scripture is given here, and commentators are not agreed as to what passage or passages may be alluded to. Accordingly, the words whoever believes in me may be taken as a part of the scripture quotation, or they may be understood as being outside the quotation.

Those who accept the second alternative naturally exclude these words from the scripture quotation. Those who accept the first have the choice: either to include or to exclude these words. TEV includes them (whoever believes in me) as a part of the scripture quotation; that is, As the scripture says, 'Whoever believes in me, streams of living water will pour out from his heart.' But the translation could also read, "Whoever believes in me, as the scripture says, 'Streams of living water will pour out from his heart.'" The alternative followed by TEV is more natural. It is also the one generally followed by translators and commentators who accept the first alternative discussed above.

As noted in other passages, it is not possible in some languages to say the scripture says, for one cannot speak of "writings" as "speaking." This phrase may be rendered as "as one may read in the writings" or "in accordance with the words of the writings."

The phrase living water means "life-giving water."

Some commentators take the phrase from his heart as a Christological reference. That is, since this is taken as a quotation, they understand these words as a reference to Jesus, from whom streams of living water pour out for the believer. The basis for this viewpoint is that throughout John's Gospel Jesus is the source of living water and of life in general. However, it seems more probable that in this particular context the believer is the source of life-giving water. Once a man has come to Jesus to drink, he himself becomes the source of life-giving water for others. This also is a more natural reading of the grammar of the Greek text. If the receptor language requires the translation to be explicit, it is suggested that the reference be to the believer. If, however, the receptor language does not require the translation to be explicit, a third person reference (his heart) may be used, thus allowing either interpretation. However the best solution may be to place one interpretation in the text and indicate the possibility of the other in a marginal note.

From his heart is literally "from his stomach." Some translators render it literally. Others translate as TEV does. Some have "from his body" and others "from within him." In support of TEV is the observation that in Hebrew thought the "stomach" was often considered the seat of emotions, but for English speakers the "heart" symbolically has that function. Others point out that the Hebrew word "stomach" is restricted to passages where strong emotions are involved, and so they believe that heart is not an adequate translation here. However, in the present context is seems doubtful that "stomach" has an emotive connotation. Since most commentators agree that there is a tie between this verse and 19.34, where blood and water poured from Jesus' side, a more general phrase, such as "from within him," would seem to be the best rendering.

The order of elements in the quotation 'Whoever believes in me, streams of life-giving water will pour out from his heart' is awkward in English. The introductory phrase Whoever believes in me is an element which should be in focus, but this arrangement can be misleading, especially if it is translated literally into another language. It may be more satisfactory to say "Streams of life-giving water will pour out from the one who believes in me" or "...from anyone who believes in me."

As suggested above, streams of life-giving water may be rendered "streams with water which causes life" or "...causes people to really live."

Since in some languages the idea of a stream flowing from a source would indicate a "spring," it may be more satisfactory to say "springs of water which give life."

7.39   Jesus said this about the Spirit, which those who
          believed in him were going to receive. At that time
          the Spirit had not yet been given, because Jesus had
          not been raised to glory.

In translating it may be more satisfactory to indicate specifically "Spirit of God," rather than Spirit, especially in languages in which a term for "Spirit" may be associated with either neutral or mischievous spirits.

Jesus said this about the Spirit may be rendered 'When Jesus was talking, he was talking about God's Spirit."

In place of the aorist tense believed, some Greek manuscripts have the present "believe." Although the evidence is not conclusive, the UBS Committee on the Greek text judges that a scribe would tend to replace the aorist with the present tense of the verb, since doing so makes an easier reading in the present context.

Which those who believed in him were going to receive may be rendered as a separate sentence, for example, "Those who put their trust in Jesus were later going to receive God's Spirit" or "This is the Spirit which those who put their trust in Jesus were going to receive" or "...were those upon whom the Spirit of God was going to come."

The Spirit had not yet been given (similarly RSV, NEB, Segond, Phps) is more literally "for there was no Spirit as yet" (JB; see NAB, Luther Revised, and Mft). It was not John's intention to deny the previous existence of God's Spirit; in 1.32 he explicitly stated that God's Spirit descended on Jesus at the beginning of his ministry. What John meant is that the Holy Spirit had not yet been given in the specifically Christian sense, since this depended on the glorification of

Jesus Christ. That is, the experience of God's Spirit in the life of the believers is dependent upon Jesus' having <u>been raised to glory</u>.

The passive expression <u>the Spirit had not yet been given</u> may be made active by saying "God had not yet given the Spirit to those who believe."

<u>Raised to glory</u> is rendered "glorified" in most translations. In particular, 12.23 and 17.1 refer to the glorification of Jesus; and, according to the Gospel of John, Jesus' glorification always comes by his being "lifted up." Moreover, this "lifting up" always has a double connotation in John's Gospel: it refers to his being lifted up on the cross and to his being lifted to the presence of the Father (see 3.14). In some languages the double significance of "being lifted up" and "given glory" may be rendered as "lifted up and given honor" or "lifted up and made wonderful."

TEV	(7.40-44)	RSV

DIVISION AMONG THE PEOPLE

40 Some of the people in the crowd heard him say this and said, "This man is really the Prophet!"⁰ 41 Others said, "He is the Messiah!" But others said, "The Messiah will not come from Galilee! 42 The scripture says that the Messiah will be a descendant of King David and will be born in Bethlehem, the town where David lived." 43 So there was a division in the crowd because of Jesus. 44 Some wanted to seize him, but no one laid a hand on him.	40 When they heard these words, some of the people said, "This is really the prophet." 41 Others said, "This is the Christ." But some said, "Is the Christ to come from Galilee? 42 Has not the scripture said that the Christ is descended from David, and comes from Bethlehem, the village where David was?" 43 So there was a division among the people over him. 44 Some of them wanted to arrest him, but no one laid hands on him.

⁰THE PROPHET: *See 1.21.*

These verses take up once again the theme of the reaction of the people towards Jesus and his teaching. While some felt that he must be the Prophet or the Messiah, others were convinced that he could not be the Messiah, because they understood that the Messiah would come from Bethlehem, and they supposed that Jesus was not from there. This argument brought a division in the crowd, and some of the people wanted to arrest him.

The section heading, <u>Division Among the People</u>, may be transformed into a verb expression, for example, "The people are divided" or "The people say different things about Jesus."

7.40   Some of the people in the crowd heard him say
            this and said, "This man is really the Prophet!"[o]

[o]THE PROPHET: *See 1.21.*

Some of the people in the crowd is literally "from the crowd," to
which a subject must be supplied in translation. In 16.17 a similar
expression occurs (literally "from the disciples") which TEV translates
some of his disciples.
        Heard him say this and said is literally "having heard these words,
they said." TEV transforms a participle, "having heard," into a finite
verb, heard, and changes the vague noun phrase, "these words," into a
more explicit verb phrase, him say this. The relation between the
events of hearing and speaking may be indicated as "After some of the
people in the crowd had heard him say this, they said."
        In 1.21 also the Prophet is mentioned, and there also he is dis-
tinguished from the Messiah. To indicate that the Prophet is a recognized figure in Jewish eschatological thought, TEV translates "prophet"
with a capital "P"; NEB translates this term "the expected prophet." In
6.14 the Prophet is referred to as the Prophet who was to come to the
world. In translation one may use such terms as "the expected prophet,"
"the prophet whom we had been led to expect," "the prophet whom we have
been expecting" or even "...have been waiting for" or "...looking
forward to."

7.41   Others said, "He is the Messiah!"
            But others said, "The Messiah will not come
            from Galilee!

The Messiah is a translation of the Greek "the Christ" (see RSV),
not the transliteration of the Hebrew term "Messiah." However, whenever
"the Christ" is used of the expected Messianic figure in Jewish thought,
TEV translates this term the Messiah (see also NEB and NAB). As in other
contexts, Messiah may be rendered "the specially chosen one" or "the
one whom God has specially chosen" or "...designated." Some translations,
however, use "the promised Savior" or "the Savior whom God had promised."
A number of translations simply employ a transliteration of "Messiah."
        The Messiah will not come from Galilee! is actually a question ex-
pecting a negative answer in the Greek text. In NEB it is indicated by
"Surely the Messiah is not to come from Galilee?" As it is translated
in RSV ("Is the Christ to come from Galilee?"), the reader is not made
to see that a negative reply is expected. In some languages it is possible to preserve the rhetorical question if an answer is given immediately following, for example, "Will the Messiah come from Galilee?
No, indeed."

7.42   The scripture says that the Messiah will be a
            descendant of King David and will be born in
            Bethlehem, the town where David lived."

In Greek, this entire verse is in the form of a question, which
this time expects a positive response. That is, the question is so
phrased as to assume that the Messiah would be a descendant of David
and that he would be born in Bethlehem. NEB retains the question form,
"Does not Scripture say that the Messiah is to be of the family of
David, from David's village of Bethlehem?" Matthew 2.5-6 also refers
to the popular Jewish belief of the first century that the Messiah
would be born in Bethlehem. The Old Testament passage referred to is
Micah 5.2. John's style here is ironical. He implies by this quotation
that Jesus was born in Bethlehem, though he was brought up in Galilee.
The crowds were unable to fathom the truth that Jesus had come from
God.

For a treatment of the phrase The scripture says, see the discussion
under verse 38.

The Messiah will be a descendant of King David is expressed in some
languages as "King David will be the ancestor of the Messiah." In other
languages one may use a term for lineage, for example, "the Messiah will
belong to the lineage of King David"; and for lineage some languages use
rather extensive figurative expressions, for example, "the root of King
David," "the rope of King David" or "the vine of King David." Although
the Greek text does not include the marker King before David, TEV has
done so because its readers may not be familiar with this figure in
Jewish history. The second time he is referred to he is spoken of merely
as David, since the reference to David is then old information.

A literal translation of the town where David lived could be misleading, since it might suggest that David lived in Bethlehem throughout his life. The real meaning is that Bethlehem was "the hometown of
David," the town from which he came.

7.43   So there was a division in the crowd because
        of Jesus.

John introduces this verse (as well as verses 6,11,25,28,30,33,35,
40,45, and 47) with his favorite particle (oun). Here that particle
indicates a climax in the narrative, and so TEV introduces the verse
by so.

The word division occurs in several key places in the Gospel (7.43;
9.16; 10.19). It is used to describe the inevitable results of Jesus'
coming into the world, since some believe and some do not. In some
languages one can speak of a "division in a crowd," but this expression
is often understood merely in terms of a physical division, the split-
ting of a crowd into two groups. What is really involved here is a
serious difference of opinion among the people in the crowd; therefore
one can more effectively translate in some languages as "Some of the
people in the crowd spoke in favor of Jesus, but others spoke against
him."

7.44   Some wanted to seize him, but no one laid
        a hand on him.

Some is literally "some from them." "From them" is the same type of grammatical construction that was used in verse 40 ("from the crowd"). Here the indefinite pronoun some is explicitly used in the Greek text with this construction.

No one laid a hand on him translates the same expression used in verse 30, except that here the Greek text uses the plural "hands" in place of a hand. Some translations show this distinction (NEB "no one laid hands on him"), but the meaning is the same whether the singular or plural is used. It is simply a matter of which alternative is more acceptable in a receptor language.

TEV	(7.45-52)	RSV

THE UNBELIEF OF THE JEWISH AUTHORITIES

45 When the guards went back, the chief priests and Pharisees asked them, "Why did you not bring him?"

46 The guards answered, "Nobody has ever talked the way this man does!"

47 "Did he fool you, too?" the Pharisees asked them. 48 "Have you ever known one of the authorities or one Pharisee to believe in him? 49 This crowd does not know the Law of Moses, so they are under God's curse!"

50 One of the Pharisees there was Nicodemus, the man who had gone to see Jesus before. He said to the others, 51 "According to our Law we cannot condemn a man before hearing him and finding out what he has done."

52 "Well," they answered, "are you also from Galilee? Study the Scriptures and you will learn that no prophet ever comes[p] from Galilee."

[p]no prophet ever comes; one manuscript has the Prophet will not come.

45 The officers then went back to the chief priests and Pharisees, who said to them, "Why did you not bring him?" 46 The officers answered, "No man ever spoke like this man!" 47 The Pharisees answered them, "Are you led astray, you also? 48 Have any of the authorities or of the Pharisees believed in him? 49 But this crowd, who do not know the law, are accursed." 50 Nicodemus, who had gone to him before, and who was one of them, said to them, 51 "Does our law judge a man without first giving him a hearing and learning what he does?" 52 They replied, "Are you from Galilee too? Search and you will see that no prophet is to rise from Galilee."

The previous section (40-44) shows how the crowd was divided in its reaction towards Jesus and how some in the crowd wanted to arrest him. This section shows how the chief priests and Pharisees wanted to arrest Jesus, though one of their own number, Nicodemus, was opposed to such action.

[251]

The section heading, The Unbelief of the Jewish Authorities, may be changed to read "The Jewish authorities do not believe in Jesus" or "...refuse to believe in Jesus."

7.45   When the guards went back, the chief priests
             and Pharisees asked them, "Why did you not bring him?"

Guards is the same word used in verse 32, and this verse refers back to that verse. If John's chronology is exact, this verse describes what took place on the last day of the festival. The last time reference to verse 37 comes in verse 14: The festival was nearly half over. This reference suggests that there was a lapse of four days between the time that the guards were sent out to arrest Jesus (verse 32) and the last...day of the festival (verse 37) when they returned (verse 45). However, throughout this chapter it appears that John was more interested in the continuity of thought than in strict chronological sequence; the complexities of time sequence were obviously not of as much a concern to him as they may be to some modern readers.

The subject and object of the verb asked are actually ambiguous in Greek (literally "and those ones said to them"), but most translations clear up this ambiguity. In some languages the chief priests and Pharisees asked them may be better rendered as a passive, for example, "The guards went back to the chief priests and Pharisees and were asked by them." One may also say "The guards went back to the chief priests and Pharisees; these asked the guards."

In some languages it is necessary to be precise about the terms used for "bringing." In this context it may be necessary to translate Why did you not bring him? as "Why did you not lead him along" or "...force him to come with you?" A term which may mean "to carry" should be avoided.

7.46   The guards answered, "Nobody has ever talked
             the way this man does!"

In the reply of the guards this man seems to be emphatic.

Their response must be understood as a reference to the content of what Jesus had said. It would be wrong to suggest that there was something unusual about Jesus' manner of speech or his accent or pronunciation. One may say in some languages "No one has ever said the things this man has said" or "What this man has said is different from what all other men have said."

7.47   "Did he fool you, too?" the Pharisees asked
             them.

In the question of the Pharisees, you is emphatic. RSV therefore translates the question "Are you led astray, you also?"

Did he fool you, too? is actually a passive construction in Greek, which is more literally "Were you also led astray?" The implied agent

[252]

of the passive verb "were led astray" is Jesus (he). TEV changes the
passive construction into an active one, and makes the agent he the
subject. The questions raised by the Pharisees here and in verse 48
are so formed as to expect the answer "No." In order to indicate the
negative response to this question, it is possible to translate in
some languages "We hope he did not fool you" or "...deceive you" or
"...lead you in the wrong way."

7.48   "Have you ever known one of the authorities
          or one Pharisee to believe in him?

Authorities is the same word used to describe Nicodemus in 3.1
(TEV a leader). The reference is to the Jewish religious authorities,
not to political leaders, as "rulers" (NEB) might imply. NAB ("any of
the Sanhedrin") sees a specific reference to the Jewish body that had
final authority in matters of religion and was presided over by the
High Priest. See the comments on 3.1.
    A literal rendering of Have you ever known might suggest a personal
acquaintance with one of the authorities or Pharisees. Since this meaning
is not intended, it may be necessary to translate this verse "Have you
ever heard of any one of the authorities or any Pharisee who believed
in Jesus?"

7.49   This crowd does not know the Law of Moses,
          so they are under God's curse!"

This crowd is no doubt equivalent to the rabbinical phrase "the
people of the land," used to describe the masses of the people, as opposed to the "students of the law." As a rule this expression had
derogatory connotations.
    The Law of Moses is literally "the Law." It is extremely important
that the reader be made to see that the religious law, not the law of
the state, is referred to. Some translators try to make this information
explicit by translating "law" with a capital "L," but this device is of
no help to those who only hear the Scripture read.
    So they are under God's curse is literally "they are under a curse,"
but obviously God's curse is referred to, and TEV makes this information
explicit. Other translations attempt to do this in other ways. Note, for
example, NAB "they are lost anyway!"; Phps "is damned anyway!"; JB "they
are damned." It is important that the reader recognize that this curse
is not imposed by the authorities or by the Pharisees, and that it is
not such a curse as one experiences in voodoo, for example.
    In order to render the term curse it is necessary in some languages
to say "to cause people to be destroyed by God," for when a person curses
another, he calls upon God to destroy such an individual. It is, of
course, impossible for God to curse in the sense of putting a person
under God's curse. The closest equivalent may simply be "God will destroy
them anyway" or "God will cause them to perish."

7.50   One of the Pharisees there was Nicodemus, the
             man who had gone to see Jesus before. He said to
             the others,

One of the Pharisees there was Nicodemus represents a rather radical
but necessary restructuring in TEV. Note, for example, the possible ambiguity in RSV: "Nicodemus...who was one of them, said to them." Some
persons might understand RSV to indicate that Nicodemus was one of the
crowd that was under God's curse (verse 49), rather than that he was
one of the authorities or one of the Pharisees mentioned in verse 48.
Other translations reflect this same ambiguity. Note, for example, NEB
"'...As for this rabble, which cares nothing for the Law, a curse is
on them.' Then one of their number, Nicodemus...'" It is certainly
preferable at this point to indicate that Nicodemus was one of the
Pharisees. One may say, for example, "Nicodemus was one of the Pharisees" or "...leaders" rather than "...one of them."

7.51   "According to our Law we cannot condemn a man
             before hearing him and finding out what he has
             done."

TEV renders this verse as a statement, but in Greek it is a question expecting the answer "No."
    As elsewhere, references to the Law must be made plural in order
to indicate the entire body of laws, for example, "in accordance with
our laws."
    In this context we cannot condemn a man may be expressed as a
matter of necessity, rather than potentiality or ability, for example,
"we should not condemn a man" or "we must not condemn a man."
    Before hearing him may be rendered "before we hear what he has to
say." This reference is to a formal defense rather than merely getting
a report of what he may have said.
    Finding out what he has done is the meaning of Nicodemus' words in
the last part of this verse. RSV implies that they were to find out
what vocation Jesus was engaged in ("and learning what he does?"). JB
("discovering what he is about?") is rather high level, as is Mft
("ascertaining his offence?"); NEB translates as "learned the facts?"

7.52   "Well," they answered, "are you also from
             Galilee? Study the Scriptures and you will learn
             that no prophet ever comes^p from Galilee."

        ^{p}no prophet ever comes; *one manuscript has* the
        Prophet will not come.

Well, they answered is literally "they answered and said to him."
John's style here reflects Semitic Greek structure. TEV attempts to
give an equivalent meaning in contemporary English style. JB translates
"To this they answered." NEB "they retorted" sounds bookish.
    In the question are you also from Galilee? the pronoun you is

emphatic. It is not possible to know what the other Jewish authorities meant in asking Nicodemus this question. Obviously, they would have known the place from which Nicodemus had come, since the Sanhedrin was formed of a relatively small and well-integrated group of men who undoubtedly knew about one another. The question may have been intended to mean "Are you a partisan of Galilee as far as the origin of the Messiah is concerned?" or "Are you one who favors Galilee?" However, rather than attempt to introduce into the translation something of the apparent intent of the question, it is probably best simply to reproduce the question and leave the interpretation of intent to the context as a whole. There seems to be little chance of serious misunderstanding.

Study the Scriptures (so also NEB) is more literally "Search" (RSV). In 5.39 this same verb "to search" is used with the Scriptures as its stated object, and there TEV translates You study the Scriptures. The verb "to search" was a technical term used by the rabbis when referring to a study of the Scriptures. For that reason TEV and NEB make this information explicit. NAB also makes an attempt in this direction, "Look it up." JB "Go into the matter" and Phps "Look where you will" are misleading.

Most Greek manuscripts have the general statement that no prophet ever comes from Galilee, while the original reading of one reliable Greek manuscript makes the specific statement that "the Prophet will not come from Galilee" (see TEV note). Most modern translations (NAB is an exception) follow the reading no prophet ever comes from Galilee. Mft follows this same Greek text, but his rendering is rather amusing, "no prophet ever springs from Galilee."

In some languages there is a problem in relating the studying of the Scriptures to what is to be learned from them. This concept may be best expressed as a conditional, for example, "If you study the Scriptures, you will learn that" or "By studying the Scriptures you will learn that."

A further problem is involved in the tense of the verb comes. If this is understood as a general truth, always applicable and then placed in a historical tense (for example, "no prophet has ever come from Galilee"), there are obvious exceptions, since Jonah had come from a town in Galilee (2 Kgs 14.25). Some translators have therefore wished to employ the expression "no prophet is ever to come from Galilee" as a reference to a predicted prophet. However, it is possible to say "you cannot expect a prophet to come from Galilee." This translation preserves the general meaning of the Greek form of the statement, and at the same time has reference to future events, rather than to past situations.

7.53   [Then everyone went home,

In the Greek text 7.53 and 8.1 form a single sentence; TEV omits the verse number 53 and places both verses together under 8.1.

CHAPTER 8

THE WOMAN CAUGHT IN ADULTERY

8 [Then everyone went home, but Jesus went to the Mount of Olives. 2 Early the next morning he went back to the Temple. All the people gathered around him, and he sat down and began to teach them. 3 The teachers of the Law and the Pharisees brought in a woman who had been caught committing adultery, and they made her stand before them all. 4 "Teacher," they said to Jesus, "this woman was caught in the very act of committing adultery. 5 In our Law Moses commanded that such a woman must be stoned to death. Now, what do you say?" 6 They said this to trap Jesus, so that they could accuse him. But he bent over and wrote on the ground with his finger. 7 As they stood there asking him questions, he straightened up and said to them, "Whichever one of you has committed no sin may throw the first stone at her." 8 Then he bent over again and wrote on the ground. 9 When they heard this, they all left, one by one, the older ones first. Jesus was left alone, with the woman still standing there. 10 He straightened up and said to her, "Where are they? Is there no one left to condemn you?"

11 "No one, sir, " she answered.

"Well, then," Jesus said, "I do not condemn you either. Go, but do not sin again."][r]

[r]*Many manuscripts and early translations do not have this passage (8.1-11); others have it after Jn 21.24; others have it after Lk 21.38; one manuscript has it after Jn 7.36.*

8 53 They went each to his own house, 1 but Jesus went to the Mount of Olives. 2 Early in the morning he came again to the temple; all the people came to him, and he sat down and taught them. 3 The scribes and the Pharisees brought a woman who had been caught in adultery, and placing her in the midst 4 they said to him, "Teacher, this woman has been caught in the act of adultery. 5 Now in the law Moses commanded us to stone such. What do you say about her?" 6 This they said to test him, that they might have some charge to bring against him. Jesus bent down and wrote with his finger on the ground. 7 And as they continued to ask him, he stood up and said to them, "Let him who is without sin among you be the first to throw a stone at her." 8 And once more he bent down and wrote with his finger on the ground. 9 But when they heard it, they went away, one by one, beginning with the eldest, and Jesus was left alone with the woman standing before him. 10 Jesus looked up and said to her, "Woman, where are they? Has no one condemned you?" 11 She said, "No one, Lord." And Jesus said, "Neither do I condemn you; go, and do not sin again."[r]

[r]The most ancient authorities omit 7.53-8.11; other authorities add the passage here or after 7.36 or after 21.25 or after Luke 21.38, with variations of text

This passage was doubtless not an original part of the Gospel of
John, and for that reason TEV places it in brackets. Several other
translations also do so, or else place the entire passage in a marginal
note. It is not found in the earlier and better Greek manuscripts, it
differs in style and vocabulary from the rest of John's Gospel, and it
interrupts the sequence of 7.52 and 8.12 and following. But it was evidently a widely circulated account in certain parts of the early
church, and finally found its place in various ancient manuscripts. In
terms of style and vocabulary it is closer to the Lukan writings than
it is to John, and in some ancient manuscripts it is even found after
Luke 21.38.

The section heading, The Woman Caught in Adultery, may present
certain difficulties in translation, in view of its grammatical structure, as well as certain complications in vocabulary. If it is necessary
to transform the passive expression into an active one, it may be possible to say "Some men catch a woman in adultery" or, perhaps better in
some languages, "...arrest a woman..." In some languages a clear distinction is made between "adultery" (illicit sexual intercourse with a
married person) and "fornication" (sexual intercourse which does not
violate the marriage relationship). In some languages adultery is
spelled out in considerable detail, for example. "sleeping with a man
who is not her husband." In others adultery may be identified by some
idiomatic expression, for example, "to live like a dog," "to receive
men guests," "to welcome intruders," or "to earn a living on one's bed."

8.1   [Then everyone went home, but Jesus went to the
           Mount of Olives.

Then everyone went home is verse 53 of Chapter 7 in most texts;
but Jesus went to the Mount of Olives is verse 1 of Chapter 8. Obviously, this chapter division takes place in an extremely awkward place,
in the middle of a sentence! TEV simply omits verse number 53 from
Chapter 7 and joins the short statement Then everyone went home to
verse 1 of Chapter 8.

Then everyone went home is more literally "and they went each one
to his own home." JB translates "They all went home."

Because of the textual problems involved, paragraphing of this
section concerning the woman caught in adultery normally begins with
7.53. However, a more logical break in content occurs between verses 1
and 2. Certainly the fact that "everyone went home" is more satisfactorily combined with the preceding account of the reaction of Jewish
authorities to Jesus.

The Mount of Olives is mentioned three or four times in each of
the Synoptic Gospels but only here in the Gospel of John. It was a hill
east of Jerusalem, named for its extensive olive groves, and separated
from the city by the deep Kidron Valley. The expression the Mount of
Olives should not be so translated as to suggest a mountain consisting
of olives. A more satisfactory rendering is found in such a phrase as
"a mountain known for its olive trees" or, better still in most languages, "a hill known for its olive trees." Usually such place names
are formed rather succinctly, for example, "Olive Tree Hill."

8.2   Early the next morning he went back to the
Temple. All the people gathered around him,
and he sat down and began to teach them.

Early the next morning (NEB, JB "At daybreak") translates one word
in Greek, which is found elsewhere in the New Testament only in Luke
24.1 and Acts 5.21.
In Greek this verse is one sentence which TEV makes into two. The
Greek sentence structure reflects Semitic style with a series of three
connectives: "but again...and...and...," which should not be expressed
in translation.
In some languages it may be necessary to be specific about the
place to which Jesus went. If one translates literally "he went back
to the Temple," it may imply he went back only to the outside of the
Temple. At the same time, one should not give the impression that Jesus
went into the sanctuary. It may be necessary to say "Jesus went back
into the Temple area" or "...into the courtyard around the Temple."
He sat down is actually a participle in Greek. A number of translations have it as a finite verb, as TEV does. Began to teach is the
force that many translators see in this verb; some translate simply
"taught," while NEB has "was engaged in teaching."

8.3   The teachers of the Law and the Pharisees brought in
a woman who had been caught committing adultery, and
they made her stand before them all.

The teachers of the Law and the Pharisees is a common expression
in the other Gospels, though it occurs only here in the Gospel of
John. Most translations render teachers of the Law as "scribes" (NEB
"the doctors of the law"). To translate as "scribes" is misleading.
Originally one of the main functions of these men was to make copies of
the Law, but by New Testament times they were the recognized authorities
on the Law. The teachers of the Law and the Pharisees is apparently a
set phrase. Most of the teachers of the Law probably belonged to the
Pharisaic party.
Teachers of the Law may also be rendered "those who explained the
Law" or "those who interpreted the Law," in the sense of "showed what
the Law meant." Note, however, that it may be necessary to employ a
plural, namely, "laws," since some receptor languages lack a singular
form which would be interpreted as a collective.
In some languages certain problems are encountered in using definite articles, such as "the teachers" and "the Pharisees," because
this usage would imply that all the teachers and all the Pharisees
were involved. Therefore, it may be necessary in some languages to
use an equivalent such as "some teachers of the Law and some Pharisees."
In some ancient manuscripts committing adultery appears as "committing sin," perhaps in anticipation of the close of verse 11. No translations seem to follow this alternative reading. As suggested in connection with the title of this section, it may be necessary to say "who
had been arrested while sleeping with a man who was not her husband."
They made her stand before them all (JB "making her stand there in

full view of everybody"; Mft "making her stand forward") is translated
rather literally in RSV "placing her in the midst" (see NEB "Making
her stand out in the middle"). The meaning is that the woman was made
to stand before the people before whom she was to be tried. (The same
expression is used in Acts 4.7: They made the apostles stand before
them.) It should be noted that, contrary to the Law of Moses (Lev 20.10;
Deut 22.22), only the woman was brought to trial.

8.4 "Teacher," they said to Jesus, "this woman was
    caught in the very act of committing adultery.

To Jesus is literally "to him." TEV makes the pronominal reference
explicit.

This woman would have been a married woman, because according to
the Jewish Law adultery had to do with the unfaithfulness of the wife.
An unmarried woman who had sexual relations with a married man was not
considered an adulteress. In the ancient world the woman was looked
upon as the property of her husband, and so originally the basic sin
in adultery was the sin against the woman's husband. Her sin was that
she had allowed herself to be used by another man.

8.5 In our Law Moses commanded that such a woman
    must be stoned to death. Now, what do you say?"

Moses commanded that such a woman must be stoned to death is literally "Moses commanded us to stone such ones." The Greek phrase "such
ones" is feminine and so equivalent to "such women" (NEB); RSV translates
merely "such" and Mft "such creatures." TEV shifts to the singular for
the sake of English style. Whether one chooses singular or plural, it
should be indicated that "such" refers to women. The command "to stone"
such women was a command to put them to death, and TEV makes this clear.
JB does the same, "to condemn women like this to death by stoning."

There may be a complication involved in combining the phrases
In our Law and Moses commanded, for in a sense Moses also gave the Law.
Therefore it may be necessary to translate "When Moses gave us our laws,
he commanded us" or "Moses gave a commandment to us in our laws, saying."
Or it may be necessary to state the content of the commandment as direct
discourse, for example, "Moses commanded us, You must stone such a
woman to death."

Several translations fill out the question Now, what do you say?
RSV translates "What do you say about her?"; NEB "What do you say about
it?"; and NAB "What do you have to say about the case?" In this question
the pronoun you is emphatic; the questioners are attempting to set Jesus
over against Moses. The conjunctive adverb Now is not to be understood
in a temporal sense but as a kind of adversative, for example, "But
what do you say?" or "On the other hand, what do you say?"

8.6 They said this to trap Jesus, so that they could accuse
    him. But he bent over and wrote on the ground with his finger.

They said this to trap Jesus is similar to the Greek of 6.6, but
the context indicates that the meaning is different. In 6.6 Jesus is
not trying to trap Philip but only to test him; here it is obvious that
the people are trying to catch Jesus in his words. TEV and NAB come
closer to giving the real impact of the passage than translations which
render "to test him." The fact that the Jews were not simply trying to
test Jesus but to trap him is made clear by what is said in the last
part of the sentence: so they could accuse him. To trap him may be expressed as "to catch Jesus saying the wrong thing" or "to hear Jesus
say words which could be used to condemn him."

So they could accuse him may need some further clarification or expansion in some languages, for example, "so that they could accuse him
before the officials" or "so that they could go to the officials saying,
This man spoke wrong" or "...this man spoke against our laws."

Bent over is actually a participle in Greek, not a finite verb, but
most translations prefer to use a finite verb and to join it by and to
the verb wrote.

What Jesus wrote on the ground and why he wrote have been sources of
much speculation. None of this speculation is profitable, and fortunately
these questions need not be answered in translating the passage. If what
Jesus wrote on the ground had been of importance as far as the account
itself is concerned, doubtless the author would have included it.

In some languages the very process of "writing" implies some kind
of instrument together with the result; here it may be necessary to say
"wrote words in the dust with his finger" or "wrote some words in the
dust, using his finger." An expression for "dust," rather than "ground,"
may be used to avoid the impression that there was tillable ground
within the Temple area.

8.7   As they stood there asking him questions, he
         straightened up and said to them, "Whichever
         one of you has committed no sin may throw the
         first stone at her."

As they stood there asking him questions is translated by Mft and
JB "as they persisted with their question" and by NEB "when they continued to press their question." This phrase is more literally translated "but as they remained asking questions." TEV understands the verb
"remained" to have the force of "remained standing," while the other
two translations connect it more closely with the participle "asking
questions." Both choices are grammatically possible. RSV translates
"And as they continued to ask him." The inclusion of the pronoun "him"
is apparently not a translational matter with RSV, but a textual matter
since "him" is possibly, though not probably, an original part of the
Greek text.

Whichever one of you has committed no sin (JB "If there is one of
you who has not sinned"; RSV "Let him who is without sin") is an
accurate representation of what Jesus said. The point of reference is
one who has not committed sin, rather than one "who is faultless" (NEB).
One might wrongly infer from reading Mft that some in the group were
children, "Let the innocent among you throw the first stone." Has

committed no sin may be translated "has never sinned" or "has never done anything wrong."

Instead of saying may throw the first stone at her, it may be necessary to say "may be the first one to throw a stone at her." In some languages it may be necessary to indicate that the hurling of the stones was designed to injure and harm. If so, one may say "may be the first one to throw a stone in order to harm her" or "to cause her to suffer" or "to cause her death."

According to the teaching of Deuteronomy 17.6-7, a person could not be given the death penalty apart from the testimony of two or three witnesses. The witnesses themselves were to throw the first stones at the condemned person. That is obviously the law to which Jesus has reference here, though he qualifies it by stating that only a witness who himself has not sinned may be the first to throw a stone at the woman.

8.8   Then he bent over again and wrote on the ground.

At least one ancient scribe was not satisfied with the Greek text as it came to him, and so he added the words "the sins of each one of them," to explain what Jesus wrote on the ground. This phrase should not of course be included in the translation, since it is not a part of the original text.

8.9   When they heard this, they all left, one by one,
        the older ones first. Jesus was left alone, with
        the woman still standing there.

As NEB points out, some ancient manuscripts add "convicted by their conscience" after they all left. However, this phrase also is recognized as an ancient scribe's addition to the text, and should not be included. These are only two of the many textual variations in this passage.

The older ones first is literally "beginning from the older ones." The Greek expression "beginning from" may simply mean "including," but apparently all translations follow the same meaning suggested by TEV. In some languages it may be necessary to say "The older men left first and then the younger men" or "The older men were the first ones to leave, and then the younger men followed them."

In Greek this verse is one sentence. TEV makes it two sentences and at the beginning of the second changes the Greek pronoun "he" to Jesus.

There is literally "in the midst," the same expression used in verse 3. NEB, JB and GeCL also translate this expression there, while RSV, Mft, and NAB "before him."

It is not possible in some languages to translate "Jesus was left alone." Obviously the woman was still standing there, and there may have been a crowd of onlookers, for the scribes and Pharisees had intruded upon Jesus as he was teaching the people. An equivalent expression in some languages is "they left Jesus there with the woman still standing where she had been."

8.10   He straightened up and said to her, "Where are they?
Is there no one left to condemn you?"

In the Greek text he is literally "Jesus," but TEV changes the
noun to a pronoun, since Jesus is mentioned explicitly in the previous
sentence. As NEB indicates, some ancient manuscripts read "seeing no
one but the woman" after the words He straightened up. This addition
represents one of several attempts by early scribes to expand the text
and is recognized not to be an original part of the story.

Where are they...? is the reading of the best manuscripts. Some
ancient manuscripts read "where are your accusers?"--another expansion
of the original story. In some languages, a literal translation of
Where are they...? may be confusing. It may be better to say "Where are
the men?" or even "Where are those who were accusing you?"

"Woman" of the Greek text (so most translations) is the same noun
of address used by Jesus in 2.4 and 19.26. Its use does not indicate
that Jesus is speaking disrespectfully, but in English it may sound
disrespectful, so TEV has deleted it.

Is there no one left to condemn you? is more literally "Has no one
condemned you?" (RSV, NEB, NAB, JB, Mft). In the context the point is
that no one was left there to condemn the woman; TEV makes this information explicit (so also GeCL). Is there no one left...? may be rendered "Is there still no one here...?" or "Has no one remained...?"
To condemn you may be rendered "to denounce you," to say that you have
sinned," or even "to say that you deserve death."

8.11   "No one, sir," she answered.
"Well, then," Jesus said, "I do not condemn you
either. Go, but do not sin again."]^{r}

> ^{r}Many manuscripts and early translations do not have
> this passage (8.1-11); others have it after Jn 21.24;
> others have it after Lk 21.38; one manuscript has it
> after Jn 7.36.

In some languages it is not sufficient to say No one. Such an
expression must be combined with a verb, for example, "There is no one
who condemns me" or "No one remains to condemn me."

Sir may be taken either as a form of polite address (as in TEV and
most other translations) or with the Christian meaning of "Lord" (RSV).
In the present context the evidence for sir seems conclusive.

Well, then is a transitional device, but the force of this expression is implicit in Jesus' response to the woman. That is, his words
represent a response to the situation in which the accusers of the
woman have left.

Go translates a Greek imperative; NEB and NAB translate "You may
go."

In the Greek text the command do not sin again has some built-in
redundancy: "from now on no longer sin." Most translations, like TEV,
combine the force of "from now on" and "no longer." NEB has the same
expression as TEV and JB has "don't sin any more." Mft maintains the

two adverbial expressions, "and never sin again." Some translators take the command <u>do not sin again</u> as a specific reference to the sin of adultery and so render "avoid this sin" (NAB).

TEV   (8.12-20)   RSV

JESUS THE LIGHT OF THE WORLD

12 Jesus spoke to the Pharisees again. "I am the light of the world," he said. "Whoever follows me will have the light of life and will never walk in darkness."

13 The Pharisees said to him, "Now you are testifying on your own behalf; what you say proves nothing."

14 "No," Jesus answered, "even though I do testify on my own behalf, what I say is true, because I know where I came from and where I am going. You do not know where I came from or where I am going. 15 You make judgments in a purely human way; I pass judgment on no one. 16 But if I were to do so, my judgment would be true, because I am not alone in this; the Father who sent me is with me. 17 It is written in your Law that when two witnesses agree, what they say is true. 18 I testify on my own behalf, and the Father who sent me also testifies on my behalf."

19 "Where is your father?" they asked him.

"You know neither me nor my Father," Jesus answered. "If you knew me, you would know my Father also."

20 Jesus said all this as he taught in the Temple, in the room where the offering boxes were placed. And no one arrested him because his hour had not come.

12 Again Jesus spoke to them, saying, "I am the light of the world; he who follows me will not walk in darkness, but will have the light of life." 13 The Pharisees then said to him, "You are bearing witness to yourself; your testimony is not true." 14 Jesus answered, "Even if I do bear witness to myself, my testimony is true, for I know whence I have come and whither I am going, but you do not know whence I come or whither I am going. 15 You judge according to the flesh, I judge no one. 16 Yet even if I do judge, my judgment is true, for it is not I alone that judge, but I and he[s] who sent me. 17 In your law it is written that the testimony of two men is true; 18 I bear witness to myself, and the Father who sent me bears witness to me." 19 They said to him therefore, "Where is your Father?" Jesus answered, "You know neither me nor my Father; if you knew me, you would know my Father also." 20 These words he spoke in the treasury, as he taught in the temple; but no one arrested him, because his hour had not yet come.

[s]Other ancient authorities read *the Father*

Almost all scholars agree that these verses originally came immediately after Chapter 7 (see the explanation at the beginning of this chapter). There is clearly a close tie between Chapters 7 and 8. The Festival of Shelters was more popularly known as "the Feast of Lights," and in this chapter Jesus stands up and says <u>I am the light of the world</u>.

Moreover, 7.10 states that Jesus went to the feast secretly, while 8.59 says that Jesus hid himself and left the Temple. There is also a connection between the theme of light mentioned in verse 12 and the healing of the blind man in Chapter 9. That is, the giving of sight to the blind man must be understood as a sign pointing to Jesus as the light of the world. Within this section several themes are woven together. The theme of light mentioned in verse 12 is not mentioned again until the following chapter. There are also the themes of Jesus' relationship to the Father and of the Father's witness to who Jesus is.

The section heading, Jesus the Light of the World, may require some modification, for example, "Jesus as the light for people in the world" or "Jesus as the one who enlightens people in the world." Or it may also be possible to use a simpler title such as "Light for those in the world" or even "Light which causes people to live" (based on a phrase in verse 12).

8.12   Jesus spoke to the Pharisees again. "I am the
             light of the world," he said. "Whoever follows
             me will have the light of life and will never
             walk in darkness."

Jesus spoke to the Pharisees again may be more literally rendered "therefore Jesus spoke to them again saying." "Therefore" represents a transitional particle (oun), and the participle "saying" after the finite verb "to speak," indicates that direct discourse is to follow. TEV specifically identifies the persons referred to by the pronoun "they" (the Pharisees), since a new section begins here.

The locale and the persons to whom Jesus is speaking are both vague, though in verse 20 we learn that Jesus said all this as he taught in the Temple, in the room where the offering boxes were placed. The last time Jesus was indicated as speaking was in 7.38 (considering, of course, that 8.1-11 is completely parenthetical). There he was apparently addressing the crowds who had come to the Temple for the feast. However, the crowd which was mentioned some eight times in Chapter 7 is not mentioned at all in Chapter 8. So it is possible that the present discourse is addressed to the Pharisees, the last group mentioned (7.47). They are mentioned again in the following verse, but the translations which make the pronominal reference of "them" explicit generally supply "the people" (so Phps, NEB, JB).

The I am statement of Jesus is here followed by a predicate, the light of the world. (On the use of I am in the Gospel of John, see comments at 4.26.) I am the light of the world is often rendered "I am the one who gives light to people in the world" or "I am the one who causes light for people of the world." It is important to avoid a translation which would equate Jesus with the sun. Unfortunately, such a thing has happened in some literal translations of this passage.

Whoever follows me must be understood in the sense of "whoever becomes my disciple." It is often expressed more clearly in some languages as "if anyone becomes my adherent" or "...joins himself with me."

The light of life means "the light that gives life (GeCL "the light that leads to life"). In some languages the light of life may be rendered "the light that causes people to really live" or "the light that shows people how they may live."

In Greek the negative statement <u>will never walk in darkness</u> precedes the positive statement <u>will have the light of life</u>; but for English style it is more natural to state the positive first and then the negative. (On the meaning of <u>light</u> and <u>darkness</u> see 1.4-5.) <u>Will never walk in darkness</u> may be rendered in some languages "will never walk where it is dark" or even "will never walk in places where they cannot see." Some translators want to express <u>will never walk in darkness</u> as "will never live in ignorance" or "...in ignorance of what God wants them to do." However, this is not really the meaning of the contrast between light and darkness in this special biblical sense. It is not advisable to change completely these figurative meanings, based upon such pervasive usage as the contrast between <u>light</u> and <u>darkness</u> suggested in the biblical message.

<u>8.13</u>　　　　　The Pharisees said to him, "Now you are testifying
　　　　　　　　on your own behalf; what you say proves nothing."

The force of the Greek particle (<u>oun</u>) which introduces this verse is implied by the context itself. The theme of light is now dropped, and it is not resumed again until 9.5. The real heart of this chapter is the question regarding the authority of Jesus.

<u>Now</u> does not actually appear in the Greek text. TEV uses it as a translational technique to emphasize the pronoun <u>you</u>, which is emphatic in the Greek text. <u>Now</u> should not be understood here in a temporal sense.

<u>You are testifying on your own behalf</u> may be rendered, in this particular context, "you are speaking about yourself only on the basis of your own authority" or "you are just talking about yourself without anyone to confirm what you say." (On the verb <u>testifying</u>, see 1.7.)

<u>What you say proves nothing</u> translates the same expression used in 5.31 (<u>what I say is not to be accepted as real proof</u>), except for the substitution of the pronoun <u>you</u> for <u>I</u>. NEB ("your testimony is not valid") is representative of a number of translations. The adjective "valid" appears in the RSV as "true." It is the same word translated <u>honest</u> in TEV at 7.18. <u>What you say proves nothing</u> may be rendered in some instances "what you say has no value" or "what you say does not convince anyone" or "...cannot convince anyone."

<u>8.14</u>　　　　　"No," Jesus answered, "even though I do testify
　　　　　　　　on my own behalf, what I say is true, because I know
　　　　　　　　where I came from and where I am going. You do not
　　　　　　　　know where I came from or where I am going.

<u>Jesus answered</u> is literally "Jesus answered and said to them," again representing a Semitic style of introducing direct discourse (see verse 12).

TEV introduces the word <u>No</u> into Jesus' response to indicate the intended effect of Jesus' words. That is, his reply must be understood as a denial of the Pharisees' position as well as an affirmation of his own. GeCL achieves this effect by beginning Jesus' reply with "What I say is true." To make clear the significance of the adversative expression No, it may be necessary to translate "but you are wrong" or "what you say is not so."

Even though I do testify on my own behalf is translated by JB "It is true that I am testifying on my own behalf" and by Mft "Though I do testify to myself." The purpose of these renderings is to indicate that the force of the clause is to show that Jesus did in fact testify in behalf of himself. The more literal "if I testify about myself" might wrongly suggest to the English reader that Jesus did not testify in his own behalf.

Jesus' words even though I do testify on my own behalf, what I say is true are, in form, a contradiction of 5.31: If I testify on my own behalf, what I say is not to be accepted as real proof. However, in each instance Jesus' argument is directed against the arguments of his opponents at the particular time. Although there is a formal contradiction between these two verses, the real thought is the same: Jesus' testimony is true and valid because the Father himself verifies it.

In some languages it is difficult to express what is called concession, represented in English by the conjunctions "although" and "even if." The closest equivalent may be "suppose that I do testify on my own behalf..." or "let us admit that I do testify on my own behalf..." or "I do testify on my own behalf, but nevertheless what I say is true."

What I say is true are the same words Jesus used in 5.31, except that in the earlier passage they are used with a negative.

I know where I came from and where I am going resumes the theme of Jesus' origin and destiny, mentioned in the preceding chapter (see 7.27-28). This theme is found again in 9.29.

8.15 You make judgments in a purely human way; I pass judgment on no one.

The pronoun you is emphatic.

In a purely human way is literally "according to the flesh." Phps and JB translate "by human standards"; NEB "by worldly standards"; and NAB "according to appearances." "According to the flesh" is a term found frequently in Paul's writings. It is used only here by John; no other New Testament writer uses it. In 7.24 Jesus had warned the crowd not to judge by external standards. It may be that in a purely human way and by external standards are very close. The first throws emphasis on what something seems to be, while the second phrase stresses the subjective aspect of the person making the judgment. That is, he judges as he does because he is "flesh" and not God, and his judgments are therefore neither adequate nor valid. In a purely human way may be rendered "following people's customs" or "in the way in which people generally judge" or "in the way in which people usually condemn others."

Many believe that Jesus' words I pass judgment on no one prompted the addition of the story of the woman caught in adultery. Elsewhere Jesus says he does judge (9.39), and the very heart of the Gospel of John is to proclaim to the world that it is judged in the light of who

Jesus is. However, there is no essential contradiction in the truth stated here. Jesus is merely stating in another way his perfect unity with the Father. Thus any judgment that Jesus makes is not made on his own, as though in a purely human way; rather, it is a judgment made on the basis of his absolute relationship with God. So then, any judgment that Jesus makes actually originates from God.

Usually in translating I pass judgment on no one, it is useful to employ a neutral word of "judging." However, in this particular context it is possible to employ a term which may suggest primarily "condemning," that is, "I am not condemning anyone."

8.16   But if I were to do so, my judgment would be true, because I am not alone in this; the Father who sent me is with me.

My judgment would be true may be rendered "the way in which I judge would be right."

I am not alone in this may be translated "I'm not doing this just on my own."

Some ancient manuscripts omit Father from this verse, and so read "because I am not alone in this; the one who sent me is with me." Accordingly, JB, NEB, and Luther Revised do not include Father. The term appears in NAB in brackets and in RSV only in a footnote. Those who assume that it was not an original part of the Greek text believe that it crept into several ancient manuscripts by way of assimilation to verse 18. However, the best and most reliable ancient Greek manuscripts do include the word. The UBS Committee on the Greek text believes that its omission from four or five manuscripts is due to a scribal error.

It may not be enough in some languages to say the Father who sent me is with me. What is important here is that the Father participates in the process of judging. Therefore, it may be necessary to say "my Father, who sent me, joins with me in what I do" or "...in my judging."

8.17   It is written in your Law that when two witnesses agree, what they say is true.

It is written in your Law may be translated "there are words in your laws which say" or "your Law contains these words." What follows must then normally be given as direct discourse.

The pronoun your (NEB "your own") is emphatic. Jesus is pictured as at once hostile to their law and superior to it.

In the Jewish context the two witnesses would normally be taken to be two witnesses other than the person actually concerned. However, in the following verse Jesus makes himself one of the witnesses on his own behalf. The Scripture passages referred to are Deuteronomy 17.6 and 19.15.

When two witnesses agree, what they say is true is literally "the testimony of two men is true"; GeCL renders "If two witnesses agree in their testimony, the truth results." TEV restructuring transforms the noun-oriented structure "the testimony of two witnesses" to a verb phrase

[267]

when two witnesses agree, which then requires the inclusion what they
say.
     The clause when two witnesses agree may be rendered as a condition,
"if two witnesses agree" or "if two witnesses say the same thing" or "if
the words of two witnesses match one another."

8.18   I testify on my own behalf, and the Father who sent
              me also testifies on my behalf."

     For the Father as one who testifies on behalf of the Son, see 5.37.
     Since the Father who sent me must be rendered in many languages as
"my Father, who sent me," note that the clause who sent me becomes non-
restrictive, that is, it simply describes an aspect of the Father, without indicating which particular Father is to be understood. In many languages such a clause must be treated quite differently from a normal
relative clause which specifies a particular individual, for example, it
may be necessary to say "my Father (he is the one who sent me)."

8.19   "Where is your father?" they asked him.
              "You know neither me nor my Father," Jesus answered.
              "If you knew me you would know my Father also."

     The question Where is your father? is yet another instance in the
Gospel where Jesus' hearers misunderstand him, and where, on the basis
of their misunderstanding, Jesus gives further teaching. This question
may be raised by the Jews as a means of trapping Jesus, since they
assume that they know where he comes from (7.27).
     TEV rearranges this verse slightly for the sake of English style,
and the same restructuring is followed by GeCL. In the Greek text, the
words they asked him come first in the sentence and are followed by the
question Where is your father? Then come the words Jesus answered, and
his answer is given in one part, not broken into by these two words.
This verse is a good example of one where restructuring is necessary to
achieve good style in the receptor language. In deciding on the kind of
restructuring, the translator must always consider his audience. In
many languages it would be more natural to follow the order of the Greek
text and to translate, for example, "They asked him, Where is your
father?" The response would then be "Jesus answered, You know neither
me nor my Father."
     Jesus' words You know neither me nor my Father represent a basic
theme of the Fourth Gospel, namely, that one can know the Father only
through the Son, and that those who do not know the Son cannot possibly
know the Father.
     In some languages it would seem anomalous to say "you do not know
me," for obviously his audience was acquainted, in a sense, with Jesus.
What needs to be emphasized here is "you do not really know me" or "you
do not really know who I am" or "you do not know who I really am." This
would then form the basis for the final statement in verse 19, "if you
really knew who I was, you would also be acquainted with my Father" or
"...recognize who my Father is."

8.20   Jesus said all this as he taught in the Temple,
in the room where the offering boxes were placed.
And no one arrested him, because his hour had not
come.

The Greek reads "he said," which TEV renders Jesus said (so also
GeCL). NEB makes this fact explicit in another manner: "These words
were spoken by Jesus." Although the reader would probably understand
that "he" refers to Jesus, it is more natural to introduce this paragraph with the noun Jesus than with the pronoun "he," since it is a
summary verse and departs from the topic discussed in 12-19.
In the room where the offering boxes were placed (so also GeCL)
appears in most translations as "in the treasury." The Jewish historian
Josephus uses this word "treasury" (in the plural) to describe a number
of small rooms in the Temple where valuables were stored. It is not likely
that Jesus was teaching in one of these "storage rooms." There were, however, some thirteen offering boxes in the Temple. It is not known exactly
where they were located, but quite possibly they were in the court of the
women, since women seemed to have had access to them (see Mark 12.41-42).
In some languages the verb were placed may be taken to mean "were
stored," thus indicating a storage room. Therefore, it may be better to
translate "near the place where the offering boxes were located" or
simply "near the offering boxes." This translation is supported by the
Greek text, since the Greek preposition that TEV translates in may have
the less precise meaning of "near" (NAB "at the temple treasury").
As he taught in the Temple may be rendered "as he taught the people
in the Temple" or "as he was there in the Temple teaching the people."
The more specific indication, in the room where the offering boxes were
placed, may be interpreted as an explanation and rendered "He was there
in the room where the offering boxes were placed."
Offering boxes may be rendered "boxes where people placed their
offerings to God" or "boxes in which people put money as gifts to God."
His hour had not come translates the same phrase used in 7.30 (see
also 2.4).

<table>
<tr><td>TEV</td><td>(8.21-30)</td><td>RSV</td></tr>
</table>

YOU CANNOT GO WHERE I AM GOING

21 Again Jesus said to them, "I
will go away; you will look for me,
but you will die in your sins. You
cannot go where I am going."

22 So the Jewish authorities
said, "He says that we cannot go
where he is going. Does this mean
that he will kill himself?"

23 Jesus answered, "You belong
to this world here below, but I
come from above. You are from this
world, but I am not from this

21 Again he said to them, I go
away, and you will seek me and die
in your sin; where I am going, you
cannot come."

22 Then said the Jews, "Will he
kill himself, since he says, 'Where
I am going, you cannot come'?" 23
He said to them, "You are from below, I am from above; you are of
this world, I am not of this world.
24 I told you that you would die in
your sins, for you will die in your

world. 24 That is why I told you that you will die in your sins. And you will die in your sins if you do not believe that 'I Am Who I Am'."

25 "Who are you?" they asked him.

Jesus answered, "What I have told you from the very beginning.[8] 26 I have much to say about you, much to condemn you for. The one who sent me, however, is truthful, and I tell the world only what I have heard from him."

27 They did not understand that Jesus was talking to them about the Father. 28 So he said to them, "When you lift up the Son of Man, you will know that 'I Am Who I Am'; then you will know that I do nothing on my own authority, but I say only what the Father has instructed me to say. 29 And he who sent me is with me; he has not left me alone, because I always do what pleases him."

30 Many who heard Jesus say these things believed in him.

[8]What I have told you from the very beginning; *or* Why should I speak to you at all?

sins unless you believe that I am he." 25 They said to him, "Who are you?" Jesus said to them, "Even what I have told you from the beginning.[t] 26 I have much to say about you and much to judge; but he who sent me is true, and I declare to the world what I have heard from him." 27 They did not understand that he spoke to them of the Father. 28 So Jesus said, "When you have lifted up the Son of man, then you will know that I am he, and that I do nothing on my own authority but speak thus as the Father taught me. 29 And he who sent me is with me; he has not left me alone, for I always do what is pleasing to him." 30 As he spoke thus, many believed in him.

[t]Or *Why do I talk to you at all?*

In verse 21 Jesus resumes his dialogue with the Jews. Structurally this verse is similar to verse 12, for both introduce the discourse with the word again. Jesus begins by indicating to the Jews that he will go away, and they will die in their sins, because they cannot go where he is going (verse 21). In the previous chapter the Jews misunderstood where Jesus was going (7.35), and here again they misunderstand him (verse 22). In verses 23 and 24 Jesus stresses the importance of knowing where he has come from (verse 23) and of believing who he is (verse 24). But again the Jews do not understand who he is (verse 25); and so once more Jesus speaks to them about the Father (verse 26), but they do not recognize that he is talking to them about the Father. In verse 28 Jesus indicates that his return to the Father by way of the cross will show who he is, and that he has taught them only what he received from his Father. He closes by affirming that the Father is always with him, because he always does what pleases the Father (verse 29). As a result, many of his hearers believe in Jesus (verse 30).

The direct quotation, You Cannot Go Where I Am Going, constitutes an effective section heading for this next series of paragraphs, but in some languages the use of direct quotation may be misleading. Some persons may prefer such an expression as "The Son of Man will be lifted up" or "Jesus declares that he comes from above."

<u>8.21</u>   Again Jesus said to them, "I will go away; you
will look for me, but you will die in your sins.
You cannot go where I am going.

<u>Again Jesus said to them</u> is literally "therefore (Greek <u>oun</u>) he
said to them again." Since this verse begins a new section, TEV introduces the noun <u>Jesus</u> in place of the pronoun "he" of the Greek text.

In Jesus' statement <u>I will go away</u> (so also GeCL), the pronoun <u>I</u>
is emphatic. <u>I will go away</u> is more literally "I am going away" (NEB)
or "I go away" (RSV). As NEB and RSV indicate, the Greek text uses the
present tense, but the implication is that of a future going away,
since Jesus is not presently leaving the persons to whom he is speaking.

<u>You will die in your sins</u> (so also NAB) is literally "you will die
in your sin." The Greek text of this verse has the singular "sin," but
later (verse 24), when Jesus refers to what he has said in this verse,
the plural <u>sins</u> is used. In the present verse it seems preferable to
translate by the singular "sin," since here the focus is on the absolute sin of rejecting Jesus. It may be meaningless to translate literally
<u>you will die in your sins</u>. In some languages the closest equivalent may
be "as you continue to sin, you will die" or "you will die with all of
your sins." In some instances <u>in your sins</u> may be interpreted as a cause,
for example, "you will die since you insist on continuing to sin."

<u>Go away</u> is the same verb used in 7.33. This verb is generally used
by John to refer to the death of Jesus, by which he would return to
the Father. This same verb is translated <u>go</u> in the second part of the
verse.

In the statement <u>You cannot go where I am going</u>, the pronouns <u>you</u>
and <u>I</u> are emphatic.

<u>8.22</u>   So the Jewish authorities said, "He says that
we cannot go where he is going. Does this mean
that he will kill himself?"

<u>So</u> translates the particle <u>oun</u>, so frequently used by John (see 2.18).

<u>The Jewish authorities</u> is literally "the Jews" (see Appendix I). It
seems, however, that in the present verse a larger group than the Jewish
authorities is intended, since later (verse 30) it is stated that <u>many
who heard Jesus say these things believed in him</u>. However, it is possible
to understand that Jesus is here addressing the Jewish authorities in
particular, but that a larger group is listening and that those who believe in him are from the larger group. Our inability to define precisely
who "the Jews" are in this particular verse reflects the loose style of
John as far as temporal and locational markers are concerned. His primary
concern is to teach certain truths about Jesus, rather than to indicate
persons and places, except where such information is important to his
purpose.

<u>So the Jewish authorites said</u> must be understood as a statement
which the Jewish authorities made to one another, for example, "So the
Jewish officials said to one another" or "...said among themselves."

TEV reorders the elements in the main part of this verse. In Greek,
the question <u>Does this mean that he will kill himself?</u> comes first and is

followed by the words "because he says." These words introduce Jesus'
statement "You cannot go where I am going." TEV changes this statement
from a direct to an indirect quotation, to achieve a more natural style.
The Greek particle used to introduce the question of the Jews (mēti) is
the same one used to introduce the question in 4.29. It indicates a degree of hesitancy in the questioners; that is, they are raising the
question, though they really doubt that it is valid. Does this mean...?
may be translated "Is he trying to say?" or "Does he mean that...?" or
"Is this what his words are saying?"

8.23   Jesus answered, "You belong to this world here
        below, but I come from above. You are from this world,
        but I am not from this world.

Jesus answered is literally "and he said to them." In both sentences of this verse the pronouns you and I are emphatic.
    You belong to this world here below, but I come from above is lit-
erally "You are from below, I am from above" (RSV). In the last part of
this verse "from below" is explained as meaning from this world; it stands
in contrast to the world above, where God is. TEV makes "from below" explicit by rendering you belong to this world. The same contrast is found
in 3.31, where the words from above are contrasted with from the earth.
    In some languages it may not make sense to say "You are from here
below," for that would be saying that Jesus' listeners had come from a
place where they already were, or from a place even lower than that!
Likewise, it is almost meaningless to say "you come from this world."
What is evidently intended by Jesus is to say that, in contradistinction
to himself, the people to whom he was speaking were associated with this
world, while he himself had his true connection with heaven. The contrast
may be expressed in some languages as "You belong to this world below,
while I belong to the world above" or "...to heaven above." The contrast
may also be expressed in some languages as "you belong to this world
below, while I come from above" or "...I come from heaven." The final
statement in verse 23 may then be rendered "You belong to this world, but
I do not belong to this world."

8.24   That is why I told you that you will die in your sins.
        And you will die in your sins if you do not believe
        that 'I Am Who I Am'."

That is why I told you is more literally "therefore (Greek oun) I
told you." Since this verse lays the basis for Jesus' affirmation in
verse 23, TEV introduces it by the words That is why. NEB and NAB also
handle the text in this way.
    As indicated in the comments on verse 21, the Greek has the plural
sins here, while there it has the singular "sin." TEV translates by
sins in both places. Here the reference is not solely to the cardinal
sin of rejecting Jesus, but to the totality of sins that these people
have committed. In some languages you will die in your sins may be
rendered "You will die with your sins" or "...with your sinning."

On the meaning of the phrase I Am Who I Am, see 4.26. In this passage, as in some others in John's Gospel, the statement "I Am" is used
absolutely, without a predicate. In such instances this expression
identifies Jesus with God. The Greek order of this last sentence is the
reverse of the order in TEV ("for if you do not believe that 'I Am,'
you will die in your sins").

In some languages it is almost meaningless to say "I am who I am."
One may be obliged to say "I am really the person who I am" or "I am
the one I claim to be." Since such a translation obviously obscures the
underlying allusion, it may be necessary to introduce a marginal note
to explain the meaning which underlies the form of the Greek text.

8.25   "Who are You?" they asked him.
             Jesus answered, "What I have told you from
         the very beginning.⁸

             ⁸What I have told you from the very beginning; *or*
         Why should I speak to you at all?

Although for the believer Jesus' affirmation I Am Who I Am clearly
identifies him with God, it is not so for the unbeliever, and so the
Jews ask Who are you? The exact meaning of Jesus' reply is not clear.
The older Greek manuscripts lack punctuation and do not have spaces be-
tween words. Thus it is possible to interpret Jesus' reply in three dif-
ferent ways. Most translations, including TEV, understand it to be a
statement: What I have told you from the very beginning (NAB, RSV, JB,
Phps, Segond). Some others understand Jesus' reply to be a question:
"Why should I speak to you at all?" (TEV alternative rendering; NEB,
GeCL, Mft, RSV alternative rendering). Finally, it is possible to take
Jesus' words as an explanation: "That I should speak to you at all!"
(see Luther Revised). One important ancient Greek manuscript reads:
"I told you at the beginning what I am also telling you," and some
modern scholars believe that this reading makes the best sense in the
context.

On the whole, the context seems to lend stronger support to taking
Jesus' words as a statement. If Jesus' words are taken either as a
question or as an explanation, what he says in verse 26 seems pointless:
I have much to say about you, much to condemn you for. Moreover, the
Greek phrase translated "at all" does not mean "at all" except when used
with a negative. No absolute judgment is possible, and there is strong
scholarly opinion in support of each point of view, including the reading
of the manuscript that has the longer text.

If one interprets the response of Jesus to mean What I have told
you from the very beginning, it may be possible to translate "I am
precisely that person that from the very beginning I told you I was."
Since it may be awkward to introduce the phrase from the very beginning,
two statements may be necessary, for example, "I am that very person I
have told you I was. I have told you that from the very beginning."

8.26   I have much to say about you, much to condemn you
for. The one who sent me, however, is truthful, and
I tell the world only what I have heard from him."

The connection between the two halves of this verse is not altogether
clear, but it becomes more so, if the verb have is given the force of
"could" or "can." By including however and only in the second sentence,
TEV makes this meaning implicit, as it appears to be in other translations which introduce the second sentence by "but" (which is actually
a part of the Greek text). NAB does so by translating have as "could."
Apparently Jesus means that there are many things he could say and
judge about them, but he will not speak his own opinion; he will speak
only what he has heard from the one who sent him, and that one is truthful. It does seem more satisfactory in most languages to introduce in
the first sentence some suggestion of "can" or "could," for example,
"There is much that I could say about you and much that I could judge
concerning you." The implication of such a statement must be "but I'm
not saying that."

On the word truthful, see Appendix II.

The world in this verse is obviously the world of mankind (see 1.10).
Since these words are addressed to the people (note the plural you in
the preceeding sentence), it is necessary to indicate in some languages
that the people themselves are a part of this world, for example, "I tell
you here in this world only what I have heard from him." If this is not
done, one may assume from Jesus' statement that he could have spoken
much about those who were interrogating him, but he preferred to talk
to people in the world, that is, to others. Such a meaning must be
avoided.

Only (see also NAB, Phps, GeCL) is clearly implied by the Greek
sentence structure.

The meaning I tell (so most translations) is more natural than the
rather formal "I report to the world" (NEB).

8.27   They did not understand that Jesus was talking
to them about the Father.

Once again the Jews misunderstand Jesus' words: They did not understand that Jesus was talking to them about the Father. In many languages
one must say "he was speaking to them about his Father." However, it may
be necessary to say "his Father in heaven," in order to avoid the implication that in some way or other Jesus was talking about his reputed
father, Joseph. The use of the definite article before "Father" in the
Greek text indicates clearly that the reference is to the heavenly
Father.

8.28   So he said to them, "When you lift up the Son of Man,
you will know that 'I Am Who I Am'; then you will know
that I do nothing on my own authority, but I say only
what the Father has instructed me to say.

As in verse 22, so translates the Greek particle oun.

It is difficult to know how to translate the verb lift up. In many translations it sounds as though the Son of Man had fallen down and the people were helping him up. This same verb is used of the Son of Man in 3.14. Generally, if not always, it has a double connotation: Jesus' crucifixion and his ascension to the Father. Both in 3.14 and here the primary focus seems to be on his crucifixion, and so it may be best to translate "when you lift up the Son of Man on a cross." By making explicit the mention of the cross, the reader may miss the further implication of Jesus' exaltation to the Father. However, to translate merely lift up may leave the reader totally ignorant of either of these two meanings. Since in the context the focus is upon the cross rather than the exaltation, it is better to make that meaning explicit, for example, "to be put up on a cross," rather than for the reader to be left completely ignorant by a translation such as "lift up" or "put up."

Son of Man was discussed in 1.51.

I Am Who I Am again translates the absolute use of "I Am" in John's Gospel (see 4.26). As in verse 14, it may be necessary to translate I Am Who I Am as "I am the one who I really am" or "I am the one who I have said I am."

Jesus' words I do nothing on my own authority complements what he said in verse 26: I tell the world only what I have heard from him.

On my own authority is the same expression used in 5.30, which, along with 6.38, is parallel in meaning to this verse. It may be necessary to render it differently in some languages, for example, "whatever I do is not just because I myself want to do it" or "if I do something, it is not merely because I myself have determined to do it."

8.29   And he who sent me is with me; he has not left me
        alone, because I always do what pleases him."

He who sent me is with me may be rendered "the one who sent me accompanies me" or "...continually remains with me."

This verse is essentially the same as verse 16, except that here the qualifying statement is added, because I always do what pleases him. The phrase what pleases him may be rendered "what causes him to be happy" or "what brings him joy" or "what causes his approval."

8.30   Many who heard Jesus say these things believed
        in him.

For the first part of this verse the Greek text has "as he was saying these things." In this summary verse, as in verse 20, TEV makes the pronominal reference ("he" = Jesus) explicit for stylistic reasons. It also reverses the order of the two clauses as they appear in Greek (see RSV, for example, "As he spoke thus, many believed in him").

[275]

TEV (8.31-47) RSV

FREE MEN AND SLAVES

31 So Jesus said to those who believed in him, "If you obey my teaching, you are really my disciples; 32 you will know the truth, and the truth will set you free."

33 "We are the descendants of Abraham," they answered, "and we have never been anybody's slaves. What do you mean, then, by saying, 'You will be free'?"

34 Jesus said to them, "I am telling you the truth: everyone who sins is a slave of sin. 35 A slave does not belong to a family permanently, but a son belongs there forever. 36 If the Son sets you free, then you will be really free. 37 I know you are Abraham's descendants. Yet you are trying to kill me, because you will not accept my teaching. 38 I talk about what my Father has shown me, but you do what your father has told you."

39 They answered him, "Our father is Abraham."

"If you really were Abraham's children," Jesus replied, "you would do^t the same things that he did. 40 All I have ever done is to tell you the truth I heard from God, yet you are trying to kill me. Abraham did nothing like this! 41 You are doing what your father did."

"God himself is the only Father we have," they answered, "and we are his true sons."

42 Jesus said to them, "If God really were your Father, you would love me, because I came from God and now I am here. I did not come on my own authority, but he sent me. 43 Why do you not understand what I say? It is because you cannot bear to listen to my message. 44 You are the children of your father, the Devil, and you want to follow your father's desires. From

31 Jesus then said to the Jews who had believed in him, "If you continue in my word, you are truly my disciples, 32 and you will know the truth, and the truth will make you free." 33 They answered him, "We are descendants of Abraham, and have never been in bondage to any one. How is it that you say, 'You will be made free'?"

34 Jesus answered them, "Truly, truly, I say to you, every one who commits sin is a slave to sin. 35 The slave does not continue in the house for ever; the son continues for ever. 36 So if the Son makes you free, you will be free indeed. 37 I know that you are descendants of Abraham; yet you seek to kill me, because my word finds no place in you. 38 I speak of what I have seen with my Father, and you do what you have heard from your father."

39 They answered him, "Abraham is our father." Jesus said to them, "If you were Abraham's children, you would do what Abraham did, 40 but now you seek to kill me, a man who has told you the truth which I heard from God; this is not what Abraham did. 41 You do what your father did." They said to him, "We were not born of fornication; we have one Father, even God." 42 Jesus said to them, "If God were your Father, you would love me, for I proceeded and came forth from God; I came not of my own accord, but he sent me. 43 Why do you not understand what I say? It is because you cannot bear to hear my word. 44 You are of your father the devil, and your will is to do your father's desires. He was a murderer from the beginning, and has nothing to do with the truth, because there is no truth in him. When he lies, he

the very beginning he was a murderer and has never been on the side
of truth, because there is no truth
in him. When he tells a lie, he is
only doing what is natural to him,
because he is a liar and the father
of all lies. 45 But I tell the
truth, and that is why you do not
believe me. 46 Which one of you can
prove that I am guilty of sin? If I
tell the truth, then why do you not
believe me? 47 He who comes from
God listens to God's words. You,
however, are not from God, and that
is why you will not listen."

speaks according to his own nature,
for he is a liar and the father of
lies. 45 But, because I tell the
truth, you do not believe me. 46
Which of you convicts me of sin?
If I tell the truth, why do you
not believe me? 47 He who is of God
hears the words of God; the reason
why you do not hear them is that
you are not of God."

^{t}If you really were...you would do;
some manuscripts have If you are...
do.

Although TEV divides John 8.31-59 into two smaller sections (31-47
and 48-59), this passage is essentially one discourse centered around
the theme of Jesus and Abraham. Abraham is mentioned first in verse 33
and again in 37, 39, 40, 52, 53, 56, 57, and Jesus closes the discourse
with the affirmation Before Abraham was born, I Am (58). The entire passage, beginning with verse 31 and proceeding through verse 58, is skillfully developed along the line of the Jewish objections to what Jesus
says. Jesus affirms that if they obey his teachings they will know the
truth and the truth will set them free. His hearers object to this by
asserting that they are the descendants of Abraham and have never been
anybody's slaves (verse 33). The interpretation of verse 38 is problematic, but, on the basis of the rendering of TEV, Jesus intimates that,
although his hearers are Abraham's descendants, he is not their true father. Again they object and reply Our father is Abraham (verse 39). Jesus' judgment against them then becomes even stronger. Not only do their
actions indicate that they are not Abraham's children, but what they have
done suggests that they are children of the devil (40-41a). With extreme
hostility these men reply that they are God's true sons, perhaps intimating that Jesus himself is of illegitimate origin (see exegesis, verse
41b). Jesus now denies that they are God's children just as he denied
that they were the children of Abraham (42-43). He openly affirms that
they are the children of the Devil, since the Devil is the father of
all murderers and all liars (44). The people reject Jesus because he
tells them the truth and because he comes from God. Since they are not
from God and their father is the father of lies, they will not listen
to Jesus (45-47).

In response the people make a frontal attack against Jesus, declaring that he has a demon in him (48). Jesus denies that he has a demon,
and affirms that he honors God, his Father (49-50). He further affirms
that whoever obeys his message will never die (51). This statement makes
his antagonists certain that he has a demon (52). They interpret Jesus'
words to imply that he is superior to Abraham and the prophets who have

died (52-53). To this Jesus responds by indicating that if he denied
the truth of his relationship to God, he would be a liar, as they are
liars (54-55). At the same time he affirms his pre-existence (verse 56).
His antagonists raise a final objection, indicating that what he says
is impossible, since he is not yet fifty years old. Jesus' words are
climaxed by the affirmation Before Abraham was born, I Am (58).

It is easy to see throughout this section the developing hostility
to Jesus. At first his hearers merely deny what he says and intimate
that he is not truthful. Then in verse 41 they imply that he is of illegitimate birth, and in 48 and 52 they affirm that he has a demon in
him. Finally, their opposition to him becomes so strong that they pick
up stones to kill him (verse 59).

Verse 31 is problematic, for it indicates that in this section
Jesus was addressing himself to the Jews who believed in him. It appears
that the dialogue which follows is not between Jesus and those who believed in him, but between Jesus and the Jews who were out to kill him.
There is no really satisfactory solution to this problem. It is possible
that verse 30 was inserted as a means of dividing the discourse, and so
it was necessary to add in verse 31 a phrase introducing Jesus' words.
Whatever solution one accepts, it seems fairly certain that Jesus' words
are not such as would have been addressed to people who believed in him.

In place of the section heading, Free Men and Slaves, some translators prefer such expressions as "The truth will make you free" or "Abraham and Jesus" or "God's Son sets men free."

8.31   So Jesus said to those who believed in him,
            "If you obey my teaching, you are really my disciples;

If you obey my teaching (GeCL "if you obey my word") is literally
"If you remain in my word." NAB translates "If you live according to my
teaching," while NEB is rather high level, "If you dwell within the revelation I have brought." JB is also difficult, "If you make my word your
home." Phps translates "If you are faithful to what I have said." It is
also possible to render this expression "If you do what I have told you"
or "If you continue to practice what I have taught you."

Evidently JB and NEB attempt to retain the figure of "remaining
in," but in this context "to remain in" is equivalent to "to obey" or
"to be faithful to." Chapter 15 contains several similar expressions and
5.38 says literally "you do not have his word remaining in you." Whether
John speaks of the word remaining in the believer or the believer remaining in the word, the meaning is essentially the same.

In this context my disciples must be understood in terms of the
larger group of Jesus' followers, and one may render here "my followers"
or "my adherents."

8.32   you will know the truth, and the truth will set
            you free."

According to Jewish teaching, the truth was found in their Law, and
the study of the Law made a man free. Here the truth referred to is the

revelation of God that Jesus brings. The intention once again is to contrast the revelation Jesus brings with the Law of Moses.

In the phrase know the truth, most translators prefer to render the Greek verb know; but Mft gives it the meaning "understand," and in JB it is rendered "learn."

On truth, see Appendix II.

In many languages it is not possible to speak about "knowing the truth." Since the abstract "truth" must refer to some type of content, it is necessary to say "you will know what is true about God." Similarly, in the following clause, one may say "and what is true about God will make you free" or "...will cause you to become free." "Become free" may be understood in the sense of "be released" or "cause you to no longer be in bondage" or "...to be chained." In some languages it may be expressed "this will cause you no longer to be slaves." Such a translation fits well with the following verse.

8.33   "We are the descendants of Abraham," they answered,
         "and we have never been anybody's slaves. What do you
         mean, then, by saying, 'You will be free'?"

In Greek this verse begins with "they answered him," which appears in TEV they answered. As in verse 19, the restructuring is for the sake of English style.

We are the descendants of Abraham (so most translations) is literally "We are Abraham's seed." Anchor Bible translates "descendant from Abraham." It is true that the Greek word is singular ("seed"), and that in Galations 3.16 Paul argues on the basis of the singular "seed" that Jesus is the only real descendant of Abraham. However, the singular "seed" is sometimes used collectively in the New Testament (see Rom 9.7; 2 Cor 11.22) with the meaning "descendants." It seems oversubtle to indicate that John, like Paul in Galatians 3.16, is making a play on the singular "seed" to indicate that Jesus is the only true descendant of Abraham. We are the descendants of Abraham may be rendered "we are Abraham's children" or "We have come from the lineage of Abraham" or "Abraham was our forefather." In some languages "ancestor" is expressed as "the one who began our tribe" or "...clan."

We have never been anybody's slaves is taken by some commentators to suggest that these Jews are disclaiming that they have ever been in political subjection to any other people. This argument seems ridiculous, since the history of the Jewish nation would have been a flat denial of this affirmation, unless they interpreted political subjection not so much as a matter of their being slaves as of God's punishing them for their sins. On the other hand, it is possible to understand their affirmation in reference to an assumed inner freedom. That is, though they had been enslaved by other nations at various times in their history, they had never really lost their freedom of soul and of life. Whatever the background of their affirmation, Jesus' argument in the following verses indicates that the Jews were in fact "spiritual slaves," since they were in slavery to sin (see verse 34), and once again his hearers miss the point of what he is saying.

In languages in which there is no technical term for "slave," or in which such a term may be inappropriate, it is possible to say "we have never been completely dominated by anyone" or "no one has ever controlled us completely." This meaning may even be expressed idiomatically as "we have never completely bowed our hearts to anyone" or "we have not made our hearts the slaves of anyone."

8.34   Jesus said to them, "I am telling you the truth; everyone who sins is a slave of sin.

Some Greek manuscripts omit the words of sin, but the UBS Committee on the Greek text judges that these words are a part of the original text, though rating their decision a "C" choice. The phrase was perhaps omitted from some ancient manuscripts in an attempt by a scribe to make a stylistic improvement, since the omission would place the two mentions of a slave closer together. Mft, Phps, and NEB omit of sin. Whether or not this phrase was an original part of the text, its meaning is implied. In some translations it may have to be necessary to say explicitly that the slavery to which Christ refers is slavery to sin.

It may be difficult in some languages to speak of "a slave of sin." If so, such an expression as "just like a slave obeying sin" may be employed. However, to do so requires personification of "sin." It is more likely that one can translate "a slave to his desire to sin" or "a slave controlled by his desires to sin."

8.35   A slave does not belong to a family permanently, but a son belongs there forever.

The relation of this verse to the context is not at all clear. Some believe it is a parenthetical insertion, since the slave of verse 34 is quite different from the slave mentioned in this verse. NAB places it in curved brackets, indicating that it is a parenthetical statement. However, it is possible to see a relation between this verse and the total context. In verse 33 a discussion regarding the descendants of Abraham was initiated, and this recalls Genesis 21.10 (see Gal 4.30). Isaac remains a member of the household, while Ishmael, who was born of a slave woman, is driven out. The Jews claim to be the true sons of Abraham, while in fact they are the sons of sin, and so have lost their status as sons. In this brief parable, then, the Jews are spoken of as a slave, while Christ is referred to as the son, as elsewhere in John's Gospel. By their rejection of the son, the Jews have lost their status in God's household, but the son will remain there forever.

The verb belong to is literally "remains in," the same verb discussed in verse 31.

In some languages it may not make sense to say A slave does not belong to a family. He has his own family, of course, but what is involved here is the household he serves. Therefore one may translate "A slave does not continue as a permanent member of a household" or "...may not necessarily continue as a member of a household."

The final clause may then be translated "but a son is always a member of such a household." In some languages, however, it is not possible

to say "a son." Such a person must be in a possessed relationship to
someone. Therefore one may have to say "a man's son always belongs to
the father's household" or "...the father's family" or in some languages,
"...his parents' family." There are, of course, certain problems involved
in such expressions, particularly in matrilineal societies, where it
would be necessary to speak of "a son belonging to his mother's family."

8.36   If the Son sets you free, then you will be really
        free.

The If clause in this verse relates back to verse 34. NEB translates the Greek particle introducing this verse "If then" and NAB
"That is why, if."
    The Jews considered themselves free, but they were not really free;
real freedom comes only as the Son makes one free. GeCL translates the
Son as the Son of God, making explicit for its readers what TEV and
other translations try to achieve by capitalizing the word Son. To do
so is translationally legitimate, and it may be an especially helpful
device to German readers, since all nouns, without distinction, are
capitalized in German. In some languages it is necessary to employ the
phrase "God's Son," since the kinship term "Son" must be possessed.
    The adverb really of this verse (ontōs), though not the same as the
one used in verse 31 (alēthōs), is synonymous in meaning.

8.37   I know you are Abraham's descendants. Yet you are
        trying to kill me, because you will not accept my
        teaching.

I know you are Abraham's descendants may be equivalent to "I recognize that you are Abraham's descendants" or "...that you have descended
from Abraham" or "...that Abraham was your ancestor."
    In the expression you are trying to kill me, the pronoun you in-
cludes all the persons Jesus is addressing; Phps tries either to soften
the words of Jesus or to make this verse fit with verse 31 by rendering
"some of you," but this distinction has no basis in the Greek text.
    Because you will not accept my teaching is more literally "because
my word finds no place in you" (RSV). NEB translates "because my teaching makes no headway with you" (see Mft); JB "because nothing I say has
penetrated into you"; and NAB "because my word finds no hearing among
you." To speak of a word or a teaching as not "having room" in someone
is simply another way of saying that that person will not accept the
word or the teaching. The restructuring of TEV is an attempt to simplify
this rather difficult Greek construction.
    Because you will not accept my teaching may be rendered "because
you will not believe what I have taught you" or "because you will not
follow what I have taught." One may in some languages translate "...obey
what I have taught."

8.38   I talk about what my Father has shown me, but you
                do what your father has told you.

In Greek the pronouns I and you are in focus.

I talk about what my Father has shown me is more literally "I talk about what I have seen with the Father." NEB translates "I am revealing in words what I saw in my Father's presence"; JB has "What I, for my part, speak of is what I have seen with my Father." There is no problem in translating "the Father" as my Father. It is done by TEV, NEB, JB, and GeCL, and in this context, "the Father" obviously means my Father. TEV attempts to make this verse easier for its readers to understand by following several other translational techniques. First, it reverses the Greek order of the clauses what my Father has shown me and I talk about, to achieve a more natural English sentence structure. Second, it takes the Greek expression "what I have seen with the Father" to mean what my Father has shown me. Thus TEV takes the phrase "with the Father" (NEB "in my Father's presence") to have the force of agency, or means. The subject of this clause in Greek ("I") can be shifted into the object position in English (TEV me), and my Father can be made into the subject of the clause by the use of a causative verb (TEV has shown), in place of the simple verb ("have seen") of the Greek text. The only problem in doing so is that, in the Greek text, the focus is more on "what I have seen" than on what my Father has shown. It may be argued that TEV is here reading an alternative Greek text ("from the Father"), on the basis of which one could more easily support its exegesis of this verse, but that is not really so.

Two observations are necessary regarding the clause but you do what your father has told you. (1) The verb which TEV translates as an indicative (you do) may also be taken as an imperative ("do"), since the form would be the same in Greek. (2) The phrase your father is literally "the father"; it may mean either "the father" in an absolute sense (="God the Father") as in the first half of the verse, or as the father of the Jews (your father = "the Devil"). It is possible to translate the verb as an imperative and combine it with the interpretation that "the father" refers to God: "Do what God the Father has told you." TEV takes the other possible combination (indicative plus reference to the father of the Jews = "the Devil"); most other modern translations agree with this interpretation (for example, NEB, NAB, JB, Mft, Phps, Segond, Luther Revised, GeCL).

The perfect tense of the verb (Greek "I have seen"; TEV my Father has shown) and the phrase "with my father" both imply a pre-existent knowledge possessed by Jesus which continues into the present. This is contrasted with the aorist verb (Greek you "heard"; TEV has told) which would refer to some moment in history, either to the giving of the Law through Moses or the proclamation of God's truth through Jesus Christ. However, most translators seem to prefer to make no distinction between the tense of these verbs, rendering both in the perfect tense.

8.39   They answered him, "Our father is Abraham."
             "If you really were Abraham's children," Jesus
         replied, "you would do[t] the same things that he did.

         [t]If you really were...you would do; *some manuscripts have*
         If you are...do.

They answered him is literally "they answered and said to him," reflecting a Semitic Greek style that is redundant in English.

Our father is Abraham must be rendered in some languages as "our forefather is Abraham" or, possibly, "our forefather was Abraham." Since, however, the term Abraham might be understood as the given information, the components of this equational sentence may be reversed in some languages as "Abraham was our forefather."

In Greek, conditional clauses ("if" clauses) may be so stated as to indicate that the condition is either true or is contrary to fact. Sometimes these clauses are greatly mixed with the result that an even greater vividness is achieved, as in the Greek text followed by TEV. Here the Greek conditional sentence is of a "mixed" type, so that the force is If you really were Abraham's children, rather than simply "if you were Abraham's children." Two important Greek manuscripts have an imperative in the conclusion of this if clause, which results in the reading, "If you are Abraham's children, do the same works that he did." Mft accepts the imperative as the better choice of text, and this possibility is given by TEV and NEB in a footnote as an alternative rendering. However, it is more logical to assume that the imperative was introduced by ancient scribes who attempted to do away with the grammatical difficulties of the mixed type of conditional clause. For this reason the UBS Committee on the Greek text gives its primary support to the reading followed by TEV, though evaluating their choice as "C," indicating considerable doubt regarding the original reading of the text.

To indicate clearly that a condition is contrary to fact, it may be necessary in some languages to employ a supplementary clause, for example, "If you were Abraham's children--and obviously you are not--you would do the same things that he did."

You would do the same things that he did may be translated "you would work in the same way that he did" or "you would behave as he behaved." It is obviously necessary in this type of expression to avoid a term which would apply merely to physical labor. Customary behavior, rather than physical labor, is meant in this context.

8.40   All I have ever done is to tell you the truth I heard
              from God, yet you are trying to kill me. Abraham did
              nothing like this!

For a literal translation of this verse, see RSV: "but now you seek to kill me, a man who has told you the truth which I heard from God; this is not what Abraham did." TEV restructures this verse by inverting the order of the first two clauses; thus the clause "but now you seek to kill me" is placed immediately before the statement "this is not what Abraham did." Without this restructuring, the text may be ambiguous; the reader could possibly connect "a man who has told you the truth which I heard from God" with the clause "this is not what Abraham did."

In TEV Jesus refers to himself in the first person throughout this verse, while in the Greek text he refers to himself in the third person ("a man who has told you the truth") and in the first person ("which I heard from God"). It is common in Hebrew, and so in the Greek influenced by Hebrew grammatical style, to shift from third to first person in the same discourse, when referring to the same individual. However, to do so is not natural in English, and TEV restructures the sentence to achieve a smoother and more understandable English style.

Finally, in Greek the verb "have told" is in the perfect tense, indicating that Jesus had been and was continuing to tell the truth that he heard from God. TEV therefore translates All I have ever done is to tell.

The truth I heard from God must be rendered in some languages "the true words which I heard from God" or "the true words which God told me."

In the last sentence of this verse the demonstrative pronoun this refers back to the totality of the verse, indicating that Abraham never tried to kill anyone who spoke to him the truth that had come from God. Abraham did nothing like this! may be rendered in some languages "Abraham never behaved that way" or "Abraham never acted in such a manner."

8.41   You are doing what your father did."
            "God himself is the only Father we have," they
            answered, "and we are his true sons."

Your father is obviously a reference to the Devil, (verse 44), but it is better not to make this information explicit until it is done so in the Greek text.

TEV inverts the order of the last two clauses of this verse. God himself is the only Father we have is obviously the meaning of the Greek "we have one Father, God." NEB translates "God is our father, and God alone." One may also render this expression "our only father is God" or "God alone is our father" or "we do not have another father; God is our father."

We are his true sons is literally "We were not born of fornication." Since the word "fornication" is not commonly used in English, TEV and most other modern translations avoid its use. The force of what these Jews are saying is expressed vividly by Mft, "We are no bastards." Phps is also accurate, "We are not illegitimate"; NAB has "We are no illegitimate breed!" JB translates "We were not born of prostitution." It is difficult to imagine men in the heat of agrument saying "We are not base-born" (NEB). TEV simply changes the Greek negative statement ("We are not...") into a positive one (We are his true sons). One may also say "We are his real sons." In expressing the statement negatively, some languages may employ an idiom. Instead of "We are not bastards," they may say "We are not secret children" (that is, children that one doesn't speak about). Other languages may have such expressions as "We are not refused children" or "We are not children from other women."

These antagonists may be making an insinuation about Jesus himself; in affirming that they are not illegitimate, they may be suggesting that he is. In the Greek clause "We were not born of fornication" the pronoun we is emphatic, suggesting a contrast between themselves and Jesus. ("We were not born of fornication, but you were.") Many commentators tend to feel that such a barb is intended.

8.42   Jesus said to them, "If God really were your
         Father, you would love me, because I came from God
         and now I am here. I did not come on my own authority,
         but he sent me.

It is obvious that Jesus' words If God really were your Father are
intended to affirm that God is not their father. They are not Abraham's
true children, because they do not do the same works that Abraham did;
and they are not God's true children, because they do not love the one
who has come from God. This contrary-to-fact condition, If God really
were your Father, you would love me, must be expressed in some languages
by negative supplementary statements, for example, "If God is your father,
but he isn't, you will love me, but you do not." In this type of context,
the receptor language's equivalent of love is likely to be a term which
would reflect love between members of a family. If such a term is not
appropriate, an expression indicating "deep appreciation for" may be
satisfactory.

I came from God (JB "I have come here from God"; Phps "For I came
from God") is best taken as a reference to the coming of Jesus into the
world, since the verb came is in the aorist tense, pointing to a specific
moment in time. Some theologians see in Jesus' words a statement regarding
the internal life of the Trinity and this idea seems to be the basis for
NEB ("God is the source of my being"). However, this interpretation reads
too much into the passage. It fails to take account of the aorist tense,
often used in John's Gospel to refer to the mission of the Son, either of
his coming into the world or of God's sending him into the world.

I came from God and now I am here actually expresses one idea, and
so Mft translates "for I came here from God." Even though the two verbs
(came...am here) are closely related in meaning, most translations, like
TEV, render them separately, rather than combine them, as Mft does. I
came refers to the Son's initial moment of coming into the world, and
I am here focuses attention on his presence with his hearers at the moment that he is speaking. The latter verb is used in pagan sources to
describe the arrival of a divine prophet, or even the manifestation of a
god himself.

On my own authority (see 5.30) is emphatic, and it is set in opposition to the pronoun he (Greek literally "that one"), which is also in
the emphatic position.

I did not come on my own authority may be rendered in some languages "The decision for me to come was not mine" or "I was not the
one who decided that I should come." Under such circumstances the final
clause but he sent me may be rendered "but my Father was the one who
sent me."

8.43   Why do you not understand what I say? It is because
         you cannot bear to listen to my message.

In Greek there is a definite contrast between what I say (lalia) and
my message (logos). The first focuses attention on the audible or spoken
word, while the second emphasizes the meaning or the message involved in
these words. Phps translates the first "my words" and the second "what

I am saying." NEB attempts to make the same distinction, though at a rather high level of speech: "Why do you not understand my language? It is because my revelation is beyond your grasp."

The verb rendered cannot bear in TEV (so also RSV, NAB) is literally "unable to hear" (Phps "cannot hear"). The question is whether the verb "to hear" has the force of "to grasp" (NEB "beyond your grasp"; JB "cannot take in") or "to listen to" (Mft "unable to listen to"). Most translations, including TEV, prefer the latter meaning. That is, the focus is on the unwillingness of these people to accept Jesus' message, rather than on their inability to understand its meaning. Though the Greek text literally says "you are not able to hear my message," there was obviously nothing wrong with the people's hearing or even with their capacity to listen. It was their fundamental unwillingness to accept the message which prevented their understanding what Jesus was talking about. Therefore, in many languages you cannot bear to listen to my message may be rendered "you refuse to listen to my message."

<u>8.44</u>   You are the children of your father, the Devil, and you want to follow your father's desires. From the very beginning he was a murderer and has never been on the side of truth, because there is no truth in him. When he tells a lie, he is only doing what is natural to him, because he is a liar and the father of all lies.

You are the children of your father, the Devil is literally "You are of your father, the Devil." It is obvious that the expression "of your father, the Devil" means the children of your father, the Devil. Phps and NEB both translate "Your father is the devil" (JB "The devil is your father"). It is best to translate as TEV does, since the pronoun you is emphatic in the Greek sentence structure.

Underlying the expression the children of your father is the concept that a son partakes of the characteristics of his parents, especially of the father; but this concept may be utterly lost in some languages. In fact, it may be preferable to shift the focus and say "the Devil himself is your father." In other languages it may be better to indicate likeness by saying "you are just like your father, the Devil."

And you want to follow your father's desires is literally "And you are willing to do the desires of your father." In some languages this clause may be rendered "and you like to do the same things your father likes to do."

In some languages it is difficult to speak of from the very beginning without indicating precisely what began. At the same time, one should not use a translation of from the very beginning which would suggest the eternal existence of the Devil. The closest equivalent in many languages is "he has always been a murderer" or, in some languages, "...one who destroys people" or "...one who kills people."

And has never been on the side of truth is more literally "And he was not standing (some Greek manuscripts, "has not stood") in the truth." On truth, see Appendex II. The UBS Committee on the Greek text indicates

that there is a high degree of doubt concerning the reading selected
for the text, and it is almost impossible to determine which of the
two Greek texts the various translations follow. However, the meaning
comes out essentially the same,whether the imperfect ("was not standing";
"did not stand") or the perfect ("has not stood") is followed. RSV translates this clause "and has nothing to do with the truth"; NEB "and is not
rooted in the truth"; JB "he was never grounded in the truth"; and Mft
"he has no place in the truth." In some languages one may say "he has
never encouraged that which is true" or "he has never favored that which
is true."

Because there is no truth in him is essentially the same translation
as a number of others (see RSV, NEB, JB). Phps changes the focus considerably by rendering "since the truth will have nothing to do with him."
The purpose of this verse is to indicate that God and truth are one, and
that the Devil has no relation with God because he has nothing in common
with truth. In some languages because there is no truth in him may be
rendered "because he has never spoken the truth" or "because he has never
said that which is true."

Jesus' judgment against the Devil proceeds a step further. He has
already affirmed that the Devil has nothing in common with truth, and
now he declares that it is the Devil's very nature to lie. TEV (he is
only doing what is natural to him), RSV ("he speaks according to his
own nature"), Mft ("he is expressing his own nature"), and Phps ("he
speaks in character") all express, at various levels of language, the
same meaning. NEB ("he is speaking his own language"), JB ("he is drawing on his own store"), and NAB ("Lying speech is his native tongue")
make it difficult for the reader to see immediately what Jesus is talking about. It is not that these translations miss the point, but rather
that they fail to communicate clearly and readily the meaning of Jesus'
words. In some languages the closest equivalent of the clauses When he
tells a lie he is only doing what is natural to him may be best expressed
in a single clause, for example, "because of his own character he habitually lies." One may, of course, also translate "Whenever he tells
a lie, he is only behaving in accordance with his own character" or
"...he is true to his own heart" or "...he is speaking from his own
heart."

Because he is a liar and the father of all lies is literally "because
he is a liar and the father of it (him)." As the literal rendering of
this clause indicates, the phrase translated of all lies by TEV may
be taken either as neuter ("of it") or as masculine ("of him"). If it
is taken as masculine, the meaning is "the father of all liars." Most
translators take this phrase to be neuter, and so translate "the father
of lies." In most languages it is easy enough to say "he is the father
of all liars," but difficult to say "he is the father of lies." One can,
of course, say "he is the one who causes people to lie" or "he is the
one who prompts lies," but this translation loses the figure of speech
involved in the use of "father."

8.45   But I tell the truth, and that is why you do not
            believe me.

8.45

In the clause I tell the truth the pronoun I is emphatic. Jesus
declares that these people to whom he speaks are not children of Abraham or children of God; rather they are children of the Devil, the
source of all lies, and so they cannot believe the truth when they hear
it.

The phrase believe me must be taken with the meaning "to believe
what I say" rather than "to have faith in me."

8.46   Which one of you can prove that I am guilty of sin?
           If I tell the truth, then why do you not believe me?

The verb prove...guilty is translated "convict" by most translators.
When used with a personal object, the verb basically means "to show
(somebody) up for what he is." Here the personal object is "me," which
is followed by the phrase "concerning sin," and so the entire expression
means "to show that I am guilty of sin." This meaning is also conveyed
by such a translation as "convict me of sin," but this expression may
prove ambiguous to the average reader. NEB reads "convicts me of sin"
in its footnote, but in the text it has "can prove me in the wrong."
The question is whether Jesus is claiming to be sinless in an absolute
sense, or that he is right in what he is saying in this particular controversy. Although either viewpoint is justified by the context, John
could have expressed himself more clearly and unambiguously if he had
intended the second meaning. The word sin seems to be used here as it
is used elsewhere in John's Gospel, and not merely in the sense of "to
be in the wrong." This opinion is evidently held by most commentators
and translators.

Believe me has the same force here as in the previous verse.

8.47   He who comes from God listens to God's words. You,
           however, are not from God, and that is why you will
           not listen."

These men who oppose Jesus do not come from God, and so they do
not listen to God's words (see verses 42-43).

The last sentence of this verse reads literally "because of this
you do not listen, because you are not from God." TEV and NEB invert the
order of the two clauses to attain a more natural English structure.
NEB reads "You are not God's children; that is why you do not listen."
You will not listen is literally "you do not listen," but it is obvious that the idea of willfulness is involved (note JB "if you refuse
to listen").

In this context listen must be understood in the sense of "pay
heed to." It is not merely a matter of hearing what is said but of responding positively to it. One may translate therefore this passage "The
one who comes from God pays attention to what God has said; but you are
not from God, and that is why you refuse to pay attention."

TEV   (8.48-59)   RSV

JESUS AND ABRAHAM

48 They asked Jesus, "Were we not right in saying that you are a Samaritan and have a demon in you?"

49 "I have no demon," Jesus answered. "I honor my Father, but you dishonor me. 50 I am not seeking honor for myself. But there is one who is seeking it and who judges in my favor. 51 I am telling you the truth: whoever obeys my teaching will never die."

52 They said to him, "Now we know for sure that you have a demon! Abraham died, and the prophets died, yet you say that whoever obeys your teaching will never die. 53 Our father Abraham died; you do not claim to be greater than Abraham, do you? And the prophets also died. Who do you think you are?"

54 Jesus answered, "If I were to honor myself, that honor would be worth nothing. The one who honors me is my Father--the very one you say is your God. 55 You have never known him, but I know him. If I were to say that I do not know him, I would be a liar like you. But I do know him, and I obey his word. 56 Your father Abraham rejoiced that he was to see the time of my coming; he saw it and was glad."

57 They said to him, "You are not even fifty years old--and you have seen Abraham?"*u*

58 "I am telling you the truth," Jesus replied. "Before Abraham was born, 'I Am'."

59 Then they picked up stones to throw at him, but Jesus hid himself and left the Temple.

*u*you have seen Abraham?; *some manuscripts have* has Abraham seen you?

48 The Jews answered him, "Are we not right in saying that you are a Samaritan and have a demon?" 49 Jesus answered, "I have not a demon; but I honor my Father, and you dishonor me. 50 Yet I do not seek my own glory; there is One who seeks it and he will be the judge. 51 Truly, truly, I say to you, if any one keeps my word, he will never see death." 52 The Jews said to him, "Now we know that you have a demon. Abraham died, as did the prophets; and you say, 'If any one keeps my word, he will never taste death.' 53 Are you greater than our father Abraham, who died? And the prophets died! Who do you claim to be?" 54 Jesus answered, "If I glorify myself, my glory is nothing; it is my Father who glorifies me, of whom you say that he is your God. 55 But you have not known him; I know him. If I said, I do not know him, I should be a liar like you; but I do know him and I keep his word. 56 Your father Abraham rejoiced that he was to see my day; he saw it and was glad." 57 The Jews then said to him, "You are not yet fifty years old, and have you seen Abraham?"*u* 58 Jesus said to them, "Truly, truly, I say to you, before Abraham was, I am." 59 So they took up stones to throw at him; but Jesus hid himself, and went out of the temple.

*u*Other ancient authorities read *has Abraham seen you?*

The analysis of verses 48-50 is given in the analysis of verses 31-34; see there.

The section heading, Jesus and Abraham, is appropriate in some languages, but in others the use of the conjunction "and" may suggest that Jesus and Abraham together did something--which, of course, is not the meaning intended. It is possible to use such a heading as "Jesus existed before Abraham" or simply "Some Jews denounce Jesus."

8.48   They asked Jesus, "Were we not right in
        saying that you are a Samaritan and have a
        demon in you?"

They asked Jesus is literally "The Jews answered and said to him." Since a new section begins here, TEV makes clear that the pronoun "him" refers to Jesus, and on stylistic grounds the Semitic redundancy "answered and said" is reduced to asked.

The question raised by Jesus' antagonists indicated that they assume the answer is "Yes." It is a rhetorical question and in some languages may be made a strong declarative statement, for example, "We were certainly right when we said that you are a Samaritan and have a demon in you."

It is not known precisely what is meant by the accusation that Jesus was a Samaritan. Some commentators believe that it indicates that his accusers thought Jesus was heretical, while others believe it is the equivalent to the accusation that he was demon-possessed. The second of these two judgments is probably the true one, especially in light of the fact that only the charge of being demon-possessed is replied to by Jesus (verse 49).

You...have a demon in you is literally "you have a demon" (so RSV). JB translates the accusation "possessed by a devil" (GeCL "possessed by an evil spirit") and Jesus' answer "I am not possessed." Mft renders the charge "you are mad" (see also Phps). NAB translates the whole accusation "you are a Samaritan, and possessed besides." To translate "you are mad" fails to convey the proper cultural impact, since in biblical times the Jews believed that madness and insanity were brought on by demon possession. JB makes clear that demon possession was the charge brought against Jesus, and this information is implicit in the way Jesus' answer to the accusation is structured. It is possible that a reader of NEB might fail to understand what is indicated by the accusation "you are possessed." It is important that the aspect of demon possession be made clear for the reader, since this belief was an essential part of the cultural situation of Jesus' day.

As already noted, different languages refer to demon possession in different ways, for example, "he is commanded by a demon," "a demon controls him," "a demon marches inside of him," or "a demon occupies his heart."

8.49   "I have no demon," Jesus answered. "I honor
        my Father, but you dishonor me.

In this verse Jesus replies to the accusation that he is demon-possessed. He says that this charge cannot be true, because he honors the Father. Then Jesus brings a charge against his opponents (but you dishonor me), which implies that by dishonoring him, they have dishonored the Father. JB may suggest that they are not yet dishonoring Jesus ("but you want to dishonour me"). Some commentators believe that the verb dishonor more nearly means "you fail to respect me" (NAB) or "you fail to honor me" (Anchor Bible). It is true that his antagonists fail to give proper honor to Jesus as God's only Son, but in the present context they also dishonor him by accusing him of being demon-possessed. It is not merely something they would like to do, as JB suggests, but something they are actually in the act of doing.

In some languages honor is often expressed in terms of "praise," for example, "I cause my father to be praised." The final clause in this verse would then be translated "but you speak against me" or "say disgraceful things about me."

8.50   I am not seeking honor for myself. But there
        is one who is seeking it and who judges in my
        favor.

I am not seeking honor for myself may be rendered "I am not trying to cause myself to be praised" or "I am not seeking to have people praise me" or "I am not asking people to honor me."

The second sentence of this verse is literally "there is one seeking and judging," and the one referred to is God the Father. It is obvious that the understood object of the verb seeking is Jesus' honor, referred to in the first half of this verse, and most modern translations make this reference explicit. What is meant by the verb judges is more difficult. Most translations are fairly literal at this point, though Phps renders "he is the true judge" and JB "and is the judge of it" (that is, of Jesus' glory). TEV understands it to mean judges in my favor. The meaning appears to be that God judges fairly by giving Jesus the honor due to him and by condemning those who refuse to give him proper honor. The entire verse appears in GeCL as "I seek no honor for myself. Another seeks it, and he is the judge." But there is one who is seeking it may be expressed as "there is someone else who seeks to have me praised" or "...desires that I should be honored."

The final expression, judges in my favor, may be rendered "decides in my favor" or "judges advantageously to me." Or it may be possible to say "he is the one who judges rightly." Such a translation suggests, of course, that God's judgment is correct in finally assigning honor to Jesus.

8.51   I am telling you the truth: whoever obeys my
        teaching will never die."

The thoughts of this verse are similar to those in 5.24; 6.40,47; and 11.25. Obeys my teaching (so also NEB) is literally "keeps my word" (JB). It may be translated in some languages "does what I teach him to do," "behaves in accordance with what I have taught," or even "does what I have told him."

Will never die is literally "will never see death" (JB). When these Jews take up Jesus' words in the next verse, they change the metaphor somewhat by saying "will never taste death" (RSV). "To see death" and "to taste death" are both idiomatic expressions meaning "to die"; "To see death" is a Hebraism, but the expression "to taste death" is not found in the Old Testament. However, it is found in other places in the New Testament (see Heb 2.9, for example). The death referred to in this verse is spiritual death, a fact which is misunderstood by Jesus' opponents in the following dialogue.

In most languages one cannot preserve the literal idioms "to see death" and "to taste death." "To see death" has sometimes been understood as "to see dead bodies." Even worse, "to taste death" has been taken to mean "to eat a corpse" or "to partake of human flesh." The translation will never die can lead to misinterpretation (especially if such a verse is completely isolated from its context). However, this bold figure of speech used by Jesus must be understood in terms of its wider context, which ultimately serves as a basis for understanding what he has said. Unless this expression is translated rather literally, it will be impossible for the reader to comprehend the reactions of Jesus' opponents mentioned in the following verse.

8.52   They said to him, "Now we know for sure that you have a demon! Abraham died, and the prophets died, yet you say that whoever obeys your teaching will never die.

Again Jesus' antagonists take his words as a reference to physical death, and so their conviction that Jesus has a demon becomes stronger. We know for sure is literally "we have known" (a perfect tense in Greek), which carries the implication of strong assurance. JB renders these words "Now we know for certain that you are possessed" (NEB "Now we are certain..."). Mft translates "Now we are sure you are mad."

Whoever obeys your teaching is literally "if anyone obeys your teaching message," a form which may be retained in some languages.

8.53   Our father Abraham died; you do not claim to be greater than Abraham, do you? And the prophets also died. Who do you think you are?"

Some ancient manuscripts omit Our father, probably because these words contradict what was said in verse 44 (you are the children of your father, the Devil). The UBS Committee includes these words, but they rate their decision a "C" choice. In the present context our father seems to be the more difficult reading, and there is no apparent reason why an ancient scribe would have included the phrase had it not been in the original text. On the other hand, if the words were not originally a part of the text, they may have been added on the basis of your father Abraham in verse 56.

Our father Abraham died; you do not claim to be greater than Abraham, do you? is literally "Are you greater than our father Abraham, who died?" In Greek this sentence is so constructed as to expect the answer "No." This emphatic rhetorical question can be shifted into an exclamation in some languages, for example, "How can you say that you are greater than Abraham!"

To be greater than Abraham may be expressed in some languages as "surpass Abraham in importance." In others the comparison may be expressed "that you are great and that Abraham is not great." This positive-negative distinction does not imply that Abraham was not great, but simply that the person identified in the positive statement is greater than the one mentioned in the negative statement.

And the prophets also died seems to have little relation to the context; it comes almost as an afterthought.

Who do you think you are? is translated "Who do you claim to be?" by Mft and RSV (see JB "Who are you claiming to be?") and "What do you claim to be?" by NEB.

8.54   Jesus answered, "If I were to honor myself, that honor would be worth nothing. The one who honors me is my Father--the very one you say is your God.

Jesus' answer to his opponents indicates that he is not trying to honor himself; if he were, that honor would be worth nothing. The verb translated to honor and the noun rendered honor are literally "to glorify" and "glory." Both are used in a variety of ways in John's Gospel. In the present context the idea of "to bring honor to" and "honor" are perhaps the nearest English equivalents. The closest equivalent of honor in some languages may be "praise" or "causing praise." The response of Jesus may then be translated "If I were merely praising myself, such praise would be worth nothing."

Worth nothing is literally "nothing"; NEB translates "worthless." This expression may be rendered in some instances "would have no value at all" or "would not equal the smallest coin."

Some ancient Greek manuscripts read your God, using indirect discourse, while others read "our God," using direct discourse. TEV uses indirect discourse (the very one you say is your God); NEB uses direct discourse ("he of whom you say, 'He is our God'"). Although the Greek manuscripts vary between indirect and direct discourse, there is no difference in meaning. The translator should use the structure that is natural for the language into which he is translating.

The very one you say is your God is equivalent in some languages to "he is the same one that you say is your God" or "he is the same one you claim as your God" or "...you address as God."

8.55   You have never known him, but I know him. If I were to say that I do not know him, I would be a liar like you. But I do know him, and I obey his word.

Two different Greek verbs are translated known and know in this

[293]

verse, though they are used synonomously. Compare, for example, 7.28-29 (you do not know him, but I know him), which uses the second (oida) of these verbs twice, with 10.15 (The Father knows me and I know the Father), which uses the first (ginōskō) of these verbs twice. Both verbs also occur here in the perfect tense, but the verb oida, though perfect in form, has a present meaning. This explains the basis for TEV: have...known and know.

But I do know him, and I obey his word indicates that, according to the theology of John's Gospel, obedience is an essential part in "knowing God." In fact, this teaching is a basic affirmation of the Old and New Testaments alike. To know God means that one follows him in faithful obedience. In 15.10 and 17.6 obedience is again stressed as an important element in this relation.

As the result of this distinctive meaning of the verb know in biblical contexts, it is important to avoid a receptor language term which will merely suggest "knowledge about." The emphasis is upon "personal acquaintance with" or direct involvement in an interpersonal relation. This type of context requires a term for "know" which will suggest the most intimate interpersonal acquaintance and involvement.

8.56   Your father Abraham rejoiced that he was to see
        the time of my coming; he saw it and was glad."

The verb translated rejoiced is a strong verb; it appears only here and in 5.35 in John's Gospel. In 5.35 the phrase is literally "to rejoice in his light," and TEV translates it to enjoy his light.

That he was to see the time of my coming gives the reason for Abraham's rejoicing. The time of my coming (GeCL "my coming") is literally "my day," which is the rendering used by most translations. This expression, however, is either meaningless or misleading in many languages, and translators are therefore advised to follow TEV.

He saw it may be rendered "he saw that event" or "he foresaw my coming."

8.57   They said to him, "You are not even fifty years
        old--and you have seen Abraham?"ᵘ

        ᵘyou have seen Abraham?; some manuscripts have has
        Abraham seen you?

In some Greek manuscripts you have seen Abraham is "Abraham has seen you," which probably represents a scribe's attempt to harmonize the Jews' question with Jesus' statement of verse 56, he saw it. The reading followed by TEV has the best manuscript support, and it is more natural in the context. Because the Jews assumed that Abraham is superior to Jesus (verse 53), they would more naturally speak of Jesus as seeing Abraham than of Abraham as seeing Jesus. Most modern translations are based upon the Greek text followed by TEV. Mft and Phps base their translations on the alternative Greek text.

In some languages it may be necessary to modify the exclamatory

question you have seen Abraham? One may translate, for example, "You
are not even fifty years old yet; therefore how can you say you have
seen Abraham?" or "...how is it possible that you have seen Abraham?"

8.58   "I am telling you the truth," Jesus replied.
          "Before Abraham was born, 'I Am'."

Jesus replied is literally "Jesus said to them."
The verb translated was born (so also NEB, Mft) may have the general sense of "come into being" (NAB "before Abraham came to be"; RSV
"before Abraham was"). It is the same verb used in 1.3 (see there).
In the present context the more specific sense of "to be born" is "to
be preferred." The passive expression was born may be modified in some
languages as "before Abraham's mother gave birth to him." However, it is
better in many instances to translate "before Abraham existed."
Here again I Am is used in the absolute sense in which it identifies
Jesus with God the Father. The same distinction is made in this verse
between Jesus and Abraham as was made in the prologue between the Word
and the created order (John 1.1-2).
In many languages it is impossible to preserve the expression I Am
in this type of context, for the present tense of the verb "to be" would
be meaningless. To make sense, one must say "Before Abraham existed, I
existed" or "...I have existed." It may be useful to introduce a marginal
note calling attention to the special form of the Greek text and its relation to other passages containing I Am.

8.59   Then they picked up stones to throw at him,
          but Jesus hid himself and left the Temple.

They refers back to those who believed in him (verse 36).
Since this scene takes place in the Temple area, it is possible
that the stones referred to were building stones, intended for use in
the Temple Herod was having constructed. In 10.31 the people again pick
up stones to throw at Jesus, on the accusation that he had made himself
equal with God, a charge they equate with blasphemy (verse 33). Here
the people's reaction is prompted by Jesus' use of the divine name I Am
(verse 58), which also would have been interpreted by them as blasphemy,
though the charge is not explicitly stated.
Hid himself (many translations) is most probably the meaning of the
Greek text, rather than "was not to be seen" (NEB; Phps "disappeared"),
which seems to suggest a miracle and at the same time may represent an
attempt to avoid making Jesus look cowardly by hiding himself. A few
ancient Greek manuscripts expand the text at this point by the additional
statement "he walked through the middle of the crowd," which is definitely an attempt to incorporate a miraculous element into the text.
However, there is no suggestion of anything miraculous here or in 12.36,
where the same Greek verb occurs.

CHAPTER 9

JESUS HEALS A MAN BORN BLIND

9 As Jesus was walking along, he saw a man who had been born blind. 2 His disciples asked him, "Teacher, whose sin caused him to be born blind? Was it his own or his parents' sin?"

3 Jesus answered, "His blindness has nothing to do with his sins or his parents' sins. He is blind so that God's power might be seen at work in him. 4 As long as it is day, we must do the work of him who sent me; night is coming when no one can work. 5 While I am in the world, I am the light for the world."

6 After he said this, Jesus spat on the ground and made some mud with the spittle; he rubbed the mud on the man's eyes 7 and told him, "Go and wash your face in the Pool of Siloam." (This name means "Sent.") So the man went, washed his face, and came back seeing.

8 His neighbors, then, and the people who had seen him begging before this, asked, "Isn't this the man who used to sit and beg?"

9 Some said, "He is the one," but others said, "No he isn't; he just looks like him."

So the man himself said, "I am the man."

10 "How is it that you can now see?" they asked him.

11 He answered, "The man called Jesus made some mud, rubbed it on my eyes, and told me to go to Siloam and wash my face. So I went, and as soon as I washed, I could see."

12 "Where is he?" they asked.

"I don't know," he answered.

9 As he passed by, he saw a man blind from his birth. 2 And his disciples asked him, "Rabbi, who sinned, this man or his parents, that he was born blind?" 3 Jesus answered, "It was not that this man sinned, or his parents, but that the works of God might be made manifest in him. 4 We must work the works of him who sent me, while it is day; night comes, when no one can work. 5 As long as I am in the world, I am the light of the world." 6 As he said this, he spat on the ground and made clay of the spittle and anointed the man's eyes with the clay, 7 saying to him, "Go, wash in the pool of Siloam" (which means Sent). So he went and washed and came back seeing. 8 The neighbors and those who had seen him before as a beggar, said, "Is not this the man who used to sit and beg?" 9 Some said, "It is he"; others said, "No, but he is like him." He said, "I am the man." 10 They said to him, "Then how were your eyes opened?" 11 He answered, "The man called Jesus made clay and anointed my eyes and said to me, 'Go to Siloam and wash'; so I went and washed and received my sight." 12 They said to him, "Where is he?" He said, "I do not know."

John intentionally places this passage immediately after the events that occurred in Jerusalem during the Festival of Shelters, which was popularly known as "the Festival of Lights," and during which Jesus affirmed: I am the light of the world. Whoever follows me will have the light of life and will never walk in darkness (8.12). The healing of the man born blind illustrated what Jesus meant (see 9.5).

The story itself, a closely knit unit, is perhaps the most artistic creation in John's Gospel. It opens with the mention of a man who was born blind, and concludes with Jesus' judgment against the Pharisees because of their spiritual blindness. The main body of the story (verses 8-34) shows the gradual development of faith in this blind man, a faith which grows under the pressure of interrogation. When first questioned about the one who has healed him of his blindness, he refers to him simply as the man called Jesus (verse 11). Then, when the Pharisees ask the man what he has to say about the one who has healed him, he says He is a prophet (verse 17). Not satified with the answers the man gives them, the Pharisees call him back a second time, and this time the man says of Jesus, ...this man came from God... (verse 33). Finally, after the religious leaders have thrown him out of the synagogue and Jesus finds him, he confesses, I believe, Lord! (verse 38).

The story also shows the increasing spiritual blindness of the Pharisees. In their first interrogation they are willing to accept the fact that a miracle has been performed, though some are not willing to admit that the one who performed it came from God. However, there is at least a suggestion that a few of them have come close to believing (verses 13-16). But in their second interrogation they even express doubt that the man was born blind, and so they call in his parents and question them (verses 17-23). Finally, when there can be no doubt regarding his cure, they accuse him of having been born and raised in sin, and so they throw him out of the synagogue (verses 24-34).

Verses 1-7 give the setting for the story and the account of the cure. Verses 35-41 describe the final result of the cure: spiritual light for the man born blind and spiritual darkness for the Pharisees who claim they can see.

The section heading, Jesus Heals a Man Born Blind, may cause difficulties because of the passive expression Born. However, such a heading may be employed as "Jesus heals a man who has always been blind," "Jesus heals a blind man," "A blind man receives his sight," or "A blind man is made to see."

9.1   As Jesus was walking along, he saw a man who had been born blind.

In Greek, Jesus is literally "he." Since this verse opens a new section and a new chapter, TEV makes the reference to Jesus explicit. Phps and GeCL do essentially the same thing, and NEB has "As he went on his way Jesus saw a man blind from his birth." In a self-contained unit like this chapter, it is more natural in English to introduce the participant first by his name and then to refer to him by a pronoun, rather than the other way around, as in NEB.

Who had been born blind is literally "blind from birth." The expression "from birth" is a good Greek idiom; the equivalent Hebrew idiom would be "from his mother's womb." In English it is more natural to speak of a man <u>born blind</u> than to speak of a man "blind from birth" (as in most translations). For this reason TEV restructures the sentence. As suggested, it would be possible to translate "who had always been blind." It is also possible to fill out the meaning expressed in <u>born</u> by saying "who had been blind from the very time his mother gave birth to him" or "...caused him to come into the world" or "...caused him to be born."

9.2   His disciples asked him, "Teacher, whose sin
      caused him to born blind? Was it his own or
      his parents' sin?"

In the phrase <u>his disciples</u>, the pronoun <u>his</u> refers back to Jesus. In many languages it may be necessary to make this fact specific, that is, "Jesus' disciples," since in the discourse the blind man is the last person mentioned.

  <u>Asked him</u> is literally "asked him, saying." The participle "saying" is merely a means of introducing direct discourse in Semitic Greek, and modern English translations omit it from the text.

  <u>Teacher</u> is literally "rabbi" (see 1.38).

  This verse reflects the Jewish belief that every illness was due to someone's sin. Generally, if a man was born with some deformity, his condition was attributed to a sin his parents had committed. However, certain rabbis taught that it was possible for a baby to sin while still in its mother's womb, and that belief is also reflected here. In Greek <u>whose sin was it that caused him to be born blind? Was it his own or his parents' sin?</u> is literally "who sinned, this man or his parents, in order that he should be born blind?" TEV reorders the elements in the question and divides them into two questions, thus simplifying the passage for the reader.

  The question posed by Jesus' disciples may cause difficulties in some languages, owing to the necessity of indicating clearly the relation between the person presumed to have sinned and the causing of the man to be born blind. The idea of sin causing blindness is fairly widespread in the world, but the grammatical ways in which this idea may be expressed differ considerably. In some languages one may say "Why was this man born blind? Was it because he sinned or because his parents sinned?" or "Who caused this man to be born blind? Was it because he himself sinned or because his parents sinned?" or "What caused this man to be born blind? Was it the evil which he did or was it the evil which his parents did?"

9.3   Jesus answered, "His blindness has nothing to do
      with his sins or his parents' sins. He is blind so
      that God's power might be seen at work in him.

<u>His blindness has nothing to do with his sins or his parents' sins</u> is literally "neither this man sinned nor his parents." A literal translation of this clause (JB "Neither he nor his parents sinned") could possibly sound like an absolute statement: neither this man nor his parents had ever sinned. Actually, Jesus is answering a question about

a specific situation, and a translation should make it immediately clear that his answer relates only to the specific question (Phps "He was not born blind because of his own sin or that of his parents"). In some languages one may say "His sin did not cause him to be blind, nor did his parents' sin cause him to be blind" or "The fact that he is blind was not caused by what he did that was wrong or what his parents did that was wrong."

The next clause in this sentence is literally "but that the works of God might be revealed in him." The Greek word "that" (hina) frequently indicates purpose, and most translations evidently take it in that sense here (TEV He is blind so that; JB, NEB "he was born blind so that"). But the same Greek word may indicate result, and result is possibly the meaning here. This interpretation is supported by the observation that in the previous verse "that" (hina) clearly does indicate result ("who sinned, this man or his parents, that [= with the result that] he was born blind"). If this present clause indicates result, the meaning is that this man's blindness offered an occasion for the power of God to be revealed. But, if this clause indicates purpose, it means that he was born blind so that Jesus could heal him of his blindness and so reveal the power of God at work. Some commentators quote Romans 9.17, which cites Exodus 9.16, as a parallel example of how God works in history to glorify his name. But the parallel is not very close, except that both passages indicate God's ultimate control over history and the affairs of men. There are really more differences than similarities. In the Exodus account the plagues are a result of Pharaoh's willful rejection of God's rule, while in this instance of a man born blind, the man's blindness cannot be due to his own sin.

That the man was born blind so that God's healing power could be manifested in him may be expressed clearly in some languages as "the fact that he is blind means that God's power may be seen at work in him" or "his being blind makes possible seeing God's power at work in him" or "...seeing how God's power can do something for him."

It is, however, possible to translate this passage in a way that God does not appear as one who arbitrarily makes a man blind so that he can later show his power in healing him. In TEV the words He is blind so that actually translates "but that" of the Greek text. The last part of verse 3 may be joined with the first part of verse 4 by placing a comma after him. The following translation would then result: "His blindness has nothing to do with his sins or his parents' sins. But that God's power might be seen at work in him, (4) we must keep on doing the works of him who sent me as long as it is day." On the basis of the Greek, it is not only grammatically possible to translate in this way; it also suits the context well. Jesus' answer to the disciples then becomes a rejection of their belief that the man's blindness was due either to his parents' sin or to his own sin, but he makes no judgment as to the reason that the man was born blind. He simply says that the man's blindness offers an opportunity to show God's power at work in him, and that Jesus himself has come to reveal that power at work in history. Apparently no modern translations follow this exegesis. It is not even discussed in the better commentaries, but it does make good sense, and it is grammatically possible. This arrangement of relations between clauses may be rendered in some languages "but in order that people may see God's

power doing something for him, we must keep on doing the works of the
one who sent me as long as it is day."

"The works of God" is taken by several other translations with the
meaning of God's power (NEB, Phps; Mft "the work of God"). The term
"work" is often used in John's Gospel to refer to Jesus' miracles, and
even though the plural "works" is used in the present context, it is
better translated by the singular "work," in light of the observation
that it refers to the particular miracle performed on this man. In some
languages "the works of God" may be expressed as "the kind of works
which only God does" or "...that only God can do." The passive expression
might be seen may, of course, be translated into an active, "people may
see." One may therefore translate this entire final clause "in order
that people may see in this man the kind of work that only God could do"
or "...the kind of miracle that only God can make possible" or "...per-
form."

9.4   As long as it is day, we must do the work of him
           who sent me; night is coming when no one can work.

The phrase As long as it is day, which must be understood figuratively, in general should be placed close to the expression of "doing."
It may be better to place it at the beginning of the sentence, for example, "as long as it is day, we must keep on doing the works of him
who sent me." Otherwise, the reader might understand it as a qualification of him who sent me.

In Greek an impersonal construction (literally "it is necessary for
us to do") is used, which TEV transforms into a more natural English
expression (We must do).

In place of the first person plural we, some manuscripts have the
singular "I," while in the latter half of the verse some Greek manuscripts read "us" in place of me. TEV accepts the reading we because it
has the best manuscript support, and because, since Jesus is the speaker,
it is more likely that a scribe would change the plural we to the singular "I" than the other way around. The reading "us" is supported by
good manuscript evidence, but the UBS Committee on the Greek text suggests that the translator follow the reading me on the assumption that
"us" was introduced into the manuscripts in order to conform with we in
the first part of the verse. Mft, RSV, Phps, NAB, and NEB all follow the
same text as TEV; JB, Segond, GeCL, and Luther Revised accept the reading
of the first person singular in both places ("I...me"). The choice of
text is not easy, and the UBS Committee has rated its decision "C," indicating considerable doubt concerning the reading selected.

Him who sent me clearly refers to God; see GeCL "I must accomplish
the works for which God has sent me."

It may not be easy to reproduce effectively the meaning of the
clause we must do the work of him who sent me. Work refers, of course,
to miracles, or "only such works as God himself can do." It may be possible in some languages to translate "We must keep on doing such wonderful works as only God who sent me can do" or "We must keep on doing what
the one who sent me ordered me to do."

Night is coming, when no one can work may be rendered in some languages "It will soon be night, and then no one can work." Such a modification must be introduced in languages in which one cannot speak of night "coming." It is also necessary in this type of context to avoid a term for work which would mean only physical labor. Thus the final clause of the verse may be translated "then no one will be able to do anything."

9.5   While I am in the world, I am the light for the world."

In Greek for the world is a genitive expression, literally "of the world," but the preposition for expresses the meaning more clearly. Mft translates this verse in the same way. In some languages I am the light for the world may be rendered "I am the one who causes light for people in the world." It is important to avoid a literal translation which would suggest that Jesus is the sun.

9.6   After he said this, Jesus spat on the ground and made some mud with the spittle; he rubbed the mud on the man's eyes

The connection between this verse and the preceding one is evident. Having stated that he is the light for the world, Jesus now illustrates what that means by healing the man's blindness.
The expression made some mud with the spittle may require a more specific indication of how the mud was made, for example, "mixed the dirt with the spittle" or "by means of his fingers mixed the dirt with the spittle to make mud."
In place of the verb rubbed...on (NEB "spread on"; Mft, NAB "smeared on"; RSV "anointed"), one ancient Greek manuscript reads "put on." This reading may be the basis for JB "put this over" and Phps "applied to." In verse 15 the verb put...on is used when the man describes what Jesus did to him. It is probably the basis for the reading "put on" in verse 6 of one Greek manuscript.
In rendering he rubbed the mud on the man's eyes it is important to avoid the suggestion that he "rubbed the mud into the man's eyes." What apparently happened was that Jesus smeared the mud over the man's eyelids. This fact must be made clear in some languages, to avoid the impression that the mud was rubbed on the eyeballs.

9.7   and told him, "Go and wash your face in the Pool of Siloam." (This name means "Sent.") So the man went, washed his face, and came back seeing.

In Greek the verb wash has no stated object, but it is obvious that the man is not told to go take a bath. In order to remove the ambiguity in the verb wash, TEV translates wash your face and Mft "wash them," referring to "eyes" of the previous verse.
The Pool of Siloam was the pool from which the water was drawn for the ceremonies connected with the Festival of Shelters. It was located within the walls of Jerusalem, at the southern extremity of the eastern hill of the city, near the point where the Kidron and Tyropean valleys

came together. In Hebrew the pool is named Shiloah (Isa 8.6), which is derived from the Hebrew verb "to send." This is the basis for John's remark, This name means "Sent."

The Pool of Siloam may be rendered "the pool called Siloam" or "Siloam pool." A translator should adapt the orthography of Siloam to reflect the pronunciation of this term in the dominant language of the area or to follow traditional practice there.

This name means "Sent." may be rendered in some languages as "the word 'Siloam' means 'sent'" or "in our language the word Siloam means 'sent.'"

So the man went, washed his face is literally "so he went and washed." Here again TEV (so also GeCL) makes explicit that the man did not take a bath.

Came back seeing may be expressed in some instances as "came back, and he could see," since the coming and the seeing are often treated as coordinate elements, rather than one being subordinate to the other. Since in terms of the events of this story, the seeing is more important than the return, it may be necessary in some languages to translate "and he was able to see as he came back."

A difficulty may be involved in translating came back, since in some languages this expression can only be understood to mean that he came back to where Jesus was. That is obviously not the case, since Jesus finally went looking for the man and found him (verse 35). The apparent meaning is that he returned to his home, for it is his neighbors who begin to comment about the change in his condition. It may be necessary, therefore, to translate "and went back home, being able to see" or "since he was able to see, he went back home."

9.8   His neighbors, then, and the people who had seen
             him begging before this, asked, "Isn't this the man
             who used to sit and beg?"

This verse initiates a series of dialogues concerning the healing, which continue through verse 34.

Who had seen him begging before this refers to habitual action, as indicated by NAB ("who had been accustomed to see him begging") and Mft ("to whom he had been a familiar sight as a beggar"). From JB ("who earlier had seen him begging") one could gain the impression that they had seen him begging only once, immediately before the healing.

The question Isn't this the man...? expects the answer "Yes." Who used to sit and beg (so many translations) expresses accurately the force of the Greek particles ("the one sitting and begging").

There is no indication to whom the question in verse 8 is posed; however, one may say "asked one another." Since the question does expect a positive answer and to this extent is an exclamation, it may be appropriate in some languages to introduce it by a type of exclamatory statement, for example, "exclaimed to one another" or "asked with wonder."

9.9   Some said, "He is the one," but others said, "No
     he isn't, he just looks like him."
     So the man himself said, "I am the man."

Some said may be rendered "some people said." He is the one may
require more specific identification to make the reference perfectly
clear. For example, one may say "he is the one who begged" or "...used
to beg."

In some languages a literal rendering of No, he isn't would have
a positive meaning "he is"; therefore it may be necessary to render this
expression as "he is not that beggar."

He just looks like him is equivalent to a reason for the first
statement, and so may be rendered "it is only that he resembles the
beggar." In some languages it may be better to treat the two closely
related expressions No, he isn't and he just looks like him as two
separate sentences.

The man himself (so also JB, NAB, NEB) is literally "that one."
This translation correctly brings out the force of the Greek and avoids
ambiguity.

I am the man is literally "I am," the same expression by which
Jesus sometimes identifies himself with God the Father. Here it is obviously no more than a simple statement of identity. I am the man may
be expressed in some languages as "I am the man who used to beg."

9.10   "How is that you can now see?" they asked him.

In Greek the words they asked him (literally "therefore they were
saying to him") come first in the sentence. The verbs said in verse 9
and asked in this verse are in the imperfect tense in Greek, perhaps
for the sake of making the action more vivid.

The Greek text has literally "How were your eyes opened?" Such
an expression, however, may have little relation to the meaning of
"being able to see," since the opening of the eyes might be understood
merely as the opening of the eyelids, rather than as the ability to
see. How is it that you can now see? must be rendered in some languages
by a causative expression, for example, "What is it that caused you now
to see?" or "What happened to cause you to see?" or "...to be able to
see?"

9.11   He answered, "The man called Jesus made some
     mud, rubbed it on my eyes, and told me to go to
     Siloam and wash my face. So I went, and as soon
     as I washed, I could see."

The words He answered, "The man called Jesus..." appear in a variety
of ways in the various Greek manuscripts. But the textual variations do
not affect translation at this point. The translator is obligated to
translate in a way that is stylistically most acceptable to his readers.

Rubbed on is the same verb as the one used in verse 6. Here in
verse 11 there is no variation in the Greek manuscripts, as there is in

verse 6. Those who believe that the original text in verse 6 reads "put on" assume that rubbed on came into the text there on the basis of its use here. The verb translated rubbed on is used nowhere in the New Testament apart from these two verses.

In Greek the verb I went is actually a participle, but rendered as a finite verb in TEV and several other translations. In translation from Greek to English, a participle must often be changed to a finite verb to avoid having a large number of subordinate clauses. However, it is sometimes necessary to change a finite verb in Greek to a participle or a subordinate clause, to meet the demands of English discourse structure.

In many languages the command of Jesus must be interpreted as a quotation within a quotation, for example, "told me, Go to Siloam and wash your face."

9.12   "Where is he?" they asked.
        "I don't know," he answered.

They refers back to the people mentioned in verse 8. The official opposition to Jesus is introduced in the next verse, when the man is taken before the Pharisees.

TEV   (9.13-16)   RSV

THE PHARISEES INVESTIGATE
THE HEALING

13 Then they took to the Pharisees the man who had been blind. 14 The day that Jesus made the mud and cured him of his blindness was a Sabbath. 15 The Pharisees, then, asked the man again how he had received his sight. He told them, "He put some mud on my eyes; I washed my face, and now I can see."

16 Some of the Pharisees said, "The man who did this cannot be from God, for he does not obey the Sabbath law."

Others, however, said, "How could a man who is a sinner perform such miracles as these?" And there was a division among them.

13 They brought to the Pharisees the man who had formerly been blind. 14 Now it was a sabbath day when Jesus made the clay and opened his eyes. 15 The Pharisees again asked him how he had received his sight. And he said to them, "He put clay on my eyes, and I washed, and I see." 16 Some of the Pharisees said, "This man is not from God, for he does not keep the sabbath." But others said, "How can a man who is a sinner do such signs?" There was a division among them.

For a general discussion and analysis of this passage, see the beginning of this chapter.

Instead of The Pharisees Investigate the Healing, it is possible to use as a section heading "The Pharisees question the man who was healed" or "...the man who became able to see."

<u>9.13</u>   Then they took to the Pharisees the man who
                  had been blind.

In Greek the verb <u>took</u> is in the present tense, often used in
narratives for the sake of vividness. NEB translates as a passive ("was
brought"), but since the Greek specifically identifies the subject as
<u>they</u> (a reference back to verse 8 and 12), it is better to keep the
active verb, with <u>they</u> as the subject.
    The persons who questioned the man who was born blind are called
Pharisees in verses 13, 15, and 16; in verses 18 and 22 they are called
"the Jews" (TEV <u>Jewish authorities</u>). In verse 40 the Pharisees are
again mentioned (<u>TEV some Pharisees</u>); and the chapter concludes on the
note of Jesus' judgment against them (verse 41).
    In some languages the manner in which the people took the man before
the Pharisees must be made specific. It is important to avoid a term for
<u>took</u> which would suggest "arrested him" or "dragged him before." The
implication is probably "they insisted that the man accompany them to
the Pharisees."

<u>9.14</u>   The day that Jesus made the mud and cured him of his
                  blindness was a Sabbath.

This verse states the basis for the controversy that follows. The
day that Jesus healed the blind man was a Sabbath, and the Jews had
strict rules regarding what could or could not be done on the Sabbath.
For example, to heal someone on the Sabbath day was considered unlawful
unless life was in danger. Obviously, this man's life was not in danger,
since he had been blind from birth. It was also forbidden to knead bread
or clay on the Sabbath, and Jesus had done so when he made mud to rub on
the man's eyes. So the Pharisees accused Jesus of failing to obey the
Sabbath law (verse 16).
    Some translations treat this verse as a parenthetical statement.
Both Phps and NAB set it off in parentheses. In Phps it is introduced
by "It should be noted that" and in NAB by "Note that it was." Mft ties
this verse to the following one, "As it was on the sabbath day that
Jesus had made clay and opened his eyes, the Pharisees asked him..." It
is also possible to interpret this parenthetical statement as explaining
why the people took the man to the Pharisees. No doubt they would have
been concerned about a healing which had taken place on the rest day.
However, it is probably better not to try to identify a specific causal
relation with either the preceding or the following sentence. It is this
activity on the Sabbath which colors the entire story and makes the
event a religious issue.

<u>9.15</u>   The Pharisees, then, asked the man again how he had
                  received his sight. He told them, "He put some mud on
                  my eyes; I washed my face, and now I can see."

Most translations render the Greek verb (imperfect tense) by <u>asked</u>,
though NAB translates "began to inquire." The verb may have either force.

The adverb <u>again</u> must not be taken to imply that the Pharisees were
asking the man a second time how he had received his sight. <u>Again</u> refers
back to the question raised by the people in verse 10. To avoid the implication that the Pharisees had previously interrogated the man, it
may be necessary to introduce the meaning of <u>again</u> as a separate sentence, for example, "The Pharisees then asked the man how he had been
cured of his blindness. This was the second time the man had been questioned" or "...the Pharisees also questioned the man, just as the other
people had."

Only rarely can one translate literally <u>received his sight</u>, since
a verb meaning "receive" normally refers to the receipt of some kind of
object, while "sight" refers to a state of being, that is, the capacity
to see. In many languages one must say "how he had become able to see"
or "how he was caused to see."

The verb <u>washed my face</u> is the same verb used in verses 7 and 11.
Mft again translates "I washed them," referring back to "my eyes."

<u>And now I can see</u> (so also NEB; JB "and I can see") is literally
"and I see." The adverb <u>now</u> is used as a literary device to emphasize
the contrast between the present condition of the man and his previous
blindness.

<u>9.16</u>   Some of the Pharisees said, "The man who did this
    cannot be from God, for he does not obey the Sabbath
    law."
    Others, however, said, "How could a man who is a
    sinner perform such miracles as these?" And there was
    a division among them.

This verse indicates the division that developed among the Pharisees
because of the different responses towards Jesus and what he had done.

<u>The man who did this cannot be from God</u> is literally "this man is
not from God." TEV includes the qualifying phrase <u>who did this</u> in order
to link the words of the Pharisees to the act of healing on the Sabbath
day. The phrase "is not from God" is correctly taken by TEV, JB, and
NAB with the force <u>cannot be from God</u>; NEB expresses the same meaning
in different words, "is no man of God." Deuteronomy 13.1-5 is perhaps
the point of reference for the Pharisees' judgment. This passage teaches
that if a prophet or a miracle worker leads people away from God, he
must be stoned to death. The Pharisees are not denying the reality of
the miracle; rather they are affirming that Jesus is not from God because <u>he does not obey the Sabbath law</u>. <u>Does not obey the Sabbath law</u>
is literally "does not keep the Sabbath," but for the English reader
TEV states it more clearly and naturally.

<u>Cannot be from God</u> may be rendered "cannot have come from God" or
"cannot be one whom God has sent."

<u>He does not obey the Sabbath law</u> may be rendered "he does not do
what one should do on the Sabbath day" or "...the rest day." However,
it may be necessary to indicate clear violation of the Sabbath law by
saying "he does on the Sabbath day what he must not do" or "he violates
the laws which apply to the Sabbath day." In some languages the appli-
cability of laws to particular days or events may be expressed as

"binding," for example, "the laws that tie one on the Sabbath day." In other languages it may be expressed in terms of their "strength," for example, "the laws that are strong on the Sabbath day."

Those who defend the action of Jesus speak of "miracles" and not merely "a miracle," which suggests that the Pharisees must have had in mind not only this one particular healing but also other miracles of which they were aware. To translate accurately such miracles as these, it may be necessary to say "this and other miracles like this."

There was a division among them may be rendered "they had different thoughts," "they opposed one another," or "their decisions did not agree."

TEV	(9.17-34)	RSV

17 So the Pharisees asked the man once more, "You say he cured you of your blindness--well, what do you say about him?"

"He is a prophet," the man answered.

18 The Jewish authorities, however, were not willing to believe that he had been blind and could now see, until they called his parents 19 and asked them, "Is this your son? You say that he was born blind; how is it, then, that he can now see?"

20 His parents answered, "We know that he is our son, and we know that he was born blind. 21 But we do not know how it is that he is now able to see, nor do we know who cured him of his blindness. Ask him; he is old enough, and he can answer for himself!" 22 His parents said this because they were afraid of the Jewish authorities, who had already agreed that anyone who said he believed that Jesus was the Messiah would be expelled from the synagogue. 23 That is why his parents said, "He is old enough; ask him!"

24 A second time they called back the man who had been born blind, and said to him, "Promise before God that you will tell the truth! We know that this man who cured you is a sinner."

25 "I do not know if he is a sinner or not," the man replied.

17 So they again said to the blind man, "What do you say about him, since he has opened your eyes?" He said, "He is a prophet."

18 The Jews did not believe that he had been blind and had received his sight, until they called the parents of the man who had received his sight, 19 and asked them, "Is this your son, who you say was born blind? How then does he now see?" 20 His parents answered, "We know that this is our son, and that he was born blind; 21 but how he now sees we do not know, nor do we know who opened his eyes. Ask him; he is of age, he will speak for himself." 22 His parents said this because they feared the Jews, for the Jews had already agreed that if any one should confess him to be Christ, he was to be put out of the synagogue. 23 Therefore his parents said, "He is of age, ask him."

24 So for the second time they called the man who had been blind, and said to him, "Give God the praise; we know that this man is a sinner." 25 He answered, "Whether he is a sinner, I do not know; one thing I know, that though I was blind, now I see." 26 They said to him, "What did he do to you? How did he open your eyes?" 27 He answered them, "I have told you already, and you would not listen. Why do you want to hear it again? Do you too want to become his

"One thing I do know: I was blind, and now I see."

26 "What did he do to you?" they asked. "How did he cure you of your blindness?"

27 "I have already told you," he answered, "and you would not listen. Why do you want to hear it again? Maybe you, too, would like to be his disciples?"

28 They insulted him and said, "You are that fellow's disciple; but we are Moses' disciples. 29 We know that God spoke to Moses; as for that fellow, however, we do not even know where he comes from!"

30 The man answered, "What a strange thing that is! You do not know where he comes from, but he cured me of my blindness! 31 We know that God does not listen to sinners; he does listen to people who respect him and do what he wants them to do. 32 Since the beginning of the world nobody has ever heard of anyone giving sight to a blind person. 33 Unless this man came from God, he would not be able to do a thing."

34 They answered, "You were born and brought up in sin--and you are trying to teach us?" And they expelled him from the synagogue.

disciples?" 28 And they reviled him, saying, "You are his disciple, but we are disciples of Moses. 29 We know that God has spoken to Moses, but as for this man, we do not know where he comes from." 30 The man answered, "Why, this is a marvel! You do not know where he comes from, and yet he opened my eyes. 31 We know that God does not listen to sinners, but if any one is a worshiper of God and does his will, God listens to him. 32 Never since the world began has it been heard that any one opened the eyes of a man born blind. 33 If this man were not from God, he could do nothing." 34 They answered him, "You were born in utter sin, and would you teach us?" And they cast him out.

<u>9.17</u>   So the Pharisees asked the man once more, "You say he cured you of your blindness--well, what do you say about him?"
"He is a prophet," the man answered.

The Pharisees is literally "they." More specifically, the reference is probably to the group of Pharisees who were opposed to Jesus (16a).

NEB combines the adverb once more (most translations "again") with the verb asked (literally "said") and so translates "continued to question."

TEV inverts the order of the two remarks made by the Pharisees. NAB likewise inverts and translates "Since it was your eyes he opened, what do you say about him?" The Greek has a particle (hoti) that TEV renders with the function of a marker of direct discourse You say and NAB with the meaning "Since." Scholars are not agreed on the interpretation of this particle in the context, and some have even conjectured that an Aramaic original lies behind the Greek text, so that the particle must be given the force of the relative pronoun "who." If that is so, the meaning would be either "what do you say about him who opened your eyes?" or "what do you say about him, you whose eyes he opened?" It is possible that this supposed Aramaic original is the basis for the translation of Mft ("What do you say about him, you whose eyes he has opened?"), Phps ("And what do you say about him? You're the one whose sight was restored."), and NEB ("What have you to say about him? It was your eyes he opened."). However, there is evidence that the particle hoti is used with the force of "with regard to the fact that," so that there is no need to assume an Aramaic original for these three translations; they may simply be based upon this third possible use of the Greek particle. Actually the meaning of TEV and NEB are essentially the same, although each apparently assigns a different grammatical function to hoti; that is, you say of TEV carries the full meaning "since you say that," while the full meaning of "since" in NEB is "since it happened that." In both translations the point of reference is the man's own testimony, given earlier to the crowds who questioned him.

If the response of the Pharisees in verse 17 is given first as a statement and then as a question (in the form of two separate sentences), it may not be possible in some languages to introduce both by a verb meaning "ask." It may be necessary to say "So the Pharisees said to the man, You say he cured you of your blindness. Then they asked, What do you say about him?" However, it seems preferable to combine the two statements, one constituting the reason for the other, for example, "Since you say that he cured you of your blindness, what do you say about him?"

When the Pharisees press the man for a decision regarding Jesus, he makes a judgment which goes beyond his previous affirmation. Earlier he referred to the man named Jesus (11), but now he confesses that he is a prophet. This is not a confession that Jesus is "the Prophet" (6.14; 7.40), but that he is a prophet (see 4.19). However, the man's faith will develop further.

9.18   The Jewish authorities, however, were not willing to believe that he had been blind and could now see, until they called his parents

The Jewish authorities is literally "the Jews"; See Appendix II.

Were not willing to believe is literally "did not believe" (RSV), but several translations see this meaning in John's words (Mft, JB, NEB, GeCL "would not believe"; NAB "refused to believe").

A literal translation of were not willing to believe that he had been blind and could now see may seem anomalous in some languages, since it was perfectly clear to the Jewish authorities that the man could now see. It may therefore be necessary to translate "were not willing to believe that this man who could at that time see had previously been blind." In English the adverb now can indicate contemporaneous time as well as present time, but in this type of context it may be necessary to translate now as "at that particular time."

They called his parents must not be so translated as to imply that they shouted to them. Since the process of "calling" in this type of context is rather complex, it may be necessary to translate with two different verbs, for example, "ordered the man's parents to come before them" or "commanded that the man's parents be brought before them."

9.19   and asked them, "Is this your son? You say that
          he was born blind; how is it, then, that he can
          now see?"

And asked them is literally "and they asked them saying." Again the participle "saying" reflects Semitic structure. It is equivalent to quotation marks in modern English.
In Greek Is this your son? You say that he was born blind is actually one sentence. NEB also translates by two sentences ("Is this your son? Do you say that he was born blind?" while RSV maintains the formal structure of the Greek: "Is this your son, who you say was born blind?" This shift into two questions is for stylistic reasons. Note NAB "'Is this your son,' they asked, 'and if so, do you attest that he was blind at birth?'"
It may even be necessary in some languages to make this read as three questions, for example, "Is this your son? Do you say he was born blind? How is it that he now is able to see?" Since this series of questions presupposes a series of conditioned answers, it may be necessary to link them on the basis of the conditions, for example, "Is this your son? And if he is, do you declare that he was born blind? And if that is so, how is it that he can now see?"

9.20   His parents answered, "We know that he is our
          son, and we know that he was born blind.

His parents answered is literally "therefore his parents answered and said." The redundancy "answered and said" reflects Semitic style, while the use of the particle translated "therefore" (oun) is characteristic of John's style. For stylistic reasons TEV repeats the verb we know (so also JB). Mft restructures by translating "This is our son, and he was born blind; we know that."

9.21   But we do not know how it is that he is now able
          to see, nor do we know who cured him of his blindness.
          Ask him; he is old enough, and he can answer for
          himself!"

Most translations maintain the literal Semitic expression "to open one's eyes" when referring to the healing of blindness. Phps translates "made him able to see." The statement of the parents may be translated succinctly "We do not know how he is now able to see, and we do not know who caused him to be able to see."
The expression he is old enough (so also JB, NAB; Mft, NEB "he is of age") is perhaps a reference to the age of legal responsibility. Phps translates "He is a grown-up man." In many languages it is sufficient to say "he is a man," though it would be more typical to say

in some languages "he is no longer a child."

He can answer for himself (Mft "he can speak for himself") is actually in the future tense "he will speak for himself" (RSV, NEB). The
meaning is that the man is old enough to speak for himself as a legally
responsible person. The NAB rendering, "he is old enough to speak for
himself," leaves implicit the meaning "he can speak."

9.22   His parents said this because they were afraid
of the Jewish authorities, who had already agreed
that anyone who said he believed that Jesus was
the Messiah would be expelled from the synagogue.

Here also Jewish authorities is literally "the Jews." In Greek
"the Jews" is repeated, but TEV replaces its second occurrence by the
relative pronoun who. The Greek expression "if anyone" is rendered as
anyone who, and the pronoun "he" as Jesus. Jesus has not been mentioned
for several verses while the man born blind has been the topic of conversation. For that reason TEV and some other translations (see JB, NEB,
NAB, GeCL) make the pronominal reference "he" explicit.

In some languages it may be necessary to stipulate the basis of the
parents' fear of the Jewish authorities, for example, "They were afraid
of what the Jewish authorities might do to them." The relative clause
beginning who had already agreed... may then be expressed as causative,
for example, "because the Jewish authorities had already agreed that..."

Messiah translates the Greek word "Christ" (see RSV), but in the
present context this word is used as a reference to the Messiah of
Jewish hope (see 1.20).

The point is that the Jews had already agreed that anyone who said
he believed that Jesus was the Messiah, not that anyone "who admitted
that Christ had done this thing" (Phps), would be expelled from the
synagogue. Who said he believed that Jesus was the Messiah may be rendered "who said to others that Jesus was the Messiah" or "who told
other people, Jesus is the Messiah," since the Greek verb translated
believed that literally is "confess that."

Would be expelled from the synagogue appears in NEB as "should be
banned from the synagogue"; RSV has "was to be put out of the synagogue."
The intensity of the threatened punishment is not indicated by John. There
was a type of suspension, lasting for thirty days, during which time the
suspended man was forbidden to have any dealings with Israelites except
those of his immediate family. He could, however, attend the religious
services of the community. But John seems to suggest a permanent excommunication, by which it would be impossible for the man even to attend the religious services of the synagogue.

In view of the evident intent of the author of this Gospel to suggest a more permanent exclusion from the synagogue, it may be necessary
in some languages to say "to cause them to no longer be members of the
synagogue" or "to exclude them from ever coming to the synagogue" or
"to forbid them ever in the future to join with those of the synagogue."
Note that in this passage synagogue must be understood not as a building
but as a group of people, though it may be possible to express the concept of "excommunication" in terms of exclusion from a particular place
of worship.

9.23   That is why his parents said, "He is old enough;
       ask him!"

The man's parents are afraid to answer in his behalf, for fear that
they themselves would be put out of the synagogue.

9.24   A second time they called back the man who had
       been born blind, and said to him, "Promise before
       God that you will tell the truth! We know that this
       man who cured you is a sinner."

In the introductory statement, A second time they called back the
man, there is a slight difficulty in the transitional development of
the account. In the preceding section there was no indication that the
man born blind had been excluded from the session in which the Pharisees
interrogated his parents. One can, however, assume from the way in which
they spoke (that is, when they insisted that the Pharisees could inter-
rogate their son) that he was not present. It may be possible in some
languages to say "again they called the man back in." However, this rendering may suggest that he had been called back before, thus implying
three sessions of interrogation. Hence, it may be sufficient to say
"they called back the man who had been born blind."
    The man who had been born blind is literally "the man who was blind,"
but the reference is obviously to his previous blindness, and TEV makes
this explicit by translating who had been born blind. Otherwise it sounds
as if the man was still blind at the time of these events.
    Promise before God that you will tell the truth is literally "give
glory/praise to God." This represents a formula used in taking an oath,
especially one involving confession of guilt (see Josh 7.19). The meaning is "Speak the truth before God" (NEB), and not "You should give God
the glory for what has happened to you" (Phps). JB translates "Give glory
to God," but adds a footnote indicating that the man was put under oath.
In some languages the closest equivalent is "promise under oath that you
will tell the truth," while in others the equivalent may be "promise
under a curse," that is, the man was forced to affirm that he was telling the truth, and if what he said was not the truth, he was exposing
himself to a curse from God. In some languages one may say "Call upon
God to witness that you are telling the truth" or "Make God a witness
of what you are going to say, so that we may be sure it is the truth" or
"...that what you are saying is the truth."
    This man who cured you translates "this man" of the Greek text.
TEV includes this explanation, for stylistic reasons.

9.25   "I do not know if he is a sinner or not," the
       man replied. "One thing I do know: I was blind, and
       now I see."

In Greek the man replied is literally "therefore (Greek oun) that
man replied" and this clause is first in the sentence structure. The
implication behind the man's answer is that Jesus is superior to the

[312]

Law of Moses. That is, the Jews have accused Jesus of breaking their Law (verse 16), but the man born blind knows that Jesus has healed him of his blindness. The only logical conclusion is that Jesus has power beyond the Law of Moses, a conclusion the Jewish authorities are not prepared to accept.

9.26   "What did he do to you?" they asked. "How did
          he cure you of your blindness?"

Because of the two questions, it may be necessary in some languages to place the introductory expression they asked at the beginning of the verse. The two questions, moreover, may seem repetitious, since the first is a general statement and the second refers specifically to the curing of the blindness. Sometimes the two can be effectively combined into a single question, for example, "What did he do to you in order to cure you of your blindness?"

9.27   "I have already told you," he answered, "and you
          would not listen. Why do you want to hear it again?
          Maybe you, too, would like to be his disciples?"

He answered is literally "he answered them," and stands at the beginning of the verse. In TEV's restructuring "them" is implicit information.
TEV, together with a number of other translations (RSV, Mft, NAB, GeCL), understands the Greek "did not listen" to carry the meaning would not listen. In some languages would not listen may be rendered "did not want to listen to what I was saying" or "did not want to pay attention."
To hear it again may be rendered "to hear me say it again" or "to hear me again say what happened."
Maybe you, too, would like to be his disciples? is so stated in Greek as to expect the answer "No" (see 4.29). The question is ironical. As a rhetorical question, expecting a negative answer, it may be reproduced as a statement in some languages: "It could not be possible that you would like to be his disciples" or the negative implication may be brought out as "Surely you would not like to be his disciples, would you?"

9.28   They insulted him and said, "You are that fellow's
          disciple; but we are Moses' disciples.

The verb translated insulted (NEB "they became abusive"; JB "they hurled abuse"; Mft "they stormed at him"; NAB "They retored scornfully"; Phps "they turned on him furiously") is a word indicating very strong verbal abuse. They insulted him and said must be rendered in some languages "they insulted him by saying" or simply "they insulted him." A literal rendering may suggest that the insulting was done in some way other than by words.

[313]

Many believe that fellow's is used in a derogatory sense, especially since that fellow's disciple is set over against Moses' disciples. That fellow's disciple may be rendered "a follower of that man" or "an adherent of that man." In order, however, to express clearly the contrast between that fellow's disciple and Moses' disciples, it may be more appropriate to say "You are one who obeys what that fellow has said, while we obey what Moses has said."

9.29   We know that God spoke to Moses; as for that fellow, however, we do not even know where he comes from!"

One of the basic Jewish doctrines was that God had spoken directly to Moses. John here uses a bit of satire. The Pharisees now admit that they do not know where Jesus comes from, even though in 7.27 they claimed to know his origin. Jesus has come from God, as the healing of the blind man ought to indicate, but the Pharisees are blind to this truth.

We know that God spoke to Moses is equivalent in some languages to "we are sure that God spoke to Moses."

For the phrase as for that fellow, it may be necessary to introduce the name of Jesus, for example, "as for that man Jesus." As in verse 28, that fellow is most probably derogatory.

Where he comes from must be related to the hometown of Jesus; for example, "we do not even know where his hometown is" or "we are not even sure of the town where he was born."

9.30   The man answered, "What a strange thing that is! You do not know where he comes from, but he cured me of my blindness!

The man answered is literally "the man answered and said to them," again reflecting John's Semitic Greek style.

What a strange thing that is! translates an expression which indicates a high degree of amazement on the part of the speaker. It is rendered in a variety of ways in modern English translations. For example, NEB "What an extraordinary thing!"; JB "Now here is an astonishing thing"; Mft "Well, this is amazing!"; NAB "Well, this is news!"; Phps "Now here's the extraordinary thing..." In other languages it may be necessary to indicate more closely the relation between the astonishment and the speaker. One may need to translate "I am amazed," "I am so surprised," or "Why, I cannot even understand this!"

9.31   We know that God does not listen to sinners; he does listen to people who respect him and do what he wants them to do.

It should be noted that in this verse the man born blind picks up the phrase used by the Pharisees themselves, we know (see verse 29).

The affirmation that God does not listen to sinners means that God will not answer ordinary petitions in the prayers of sinners, not that God will not hear a prayer of repentance. Does not listen to sinners may be translated "does not respond to the petitions of sinners" or "does not give to sinners what they ask for when they pray."

People who respect him (most translations "devout"; Phps "the man who has a proper respect for God") translates a word that occurs only here in the New Testament, though it is from the same stem as the word translated religious in 1 Timothy 2.10. RSV translates this word "a worshiper of God." People who respect him may often be rendered "people who worship him" or even "people who pray to him." Such persons may be described in some languages as "those who regularly bow before him."

What he wants them to do is a noun phrase in Greek (literally "his will").

9.32   Since the beginning of the world nobody has ever heard of anyone giving sight to a blind person.

Since the beginning of the world is literally "from the age." Most translations give the same meaning that TEV gives this phrase. Since the beginning of the world may be rendered "since the world was created" or "from the very time that the world was first created."

Nobody has ever heard of anyone giving sight to a blind person may require restructuring in light of 9.1, which states that the man had been born blind. For example, "people have never heard that anyone ever gave sight to a person who had been blind from the day he was born" or "...caused a man who had always been blind to see" or "...caused that a man who was blind from birth would be able to see."

9.33   Unless this man came from God, he would not be able to do a thing."

The truth stated in this verse is also expressed by Nicodemus (see 3.2).

This man is obviously a reference to Jesus and may be rendered "this man who healed me."

The condition in verse 33 is contrary to fact, that is, it has an "if" clause the content of which is not true. As noted in other contexts, it may be necessary to indicate this fact clearly by the introduction of parenthetical clauses, for example, "If this man did not come from God (but he did), he would not be able to do a thing (but he has been able to)."

9.34   They answered, "You were born and brought up in sin--and you are trying to teach us?" And they expelled him from the synagogue.

They answered is literally "they answered and said to him." You were born and brought up in sin is literally "you were born in sin altogether." NEB, JB, NAB, and GeCL all understand this phrase as TEV does. NEB translates "born and bred in sin as you are"; JB "and you a sinner through and through, since you were born"; NAB "You are steeped in sin from your birth." Others take this statement, not as a reference to the man's sinfulness from the time he was born until the present time, but as an indication of the degree of his sinfulness even at the time of his birth, that is, to his absolutely sinful condition even before he was born into this world (RSV "You were born in utter sin"; Mft "you, born in utter depravity"; Anchor Bible "You were born steeped in sin"). The closest equivalent to You were born and brought up in sin may be "You have always been a sinner, right from the time you were born" or "You are completely a sinner and always have been."

And you are trying to teach us? is literally "and you are teaching us," but commentators point out that trying to teach is the real meaning of the verb in the present passage; a number of translations make this information explicit. NEB ("Who are you to give us lessons?") and NAB ("and you are giving us lectures") are both rather high level. The force of the question may be more effectively indicated in some languages by "How is it that you are trying to teach us?" or "How can you try to teach us?"

And they expelled him from the synagogue (NEB "Then they expelled him from the synagogue") is literally "and they threw him out." Some commentators understand the meaning to be that of physically throwing the man out of their presence rather than that of excommunication. Thus NAB translates "With that they threw him out bodily." JB also goes in this direction "And they drove him away." A literal translation of expelled him from the synagogue may suggest something more violent than what really happened. It seems clear that they did not hurl him out the door of the synagogue. A generic expression, such as "expelled him..." or "forcibly made him leave the synagogue," may be used. Or such an expression as "rushed him..." or "violently pushed him out of the synagogue" may be used.

TEV   (9.35-41)   RSV

SPIRITUAL BLINDNESS

35 When Jesus heard what had happened, he found the man and asked him, "Do you believe in the Son of Man?"

36 The man answered, "Tell me who he is, sir, so that I can believe in him!"

37 Jesus said to him, "You have already seen him, and he is the one who is talking with you now."

38 "I believe, Lord!" the man said, and knelt down before Jesus.

39 Jesus said, "I came to this world to judge, so that the blind should see and those who see

35 Jesus heard that they had cast him out, and having found him he said, "Do you believe in the Son of man?"[v] 36 He answered, "And who is he, sir, that I may believe in him?" 37 Jesus said to him, "You have seen him, and it is he who speaks to you." 38 He said, "Lord, I believe"; and he worshiped him. 39 Jesus said, "For judgment I came into this world, that those who do not see may see, and that those who see may become blind." 40 Some of the Pharisees near him heard this, and they said to him, "Are we also blind?" 41 Jesus said

should become blind."

40 Some Pharisees who were there with him heard him say this and asked him, "Surely you don't mean that we are blind, too?"

41 Jesus answered, "If you were blind, then you would not be guilty; but since you claim that you can see, this means that you are still guilty."

to them, "If you were blind, you would have no guilt; but now that you say, 'We see,' your guilt remains.

*v*Other ancient authorities read *the Son of God*

The setting and the account of the healing of the blind man given in 9.1-7 are followed by an account of the controversy which arose as a result of the healing (verses 8-34). The present section (verses 35-41) forms the conclusion of the story, giving an account of the blind man's faith and the Pharisees' spiritual blindness.

The section heading, Spiritual Blindness, may be rendered in some languages "Blindness of the heart" or "Those whose hearts are blind." Or it may be effective to use such a title as "Those who insist they are not blind."

9.35   When Jesus heard what had happened, he found the man and asked him, "Do you believe in the Son of Man?"

In Greek this verse is a single sentence (note RSV "Jesus heard that they had cast him out, and having found him he said..."), which NEB divides into two sentences ("Jesus heard that they had expelled him. When he found him he asked..."). TEV translates as one sentence but re-structures the verse. Such differences between the Greek and English sentence divisions reflect the efforts of translators to achieve a natural sounding English style.

In translating he found the man, it is important to note that some languages have several different words for "find." Sometimes the meaning is "to come upon something accidentally," but in this particular context the implication is that Jesus, having heard about the man's being expelled from the synagogue, went to find him, that is, "looked for him and then found him."

Instead of the reading the Son of Man, some ancient manuscripts have "the Son of God," but the manuscript evidence is strongly in favor of the reading the Son of Man. If "the Son of God" had been the original reading, it is doubtful that a scribe would have changed it to read the Son of Man. No modern translation follows the reading "the Son of God." In many contexts it is important to introduce the first person singular when Jesus speaks of the Son of Man, but to do so in this context would not make sense, since immediately afterward the man asks who the Son of Man is.

9.36   The man answered, "Tell me who he is, sir, so I can believe in him!"

The man answered is literally "that one answered and said."
In Greek Tell me who he is, sir is literally "And who is he,
sir...?" (RSV). NEB translates exactly as TEV does, and JB is similar,
"'Sir,' the man replied 'tell me who he is...'" Sir in this verse is
the same as the word translated Lord in verse 38. But most translators
and commentators see a development from verse 36 to verse 38. In verse
36 the man merely addresses Jesus with a polite form of address, but in
verse 38 he confesses that Jesus truly is Lord.

9.37   Jesus said to him, "You have already seen him, and
         he is the one who is talking with you now."

Already and now are not in the Greek text. TEV incorporates these
adverbs to bring out as effectively as possible the contrast in meaning
in the Greek text between the perfect tense (have...seen) and the present tense (is talking). Phps and NAB include the adverb now in the
second clause of this sentence, while NEB translates "Indeed, it is he
who is speaking to you." Since this reference to the third person is
clearly a reference to Jesus himself, it may be necessary to introduce
the first person singular, for example, "You have already seen him, and
I am that very one, the one who is talking with you now."

9.38   "I believe, Lord!" the man said, and knelt down
         before Jesus.

Some consider this verse not to be an original part of John's Gospel,
but rather a later addition connected with a baptismal liturgy. It is
true that the verse is omitted in more than one important Greek manuscript, but most commentators and translators consider it an integral
part of John's Gospel. NAB includes it in brackets, with a note suggesting that it may not have been an original part of the text. The manuscript evidence is strongly in favor of the inclusion of this verse. Its
omission from some ancient manuscripts is perhaps explained by a desire
of some scribes to unite the teaching of verses 37 and 39.
The words the man said come first in Greek but TEV changes the word
order for stylistic reasons.
Knelt down before (NEB "bowed before") is the same verb often translated "worshiped" (RSV, JB). In some languages it may be necessary to
translate "bowed before Jesus and worshiped him."

9.39   Jesus said, "I came to this world to judge, so
         that the blind should see and those who see should
         become blind."

In Greek this verse begins "and Jesus said," again representing
Semitic style.
The TEV verb phrase to judge translates a noun phrase in Greek (lit-
erally "for judgment"), and it is emphatic in the sentence structure.
There is a contrast between this verse and 3.17 (For God did not send

his Son into the world to be its judge, but to be its savior), but there
is no real contradiction. The earlier verse affirms that the ultimate
purpose of God's sending his Son into the world was to be its savior.
This verse speaks of the inevitable results of the Son's coming: judgment
on those who refuse to open their eyes to the light.

A term for judge which means essentially "to indicate distinctions
between people" may be satisfactory in this context. However, the term
judge does not refer here to pronouncing condemnation or innocence, nor
is it a reference to final judgment. It is a reference to the exposure
of sins. In some languages this statement by Jesus may be rendered as
"I have come into the world in order that people's sins will be found
out" or "...be exposed." In one language this passage is translated
"I came into this world to be a means of dividing up people." The meaning of "dividing up" is clearly a reference to a process of judgment.

The contrast between sight and blindness in those who see should
become blind has its roots in the Old Testament. See especially Isaiah
29.18; 35.5; 42.7, but also Isaiah 6.10; 42.18-19. Here the point is
that those who reject Jesus reject the light of the world, while those
who accept him have the light of life.

9.40   Some Pharisees who were there with him heard
            him say this and asked him, "Surely you don't mean
            that we are blind, too?"

The phrase with him is translated in a variety of ways: RSV and
Phps "near him"; JB "who were present"; NEB "in his company"; NAB "around
him"; Mft "beside him."

The question raised by some Pharisees expects the answer "No." They
do not believe that they are blind.

9.41   Jesus answered, "If you were blind, then you
            would not be guilty; but since you claim that you
            can see, this means that you are still guilty."

Jesus answered is literally "Jesus said to them." You would not be
guilty is literally "you would not have sin." In light of the Old Testament, where sin may refer either to the deed itself or to guilt resulting from it, it is possible to take the word "sin" with the more specific
meaning of "guilt" in this context. Mft, JB, NEB, and RSV seem to feel
that the meaning of "guilt" is better suited to the context. Phps misses
the meaning by translating "nobody could blame you."

You are still guilty is literally "your sin/guilt remains" (see
RSV, JB, NEB). The verb "to remain," one of John's favorite terms, is
generally used in a positive sense; here, its connotation is clearly
negative.

In some languages a clear distinction is made between "sin" and
"guilt." "Sin" refers to the process of doing what is wrong, while "guilt"
refers to the condemnation which rests upon the individual who has done
wrong. In some languages guilt is expressed as "the weight of one's
sins" or "the counting of one's sins." In others it may be necessary to

explain guilt as a declaration of having sinned, for example, "If you were blind, you could not be condemned for having sinned" or "...you would not be condemned even though you had sinned."

CHAPTER 10

THE PARABLE OF THE SHEPHERD

10 Jesus said, "I am telling you the truth: the man who does not enter the sheep pen by the gate, but climbs in some other way, is a thief and a robber. 2 The man who goes in through the gate is the shepherd of the sheep. 3 The gatekeeper opens the gate for him; the sheep hear his voice as he calls his own sheep by name, and he leads them out. 4 When he has brought them out, he goes ahead of them, and the sheep follow him, because they know his voice. 5 They will not follow someone else; instead, they will run away from such a person, because they do not know his voice."

6 Jesus told them this parable, but they did not understand what he meant.

10 "Truly, truly, I say to you, he who does not enter the sheepfold by the door but climbs in by another way, that man is a thief and a robber; 2 but he who enters by the door is the shepherd of the sheep. 3 To him the gatekeeper opens; the sheep hear his voice, and he calls his own sheep by name and leads them out. 4 When he has brought out all his own, he goes before them, and the sheep follow him, for they know his voice. 5 A stranger they will not follow, but they will flee from him, for they do not know the voice of strangers." 6 This figure Jesus used with them, but they did not understand what he was saying to them.

Many commentators conclude that Chapter 10 does not logically follow Chapter 9; consequently a number of rearrangements have been suggested. Some of them are radical, while others involve only minor rearrangements. Very few translators rearrange the sequence of the text, but Mft places 10.19-29 at the end of Chapter 9, in what he believes to be a more logical sequence.

Actually the beginning of Chapter 10 follows naturally after 9.41. Chapter 10, an excellent commentary on Chapter 9, is connected closely with it. John gives no hint that Jesus is addressing a new audience, and it is best assumed that Jesus is continuing to speak to the Pharisees (see 9.40-41). Moreover, 10.21 presupposes the cure of the blind man and refers back to that event. The parable at the beginning of this chapter speaks not only of the good shepherd but also of thieves and robbers and of hired hands who do not care for the sheep. The theme of Chapter 10 is essentially that of Chapter 9: the denunciation of the Jewish authorities.

The parable (or perhaps better, parables) is given in verses 1-5, while verses 7-18 explain the meaning of the gate (verses 7-10) and of the shepherd (verses 11-18). The reaction to the parable itself is given in verse 6, and the reaction to the explanation of the parable is given in verses 19-21. Verses 1-5 are perhaps better taken as containing "twin parables," rather than a single parable. The first parable (verses 1-3a) concerns the proper way to come to the sheep, while the second (verses

3b-5) speaks of the responses of the sheep to the true shepherd and the false shepherd. The second parable is perhaps another denunciation of the Pharisees, pointing back to the man born blind of Chapter 9, who refused to obey the Pharisees but responded to the voice of the true shepherd.

Several complications, both grammatical and lexical, are involved in translating the section heading, The Parable of the Shepherd. First, some languages do not possess such a term as parable, and it may be necessary to use some kind of descriptive equivalent, for example, "a comparison story" or "a story which shows a comparison." The best equivalent may be "a story" or "an account." Rather than use a definite article, implying that the parable is already known, an indefinite article such as "a" may be used. The same applies to the Shepherd; an indefinite article such as "a" would be better.

One of the complications of translating Parable by "story" is that in this passage there is no real narrative but merely a description of what takes place in connection with the keeping of sheep in a pen.

10.1 **Jesus said, "I am telling you the truth: the man who does not enter the sheep pen by the gate, but climbs in some other way, is a thief and a robber.**

The details of this chapter regarding sheep and shepherd agree accurately with what is known of sheep herding in Palestine. Although sheep pens were sometimes located on hills and enclosed by stone walls, the one referred to here is apparently of a yard in front of a house and surrounded by a stone wall. It may be difficult to find an adequate term for sheep pen, which must often be described as "a place for the protection for sheep" or "a place where sheep are kept." The only equivalent in some languages is "a corral for sheep."

The Greek text has "door," but a number of translators find gate to be more appropriate.

There may be problems in rendering climbs in some other way. The only way that a thief or robber could get into the sheep pen would be by climbing over the wall, since the gate would obviously be guarded and there was no other opening. It may be necessary to say "but climbs over the wall" or "climbs over at some other place" (implying some place other than the gate). However, it may be possible to use a less specific expression, for example, "but gets into the sheep pen by some other means."

In some languages it is almost obligatory to employ the positive expression before the negative; therefore, it may be necessary to say "the man who gets into the sheep pen over the wall rather than by entering through the gate is a thief..."

In the phrase a thief and a robber most translations render the first noun as TEV does (it is used of Judas in 12.6), but there is considerable difference in the translation of the second word. RSV and NEB also have "robber," but NAB has "marauder"; Phps "rogue"; JB "brigand"; and Anchor Bible "bandit." Since the two Greek nouns which TEV renders thief and robber are not normally synonyms, it is suggested by some commentators that the Greek word "and" (kai) should here be translated "or." However, most translators prefer "and." In 18.40 the word here translated robber is used of Barabbas, but TEV renders it bandit. Bandit is quite possibly also the meaning in the present context, especially in light of the fact that this discourse on the good shepherd was probably connected with the Festival of Dedication (see verse 22). This festival celebrated the restoration and rededication of the Jewish Temple by Judas Maccabeus in 165 B.C. If the Maccabean leaders are the persons referred to in verse 8, the designation bandit fits the context of both verse 1 and verse 8 very well. Jesus is comparing the Pharisees to the leaders of the Maccabean revolt, whom the people willingly followed with Messianic expectations. These people were indeed thieves and bandits, and Jesus is affirming that the Pharisees are no better. They have come only to steal, kill, and destroy, but Jesus has come to give people life.

In general, the distinction between thief and robber is the fact that the thief employs stealth while the robber uses violence, to obtain what he takes away from other people. Most languages have ways of marking the distinction. A thief may be described as "one who takes away stealthily" and a robber as "one who takes away by threats or weapons" or "...by threat of injury or harm."

10.2   The man who goes in through the gate is the
            shepherd of the sheep.

The imagery of this verse is somewhat mixed, since later Jesus is pictured both as the gate (verse 7) and as the good shepherd (verse 11). The Greek text does not have the definite article before "shepherd," and so NAB renders "is shepherd of the sheep"; all other translations seem to prefer is the shepherd of the sheep.

A shepherd may be described as "one who takes care of the sheep." In some instances an expression for "takes care of" will focus upon the protection given to the sheep. In others a language may focus upon the provision made for the sheep in the sense of taking them out to pasture. There is no doubt that in some parts of the world it is anomalous to speak of a shepherd, since in certain tropical areas (for example, certain parts of Africa) sheep are primarily scavengers. However, the concept of protecting and providing for sheep is not an impossible one, though the translator may find it useful in some instances to provide a supplementary note telling something about the care and concern which ancient Semitic peoples had for their sheep.

10.3   The gatekeeper opens the gate for him; the sheep
            hear his voice as he calls his own sheep by name,
            and he leads them out.

In the Greek of this verse the verb opens does not have an expressed object, and the phrase for him is emphatic in the sentence structure. RSV translates literally "To him the gatekeeper opens." TEV supplies an object (the gate), since this information is implicit in the Greek text. JB ("the gatekeeper lets him in") and NEB ("The

[323]

door-keeper admits him") so restructure that no object is necessary.

It is necessary to make a clear distinction between the person who guarded the gate leading into the sheep pen and the shepherd. The gate-keeper was responsible for protecting the sheep during the night. The shepherd was one who came in the early morning and called his sheep, and then followed him out of the pen to pasture. The gatekeeper can always be described as "one who guarded the entrance to the sheep pen."

There may be serious complications in shifting from gate to "door." In some languages such a term as "door" refers only to the entrance to an enclosed building, such as a house, while gate indicates an entrance to an open area. In most languages it is better to use only one term, and preferably one that means gate, since a sheep pen was normally an open enclosure.

Evidently Palestinian shepherds often had pet names for their sheep, and that custom is referred to in the second part of verse 3; he calls his own sheep by name. In Greek this whole verse is one sentence connected by the conjunction "and" at three points. The first of these "ands" is replaced in TEV by a semicolon, the second is translated as, while the last does appear as and.

The verb translated leads them out is also used in the Septuagint of Numbers 27.17 and Ezekiel 34.13, both passages referring to shepherds.

10.4   When he has brought them out, he goes ahead of
            them, and the sheep follow him, because they know
            his voice.

This verse may imply that there are other sheep in the fold that do not recognize the shepherd's voice and so will not follow him. If so, this parable has a cutting edge. Jesus is not only speaking of those who hear his voice and follow him; he is also directing a polemic against those who refuse to acknowledge him and obey his voice.

In the clause when he has brought them out, the pronoun them actually translates "all his own" (RSV). TEV uses a pronoun in this verse because the pronoun follows the noun phrase his own sheep of the preceding verse.

The verb brought...out translates the same verb used in 9.34, where it means "to put out (of the synagogue)." Obviously the meaning "to bring out" or "to lead out" is intended here.

10.5   They will not follow someone else; instead, they
            will run away from such a person, because they do
            not know his voice.

The possibility that there were sheep that belonged to other shepherds in the same sheep pen evidently reflects an ancient custom, in which various shepherds brought their sheep to the same pen in the evening, to be guarded during the night by the gatekeeper. In the morning each shepherd would come to the pen and call his own sheep, and they would then follow him. Though in many parts of the world sheep are herded (that is, driven by shepherds), in the Middle East shepherds still walk ahead and their sheep follow them. It may be necessary to indicate by means of a marginal note these facts concerning shepherding in ancient times; otherwise, the story may appear to be anomalous and the analogies misleading.

In the Greek sentence structure, someone else is in the emphatic position. The word means literally "stranger," and it appears as such in most translations. TEV translates someone else, because in the present context the emphasis is not that the person involved is a stranger, but that he is not the sheep's own shepherd.

Because they do not know his voice is literally "because they do not know the voice of strangers." In Greek the first clause has the singular "stranger" (TEV someone else), while here it has the plural "strangers." In English it is more natural to be consistent throughout, using either a singular or a plural in both instances. Thus TEV uses a singular in both places: someone else...his (voice).

In this context know must be understood in the sense of "recognize," for example, "because they do not recognize his voice" or "because they do not recognize the voice as being that of their shepherd" or "...the one who takes care of them."

10.6   Jesus told them this parable, but they did not
              understand what he meant.

The pronoun them is best taken to refer back to the Pharisees of 9.40. JB indicates in a footnote that this is the noun to which the pronoun refers. GeCL renders "Jesus told this parable." In some languages it may be necessary to say "Jesus told the people there."

The word here translated parable (Greek paroimia) is not the word rendered parable (Greek parabolē) elsewhere in the Gospels. This particular word is used only here and in John 16.25,29 and 2 Peter 2.22. Although different translations use other terms for this word (for example, RSV, NAB "figure"; Mft "allegory"; Phps "illustration"), it is doubtful that in biblical Greek any distinction should be made between this term and the word normally used for parable, and so TEV, NEB, and JB all translate parable. In the Septuagint both words (parabolē and paroimia) are used to translate the Hebrew word mashal, a broad term referring to all types of figurative speech. There seems to be no perceptible difference between the term as John uses it here and the word the other Gospels use for "parable," and so it is probably best to translate both by the same term.

In translating Jesus told them this parable, one verb that specifies the act of telling a parable may be used; but in translating what he meant it may be necessary to use a verb that primarily means communicating, for example, "they did not understand what he was trying to say to them" or "...trying to communicate to them."

JESUS THE GOOD SHEPHERD

7 So Jesus said again, "I am telling you the truth: I am the gate for the sheep. 8 All others who came before me are thieves and robbers, but the sheep did not listen to them. 9 I am the gate. Whoever comes in by me will be saved; he will come in and go out and find pasture. 10 The thief comes only in order to steal, kill, and destroy. I have come in order that you might have life--life in all its fullness.	7 So Jesus again said to them, "Truly, truly, I say to you, I am the door of the sheep. 8 All who came before me are thieves and robbers; but the sheep did not heed them. 9 I am the door; if any one enters by me, he will be saved, and will go in and out and find pasture. 10 The thief comes only to steal and kill and destroy; I came that they may have life, and have it abundantly.

10.7   So Jesus said again, "I am telling you the truth:
          I am the gate for the sheep.

Verses 7-21 is the subject of analysis at verse 1.
The section heading Jesus the Good Shepherd may be rendered in some languages "Jesus likens himself to a good shepherd" or "Jesus says that he is like a good shepherd." It is also possible to use the phrase "a good shepherd" or "one who takes good care of the sheep." In this type of phrase the term "good" does not qualify the moral character of the shepherd but the efficiency and dedication with which he does his work.
I am the gate for the sheep is literally "I am the door of the sheep." By translating the Greek phrase "of the sheep" as for the sheep (so also Phps), TEV makes explicit the meaning of this genitive expression. Here the expression I am is followed by a noun in the predicate position (see comments at 4.26), and so the structure is similar to I am the bread of life (6.35).
Instead of the reading "door," one ancient Greek manuscript of the New Testament and one ancient translation read "shepherd." Among modern translations Mft appears to be the only one to accept this alternative reading. The reading "door" was probably changed to "shepherd" by some scribe in an attempt to make the parable appear more self-consistent. It seems difficult to think of Jesus as both door (verse 7) and shepherd (verses 11,14) in the same parable, and so the scribe may have deleted the reference to door from this verse.
In the statement I am the gate for the sheep it may be necessary to change the metaphor to a simile in some languages to make clear the intention of this passage, for example, "I am just like a gate for the sheep." However, as noted in the discussion of the differences between "door" and gate, it may be necessary to continue the use of such a term as gate. Otherwise there may be disruption and confusion in the meaning.
In some languages it may be important to indicate more clearly the relation between the gate and the sheep, for example, "I am like a gate for the sheep to use" or even "...for the sheep to come in and go out of" or "...to pass through."

<u>10.8</u>   All others who came before me are thieves and
            robbers, but the sheep did not listen to them.

It is difficult to determine precisely who is referred to in <u>all
others who came before me</u>. Evidently this expression was taken by some
scribes as a reference to the Old Testament period, and so one ancient
Greek manuscript and several other ancient sources omit the word <u>all</u>
from the text. However, the evidence for the omission of this word is
very weak. It is readily seen why a scribe would delete it from the
text, but it is difficult to see any possible reason for adding it, if
it was not there originally. On the other hand, the words <u>before me</u>
are problematic, and the UBS Greek text places them in brackets to
indicate their uncertainty. It may be that these words were added in
an attempt to explain the meaning of the verb <u>came</u>, or it may be that
they were omitted to help resolve the difficulty mentioned in connection
with the word <u>all</u>. Even though the inclusion of <u>before me</u> remains problematic, most modern translations include this phrase.
    In spite of the textual difficulties, there is no real problem in
the interpretation of the text as it stands, provided one takes the reference to <u>thieves and robbers</u> to be the same here as in verse 1. It is
not, of course, a blanket reference to all leaders of the Old Testament
period. It would include any leaders, including prophets, priests, or
kings, who had taken advantage of the people God had placed in their
care; it would also include the false Messianic pretenders, as well as
the Pharisees and Sadducees of Jesus' own day. <u>Thieves</u> and <u>robbers</u> are
the same words used in verse 1.
    <u>All others who came before me</u> may be rendered in some languages
"All others who have come in the past." It may, however, be necessary
to indicate clearly just who "all others" are, for example, "All others
who have come pretending to take care of the sheep." It is also possible
to make this meaning clear by means of a marginal note.
    The Greek verb "to hear" covers a broad area of meaning. TEV takes
it here to mean <u>did...listen to</u>. RSV translates "did...heed"; NEB "paid
...heed to"; JB "took...notice of"; and Mft "would...listen to."

<u>10.9</u>   I am the gate. Whoever comes in by me will be saved;
            he will come in and go out and find pasture.

It is obvious from this verse that Jesus is <u>the gate</u> by which one
enters into the Kingdom. In the Greek sentence construction the phrase
<u>by me</u> is emphatic, thus emphasizing that Jesus is the only one through
whom one enters the Kingdom. The one who enters through Jesus is saved,
and he has freedom, which is expressed by the phrase <u>come in and go out</u>.
The expression <u>find pasture</u> describes the life-sustaining force that is
given to the believer. Jesus is the bread of life and the water of life,
and he provides his sheep with pasture that sustains them.
    As in verse 7, it may be necessary to introduce a simile, for ex-
ample, "I am just like a gate" or "I am just like the gate for the
sheep."
    <u>Will be saved</u> may in this context be translated "will become safe."
Or it may be expressed negatively as "will be kept from danger."

10.10   The thief comes only in order to steal, kill, and
               destroy. I have come in order that you might have
               life--life in all its fullness.

The Greek text literally reads "the thief," and TEV and most other
translations maintain this expression exactly as the Greek has it. The
definite article the does not point to any specific thief, but is simply
a part of the parabolic style. The reference is generic, and such an
expression as "a thief" or "thieves" may also be used.

TEV and several other translations change the Greek negative expression (literally "does not come except in order to") into a positive
one: comes only in order to.

The verb translated kill is used only here in John's Gospel; it
refers specifically to the killing of animals and literally means
"slaughter" (NAB). The word destroy is a frequently used Johannine term.
In John 3.16 this verb is used intransitively, where it is translated
die in TEV. In 6.39 Jesus, speaking of those whom the Father has given
him, says I should not lose any of all those he has given me. There the
verb "to destroy" is used with the meaning of lose. It may be that here
the verb carries more overtones of meaning than its companion verb "to
kill"; that is, it may well connote eternal destruction. However, this
idea is merely intimated, and should not be expressed in translation.
It is better to translate by a general term, such as "to destroy," rather
than to specify "to destroy eternally," even though this idea may be involved here. In some languages it may be difficult to find a term meaning "destroy" which will contrast with or at least amplify the concept
of "kill." In speaking of the destruction of an animal, "kill" seems to
be the strongest term which could be employed, but in some languages a
general term, such as "to get rid of" or "to ruin" or "to cause to be
no more" may be used.

TEV shifts to the second person you, in place of the Greek third
person "they." This is an important shift, since the persons referred
to are Jesus' followers rather than the Pharisees to whom the parable
is addressed (verse 6). GeCL translates "they" by "my sheep." It may
be possible also to render "people" or "they who hear my voice." The
life referred to is eternal life, a central and basic theme of this
Gospel.

The expression life in all its fullness (NEB "and may have it in
all its fullness") is translated in various ways. RSV ("and have it
abundantly") and NAB ("and have it to the full") are fairly close to
the form of the Greek. Since in many languages life must be translated
by a verb meaning "to live," it may be necessary here to translate
"that they might really live." The final phrase life in all its
fullness may then possibly be translated "that they may live completely"
or even "...completely and wonderfully." Or this idea may be expressed
by the use of a negation, for example, "that there may be nothing lacking in their living."

TEV   (10.11-16)   RSV

11 "I am the good shepherd, who
is willing to die for the sheep.
12 When the hired man, who is not
a shepherd and does not own the
sheep, sees a wolf coming, he
leaves the sheep and runs away; so
the wolf snatches the sheep and
scatters them. 13 The hired man
runs away because he is only a
hired man and does not care about
the sheep. 14-15 I am the good
shepherd. As the Father knows me
and I know the Father, in the same
way I know my sheep and they know
me. And I am willing to die for
them. 16 There are other sheep
which belong to me that are not in
this sheep pen. I must bring them,
too; they will listen to my voice,
and they will become^v one flock
with one shepherd.

11 I am the good shepherd. The
good shepherd lays down his life
for the sheep. 12 He who is a
hireling and not a shepherd, whose
own the sheep are not, sees the
wolf coming and leaves the sheep
and flees; and the wolf snatches
them and scatters them. 13 He
flees because he is a hireling
and cares nothing for the sheep.
14 I am the good shepherd; I know
my own and my own know me, 15 as
the Father knows me and I know
the Father; and I lay down my life
for the sheep. 16 And I have other
sheep, that are not of this fold;
I must bring them also, and they
will heed my voice. So there shall
be one flock, one shepherd.

^{v}they will become; *some manuscripts
have* there will be.

10.11   "I am the good shepherd, who is willing to die
               for the sheep.

Jesus speaks of himself as the good shepherd. The meaning of the
adjective translated good (Greek kalos) here and in verse 14 depends on
the context more than on the etymology of the word itself. Jesus is the
good shepherd, the one who is willing to die for the sheep, in contrast
to thieves, robbers, and hired men, who either destroy the sheep themselves or allow them to be destroyed. In this context good may therefore be understood in the sense of "dedicated" or "devoted," that is,
"the shepherd who is devoted to his sheep" or "...gives himself for
his sheep."
          Is willing to die for the sheep is more literally "lays down his
life for the sheep" (RSV, NEB, NAB). The expression "to lay down one's
life" is used also in 13.37 and in 15.13, as well as in 1 John 3.16. In
13.37 the future form is used, and it is translated by TEV I am ready
to die for you! In 15.13 TEV translates to give his life. In the present
passage TEV and Phps ("The good shepherd will give his life for the sake
of his sheep") take Jesus' words as a reference to a general truth, describing what a good shepherd is like, rather than as a specific reference to what Jesus as the good shepherd will eventually do for his
sheep. Some commentators point out that, though this meaning is possible for the present verse, it is made difficult by the explicit reference to Jesus' own death in verses 17-18. But this conclusion is not
required. It is possible to take both passages (this verse and 17-18) as

a statement of the good shepherd's willingness to die for his sheep,
as TEV does. In some languages it is necessary to indicate specifically
how or why the shepherd dies for the sheep, for example, "is willing to
die in order to protect the sheep" or "...to keep the sheep from harm."

10.12   When the hired man, who is not a shepherd and does
not own the sheep, sees a wolf coming, he leaves the
sheep and runs away; so the wolf snatches the sheep
and scatters them.

In Greek this verse begins with an absolute statement "the hired
man...," which TEV has changed to a dependent clause (when the hired
man...) for stylistic reasons.

The hired man may be rendered as "the man who is just paid to take
care of sheep" or "the man who is paid to take care of other people's
sheep."

Who is not a shepherd may be translated "whose real work is not
that of taking care of sheep" or "who is not a shepherd by profession."

The phrase does not own the sheep must be translated in some languages "the sheep do not belong to him."

So the wolf snatches the sheep and scatters them is translated
"Then the wolf harries the flock and scatters the sheep" by NEB; JB
translates "and then the wolf attacks and scatters the sheep." The
verb translated snatches in TEV is used frequently in Greek to refer
to wild animals carrying away their prey. It may be awkward in some
languages to speak of both snatching and scattering the sheep, as though
the two activities affect all the sheep in the same way. What happens
is that the wolf grabs one of the sheep and causes the rest of them
to scatter. This meaning may be expressed as "pounces upon one of the
sheep and scatters the rest."

In languages that have no indigenous term for wolf, some translators
prefer a term identifying another kind of animal which may attack sheep,
for example, a "leopard." Others prefer to use a term which would designate an animal either resembling or belonging to the dog family, for
example, "hyena" or "wild dog." Translators sometimes use a generic
term, such as "dog," but qualify it as "fierce."

10.13   The hired man runs away because he is only a
hired man and does not care about the sheep.

In Greek this verse is literally "because he is a hired man and
does not care about the sheep." If one puts a full stop at the end of
verse 12, as most translations do, some information must be introduced
at the beginning of verse 13. RSV begins this verse by "He flees because..."; NEB "The man runs away because..."; JB "this is because...";
and NAB "That is because..." The purpose of this information is to make
it clear to the reader that the because clause refers back to the first
half, not to the second half, of verse 12. Otherwise, the second half
of verse 12 and the first part of verse 13 would read "so the wolf
snatches the sheep and scatters them, because he is a hired man and

does not care for the sheep." TEV (also JB) introduces the adverb <u>only</u> (because <u>he is only a hired man</u>), thus conveying more clearly the intent of the Greek.

<u>Does not care about the sheep</u> must be translated in some languages "has no love for the sheep." More is intended than mere failure to provide for the sheep. The meaning may be expressed in some languages as "he is not concerned for the sheep" or "the sheep make no difference to him" or "it's all the same to him, no matter what happens to the sheep."

10.14-15   I am the good shepherd. As the Father knows me
                  and I know the Father, in the same way I know my
                  sheep and they know me. And I am willing to die
                  for them.

In Greek these two verses are one sentence, which undergoes some restructuring in TEV. The opening statement, <u>I am the good shepherd</u>, is followed in Greek by "and I know my own, and my own know me, just as the Father knows me, and I know the Father." TEV inverts the order of comparison by placing first the comparative clause <u>as the Father knows</u> <u>me and I know the Father</u> and then introducing the main clause (<u>in the</u> <u>same way I know my sheep</u> and they know me). In this clause TEV translates the first Greek "my own" as <u>my sheep</u>, and the second by the pronoun <u>they</u>. This change is legitimate, since in the last clause in Greek <u>sheep</u> are explicitly referred to (literally "and I give my life for the <u>sheep</u>"). TEV introduces earlier the information that those whom Jesus calls his own are his sheep; therefore, TEV is able to render the second reference to sheep by the pronoun <u>them</u>. In this context the verb translated <u>know</u> should be understood in the sense of "intimate acquaintance with." The meaning is not "knowing about," but personal knowledge, based upon acquaintance and familiarity.

<u>I am willing to die for them</u> is similar in construction to the Greek of verse 11 (<u>the good shepherd is willing to die for the sheep</u>). The element of willingness, which TEV includes, finds its basis in verse 18 (<u>I give it up of my own free will</u>). <u>To die for them</u> must be expressed in some languages as "to die in order to protect them." However, in others it is possible to employ a kind of benefactive, for example, "to die for their benefit" or "to die in order to help them." In one language the expression <u>to die for them</u> is rendered literally "to give my heart for them," indicating not only death, but also emotional concern.

10.16   There are other sheep which belong to me that
                  are not in this sheep pen. I must bring them,
                  too; they will listen to my voice, and they
                  will become^v one flock with one shepherd.

                  ^{v}they will become; *some manuscripts have* there
                  will be.

The sheep that are not in this sheep pen is taken by most commentators as a reference to Gentile believers. However, this is not the kind of information which a translator should introduce into the text.

As TEV points out in footnote "v," they will become one flock with one shepherd reads in some manuscripts "there will be one flock with one shepherd." There is strong Greek manuscript evidence for each of these readings, but "they will be" has slightly stronger support. The UBS Committee on the Greek text judges that "there will be" was introduced as a stylistic correction. It should at least be pointed out that most modern English translators favor "there will be." In fact, TEV is definitely in the minority with its reading they will become. Fortunately, as far as ultimate meaning is concerned, there is no basic difference.

They will become one flock implies that the other sheep, as well as those of the sheep pen of which Jesus is speaking, will together become one flock. It may therefore be necessary to say in some languages "they all will become one flock," since they must refer both to the sheep within the sheep pen and to the other sheep.

With one shepherd may be expressed as a separate clause, for example, "they will become one flock and they will have one shepherd" or "...and one shepherd will take care of them."

TEV	(10.17-18)	RSV

17 "The Father loves me because I am willing to give up my life, in order that I may receive it back again. 18 No one takes my life away from me. I give it up of my own free will. I have the right to give it up, and I have the right to take it back. This is what my Father has commanded me to do."

17 For this reason the Father loves me, because I lay down my life, that I may take it again. 18 No one takes it from me, but I lay it down of my own accord. I have power to lay it down, and I have power to take it again; this charge I have received from my Father."

10.17   "The Father loves me because I am willing to give up my life, in order that I may receive it back again.

In Greek the first part of this verse reads literally "because of this the Father loves me because I give up my life." TEV combines the two "because" constructions and introduces the English sentence with the Father, the subject of the Greek sentence. NEB and JB do exactly the same. Here again, as in verses 11 and 14, TEV takes the Greek expression as indicating Christ's willingness to die.

It is best to take the Greek conjunction (hina) with its full force, indicating purpose (TEV in order that). According to the teaching of the Gospel of John, the death, resurrection, and exaltation of Jesus are looked upon as one event, not as single isolated actions. JB makes clear the notion of purpose ("in order to take it up again"), while NAB translates "to take it up again," and RSV "that I may take it again."

In some languages it is impossible to say give up my life. The only equivalent would be "voluntarily die" or "die, not being forced by someone else to do so." Similarly it may be impossible to say "receive life back again." One can normally receive material things, but not a state of being, such as life. Therefore it may be necessary to translate the purpose clause "in order that I may live again" or "...become alive again."

10.18   No one takes my life away from me. I give it up
                of my own free will. I have the right to give it
                up, and I have the right to take it back. This is
                what my Father has commanded me to do."

In Greek my life is literally a pronoun "it," which TEV makes explicit by translating as a noun.

In place of the present tense, takes...away, some ancient Greek manuscripts have the past tense "took away" (NEB "No one has robbed me of it"). The past tense is obviously the more difficult reading. It is best taken, not as a reference to past attempts on Jesus' life, but rather to the crucifixion viewed from the time the Gospel was written, rather than from the time Jesus was speaking. The UBS Committee prefers the present tense, because the manuscript evidence supporting the past tense is too limited in its range and represents only the Egyptian family of manuscripts. Evidently most translators prefer the present tense, but modern commentators tend to consider the past tense as the original reading.

The present tense in No one takes my life away from me is entirely acceptable in English, since it refers to a process reported as already begun or contemplated. However, in some languages the present tense would not be acceptable, since it would imply that Jesus was at that very time in process of dying. Therefore it may be necessary to say "No one will take my life away from me." A literal translation of "take my life away from me" may be misleading or even impossible. One may translate "kill," but it is not the meaning of this passage to say "no one will kill me." The meaning must be expressed in some languages as "No one will kill me unless I let him do so" or "...unless I permit him to kill me."

Of my own free will (so also NEB and JB) is the meaning most translations give to Jesus' words. The same expression is used in 5.30 (TEV on my own authority). I give it up of my own free will may be rendered in some languages "I am the one who allows myself to be killed" or "I am the one who permits my life to cease."

The noun translated right (so also NEB) is rendered "power" in most translations. The same word is used in 1.12, and its primary meaning is right or "authority," though some commentators believe that in this context it is equivalent to "power." Here the meaning right seems more in keeping with the context, since it is something the Father has commanded Jesus to do. That is, the meaning right or "authority" is more in keeping with the idea of a command than is the meaning "power." In some languages the closest equivalent to right is "ability," for example, "I am able to give up my life and I am able to take it back again" or "I am able to permit myself to be killed, and I am able to come back to life."

My Father has commanded me to do translates substitute passive construction in Greek (literally "this command I received from my Father"). TEV makes it into an active construction. It may be necessary to restructure the final sentence of verse 18 as direct discourse, for example, "My Father has commanded me, 'This is what you shall do.'"

TEV	(10.19-21)	RSV

19 Again there was a division among the people because of these words. 20 Many of them were saying, "He has a demon! He is crazy! Why do you listen to him?"

21 But others were saying, "A man with a demon could not talk like this! How could a demon give sight to blind people?"

19 There was again a division among the Jews because of these words. 20 Many of them said, "He has a demon, and he is mad; why listen to him?" 21 Others said, "These are not the sayings of one who has a demon. Can a demon open the eyes of the blind?"

10.19   Again there was a division among the people because of these words.

The presence of the adverb again makes this verse more difficult to translate than may be apparent. For example, NEB sounds as if the same words had previously caused a division among the Jews ("These words once again caused a split among the Jews"). GeCL resolves the problem of "again" by rendering "Because of this assertion the Jews were again divided in their opinion regarding Jesus."

In some languages one must make specific the causal relation between the words and the resulting division, for example, "These words of Jesus caused the Jews to be divided again."

It is important to avoid giving the impression that there was a physical division or separation in the group. It may be necessary to specify that the division was one of argument or viewpoint, for example, "again they argued among themselves" or "again they had two different opinions."

10.20   Many of them were saying, "He has a demon! He is crazy! Why do you listen to him?"

Verses 20 and 21 explain the division caused among the Jews by Jesus' words. Some thought he was demon-possessed (verse 20), while others suggest that it was impossible for a demon to open the eyes of blind men (verse 21).

Also in 7.20 and in 8.48 Jesus is accused of being demon-possessed. He has a demon! He is crazy! in reality represents a single accusation, for according to ancient Jewish thought, demon possession caused insanity. Because of the causal relation between having a demon and being crazy, it may be possible to say "Because he has a demon, he is crazy" or "He has a demon and therefore he is crazy." As has already been pointed out in other contexts, it may be necessary to use different expressions for He has a demon, for example, "A demon has him" or "...is riding him" or "...lives within him." Different languages possess various idioms for being crazy, for example, "His mind is twisted," "His mind has left him," "He doesn't have the world," and "He has become another person."

Listen to translates the same verb used in verse 16. In the present context it may be translated "pay any attention to."

10.21   But others were saying, "A man with a demon could not talk like this! How could a demon give sight to blind people?"

Could not talk like this must refer to content, not to manner of speech, for example, "could not say things like this" or "could not communicate a message such as he has communicated."

How could a demon give sight to blind people? is more literally "Can a demon open the eyes of blind men?" In Greek the expected answer is "No." This exclamatory question may be changed into a statement: "A demon could certainly not give sight to blind people" or "...cause blind people to see."

TEV   (10.22-30)   RSV

JESUS IS REJECTED

22 It was winter, and the Festival of the Dedication of the Temple was being celebrated in Jerusalem. 23 Jesus was walking in Solomon's Porch in the Temple, 24 when the people gathered around him and asked, "How long are you going to keep us in suspense? Tell us the plain truth: are you the Messiah?"

25 Jesus answered, "I have already told you, but you would not believe me. The deeds I do by my Father's authority speak on my behalf; 26 but you will not believe, for you are not my sheep. 27 My sheep listen to my voice; I know them, and they follow me. 28 I give them eternal life, and they shall never die. No one can snatch them away from me. 29 What my Father has given me is greater^w than everything, and no one can snatch them

22 It was the feast of the Dedication at Jerusalem; 23 it was winter, and Jesus was walking in the temple, in the portico of Solomon. 24 So the Jews gathered round him and said to him, "How long will you keep us in suspense? If you are the Christ, tell us plainly." 25 Jesus answered them, "I told you, and you do not believe. The works that I do in my Father's name, they bear witness to me; 26 but you do not believe, because you do not belong to my sheep. 27 My sheep hear my voice, and I know them, and they follow me; 28 and I give them eternal life, and they shall never perish, and no one shall snatch them out of my hand. 29 My Father, who has given them to me,^{w} is greater than all, and no one is able to snatch them out of the Father's hand. 30 I and the Father

[335]

away from the Father's care. 30
The Father and I are one."

*w*What my Father has given me is
greater; *some manuscripts have*
My Father, who gave them to me,
is greater.

are one."

*w*Other ancient authorities read
What my Father has given to me

The Festival of Dedication is the last in the series of four
important Jewish holy days mentioned in John's Gospel, beginning in
Chapter 5 (the Sabbath, Passover, Shelters, and Dedication). By healing
the lame man on the Sabbath day, Jesus indicated his superiority over
the Sabbath; by the teaching given in connection with the healing (5.17),
he identified himself and his activity with God and with God's work.
During the Passover Festival Jesus fed the multitude and so revealed
that he was the life-giving bread that God had sent down from heaven.
And at the Festival of Shelters, Jesus revealed himself as the life-
giving water and the light for the world, thus fulfilling the meaning
of the water and light ceremonies connected with that festival. Now,
at the Festival of Dedication, Jesus affirms that he is the one whom
God has dedicated and sent into the world (see comments at verse 36).
        Verses 40-42 conclude the series of events which began in Chapter
5. In fact, these verses form a conclusion to the entire public ministry of Jesus.
        The rest of the chapter (verses 22-39) is in the form of two
parallel accounts. The first (verses 22-30) revolves about the question
are you the Messiah? (verse 24). This question is actually related to
Jesus' claim to be the good shepherd, and in answering the question
Jesus again describes his followers as sheep (verses 26-27). In the
Old Testament, the Davidic King is often represented as the shepherd
of his people, and so the affirmation that Jesus is the good shepherd
has Messianic overtones. In answering this question in verse 24, Jesus
appeals to the works that he had done by his Father's authority (verse
25). He points out that the reason the people will not believe is because they are not his sheep, and they do not belong to him (verse 26).
The analogy between shepherd and sheep is further developed in the following verses. Jesus speaks of the security of his sheep by affirming
no one can snatch them away from me (verse 28). This short account
concludes with the statement of Jesus' identity with the Father (verse
30). Then the Jews once more pick up stones to throw at him (verse 31),
which introduces the second account.
        The first of the two parallel accounts (verses 22-30) is centered
around the question of Jesus' Messiahship (verse 24); the second (verses
31-39) around the statement you are trying to make yourself God (verse
33). Jesus quotes from Scripture to show that this accusation is not
valid (verse 34). Then he argues from this Scripture text to validate
his claim to be the Son of God (verses 35-36). Again he appeals to the
things he has done as a witness to who he really is (verse 37), and he
concludes with a statement affirming his unity with the Father (verse
38). This second narrative section ends with the reaction of the Jews,
who try to arrest Jesus (verse 39).
        The section heading, Jesus is Rejected, may be transformed into an

active expression, for example, "The people reject Jesus" or, in many
languages, "The people rejected Jesus," using a past rather than a present tense form.

10.22   It was winter, and the Festival of the
             Dedication of the Temple was being celebrated
             in Jerusalem.

The Festival of Dedication was known also as Hanukkah, or "Tabernacles of the month of Kislev"(2 Macc 1.9). This month was approximately equivalent to December. The festival celebrated the rededication
of the Temple in 164 B.C., after the Syrians had profaned it for three
years (Macc 4.54). It began on the 25th day of the month and lasted for
eight days, and it was a time of great happiness for the Jews. For
Festival a term meaning "feast" may be used, but the focus of meaning
should be not upon eating, but upon the joy that accompanied the celebration. It may be possible to translate the Festival of the Dedication
...was being celebrated in a combined expression meaning "celebrate the
time for remembering the dedication of the Temple."
   Winter in Jerusalem can be cold, and this fact perhaps explains
why Jesus was walking in Solomon's Porch in the Temple (verse 23). In
some languages it is better to employ such a term as "a cold time" or
"a cold season," rather than attempt to define winter in terms of a
particular period of the year. If one must use a term for winter which
depends upon the annual calendar, it may be necessary, especially in
the tropics or in the southern hemisphere, to provide a marginal note
explaining that at this time of the year the weather was cold.

10.23   Jesus was walking in Solomon's Porch in the
             Temple,

The Temple area was surrounded on all four sides by covered porches
which were open on the inside, facing the Temple, but closed on the outside. It is generally believed that Solomon's Porch was the one on the
eastern side, but there is no certainty as to that.
   Verse 23 is a continuation of the sentence which begins in Greek
with verse 22; it literally begins "and Jesus was walking..." It is better
to take the verb as a simple past progressive (was walking) than to see
in it a customary action of Jesus (Mft "used to walk"). JB sounds as if
Jesus was pacing the floor: "and Jesus was in the Temple walking up and
down in the Portico of Solomon." The word translated Temple does not
refer to the sanctuary proper, but to "the Temple precincts" (NEB). NAB
has "in the temple area." TEV restructures verses 23 and 24 slightly,
making verse 23 an independent clause and verse 24 a dependent clause.
In Greek, verse 24 is an independent sentence in itself.
   In some languages the choice of a verb to translate was walking
depends upon the way one interprets this manner of walking. Often there
are three distinct verbs for walking: one would mean walking through the
Temple, the second would imply strolling around in the Temple looking at
various objects, while the third would suggest walking back and forth in

the area. Either the second or the third meaning seems appropriate for this particular context.

The phrase Solomon's Porch can be misconstrued if translated literally, since it may suggest a porch belonging specifically to Solomon. It was, of course, a porch associated with the name of Solomon. Therefore it may be best to translate as "Jesus was walking in a porch called Solomon's Porch" or "...in a place called Solomon's Porch." Such an expression will avoid the misunderstanding that Jesus was walking in a porch which actually belonged to Solomon.

10.24   when the people gathered around him and asked,
          "How long are you going to keep us in suspense?
          Tell us the plain truth: are you the Messiah?"

When the people gathered around him and asked is literally "therefore the Jews gathered around him and said to him." On "the Jews," see Appendix I.

In some languages it would be preferable to make verse 23 the dependent temporal clause, and change the contents into the main clause, for example, "while Jesus was walking in Solomon's Porch in the Temple, the people gathered around him..."

In some instances it may be necessary to use such a phrase as "some people," since "the Jews" could be misunderstood to mean that all the Jews gathered around him. Moreover, these particular Jews have not been specifically identified, and it would be wrong to suggest that they were precisely the same ones who confronted Jesus in earlier accounts.

Keep...in suspense is the meaning that most translators give the phrase that John uses here, though some commentators suggest that it may mean "to annoy," a meaning it has in modern Greek. This question may be rendered in some languages "How long are you going to delay in telling us the truth?" or "How long are you going to keep us wondering?"

The plain truth, actually an adverb in Greek, means more literally "plainly" (Mft, RSV, NEB, JB). NAB translates it "in plain words." In Greek this last part of verse 24 literally reads "if you are the Christ, tell us plainly." To give it more effect in English, TEV places the question last and precedes it with the statement Tell us the plain truth. This expression may be rendered in some languages "Tell us clearly" or "...so that we can understand well" or "...so that we will not misunderstand."

Here again the Greek term "the Christ" (RSV) is a technical term referring to the Jewish Messiah, and so TEV and some other English translations (NEB, NAB) render it "the Messiah." It is impossible to determine precisely who raised this question or what motives were involved. The question may have come from those who were truly puzzled (see verse 21), but more likely it came from those who had already made up their minds regarding Jesus.

10.25   Jesus answered, "I have already told you, but
          you would not believe me. The deeds I do by my Father's
          authority speak on my behalf;

Jesus answered is literally "Jesus answered them," but here again the indirect object is clearly implied in the TEV rendering.

I have already told translates a simple past in Greek (RSV "I told"), rendered in some English translations "I have told" (NEB,JB). There is no indication in John's Gospel that Jesus explicitly told the Jews that he was the Messiah (only to the Samaritan woman did he clearly declare this, 4.26). On the other hand, his actions and teachings were such that there should have been no doubt among the Jews concerning his identity. In this very verse Jesus refers to the works that he has done as testimony to who he is.

Jesus literally says "you do not believe," which TEV takes to have the force of you would not believe (so GeCL). An equivalent of you would not believe in some languages is "you didn't want to believe" or "you refused to believe."

By my Father's authority is literally "in my Father's name" (so most translations). In Jewish thought the name of a person can represent that person and his authority, and so TEV translates by a more natural English equivalent (see 1.12). (See 14.13 for a discussion of "in my name.") In some languages by my Father's authority may best be rendered "just as my Father told me to do" or "this is precisely what my Father ordered" or "this is just what my Father said I could say."

Speak on my behalf is literally "testify concerning me." (On the use of the verb "to testify" or "to witness" see 1.7.)

10.26   but you will not believe, for you are not my
               sheep.

In the phrase you will not believe the pronoun you is emphatic, as is the pronoun I in the last sentence of verse 25. A sharp contrast is drawn between the I of verse 25 and the you of verse 26.

You will not believe is more literally "you do not believe" (so most translations); NAB has "but you refuse to believe," and GeCL "you would not believe." The idea of will may also be involved here, as it is in the first part of verse 25 (you would not believe).

After the clause because you are not my sheep, some ancient manuscripts add "just as I told you." No modern translations include this clause in their text, and the UBS Committee on the Greek text considers it a scribal addition. It is possible that it was deliberately omitted by some scribes because they could not find in the earlier account any saying of Jesus that these Jews were not his sheep. Absolute certainty cannot be achieved, but it is suggested that the translator follow the decision of the UBS Committee, which also is the conclusion of most modern translators.

At this point John reintroduces the metaphor of the sheep, and it may be necessary to mark this figurative usage as a simile, for example, "because you are not my sheep, so to speak" or "because you are not my sheep, as it were."

10.27   My sheep listen to my voice; I know them, and
               they follow me.

This verse reiterates themes found in verses 4 (the sheep follow him, because they know his voice) and verse 14 (I know my sheep).
There may be some confusion in rendering My sheep listen to my voice, since if one were speaking literally of sheep, the translation would probably be "listen to the sound of my voice," while if one were speaking about people, it would probably be "listen to what I say." Note, however, that beginning with verse 28, there is a definite shift back to speaking about people rather than sheep. Therefore it may be preferable to use a form which means essentially "listen to what I say."

<u>10.28</u>   I give them eternal life, and they shall never
              die. No one can snatch them away from me.

I give them eternal life is similar to verse 10: I have come that you may have eternal life (on the concept of eternal life see 1.4 and 3.15). The verb translated die is the same verb used in 3.16.
Because sheep have been specifically identified in verse 27, it may be misleading to use the pronoun them in verse 28, since it would imply that sheep were to have eternal life. This difficulty may often be avoided by translating "I give to my followers eternal life" or "...those people who follow me..."
No one can snatch them away from me has its counterpart in verse 12. From me (so also JB) is literally "from my hand." NEB translates "from my care."

<u>10.29</u>   What my Father has given me is greater[w] than
              everything, and no one can snatch them away
              from the Father's care.

              [w]What my Father has given me is greater; *some*
              manuscripts have My Father, who gave them to
              me, is greater.

There are serious textual problems in the first part of this verse. A detailed discussion of the problems is beyond the scope of this commentary. The real possibilities finally resolve themselves basically into two choices. The text may read either (1) what my Father has given me is greater than everything (literally "all") or (2) "my Father, who gave them to me, is greater than everything." TEV accepts the first alternative. It is certainly the more difficult reading, but from it the origin of the other readings can be explained. The antecedent of the relative pronoun what must be taken to be the sheep of verse 27. Elsewhere in John the singular neuter relative pronoun (what) is used in a collective sense of the disciples God gave to Jesus (see 17.2). To assume that these people (sheep in the present passage) are greater than everything is a difficult thought, and for that reason the reading was changed in some manuscripts to "my Father, who gave them to me, is greater than all."
A literal translation of "What my Father has given me is greater than all" may be misleading, since it may imply that a particular

present which the Father had given to his Son was greater than all other presents. To make clear that the content of what is given refers to people, it may be necessary to translate "those whom my Father has given me are greater than all." However, such an expression does not make much sense, for it is extremely difficult to determine just what greater could mean in this context. The Greek term simply means "more than," but it is difficult to understand what could be compared with those who are given to Jesus by the Father. Yet the second clause of verse 29 does suggest a comparison between the Father's power and that of someone else who might presumably want to snatch these persons out of the care of the Father. For that reason many translators follow the second interpretation, namely, "My Father who gave them to me is greater than everything."

In Greek the verb snatch has no expressed object, but TEV includes the object them (so also a number of other translations). JB translates without an object ("and no one can steal from the Father"). Thus also NAB ("and there is no snatching out of his hand"); Gdsp and Phps have "anything." If one follows TEV's choice of Greek text for the first part of this verse, them is the best object to supply, since it can refer back to what my Father has given me. However, if the alternative text is followed, it may be necessary to supply an indefinite object, such as "anything" or "anyone," or else leave the object unexpressed.

From the Father's care is literally "from the hand of the Father." Some Greek manuscripts read "...my Father." There is no serious difference in meaning, and the use of the definite article "the" before Father in such a context may well be the equivalent of "my." It may not be possible in some languages to speak of "snatching them away from the Father's care," but it is almost always possible to speak of "snatching them away from my Father who cares for them" or "...who watches over them" or "...provides for them."

10.30   The Father and I are one."

In the overall context of this passage, the oneness which Jesus shares with the Father grows out of his obedience to the Father, by which he is able to do the same deeds as the Father. Elsewhere in John's Gospel the oneness of nature or being that Christ shares with the Father is emphasized, but in the present context the emphasis seems to be that Christ reflects the Father in all that he says and does.

In some languages it is grammatically impossible to say The Father and I are one, particularly in languages which require a concord between a plural subject and a predicate numeral such as "one." For example, in most Bantu languages it is impossible to pluralize the numeral "one." One can, however, say "the Father and I are just like one person" or "...are the same as one person." One may in some languages also say "are joined together as one person."

	TEV	(10.31-39)	RSV

31 Then the people again picked   31 The Jews took up stones again
up stones to throw at him. 32 Jesus   to stone him. 32 Jesus answered

said to them, "I have done many good deeds in your presence which the Father gave me to do; for which one of these do you want to stone me?"

33 They answered, "We do not want to stone you because of any good deeds, but because of your blasphemy! You are only a man, but you are trying to make yourself God!"

34 Jesus answered, "It is written in your own Law that God said, 'You are gods.' 35 We know that what the scripture says is true forever; and God called those people gods, the people to whom his message was given. 36 As for me, the Father chose me and sent me into the world. How, then, can you say that I blaspheme because I said that I am the Son of God? 37 Do not believe me, then, if I am not doing the things my Father wants me to do. 38 But if I do them, even though you do not believe me, you should at least believe my deeds, in order that you may know once and for all that the Father is in me and that I am in the Father."

39 Once more they tried to seize Jesus, but he slipped out of their hands.

them, "I have shown you many good works from the Father; for which of these do you stone me?" 33 The Jews answered him, "It is not for a good work that we stone you but for blasphemy; because you, being a man, make yourself God." 34 Jesus answered them, "Is it not written in your law, 'I said, you are gods'? 35 If he called them gods to whom the word of God came (and scripture cannot be broken), 36 do you say of him whom the Father consecrated and sent into the world, 'You are blaspheming,' because I said, 'I am the Son of God'? 37 If I am not doing the works of my Father, then do not believe me; 38 but if I do them, even though you do not believe me, believe the works, that you may know and understand that the Father is in me and I am in the Father." 39 Again they tried to arrest him, but he escaped from their hands.

<u>10.31</u>   Then the people again picked up stones to throw at him.

This verse may be understood either as the conclusion of the preceding section or as an introduction to the following section. It is really both, serving a transitional role. The claim that Jesus and the Father are one led the Jews to pick up stones to throw at him, and that in turn led Jesus into a new dialogue with them.

<u>The people</u> translates "the Jews." See Appendix I.

<u>10.32</u>   Jesus said to them, "I have done many good deeds in your presence which the Father gave me to do; for which one of these do you want to stone me?"

<u>I have done...in your presence</u> is literally "I have shown you" (RSV). NEB translates "I have set before you"; and JB "I have done...for you to see." Certain problems may be involved in a more or less literal translation of <u>I have done...in your presence</u>. The rendering of JB "I

have done...for you to see" might suggest that Jesus had performed miracles only in order to show off his power. This was evidently not Jesus' intent, for he was not concerned with performing spectacles. It is possible to translate "I have done many good works which you have seen" or "you have seen many good works which I have done."

Which the Father gave me to do is literally "from the Father" (RSV, NAB, "from my Father" JB). Most translations render this clause literally, though NEB has "done by my Father's power" and GeCL "at the command of my Father." The clause is meant to emphasize that what Jesus has done he has done either at the Father's command or through the Father's power. This clause may be rendered "which my Father told me to perform." Depending, however, upon the construction of the first part of this verse, one may employ a complete sentence, for example, "my Father told me to do these works" or "it was my Father's power which made me able to do these works."

Do you want to stone me? is literally "do you stone me?" (RSV). In the present context the verb "to stone" denotes intention, and so NEB translates "for which of these would you stone me?" The RSV rendering (so also JB "for which of these are you stoning me?") could imply that the persons are actually in the process of stoning Jesus while he is speaking to them. The causal relation between the good works and the stoning may be expressed in some languages as "because of which of these works do you want to stone me to death?" or "which one of these good works has caused you to want to stone me to death?"

10.33   They answered, "We do not want to stone you because of any good deeds, but because of your blasphemy! You are only a man, but you are trying to make yourself God!"

They answered is literally "the Jews answered him." In Greek the first part of the Jews' answer to Jesus is literally "concerning a good work we are not stoning you but concerning blasphemy." TEV takes the verb "we are...stoning" to mean we...want to stone, and places it at the beginning of the sentence. "Good work" of the Greek text is rendered in the plural by TEV good deeds, making the phrase more generic.

In most languages there is no technical term for blasphemy in the sense of a person insulting God by means of preempting some of the qualities or attributes of God. However, blasphemy may be rendered in some languages "the way in which one insults God." Accordingly, one may translate the statement of the Jews "We do not want to stone you because of any of the good works which you have done, but because of the way in which you insult God." In Jewish thought blasphemy consisted primarily of speaking evil against God, though the word could also be used of abusive speech against people or sacred objects. In the present context Jesus is accused of insulting God because, although merely a man, he is trying to make himself God.

In Greek the pronoun you in the statement you are only a man is emphatic. Are only a man is literally "being a man" (RSV), but the adverb only brings out the impact of the Greek. NEB translates "You, a mere man..." JB and GeCL translate exactly as TEV does.

[343]

You are trying to make expresses accurately the force of the Greek, literally "you are making." JB and NEB translate "you claim to be." It is important to avoid a translation of you are trying to make yourself God which would suggest that Jesus was "making himself into God," that is, "changing himself into God." In most instances it seems better to translate "because you claim to be God" or "because you say that you are God."

In the clause but you are trying to make yourself God the Greek does not have the definite article "the" before the noun God. Normally in the New Testament when God the Father is referred to, the definite article "the" is used before the noun God. Purely on the basis of the Greek text, therefore, it is possible to translate "a god," as NEB does, rather than to translate God, as TEV and several other translations do. One might argue, on the basis of both the Greek and the context, that the Jews were accusing Jesus of claiming to be "a god" rather than "God." But to do so is certainly not in keeping with the theology of John's Gospel, nor with the accusation of blasphemy brought against Jesus. Jesus does quote from Psalm 82.6, which says "you are gods," (see verse 34) but to assume that Jesus is doing no more than claiming an equal status with the people addressed in that Psalm is to miss the entire point of the passage. Jesus' argument is, in fact, a typically rabbinical one by which the speaker argues from the lesser to the greater. According to the rabbis, Psalm 82 was addressed to Israel when they received the Law at Mount Sinai. Jesus' argument proceeds in this way. If those persons who received God's Law on Mount Sinai could be spoken of as "gods," how much more can the one whom the Father has chosen and sent into the world claim to be "the Son of God." In verse 36 the Greek does not have the article "the" before "Son," and so it is possible to translate as NEB does "I am God's son" ("son" with lower case "s"). However, once again this interpretation is not in keeping with the theology of the Gospel of John. Moreover, it does not fit well with the context. Jesus is not claiming to be a divine being among many others; he is claiming a unique prerogative, and the Jews recognize this. Accordingly, it is best to follow TEV and most other translations.

10.34   Jesus answered, "It is written in your own
          Law that God said, 'You are gods.'

Jesus answered is literally "Jesus answered them." In Greek this verse is in the form of a rhetorical question which expects the answer "yes" (RSV "Is it not written in your law...?"). A capital "L" is used by TEV in its spelling of the word Law, for the reference is to the Jewish Scriptures. As mentioned in the preceding verse, the quotation is from Psalm 82.6, and John follows the Septuagint exactly (literally "I said, 'You are gods'"). TEV makes the pronoun "I" explicit as a reference to God (God said), since in the Psalm it is God who is speaking. This enables the person who reads this passage to himself, or who hears the passage read aloud, to know immediately that God is the one who said this in the Scripture. That is, since in this context Jesus is the one speaking, it may sound as if Jesus himself said this in their Law unless one introduces God in place of the pronoun "I" in the statement "I said."

As noted elsewhere, the expression It is written in your own Law
may be difficult to express in some languages. One may sometimes say "The
following words are in your laws" or "These are the words written in your
Law."

You are gods: see comments at verse 33.

10.35   We know that what the scripture says is true
               forever; and God called those people gods, the
               people to whom his message was given.

This verse has undergone a good deal of restructuring in TEV. The
form is, in fact, very much different from that of the Greek, which
reads: "If he called them gods, to whom the word of God came, and the
scripture cannot be broken." The order of the two major clauses in
Greek ("if he called them gods" and "the scripture cannot be broken")
has been reversed, and the initial clause of TEV introduced with the
words we know that, since the clause represents a well attested Jewish
conviction. In this same first clause of TEV the Greek negative expression "cannot be broken" is stated positively: is true forever (GeCL
"remains valid"). In the Jewish setting the verb "to be broken," when
applied to Scripture, would indicate that the meaning could not be
changed, nor could the words be declared invalid. In Greek the "if"
clause actually introduces a statement of fact, not of doubt, as would
normally be implied by a literal rendering into English; this is why
TEV transforms "if" into "and" at the beginning of the clause. Within
this same clause TEV makes explicit the meaning of the pronouns "he"
(= God) and "them" (= those people), and at the same time introduces
the people in a position after those people and before to whom in order
to make immediately evident the connection between people and whom. Behind the structure "to whom the word of God came" lies the meaning "to
whom God gave his word," which TEV has transformed into a passive structure: to whom his message was given. Him represents "of God," and has
been chosen by TEV for stylistic reasons. "Word" carries a broader meaning in the context of Scripture than the English equivalent, and so TEV
uses message, which also has the extra advantage of avoiding the construction "his word was given," in which "word" would suggest the
meaning of "promise."

It may not be sufficient to translate the scripture merely as "the
writings." In some languages it is essential to translate "the holy
writings" or "the writings relating to God." An expression which would
mean "God's writings," in the sense that God himself did the writing,
should be avoided.

God called those people gods may be rendered "God applied the name
of gods to those people" or "God spoke of those people as gods."

To whom his message was given is literally "to whom the word of
God came." JB translated "to whom the word of God was addressed," while
NEB has "to whom the word of God was delivered." In the Old Testament
the expression "the word of God came to...," used by some of the prophetic books (note Jer 1.2 and Hos 1.1), was simply a Jewish way of
saying "God spoke his message to..."

The people to whom his message was given may be treated as a completely separate sentence, for example, "These are the people to whom his message was given" or "...to whom God spoke his message."

10.36   As for me, the Father chose me and sent me
    into the world. How, then, can you say that
    I blaspheme because I said that I am the Son
    of God?

In Greek verse 36 is the continuation of the rhetorical question begun with verse 35 (note RSV). As for me...me...me translates a relative pronoun ("whom") which is emphatic in the Greek sentence structure. It is obvious from what follows that Jesus is using the third person relative pronoun ("whom") as a reference to himself. TEV changes it to me in English, which is more natural for the English reader. Moreover, this part of the rhetorical question is changed into a statement, as also is all of verse 35.

The verb translated chose (Greek hagiazō) is rendered "consecrate" by most modern translators. It literally means "to make holy," in the sense of setting aside someone or something to God's service, and it may well be that this verb was used specifically because of the setting of the Festival of Dedication. That is, Jesus has shown that he is the fulfillment of the Sabbath Day, Passover, and the Feast of Shelters. Now the context suggests that he is claiming to be the fulfillment of the Festival of Dedication. As the Jews are celebrating the time when the Temple was "made holy" again, after its desecration by the Syrians, Jesus alludes to himself as the one whom God has "made holy" and sent into the world. In John 17.17,19 this same verb is translated dedicate in TEV; in the Septuagint of Numbers 7.1 it is used to describe Moses' consecration of the Tabernacle, while in Numbers 7.10-11 a noun (egkainismos) related to the noun used of the Festival itself in John 10.22 (egkainia) is used of Moses' dedication of the altar. This suggests that the two Greek verbs and their related nouns are essentially synonyms. In 6.69 Jesus is called the Holy One from God (ho hagios tou theou).

The equivalent of "consecrate" in some languages is "select and give a special function to" or "select for a particular task." However, certain dangers are inherent in translating merely "set aside" or "set apart." More often than not, setting something aside means taking something inferior out of a group of superior objects. Consecration is the exact opposite; it is setting aside a particularly significant object for a special function of a religious nature.

See verse 33 for a discussion of the remainder of this verse.

10.37   Do not believe me, then, if I am not doing
    the things my Father wants me to do.

TEV inverts the order of this sentence from the order in Greek ("if I am not doing my Father's works, then do not believe me"). Jesus appeals to his works as evidence of who he is; he and the Father are one (verse 30) because they both do the same works.

10.38   But if I do them, even though you do not
               believe me, you should at least believe
               my deeds, in order that you may know once
               and for all that the Father is in me and that
               I am in the Father.

     In Greek the clause But if I do does not have an object expressed,
but TEV and some other translations express the object as them, referring
back to deeds in verse 37.
     You should at least believe my deeds is literally "believe the
works" (RSV). In Greek the verb believe is imperative, but it expresses
more an appeal than a command, and so TEV translates you should...believe.
The inclusion of the adverbial phrase at least (so also JB and GeCL)
helps to indicate more fully the connotation of Jesus' words. Finally,
"the works" is obviously a reference to Jesus' works, and so it is legit-
mate to translate my deeds (so NEB). In the Greek of this verse, forms
of the verb "to know" are used twice. The first is an aorist, meaning
"that you may begin to know," while the second is a present meaning
"and that you may keep on knowing." TEV combines the two verbs into one
and translates that you may know once and for all. JB also uses one verb
plus an adverbial expression, "then you will know for sure." The decision of TEV and JB is certainly valid, because the two verbs are apparently used simply to reinforce one another. To translate by two different
verbs meaning "to know," as most translators do, is not necessary.
     The last words of this verse (that the Father is in me, and I am in
the Father) refer back to the words of Jesus in verse 30 that initiated
this controversy between him and the Jews. It is, of course, an essential
theme of the Gospel of John that Jesus and the Father are one. GeCL has
"that the Father lives in me, and I live in the Father."
     The grammatical structure of verse 38 is rather complex. It consists
of several clauses bound closely together. The first is a condition, if
I do them; the second, a concession, even though you do not believe me;
the third is the main clause, you should at least believe my works; the
fourth is a purpose clause, in order that you may know, which has as its
content object the indirect statement, that the Father is in me, and I
am in the Father. In some languages it is not possible to combine so
many complex clausal relations within a single sentence. But this rather
complex grouping may be broken up as follows: "But if I do my Father's
works, you should at least believe what I have done. You should believe
these works even though you do not believe me. You should believe in
what I have done in order that you may know once and for all that the
Father is in me and I am in the Father." In some languages, however, it
is difficult to use the same type of expression in speaking of "believing
a person" and "believing works." "To believe a person" would mean "to
trust what a person has said" or "to believe that what a person has said
is true." On the other hand, "believe my works" may be more or less
equivalent to "take seriously my works" or "have confidence in what I
say because of what I have done."
     That the Father is in me, and I am in the Father may require modi-
fication because of the problem of a so-called possessive relation with
Father, for example, "that my Father is in me and I am in my Father."
However, this expression may seem meaningless in some languages, and

therefore one may say "that my Father and I are completely joined together as one" or "that my Father and I are just like one person." This expression is therefore equivalent to the expression "my Father and I are one."

10.39   Once more they tried to seize Jesus, but he
               slipped out of their hands.

As verse 31 describes the response of the Jews to Jesus' previous debate, so this verse describes their reaction towards the present debate. For similar passages see 7.30; 8.20,59.

John seems to indicate a miraculous escape by Jesus. The Jews have no authority over him, because his hour has not yet come.

He slipped out of their hands is literally "he went out from their hand." NEB sounds rather high level, "But he escaped from their clutches." JB translates "but he eluded them" and NAB "but he eluded their grasp." It would be a serious mistake in most languages to translate literally he slipped out of their hands; this could be applicable to a pot, spear, or knife, but certainly not to a person. An appropriate equivalent in some languages is "he escaped" or "he disappeared."

TEV	(10.40-42)	RSV
40 Jesus then went back again across the Jordan River to the place where John had been baptizing, and he stayed there. 41 Many people came to him. "John performed no miracles," they said, "but everything he said about this man was true." 42 And many people there believed in him.		40 He went away again across the Jordan to the place where John at first baptized, and there he remained. 41 And many came to him; and they said, "John did no sign, but everything that John said about this man was true." 42 And many believed in him there.

These verses bring to a conclusion the section of the Gospel dedicated to showing that Jesus is the fulfillment of the Jewish feasts (Chapters 5-10). In fact, it is possible to look upon these verses as a conclusion to the entire public ministry of Jesus. It is worth noting that, if these verses do indeed indicate the end of Jesus' public ministry, the account of his ministry is included within two incidents that mention the ministry of John the Baptist (1.19-28 and 10.40-42). However, some scholars see in these verses, not a conclusion to the previous section, but an introduction to Chapter 11 (see, for example, the arrangement of NEB).

10.40   Jesus then went back again across the Jordan
               River to the place where John had been baptizing,
               and he stayed there.

The Greek of this verse does not explicitly mention Jesus, but it is obvious that the pronoun "he" of the Greek text refers to him; TEV and NEB make this information explicit in the text. JB does so by means of a section heading ("Jesus withdraws to the other side of the Jordan").

The Greek of this verse and the two following verses reflects Semitic style in the use of the coordinating conjunction "and." Literally these verses are introduced, "(40) And he... (41) And many people...(42) And many people." Naturally, it is not necessary to retain all these "ands" in the receptor language. TEV, for example, has _and_ only in verse 42.

The Greek has "across the Jordan"; TEV adds the classifier River.

Where John had been baptizing is more literally "where John at first baptized" (RSV) or "Where John was baptizing earlier." By the use of the past perfect tense (had been baptizing). TEV retains the force of the Greek past linear tense "was baptizing" in combination with the adverb "earlier." If a choice must be made between the rendering "at first" and "earlier," then "earlier" is to be preferred. To translate "at first" may suggest that John at first baptized at this place and later baptized somewhere else. Rather, the force of the Greek is merely to throw back the point of action to an earlier time (see NEB "where John had been baptizing earlier"). The place referred to is Bethany (see 1.28).

In selecting the form of the verb stayed it may be necessary in some languages to imply the time approximately involved, whether a few days, a few weeks, or several months. In view of the context, a form suggesting a period of several weeks may be preferable.

10.41   Many people came to him. "John performed no
           miracles," they said, "but everything he said
           about this man was true."

The many people referred to in this verse may have been disciples of John the Baptist, but the translator should not attempt to make explicit this sort of information.

The Gospels do not indicate that John the Baptist performed any miracles (literally "signs"; see 2.11). Not only did John perform no miraculous works, but he refused to accept any of the Jewish Messianic titles (see 1.19-23).

It is impossible to determine precisely the point of reference in the people's affirmation everything he had said about this man was true, since John the Baptist had referred to Jesus both as the Lamb of God, who takes away the sin of the world (1.29) and as the one who baptizes with the Holy Spirit (1.33). The declaration should perhaps be interpreted in the more general sense that Jesus had fulfilled all the Old Testament predictions and all the hopes of John the Baptist.

It may be necessary to indicate to whom the people spoke when they said everything he said about this man was true. In view of the fact that Jesus is referred to as this man, it is best to translate "they said to one another," thus avoiding the possible misunderstanding that they said it to Jesus.

10.42   And many people there believed in him.

It is not known who the many people are, since we are told nothing further about these believers. However, in 2.23 and 8.30 we are also told that many people believed in Jesus. It is interesting to note that the public ministry of Jesus is brought to a close at the Jordan River, the same geographical point where it began. No longer will the revelation of Jesus' power to give life be confined to the use of symbols, such as bread, water, and light. In the scene to follow he will actually raise Lazarus from death and thereby affirm both in word and deed that he is the resurrection and the life (11.25). The remainder of the Gospel will show how the reality of this life is made available to his followers.

CHAPTER 11

TEV   (11.1-16)   RSV

THE DEATH OF LAZARUS

11 A man named Lazarus, who lived in Bethany, became sick. Bethany was the town where Mary and her sister Martha lived. (2 This Mary was the one who poured the perfume on the Lord's feet and wiped them with her hair; it was her brother Lazarus who was sick.) 3 The sisters sent Jesus a message: "Lord, your dear friend is sick."

4 When Jesus heard it, he said, "The final result of this sickness will not be the death of Lazarus; this has happened in order to bring glory to God, and it will be the means by which the Son of God will receive glory."

5 Jesus loved Martha and her sister and Lazarus. 6 Yet when he received the news that Lazarus was sick, he stayed where he was for two more days. 7 Then he said to the disciples, "Let us go back to Judea."

8 "Teacher," the disciples answered, "just a short time ago the people there wanted to stone you; and are you planning to go back?"

9 Jesus said, "A day has twelve hours, doesn't it? So whoever walks in broad daylight does not stumble, for he sees the light of this world. 10 But if he walks during the night he stumbles, because he has no light." 11 Jesus said this and then added, "Our friend Lazarus has fallen asleep, but I will go and wake him up."

12 The disciples answered, "If he is asleep, Lord, he will get well."

13 Jesus meant that Lazarus had died, but they thought he meant natural sleep. 14 So Jesus told them plainly, "Lazarus is dead,

11 Now a certain man was ill, Lazarus of Bethany, the village of Mary and her sister Martha. 2 It was Mary who annointed the Lord with ointment and wiped his feet with her hair, whose brother Lazarus was ill. 3 So the sisters sent to him, saying, "Lord, he whom you love is ill." 5 But when Jesus heard it he said, "This illness is not unto death; it is for the glory of God, so that the Son of God may be glorified by means of it."

5 Now Jesus loved Martha and her sister and Lazarus. 6 So when he heard that he was ill, he stayed two days longer in the place where he was. 7 Then after this he said to the disciples, "Let us go into Judea again." 8 The disciples said to him, "Rabbi, the Jews were but now seeking to stone you, and are you going there again?" 9 Jesus answered, "Are there not twelve hours in the day? If any one walks in the day, he does not stumble, because he sees the light of this world. 10 But if any one walks in the night, he stumbles, because the light is not in him." 11 Thus he spoke, and then he said to them, "Our friend Lazarus has fallen asleep, but I go to awake him out of sleep." 12 The disciples said to him, "Lord, if he has fallen asleep, he will recover." 13 Now Jesus had spoken of his death, but they thought that he meant taking rest in sleep. 14 Then Jesus told them plainly, "Lazarus is dead; 15 and for your sake I am glad that I was not there, so that you may believe. But let us go to him." 16 Thomas, called the Twin, said to his fellow

15 but for your sake I am glad that
I was not with him, so that you
will believe. Let us go to him."
16 Thomas (called the Twin)
said to his fellow disciples, "Let
us all go along with the Teacher,
so that we may die with him!"

disciples, "Let us also go, that
we may die with him."

The account of the death and resurrection of Lazarus, which comes
almost midway in the Gospel of John, emphasizes a theme that is the
heart of this Gospel: Just as the Father raises the dead and gives them
life, in the same way the Son gives life to those he wants to (5.21).
The raising of Lazarus from the dead is a confirmation of Jesus' claim
to be the resurrection and the life (11.25), and at the same time an
anticipation of what will take place on the last day. In this account
the symbols--water, bread, and light--give way to the reality.

The story itself is told in simple, straightforward fashion. Verses
1 and 2 serve to introduce Lazarus, around whom the narrative revolves.
He is defined in terms of both the place where he lived and his kinship
to Mary and Martha (verse 1). Verse 2 further identifies the Mary spoken
of in verse 1 and reemphasizes the illness of Lazarus. Following the
setting in these verses the action of the story begins in verse 3, when
the sisters send a message to Jesus to tell him that Lazarus is sick.
Verse 4 gives Jesus' response to the news; he declares that the final
result of Lazarus' illness will be not his death, but the means by which
the Son will receive glory. In this verse the primary meaning of will
receive glory is not that he will receive praise. Rather, it indicates
that, as a result of what will happen to Lazarus, Jesus' true life-giving
power will be revealed. According to Jesus' teaching elsewhere in the
Gospel of John, his glorification comes through his death, resurrection,
and exaltation. And that teaching is involved here. In the framework of
John's Gospel, the raising of Lazarus from the dead is the primary event
that caused the Jews to decide to put Jesus to death. So the death of
Lazarus leads to the glorification of Jesus by another route also. Not
only is he "glorified" by raising Lazarus from the dead; but the raising
of Lazarus leads to Jesus' own death, resurrection, and exaltation.

The statement in verse 5 is to preclude the misunderstanding that
Jesus' failure to go immediately to Bethany is due to a lack of love for
Lazarus. On the basis of verse 6 alone, it would be possible to interpret
Jesus' delay in going to Bethany as a lack of concern. Verse 5 makes
such a misinterpretation impossible. Verses 7-16 indicate that there are
two reasons for Jesus' going to Bethany. (1) As the reader may suspect,
Jesus is going there in order to help Lazarus (verses 11-15). (2) But
there is another reason. Bethany is very near to Jerusalem. In going to
Bethany, Jesus must go to Jerusalem; and he goes there to die (verses 7-
10, 16). Both events--the raising of Lazarus from the dead and the death
of Jesus--will be means by which the Son of God is glorified.

Verses 17-19 are transitional; they introduce Jesus and his disciples,
now at Bethany. Verses 20-27 are parallel with verses 28-33. The first
section tells how Martha came out of the house to greet Jesus, and the
second how Mary did the same. The accounts are similar, and Martha and
Mary greet Jesus in precisely the same way (verses 21, 32). When Martha

comes out to meet him, he tells her that Lazarus will rise to life
(verse 23). She takes this statement as a reference to the Jewish hope
in the final resurrection of the dead (verse 24), but Jesus declares
that he himself is the one who raises people from the dead and gives
them eternal life (verses 25-26). This statement is followed by Martha's
confession of faith (verse 27).

The account of Mary's going to meet Jesus (verses 28-37) does not
actually carry forward the action of the story. In it is included Jesus'
response to her weeping and to the grief of the Jews (verse 33), and a
question from the Jews which sets the stage for what follows: Could he
not have kept Lazarus from dying? (verse 37).

Verses 38-44 give the account of the raising of Lazarus from the
dead. The miracle itself is described very simply, and it is accomplished solely by the words of Jesus: Lazarus, come out! (verse 43).

Finally, the chapter concludes with the plot against Jesus (verses
45-57). The Jewish leaders are afraid that Jesus may mislead the people
into bringing about a revolt against the Roman government, and so be
responsible for the complete destruction of their nation (verse 48).
Caiaphas, the High Priest that year (verse 49), points out that it is
better for one man to die for the people than that the whole nation be
destroyed (verse 50). The Gospel writer sees in these words of Caiaphas
a prediction that Jesus is about to die for the Jewish people (verses
51-52). From that day on the Jewish authorities make plans to kill Jesus (verse 53), and so Jesus no longer travels openly in Judea (verse
54). The account of the plot against Jesus' life concludes with an order
from the Jewish leaders that if anyone knows where Jesus is, he must
report it, so they can arrest him (verse 57).

In some languages the nominal form of the section heading, The Death
of Lazarus, should be changed to a verbal form, for example, "Lazarus
dies" or "Lazarus died."

11.1   A man named Lazarus, who lived in Bethany,
              became sick. Bethany was the town where Mary and
              her sister Martha lived.

The story of the death of Lazarus (verses 1-16) is a self-contained
unit, and so the first two verses serve primarily to introduce Lazarus.
Verse 1 gives his name and the town where he lived, while verse 2 relates
him to Mary, whom the Gospel writer intimates his readers will know.
Verse 1 is considerably reordered in TEV and in most modern translations
(see Phps, NEB, JB, NAB). This reordering is intended to achieve a more
natural construction in English. Compare, for example, the rather literal
rendering of RSV with TEV and NEB. RSV reads "Now a certain man was ill,
Lazarus of Bethany, the village of Mary and her sister Martha." TEV
renders this verse A man named Lazarus, who lived in Bethany, became
sick. Bethany was the town where Mary and her sister Martha lived. NEB
reads "There was a man named Lazarus who had fallen ill. His home was
at Bethany, the village of Mary and her sister Martha."

Lazarus is the Greek form of the Hebrew name Eleazar, which means
"God helps." It appears elsewhere in the New Testament only in Luke
16.19-31, the parable of Lazarus and the rich man. It may be that the

meaning of the name Lazarus was in John's mind, though he makes no attempt to explain it to his readers.

A man named Lazarus is a typical way in which a character is introduced in a narrative in English. Languages differ considerably in the ways in which names may be introduced, for example, "a man the people called Lazarus," "a man whose name was Lazarus," "a man who had the name Lazarus," or "a man Lazarus."

The Bethany referred to here is not the Bethany of 1.28. The Bethany of this verse is identified with the modern town of El 'Azariyeh, just east of Jerusalem. The modern name of the town is itself derived from the name Lazarus.

Except in the Gospel of John the two sisters, Martha and Mary, are mentioned only in Luke 10.38-42. Luke does not identify where they lived. John seems to mention the names of the two sisters with the expectation that their names will be known to the reader, even if that of Lazarus is not. It may appear quite anomalous, or even contradictory, in some languages to introduce Mary and her sister Martha in verse 1 and then indicate in verse 2 that Lazarus is the brother of Mary. He would obviously be the brother of Martha as well, and not to have said so in verse 1 may leave readers in some receptor languages dubious as to what the relations really were. It may be necessary in some languages to introduce into verse 1 the statement "These were Lazarus' sisters" or "Bethany was the town where his sisters Mary and Martha lived."

11.2   (This Mary was the one who poured the perfume
          on the Lord's feet and wiped them with her hair;
          it was her brother Lazarus who was sick.)

Several modern translations, including TEV, assume that this verse is a parenthetical explanation, and so enclose it in parentheses (NEB, NAB, Mft, Phps). In this verse John makes reference to an episode which will be described in 12.1-8. The fact that he refers to an event not yet recorded in his Gospel may indicate that John believes his readers are familiar with the story, perhaps from some other Gospel.

In some languages one cannot say This Mary; however, it may be possible to say "Mary just referred to" or "Mary the sister of Lazarus." In other languages it may be better to start verse 2 "Mary was the one who poured the perfume on the Lord's feet."

The word translated perfume may also mean "ointment." The Greek word used here (muron) refers to a perfume or ointment, which was used as incense and in cosmetics, medicine, and preparation for burial. In the present passage the word probably is used in a more generic sense, and may mean either perfume or "ointment." The verb of which this noun is the object is literally "anointed" (most translations), but since this term is difficult for modern readers, both TEV and Phps translate it poured. In almost all languages there are expressions for perfume. In some instances a descriptive expression is used, for example, "that which smells nice." In others, however, perfume is included in the general category of medicines, for example, "a sweet-smelling medicine."

11.3   The sisters sent Jesus a message: "Lord, your
            dear friend is sick."

The sisters sent Jesus a message is more literally "So the sisters
sent to him, saying." The participle "saying," a Semitic way of introducing direct discourse, need not be translated. The word translated
"so" by RSV represents John's favorite particle (oun), which also need
not usually be translated by a given word. TEV makes explicit the reference to Jesus in this verse, since the preceding two verses are focused
on Lazarus, with a passing mention of the Lord in verse 2. JB also makes
explicit the reference to Jesus ("The sisters sent this message to Jesus"), and so does NAB ("The sisters sent word to Jesus to inform him").
The same is true of Phps ("So the sisters sent word to Jesus"). In some
languages the only way one can "send a message" is "send a person with
a message" or "send a person to tell" or "send a messenger who is to say."
    The word translated Lord may merely be the equivalent of "Sir" (NEB).
However, most commentators and translators take this word here to have
the full Christian sense of Lord. Receptor languages tend to employ three
different ways of expressing the Christian sense of Lord: (1) Some use a
term which designates primarily "leader," "ruler," "one who commands,"
or "chief." (2) Others use a term which designates primarily a religious
attitude toward, for example, "the one whom we worship" or "the one we
reverence." (3) Still other languages use an expression which indicates
the majesty or glory of the person referred to, for example, "the glorious one," "the wonderful one," or "the one who has majesty."
    Your dear friend (Phps, NEB "your friend") is literally "he whom
you love" (JB "the man you love"), a descriptive phrase for speaking of
a close friend. To translate literally, as many translators do, may connote something evil, and this danger should be guarded against. On the
basis of this phrase, some have taken Lazarus to be the disciple whom
Jesus loved (13.23; 19.26; 20.2; 21.7), but there is little ground for
this conclusion. In some languages the closest equivalent to your dear
friend is "your close friend," "your cherished friend," or "one who is
truly your friend."

11.4   When Jesus heard it, he said, "The final result
            of this sickness will not be the death of Lazarus;
            this has happened in order to bring glory to God,
            and it will be the means by which the Son of God will
            receive glory."

The Greek expression "this sickness is not to death" means that
"death will not be the final result of this sickness." Several translations make this meaning clear, but only TEV makes explicit the reference to the death of Lazarus: ...will not be the death of Lazarus. It
is possible that more than the death of Lazarus is referred to here.
There may be a double reference--to the death of Lazarus and the death,
resurrection, and exaltation of Jesus. Such an interpretation is
strengthened by the observations regarding the meaning of the phrase
the means by which the Son of God will receive glory. However, while
there may be a double meaning here, the primary focus is obviously the

death of Lazarus. It is suggested that the translator either make explicit
the reference to the death of Lazarus or translate "death will not be the
final result of this sickness," without specifying whose death is meant.
To make explicit the reference to the death of Jesus is beyond the bounds
of translation.

In some languages it may be difficult to say The final result of
this sickness will not be the death of Lazarus, for result can be expressed only in terms of cause and effect, for example, "Because Lazarus
is sick does not mean that he will die." Such a translation may seem to
be contradictory, because Lazarus did die. However, even in the form
which Jesus spoke to his disciples (literally "this sickness is not to
death"), there is anomaly, since the sickness did result in Lazarus'
death, though not in a permanent state of death. In some languages this
aspect of permanence may be expressed by a particular form of the verb
"to die."

The last part of this verse is literally "but for the glory of God,
in order that the Son of God might be glorified through it." Rather than
use the conjunction "but" to indicate the contrast, TEV introduces the
words this has happened (Mft "the end of it is"; NEB "it has come"; Phps
"it is going to"; NAB "rather it is"). Then TEV transforms the noun phrase
"for the glory of God" into a verb phrase to bring glory to God (so also
Phps). Some commentators understand the phrase "for the glory of God" to
have the meaning "to reveal God's glory." Either meaning (to bring glory
to God or "to reveal the glory of God") is legitimate in light of the
context. To bring glory to God means "to cause people to praise God,"
which may not be the focus in the context. "To reveal God's glory" may
mean, "to reveal how powerful God is" (GeCL), which seems to be more in
keeping with the words of Jesus in verse 40 (Didn't I tell you that you
would see God's glory if you believed?) In some languages To bring glory
to God is simply "to cause people to see how glorious God is" or "...how
wonderful God is" or "in order to show people how wonderful God is."

The last clause of the Greek sentence begins with the subordinate
conjunction "so that" (Greek hina). TEV makes it into a coordinate clause
beginning with the conjunction and. In Greek the last two words of this
clause are literally "through it," which TEV takes as a reference to
Lazarus' sickness and translates by a verb phrase will be the means by
which. In the Greek phrase "through it," the pronoun "it" is feminine
and may refer either to sickness or to glory (feminine nouns in Greek).
Although a few commentators understand "it" to refer to God's glory, a
majority of commentators and most translators take "it" to refer to
Lazarus' sickness. In English the verb "to be glorified" is rather awkward. TEV transforms it into a more natural expression: the Son of God
will receive glory (GeCL "Through it God will make known his Son's
glory"). Again glory may be understood either as "praise" or as the revelation of the true nature of the Son, but here it is specifically a
reference to the revelation of the Son's power to give life. This final
clause may be expressed in some languages as "his death will also show
people how wonderful the Son of God is" or because of his death people
will see how glorious the Son of God is."

11.5   Jesus loved Martha and her sister and Lazarus.

The author of the Gospel includes this statement to indicate that Jesus' failure to go to Bethany immediately was not due to any lack of love for Lazarus. Mft, who finds it difficult to believe that the verse was originally in this place, puts it immediately after verse 2. However, in its present position, it fits in quite well with the logic of this chapter, and there is no textual basis for changing its position. The Western mind does not always narrate events in the same sequence that the Jews of the first century did, and some scholars tend to transpose verses when there is no need to do so.

The Greek verb for loved (agapaō) is not the same verb used in verse 3 (phileō), but in John's Gospel these verbs are essentially synonyms, with no distinguishable difference in meaning. (See comments at 3.35 and 5.20.)

In the choice of a term for loved it is important to avoid an expression which would suggest sexual or erotic concern. In some languages the closest equivalent may be "deeply respected" or "had great concern for" or even "appreciated very much."

In a number of languages it is extremely awkward to speak of Martha and her sister, and Lazarus. This phrase would seem to suggest that Mary was the sister of Martha but that neither of them was related to Lazarus. A more natural expression in some languages is "the siblings Martha, Mary, and Lazarus." In others one may say "Martha and Mary and their brother Lazarus." In speaking of "their brother Lazarus" one automatically identifies Martha and Mary as sisters.

In some languages it is necessary to indicate the relative ages of these three persons. Since in New Testament accounts the tendency is to place the oldest person first, one can say "Martha and her younger sister Mary and their younger brother Lazarus." We do not know what the actual relative ages were, but since Lazarus is mentioned after Martha and Mary, he was probably their younger brother. However, a term suggesting that Lazarus was a child should be avoided.

11.6 Yet when he received the news that Lazarus was
    sick, he stayed where he was for two more days.

In Greek neither Lazarus nor Jesus are mentioned by name: "when he heard that he was sick, he remained where he was..." To avoid the repetition of the pronoun "he" four times, and, at the same time, to avoid confusion to the reader, TEV renders Lazarus was sick; the first "he" is clear in light of the explicit mention of Jesus in verse 5, and by the sentence structure of TEV any possible ambiguities are removed from this verse.

In many languages received the news may be best expressed as "heard the messenger say" or "heard the report that."

No reason is given why Jesus stayed where he was for two more days, instead of going immediately to Bethany. It was certainly not for the sake of letting Lazarus die so that a greater miracle could be performed, since verses 17 and 39 suggest that Lazarus was already dead at the time Jesus received the message. More likely Jesus stayed where he was for two more days to indicate that his actions and movements were determined by divine decree, rather than by the will and desires of human beings

11.6

(compare 2.3,4; 7.3-9); but this information should not be included in the translation.

11.7   Then he said to the disciples, "Let us go back to Judea."

Then is literally "Then after this" (see RSV). NEB has "After this." The expression Let us go back to Judea must not be understood in the sense of asking permission. Technically this is a "hortatory" expression, but there is certainly no exhortation involved. It is a kind of polite command in the first person plural. The equivalent in some languages is "We must now go back to Judea" or "We should now go back to Judea."

11.8   "Teacher," the disciples answered, "just a short time ago the people there wanted to stone you; and are you planning to go back?"

Teacher is literally "Rabbi" (see 1.38). This is the final occurrence of the word in the Greek text of John's Gospel.
Just a short time ago (JB and NEB "it is not long since"; Mft "only the other day"; NAB "only recently") translates an adverb which normally means "now." However, in classical Greek this adverb was sometimes used of events that had recently happened, and that is its use here. The reference is to 8.59 and 10.31. In some languages just a short time ago is best rendered "just a few days ago" or "it has not been many days since" or "we have only passed a few days since."
And are you planning to go back? is literally "and you are going back there?" The verb at this stage expresses the intention of Jesus, since he has not yet started back. TEV (so also GeCL) includes the idea of intention (plan to). A question in the form are you planning to go back? may be misleading in some languages. A more appropriate equivalent may be "Why do you plan to go back there now?" or "Why do you go back there?"

11.9   Jesus said, "A day has twelve hours, doesn't it? So whoever walks in broad daylight does not stumble, for he sees the light of this world.

Both the Jews and the Romans divided the period from sunrise to sunset into twelve hours. Jesus' question naturally expects the answer "Yes." In a few languages there are still no terms for "hours." However, one can always speak of "twelve divisions of the day" or "twelve parts of the day."
In broad daylight is literally "in the day," an expression intended to contrast the light of day with the darkness of night. Phps and NEB have "daylight"; JB has "daytime." The closest equivalent in some languages is "while the sun is shining" or "while the sun is bright.
For he sees the light of this world is a fairly literal translation

[358]

of the Greek. JB translates "because he has the light of this world to
see by," and NAB "because he sees the world bathed in light." The meaning is obvious. This clause merely takes up the previous clause and explains it. The light of this world is clearly a reference to the sun,
but almost as clearly John intends his readers to see in this statement
a description of Jesus (8.12; 9.5). Therefore it would be wrong to translate "because he sees the sun." It is better to use such a phrase as
"the one who gives light to this world," so that the implied allusion to
Jesus himself may be seen.

11.10   But if he walks during the night he stumbles,
          because he has no light."

Evidently the people of Jesus' day believed that it was necessary
for a person to "have light in himself" in order for him to see. Accordingly the two parts of this verse supplement each other. A person stumbles
at night not only because of the lack of external light, but also because
he has no light.
He has no light can be misleading, since it may suggest that "he
has no torch." It is important to understand the passage as referring
to an internal source of light or capacity to see in the darkness.

11.11   Jesus said this and then added, "Our friend
          Lazarus has fallen asleep, but I will go and
          wake him up."

Jesus said this and then added is literally "he said these things,
and after this he says to them."
Our friend Lazarus has fallen asleep, but I will go and wake him
up may have more than one meaning, as Jesus' words often do in the
Gospel of John. Both in Greek and in Hebrew "to fall asleep" may be used
as a euphemism for "to die," but the disciples fail to see this second
meaning. The verb wake him up (exhupnizo) is the normal verb for "to
wake someone from sleep"; it is not one of the two verbs (egeiro and
anistēmi) used in the New Testament of raising people from death. Though
the readers of the Gospel will understand from the following verse what
Jesus means, the disciples do not at this time comprehend the true significance of Jesus' words. Because of the response of the disciples, it
is necessary to translate has fallen asleep and wake him up in their
first and primary meanings. If one goes beyond the primary meanings, the
response of the disciples becomes almost meaningless.
It is thought by some that by the time John's Gospel was written
the word friend had become a technical term for "Christian believer"
(see Luke 12.4; Acts 27.3; 3 John 15; and John 15.13-15). However, it
should not be so rendered in translation.

11.12   The disciples answered, "If he is asleep, Lord,
          he will get well."

The disciples answered is literally "therefore the disciples said
to him." He will get well translates a verb which literally means "to be
saved," but it can be used with the meaning "to recover from sickness."
What the disciples had in mind was that if Lazarus was sleeping, the
worst stage of his sickness had passed, and now he would gradually get
better. But the situation was otherwise, as the next verse indicates.

11.13   Jesus meant that Lazarus had died, but they
              thought he meant natural sleep.

Jesus meant that Lazarus had died is literally "but Jesus had
spoken concerning his death." TEV translates the noun phrase "concerning
his death" by a verb phrase and makes the reference to Lazarus explicit.
JB translates "The phrase Jesus used referred to the death of Lazarus."
To translate Jesus meant that Lazarus had died, it may be necessary in
some languages to introduce direct discourse, for example, "What Jesus
was really trying to say was, 'Lazarus has died'" or "What Jesus' words
really meant was, 'Lazarus has died.'" In some languages it is possible
to speak of "Lazarus' death" and to translate "Jesus was really talking
about Lazarus' death."
      Mft, Phps, NEB, and TEV all translate John's phrase natural sleep.
In RSV this is rendered as "taking rest in sleep," and in NAB "sleep in
the sense of slumber." The Greek phrase that John uses is unusual, but
its nearest meaning in English is natural sleep.
      The contrast between what Jesus meant and what the disciples thought
he meant must be indicated in some languages by an adversative conjunction, such as "but," or "on the other hand." The final clause may then
be translated "but the disciples thought he was talking about just
sleeping" or, in the form of direct discourse, "but his disciples thought,
'He is just talking about sleep.'" or "...He is just saying that Lazarus
is sleeping."

11.14   So Jesus told them plainly, "Lazarus is dead,

Plainly is the same adverb used in 7.4. Though in other passages it
may have the meaning of "in public" or "openly," it obviously has the
meaning of plainly in the present verse (Elsewhere in John's Gospel this
adverb is used in 7.4,13,26; 10.24; 11.14,54; 16.25,29; 18.20.) In some
languages "openly" may be best translated "without hiding anything" or
"without covering up the words," while in others it is best to say "Jesus told them straight" or "Jesus told them so that they could understand
well."

11.15   but for your sake I am glad that I was not with
              him, so that you will believe. Let us go to him.

TEV and most other modern translations restructure this verse radically. It reads literally "and I am glad because of you, in order that
you might believe, because I was not there. But let us go to him." In

its restructuring, NAB is close to TEV, but it retains the adverb "there," which TEV renders with him.

So that you will believe is translated "that you may learn to believe" by Gdsp and Phps, and "that you may come to believe" by NAB. These renderings represent an attempt to carry through the force of the aorist subjunctive, which in the present context may have the meaning of "begin to believe." That is, this verse is written as if 2.11 had not been included in the Gospel. Evidently, John is not so much concerned to show the development of the disciples' faith as to indicate that this miracle was a means of initiating faith in their lives. For this reason the rendering of NEB, "it will be for your good and for the good of your faith," appears not to carry through the force of the Greek aorist subjunctive.

In Greek there is no expressed object of the verb will believe, though it is obvious that Jesus is the intended object. Gdsp renders this verb "believe in me," and GeCL is similar: "in this way you will learn to trust me."

In some languages serious problems are involved in the first sentence of this verse. For your sake cannot be syntactically combined immediately with I am glad, but it is meaningfully associated with the entire expression which follows. Similarly the purpose, so you will believe, is not dependent solely on I was not with him. The belief of the disciples is dependent upon an implied miracle which is going to happen because of the fact that Jesus was not with Lazarus. In some languages the most appropriate way to combine these various concepts is to translate "but I am glad that I was not with him. Because of this you will learn to trust me. All this is for your benefit."

Let us go to him may be rendered in some languages "We must now go to him."

11.16   Thomas (called the Twin) said to his fellow
        disciples, "Let us all go along with the Teacher,
        so that we may die with him!"

The name Thomas is derived from the Hebrew word Te'oma, meaning "twin." The word Twin translates the Greek word "Didymus," which has the same meaning. Though there is some doubt whether Thomas, in its Hebrew or Aramaic form, was ever used as a proper name, Didymus evidently had wide use as such in Greek circles. Two other times in John's Gospel (20.24; 21.2) Thomas is described as "the one called the Twin." Elsewhere in the New Testament Thomas is mentioned only in lists of the apostles (Matthew 10.3; Mark 3.18; Luke 6.15; and Acts 1.13). Besides the passages already mentioned, Thomas appears also in John's Gospel in 14.5 and 20.24-29.

Thomas (called the Twin) may be translated in some languages as "Thomas, whose nickname was Twin" or "Thomas, also called Twin." However, in some languages it is important to distinguish between the older and younger twin--that is, according to the order of their birth. There is no way on the basis of the Greek text to make this distinction, but in some languages one must choose one term or the other.

The word translated fellow disciples (so most other modern translations) is found only here in the New Testament. His fellow disciples

may be translated "the rest of the disciples" or "those who were also
disciples with him."

Let us all go along with the Teacher, so that we may die with him
is literally "Let us also go, that we may die with him" (RSV). The problem of a literal rendering, in which the participants are not specifically
marked, is that a serious ambiguity may result. That is, the phrase with
him could possibly be taken as a reference to Lazarus, who in verse 15
is referred to by with him and to him. Here TEV makes it explicit that
the disciples are intending to accompany Jesus so that they may die
with him. TEV refers to Jesus by the title Teacher in this verse because
this title is the one by which the disciples address him in verse 8.
However, since they address him as Lord in verse 12, it is also possible
in translating to introduce "Lord" here instead of Teacher. As in other
contexts, a first person plural admonition may be translated "We should
all go along with the Teacher" or "...with our Teacher."

This verse introduces for the first time in John's Gospel the theme
that the destiny of the disciples must be the same as that of their Lord,
a theme further developed in the farewell discourses of Chapters 15-17.

<table>
<tr><td>TEV</td><td>(11.17-27)</td><td>RSV</td></tr>
</table>

JESUS THE RESURRECTION AND THE LIFE

17 When Jesus arrived, he found
that Lazarus had been buried four
days before. 18 Bethany was less
than two miles from Jerusalem, 19
and many Judeans had come to see
Martha and Mary to comfort them
about their brother's death.

20 When Martha heard that Jesus
was coming, she went out to meet
him, but Mary stayed in the house.
21 Martha said to Jesus, "If you
had been here, Lord, my brother
would not have died! 22 But I know
that even now God will give you
whatever you ask him for."

23 "Your brother will rise to
life," Jesus told her.

24 "I know," she replied, "that
he will rise to life on the last
day."

25 Jesus said to her, "I am the
resurrection and the life. Whoever
believes in me will live, even
though he dies; 26 and whoever
lives and believes in me will never
die. Do you believe this?"

27 "Yes, Lord!" she answered.
"I do believe that you are the

17 Now when Jesus came, he found
that Lazarus*x* had already been in
the tomb four days. 18 Bethany was
near Jerusalem, about two miles*y*
off, 19 and many of the Jews had
come to Martha and Mary to console
them concerning their brother. 20
When Martha heard that Jesus was
coming, she went and met him, while
Mary sat in the house. 21 Martha
said to Jesus, "Lord, if you had
been here, my brother would not
have died. 22 And even now I know
that whatever you ask from God, God
will give you." 23 Jesus said to
her, "Your brother will rise again."
24 Martha said to him, "I know that
he will rise again in the resurrection at the last day." 25 Jesus
said to her, "I am the resurrection
and the life;*z* he who believes in
me, though he die, yet shall he
live, 26 and whoever lives and believes in me shall never die. Do
you believe this?" 27 She said to
him, "Yes, Lord; I believe that you
are the Christ, the Son of God, he
who is coming into the world."

Messiah, the Son of God, who was
to come into the world."

^xGreek *he*

^yGreek *fifteen stadia*

^zOther ancient authorities omit
and the life

See the introductory remarks to this chapter for the relation of
these verses to the entire story of Lazarus.

Jesus the Resurrection and the Life may be transformed in some
languages to "Jesus the one who raises people back to life and causes
them to live." However, these two expressions are really redundant, and
it may therefore be better in some languages to employ only the first--
that is, "Jesus as the one who causes people to live again." The reference, of course, is to the miracle performed on Lazarus; therefore the
phrase is a fitting section heading. (For futher discussion of the
resurrection and the life, see verse 25.)

11.17   When Jesus arrived, he found that Lazarus had
               been buried four days before.

The statement that Lazarus had been buried four days before is to
affirm the certainty of his death. Jewish rabbis held the belief that
the soul hovered near the body for three days, but after that there was
no hope for restoration of life.

In Greek, Lazarus is literally "he," but several modern translations
make the reference explicit. RSV does so by way of a note indicating that
the Greek has "he." A footnote is unnecessary, however, since the meaning
can be handled translationally.

He found that must be rendered in some languages "he learned that,"
while the passive expression Lazarus had been buried four days before
must be changed in some languages to an active one, for example, "people
had put Lazarus in a tomb four days before." However, in some languages
it would be improper to speak of "putting Lazarus in the tomb"; it is
necessary to say "put the body of Lazarus in a tomb," to avoid the impression that Lazarus was put in a tomb while he was still alive.

It is essential in choosing a word for buried to indicate that Lazarus was not put beneath the ground in a grave, but rather was placed in
a kind of cave. Otherwise, the miracle of his resurrection and coming
forth from the tomb would be even more astounding, and, of course, quite
inconsistent with what occurs later in this same chapter.

11.18   Bethany was less than two miles from Jerusalem,

For Bethany, see the comments at 11.1.
Less than two miles (NEB "just under two miles"; RSV, JB "about
two miles") is literally "fifteen stadia." A "stade" was a Roman measurement of a little more than six hundred feet, and so fifteen "stadia"
is a little less than two miles or "about three kilometers." It seems
probable that the close distance between Bethany and Jerusalem is

indicated to explain the large number of Jews in Bethany (see verse 19).

11.19   and many Judeans had come to see Martha and
               Mary to comfort them about their brother's death.

In Greek verses 18 and 19 are two separate sentences. TEV combines
them into one, thus bringing together the motifs of the short distance
between Bethany and Jerusalem and the visit of the many Judeans. In
some languages many Judeans can be best expressed as "many people from
Judea" or even "many people from that part of the country."
      To comfort them about their brother's death (Phps "to offer them
sympathy over their brother's death"; NEB "to condole with them on their
brother's death") is literally "to comfort them concerning the brother."
Either rendering (about their brother's death or "about their brother")
is legitimate, as is also the rendering of GeCL ("to comfort the two of
them").
      The verb rendered to comfort appears again in verse 31; elsewhere
in the New Testament it is used only in 1 Thessalonians 2.11 (2.12 in
TEV) and 5.14, where it seems to have the meaning "to encourage" or "to
cheer up." In some languages an equivalent of comfort may be "to speak
helpful words." If one translates in this manner, it will be possible
to translate the final phrase, more or less literally, "about their
brother's death" or "about the fact that their brother had died." However, if one uses a verb meaning "to encourage" or "to cheer them up,"
it may be necessary to indicate the brother's death as cause, for example, "to cheer them up because of the fact that their brother had
died."
      Embalming was not practiced in ancient Palestine, and so burial
took place on the day of death. It was common, therefore, for the mourn-
ers to remain and offer their comfort to the bereaved after the time
of burial.

11.20   When Martha heard that Jesus was coming, she went
               out to meet him, but Mary stayed in the house.

In this verse John states that Martha went out to meet Jesus, and
in verse 30 that she met him before he came into the village. One cannot say for certain how Martha heard that Jesus was coming; verse 29
seems to imply that Mary had not heard of Jesus' arrival.
      When Martha heard that Jesus was coming must be understood in
terms of hearing a report that Jesus was coming. It would be wrong to
translate in a way that would suggest that Martha actually heard the
noise of Jesus' approach. One may translate, for example, "when Martha
heard someone say that Jesus was coming" or "...had arrived nearby."
      Stayed in the house is literally "was sitting at home." It was
customary for persons in mourning to sit (Job 2.8; Ezek 8.14), as it
was for these persons who came to offer comfort (Job 2.13).

11.21   Martha said to Jesus, "If you had been here, Lord,
           my brother would not have died!

Both Martha and Mary (verse 32) greet Jesus with the same words:
If you had been here, Lord, my brother would not have died! Some commentators take these words as a reproach, suggesting that Jesus should
have been there to prevent the death of Lazarus. However, it is better
to take them as an expression of painful regret, at the same time revealing faith in the power of Jesus to heal.

The condition contrary to fact may be expressed in some languages
as "You should have been here, Lord; then my brother would not have
died." But in some languages the clear expression of a condition contrary to fact must be made explicit by appropriate negations, for example, "If you were here, Lord (but you were not), my brother would not
have died (but he did)."

11.22   But I know that even now God will give you whatever
           you ask him for."

This verse carries the expression of Martha's faith even further.
She is confident, not only that Jesus could have kept Lazarus from
dying, but that even now he has the power to ask God to raise her brother
from the dead. Martha's words are a confession of faith in Jesus (I
know), but at the same time they imply a request that Jesus would ask
God to raise her brother from the dead. Even now is the way most modern
English translations render John's particles here; it is also possible
to translate "but nevertheless."

TEV slightly restructures the last part of this verse. God will give
you whatever you ask him for is literally "whatever you ask God, God will
give to you." The words "to you" are possibly emphatic in Greek.

In rendering the clause whatever you ask him for it is important to
indicate clearly that this "whatever" may be an event or a happening,
not an object. The inherent difficulty in the expression of whatever may
be resolved in some languages by translating "But I know that even now,
if you pray to God, he will cause you to be able to do whatever you ask."
In this way the reference may be to a possible miracle, rather than to
some particular object.

11.23-24   "Your brother will rise to life," Jesus told her.
           24 "I know," she replied, "that he will rise to life
           on the last day."

In Greek verse 23 is introduced by the words "Jesus told her," but
TEV places the words of Jesus first to make them more emphatic. Most
translations render the Greek verb "will rise again," but TEV makes it
explicit by translating will rise to life. Martha immediately assumes
that Jesus refers to the Jewish belief in the resurrection, which is to
take place on the last day, when all God's people will rise again to
life. Once again the misunderstanding of one of Jesus' hearers enables
him to present a deeper truth. Martha accepts the doctrine of resurrection

on the last day, but this is of no immediate hope and consolation to her, and so Jesus makes explicit in the following verse what he meant by his statement Your brother will rise to life. These words may be translated simply "Your brother will live again" or "...will become alive again."

She replied is literally "Martha says to him," but better English style is achieved by the use of a pronoun in place of a noun.

In many languages one cannot say the last day without indicating the relation of the day to a given event. In some languages one may use the expression "the last day of the world" or "at the end of the world" or "at the end of the age" or even "...of time."

11.25   Jesus said to her, "I am the resurrection
               and the life. Whoever believes in me will live,
               even though he dies;

Most translations render Jesus' words literally, as TEV does, I am the resurrection and the life. NEB translates "I am the resurrection and I am life"; Gdsp "I myself am Resurrection and Life"; Mft "I am myself resurrection and life"; Phps "I myself am the resurrection and the life." It may be necessary in most languages to use verb phrases in place of nouns resurrection and life, for example, "I am the one who raises people from the dead and gives them life." GeCL translates "I am he who brings resurrection and life." In several languages the closest equivalent is "I am the one who causes people to live again." With this expression, however, it is rather difficult to add "and to live" as an equivalent for and the life. Therefore, it may be necessary to reverse the order, for example, "I am the one who causes people to live and to live again."

One important ancient Greek manuscript and several other ancient witnesses omit the words "and the life" and read merely "I am the resurrection." Among modern translations this choice of text is followed only by JB, but it adds "and the life" in a note. It is difficult to explain why the phrase was omitted, if it was indeed an original part of the Greek text. It is possible that some scribe accidentally omitted it, or it may be that it was omitted because verse 24 makes mention only of the resurrection and not of life. On the other hand, it is possible that it was not a part of the original text and was added in anticipation of will live and whoever lives in verses 25 and 26. The UBS Committee on the Greek text retains these words in view of the fact that they are in many of the more important manuscripts representing different family groups and different geographical areas.

Even though he dies must be taken as a reference to physical death, rather than to spiritual death in sin.

In some languages it may be necessary to alter the order of concessive and conditional clauses, for example, "even if a person dies, he will continue to live if he believes in me." In others a concessive clause must be rendered by some expression of mental activity, and somewhat separated from the rest of the sentence, for example, "Suppose a man dies; if he believes in me, he will continue to live."

11.26   and whoever lives and believes in me will
        never die. Do you believe this?"

Some commentators understand verse 26 to be merely a repetition of
verse 25 in other words. They take whoever lives as a reference to
physical life and will never die to physical death. The following translation results: "No living person who believes in me will ever die."
For the commentators who accept this viewpoint, the impact of the verse
is to indicate that, for the believer, the only death that is really
worth considering has no effect on his life.

It seems better, however, to take whoever lives to be a reference
to spiritual or eternal life, and will never die as a reference to
spiritual or eternal death. The meaning is, then, "the believer who is
spiritually alive will never die spiritually." This meaning seems to
be the most in keeping with John's theology, since in the Gospel of
John the word "life," when unqualified, must always be taken as a reference to spiritual or eternal life. Moreover, the double use of death in
verses 25-26 is to be found also in 6.49-50; in verse 49 death is physical, but in verse 50 it is spiritual. It seems best therefore to suggest that the death in verse 25 is physical, while death in verse 26 is
spiritual, and life in verses 25-26 is spiritual.

It is possible, on the basis of the Greek sentence, to take in me
both with lives and believes. If so, then one may translate "whoever
lives in me and believes in me will never die." However, most commentators and translators evidently take in me only with the verb believes.

The relative clause introduced by whoever may be made conditional,
for example, "if a man lives and believes in me." In order to suggest
that lives indicates a quality of living, and not mere existence, one
may in some languages use such an expression as "really," for example,
"if a person really lives and believes in me." The final part of the
condition will never die may then be rendered "will really never die"
or, to indicate that these words are to be understood figuratively, "he
will really never die, so to speak" or "it is just as though he will
never die."

Do you believe this? must be taken as a reference to the full content of verses 25-26.

11.27   "Yes, Lord!" she answered. "I do believe that you
                are the Messiah, the Son of God, who was to come into
                the world."

"Yes, Lord!" she answered is literally, "she says to him, 'Yes,
Lord.'" A more dramatic effect is attained by placing Martha's answer
first, and then the words she answered; and so TEV rearranges the sentence order. (See also verse 23.)

I do believe translates a verb in the perfect tense in Greek, which
most translations render "I believe." John often uses the perfect tense
of the verb "to believe" where one might expect the present tense (see
6.69, for example). If the use of the perfect tense has any significance
here, it is to indicate that Martha continues in her belief that Jesus
is the Messiah, the Son of God. On the other hand, it may indicate

[367]

nothing more than an emphatic force, as suggested by the TEV rendering I do believe.

On the use of the term Messiah, see comments at 1.41. GeCL, which does not use the technical term Messiah, translates "Yes, I believe that you are the promised Savior."

For Jesus as the Son of God, see 1.49.

Who was to come into the world (so also NEB, Gdsp, Mft) is literally "The one coming into the world." In 6.14 Jesus is spoken of as the prophet who was to come to the world, the same descriptive phrase used here of Jesus as the Son of God. Was to come into the world is difficult in some languages, since it involves a past reference was and a future reference to come. It is sometimes possible to translate "who was destined to come into the world," but such a passive expression may not be possible in some languages. Therefore it may be necessary to employ a full and explicit statement of what is meant, "whom God promised would come into the world" or "of whom God said,'He will come into the world.'"

<table>
<tr><td>TEV</td><td>(11.28-37)</td><td>RSV</td></tr>
</table>

JESUS WEEPS

28 After Martha said this, she went back and called her sister Mary privately. "The Teacher is here," she told her, "and is asking for you." 29 When Mary heard this, she got up and hurried out to meet him. (30 Jesus had not yet arrived in the village, but was still in the place where Martha had met him.) 31 The people who were in the house with Mary comforting her followed her when they saw her get up and hurry out. They thought that she was going to the grave to weep there.

32 Mary arrived where Jesus was, and as soon as she saw him, she fell at his feet. "Lord," she said, "if you had been here, my brother would not have died!"

35 Jesus saw her weeping, and he saw how the people with her were weeping also; his heart was touched, and he was deeply moved. 34 "Where have you buried him?" he asked them.

"Come and see, Lord," they answered.

35 Jesus wept. 36 "See how much he loved him!" the people said.

28 When she had said this, she went and called her sister Mary, saying quietly, "The Teacher is here and is calling for you." 29 And when she heard it, she rose quickly and went to him. 30 Now Jesus had not yet come to the village, but was still in the place where Martha had met him. 31 When the Jews who were with her in the house, consoling her, saw Mary rise quickly and go out, they followed her, supposing that she was going to the tomb to weep there. 32 Then Mary, when she came where Jesus was and saw him, fell at his feet, saying to him, "Lord, if you had been here, my brother would not have died." 33 When Jesus saw her weeping, and the Jews who came with her also weeping, he was deeply moved in spirit and troubled; 34 and he said, "Where have you laid him?" They said to him, "Lord, come and see." 35 Jesus wept. 36 So the Jews said, "See how he loved him!" 37 But some of them said, "Could not he who opened the eyes of the blind man have kept this man from dying?"

37 But some of them said, "He
gave sight to the blind man,
didn't he? Could he not have kept
Lazarus from dying?"

See the introductory comments to this chapter for the part these
verses play in the overall account.

The section heading, Jesus Weeps, may require expansion in some
languages as "Jesus weeps because of Lazarus." It would be possible to
say that Jesus wept because of his sympathy for Martha, Mary, and the
others who were there (verse 33). However, Jesus' weeping was interpreted by the Jews as being an expression of his love for Lazarus.

11.28   After Martha said this, she went back and
               called her sister Mary privately. "The Teacher
               is here," she told her, "and is asking for you."

In this verse TEV makes explicit the subject of said (Greek "she"),
that is, Martha.

Called her sister Mary privately may be translated as "spoke to
her sister so that others would not hear, telling her to come." To
translate called literally may suggest a rather loud noise, which could
hardly be done privately.

The word translated Teacher in this verse is the Greek word for
"teacher" (as in 3.2,10; 13.13-14); it is not a translation of the word
"rabbi," used in verse 8.

"The Teacher is here," she told her, "and is asking for you" is
literally "saying, 'the Teacher is here and is calling you.'" TEV restructures this part of the verse for stylistic reasons (note also
verses 23 and 27); Mft and RSV translate "is calling for you."

The Teacher is here must be expressed in some languages as "the
Teacher is nearby." It would be inappropriate to use an expression
meaning "here," which would indicate his presence in the same room.

The Teacher must be translated "our Teacher" in languages in which
the term Teacher must be possessed.

Is asking for you must be rendered in some languages "is asking
that you come" or "is saying,'Have her come'" or "...'have Mary come.'"

11.29   When Mary heard this, she got up and hurried
               out to meet him.

In Greek the subject of this verse is "that one," which TEV renders
Mary.

Hurried out is literally "went quickly." However, most translations
connect the adverb "quickly" with the verb got up rather than with
"went." This translation is more in keeping with the Greek sentence
structure (NEB "she rose up quickly and went to him").

To meet him is literally "to him" (so most translations).

[369]

11.30 (Jesus had not yet arrived in the village, but was
     still in the place where Martha had met him.)

  Since this verse interrupts the flow of the narrative, TEV and NAB
place it as a parenthetical statement. This verse indicates, as mentioned
in verse 20, that Martha met Jesus outside the village.

  In some languages a subtle but complex problem is involved in the
statement Jesus had not yet arrived in the village. A literal translation
would suggest that Jesus was moving very slowly, since Martha was able
to go out and meet him, return home, and speak to Mary while Jesus was
approaching the village. There is no indication of whether Jesus was
traveling slowly or remaining somewhere outside the village, but it may
be necessary in some languages to say "Jesus had not yet come into the
village." This translation would focus upon Jesus' location, rather than
his rate of travel.

11.31 The people who were in the house with Mary comforting
     her followed her when they saw her get up and hurry
     out. They thought that she was going to the grave to
     weep there.

  In Greek this verse is one sentence, which TEV divides into two. In
English it is more natural to refer to a person by name the first time
he is introduced in a narrative, and then to refer to him by pronouns.
TEV does so, introducing Mary in the first part of verse 31 and then referring to Mary as her...her...her...she. This practice is not in keeping
with the Greek structure, which introduces the noun Mary about midway in
the verse. However, in translating one must give attention to the struc-
tural requirements of the receptor language.

  The same comments can be made of get up and hurry out as were made
of got up and hurried out in verse 29. Here, too, it is more natural to
put the adverb "quickly" with the verb get up than with the verb "went."

  They thought is actually a participle in Greek ("thinking") which is
dependent upon the main clause in the sentence. The infinitive phrase to
weep there translates a clause of purpose in Greek, literally, "in order
that she might weep there."

  The grave, to which reference is made in this verse, was actually a
cave with a stone placed at the entrance (verse 38). The word "tomb" (so
most translations) is slightly archaic, and grave implies to most English
readers something other than a cave with a stone rolled in front of the
entrance. However, the word grave is a more natural English term, and a
description of this grave is given in verse 38.

11.32 Mary arrived where Jesus was, and as soon as
     she saw him, she fell at his feet. "Lord," she
     said, "if you had been here, my brother would not
     have died!"

  In Greek this verse is one sentence, which TEV makes into two sentences. Mary's words to Jesus are the same as those of Martha in verse 21.

Jesus saw her weeping, and he saw how the
people with her were weeping also; his heart
was touched, and he was deeply moved.

Weeping is the rendering of most English translations. Mft has
"wailing," and JB "At the sight of her tears." This strong verb is the
same one that describes Mary Magdalene's behavior at the tomb (20.11,15).
The closest equivalent in most languages is the regular expression used
of mourning for the dead.

It is difficult to know exactly what is meant by the phrase his
heart was touched. RSV translates "deeply moved in spirit"; NEB "he sighed
heavily"; NAB "he was troubled in spirit"; JB "said in great distress";
Gdsp "repressing a groan"; Mft "chafed in spirit"; Phps "deeply moved."
Etymologically the words mean "to snort like a horse," and in the Septuagint of Daniel 11.30 it means "to be enraged" or "to be greatly angry." This same verb appears again in verse 38; elsewhere it is used
of Jesus in addressing the leper whom he afterward cleansed (Mark 1.43),
and in addressing the blind man whose sight he had restored (Matt 9.30).
In both these instances TEV renders with the meaning "to speak harshly
to." In Mark 14.5 this verb is used of the anger of the guests in the
house of Simon the leper toward the woman who poured the expensive perfume on Jesus' head (TEV they criticized her harshly). In the present
context GeCL, Zür, and Luther Revised all have the idea of "to become
angry"; NAB provides a note: "he was troubled in spirit...deepest emotions: probably signifies that Jesus was angry, perhaps at the lack of
faith or at the presence of evil (death)." It is impossible to conclude
that anything less than anger is meant here or in verse 38. The use of
this verb and its cognates, both in the New Testament and elsewhere,
clearly implies anger. Evidently the translations which attempt to remove the concept of anger from these verses do so on theological rather
than linguistic or exegetical grounds. The actual basis for Jesus' anger
is not explicitly indicated, but the contents of verse 33 and verse 37
imply that it was caused by the immature faith of the Jews who were present.

In some languages the difficulty of interpretation of the expression
his heart was touched may be resolved by using an ambiguous expression,
for example, "he was very much disturbed" or "...agitated." A literal
translation, such as "was moved in spirit," may be wrongly interpreted
in some languages as "changed his mind."

He was deeply moved also appears in a variety of ways. RSV has
"was...troubled"; NEB "was deeply moved"; NAB "moved by the deepest
emotions"; JB "with a sigh that came straight from the heart"; Gdsp
"showing great agitation"; Mft "was disquieted"; Phps "visibly dis-
tressed." This verb, also used of Jesus in 12.27 (my heart is troubled)
and in 13.21 (he was deeply troubled), is literally "he stirred himself
up"). It is used by Jesus in speaking to his disciples in 14.1,27, where
it is translated worried and upset by TEV; in 5.4,7 it is used of the
stirring of the waters at the pool of Bethzatha. The particular form in
which the verb occurs in this verse is transitive with "himself" as object. It may be that this form is a kind of substitute passive (the passive form is used in 12.27 and 13.21 of Jesus), but it is also possible
that John uses the active form with an object ("he troubled himself")

in order to indicate that Jesus was master over his own emotions.

It is difficult in some languages to employ two different expressions, namely, his heart was touched and he was deeply moved. They may sometimes be combined into a single expression, provided it is in some way marked as an intensive, for example, "he was very much disturbed." These two expressions need not be interpreted as two completely different types of emotion. The two phrases may simply serve to reinforce each other.

11.34   "Where have you buried him?" he asked them.
         "Come and see, Lord," they answered.

"Where have you buried him?" he asked them is literally "and he said, 'Where have you laid him?'" (so most translations). The verb translated "laid" by most translations is used elsewhere in the New Testament of the disposal of a body, and so to translate buried is certainly legitimate. It is obvious that the body of Lazarus had not simply been laid aside somewhere, but that Jesus referred to burial in his question. The last part of this verse is also reordered in TEV; literally it reads, "They say to him, 'Lord, come and see.'" Come and see are the same words used by Jesus in 1.39.

As noted in connection with the translational problems in verse 17, it is necessary to employ a term for buried which will suggest, not a hole in the ground, but rather a place in some kind of tomb or cave. In some instances a very general expression may be used to translate buried, for example, "Where have you put his body?" or "Where is the tomb where his body has been placed?"

11.35-36   Jesus wept. (36) "See how much he loved him!"
            the people said.

No indication is given of why Jesus wept, though the Jews interpreted his weeping as a sign of his love for Lazarus. The word translated wept is used only in this verse in the New Testament. The word used of Mary in verse 33 indicates loud wailing, but the word used here comes from a noun meaning "tears."

Rather than the imperative expression See how much he loved him, one may employ an expression of possibility, for example, "You can see how much he loved him" or "...loved Lazarus." The people said may be translated "The people said to one another."

11.37   But some of them said, "He gave sight to the
         blind man, didn't he? Could he not have kept
         Lazarus from dying?"

In the Greek structure of this verse the people ask only one question; it is made into two questions by TEV. NAB translates it as a statement followed by a question: "He opened the eyes of that blind man. Why could he not have done something to stop this man from dying?" It may be

noted here that the people in this verse express no doubt regarding
the reality of Jesus' healing of the blind man, as did the Pharisees
of Chapter 9.

Some of them said may be better expressed in some languages as
"some of them said to one another."

The relation between the two questions in verse 37 may be better
expressed in some languages as a condition, for example, "If he could
give sight to the blind man, could he not have kept Lazarus from dying?"
Under such circumstances the conditional clause would not suggest any
doubt as to Jesus' ability to give sight to the blind; it is, rather,
a means of linking a known fact about Jesus' ability to their presump-
tion of what he could have done had he been present when Lazarus was
ill. The relation between these two clauses may be expressed somewhat
differently, for example, "He gave sight to the blind man, then surely
he could have kept Lazarus from dying" or "...he could have caused
Lazarus not to die."

TEV	(11.38-44)	RSV

LAZARUS IS BROUGHT TO LIFE

38 Deeply moved once more, Jesus went to the tomb, which was a cave with a stone placed at the entrance. 39 "Take the stone away!" Jesus ordered.

Martha, the dead man's sister, answered, "There will be a bad smell, Lord. He has been buried four days!"

40 Jesus said to her, "Didn't I tell you that you would see God's glory if you believed?" 41 They took the stone away. Jesus looked up and said, "I thank you, Father, that you listen to me. 42 I know that you always listen to me, but I say this for the sake of the people here, so that they will believe that you sent me." 43 After he had said this, he called out in a loud voice, "Lazarus, come out!" 44 He came out, his hands and feet wrapped in grave cloths, and with a cloth around his face. "Untie him," Jesus told them, "and let him go."

38 Then Jesus, deeply moved again, came to the tomb; it was a cave, and a stone lay upon it. 39 Jesus said, "Take away the stone." Martha, the sister of the dead man, said to him, "Lord, by this time there will be an odor, for he has been dead four days." 40 Jesus said to her, "Did I not tell you that if you would believe you would see the glory of God?" 41 So they took away the stone. And Jesus lifted up his eyes and said, "Father, I thank thee that thou hast heard me. 42 I knew that thou hearest me always, but I have said this on account of the people standing by, that they may believe that thou didst send me." 43 When he had said this, he cried with a loud voice, "Lazarus, come out." 44 The dead man came out, his hands and feet bound with bandages, and his face wrapped with a cloth. Jesus said to them, "Unbind him, and let him go."

These verses describe the events leading up to the raising of
Lazarus from the dead, and the miracle itself, which is described in
verse 44 in a simple and straightforward fashion.

The section heading, Lazarus is Brought to Life, must be rendered
in some languages as an active expression, "Lazarus lives again." It
may even be best to introduce a causative relation, for example, "Jesus
causes Lazarus to live again."

11.38   Deeply moved once more, Jesus went to the
               tomb, which was a cave with a stone placed at
               the entrance.

Deeply moved translates the same verb rendered was touched in
verse 33. In the former passage the verb is connected with the noun
phrase "in spirit," while in this verse it is connected with "in himself." Although these are different terms, their meaning is the same.
As indicated in verse 33, the sense of this verb seems to be that of
"anger." But it is difficult to know how an expression of "anger" could
be meaningfully combined with what follows, or even with what precedes.
Since the cause for this emotion is not indicated, a rendering indicating
"anger" could be misleading. Accordingly, most translations emphasize
the intensity, rather than the precise nature of the emotion.
    In Greek, verse 38 is two sentences, which TEV makes into one. The
place where Lazarus was buried is described as a cave with a stone
placed at the entrance. The Greek phrase which TEV renders at the entrance is ambiguous. It may mean "on it," in which case the shaft of the
burial tomb was vertical. Or it may mean "against it," in which case the
shaft was horizontal. Commentators are divided in their opinions, but
the weight of evidence seems to favor a horizontal cave. In either case,
the purpose of the stone was primarily to keep animals from entering the
tomb and devouring the body. A stone placed at the entrance may often be
best translated "a stone covering the opening to the cave" or "with a
large stone covering the hole of the cave."

11.39   "Take the stone away!" Jesus ordered.
               Martha, the dead man's sister, answered, "There
               will be a bad smell, Lord. He has been buried four
               days!"

Jesus ordered is literally "Jesus says." Most translations have
"Jesus said," but the Greek verb "to say" covers a large area of meaning,
and it is legitimate to see here the meaning of "to order" (GeCL "he
ordered"; NAB "Jesus directed"). In some languages it may be necessary
to specify those whom Jesus ordered to take the stone away, for example,
"Jesus ordered some of the people there, 'Take the stone away.'"
    In some languages it may seem unnecessary, or even artificial, to
use the explanation the dead man's sister, for Martha has already been
identified in the story as the sister of Lazarus. However, the translator's
task is not to edit a story but to translate it, and therefore one should
perhaps introduce this sentence as "the sister of the man who had died,"
omitting "Martha."
    There will be a bad smell is literally "already he stinks." Several
other translations likewise handle this statement impersonally: RSV "there

will be an odor"; NAB "surely there will be a stench"; NEB "by now there
will be a stench." Gdsp translates "by this time he is decaying." Mft
is quite blunt: "he will be stinking by this time." Rather than a general expression there will be a bad smell, it may be necessary in some
languages to say "you will smell a bad stink." In other languages, however, one may say "his body is already stinking."

He has been buried four days is literally "he is a four day man."
Most translations have something like "for he has been dead four days."
NAB reverses the order of the two clauses to gain effect: "Lord, it has
been four days now; surely there will be a stench!" As indicated earlier,
according to popular Jewish belief there was no hope for a person who
had been dead for four days; by then the body showed recognizable decay,
and the soul, which was thought to hover over the body for three days,
had left. The passive expression He has been buried four days may be
made active in some languages as "We buried him four days ago." In other
languages one must speak, not of "him," but of "his body," for example,
"We buried his body four days ago."

11.40   Jesus said to her, "Didn't I tell you that
        you would see God's glory if you believed?"

It is obvious from the context that the implied answer to Jesus'
question is "Yes." There is no specific place in this passage where
Jesus told Martha that she would see God's glory revealed if she believed. The reference is perhaps to the conversation Jesus had with
Martha (verses 25-26, especially verse 26). In the comments on verse
4, where Jesus speaks to his disciples, it was suggested that the clause
which TEV translates this has happened to bring glory to God may have
the meaning "this has happened to reveal how powerful God is." Although
Jesus' words in verse 40 do not refer directly back to verse 4, it is
possible to interpret these two verses in the same way; that is, to take
the phrase you would see God's glory to mean "you will see God reveal
how powerful he is" or "you will see how powerful God is." However, in
some languages the equivalent of glory would be "how wonderful God is,"
which may prove more meaningful and accurate than merely a reference to
God's "power."

11.41   They took the stone away. Jesus looked up and
        said, "I thank you, Father, that you listen to me.

From this point until the raising of Lazarus in verse 44 the narrative moves very rapidly. The reference of They is not explicit in the
Greek text, though the reference must be to the people (verse 33) and
them (verse 37), rather than to Martha and Mary. The stone would doubtless have been too heavy for the women to take away, and in their state
of mourning they would probably not in any case have been able to move
the stone. They took the stone away may be rendered "some of the people
there took the stone away." There is no indication of the particular
manner in which the stone was taken away, but if it was leaning against
the entrance to the cave, it would be possible to say "they pushed the

stone away." However, it is better to use some general expression for
movement, for example, "moved the stone away" or "caused the stone
to be moved," rather than to suggest a particular manner of removing
the stone.

Jesus looked up is literally "Jesus lifted his eyes up." As the
JB note indicates, the meaning is that Jesus "looked up to heaven," and
this meaning is expressed explicitly in Mft and GeCL. A useful equivalent in many languages is "he looked up toward heaven" or "...toward
where God was."

In TEV Jesus' words to the Father are rendered in the present tense,
and so are given a timeless meaning. In most translations these words
refer to a specific response to a request. Note, for example, JB "Father, I thank you for hearing my prayer." It is true that the verb
translated listen to in TEV is in the aorist indicative, which normally
expresses action already accomplished. However, there is no earlier
reference to a specific prayer of Jesus in this narrative, nor any mention of an answer given. It is possible to take the aorist indicative
in a timeless sense, and TEV does so, as seems best in the present context. Here the verb tense expresses, not an action already accomplished,
but Jesus' absolute confidence in knowing that the Father will accomplish
what he asks. God has already heard Jesus' prayer, even before it is
uttered, since Jesus always remains in perfect fellowship with the Father. In order to express the timeless element in the verb listen to,
it may be necessary to add a qualifying adverb, for example, "that you
always listen to me." The focus here, of course, is not merely upon
"hearing," but upon "heeding" or "responding to."

11.42   I know that you always listen to me, but I say
             this for the sake of the people here, so that
             they will believe that you sent me."

The words I know that you always listen to me support the interpretation given to verse 41.

The purpose of Jesus' prayer, as his own words indicate, is that
the people will believe that the Father sent him. Jesus is not concerned
to show the people that he is a miracle worker, but rather to reveal
through his miracles the power of God active in him. This meaning is indicated by the fact that in Greek you (in the clause you sent me) is
emphatic.

11.43   After he had said this, he called out in a loud
             voice, "Lazarus, come out!"

Since the clause After he said this refers to Jesus' statement to
his Father in heaven, it may be necessary in some languages to use a
verb for "pray," for example, "After he had prayed in this way" or
"After he had prayed these words."

The verb called out is also used of the crowds who want to crucify
Jesus (John 18.40; 19.6,15).

Come out translates two adverbs in Greek, which may literally be rendered "here, out." The first of these adverbs (deuro) is used with the force of a command, and so may legitimately be translated as in TEV and most other translations. JB seeks to maintain the adverbial emphasis of "here," and so translates as though Jesus were calling a pet, "Lazarus, here! Come out!"

11.44   He came out, his hands and feet wrapped in grave cloths, and with a cloth around his face. "Untie him," Jesus told them, "and let him go."

We are not told how Lazarus came out, and it is foolish to speculate on this point. His hands and feet were still wrapped in grave cloths, and a cloth was still around his face. The word which TEV translates grave cloths (so also Phps) literally means "bandages," and some translations use this word (RSV "bound with bandages"; Mft "swathed in bandages"). The reference is probably to strips of linen wrapped about the corpse. NAB translates "linen strips"; NEB "linen bands"; Gdsp "wrappings"; JB "bound with bands of stuff" is not entirely clear. The word translated cloth is technically a "handkerchief," used for wiping off perspiration. According to John 20.7, Jesus also had such a cloth wrapped around his face at his burial. There is some indication that in New Testament times it was customary to use handkerchiefs to wrap the faces of the poor in preparing them for burial.

Despite the difficulty of determining just how Lazarus came out of the tomb, it may be necessary to use a term which would suggest "walking." One should avoid an expression which would suggest "floating out" through the air.

Again, for stylistic reasons, TEV restructures the Greek in the last sentence of this verse. Literally it reads "Jesus says to them, 'Untie him and let him go.'" The verb told is the same verb translated ordered in verse 39. As indicated there, it covers a wide area of meaning.

If the phrase Untie him is translated literally, it may suggest that Lazarus was in some way tied up with ropes. It may therefore be necessary to employ a phrase which means "Unwind the cloths from around him" or "Take off the cloths that are wound around him" or even "Take off the cloths from his body."

TEV   (11.45-57)   RSV

THE PLOT AGAINST JESUS

45 Many of the people who had come to visit Mary saw what Jesus did, and they believed in him. 46 But some of them returned to the Pharisees and told them what Jesus had done. 47 So the Pharisees and the chief priests met with the Council and said, "What shall we do? Look at all the miracles this

45 Many of the Jews therefore, who had come with Mary and had seen what he did, believed in him; 46 but some of them went to the Pharisees and told them what Jesus had done. 47 So the chief priests and the Pharisees gathered the council, and said, "What are we to do? For this man performs many

man is performing! 48 If we let
him go on in this way, everyone
will believe in him, and the Roman authorities will take action
and destroy our Temple and our
nation!"

49 One of them, named Caiaphas,
who was High Priest that year,
said, "What fools you are! 50
Don't you realize that it is better for you to have one man die
for the people, instead of having
the whole nation destroyed?" 51
Actually, he did not say this of
his own accord; rather, as he was
High Priest that year, he was
prophesying that Jesus was going
to die for the Jewish people, 52
and not only for them, but also to
bring together into one body all
the scattered people of God.

53 From that day on the Jewish
authorities made plans to kill Jesus. 54 So Jesus did not travel
openly in Judea, but left and went
to a place near the desert, to a
town named Ephraim, where he
stayed with the disciples.

55 The time for the Passover
Festival was near, and many people
went up from the country to Jerusalem to perform the ritual of
purification before the festival.
56 They were looking for Jesus, and
as they gathered in the Temple,
they asked one another, "What do
you think? Surely he will not come
to the festival, will he?" 57 The
chief priests and the Pharisees
had given orders that if anyone
knew where Jesus was, he must report it, so that they could arrest
him.

signs. 48 If we let him go on thus,
every one will believe in him, and
the Romans will come and destroy
both our holy place^a and our nation." 49 But one of them, Caiaphas,
who was high priest that year, said
to them, "You know nothing at all;
50 you do not understand that it is
expedient for you that one man
should die for the people, and that
the whole nation should not perish."
51 He did not say this of his own
accord, but being high priest that
year he prophesied that Jesus should
die for the nation, 52 and not for
the nation only, but to gather into
one the children of God who are scattered abroad. 53 So from that day
on they took counsel how to put him
to death.

54 Jesus therefore no longer went
about openly among the Jews, but
went from there to the country near
the wilderness, to a town called
Ephraim; and there he stayed with
the disciples. 55 Now the Passover
of the Jews was at hand, and many
went up from the country to Jerusalem before the Passover, to purify themselves. 56 They were looking for Jesus and saying to one another as they stood in the temple,
"What do you think? That he will
not come to the feast?" 57 Now the
chief priests and the Pharisees had
given orders that if any one knew
where he was, he should let them
know, so that they might arrest him.

^{a}Greek *our place*

11.45   Many of the people who had come to visit Mary
saw what Jesus did, and they believed in him.

This verse gives the immediate effect of the raising of Lazarus
from the dead.

In Greek the verbs translated had come and saw in TEV are actually
participles, but TEV restructures this sentence for naturalness in

English, and makes explicit that Jesus is the subject of the verb did, whereas the Greek has only "he." It is especially important, when new sections are begun, to identify the participants by name.

To visit Mary is more literally "to Mary," but visit is obviously implied, as several translations indicate (NEB, NAB, JB, Gdsp, GeCL). The meaning is not that the people had come "with Mary" (so RSV). The reference is to verse 19. It may seem strange to have a reference to Mary without any indication of her sister Martha. Some translators, therefore, want to render this passage "to visit Martha and Mary." However, it is not the task of the translator to revise the original text.

There is a textual problem in the word that TEV translates what (in what Jesus did). Some Greek manuscripts have the singular, while the strongest evidence is in favor of the plural (literally "what things"). Evidently the majority of English translations prefer ambiguity here, and so translate what, as TEV does.

11.46   But some of them returned to the Pharisees and told them what Jesus had done.

Although some of the people believed after seeing the miracle (verse 45), others reported to the Pharisees what Jesus had done. This is significant in the Gospel of John, because now the plot against Jesus begins to take form. Here the hostile Jewish party is identified as the Pharisees; in verse 54 the hostile Jews are simply called in Greek "the Jews" (TEV in Judea). In 9.13,18 the terms "the Pharisees" and "the Jews" (TEV the Jewish authorities) are used interchangeably of the enemies of Jesus.

A literal translation of some of them returned to the Pharisees may suggest that the Pharisees had sent certain individuals to Bethany to investigate the situation. But that they did so is not implied in the Greek text. One can therefore translate "but some of them went away and went to the Pharisees" or "...returned home and went to see the Pharisees."

Since not all the Pharisees are included in this reference, it may be necessary in some languages to use a form which means "some Pharisees."

11.47   So the Pharisees and the chief priests met with the Council and said, "What shall we do? Look at all the miracles this man is performing!

TEV introduces this verse with so (Greek oun) to indicate the relation between the report of the events to the Pharisees and their action in calling together the Council. (On oun, see under 2.18.)

TEV inverts the Greek order "the chief priests and the Pharisees," since John's readers already know about the Pharisees, but in this narrative the existence of the chief priests is new information for them. Since in verse 46 the Pharisees in question may be identified as "some Pharisees," it is possible in verse 47 to translate "so these Pharisees and the chief priests." In some languages "the Pharisees" would suggest that all the Pharisees were involved.

The chief priests may be expressed in many languages as "the leaders among the priests."

Met with is more literally "called a meeting of" (see Mft, Gdsp, NAB). JB translates simply "called a meeting," without stating who were called. There is a question in many commentators' minds as to whether this meeting was a formal or informal gathering of the Jewish Council. This uncertainty may be why JB omits an explicit mention of the Council, assuming that it was an informal gathering. Only here in John's Gospel does the Greek word translated Council appear. It was the supreme religious court of the Jewish people, composed of seventy leaders and presided over by the High Priest. Most of its members were Sadducees, but some Pharisees were members (see the note on 3.1). The Council may be rendered in some languages "the gathering of the leaders." In others the Council is literally "the gathering of the old men," but not all members of this council were necessarily old men. In many languages such a phrase as "old men" may refer primarily to status rather than to age.

The question raised by the Pharisees and the chief priests (What shall we do?) may be understood in either of two ways. Most translations prefer to take this question in a deliberative sense, as TEV does. But it is possible to take the question as rhetorical (NEB and JB "What action are we taking?"; see also Luther Revised, Zür, Segond). If so, the expected answer is "Nothing" (NAB alternative rendering "Why are we doing nothing?").

In some languages such a verb as said must be changed into a verb for "questioning" if what follows is in fact a question, for example, "and they asked one another, 'What shall we do?'"

Look at all the miracles this man is performing! is literally "because this man is doing many signs." As elsewhere TEV takes "sign" in the sense of miracle. (See the comment on 2.11.)

In some languages one cannot employ such an expression as "look at" unless it is actually possible to see something going on. An equivalent would be "Think about all the miracles this man is doing" or "Remember all the miracles this man has done."

11.48 If we let him go on in this way, everyone will
    believe in him, and the Roman authorities will
    take action and destroy our Temple and our nation!"

If we let him go on in this way may be rendered "If we permit him to go on doing these things" or "If we allow him to keep on doing miracles."

Everyone (Mft, Gdsp, Phps, JB "everybody") is in Greek a plural form. NAB translates "the whole world" and NEB "the whole populace." Though the Pharisees and the chief priests may have had the Jewish people specifically in mind, as NEB and other versions indicate, it seems better in light of John's theology not to limit this reference to the Jewish people.

The Roman authorities is literally "the Romans," and the verb translated will take action is literally "will come." Here TEV simply uses a specific term in place of the more generic Greek term.

Our Temple (so also NEB; NAB "our sanctuary"; JB note "...or more probably the holiest of all places, the Temple") is literally "our place," and is rendered in most translations "our holy place." The reference may be to the city of Jerusalem; but, as the JB note indicates, it is more probably a reference to the Temple itself.

Our nation may be understood in the sense of "our people." It is interesting to note that the members of the Council identified their own power with the welfare of the nation as a whole.

11.49   One of them, named Caiaphas, who was High
          Priest that year, said, "What fools you are!

Caiaphas is mentioned again in 18.13,14,24,28. He was appointed High Priest in A.D. 18 and was deposed in A.D. 36, when Pilate also was put out of office. As John indicates in 18.13, Caiaphas was the son-in-law of Annas. Traditionally the Jewish High Priest held office for life, but in New Testament times the tenure of the High Priest depended on the favor of the Roman government. John's statement who was High Priest that year is taken by some commentators to indicate that John believed that the office of High Priest was a yearly appointment. However, this assumption is not necessarily correct. More probably John simply meant that Caiaphas was the High Priest in that memorable year in which Jesus was crucified.

The same term in Greek may be rendered either "high priest" or "chief priest" when used in the singular, but it must be rendered "chief priests" when it occurs in the plural. In the singular it may be translated "the leader of the priests" or "the one who is over all the other priests" or, as in some languages, "the first priest of all."

What fools you are! is literally "you do not know nothing," in which "you" and "nothing" are emphatic. This statement may be rendered "You don't understand what's happening" or "You don't realize what's involved" or "You don't see the problem."

11.50   Don't you realize that it is better for you to
          have one man die for the people, instead of having
          the whole nation destroyed?"

For you (so most translations) has by far the strongest manuscript support, and this reading is followed by the UBS Committee on the Greek text. Only Phps ("for us") seems to follow an alternative reading. It is better for you may be rendered "you will be better off" or "it will be to your advantage" or, idiomatically, "you will get the bigger part" or "you will be above others."

NAB is wrong in placing for the people in brackets, as if its presence in the text were doubtful. No Greek manuscript evidence favors its omission; only the evidence of some of the early Church Fathers. However, NAB note is possibly correct, in suggesting that the preposition rendered for should be understood with the meaning "instead of." In verse 51 the preposition for in the phrase for the people has its usual meaning, "for the sake of."

Nation in this verse is the same word translated Jewish people in verse 51, and both these terms are synonymous with the word translated

[381]

<u>people</u> in this verse. Technically one could say that <u>nation</u> refers to the Jewish people as a political unit, while the word <u>people</u> refers to them in their relation to God. However, this distinction is rather artificial in this passage.

The rhetorical question in verse 50 may be transformed into a statement in languages in which such a question might be misleading. For example, one may say "You should realize that it is better..."

<u>Instead of having the whole nation destroyed</u> may be treated as a causative, for example, "instead of causing the whole nation to be destroyed" or "instead of causing the Romans to destroy the whole nation." In some languages, however, it may be better to treat this expression as one which allows, rather than causes, something to happen, for example, "instead of allowing the whole nation to be destroyed."

<u>11.51</u>   Actually, he did not say this of his own accord;
                rather, as he was High Priest that year, he was
                prophesying that Jesus was going to die for the
                Jewish people,

In Greek the adverb <u>actually</u> is literally "but."

<u>He did not say this of his own accord</u> (so also RSV, NEB; Mft "... simply of his own accord") appears in a variety of ways in different translations: "Now he was not self-moved in saying this" (Gdsp); "He did not speak in his own person" (JB); "He did not make this remark on his own initiative" (Phps). The form of the word here is similar to that of the words of 14.10; <u>The words that I have spoken to you...do not come from me.</u> John is saying in these two passages that God is able to speak through a person, whether that person is conscious of it (as in 14.10), or not (as here). <u>He did not say this of his own accord</u> may be expressed in some languages "He didn't himself think up this" or "He himself didn't think of this which he said."

JB omits the phrase <u>that year</u> from this verse, though the manuscript support for the omission is very weak. Its omission from one Greek manuscript is perhaps due to the observation that it was redundant after verse 49.

The Jews traditionally ascribed a degree of prophetic ability to the High Priest, and that belief is reflected in this verse. Despite Caiaphas' unwillingness to respond to God's words in Jesus Christ, God was able to speak through him, without Caiaphas' realizing it. <u>As he was High Priest that year</u> should be treated in most languages as causative, for example, "because he was the High Priest that year."

The verb "to prophesy" in a biblical context normally has the primary meaning of "to speak forth God's message," but in the present context the meaning is obviously "to predict." In this context <u>he was prophesying</u> may be rendered "he was telling ahead of time what was going to happen; he was saying that Jesus was going to die for the Jewish people."

As indicated in the preceding verse, the phrase <u>for the Jewish people</u> is literally "for the nation," but the meaning is the same as the word translated <u>people</u> and <u>nation</u> in verse 50.

11.52   and not only for them, but also to bring together
          into one body all the scattered people of God.

For them is literally "for the nation," but in the English structure
a pronoun is more natural here. It may be necessary to fill out the ellipsis in the expression and not only for them, for example, "he was
going to die, but not only for them." The contrast in not only...but
also may be expressed in some languages as "it is true he was going to
die for them; it is also true he was going to..."
     Into one body is literally "into one" (RSV, NAB, Mft), and is trans-
lated "in unity" by JB, and "into one family" by Phps. NEB, GeCL, Zür,
and Luther Revised all have the idea of "to bring together," without
explicitly mentioning "into one." Segond has "in one (body)." In many
languages it is impossible to conserve the figure of body; hence, one
must often say "to bring them together so that they would be just like
one group" or "to bring them together so that they would act as if they
were one person."
     The Greek phrase translated children of God is used elsewhere in
this Gospel only in 1.12. The entire phrase the scattered children of
God, in a Jewish context alone, would refer to the gathering together
of the scattered Israelites to their own land. In the present context,
the reference is to the Gentiles who were destined to believe in Jesus
Christ. All the scattered people of God must often be broken into two
distinct expressions, "all the people of God who are scattered in various places." However, a literal translation of scattered may suggest
that someone had somehow thrown the people into various places. Therefore, in some languages it may be better to say "all the children of
God who were living in different lands."

11.53   From that day on the Jewish authorities made
               plans to kill Jesus.

     From that day on refers to the time that Caiaphas spoke to the
Jewish Council (verses 49-50). In order to make this fact explicit, it
may be necessary, as in NAB, to indicate that verses 51-52 are a parenthetical statement by the author of the Gospel. Or one may introduce
verse 53 by translating "So from the day that Caiaphas spoke to the
Jewish Council, they made plans to kill Jesus."
     In Greek the Jewish authorities is literally "they," while Jesus
is literally "him." Again TEV makes pronominal references explicit.
     Made plans to kill Jesus may be translated "were planning to kill
Jesus" or "were planning how they could kill Jesus."

11.54   So Jesus did not travel openly in Judea, but left
               and went to a place near the desert, to a town
               named Ephraim, where he stayed with the disciples.

     The word translated openly appears first in John 7.4, but it is
used also in 7.13,26; 10.24; 11.14,54; 16.25,29; and 18.20. Openly is
also the translation of RSV and JB; NAB has "freely," and NEB "publicly"
(Mft and Gdsp "in public").

It may be important to indicate clearly the relation of the first
part of verse 54 to what immediately precedes it. Hence, the particle
So may require expansion in some languages, for example, "As a result
of this" or "because of what the Jewish authorities were planning."

Jesus did not travel openly may be translated "Jesus did not travel
in such a way that everyone knew where he was" or "...so that everyone
would see him."

In Judea (so also NEB) is literally "among the Jews" (so most translations); NAB has "in Jewish circles."

The exact location of the town called Ephraim is not known, though
many scholars believe it to be the present Et-Taiyibeh, which is four
miles (seven kilometers) northeast of the town of Bethel.

Where (so also NEB, NAB) is literally "and there," as in most
translations.

11.55   The time for the Passover Festival was near,
            and many people went up from the country to
            Jerusalem to perform the ritual of purification
            before the festival.

The three verses 55-57 form a transition to the following section.
In this respect they are similar to 7.11,13.

The time...was near may be rendered in some languages "It was almost
the day" or "It was only a few more days before the day" or "In a few
days it would be the day."

For the third time in John's Gospel the Passover Festival is definitely mentioned (2.13; 6.14), though it may be that the festival mentioned in 5.1 is also a Passover (see there). Many people did go up to
the Passover Festival. During the Passover season the population of
Jerusalem, normally about 25,000, swelled to more than 100,000.

Went up is the same verb used in 2.13 (went to). It is the normal
word used of a pilgrimage to the Holy City.

It was customary for persons coming from the countryside to purify
themselves before a major festival. Especially was this true of persons
who lived near Gentiles or who had business dealings with Gentiles. One
may recall here Paul's actions in Acts 31.24-26.

To perform the ritual of purification (GeCL "they wanted to purify
themselves before the feast according to the prescribed regulations") is
more literally "in order that they might purify themselves." Ceremonial
purification was necessary if a man were to keep the Passover correctly
(Num 9.10); and this ritual of purification could last as long as an
entire week, depending on the degree of pollution experienced by the
worshiper. The verb "to purify" does not appear again in John's Gospel;
but it does appear in 1 John 3.3 as a reference to spiritual purification.

It may be difficult to translate perform the ritual of purification.
In some languages it is rendered simply "to do what was necessary in
order to be purified" or "...to be pure." Other languages, however, have
no word which suggests purification in the ritual sense. Some employ
such a phrase as "to be clean before God" or "to be clean in God's eyes."
However, in some languages there is no relation at all between physical
cleanliness and spiritual purity. It may be necessary to say "to do what

was necessary in order to be free from sin." But such an expression may suggest the concept of atonement. If so, one may say instead "to do what was necessary in order that God would look upon them as being good" or "...that God would accept them."

There is no textual evidence to support the omission of the phrase before the festival, as in JB.

11.56   They were looking for Jesus, and as they
          gathered in the Temple, they asked one
          another, "What do you think? Surely he
          will not come to the festival, will he?"

The word used for Temple in this verse refers to the Temple precincts, not to the sanctuary proper (see comments at 2.14).

What do you think? is the way most translations render the first question the people were asking one another. The second question (Surely he will not come to the festival, will he?) is translated in a variety of ways. NAB has "Is he likely to come for the feast?"; Mft reads "Do you think he will not come up to the festival?"; Gdsp "Do you think he will not come to the festival at all?" NEB has a statement, "Perhaps he is not coming to the festival." Phps reads "Surely he won't come to the festival?"; and JB has "Will he come to the festival or not?" It is difficult to determine precisely the meaning of the question in Greek. It may be that it expects a strong denial, or it may merely suggest doubt. The context suggests that an element of doubt is involved. Since the second question posed by the people is in essence the content of what they were thinking, the two questions are more frequently combined as one, for example, "Do you think that he will come to the Festival?" This form of question suggests in several languages an element of doubt.

11.57   The chief priests and the Pharisees had given
          orders that if anyone knew where Jesus was, he
          must report it, so that they could arrest him.

As in verse 47, the Greek text here reads the chief priests and the Pharisees. In verse 47 TEV reverses the order, mentioning the Pharisees first because they were already known to the readers and the chief priests were not. It is not necessary to reverse the order here, because both the chief priests and the Pharisees have been introduced into the discourse.

The verb translated must report it (NAB "should report it"; NEB "should give information"; JB "must inform them"; Phps "should tell them") occurs only here in John's Gospel. It is used similarly but in a passive form in Acts 23.30 (TEV when I was informed).

The content of what was ordered by the chief priests and Pharisees must be expressed as direct discourse in some languages, for example, "The chief priests and the Pharisees had commanded, 'If anyone knows where Jesus is, he must report it to us so that we can arrest him.'" He must report it may also be rendered "he must tell us what he knows."

TEV   (12.1-8)   RSV

JESUS IS ANOINTED AT BETHANY

12 Six days before the Passover, Jesus went to Bethany, the home of Lazarus, the man he had raised from death. 2 They prepared a dinner for him there, which Martha helped serve; Lazarus was one of those who were sitting at the table with Jesus. 3 Then Mary took a whole pint of a very expensive perfume made of pure nard, poured it on Jesus' feet, and wiped them with her hair. The sweet smell of the perfume filled the whole house. 4 One of Jesus' disciples, Judas Iscariot--the one who was going to betray him--said, 5 "Why wasn't this perfume sold for three hundred silver coins[x] and the money given to the poor?" 6 He said this, not because he cared about the poor, but because he was a thief. He carried the money bag and would help himself from it.

7 But Jesus said, "Leave her alone! Let her keep what she has for the day of my burial. 8 You will always have poor people with you, but you will not always have me."

12 Six days before the Passover, Jesus came to Bethany, where Lazarus was, whom Jesus had raised from the dead. 2 There they made him a supper; Martha served and Lazarus was one of those at table with him. 3 Mary took a pound of costly ointment of pure nard and anointed the feet of Jesus and wiped his feet with her hair; and the house was filled with the fragrance of the ointment. 4 But Judas Iscariot, one of his disciples (he who was to betray him), said, 5 "Why was this ointment not sold for three hundred denarii[b] and given to the poor?" 6 This he said, not that he cared for the poor but because he was a thief, and as he had the money box he used to take what was put into it. 7 Jesus said, "Let her alone, let her keep it for the day of my burial. 8 The poor you always have with you, but you do not always have me."

[b]The denarius was a day's wage for a laborer

[x]SILVER COINS: *See 6.7.*

This account of the anointing of Jesus at Bethany has its parallels in Mark 14.3-9 and Matthew 26.6-13. There are several differences among the accounts, but the primary difference is that in Mark and Matthew the woman is not named. On the other hand, in John the host is not named (the Greek text simply has "they"), while according to Mark and Matthew the anointing took place as Jesus was a guest in the house of Simon the leper. Another immediately noticeable difference is that, according to John, it is Judas Iscariot who makes the comment concerning the waste of the perfume, while in Matthew it is the disciples, and in Mark it is simply "some of the people there." Luke does not include this particular scene, but in 7.36-50 he tells of the anointing of Jesus by a sinful woman in a house of Simon the Pharisee. Not only in the details, but in the focus as well, the narrative in Luke is quite different from that of the other Gospels.

Evidently the presence of Lazarus at the feast caused a great deal of public interest. As a result, the Jewish leaders decided to kill not only Jesus, but Lazarus as well. The first two verses give the temporal setting (six days before the Passover) and the place (Bethany, where Lazarus lived...a dinner), as well as most of the participants in the narrative: Jesus, Lazarus, the unidentified "they," and Martha. In the next two verses Mary and Judas Iscariot are introduced. The development of the story is simple, with the climax coming in the words of Jesus in verses 7 and 8.

The section heading, Jesus Is Anointed at Bethany, may require restructuring as an active expression, for example, "Mary anoints Jesus" or "Mary puts expensive perfume on Jesus' feet."

12.1   Six days before the Passover, Jesus went to
                    Bethany, the home of Lazarus, the man he had raised
                    from death.

According to the Gospel of John, the Passover began on the next Friday evening (13.1; 18.28; 19.31,42), and so the anointing must have taken place on the Saturday evening preceding.

In many languages "festival" must be added whenever a reference is made to the Passover. The full phrase may be "a festival for celebrating the passing over" or "...the passing over of the angel."

For the first mention of this Bethany, see 11.1.

The home of Lazarus (so also NEB; Gdsp "where Lazarus...was living") is literally "where Lazarus was" (many translations). NAB translates "the village of Lazarus." Lazarus is specifically identified as the man he had raised from death. In some languages it is better to treat this clause as a separate sentence, for example, "Jesus had raised this man Lazarus from death" or "...had caused him to live again."

12.2   They prepared a dinner for him there, which Martha
                    helped serve; Lazarus was one of those who were
                    sitting at the table with Jesus.

There is no way to identify the they of the statement they prepared a dinner for him there. NEB makes this impersonal: "There a supper was given in his honour." According to the account in Mark and Matthew, this meal took place at the home of Simon the leper, and at least one commentator takes this Simon to be the father of Lazarus, Mary, and Martha. However, it is impossible to read that meaning into the present account. Others assume that Lazarus was the host, but from the fact that he was one of those at the table, it is better to assume that he was a guest. If it is necessary in translation to identify they, such an expression as "Jesus' friends" or "some of Jesus' friends" may be used. It would also be possible to say "some people there" or "some people in that town." The difficulty is that such a pronoun as "they" suggests a definite identification, and the reader tends to associate "they" with some preceding reference. The nearest such reference is the chief priests and the Pharisees of 11.57, which certainly would not fit the they of 12.2.

[387]

Which Martha helped serve (GeCL "Martha helped serve") is more literally "Martha served"; NEB and NAB have "at which Martha served." Mft is too limiting in his translation ("Martha waited on him"); Gdsp seems to have the proper focus ("Martha waited on them").

GeCL ("Lazarus lay at the table with Jesus and the others") is close to NEB ("Lazarus sat among the guests with Jesus"), though it retains the literal rendering "lay" instead of translating "sat." GeCL then adds a cultural note, explaining the particular situation at the time of Jesus, according to which people "lay at the table" rather than "sat at the table." If it seems necessary to give readers the proper cultural picture, this should be done in a footnote, and the text rendered in terms of the table customs of the readers. TEV (so also NEB and GeCL) substitute Jesus for the pronoun "him" of the Greek text.

12.3   Then Mary took a whole pint of a very expensive
              perfume made of pure nard, poured it on Jesus'
              feet, and wiped them with her hair. The sweet
              smell of the perfume filled the whole house.

In the Greek structure of this verse there are only two main verbs (poured...wiped), while took is a participle. For English readers it is more natural to restructure the statement as TEV and several other translations do.

A whole pint (GeCL "a bottle") is rendered in most translations "a pound" (Phps "a whole pound"). This Greek word appears only here and in John 19.39 in the New Testament. It corresponds to the Roman pound of 12 ounces, or 327.45 grams. TEV translates a whole pint because of the word perfume that follows. The word translated perfume in TEV and most other translations may also have the meaning of "ointment" (RSV, JB). It is not certain which is referred to, but the indication is that it was a liquid rather than a salve, and so most translations have perfume. It is true that perfume was sold by weight, rather than by volume, but it is more natural to speak either of "a bottle of perfume" or "a pint of perfume" than of "a pound of perfume"; and so TEV renders a whole pint...of perfume. What is important is not the kind of measurement, but the large amount involved and its high value. If the metric system is used, a whole pint may be rendered "about half a liter."

Very expensive is not the same word used in the Markan account (14.3), but the meaning is basically the same. Most translations have the meaning of either expensive or "costly." The word translated pure in TEV (Greek pistikos) is rendered "pure" or "real" ("genuine") in most translations. The word itself is of uncertain meaning, and other meanings given to it are "liquid," "spike" (referring to the hair root of the nard plant from which the oil was derived), or "mixed with pistachio oil." Among modern translators Gdsp ("liquid spikenard") is apparently the only one who gives the meaning of "liquid." He translates nard with the meaning of "spikenard," which is a synonym. The nard plant grows in the mountains of northern India, and from its root and hair stem is derived a very fragrant oil used in perfumes and ointments.

In some languages it may be necessary to specify the various attributives of the perfume by means of separate statements. The first

statement may be simply "Then Mary took a whole pint of perfume," which
may be followed by such qualifiers as "This perfume cost a great deal
of money, and it was made completely from a plant called nard" or "...
it was made only from nard." It may be useful to indicate by a marginal
note the nature of the plant called "nard." However, this cultural feature is not important. In most translations no reference is made to the
plant from which the perfume was extracted.

The term one uses to translate poured will depend primarily upon
the type of substance suggested by the translation of "perfume." If a
liquid is suggested, then obviously a term meaning "to pour" would be
appropriate. If, however, "an ointment" is indicated, then such a term
as "to put on" or "to rub on" would be required.

In rendering wiped them with her hair, the reference should be
primarily to the wiping of the feet, not the wiping off of the nard.

The sweet smell of the perfume filled the whole house translates
a passive Greek construction ("the house was filled with the fragrance
of the perfume"). It may not be possible to say "the sweet smell filled
the whole house." However, one can often say "people throughout the
house smelled this sweet odor" or "...smelled the good perfume."

12.4   One of Jesus' disciples, Judas Iscariot--the one
           who was going to betray him--said,

In Greek this sentence, like the last sentence of verse 3, is introduced by a particle (de) which often indicates a transition in a Greek
narrative. However, it may well be that in neither of these instances
does John indicate a transition. Many translations do not indicate the
presence of this particle by a particular word in the text. In verse 4
NEB translates "At this," while JB translates "Then."

It may be more natural in some languages to introduce the proper
name "Judas Iscariot" first and then identify Judas as "one of Jesus'
followers."

In Greek the verb said is actually in the present tense ("says"),
and it appears as the first word in the verse. In English it is more
natural to have the verb of speaking immediately precede the words it
introduces, and so in TEV, as in most other English translations, said
appears as the last word in the verse.

One of Jesus' disciples is literally "one of his disciples," but
TEV employs the noun Jesus to avoid possible ambiguity.

Betray is the rendering of most translations, but NAB has "hand
over." The first reference to Judas as the one who would betray Jesus
is found in 6.71.

The one who was going to betray him does not imply that Judas had
at this point already decided to betray Jesus. It is rather a comment
made by the writer, who knew the outcome of events at the time of
writing.

The double apposition preceding the verb said may prove awkward
in some languages. It may be necessary to introduce the information by
two relative clauses, for example, "One of Jesus' disciples, who was
Judas Iscariot, and who was later going to betray Jesus, said..." It is
possible also to invert certain forms, for example, "Judas Iscariot, who

was one of Jesus' disciples and who later was the one who betrayed Jesus, said..."

If the translator wishes to preserve the question in verse 5, it may be necessary to employ in verse 4 a verb meaning "asked," rather than "said." It may be necessary also to indicate of whom the question was asked; perhaps it was even posed to Jesus himself. However, it is probably best to make the statement of Judas a rather general one, directed to the guests, for example, "said to those there." But in view of the nature of the following statement, it may be possible to say "explained to those there," which would prepare the reader for the statement to follow.

12.5   "Why wasn't this perfume sold for three hundred silver coins^x and the money given to the poor?"

^{x}SILVER COINS: *See 6.7.*

Three hundred siver coins is literally "three hundred denarii." According to Matthew 20.2 a "denarius" (the singular of "denarii") is equivalent to the average daily wage of a laborer. By translating "three hundred dollars" in its earlier editions, TEV simply tried to find a cultural equivalent, like NEB, which renders "thirty pounds." Mft ("ten pounds"), Gdsp ("sixty dollars"), and Phps ("thirty pounds") likewise attempt to give a cultural equivalent. Rapid currency inflation in nearly all parts of the world quickly renders all such translations obsolete. NAB renders simply "three hundred silver pieces." Whatever term the translator uses, it should reflect a high amount in relation to the average earnings of a working-class man. In view of the rapid change in the buying power of the money in current use almost everywhere, it may be best to use such a phrase as "silver pieces," and then to provide a footnote indicating that "a silver piece" was the average daily wage of a working-class man. Some translations actually say "Why wasn't this perfume sold for the equivalent of three hundred days' wages?"

Although the Greek of this verse merely has a question (Why wasn't this perfume sold...?), Phps ("Why on earth wasn't this perfume sold? It's worth thirty pounds...") and NAB ("Why was not this perfume sold? It could have brought three hundred silver pieces...") render it by a question and a statement, thus indicating that the value of the perfume is in focus here. It is necessary to supply such a term as the money in this verse, though it does not appear in the Greek text. Otherwise the translation may end by sounding as if the perfume should be sold for three hundred dollars and at the same time given to the poor. Note, for example, RSV, which has a rather literal rendering of the Greek ("Why was this ointment not sold for three hundred denarii and given to the poor?").

Since the question posed by Judas Iscariot was essentially rhetorical (that is to say, he was not really asking for information), it may be best in some languages to transform it into a strong statement, for example, "This perfume should have been sold for three hundred silver coins, and then the money given to the poor."

12.6   He said this, not because he cared about the
poor, but because he was a thief. He carried
the money bag and would help himself from it.

This verse is introduced with the same particle (de) as verse 4.
The verb cared about is the same one used in 10.13, which speaks
of the hired man who does not care for the sheep.
Only in this verse in the Gospels is Judas described as a thief.
In languages in which it is necessary to place the positive before
the negative clause, the first part of verse 6 may be altered to read
"He said this because he was a thief; he didn't say it because he cared
for the poor" or "...he said this, not because he cared for the poor."
The word translated money bag ("purse" in many translations) was
originally used of a box used to carry mouthpieces of flutes. Later it
was used of boxes in general, but more specifically with the meaning
"money box" (so some translations). The word is used again in 13.29.
A literal translation of he carried the money bag may suggest that
Judas was a low-ranking disciple who had the burden of carrying the
money for the others. The implication, however, is simply that he was
treasurer of the group. This meaning may be expressed in some languages
as "he had charge of the money that belonged to all of them" or "he was
the man responsible for keeping the money."
Would help himself from it indicates customary or repeated action.
The translation should not imply that Judas took everything that was
placed in the money bag. The meaning is that Judas had the habit of
helping himself from the contributions given to the disciples to be dis-
persed to the poor. JB, though rather high level, conveys this meaning:
"he was in charge of the common fund and used to help himself to the
contributions." One may also say "he took money for himself from time
to time" or "from time to time he took some of the money and used it for
himself."

12.7   But Jesus said, "Leave her alone! Let her
keep what she has for the day of my burial.

In most translations the punctuation of this verse is similar to
that of TEV. That is, a break is made after Leave her alone, though it
is possible on the basis of the Greek to punctuate otherwise. Segond is
apparently the only modern translation that follows the alternative possibility: "Let her keep the perfume for the day of my burial."
Let her keep what she has for the day of my burial may be interpreted in several different ways. (1) It is possible to understand the
verb keep as meaning "keep in mind," and so to translate "On the day of
my burial, let her keep in mind what she has done." (2) In Mark the
parallel passage in 14.8 the meaning is obvious: "She did what she could;
she poured perfume on my body to prepare it ahead of time for burial."
But it is not necessary to assume that the meaning here is the same as
in Mark. If, however, the Markan meaning is seen in the present verse,
then this verse may be translated "(Unknowingly) she has kept what she
has done for the day of my burial." (3) Finally, there are those who
see in John a possible Aramaic origin for the Greek and so translate

"Should she keep the perfume till the day of my burial?" None of these possibilities is wholly satisfactory. Arguments for an Aramaic origin are not conclusive; one cannot insist that John must have the same meaning that Mark has; and to take the verb keep in the sense of "to keep in mind" seems somewhat farfetched.

There is relatively little difficulty in translating Leave her alone! It can be rendered "Do not bother her" or "Do not make it difficult for her." However, it is extremely difficult to know how to translate Let her keep what she has for the day of my burial, since, as already indicated, we really do not know what is meant by the Greek expression. None of the alternatives is completely satisfactory. It would be possible to translate this sentence "Let her keep what she has left so that she may use it on the day of my burial," but this interpretation is out of keeping with the fact that Mary had already poured the ointment on Jesus' feet. If the meaning "bear in mind" is followed, it may be possible to say "Let her bear in mind what she has done, since it was done in anticipation of the day when I would be buried." However, it may be more satisfactory to translate in a relatively obscure way, since in the original text itself the statement is obscure, and the translator should not attempt to be clearer than the original text.

12.8   You will always have poor people with you, but
          you will not always have me."

There is some weak manuscript evidence for the omission of this verse as an original part of the Greek text. It is possible that these words were added at an early date by a scribe who recalled the similar words of Jesus in Matthew 26.11 and Mark 14.7. However, in light of the overwhelming manuscript evidence in support of this verse, the UBS Committee on the Greek text felt justified in retaining it. They rate their decision a "C" choice, indicating a reasonable degree of doubt regarding its authenticity.

Although both were considered good works, the rabbis ranked the care of the dead superior to almsgiving. In this verse "the poor" and "me" are in emphatic positions in the Greek sentence, as is reflected in the rather literal rendering of NAB: "The poor you always have with you, but me you will not always have."

A literal translation of You will always have poor people with you could be misunderstood to mean "You will always have about you poor people whom you retain as helpers" or "you will always be surrounded by poor people." Obviously, such renderings should be avoided. A more satisfactory translation may be "There will always be poor people among you, but I will not always be among you" or "Poor people will always be with you, but I will not always be with you."

TEV   (12.9-11)   RSV

THE PLOT AGAINST LAZARUS

9 A large number of people heard that Jesus was in Bethany, so they

9 When the great crowd of the Jews learned that he was there, they

went there, not only because of
Jesus but also to see Lazarus,
whom Jesus had raised from death.
10 So the chief priests made plans
to kill Lazarus too, 11 because on
his account many Jews were rejecting them and believing in Jesus.

came, not only on account of Jesus but also to see Lazarus, whom
he had raised from the dead. 10 So
the chief priests planned to put
Lazarus also to death, 11 because
on account of him many of the Jews
were going away and believing in
Jesus.

These verses are transitional; they tie the Lazarus motif to the
triumphant entry of Jesus into Jerusalem (verses 17-19).

It may be necessary to expand the section heading, The Plot against
Lazarus, and to translate "The chief priests plan to kill Lazarus" or
"...decide to try to kill Lazarus."

12.9   A large number of people heard that Jesus was
            in Bethany, so they went there, not only because
            of Jesus but also to see Lazarus, whom Jesus had
            raised from death.

A large number of people represents one textual tradition (NEB,
JB, Gdsp, GeCL, Luther Revised); "the great crowd" of RSV (Zür, Mft,
Phps, NAB) represents a second textual tradition. The choice of text
is difficult, since the text that includes the definite article "the"
has such poor structure that there is doubt whether John could have
written it. On the other hand, the text which omits "the" is obviously
the easier text and could be the result of some scribe's attempt to remove the difficulty of the other text. A similar problem exists in
12.12. The UBS Committee supports the manuscript reading which includes
the definite article, but places the definite article in brackets to
indicate serious doubt regarding the text at this point. Here, as elsewhere, scholarly opinion is divided, and the translator is free to choose
either possibility.

The word rendered large number of people is mentioned in four places
here and in the following section (verses 9,12,17,18). In these verses
it is difficult to differentiate one use of the word from another. On
the whole, it may be best to identify the "crowd" of verses 9 and 17
as one group and the "crowd" of 12 and 18 as another. However, it may
be also possible to distinguish three groups: the large number of people
of verse 9, the people of verse 17, and the crowd of verses 12 and 18.

That Jesus was in Bethany is literally "that he was there." TEV
makes both person and place explicit. Similarly, whom Jesus had raised
from death is literally "whom he had raised from death."

The contrast in the phrases not only...but also is difficult in
some languages because the elements are not parallel. It may be necessary
to restructure the second part of verse 9 to read "They went because Jesus was there, and they also went in order to see Lazarus, the one Jesus
had caused to live again." It is also possible to translate because of
Jesus "in order to see Jesus." By making the two expressions parallel
("in order to see Jesus" and "in order to see Lazarus"), it is easier
to treat the contrasting elements not only...but also. However, as noted

elsewhere, it may be necessary to place the positive before the negative, that is, "They went in order to see Lazarus, whom Jesus had raised from death. They also went in order to see Jesus."

12.10   So the chief priests made plans to kill Lazarus too,

This verse reflects 11.53.

It may be necessary to make explicit the implications of the adverb too, for example, "So the chief priests made plans to kill Lazarus as well as Jesus" or "...in addition to making plans to kill Jesus."

12.11   because on his account many Jews were rejecting them and believing in Jesus.

There is some difficulty in the phrase rendered by TEV many Jews were rejecting them. The Greek phrase itself may be taken in one of three ways: (1) "Many of the Jews were going over/away (to Bethany)." Although supported by some commentators, this interpretation is apparently not accepted by any translators. (2) "Many of the Jews were going over (to Jesus)." This exegesis reads the expression "of the Jews" as a partitive genitive, indicating that part of the Jews were going over, and it understands the verb (Greek hupagō) to have the meaning of "to go over." This exegesis is followed by NEB and NAB. NAB translates "many Jews were going over to Jesus and believing in him." (3) The TEV rendering represents a third possible exegesis. It understands "from the Jews" to be a genitive of separation, and the verb to have the meaning of "to leave," a meaning which it has in 6.67, where Jesus said to his twelve disciples, And you--would you like to leave also? This definitely seems to be the meaning in the present context, and Gdsp, JB, Phps, GeCL, Segond, and RSV make it explicit. For example, Gdsp reads "many of the Jews were leaving them," in which "them" refers to the chief priests of verse 10. The wording of GeCL, and JB is almost precisely that of Gdsp.

There is a problem involved in the translation of verse 11, since there are two elements expressing cause, one introduced by because and the other by on his account, that is, the chief priests had plans to kill Lazarus because many Jews were rejecting them. At the same time, they were rejecting them because of what happened to Lazarus. These two causes must be made explicit in some languages, for example, "The chief priests made plans to kill Lazarus also because many Jews were rejecting the chief priests; they were doing this because of Lazarus" or "...because of what happened to Lazarus." Such renderings, however, are not fully acceptable, since they tend to disregard the relation between the rejection of the chief priests and the believing in Jesus. Therefore, it may be necessary to say "The chief priests made plans to kill Lazarus also, because the Jews were rejecting them and believing in Jesus. They were doing so because of what happened to Lazarus.

THE TRIUMPHANT ENTRY INTO JERUSALEM

12 The next day the large crowd that had come to the Passover Festival heard that Jesus was coming to Jerusalem. 13 So they took branches of palm trees and went out to meet him, shouting, "Praise God! God bless him who comes in the name of the Lord! God bless the King of Israel!"

14 Jesus found a donkey and rode on it, just as the scripture says,

15 "Do not be afraid, city of Zion!
    Here comes your king,
       riding on a young donkey."

16 His disciples did not understand this at the time; but when Jesus had been raised to glory, they remembered that the scripture said this about him and that they had done this for him.

17 The people who had been with Jesus when he called Lazarus out of the grave and raised him from death had reported what had happened. 18 That was why the crowd met him--because they heard that he had performed this miracle. 19 The Pharisees then said to one another, "You see, we are not succeeding at all! Look, the whole world is following him!"

12 The next day a great crowd who had come to the feast heard that Jesus was coming to Jerusalem. 13 So they took branches of palm trees and went out to meet him, crying, "Hosanna! Blessed is he who comes in the name of the Lord, even the King of Israel!" 14 And Jesus found a young ass and sat upon it; as it is written,

15 "Fear not, daughter of Zion;
    behold, your king is coming,
       sitting on an ass's colt!"

16 His disciples did not understand this at first; but when Jesus was glorified, then they remembered that this had been written of him and had been done to him. 17 The crowd that had been with him when he called Lazarus out of the tomb and raised him from the dead bore witness. 18 The reason why the crowd went to meet him was that they heard he had done this sign. 19 The Pharisees then said to one another, "You see that you can do nothing; look, the world has gone after him."

The account of the entry of Jesus into Jerusalem appears in all four Gospels (Matt 21.1-11; Mark 11.1-11; Luke 19.28-40; and John 12.12-19). All four accounts are similar, but John makes two emphases which seem to be important to him: (1) He explicitly mentions that Jesus is the King of Israel, that is, the king that God promised to send to save the people of Israel (verse 13); (2) and he makes emphatic the statement that Jesus' disciples did not understand the meaning of this at the time (verse 16), a statement similar to the notation made in 2.22.

The section heading, The Triumphant Entry into Jerusalem, can rarely be translated literally, since it involves semantic problems. First, Triumphant essentially qualifies Jesus as the victor or the person who triumphs, but no specific mention of any victory is made in this passage. The focus is primarily upon the praise the crowds give him. Secondly, it is difficult in most languages to speak about "entering

Jerusalem," for such a term as "to enter" would apply primarily to a
building, not to a city. However, Jerusalem did have a wall around it,
so that one can use a term for "entering" which would be applicable to
a person going into an enclosure surrounded by a fence. Rather than
attempt to translate literally the term Triumphant, it is probably better to focus upon the praise the people give to Jesus, for example, "The
people praise Jesus as he rides into Jerusalem" or "The crowds honor
Jesus as he enters into Jerusalem" or "...arrives in Jerusalem."

12.12   The next day the large crowd that had come to
               the Passover Festival heard that Jesus was coming
               to Jerusalem.

     The next day refers back to 12.1, and so this day was evidently a
Sunday.
     In Greek the verb had come is a participle, but many translations,
including TEV, make it a finite verb.
     The Passover Festival is literally "the feast." It is obvious, on
the basis of 12.1, that "the feast" is the Passover, and so TEV and
GeCL and French common language translation (FrCL) make this fact explicit. It is particularly important to do so here, since a new section
is introduced and this passage is often read publicly without the connection to verse 1 being made clear.
     Like the verb had come, the verb heard is also a participle in
Greek, where verses 12 and 13 are one sentence.
     In some languages it is difficult to speak of "a crowd hearing." One
can, however, say "the people of the large crowd heard."
     As mentioned under verse 9, there is a problem with the phrase the
large crowd. Here the definite article is not placed in brackets by the
UBS Committee in the Greek text. Therefore TEV has the article here,
though not in verse 8. This large crowd refers to the people who had
come to the Passover Feast as pilgrims, and so NEB translates "The next
day the great body of pilgrims who had come to the festival." However,
for American English speakers it is better not to use the term "pilgrims," because in America this word generally has a restricted meaning.
     In the translation of was coming, it is necessary to use terms con-
sistent with the fact that Jesus rode on a donkey (verse 14).

12.13   So they took branches of palm trees and went out
               to meet him, shouting, "Praise God! God bless him
               who comes in the name of the Lord! God bless the
               King of Israel!"

     The Greek phrase John uses for branches of palm trees is redundant,
but its meaning is clear. The question has been raised whether there
was an abundance of palm trees in Jerusalem. In modern times, palm
branches are brought in from the region around Jericho for the celebration of Palm Sunday in Jerusalem. However, some palms do grow in the
region of Jerusalem, and the question of how many there were in New
Testament times is not important as far as translation is concerned.

In translating they took branches of palm trees one must assume that
they "cut off branches of palm trees." A literal translation might imply
that they simply picked up branches of palm trees which were discarded
along the road.

Praise God! translates the meaning of an Aramaic phrase, which is
transliterated "Hosanna" in many translations. A literal translation
would be "Save--please!" In general "Hosanna" was a prayer for help.
During the Festival of Shelters it was a prayer for rain. But here the
term is better taken to indicate praise rather than petition. Gdsp renders "Bless him!" GeCL and FrCL render in the same way as TEV. Praise
God! cannot be translated literally in some languages, since it would
mean only that the speakers were commanding others to praise God. In
some languages the closest equivalent would be "Let us praise God" or
"God deserves our praise." In some languages, however, instead of using
a verb meaning "praise," it is better to indicate the content of the
praise, namely, "God is wonderful!"

God bless him who comes in the name of the Lord is more literally
"Blessed is the one who comes in the name of the Lord." However, the
blessing referred to or appealed for comes from God, and TEV makes this
explicit. The words come from Psalm 118.26, and the meaning of the Hebrew
is evidently "Blessed in the Lord's name is the one who comes." In the
original setting of the Psalm, the reference was to the pilgrims who
came to the Temple to worship, but the meaning for John is obviously
different. According to John's Gospel, the one who comes in the name
of the Lord is Jesus.

The third person imperative in God bless him who comes in the name
of the Lord! is essentially a type of request or prayer, and it must be
expressed as such in certain languages, for example, "We pray that God
will bless him..."

There is, however, a problem involved in the clause who comes in
the name of the Lord. If in this context "Lord" refers to Jesus Christ,
the request will seem to be for God to bless someone who has come representing Jesus. However, the blessing is requested for Jesus himself
and this meaning makes the term Lord equivalent to God. One may translate in many languages "We pray that God will bless the one that comes
in his name," that is, in the sense of "in God's name." In some languages, however, the expression "in his name" has no real meaning, and
one must translate "We pray that God will bless the one who comes representing him" or "...comes as his representative" or "...as his messenger."

God bless the King of Israel is literally, "even the king of Israel." But the force of the Greek structure is to equate him who comes in
the name of the Lord with the King of Israel, and TEV does this explicitly. This slight restructuring also makes the elements of praise in
this verse emphatic. By breaking the sentence into two parts and introducing each part with God bless, the meaning is made clearer, and the
staccato style is more in keeping with spontaneous utterances of praise.
(For Jesus as the King of Israel, see 1.49. See comments at 14.13 for
a discussion of "in my name.")

It may sometimes be best to translate the King of Israel "the one
who will rule over Israel," since Jesus was not at that time actually
ruling over Israel. King must often be translated by a verb "to rule"

rather than by a noun designating a particular kind of ruler.

12.14   Jesus found a donkey and rode on it, just
                  as the scripture says,

    This verse is introduced with the same Greek particle (de) used in
the last sentence of verse 3 and in verse 4. (See comments there.)
    In Greek, found is a participle, but many translators render it a
finite verb. In rendering this verb, it is important to avoid the suggestion that Jesus accidentally came across a donkey, or that he went
out looking for a donkey and finally was able to discover one. In some
languages a more satisfactory rendering would be "he procured a donkey"
or "he got a donkey."
    Just as the scripture says is literally "just as it has been writ-
ten," but the reference is to the scripture, and TEV makes it explicit
(see 2.17). This clause should not be so translated as to refer merely to
the manner in which Jesus rode into Jerusalem. The quotation from Zechariah qualifies, not merely the way in which Jesus rode the donkey, but
also the entire event of Jesus' entrance into Jerusalem. It may therefore be best to introduce a new sentence in verse 14, for example, "This
happened just as the scripture says" or "This happening was as the scripture says" or "...as one may read in the holy writings."
    The Greek word rendered donkey in this verse appears only here in
the New Testament. Etymologically this word (onarion) is a diminutive
form, meaning "a small donkey," but outside the New Testament the word
often means simply donkey. Mft, Gdsp, Phps, and RSV evidently prefer to
maintain the meaning of "a young donkey" and so render "a young ass."
The Greek expression in the last part of verse 15 does mean "a young
donkey," and TEV so renders it there. However, it seems doubtful that
"young donkey" is the exact meaning of the word as intended by John in
the present verse.

12.15   "Do not be afraid, city of Zion!
                  Here comes your king,
                      riding on a young donkey."

    This verse is a quotation from Zechariah 9.9, but at two points
John differs from both the Hebrew and the Septuagint texts. First, in
place of Do not be afraid the Hebrew and Spetuagint both have "rejoice
greatly." There is no obvious reason why John would have deliberately
changed the wording; the best explanation seems to be that he was quoting
loosely from memory. If so, it is possible that such a passage as Isaiah
40.9 or Zephaniah 3.16 influenced his thinking, since both these passages
have "Do not be afraid." In fact, the exhortation not to be afraid in
Zephaniah 3.16 is based on the affirmation that "the King of Israel, the
Lord, is in your midst." This affirmation may well be the basis for
John's inclusion of "the King of Israel" in verse 13.
    A second point at which John differs from the Hebrew and the Sep-
tuagint is in the mention of the animal on which Jesus rode. Whereas the
Hebrew text (followed by Matt 21.5) has a kind of parallelism in which

two animals are used synonymously, John mentions only one animal <u>a</u>
<u>young donkey</u>.

In some languages such an expression as <u>Do not be afraid</u> should
include somewhere in the context a reference to what people were not
to fear. In the present context it would be more satisfactory to translate "Do not be afraid of anything" or "There is nothing you need to
fear."

<u>Here comes your king</u> is more literally "Behold, your king is
coming." But the particle "behold" (Greek <u>idou</u>), like its Hebrew counterpart (<u>hinne</u>), is merely an interjection used for the sake of emphasis or drawing attention, and it need not be included in translation.

<u>A young donkey</u> is literally "a donkey's colt," but the meaning of
this unusual sounding expression is merely a <u>young donkey</u>.

<u>City of Zion</u> is literally "daughter of Zion," a Hebraic way of
speaking of the city of Zion, that is, Jerusalem. The problem with a
literal rendering is that most readers will not have the background to
understand "daughter" as a collective term for the people of Jerusalem.
In many translations the best rendering may simply be "city of Jerusalem" or even "people of Jerusalem."

<u>12.16</u>   His disciples did not understand this at the
                time; but when Jesus had been raised to glory, they
                remembered that the scripture said this about him
                and that they had done this for him.

<u>This</u> (so most translations; NAB "all this") is literally "these
things," and is in the emphatic position in the Greek sentence structure.
The plural form is used here in a collective sense and so many legitimately be rendered by the singular <u>this</u>.

The verb translated <u>understand</u> normally means "to know," but the
meaning "to understand" is obvious in the present context and so appears in most translations.

<u>At the time</u> (so also NEB, Gdsp, Phps, JB) is literally "at first"
(as in many translations). The phrase is used here to contrast the
disciples' understanding when these events were taking place with their
understanding when Jesus was raised to glory. For this purpose the translation "at the time" is better than "at first." In some languages it
may be necessary to make more specific the reference to <u>this</u> and to
stipulate more clearly the reference to time. Therefore one may translate "At the time these events took place his disciples did not understand what they meant" or "...did not understand all that was involved"
or "...just what all of these happenings were pointing to."

<u>When Jesus had been raised to glory</u> (GeCL "but when Jesus was
raised in the glory of God") is literally "when Jesus was glorified."
The reference is obviously to Jesus' resurrection or exaltation, and
the renderings in TEV and GeCL make this information explicit. This same
expression is used in John 7.39. Also see 2.22, where the phrase <u>was</u>
<u>raised from death</u> is used with a meaning equivalent to <u>raised to glory</u> in
this verse. To indicate clearly that <u>raised to glory</u> refers not only to
the resurrection but also to the glorious results of that event, it may be

necessary to translate in some languages "when Jesus had been brought
back to life and made wonderful" or "...been brought back to life in a
wonderful way."

That the scripture said this about him is literally "that these
things were written about him." But here, as elsewhere in the New
Testament, "was written" is a reference to the Jewish scriptures (see
verse 14 and 2.17). Said this about him may be rendered "said that this
would happen to him" or "said that this is what he would experience."

They had done this for him may be interpreted in several ways,
depending on whom the subject they is assumed to be. TEV (so also Phps,
GeCL, FrCL, Segond) takes they as a reference to his disciples at the
beginning of the verse, since they are apparently the subject throughout
the verse. Grammatically this is the simplest solution, though it is
difficult to know what action is referred to in had done this for him,
unless it is their procuring the donkey, which is not mentioned in John's
account. It is possible also to understand the crowd to be the subject
of this verse, and so to translate with NAB "they recalled that the
people had done to him precisely what had been written about him." This
may also be the meaning of JB ("but later...they remembered that this
had been written about him and that this was in fact how they had received him"), but this translation is not clear. Finally, it is possible
to take they as an impersonal construction equivalent to a passive
(Mft "then they remembered how this had been written of him and had happened to him"). This passive construction is followed also by NEB, Zür,
and Luther Revised. The simplest solution grammatically is to assume
with TEV that they refers to his disciples, even though it is not clear
precisely what the disciples had done for Jesus. It is, of course, possible to understand his disciples in the sense of the larger group of
followers, who would remember that on this occasion they had participated in praising Jesus as he entered into Jerusalem.

12.17   The people who had been with Jesus when he
              called Lazarus out of the grave and raised him
              from death had reported what had happened.

The most emphatic element in this sentence is the verb that TEV
translates had reported what had happened (literally "were witnessing"
or "were testifying"). The verb "to witness" is used in John's Gospel
in various ways; it is discussed in some detail in 1.7. NAB here translates "kept testifying to it"; NEB "told what they had seen and heard";
JB "were telling how they had witnessed it." In Greek the verb is in
the imperfect tense and perhaps indicates action in progress, as these
translations indicate.

In the Greek text Jesus is literally "he." In place of when (hote)
some Greek manuscripts read "that" (hoti), which changes the meaning
somewhat. If the reading "that" is accepted, the statement he called
Lazarus out of the grave and raised him from death becomes the content
of the verb had reported. The following translation would then result:
"The crowd that was with Jesus had reported that he called Lazarus out
of the grave and raised him from death." Most translations, however,
accept the same reading as TEV, because it is supported by better

manuscript evidence. The other reading is evidently an attempt to smooth out the difficulty concerning the mention of the various crowds in this narrative.

The order of constituent clauses in verse 17 produces some difficulty, since the linguistic and temporal orders are not parallel. The presence of the people with Jesus when he called Lazarus out of the grave and raised him from death is prior to the time in the verb had reported, but this time in turn is after what is contained in the report, namely, what had happened. However, verse 17 is prior to the content of verse 18 and also prior to the content of verse 16. Note also that the content of verse 17 constitutes the reason for the behavior of the crowd in verse 18. These problems of relative time may make it necessary to recast verse 17 as "When Jesus called Lazarus to come out of the grave and raised him from death, the people who were there with Jesus later reported what had happened to Lazarus." This rendering may then constitute an introduction to verse 18, for example, "Because of what these people said, the crowd went out to meet Jesus."

12.18   That was why the crowd met him--because they
          heard that he had performed this miracle.

This verse suggests that a crowd is following Jesus, telling about the miracle of raising Lazarus from the dead, and another crowd (the crowd of this verse) comes out from Jerusalem because of what it has heard from the first crowd.

This miracle is literally "this sign" (see 2.11). In the Greek sentence structure, the demonstrative pronoun this is in the emphatic position.

The final clause because they heard that he had performed this miracle constitutes an emphatic repetition of the reason for the crowd's meeting Jesus. In a sense it repeats the contents of verse 17. One may make the relation more specific by saying "The crowd went out to meet Jesus because they heard that he had performed this miracle."

12.19   The Pharisees then said to one another, "You see,
          we are not succeeding at all! Look, the whole
          world is following him!"

In 11.47 and in 11.57 the Pharisees and the chief priests appear together; here only the Pharisees are mentioned.

You see is the rendering of most translations, though these words may be taken as an imperative ("see").

We are not succeeding at all (so also GeCL; Phps "There's nothing one can do!") is actually a second person reference in Greek: "You can do nothing." TEV shifts from second person "you" to first person "we," since the Pharisees are speaking to one another. This is the normal way to handle the construction in English. We are not succeeding at all may be rendered negatively as "we have completely failed." One can also render this clause "we have not realized our purposes" or "we have not fulfilled our plans" or "we have not accomplished what we set out to do."

[401]

The whole world (so also NAB; NEB "all the world") is literally "the world," but, as the NAB footnote indicates, "the sense is that everyone is following Jesus..."

The various translations render is following him in several different ways, but the meaning is the same in all.

TEV   (12.20-26)   RSV

SOME GREEKS SEEK JESUS

20 Some Greeks were among those who had gone to Jerusalem to worship during the festival. 21 They went to Philip (he was from Bethsaida in Galilee) and said, "Sir, we want to see Jesus."
22 Philip went and told Andrew, and the two of them went and told Jesus. 23 Jesus answered them, "The hour has now come for the Son of Man to receive great glory. 24 I am telling you the truth: a grain of wheat remains no more than a single grain unless it is dropped into the ground and dies. If it does die, then it produces many grains. 25 Whoever loves his own life will lose it; whoever hates his own life in this world will keep it for life eternal. 26 Whoever wants to serve me must follow me, so that my servant will be with me where I am. And my Father will honor anyone who serves me.

20 Now among those who went up to worship at the feast were some Greeks. 21 So these came to Philip, who was from Bethsaida in Galilee, and said to him, "Sir, we wish to see Jesus." 22 Philip went and told Andrew; Andrew went with Philip and they told Jesus. 23 And Jesus answered them, "The hour has come for the Son of man to be glorified. 24 Truly, truly, I say to you, unless a grain of wheat falls into the earth and dies, it remains alone; but if it dies, it bears much fruit. 25 He who loves his life loses it, and he who hates his life in this world will keep it for eternal life. 26 If any one serves me, he must follow me; and where I am, there shall my servant be also; if any one serves me, the Father will honor him.

This entire section (verses 20-36) is at once a conclusion to Chapters 11-12 and to the first part of the Gospel itself. According to Jesus' words in 11.4, the purpose of Lazarus' illness was that the Son of God would receive glory (or, perhaps better, the means by which his glory would be revealed). And the real outcome of Lazarus' death was to reveal Jesus as the resurrection and the life (11.25). Now, as a result of the raising of Lazarus, events have been set in motion that will lead to the death of Jesus--which is also the means by which his glory will be revealed. As a result of his death, life will be made available to all people (12.32). Accordingly, this section is a climax to the events which began with Chapter 11. It is climactic also in that it tells of the coming of the Gentiles to see Jesus. This theme is very important in the Gospel of John, and its universal implications have already been given throughout Chapters 11 and 12.

A brief analysis of 12.20-36 will be helpful before it is discussed in detail. Verses 20-22 tell of the coming of the Greeks to see Jesus.

[402]

As a result of their coming, Jesus acknowledges that it is now time <u>for</u>
<u>the Son of Man to be given great glory</u> (verse 23). The same theme of
the hour of Jesus' glorification is renewed in verses 27-28. Here, however, the voice from heaven confirms Jesus' conviction that his hour for
glorification has come and at the same time declares that it will also
be the means by which God's name is glorified. These two sections deal-
ing with the glorification of Jesus are separated by a series of three
sayings that form a commentary on the themes of death and life. Verse
24 emphasizes that only through death can fruit be borne. The reference
is probably to the necessity of Jesus' death, both for the Gentiles and
for the people of Israel. The theme of verse 25 is the contrast between
loving and hating one's own life. And verse 26 affirms that if one is
to be with Jesus, he must follow him, with the implication that the
following involves death.

As indicated, verse 27 resumes the theme of glorification, and this
continues through verse 30. Verses 31-33 indicate that the lifting up of
the Son of Man will be the means by which the world will be judged and
the ruler of the world overthrown. In verse 34 the Jews raise the question
<u>Who is this Son of Man</u>, and Jesus' reply is contained in verses 35-36.
It comes by way of a warning, indicating that the Jews will not have the
light with them much longer. Jesus then encourages them to believe in
the light while they have opportunity, so that they can be the people
of the light.

Thus, this section brings together several important themes of John's
Gospel. It concludes with the urgency of the situation in which the Jews
find themselves. They will have the light with them only a little while
longer, because Jesus will soon hide himself (verse 36b), and the light
will no longer be available to them. Also woven into this section are the
themes of the exaltation of the Son of Man and the consequent judgment
of the world. What is most important in this section is the explicit
mention of the universal application of Jesus' message and his mission:
the Gentiles have now come to see Jesus.

The section heading, <u>Some Greeks Seek Jesus</u>, may be rendered "Some
Greeks want to talk with Jesus."

<u>12.20</u>   Some Greeks were among those who had gone
                to Jerusalem to worship during the festival.

It should be noted that the mention of the <u>festival</u> in this verse
ties this theme closely to the overall context of Passover, which has
been the background since 11.55. The term <u>Greeks</u> (see also 7.35) is not
used in a nationalistic sense; it refers rather to "non-Jews" or "Gentiles." In this instance the reference is to Gentiles who have become
proselytes to Judaism and so have come up to Jerusalem to worship during
the festival. They are mentioned only in this verse and those that follow.
It is not sufficient to translate <u>Greeks</u> merely as "Greek-speaking people," since this term could refer to many Jews who spoke only Greek. The
term <u>Greeks</u> may be expressed in some languages as "people known as
Greeks" or "Greek people" or "people who were not Jews."

It may be essential in some languages to introduce an object of
worship, for example, "to worship God." <u>During the festival</u> may be

[403]

rendered "during the time of the celebration" or even "during the
time that people were celebrating the Passover."

In the Greek text Jerusalem is not explicitly mentioned and the
verb had gone is literally "went up"; but this verb is normally used
for describing a journey to Jerusalem (see 2.13; 5.1; 7.8; and 11.55).

12.21   They went to Philip (he was from Bethsaida in
            Galilee) and said, "Sir, we want to see Jesus."

Philip is first mentioned in 1.43; Bethsaida, his home town, first
appears in 1.44. The parenthetical insertion (he was from Bethsaida in
Galilee) is restructured as a relative clause by GeCL: "Philip, who was
from Bethsaida in Galilee, and said..." Galilee may have been mentioned
because of its association with Gentiles. Perhaps the Greeks approached
Philip because he had a Greek name and, being from Galilee, was more
likely to be able to speak Greek.

Said (so most translations) is more literally "were asking him
saying" (JB, NAB "put this request to him"). The word translated Sir
can also mean "Lord" in the technical Christian sense, but its meaning
is obvious in the present context, since Philip is the one addressed.

In this context the verb to see means "to meet and to talk with."
(For a similar usage of this same verb see Luke 8.20; 9.9; Acts 28.20.)

12.22   Philip went and told Andrew, and the two of
            them went and told Jesus.

No reason is given why Philip went to tell Andrew, though it may be
noted that among the twelve disciples only these two bore Greek names.

The two of them went and told Jesus (NEB "the two of them went to
tell Jesus"; NAB "Philip and Andrew in turn came to inform Jesus") is
more literally "and they told Jesus" (RSV). But the context implies
that Jesus was not there with them, and so they had to go and tell him,
as NEB, NAB, and TEV make clear. In some languages it may be necessary
to mention the content of what they told Jesus, for example, "they told
Jesus what the Greeks had said."

12.23   Jesus answered them, "The hour has now come for
            the Son of Man to receive great glory.

Jesus answered them is literally "but Jesus answers them saying"
a Semitic form of introducing discourse; the word "saying" may be regarded as the equivalent of quotation marks in English.

There is no specific indication of what persons are referred to by
them. However, this pronoun should not be so rendered as to indicate
that Jesus would speak only with Philip and Andrew, and so reject an opportunity to talk with the Greeks. It is best to imply in translation
that Jesus' words were directed to all who were there, including the
Greeks.

A literal translation of The hour has now come might suggest that

the glory that Jesus was to receive was to take place within that very
hour. The reference, of course, is to the death and exaltation of Jesus,
and it may be necessary to use a more general expression for time, for
example, "The time has now come" or "Now is the occasion for." In some
languages the equivalent expression would be "It will soon happen that."

Receive great glory is literally "be glorified" (so most translations). GeGL translates "now must the glory of the Son of Man be revealed." In 7.39 TEV translates this same verb been raised to glory,
but there the meaning is not as difficult as in most occurrences of
the verb in John's Gospel. In 11.4 TEV translates it with the meaning
receive glory, that is, "receive praise." But, as pointed out there,
the focus seems not to be on receiving praise, as TEV intimates, but
rather on revealing the true nature of the Son of God. In that context
the reference is specifically to his power to give life. Now, the question arises as to what is meant by "to be glorified" in this verse,
which cannot be taken in isolation from verse 28 (bring glory to your
name). In both places the focus seems to be more on revealing the true
nature of the Son of Man and of the Father, than on bringing praise to
them through this revelation. For that reason, such a rendering as "the
hour has now come for the true glory of the Son of Man to be revealed"
is suggested for this verse.

In some languages, the expression to receive great glory must indicate the agent. It is then necessary to introduce God as the agent.
To do so makes possible a clear indication of the revelation involved,
for example, "for God to show how wonderful the Son of Man is." For
languages which require a first person singular reference to Jesus, it
may be necessary to say "...how wonderful I, the Son of Man, am."

12.24   I am telling you the truth: a grain of wheat
                remains no more than a single grain unless it
                is dropped into the ground and dies. If it does
                die, then it produces many grains.

I am telling you the truth is the same emphatic formula first used
in 1.51 (see there).

In the first sentence of this verse, the clause TEV renders remains
no more than a single grain (literally "remains alone") comes last, but
TEV places it first to achieve a more natural English sentence structure.
NEB translates this clause "a grain of wheat remains a solitary grain,"
and NAB "it remains just a grain of wheat."

The verb rendered is dropped in TEV is literally "falls." But since
the focus is on dying, it sounds more natural in English to speak of a
grain of wheat being dropped, rather than of its falling into the ground.
Dropped suggests purpose, while falls may suggest an accidental happening. The passive expression it is dropped into the ground must be made
active in some languages, for example, "unless someone drops it into
the ground and lets it die." However, in some languages the process of
dropping grain into the ground is expressed in a special sense of "planting grain in the ground" or "placing grain in the ground."

A serious problem is involved in understanding this passage if it
is translated literally if it does die. Obviously, if a grain really

dies, it produces no fruit at all. However, it is difficult to remove
the figure of speech involved in dying, and it may be necessary in
some languages to translate "if it does, as it were, die" or "if it
dies, so to speak."

Many grains is literally "much fruit." But when speaking of a
grain harvest, one does not speak of "much fruit" but of "much grain"
or "many grains." Perhaps it should be noted that the word rendered
wheat may refer either to wheat in particular or to grain in general
(it is used in the parable of the weeds, Matt 13.25). As indicated in
the introductory remarks to this section, the reference is to the death
of Jesus, which makes possible the gathering in of the Gentile believers.

12.25   Whoever loves his own life will lose it; whoever
             hates his own life in this world will keep it for
             life eternal.

His own life is literally "his soul," but it is rendered "his life"
by most modern translations. NEB renders "The man who loves himself is
lost." The reason for translating "life" rather than "soul" is that the
rendering "soul" does not give a true reflection of the Jewish concept
of the nature of man. For the Jews there was no body-soul dualism in
the way that is familiar to us, and so this word refers to one's natural
life. The same word is used in 10.15, and there TEV renders the Greek
"I lay down my soul" I am willing to die.

The contrast between loves and hates also reflects Semitic thought.
The meaning of "to hate" in such a context means that a person considers
the object he "hates" as less desirable and important than the one he
"loves" (See Deut 21.15; Gen 29.31,33; Matt 6.24; Luke 14.26).

Lose is the verb translated die in 3.16 and 10.28. It is used in
17.12 with the same meaning that it has here (see note at 3.16).

For the concept of eternal life see comments at 1.4 and 3.15. Will
keep it for life eternal is rendered in Anchor Bible "preserves it to
live eternally."

The translation of verse 25 involves several serious problems. In
the first place, a literal rendering may be quite misleading. For example, in one language the expression "loves his own life" means that
the person is kind, while "hates his own life" means that he is mean
and unjust. Furthermore, in many languages one cannot speak about "loving life" or "hating life," for the term life must itself be rendered
as a verb. In some instances loves his own life may be rendered "lives
just for himself." By way of contrast, hates his own life may then be
rendered "but rather lives for others." In some languages loves his
own life may be expressed idiomatically as "keeps hanging onto his
own life." The contrast then may be set up as "lets go of his own life."

Only rarely can the radical contrast between "loves" and "hates"
be employed. It is nearly always necessary to indicate that hates refers to "loving less" or "having no regard for."

It may also be difficult in some languages to speak about "losing
life." Such an expression can be understood only in the sense of "die,"
but evidently in this verse the focus is more upon the quality of life
which is lost, and not upon death. Furthermore, it is important to

avoid a verb meaning "lose" which would suggest an accidental loss. The loss of real life is the direct result of one's wishing to hang onto his own way of life. It may be possible to translate the first part of verse 25 "Whoever loves only himself will lose out completely" or "Whoever loves to do only what he wants to do will end up with nothing" or "...will come to an end" or "...will finally have nothing." To show the contrast between loves and hates, it may be better to employ a negation, for example, "Whoever doesn't love his own life" or "Whoever doesn't just love himself." The difficulty with a term meaning "hate" is that it carries too many additional connotations and in some languages may even suggest suicide.

12.26   Whoever wants to serve me must follow me, so that
            my servant will be with me where I am. And my
            Father will honor anyone who serves me."

Whoever wants to serve me is literally "if anyone serves me." But the Greek "if" followed by an indefinite pronoun ("anyone" or "someone") is equivalent to whoever in English.

In some languages it may be necessary to invert the concept of "serving" by saying "If any of you want me to be your master." Otherwise "serving" might refer merely to "serving meals."

So that my servant will be with me where I am is a restructuring of the Greek, which reads literally "and where I am, there also my servant will be." Jesus is on his way to death, and this observation, taken in conjunction with verse 25, indicates that the route the servant must follow is also that of death.

It is necessary to make clear that my servant refers to the individual who wishes to serve his master. By changing the conditional relative clause introduced by whoever into a conditional sentence with "if" and using the second person plural to identify the persons involved, one may translate "If any of you want me to be your master (or "serve me"), you must follow me so that you, as my servants, will be with me wherever I am."

In Greek my Father reads literally "the Father"; but see comments at 5.19. It should be noted that according to the Greek sentence structure the pronouns "him" (TEV anyone) and "me" are emphatic. Nowhere else in his Gospel does John speak of the Father honoring someone, but we do read of the honor that people pay either to Jesus or to the Father (5.23; 8.49). Here the honor that the Father shows to the believer is a reward for his faithful service to Jesus. At the same time it suggests that a mutual relationship exists between the Father and the believer, in a way similar to that which exists between the Father and the Son.

In some instances it may be important to render serve in the sense of "help" or "assist." The final part of verse 26 would then be rendered as "and hence my Father will honor anyone who helps me."

JESUS SPEAKS ABOUT HIS DEATH

27 "Now my heart is troubled--
and what shall I say? Shall I say,
'Father, do not let this hour come
upon me'? But that is why I came--
so that I might go through this
hour of suffering. 28 Father, bring
glory to your name!"

Then a voice spoke from heaven,
"I have brought glory to it, and I
will do so again."

29 The crowd standing there
heard the voice, and some of them
said it was thunder, while others
said, "An angel spoke to him!"

30 But Jesus said to them, "It
was not for my sake that this
voice spoke, but for yours. 31 Now
is the time for this world to be
judged; now the ruler of this
world will be overthrown. 32 When
I am lifted up from the earth, I
will draw everyone to me." (33 In
saying this he indicated the kind
of death he was going to suffer.)

34 The crowd answered, "Our Law
tells us that the Messiah will live
forever. How, then, can you say that
the Son of Man must be lifted up?
Who is this Son of Man?"

35 Jesus answered, "The light
will be among you a little longer.
Continue on your way while you have
the light, so that the darkness will
not come upon you; for the one who
walks in the dark does not know
where he is going. 36 Believe in
the light, then, while you have it,
so that you will be the people of
the light."

27 "Now is my soul troubled. And
what shall I say? 'Father, save me
from this hour'? No, for this purpose I have come to this hour. 28
Father, glorify thy name." Then a
voice came from heaven, "I have
glorified it, and I will glorify
it again." 29 The crowd standing
by heard it and said that it had
thundered. Others said, "An angel
has spoken to him." 30 Jesus answered, "This voice has come for
your sake, not for mine. 31 Now is
the judgment of this world, now
shall the ruler of this world be
cast out; 32 and I, when I am
lifted up from the earth, will
draw all men to myself." 33 He
said this to show by what death he
was to die. 34 The crowd answered
him, "We have heard from the law
that the Christ remains for ever.
How can you say that the Son of
man must be lifted up? Who is this
Son of man?" 35 Jesus said to them,
"The light is with you for a little
longer. Walk while you have the
light, lest the darkness overtake
you; he who walks in the darkness
does not know where he goes. 36
While you have the light, believe
in the light, that you may become
sons of light."

For the section heading, Jesus Speaks about His Death, it may be
necessary in some languages to use a verbal form for death. To do so will
require some restructuring, for example, "Jesus speaks about the fact that
he is to die" or "Jesus says that he is going to die" or "Jesus says, 'I
am going to die'" or "...'I am going to be killed.'"

"Now my heart is troubled--and what shall
I say? Shall I say, 'Father, do not let this
hour come upon me'? But that is why I came--
so that I might go through this hour of suffering.

Now my heart is troubled (so also Gdsp) is more literally "Now my
soul is troubled." The word "soul" is the same word translated life in
verse 25, and so the translation here could read "Now I am troubled."
However, for English readers heart expresses more of the emotional
overtones involved, and that is the reason for TEV rendering. The verb
troubled is used of the stirring of the water in 5.4. Now my heart is
troubled may be expressed idiomatically in some languages, for example,
"Now my liver is moving within me" or "Now my spleen is swollen." However, one may also employ such an expression as "Now what shall I
think?" This type of rendering often goes well with the expression that
follows--and what shall I say? In other languages it may be more satisfactory to use such an expression as "Now what shall I do?" For languages in which the form of a question might be misunderstood, it is
always possible to say "Now I do not know what to think, I do not know
what to say. I could say, 'Father, do not let this hour come upon me.'"
Father, do not let this hour come upon me may be punctuated either
with a question mark, as in TEV, or as a statement, as in some other
translations. TEV takes this sentence as a deliberative question and
so introduces it with Shall I say and then concludes it with a question
mark. That is, TEV understands it as a thought that Jesus considered
but dismissed from his mind. Support for this interpretation is found
by the way these words are introduced in Greek (and what shall I say?).
However, some translations understand this sentence to be a genuine petition, and so make it a statement. Note, for example, Gdsp "Now
my heart is troubled; what can I say? Father, save me from this trial!
And yet it was for this very purpose that I have come to this trial."
In the final analysis the meaning is essentially the same, though there
is some difference of emphasis. If the clause in question is taken to be
a question, then in the mind of Jesus the answer all along is "No." But
if it is taken as a genuine petition, then Jesus is seen asking the Father
to save him from this hour, but then changing his mind as he realizes
that it was for this hour of suffering that he came into the world. All
in all, no final decision can be made in favor of one position or the
other.
It would be an unusual language in which one could translate literally do not let this hour come upon me. In the first place, it would
be unusual to speak of an hour "coming." In the second place, a term
such as "hour" would rarely suggest a time of trial or difficulty. In
some languages one may say "do not permit this testing of me to come"
or "do not allow me to be tested in this way." In some languages an
equivalent of "trial" may be "suffering." Accordingly, one may translate
"do not make me suffer as I know I will have to."
But that is why I came--so that I might go through this hour of
suffering is literally "But because of this I came to this hour." TEV
makes explicit the meaning of "this hour" by rendering this hour of suffering. Though the Greek text does not indicate the point to which Jesus
had come, it may, however, be necessary in some languages to say "this is

why I came to earth"; otherwise, the context might suggest that Jesus
was only speaking of his immediate entry into Jerusalem. Similarly, it
may be necessary to translate so that I might go through this hour of
suffering in such a manner that this clause will refer not to what has
passed but to what is going to take place, for example, "in order to
suffer as I will."

12.28   Father, bring glory to your name!"
                 Then a voice spoke from heaven, "I have
             brought glory to it, and I will do so again."

   Father, bring glory to your name! is changed in some late manuscripts to read "Father, bring glory to your Son"--evidently changed on
the basis of Jesus' prayer in 17.1. One ancient manuscript reads "Father,
bring glory to your name with the glory that I had with you before the
world was created"--obviously inserted on the basis of 17.5. Evidently
all modern translations follow the reading of the UBS Greek text, as
reflected in TEV. Bring glory to your name may be rendered "reveal how
glorious you are" or "show people how wonderful you are."
   The expression of direct address Father must be rendered in some
languages as "my Father."
   According to the Synoptic Gospels a voice spoke from heaven at
Jesus' baptism (Matt 3.17; Mark 1.11; Luke 3.22) and from a cloud at his
transfiguration (Matt 17.5; Mark 9.7; Luke 9.35). Also Acts 11.7 and Revelation 10.4 mention voices speaking from heaven. In each one of these
New Testament instances, the voice from heaven is understood as the directly heard voice of God.
   It may appear strange, if not impossible, to say in some languages
a voice spoke. A person may speak, but not a voice. The reference, of
course, is to God, but here, as elsewhere, a direct mention of God is
avoided. In some languages, however, it may be necessary to say "God
spoke from heaven." Some translators try to reproduce the indefiniteness
of a voice spoke by translating "someone said." This type of rendering,
however, would lead some to think it was someone other than God who
spoke.
   I have brought glory to it, and will do so again appears in most
translations "I have glorified it and will glorify it again." TEV avoids
the use of the archaic "glorify" and translates the second occurrence of
the verb by and will do so again, for stylistic reasons. The meaning of
"glorify" in this verse must be taken in light of the conclusions reached
in verse 23 (see also 13.31,32). That is, Jesus' prayer is for God to
reveal the true glory of his name, his own true glory. In the signs Jesus
performs (see especially 11.40; God does reveal his true glory; and in the
death and exaltation of Jesus, he will reveal it again. In some languages
an equivalent of I have brought glory to it, and I will do so again is
"I have shown how glorious I am and I will do it again" or "I have shown
people my wonderfulness...."

12.29   The crowd standing there heard the voice, and some
             of them said it was thunder, while others said, "An
             angel spoke to him!"

In Greek <u>heard</u> is a participle, rather than a finite verb, and has no expressed object. Most translations render it as a finite verb and supply an object (TEV <u>the voice</u>; RSV "it"). NEB does not render the object explicitly, but assumes the information to be implicit: "28...A voice sounded from heaven:...29 The crowd standing by said it was thunder." <u>Said it was thunder</u> is also indirect discourse in Greek, and is retained as such in most translations. In earlier editions of TEV direct discourse was used: "and said, 'It was thunder.'" In the second sentence in this verse direct discourse is used in Greek as well as in TEV. In the Old Testament thunder is frequently spoken of as the voice of God (see, for example, 2 Sam 22.14; Job 37.4; Psa 29.3; Jer 10.13). Perhaps John intends his readers to assume that the sound of the voice was mistaken for thunder, or that thunder accompanied the voice. Evidently the people who said <u>An angel spoke to him!</u> recognized that the sound was speech, though they did not recognize the origin. But it seems obvious that, in either case, neither group of persons understood the content of what was said, and so Jesus' words in the following verse, where he says that the voice spoke for the benefit of the people, and not for his own benefit, are difficult to understand.

Thus it may be difficult to employ a literal translation of <u>heard the voice</u>, for it would suggest that the people actually heard the words and understood their meaning. A more appropriate equivalent in some languages would be "the crowd standing there heard the sound."

The Greek mentions only two groups, "the crowd" and "others." However, "others" are actually included within "the crowd," and so TEV translates <u>The crowd...heard the voice...some of them said...Others said</u>. In this type of context <u>An angel</u> could be rendered "a heavenly messenger" or "a messenger from heaven" or "one of God's messengers."

<u>12.30</u>　　　　But Jesus said to them, "It was not for my sake that this voice spoke, but for yours.

<u>But Jesus said to them</u> is literally "and Jesus answered and said," once again reflecting a Semitic introductory formula.

As mentioned in the discussion of verse 29, these words of Jesus are difficult to understand. The suggestion that John had in mind a third group, probably Jesus' disciples, who did not recognize the content and origin of the voice, seems improbable.

In order to avoid the complication of "a voice speaking," it is possible to render the statement of Jesus "these words were spoken not for my sake but for yours." The rendering of <u>not for my sake...but for yours</u> may be expressed "not in order to help me...but in order to help you."

<u>12.31</u>　　　　Now is the time for this world to be judged; now the ruler of this world will be overthrown.

<u>Now is the time for this world to be judged</u> is literally "Now is the judging of this world." This verse is introduced by the adverb <u>now</u>

(so also verse 27), which gives strong emphasis. NEB translates "Now is the hour of judgment for this world" and JB "Now sentence is being passed on this world." TEV transforms the noun "judging" into a verb phrase, to be judged. The theme of judgment, frequent in John's Gospel, is discussed at some length at 5.22-30.

In languages which do not permit such a passive expression as to be judged, it may be necessary to introduce an agent. In terms of this context, it is probably best to introduce "God" as the agent, for example, "Now is the occasion when God will judge the world" or "...the people of the world." One should not, however, employ an expression which would suggest the so-called "final judgment." Such a variant as "pass judgment on the world" or "pronounce a sentence of condemnation on the world" may be employed.

The ruler of this world appears also in 14.30 and 16.11, but nowhere else in the New Testament. A related phrase, "the god of this age," is used in 2 Corinthians 4.4; note also such passages as 1 Corinthians 2.6-8; Ephesians 2.2; 6.12. The ruler of this world, obviously Johannine, is used to refer to the Devil.

Will be overthrown (JB "is to be overthrown") is literally "will be thrown out" and appears in many translations as "will be expelled" or "will be driven out." The reference is to the defeat of the Devil. This same verb is used in different settings in 6.37; 9.34; and 15.6. For languages in which the passive expression will be overthrown cannot be employed, it is possible to introduce God as the agent, for example, "God will overthrow the one who rules this world."

12.32 When I am lifted up from the earth, I will draw everyone to me."

When I am lifted up from the earth refers to Jesus' crucifixion but also includes his exaltation. (See comments on 3.14.)

Everyone (Greek masculine accusative plural, pantas, = "all men") is the reading of most modern English translations, and it has the best manuscript support. However, in some manuscripts the Greek neuter plural (panta) appears. This neuter form in Greek is ambiguous and may have the meaning of "everyone," "all things," or "all." The stronger manuscript evidence is in support of the masculine plural ("all men"). The idea of a cosmic redemption, suggested by the neuter plural, represents more closely the theology of such a passage as Colossians 1.16-17. The UBS Committee on the Greek text decided in favor of the reading "all men," evaluating their decision as a "D" choice, which indicates a very high degree of doubt concerning the reading selected.

I will draw everyone to me may be rendered in some instances "I will cause everyone to come to me." Unfortunately, some translators attempt to reproduce literally the meaning of draw, and produce expressions which literally mean "I will drag everyone to me."

12.33 (In saying this he indicated the kind of death he was going to suffer.)

To indicate that this statement is parenthetical, TEV and several other translations (Mft, NAB, Phps) include these words in parentheses. A similar explanatory comment is included in 18.32.

The kind of death he was going to suffer is more literally "by what kind of death he was going to die." GeCL is close to TEV, but most translations have the verb "to die" instead of "to suffer."

The parenthetical explanation may be rendered in some languages "when Jesus said this, he was talking about how he was going to die" or "...how he was going to be killed."

12.34   The crowd answered, "Our Law tells us
            that the Messiah will live forever. How, then,
            can you say that the Son of Man must be lifted
            up? Who is this Son of Man?"

The crowd answered is more literally "therefore (oun) the crowd answered him."

Our Law tells us translates a false passive construction in Greek ("we heard from the Law"). TEV makes it an active construction and specifies that the reference is to the Jewish (Our) Law. Our Law in this context is best understood as a reference to the entire Jewish Bible, not just to the section traditionally known as "the Law." If any specific passage is in the minds of the people, it is probably Psalm 89, which both the New Testament (Acts 13.22; Rev 1.5; 3.14) and Jewish rabbinical sources interpret Messianically. For example, Psalm 89.36 states "his seed (= David's descendant) remains forever," while in verse 51 of that same Psalm interprets the "seed" as the Lord's "anointed" (= the Messiah). However, it is impossible to be this precise; more than likely this teaching is a general conclusion derived from the total Old Testament.

In a number of languages it is not possible to say "our Law tells us," for one cannot speak of a collection of ordinances as doing any kind of talking. But it is possible to say "in our laws we read that" or "from our laws we learn that."

It should be noted that it is not Jesus, but the people who introduce the mention of the Son of Man. For the crowd, at least in this context, the Messiah is identified with the Son of Man. If the Messiah will live forever, how then can Jesus say that he will be lifted up (that is, be put to death)? Who is this Son of Man? may be taken either as a question regarding the identity of the Son of Man, or as one regarding his relation to the Messiah.

For languages in which the Son of Man is made specific with a first person reference when Jesus himself is speaking, it may be appropriate here to identify the Son of Man with a second person singular pronoun, for example, "you as the Son of Man." However, if one uses this expression, the question which follows may seem strange, for Who is this Son of Man? seems to be asked about the identity of that person. One possible interpretation of the phrase Son of Man may be "What do you mean by the expression Son of Man?" However, real dangers are involved in attempting to be too specific, either in identifying the referent of the Son of Man in the first of the two questions, or in trying to suggest too clearly the relation between the phrase Son of Man and Messiah. Since the crowd was not certain of what was meant or intended, there is nothing wrong in leaving the questions somewhat obscure. In fact, introducing some measure of obscurity would be completely in keeping with this context.

Perhaps it should be noted that, whereas most translations render with the meaning will live forever, GeCL has "will remain with us forever." This translation represents a slight shift in emphasis, and it seems that the interpretation of TEV and most other translations is more in accord with what is meant in this particular passage. Here again GeCL translates "Messiah" by "the promised Savior," which is a definite improvement over most other translations. (See comments at 1.20.)

12.35 Jesus answered, "The light will be among you a little longer. Continue on your way while you have the light, so that the darkness will not come upon you; for the one who walks in the dark does not know where he is going.

Jesus answered is literally "therefore (oun) Jesus said to them." A little longer is emphatic in the Greek sentence structure. The reference is to the remainder of Jesus' ministry. The light (see 1.4; 8.12) is a reference to Jesus himself, but it is not necessary to identify the light as Jesus, since the context makes the identity relatively clear. What is more, the statement Jesus makes is obscure. It may not be possible to say in some languages "the light will be among you." It may be necessary to say "you will have light" or "light will be with you" or "you will experience light."

Continue on your way while you have the light is translated by NEB "Go on your way while you have the light" and by Gdsp "Go on while you still have the light." The verb is literally "walk" (many translations), and the force of the present imperative in Greek is to encourage the continuation of an action already begun (TEV Continue; NEB "Go on").

Jesus will not be among the Jews forever, so he appeals to them to walk in the light, that the darkness may not come upon them. The verb translated come upon is used in 1.5, where it is rendered put out (see comments at 1.5). A number of translations render this verb by "overtake" (Mft, Gdsp, NEB, JB, RSV), while NAB translates "come over" and Phps as "comes down upon." This same verb is used in 1 Thessalonians 5.4 with the meaning it has in this passage.

In some languages one cannot speak of "darkness coming upon a person." One can often say "you will be suddenly in the dark" or "you will suddenly experience darkness."

Instead of saying one who walks in the dark, it may be necessary to say "one who walks when it is dark" or "...in places where it is dark." In some languages the most satisfactory equivalent of dark is "where there is no light" or "where it is not light."

The word rendered for is literally "and," but a causative connection is indicated in this context. Some translations indicate the causative relation otherwise (RSV "...lest the darkness overtake you; he who walks in the darkness does not know where he goes").

<u>12.36a</u>   Believe in the light, then, while you have
             it, so that you will be the people of the
             light."

    <u>Believe in the light, then, while you have it</u> is inverted from
the Greek word order, which reads "while you have the light, believe in
the light" (RSV). Here <u>Believe</u> is made the equivalent of <u>Continue on
your way</u> of verse 35. In both instances the appeal is for the Jews to
receive the light.
    In certain languages a literal rendering of <u>Believe in the light</u>
may be very difficult, since these words may be taken as an exhortation
to put one's trust in the sun or in the sun god. The only satisfactory
alternative may be "Believe in the one who causes light," which can
more readily be interpreted as an indirect reference to Jesus. If such
a rendering is adopted, it is necessary to modify the second clause
<u>while you have it</u> to read "while you have him still with you" or "while
he is still with you."
    <u>The people of the light</u> is literally "sons of light" (so most
translations). GeCL translates "then you will become men who live in
the light," and NEB "so that you may become men of light." In Semitic
thought such an expression as "sons of (noun/adjective)" means "people
who are characterized by (noun/adjective)." Here, then, "sons of light"
are either people who live in the light or people who belong to the
light.

              TEV   (12.36b-43)   RSV

        THE UNBELIEF OF THE PEOPLE

    After Jesus said this, he went
off and hid himself from them. 37
Even though he had performed all
these miracles in their presence,
they did not believe in him, 38 so
that what the prophet Isaiah had
said might come true:
    "Lord, who believed the
        message we told?
    To whom did the Lord
        reveal his power?"
    39 And so they were not able to
believe, because Isaiah also said,
    40 "God has blinded their eyes
        and closed their minds,
    so that their eyes would not
        see,
    and their minds would not
        understand,

    When Jesus had said this, he de-
parted and hid himself from them.
37 Though he had done so many signs
before them, yet they did not believe
in him; 38 it was that the word spoken by the prophet Isaiah might be
fulfilled:
    "Lord, who has believed our
        report,
    and to whom has the arm of the
        Lord been revealed?"
39 Therefore they could not believe.
For For Isaiah again said,
    40 "He has blinded their eyes and
        hardened their heart,
    lest they should see with their
        eyes and perceive with
        their heart,
    and turn for me to heal them."

[415]

and they would not turn to
me, says God,
for me to heal them."
41 Isaiah said this because he
saw Jesus' glory and spoke about
him.

42 Even then, many Jewish authorities believed in Jesus; but because
of the Pharisees they did not talk
about it openly, so as not to be
expelled from the synagogue. 43 They
loved the approval of men rather than
the approval of God.

41 Isaiah said this because he saw
his glory and spoke of him. Nevertheless many even of the authorities believed in him, but for fear
of the Pharisees they did not confess it, lest they should be put
out of the synagogue: 43 for they
loved the praise of men more than
the praise of God.

This entire section is a commentary on the unbelief of the Jews
(verse 37). Why had they rejected Jesus? Why was it that his own people
did not receive him (1.11)? It was so that the words of Isaiah the prophet might come true (verse 38), and it was in keeping with the purpose
of God, who had blinded their eyes, and closed their minds (verse 40).
Evidently Isaiah 6.10 (quoted in verse 40) was the typical early Christian answer to this burning question, as Luke's use of this same verse
in Acts 28.26-27 suggests (note also Matt 13.13-15; Mark 4.12; Luke
8.10).

Yet, even though the majority of the Jews rejected Jesus, many
of the Jewish authorities did believe in him, but they were not willing
to confess him openly for fear of being put out of the synagogue (verse
42). John closes this section with his own explanation of why the Jewish
authorities were not willing to confess Jesus openly: They loved the
approval of men rather than the approval of God (verse 43).

The section heading, The Unbelief of the People, may be made more
specific by saying "Most of the Jewish people did not believe in Jesus"
or "Most of the Jewish people refuse to believe in Jesus."

12.36b   After Jesus said this, he went off and hid
     himself from them.

TEV, following in the tradition of Gdsp (see also Phps and GeCL)
begins a new paragraph with verse 36b. After Jesus said this is more
literally "These things Jesus said." The reference is best taken to what
Jesus has just said (verses 23-28, 30-32, 35-36). Gdsp translates "With
these words"; NEB "After these words"; JB "Having said this."

In Greek, went off is a participle dependent on the main verb hid,
but most translations, including TEV, render it as a finite verb. NEB
"Jesus went away from them into hiding" actually changes the main verb
(hid himself) to a noun, while making the participle the main verb. In
8.59, after the Festival of Shelters, it is said that Jesus hid himself
and left the Temple. In 12.36b the statement is very appropriate; the
light has now disappeared, and there is no chance for the Jews to believe in the light.

In translating hid himself from them, it is important to avoid the
impression that Jesus was playing a kind of game of hide and seek. One

may, for example, render it "stayed where they could not find him" or "stayed where they did not know where he was."

12.37   Even though he had performed all these miracles
               in their presence, they did not believe in him,

All these miracles is literally "these many signs." (For "sign" as a mighty work, see 2.11.)

In their presence is more literally "before them." In some languages in their presence is best rendered "with them looking on" or "while they were themselves seeing what was happening."

They did not believe is the rendering of most translations, though NAB has "they refused to believe" and Gdsp and NEB have "they would not believe in him." In light of verse 40, these may be legitimate renderings, but it seems best to use a more neutral verb, such as "did not."

12.38   so that what the prophet Isaiah had said might
               come true:
                    "Lord, who believed the message we told?
                    To whom did the Lord reveal his power?"

In order to show clearly the purpose involved in verse 38 and its relation to the preceding statement, it may be necessary to begin this verse as a separate sentence, introduced by the expression "All this happened so that what the prophet Isaiah had said might come true."

What the prophet Isaiah had said is more literally "the word of the prophet Isaiah." TEV makes the Greek noun phrase into an English verb phrase.

Might come true is rendered in most translations "might be fulfilled." However, to use the imagery of "fulfilled" is to use technical biblical vocabulary to express a meaning which can be conveyed more simply in English with the words might come true. In some instances it may be expressed as "might actually happen." Such an expression may then be combined with the preceding as "All this happened so that what the prophet Isaiah said would happen, did actually happen." It may be necessary, however, to introduce another verb to indicate what Isaiah said, for example, "Isaiah had said, Lord, who believed the message we told..."

The message we told (Mft "what they heard from us"; NEB "what we reported") is more literally "our report." Here again TEV transforms a Greek noun phrase into a verb phrase in English. The Greek noun phrase "our report" can be taken to mean "what has reached our ears" (NAB) or "what we have heard said" (JB), but the focus is not on "what we have heard" but on "what we have reported."

To whom did the Lord reveal his power? is literally "to whom has the arm of the Lord been revealed?" (RSV). In Semitic thought, the use of "arm" in such a context is a symbol of power (NEB "the Lord's power"; NAB "the might of the Lord"), and "has been revealed" is a "divine passive" (that is, a way of speaking of God's activities without mentioning the name of God). It is simply another way of saying "the Lord did reveal" or "the Lord did show." It may be difficult to speak of "revealing his power." However, one can often say "reveal how powerful he is" or "show how much power he has" or even "reveal how he is able to control."

12.39   And so they were not able to believe, because
             Isaiah also said,

And so is explained by because Isaiah also said, but the TEV restructuring of this sentence does not make the connection clear. Compare, for example, NAB, "The reason they could not believe was that, as Isaiah says elsewhere..." And so could, of course, be interpreted as result, for example, "And as a result they were not able to believe." Such an expression approximates closely the idea of cause, but it may be better to make the cause more specific, for example, "The reason why they could not believe was that..." or "The reason they could not believe was because, as Isaiah had also said, 'God has blinded their eyes...'"

12.40   "God has blinded their eyes
                 and closed their minds,
             so that their eyes would not see,
                 and their minds would not understand,
                 and they would not turn to me, says God,
                 for me to heal them."

This verse is a quotation from Isaiah 6.10, though its form in John differs from both the Hebrew and the Septuagint. Probably John was quoting freely, perhaps from memory, and adapting the material to suit his purpose. In place of God (literally "he") has blinded their eyes, and closed their minds (literally "hardened their heart") the Hebrew text reads "make (imperative) the heart of this people fat, and their ears heavy, and shut their eyes..." It should be noted that John omits "ears" and speaks of the "eyes" before the "heart." (In Hebrew "heart" functions as the equivalent of "mind" for the western reader.) Also, John omits the phrase "of this people." However, the most noticeable difference is that John changes the imperatives of the Hebrew text ("make ...shut") to a statement has blinded, with God as the assumed subject, as TEV makes explicit. Quite likely John makes the changes to emphasize that the judgment on the Jews is in reality the action of God. This conclusion is supported by the observation that John's last line follows the Septuagint (literally "and I will heal them") instead of the "divine passive" of the Hebrew text ("and be healed").

It may be difficult to preserve the type of double parallelism of this verse. Note, for example, that the first line refers to the eyes and the second line to the mind, while the third line refers back to the eyes and the fourth line to the mind. It may be necessary to bring together the lines referring to the eyes and those referring to the mind, for example, "God has blinded their eyes so that they cannot see, and he has closed their minds so that they cannot understand." If it is difficult to speak of "closing minds" an equivalent may be "make their minds slow" or "make their minds hard." Or an equivalent may be "he made them stupid," in the sense that "they could not think correctly." If verse 39b is translated "God spoke further through the prophet Isaiah and said," then in verse 40, instead of the third person (God has blinded...and closed), the first person, referring to God, may be used throughout: "I have blinded their eyes, and I have closed their minds."

They would not turn to me, says God, for me to heal them is literally "lest they...turn, and I will heal them." It is clearly implied by the context that the turning is to God, and TEV makes this explicit by including to me, says God. It may be made explicit in another way. That is, if verse 39 is made to read "God spoke through the prophet Isaiah, and also said," then in verse 40 a first person reference can be made to God throughout ("I have blinded their eyes... And they would not return to me, for me to heal them").

It is important to note that the clause and they would not turn to me is still a part of the expression of purpose stated in the beginning of the third line. However, since the second part of verse 40 is to be understood as a quotation, it may be necessary to break the sentence after the fourth line and introduce the direct quotation as "God says, I did this so that they would not turn to me in order for me to heal them."

It is difficult to overestimate the significance of Isaiah 6.10 for the New Testament. It is used in the Synoptic Gospels (see Matt 13.13-15; Mark 4.12; Luke 8.10) to explain why the people did not understand Jesus' teaching in parables concerning the Kingdom. Paul quotes it in Acts 28.26-27 to explain why the Jews did not accept the gospel which he proclaimed to them. And here John uses it to explain why the Jews rejected Jesus.

12.41   Isaiah said this because he saw Jesus'
               glory and spoke about him.

Isaiah said this is literally "These things Isaiah said." But once again "these things" is best translated this for English speakers, as in most translations.

Because (hoti) appears in some Greek manuscripts as "when" (hote). The manuscript evidence is heavily in support of the reading because, and in the context it seems more probable that a scribe would have changed because to read "when" than vice versa. Most modern translations (with the exception of JB and Luther Revised) follow the reading because. Note the similar change in verse 17.

Jesus' glory is literally "his glory," but the pronominal reference is ambiguous for the English reader, and for this reason TEV makes it explicit. Note the ambiguity of NEB: "Isaiah said this because he saw his glory and spoke about him." According to the English sentence structure, it would be natural to refer the pronouns to God, who is mentioned in the last part of the preceding verse. However, John is affirming that Isaiah had seen Jesus' glory, and this information should be made explicit (note GeCL "Isaiah spoke here of Jesus. He said this because he had seen his glory"). NAB is similar to TEV, and JB makes "Jesus" explicit by reading "Isaiah said this when he saw his glory, and his words referred to Jesus."

Certain problems are involved in the translation of verse 41 because

the temporal relations are not made explicit in the Greek text. Because
he saw Jesus' glory could mean that Isaiah saw in his own day the preincarnate glory which Jesus had. However, it is better to understand
this clause as referring to Isaiah's prophetic vision of the glory that
Jesus would have as the result of his death and resurrection. One may
translate, therefore, "he saw ahead of time the glory that Jesus would
have later" or "...how wonderful Jesus would be."

12.42 Even then, many Jewish authorities believed
in Jesus; but because of the Pharisees they did
not talk about it openly, so as not to be expelled
from the synagogue.

Even then may be rendered "There were in fact" or "Actually there
were." This verse serves to emphasize what is to follow and suggests a
certain amount of contrast with what has preceded.

Many Jewish authorities is literally "many authorities." The reference is to the Jewish leaders. "The leading men" of JB seems to imply
that a number of leading citizens believed in Jesus, whereas the emphasis
is that a number of the Jewish authorities believed in Jesus (note, for
example, NAB "There were many, even among the Sanhedrin, who believed in
him"). Gdsp translates "...even among the members of the Council, many
came to believe in him." It is quite likely that authorities in this context is to be understood specifically as members of the Jewish Council
(see 3.1; 7.26,48).

The expression because of the Pharisees may require further expansion in some languages, for example, "because of fear of the Pharisees"
or "because they feared what the Pharisees might do to them."

In Jesus is literally "in him." It is necessary to make the pronominal reference explicit; otherwise it may be taken as referring back
to Isaiah in verse 41, since he is the last person mentioned by name.

Talk about it openly is the verb spoke out clearly (1.20; see also
9.22). Gdsp translates "would not acknowledge it" (NEB "would not acknowledge him"); Phps has "would not admit it" (JB "did not admit it";
NAB "refused to admit it"). It may be necessary in some languages to say
"would not say to others that they believed in Jesus."

Be expelled from the synagogue is the same expression used in 9.22.

12.43 They loved the approval of men rather than
the approval of God.

They is obviously a reference to the many Jewish authorities of
verse 42 who believed in Jesus.

Loved...rather than is rendered "loved...more than" by some translators. This idea is expressed as "cared more for...than" by Gdsp and
"preferred...to" by Mft and NEB. NEB is somewhat more sophisticated in
its language: "For they valued their reputation with men rather than
the honor which comes from God."

The word rendered approval by TEV is literally "glory." It is obvious that the reference here is to the approval or praise that comes

from men or from God. It may be necessary to restructure expressions involving <u>loved</u> and <u>approval</u>, for example, "They wanted men to praise them more than they wanted God to praise them" or "They wanted very much to have people say, 'We like you.' They were not so anxious to have God say, 'I like you.'"

	TEV	(12.44-50)	RSV

JUDGMENT BY JESUS' WORDS

44 Jesus said in a loud voice, "Whoever believes in me believes not only in me but also in him who sent me. 45 Whoever sees me sees also him who sent me. 46 I have come into the world as light, so that everyone who believes in me should not remain in the darkness. 47 If anyone hears my message and does not obey it, I will not judge him. I came, not to judge the world, but to save it. 48 Whoever rejects me and does not accept my message has one who will judge him. The words I have spoken will be his judge on the last day! 49 This is true, because I have not spoken on my own authority, but the Father who sent me has commanded me what I must say and speak. 50 And I know that his command brings eternal life. What I say, then, is what the Father has told me to say."

44 And Jesus cried out and said, "He who believes in me, believes not in me but in him who sent me. 45 And he who sees me sees him who sent me. 46 I have come as light into the world, that whoever believes in me may not remain in darkness. 47 If any one hears my sayings and does not keep them, I do not judge him; for I did not come to judge the world but to save the world. 48 He who rejects me and does not receive my sayings has a judge; the word that I have spoken will be his judge on the last day. 49 For I have not spoken on my own authority; the Father who sent me has himself given me commandment what to say and what to speak. 50 And I know that his commandment is eternal life. What I say, therefore, I say as the Father has bidden me."

Many commentators believe that these verses are not in their original place, but there is no textual evidence for placing them elsewhere. Mft, however, places verses 44-50 in the middle of verse 36 ("36 While you have the Light, believe in the Light, that you may be sons of the Light [44-50]. With these words Jesus went away and hid from them "). That is, Mft understands this passage as a part of Jesus' last appeal to the Jews. But it seems best to take it as an independent unit. It is a summary of the results of Jesus' ministry, reflecting several of its themes. That is, the entire section is best understood as a summary proclamation.

The section heading, <u>Judgment by Jesus' Words</u>, is a very condensed statement in English and an effective summary of the principal emphasis in the following paragraph. However, in other languages a somewhat different kind of statement may be needed, for example, "People will be judged by what Jesus says" or "The words of Jesus will judge people" or "My words will be his judge."

12.44   Jesus said in a loud voice, "Whoever believes
in me believes not only in me but also in him who
sent me.

Jesus said in a loud voice is literally "but (Greek de) Jesus cried
out and said." Here the words "and said" reflect a kind of Semitic redundancy, serving as the equivalent of quotation marks in contemporary
English. NAB translates "Jesus proclaimed aloud," while NEB has "So
Jesus cried aloud," and JB "Jesus declared publicly."
    Whoever believes in me is in Greek a participial construction
(note RSV "He who believes in me"). It is equivalent in English to an
indefinite relative followed by a noun (whoever believes). Him who sent
me is obviously a reference to God the Father. A basic theme of John's
Gospel is that Jesus comes from God, and that one's reaction towards
Jesus is the same as one's reaction towards God. As elsewhere, the indefinite relative clause may be rendered as a conditional, for example,
"If anyone believes in me, he believes not only in me..."
    Believes not only in me but also in him who sent me is literally
"believes not in me but in him who sent me" (RSV). However, a literal
translation sounds as if the person is actually not believing in Jesus,
but believing only in God, a meaning clearly not intended. NAB translates "believes not so much in me as in him who sent me"; and Anchor
"is actually believing, not in me, but in Him who sent me." Phps translates "Every man who believes in me is believing in the one who sent me."
Because of the possible misinterpretation in some languages of the contrast in not only...but also, this expression may be rendered "he believes both in me and in him who sent me." In some languages the order
of the clauses is best inverted in order to provide the appropriate
emphasis, for example, "he believes in him who sent me as well as believing in me." The fact that belief is both in Jesus and in God is emphasized and made clear by verse 45, which is semantically parallel to
verse 44.

12.45   Whoever sees me sees also him who sent me.

As with whoever believes in me in verse 44, so whoever sees me
is a participial construction in Greek (literally "the one seeing me").
The verb "to see" of this verse is parallel in force to the verb "to believe" in verse 44. As belief in Jesus is the same as belief in the
Father, so seeing Jesus is the same as seeing the Father.

12.46   I have come into the world as light, so that
everyone who believes in me should not remain
in the darkness.

For Jesus as the light of God come into the world, see 8.12 and
verse 35 above. In 8.12 an equation is made (I am the light of the
world), whereas in the present verse a simile is used (I have come into
the world as light). As light may be rendered "as one who causes light
for people" or "as one who causes light to shine upon people" or "as one
who causes people to be in light."

[422]

Remain in the darkness is here the contrast to the people of the
light in verse 36. Remain in the darkness may be rendered "remain in a
place which is dark" or "remain in a dark condition." In some languages
it is not possible to speak of "darkness" without indicating what this
abstract quality refers to, for example, place, condition, state, etc.

12.47   If anyone hears my message and does not obey
      it, I will not judge him. I came, not to judge
      the world, but to save it.

My message is literally "my words" (Greek rema), the same noun used
in 8.47 (of God's words). Most translations render "my words." But my
message may also be rendered in some instances "what I have said" or
"what I say."
Does not obey it may be rendered "does not do what I have said" or
"does not obey what I have told him to do."
In some places the Gospel of John indicates that Jesus does not
judge (see 3.17; 8.15), while in other passages it indicates that Jesus
is the judge (see 5.22 and 27; compare 8.16 and 26). The apparent contradiction may be resolved by the observation that Jesus' purpose in
coming into the world was to save it, not to judge it. However, the inevitable outcome of his coming into the world means judgment, because
some refuse to accept him.
I will not judge him may perhaps be best understood in this context in terms of "condemn him," since the emphasis here is upon a type
of judgment which results in condemnation.
As noted elsewhere, certain receptor languages require the positive
before the negative statement. Therefore, one may translate the last sentence of verse 47 "I came into the world in order to save people. I did
not come in order to condemn them."

12.48   Whoever rejects me and does not accept my message
      has one who will judge him. The words I have spoken
      will be his judge on the last day!

Whoever rejects me is a participial construction in Greek, similar
to whoever believes in me in verse 44, whoever sees me in verse 45, and
everyone who believes in me in verse 46. And does not accept my message
is literally "(the one) not receiving my words (rema)." The word rejects
appears only here in the Gospel of John. Whoever rejects me may be rendered "whoever refuses to have anything to do with me" or, idiomatically,
"whoever pushes me aside" or "whoever scoffs at me." Does not accept my
message is essentially equivalent to "does not do what I have said."
Here TEV changes the Greek verb phrase "will judge him" to a noun
phrase will be his judge.
The words translates a singular masculine noun. Therefore, it may
be an appropriate reference to a preceding participle rendered in TEV
one who will judge him. In the English translation the connection is
lost. If one uses the TEV text as a basis for translation, certain seeming contradictions may result in some receptor languages, for it will not

be possible to see a connection between one who will judge him and the words. The first phrase will evidently refer to a person, while the second will suggest only what was spoken. One could translate "has something which will judge him," and this clause may be followed by "what will judge him are the words I have spoken; they will judge him on the last day." In these contexts, "to judge" may be understood in the sense of "to condemn" or "to pass sentence on."

12.49   This is true, because I have not spoken on
          my own authority, but the Father who sent
          me has commanded me what I must say and
          speak.

This is true does not appear as part of the Greek text; it is used as a literary device in English, to contrast Jesus' words in 48 with those in 49.

For the meaning of the phrase on my own authority, see comments at 7.17.

Has commanded me is literally "has given me a command." The change from a noun phrase to a verb phrase is to attain a more natural equivalent in English.

In some languages there is no way to distinguish effectively between say and speak. The two expressions may be used in the Greek text simply as a means of emphasis, equivalent essentially to "just what I must say."

12.50   And I know that this command brings eternal
          life. What I say, then, is what the Father
          has told me to say."

Brings eternal life is literally "is eternal life." JB translates "and I know that his commands mean eternal life," while NAB renders "Since I know that his commandment means eternal life." The meaning of the phrase is that God's command brings eternal life to those who believe. (On the meaning of eternal life see comments at 1.4 and 3.15.)

The expression his command brings eternal life involves a complex set of semantic relations. His command is essentially equivalent to "what he has commanded." The verb brings indicates a causative relation between the subject and predicate elements, while eternal life is equivalent to "people live forever." In some languages it is necessary to translate his command brings eternal life by "what he has commanded causes people to live forever."

C H A P T E R   13

TEV	(13.1)	RSV

JESUS WASHES HIS DISCIPLES' FEET

13 It was now the day before the Passover Festival. Jesus knew that the hour had come for him to leave this world and go to the Father. He had always loved those in the world who were his own, and he loved them to the very end.

13 Now before the feast of the Passover, when Jesus knew that his hour had come to depart out of this world to the Father, having loved his own who were in the world, he loved them to the end.

As indicated at the beginning of Chapter 2, Chapters 2-12 are generally referred to as "The Book of Signs," because they describe a series of seven "signs" done by Jesus in the course of his ministry. Chapter 12 brings to an end the first division of John's Gospel, and Chapter 13 introduces the second half of the book, which may be called "The Book of Glory," since it deals primarily with the revelation of Jesus' glory. He reveals his glory first in his farewell discourses to the disciples, then in his passion, and finally in his resurrection. Thus, in the second half of John's Gospel the true glory of the Son of Man is revealed. He is now "lifted up" to the glory that he had before the world was created, but this "lifting up" is accomplished only by his being "lifted up" on the cross.

In a real sense, Chapters 13-17 form the background for understanding the passion narrative which follows them, and in this respect Jesus' washing the disciples' feet (13.1-20) plays a significant role. It prefigures the crucifixion itself, by which they will be cleansed from their sins (verses 6-10a). At the same time, it is a call to them to express the same love for one another that Jesus reveals for them in his death (verses 12-20). After the act of washing their feet (verses 2-5), which Jesus explains in his dialogue with the disciples (verses 6-10a, 12-20), he then predicts his betrayal (verses 21-29), and immediately the betrayer goes out into the night (verse 30). In a true sense, Judas' departure initiates the events by which the Son of Man's glory is to be revealed, and so Jesus gives his disciples the command to love one another, since he will not be with them much longer (verses 31-35). Jesus' departure is not understood by Peter, who asks "Where are you going, Lord?" Jesus explains that Peter is not able to follow him at present, to which Peter replies that he is willing to die for Jesus. This affirmation then leads to the prediction of Peter's denial (verses 36-38).

The only translational problem likely to be involved in the section heading, Jesus Washes His Disciples' Feet, is the choice of a term for "wash." Some languages have distinct terms for washing, depending on the kind of object washed. The washing of a body part may require a special term or phrase. In some languages it is necessary to use the distributive plural for feet, in order to indicate clearly that each disciple was washed separately.

[425]

13.1   It was now the day before the Passover
            Festival. Jesus knew that the hour had come
            for him to leave this world and go to the
            Father. He had always loved those in the world
            who were his own, and he loved them to the very
            end.

This verse serves as an introduction to the entire "Book of Glory."
It also gives the immediate setting for Jesus' Last Supper with his
disciples (verse 2).

In Greek the first verse of Chapter 13 is one sentence, which TEV,
NEB, and GeCL break into two sentences. It was now the day before the
Passover Festival is more literally "but before the Feast of Passover..."
The phrase "before the Feast of Passover" is rather vague. Anchor attempts
to make it more specific by translating "It was just before the Passover
Feast..." That John has reference to the day before the Passover Feast
is seen by 18.28; 19.14,31,42. TEV makes this information explicit in the
present verse.

John clearly distinguishes between the Last Supper and the Jewish
Passover, and in this respect he differs from the Synoptic Gospels, which
understand the last supper to be a Passover meal. It is not within the
scope of this commentary to discuss the problem of the relation between
the Johannine and the Synoptic accounts of that last meal, but it is important to point out one or two facts. The Jewish religious calendar
was a lunar calendar, and the beginning of a new day was counted from
sunset. According to Old Testament regulations (Lev 23.5), the Passover
meal was eaten on the evening that concluded the fourteenth day of Nisan
and began the fifteenth day. For the Synoptic Gospels the meal that Jesus
ate was a Passover meal (Mark 14.12 and parallels), whereas, according to
the Gospel of John, the last supper took place a day before the Passover,
and the trial and crucifixion of Jesus are clearly dated on Passover eve,
the fourteenth of Nisan (18.28; 19.14). Although the calendar dates are
different, John (19.31) agrees with the other Gospels on the day of the
week on which these events took place. That is, both for the Synoptics
and for John the meal was eaten on Thursday evening, and the crucifixion
took place on Friday.

TEV, NEB, and GeCL all have a full stop after the reference to the
"Passover" (or Passover Festival); some translations place a comma after
"Passover," but achieve essentially the same effect: "It was before the
festival of the Passover, and Jesus knew that the hour had come for him
to pass from this world to the Father" (JB). The difference of focus
between the two restructurings is slight. According to the restructuring
of TEV, the first sentence is simply a statement of time. Those translations which join the first two sentences with "and" (as JB) tie the idea
of Jesus' knowing about his hour more closely to the day before the Passover Festival. The grammar of the Greek sentence is difficult, and no
final decision can be made in favor of either viewpoint, though it seems
more natural to tie the idea of knowing to the temporal clause, rather
than separating the two as TEV, NEB, and GeCL do. In Greek the verb knew
is a participle, but most modern English translations make it a finite
verb.

It is impossible in most languages to translate literally It was now the day before the Passover Festival, for a temporal particle such as now would not fit in such a past tense sequence. Furthermore, some languages require a verb of "becoming" to indicate a progression of time, for example, "as the day before the Passover Festival became..."

In some languages the first sentence of verse 1 is best interpreted simply as a temporal setting. The identification of the day before the Passover Festival may often be indicated merely as a preposed element to the following sentence, for example, "The day before the Passover Festival Jesus knew that his hour had come..."

The hour is a reference to Jesus' death and exaltation (see 2.4). As in many languages, one cannot say literally the hour had come. In some instances one can say "Jesus knew that it was almost time for him to leave this world" or "...that soon it would be the occasion for him to leave this world." In certain instances neither "time" nor "occasion" may be employed, and one may simply say "Jesus knew that soon he would leave this world."

To leave this world and go to the Father is more literally "to go from this world to the Father." NEB also uses two verbs: "and he must leave this world and go to the Father." For languages which require an indication of kinship relations, it may be necessary to say "his Father."

Especially in the second half of John's Gospel, the world is equated with thosepeople who stand in opposition to God (see 1.10). This is a frequent term throughout John's Gospel. However, it should be noted that in these last discourses the phrase "the world" or "this world" appears some forty times.

In 14.12,28 and 16.10,28, Jesus' departure from this world is again spoken of as "going to the Father."

Although the Greek of this verse is one sentence, most modern English translations have a full stop after Father. He had always loved is a participle in Greek, rendered rather literally in RSV as "having loved." This aorist participle is to be taken as applying to the expression of Jesus' love throughout his entire ministry; and several other translations (NEB, JB, GeCL) also render this participle He had always loved. The second appearance of the verb loved in this verse translates an aorist indicative, best understood as a reference to the love he revealed in his death on the cross.

The Greek clause rendered to the very end occurs in the emphatic position. Most translations understand it in the same way as TEV does, that is, "to the very end of life." However, it may also mean "completely," the meaning given it in NEB, JB, and Segond. Although the idea of "completely" is certainly not foreign to the context, the fact that the hour of Jesus' death is in focus in this passage tends to support the other interpretation.

In rendering those in the world who were his own, it is important to avoid the impression that these individuals were his personal slaves, that is, persons who were "his own" in a commercial sense. In some languages the most appropriate equivalent of his own would be "his followers" or "those who believed in him."

He loved them to the very end must be translated in some languages "he loved them right up to the time that he died" or "...to the end of his life." Such a rendering may be necessary in languages which cannot speak of an "end" without indicating specifically what is involved.

However, to translate "he loved them as long as he lived" might imply that he did not love them after he had died. This problem may be avoided by translating "he always loved them, even to the end of his life."

TEV   (13.2-11)   RSV

2 Jesus and his disciples were at supper. The Devil had already put the thought of betraying Jesus into the heart of Judas, the son of Simon Iscariot.ʸ 3 Jesus knew that the Father had given him complete power; he knew that he had come from God and was going to God. 4 So he rose from the table, took off his outer garment, and tied a towel around his waist. 5 Then he poured some water into a washbasin and began to wash the disciples' feet and dry them with the towel around his waist. 6 He came to Simon Peter, who said to him, "Are you going to wash my feet, Lord?"

7 Jesus answered him, "You do not understand now what I am doing, but you will understand later."

8 Peter declared, "Never at any time will you wash my feet!"

"If I do not wash your feet," Jesus answered, "you will no longer be my disciple."

9 Simon Peter answered, "Lord, do not wash only my feet, then! Wash my hands and head, too!"

10 Jesus said, "Anyone who has taken a bath is completely clean and does not have to wash himself, except for his feet.ᶻ All of you are clean--all except one." (11 Jesus already knew who was going to betray him; that is why he said, "All of you, except one, are clean.")

ʸThe Devil...Simon Iscariot; or The Devil had already decided that Judas, the son of Simon Iscariot, would betray Jesus.

ᶻ*Some manuscripts do not have* except for his feet.

2 And during supper, when the devil had already put it into the heart of Judas Iscariot, Simon's son, to betray him, 3 Jesus, knowing that the Father had given all things into his hands, and that he had come from God and was going to God, 4 rose from supper, laid aside his garments, and girded himself with a towel. 5 Then he poured water into a basin, and began to wash the disciples' feet, and to wipe them with the towel with which he was girded. 6 He came to Simon Peter; and Peter said to him, "Lord, do you wash my feet?" 7 Jesus answered him, "What I am doing you do not know now, but afterward you will understand." 8 Peter said to him, "You shall never wash my feet." Jesus answered him, "If I do not wash you, you have no part in me." 9 Simon Peter said to him, "Lord, not my feet only but also my hands and my head!" 10 Jesus said to him, "He who has bathed does not need to wash, except for his feet,ᶜ but he is clean all over; and youˣ are clean, but not every one of you." 11 For he knew who was to betray him; that was why he said, "You are not all clean."

ᶜOther ancient authorites omit *except for his feet*

ˣThe Greek word for *you* here is plural

13.2   Jesus and his disciples were at supper. The
          Devil had already put the thought of betraying
          Jesus into the heart of Judas, the son of Simon
          Iscariot.*y*

     *y*The Devil...Simon Iscariot; *or* The Devil had
      already decided that Judas, the son of Simon
      Iscariot, would betray Jesus.

Jesus and his disciples were at supper is more literally "during
supper." TEV simply introduces information which is implicit from the
remainder of the account. JB has "they were at supper," but with no
antecedent to "they." GeCL translates as TEV does. The phrase were at
supper must be restructured in some languages as "were eating together
in the evening." The term supper involves two important components: (1)
the fact of eating and (2) the time of eating. It is necessary in some
languages to separate these components into two distinct expressions.
     Put the thought into the heart of Judas involves at least two
problems. First, the verb rendered put the thought into the heart is
literally "had thrown into the heart," and there is a question as to
whose heart is intended. Some Greek manuscripts read "the heart of
Judas," but others have "Judas" in the nominative case and so may be
translated literally "had thrown into the heart that Judas would betray
him." The reading of the genitive case ("the heart of Judas") is obviously the easier reading, and it is much more likely that scribes
would have changed the nominative to the genitive than the other way
around. But the translator, after solving the textual problem, is still
faced with the problem of ambiguity in the Greek text. What is meant by
the phrase "had thrown into the heart that Judas should betray him"?
Whose heart is intended? Segond and Zür understand the heart to be that
of the Devil himself, but most translators apparently understand it to
be the heart of Judas.
     Put the thought...into the heart of Judas is often expressed idio-
matically, for example, "whispered into the ear of Judas" or "touched
Judas with the thought of" or "whispered to the mind of Judas." The relation between the Devil and the mind of Judas is essentially causative,
and it is so treated in some languages, for example, "the Devil caused
Judas to think." In some instances the content of the thought must be
expressed in direct discourse, for example, "the Devil caused Judas to
think, I will betray Jesus."
     Secondly, this sentence presents a textual problem connected with
the phrase rendered Judas, the son of Simon Iscariot (so also NAB, NEB,
GeCL). Some translations render this "Judas Iscariot, Simon's son" (RSV,
Mft, Gdsp, Phps, JB, Segond, Zür). The evidence is not conclusive, but
elsewhere (6.71 and 13.26) "Iscariot" is connected with Simon, the father
of Judas, and so the UBS Committee prefers the reading adopted by TEV.
Because of the awkwardness of the appositional phrase the son of Simon
Iscariot, it may be necessary in some languages to make this expression
into a complete sentence, for example, "Judas was the son of Simon
Iscariot."

13.3   Jesus knew that the Father had given him complete
power; he knew that he had come from God and was
going to God.

In Greek verses 2-4 are one sentence. Jesus knew is simply a participle ("knowing"), which TEV makes into a finite verb with an explicit
subject. A number of other translations handle the matter similarly.
Had given him complete power is literally "gave all things into
his hand." A related expression is found in 3.35 (has put everything in
his power). NEB translates "intrusted everything to him" and NAB "had
handed everything over to him." This clause may be equivalent in some
languages to "had given him strength to do anything" or "gave him the
power to do everything."
The verb rendered was going appears also in 7.33 (see there). It
is frequently used in John's Gospel in reference to Jesus' departure
from the world.

13.4   So he rose from the table, took off his
outer garment, and tied a towel around
his waist.

The table is literally "the meal," but a number of translators render it as TEV does.
The expression he rose from the table involves what some call a
"hidden figure." In this context the table is a figurative expression
for the meal, and rose means standing up, not literally rising above a
surface. A literal translation of this statement could be understood in
some languages to mean that Jesus was floating in the air above the
table. The most convenient equivalent may be "so Jesus stood up."
Took off his outer garment is more literally "puts (aside) his outer
garments." The verb took off (Greek tithēmi) is not the normal word used
for taking off one's clothes, but it is used in 10.11,15,17, and 18 for
the laying down of one's life. By "laying down" his garments, Jesus fore-
shadows the "laying down" of his life. It may be noted in this context
that the same words rendered put...back on in verse 12 is translated
receive...back and take...back (of Jesus' life) in 10.17,18. The word
rendered outer garment may have this specific meaning, or it may simply
mean "garment" in the general sense; but John clearly intends his readers
to understand that Jesus did not completely disrobe, and so it is better
to specify an outer garment. In most languages outer garment is equivalent to "coat," but this term should not be understood in the sense of
a heavy overcoat. It would be equivalent to "robe" in some languages.
The word rendered towel appears only here and in verse 5 in the
New Testament.

13.5   Then he poured some water into a washbasin
and began to wash the disciples' feet and
dry them with the towel around his waist.

The word translated washbasin does not appear elsewhere in Greek literature; its meaning is uncertain, but most translations have "basin." It can be argued that the word means "pitcher," since in the ancient Near East peoples' feet were not generally washed in a basin of standing water but by pouring water over the feet from a pitcher. The picture would be as follows: The disciples were on couches, reclining on their left sides, and using their right arms to reach into the dishes that were on the table, or tables, placed in front of the couches. Jesus poured water into "the pitcher" (the Greek has the definite article "the," suggesting that it was a particular vessel used specifically for that purpose) and then went around behind the couches, where the disciples' feet were stretched out behind them. There he poured water from the pitcher over their feet and dried them with the towel wrapped around his waist.

13.6   He came to Simon Peter, who said to him,
          "Are you going to wash my feet, Lord?"

Some argue that Simon Peter was the first to have his feet washed and others that he was the last. On the basis of Jesus' reply in verse 10 (All of you are clean--all except one), the evidence seems to favor Simon Peter's being the last. In Greek who said to him begins a new sentence, but TEV makes it into a subordinate clause (note RSV "He came to Simon Peter; and Peter said to him...").

Are you going to wash...? (so also JB, NAB) is literally "are you washing...?" But in the present context the verb seems to suggest an action not yet initiated, rather than an action in progress. In the Greek text both pronouns (you...my) are emphatic.

Since the words of Simon Peter are a question directed to Jesus, it is often better to indicate this fact by the choice of the preceding verb, for example, "who asked him, Are you going to wash my feet?"

In most languages any form of direct address such as Lord must appear at the beginning, rather than at the end of the question, for example, "Lord, are you going to wash my feet?" Since what Peter is asking about is Jesus' intent, rather than about a future action, it may be more satisfactory to translate "Do you intend to wash my feet?" or "Is it your plan to wash my feet?"

13.7   Jesus answered him, "You do not understand
              now what I am doing, but you will understand
              later."

Jesus answered is literally "Jesus answered and said to him," reflecting once again Semitic redundancy in introducing direct discourse.

The pronouns you...I are emphatic; so also is the phrase what I am doing.

You will understand later is literally "but you will understand after these things." The phrase "after these things" is vague, but it may refer to when Jesus had been raised to glory (12.16; see also 2.22). That is, only after Jesus' death and resurrection will the disciples realize the full meaning of what he is now doing.

[431]

13.8   Peter declared, "Never at any time will
you wash my feet!"
       "If I do not wash your feet," Jesus an-
swered, "you will no longer be my disciple."

Peter declared (NAB "Peter replied") is rendered "Peter said" in
most translations. The Greek verb "to say" covers a wide spectrum of
meaning, and TEV gives it the proper shade of meaning in the context.
Never at any time expresses a very strong negation in Greek. Mft
translates "You will never wash my feet, never!" (note also JB "'Never!'
said Peter. 'You shall never wash my feet.'") In some languages this
strong negation is not properly expressed by a future tense, such as
"You will never wash." The closest equivalent would be some expression
of necessity, for example, "You must never wash."
     If I do not wash your feet is literally "If I do not wash you."
Most translations here are literal, but the reference is obviously to
Peter's feet, not to his whole body (see verse 9). TEV makes this information explicit.
     You will no longer be my disciple is more literally "You have no
part with me." Mft renders "you will not share my lot"; Phps "you cannot
share my lot"; Gdsp "You will have no share with me"; NEB "you are not
in fellowship with me"; and JB "you can have nothing in common with me."
NAB assumes that the background of the Greek word "part" is to be found
in the Hebrew term that describes the God-given heritage of Israel. That
is, NAB takes the analogy to represent the "heritage" or "share" in the
promised land that God gave to the individual tribes. In light of this
background, NAB translates "you will have no share in my heritage."
Whatever the source of the imagery, Jesus uses these words to affirm
that if Peter is not "washed" he will not share in the benefits of Jesus'
death, and so will have no place among God's people.

13.9   Simon Peter answered, "Lord, do not wash only
my feet, then! Wash my hands and head, too!"

That only Peter's feet are referred to by Jesus in verse 8 is made
clear in this verse. In its restructuring TEV supplies the verb wash;
the Greek text reads literally "not my feet only, but also my hands and
my head."

13.10   Jesus said, "Anyone who has taken a bath is
completely clean and does not have to wash himself, except for his feet.² All of you are clean--
all except one."

²Some manuscripts do not have except for his feet.

Except for his feet is considered by NEB and JB not to be part of
the original Greek text. This phrase is placed in brackets in NAB, indicating its doubtful presence in the text. However, the manuscript
evidence is in favor of its inclusion, and it is possible that the words

were accidentally, or even deliberately, omitted from some manuscript because of the difficulty of reconciling them with the statement is completely clean. The UBS Committee on the Greek text includes the words and rates its decision a "B" choice.

TEV restructures this verse slightly, introducing the phrase is completely clean after the word bath, whereas in the Greek text these words appear at the end of the sentence. Completely clean may be understood to mean either "in every respect" or "all over." In other words, completely may be an intensive qualifier of "clean," or it may mean that once a person has taken a bath, every part of his body is clean, and it is not necessary to bathe other parts of the body except the feet, which may get dirty in walking from one place to another. This fact becomes obvious when we consider that sandals were the common footwear of those times. There may seem to be a contradiction between is completely clean and does not have to wash himself. The latter expression must certainly not be understood in the sense of "having someone else wash him." It may be necessary to translate does not have to wash himself as "does not have to wash himself again soon." The final phrase, except for his feet, may be rendered "he only has to wash his feet."

All of you are clean--all except one is literally "and you (plural) are clean--but not all (masculine plural)." NEB translates "and you are clean, though not every one of you." NAB has "he is entirely cleansed, just as you are; though not all." In English "you" may be singular or plural. But since Jesus is addressing Peter, it is more likely to be taken as singular by the English reader. Especially is this true because of the ambiguity of the phrase "not all," which could mean "not all over" to a reader of English. For this reason RSV has added the words "of you" ("and you are clean, but not all of you").

All except one is often expressed as simply an adversative, for example, "but one of you is not clean."

13.11   (Jesus already knew who was going to betray him; that is why he said, "All of you, except one, are clean.")

This verse functions as a parenthetical statement, and so TEV has placed it in parentheses. In the Greek text Jesus is literally "he." Who was going to betray him (so most translations) is rendered by NAB "his betrayer." However, this translation opens the possibility for a misunderstanding (note NAB "he knew his betrayer"). That is, to translate as a noun ("betrayer"), rather than as a phrase (who was going to betray him), may imply more acquaintance with the person, rather than knowledge about the person's intentions.

As mentioned in other contexts, there is usually no difficulty in finding an appropriate term for betray, since this kind of behavior is universal. If no specific term is adequate to render betray, it is always possible to describe the action as "hand him over to enemies" or "cause him to be arrested by enemies."

All of you, except one, are clean is rendered by RSV "You are not all clean." The same observation can be made about the statement here as was made in the discussion of verse 10.

[433]

12 After Jesus had washed their feet, he put his outer garment back on and returned to his place at the table. "Do you understand what I have just done to you?" he asked. 13 "You call me Teacher and Lord, and it is right that you do so, because that is what I am. 14 I, your Lord and Teacher, have just washed your feet. You, then, should wash one another's feet. 15 I have set an example for you, so that you will do just what I have done for you. 16 I am telling you the truth: no slave is greater than his master, and no messenger is greater than the one who sent him. 17 Now that you know this truth, how happy you will be if you put it into practice!

12 When he had washed their feet, and taken his garments, and resumed his place, he said to them, "Do you know what I have done to you? 13 You call me Teacher and Lord; and you are right, for so I am. 14 If I then, your Lord and Teacher, have washed your feet, you also ought to wash one another's feet. 15 For I have given you an example, that you also should do as I have done to you. 16 Truly, truly, I say to you, a servant^d is not greater than his master; nor is he who is sent greater than he who sent him. 17 If you know these things, blessed are you if you do them.

^{d}Or *slave*

13.12   After Jesus had washed their feet, he put his outer garment back on and returned to his place at the table. "Do you understand what I have just done to you?" he asked.

The subject of all the verbs in this verse is "he," but TEV introduces the proper name Jesus.

His outer garment is the same word discussed in verse 4.

Returned to his place at the table (JB "he went back to the table") is literally "he reclined again" (NAB "reclined at table once more"). This verb, used twice in 6.10, was normally used to describe one's position while eating a meal (see 12.2). It occurs again in verse 25 and in 21.20 as well as in Matthew 9.10; 26.7,20; Mark 14.18; 16.14.

In the question Do you understand what I have just done to you? the adverb just is added by TEV in order to make Jesus' words refer explicitly to the immediate action of washing his disciples' feet. Phps and NAB do the same. It is possible to take Jesus' words as imperative ("Understand what I have just done to you!"), but no translators seem to understand them in this way.

In this context understand refers to the disciples' appreciation of the significance of what Jesus had done. This meaning may be reflected in some languages by saying "realize the meaning of what I have just done."

13.13   "You call me Teacher and Lord, and it is right that you do so, because that is what I am.

The title Teacher is frequently used of Jesus in the first half of John's Gospel (1.38; 3.2,10; 8.4; 11.28), but in the last part of the Gospel it is rare (13.13,14; 20.16). In two of these passages (1.38; 20.16) it is identified with the title "rabbi." Lord is a frequently used title of Jesus in the Gospel of John. The fact that Teacher is more common in the earlier half, while Lord is more common in the second half, may reflect a development in the disciples' understanding of Jesus.

You call me Teacher and Lord must be rendered as direct address in some languages, for example, "When you speak to me, you say Teacher, or you say Lord." This translation avoids giving the wrong impression that whenever the disciples spoke to or about Jesus they referred to him by the composite title "Teacher and Lord." What is meant is that they used both titles, but not necessarily together or in this order. In other words, the conjunction and is essentially equivalent to "or." In some instances this clause may be translated "You call me your teacher and your Lord."

And it is right that you do so (NEB "and rightly so"; NAB "and fittingly enough") is more literally "you are speaking correctly." The adverb "correctly" occurs also in 4.17, where "you are speaking correctly" is translated in TEV you are right when you say; in 8.48 "were we not speaking correctly" is translated were we not right in saying.

It is right that you do so must often be restructured as "When you do this, you are doing what is right" or "...you do right."

13.14   I, your Lord and Teacher, have just washed
         your feet. You, then, should wash one another's
         feet.

The first sentence of this verse represents a Greek clause, which indicates fact, rather than condition or supposition as "If..." might imply in English (RSV "If I then, your Lord and Teacher, have washed your feet..."). Accordingly, TEV renders it simply as a statement: I, your Lord and Teacher, have just washed your feet. Jesus is using here a recognized rabbinical type of argument, which moves from the greater to the lesser. If the greater (the Lord and Teacher) has done a certain thing, then the lesser (the disciples) are obligated to do the same. It should be noted that, while in verse 13 the order is Teacher and Lord, in this verse the order is Lord and Teacher.

Though the implied condition between the first and second halves of verse 14 may be clear in some languages, it may be necessary in others to make the relation more specific, while at the same time not making the construction too difficult, for example, "I am your Lord and your Teacher, and yet I have just washed your feet. Since I have done that to you, you should wash one another's feet."

The Greek verb here translated should appears again in 19.7; there it is translated ought.

13.15   I have set an example for you, so that you
         will do just what I have done for you.

    I have set an example for you (NEB "I have set you an example")
is more literally "I have given you an example"; in English, however,
it is more natural to speak of "setting" an example. The word translated
example also occurs in Hebrews 4.11; 8.5; 9.23; James 5.10; 2 Peter 2.6.
In some languages there is no technical term for example, but the meaning can always be expressed, for example, "I have shown you what to do
by doing it myself" or "I have shown you how you should imitate me."
    So that you will do just what I have done for you represents a
slight alteration of the Greek, which reads "in order that just as I
did to you also you should do." Both NEB ("you are to do as I have done
for you") and JB ("so that you may copy what I have done to you") invert the sentence structure in essentially the same way as TEV. It may
be necessary in some languages to indicate the goal of the action in
the first part of this second half of verse 15, for example, "so that
you will do for one another just what I have done for you" or "so that
you will act toward one another just as I have acted toward you." In
some languages a word meaning "help" or "benefit" may be required to
express the meaning of what was done.

<u>13.16</u>   I am telling you the truth: no slave is greater
             than his master, and no messenger is greater than
             the one who sent him.

    I am telling you the truth is used a number of times in John's Gos-
pel. For its first occurrence see 1.51.
    No slave is greater than...no messenger is greater than is literally
"a slave is not greater than...a messenger is not greater than..." The
word translated messenger appears only here in John's Gospel: it is the
normal word for "apostle," but all translators recognize that it does
not have that technical sense here. This verse is similar to Matthew
10.24: No pupil is greater than his teacher; no slave is greater than
his master. The meaning is obvious: the disciple is not to feel too important to perform the acts of service that his Lord performed, nor is
he to expect better treatment from the world than his Lord received.
    In this context greater may be understood in the sense of "more
important," for example, "No slave is more important than his master."
Comparison may be expressed in some languages as involving a surpassing
quality, for example, "No slave surpasses his master in being great."
For other languages a positive-negative contrast may be helpful, for
example, "No slave is great while his master is not great."

<u>13.17</u>   Now that you know this truth, how happy you
             will be if you put it into practice!

    The first part of this verse is literally "If you know these things
..." Here again, as in verse 14, the "if" clause in Greek states a condition that is true to fact. On this basis TEV transforms the "if" clause
into a statement: Now that you know this truth (JB "Now that you know
this..."). This truth translates the more generic "these things" of the
Greek text. Although the antecedent of "these things" is not altogether

clear, it is best taken as a reference to the words of Jesus in verses 13-16.

In some languages it is not possible to speak of this truth; that is, something which is true may not be spoken of simply as an abstract in a nominal (or noun) form. However, one can say "Now that you know this" or "Now that you know this is true" or "Now that you realize that what I have said is true."

How happy you will be is literally "you are happy (Greek makarios)." The Greek adjective used here is the same one used in each of the Beatitudes. It occurs once again in John's Gospel (20.29). It is a difficult word to translate with precision, but most modern English translations render it as either "happy" or "blessed." GeCL renders "joy without end." In biblical thought the ideas of "blessed" and "happy" are related, but there is a slight difference in focus. "Blessed" focuses attention on the source of the benefit, that it has come from God, while "happy" describes the state of the person who receives the benefit. In the present passage, as in most other New Testament passages where this Greek word occurs, the focus is upon the subjective state of happiness shared by persons who have received God's blessing. For this reason, the translation "happy" is preferable to "blessed."

If you put it into practice is literally "if you do these things," referring to this truth at the beginning of the verse (literally "these things"). JB translates the two clauses as "happiness will be yours if you behave accordingly," while NEB renders "happy are you if you act upon it"; and Phps has "you will find your happiness in doing them."

TEV	(13.18-20)	RSV

18 "I am not talking about all of you; I know those I have chosen. But the scripture must come true that says, 'The man who shared my food turned against me.' 19 I tell you this now before it happens, so that when it does happen, you will believe that 'I Am Who I Am.' 20 I am telling you the truth: whoever receives anyone I send receives me also; and whoever receives me receives him who sent me."

18 I am not speaking of you all; I know whom I have chosen; it is that the scripture may be fulfilled, 'He who ate my bread has lifted his heel against me.' 19 I tell you this now, before it takes place, that when it does take place you may believe that I am he. 20 Truly, truly, I say to you, he who receives any one whom I send receives me; and he who receives me receives him who sent me."

13.18   "I am not talking about all of you; I know those I have chosen. But the scripture must come true that says, 'The man who shared my food turned against me.'

I am not talking about all of you (see verses 10-11) is an obvious reference to Judas.

I know those I have chosen may be taken in one of two ways: (1) It may mean "I know those men whom I have really chosen, but I have not chosen Judas"; (2) or it may mean "I know the kind of men I chose" (NAB). The second interpretation implies that Jesus did choose Judas, though he knew all along what his character was, even as he knew the character of the other men he chose. On the basis of passages such as 6.64,70, the second alternative seems to be the meaning here. That is, even the choice of the one who would betray Jesus was within the divine purpose; Jesus did not choose him without knowing his character.

In rendering I know those I have chosen, the term for know should be chosen carefully. It should not be an expression which merely means "be acquainted with." The rendering of this clause should suggest "I know the kind of men I have chosen" or "I realize what sort of persons I have chosen."

Come true translates the same verb used in 12.38 (most translations "be fulfilled"). Must come true may be rendered in some languages "must surely happen," for example, "But what is written in the scriptures, 'The man who ate with me turned against me,' must surely happen."

In the scripture quotation, which comes from Psalm 41.9, there is a textual problem. The text may read who ate my food (TEV, Mft, Gdsp, Phps, RSV, Zür, Luther Revised); or it may read "who ate food with me" (NAB, NEB, JB, Segond). Because of the complexity of the problem, the UBS Committee on the Greek text rates the reading retained in the text a "D" choice, indicating a high degree of doubt. The manuscript evidence for "with me" is much stronger than for "my," which is also the reading of the Septuagint. But the UBS Committee prefers the latter reading, because "with me" may be an assimilation to Mark 14.18. It is difficult to explain the basis for GeCL, which seems to follow a composite reading: "with whom I have shared my bread." Whereas the specific term "bread" occurs in the Greek text, TEV substitutes the more generic term food.

Turned against me (so also NEB, GeCL) is literally "has lifted his heel against me" (RSV). JB translates "rebels against me." In the Near East to show the bottom of one's foot to someone was a mark of contempt, or even possibly a threat of violence. It was an especially treacherous thing to do after eating at someone's table, because eating a meal with a superior was a pledge of loyalty to that person (note 2 Sam 9.7,13; 1 Kgs 18.19; 2 Kgs 25.29). Turned against me may be rendered in some languages "became my enemy" or "began to fight against me."

13.19 I tell you this now before it happens, so that when it does happen, you will believe that 'I Am Who I Am.'

Now (so most translations) is literally "from now" (Gdsp "from now on"; Phps "from now onward"). In Matthew 26.29,64, the phrase is used with the meaning "from now on" or "from this time on." In John's Gospel it occurs only one other time (14.7). In the present passage the meaning must surely be "now," as the parallel in 14.29 indicates, where the adverb "now" (Greek nun) is actually used. Some scholars think that the meaning must be "surely," reaching this conclusion through a comparison with Matthew 26.29,64. (See Matt 23.39 and Rev 14.13 for the only other occurrences of this phrase in the New Testament.)

I tell you this now before it happens may require a slight expansion, for example, "I am telling you now what is going to happen before it happens."

On the absolute use of the phrase I Am Who I Am, see 4.26. When used without a predicate, this statement is a way of identifying Jesus with God. Both this passage and 8.24 are very close to the Septuagint text of Isaiah 43.10 ("in order that you might know and believe and understand that I am"), where God is the speaker. There are real complications in attempting to translate meaningfully the expression I Am Who I Am. The English rendering certainly does not do justice to the underlying meaning, for in this form it would mean to the average person "I'm just the kind of person I am, and no one else." While it is grammatically possible in English, in some languages one cannot say I Am Who I Am. In fact, in some languages there is no equational verb. Such expressions as "I am John" and "I am good" are simply "I John" and "I good." Thus a literal rendering of I Am Who I Am would be nothing more than "I who I." The closest equivalent in some languages is "I am the one who has always existed." In this way one may emphasize the aspect of "being" and relate it to the divine quality of eternal existence. This means that for the expression "I AM" in the Old Testament, one may translate "the eternally existing one."

13.20   I am telling you the truth: whoever receives
        anyone I send receives me also; and whoever
        receives me receives him who sent me."

I am telling you the truth is the same expression used in verse 16. (On the meaning of this expression, see 1.51.)

This verse, like many other passages in the Gospel of John, affirms the unity of Jesus with God the Father. At the same time, it affirms the unity of Jesus and his disciples, so that whoever accepts his followers accepts him and so accepts God. In this context receives may be understood in the sense of "to welcome." In some languages one may even say "welcomes into his heart."

                TEV   (13.21-30)   RSV

JESUS PREDICTS HIS BETRAYAL

21 After Jesus had said this, he was deeply troubled and declared openly, "I am telling you the truth: one of you is going to betray me." 22 The disciples looked at one another, completely puzzled about whom he meant. 23 One of the disciples, the one whom Jesus loved, was sitting next to Jesus. 24 Simon Peter motioned to him and said, "Ask him whom he is talking about." 25 So that disciple moved closer to Jesus' side and asked, "Who is

21 When Jesus had thus spoken, he was troubled in spirit, and testified, "Truly, truly, I say to you, one of you will betray me." 22 The disciples looked at one another, uncertain of whom he spoke. 23 One of his disciples, whom Jesus loved, was lying close to the breast of Jesus; 24 so Simon Peter beckoned to him and said, "Tell us who it is of whom he speaks." 25 So lying thus, close to the breast of Jesus, he said to him, "Lord, who

it, Lord?"

26 Jesus answered, "I will dip some bread in the sauce and give it to him; he is the man." So he took a piece of bread, dipped it, and gave it to Judas, the son of Simon Iscariot. 27 As soon as Judas took the bread, Satan entered into him. Jesus said to him, "Hurry and do what you must!" 28 None of the others at the table understood why Jesus said this to him. 29 Since Judas was in charge of the money bag, some of the disciples thought that Jesus had told him to go and buy what they needed for the festival, or to give something to the poor.

30 Judas accepted the bread and went out at once. It was night.

is it?" 26 Jesus answered, "It is he to whom I shall give this morsel when I have dipped it." So when he had dipped the morsel, he gave it to Judas, the son of Simon Iscariot. 27 Then after the morsel, Satan entered into him. Jesus said to him, "What you are going to do, do quickly." 28 Now no one at the table knew why he said this to him. 29 Some thought that, because Judas had the money box, Jesus was telling him, "Buy what we need for the feast"; or, that he should give something to the poor. 30 So, after receiving the morsel, he immediately went out; and it was night.

Verse 21 clearly introduces a new scene, for now Jesus indicates that one of his disciples will betray him. The disciples express their complete amazement at what Jesus has said (verse 22). Then Simon Peter motioned for "the disciple whom Jesus loved" (verse 23) to ask Jesus whom he meant (verse 24). He raises the question (verse 25), and Jesus indicates that it is the one to whom he will give the bread (verse 26a). Satan enters into Judas (verse 27a) as soon as he receives the bread (verse 26b), and Jesus then tells Judas to hurry out and do what he must (verse 27b). The next two verses are parenthetical, explaining why the disciples did not grasp the real purpose of Judas' departure. Verse 30 resumes the narrative with the statement that Judas took the bread and went out immediately afterward. The pericope closes with a remark that is as much theological as temporal: It was night.

The English section heading, Jesus Predicts His Betrayal, is extremely condensed. It may be necessary in some languages to expand it, for example, "Jesus tells ahead of time that he will be handed over to his enemies." If such a section heading seems unnecessarily long, one may say "Jesus tells what is going to happen to him."

13.21   After Jesus had said this, he was deeply troubled and declared openly, "I am telling you the truth: one of you is going to betray me."

After...said this is literally "having said these things," the same transitional formula used in 7.9; 9.6; 11.28,43; and 18.1.

He was deeply troubled is literally "he was troubled in spirit" (see comments at 12.27). In 14.1,27, the verb "to be troubled" is used of the disciples. Such an expression as deeply troubled may be expressed best by a figurative phrase, for example, "his thoughts made him suffer" or "he was pained in his heart" or "his liver quivered."

Declared openly is literally "he testified and said," reflecting
the redundancy of Semitic Greek style. The verb "to testify" was first
discussed in 1.7. NEB translates "Jesus exclaimed," and JB "declared."
The language of NAB is rather formal: "He went on to give his testimony."
An equivalent of declared openly may be "said clearly" or "said without
hiding anything."

I am telling you the truth is the same expression used in verses 16
and 20. See at 1.51.

The verb "to betray" first appears in 6.64.

13.22   The disciples looked at one another,
       completely puzzled about whom he meant.

The participle translated completely puzzled is also used in Acts
25.20 (TEV undecided) and in 2 Corinthians 4.8 (TEV in doubt). It is
used in Luke 24.4 in an infinitive form (TEV puzzled), and in Galatians
4.20 as a finite verb (TEV so worried). In the present passage NEB translates "in bewilderment"; JB "wondering"; NAB "puzzled"; Mft "at a loss";
and Phps "completely mystified." In some languages completely puzzled
may be best expressed in a negative phrase: "They couldn't understand
at all" or "They could not figure out."

About whom he meant (Gdsp, NAB "as to whom he could mean") is more
literally "of whom he spoke." NEB translates the entire verse as "The
disciples looked at one another in bewilderment: whom could he be speaking of?"

13.23   One of the disciples, the one whom Jesus
       loved, was sitting next to Jesus.

The one whom Jesus loved, though appearing last in the Greek sentence order, is moved to its present position in the verse in most contemporary English translations. The disciple whom Jesus loved is first
mentioned here (see also 19.26-27; 20.2; 21.7,20). Traditionally, this
disciple is identified as John, the son of Zebedee, but there is no
conclusive evidence to indicate who he was.

There is a problem in translating whom Jesus loved, since it is a
qualification of one disciple, and not simply an expression of relation
to all the disciples. In other words, whom refers to one and not to the
disciples. One might translate in some languages "one of the disciples--
it was the one Jesus loved--was sitting next to Jesus." However, this
distinction does not seem to be particularly significant, since in the
first verse of this chapter it is stated that "he loved them (all) to
the very end." Accordingly, some translators render whom Jesus loved
as "whom Jesus particularly loved." In chosing a term for loved, it is
essential to avoid an expression which would suggest improper associations. It may be necessary to employ such a phrase as "whom Jesus especially liked."

Was sitting next to Jesus is literally "was reclining on Jesus'
bosom." The word "bosom" is used here and in 1.18 (TEV at the Father's

side). The expression reflects the table posture of that day. Guests at
a feast reclined sideways on couches, resting on the left arm and keeping the right arm free for taking food. The feet were stretched out behind. The tables were probably placed in a kind of horseshoe arrangement,
with the host in the center, and the place of honor to his left. The
next highest place would be the one immediately to his right. Thus, the
person to the right of the host would be in a position with his head
close to the host's chest, and it would be easy for him to speak con-
fidentially to the host. The host would occupy a similar position in
relation to the honored guest on his left, and could easily speak to
him privately. It is impossible to define positively the positions of
the disciples at the meal, but the intimation is that the beloved disciple was on Jesus' right.

It may be impossible in translating, to maintain all the details
of the cultural situation of Jesus' day, particularly in the matter of
reclining at table. What is important is to translate in such a way that
the situation at the table sounds natural in the receptor language.

13.24   Simon Peter motioned to him and said, "Ask
     him whom he is talking about."

Motioned (NAB "signaled") is literally "nodded" (NEB). In some languages it may be necessary to indicate how Simon Peter was able to motion
to the disciple sitting next to Jesus. The Greek does not indicate precisely how this was done, though the basic meaning of the verb is "nod."
One can, if necessary, say "gestured with his hands," "motioned with his
head," or even "showed him by means of his eyes." It is important to indicate a form of gesturing which will mean a way of signaling a message
in the receptor language.

In place of Ask him whom he is talking about (TEV, NAB, NEB, GeCL,
Segond), some Greek manuscripts have the meaning "tell us who it is that
he is talking about" (Gdsp, Mft, Phps, RSV, Luther Revised, Zür). TEV
follows the reading chosen by the UBS Committee on the Greek text, which
is based on the age and diversity of the manuscript evidence. The second
reading assumes that Peter was close enough to the disciple whom Jesus
loved to speak directly to him (so why signal?), and that this disciple
in turn knew and could tell Peter about whom Jesus was speaking. The
UBS Committee rates its decision "B," indicating some degree of doubt
concerning it.

13.25   So that disciple moved closer to Jesus'
     side and asked, "Who is it, Lord?"

In Greek that disciple is "that one." Many translations simply render "he."

So that disciple moved closer to Jesus' side is more literally
"therefore (oun) that one reclined thus on the chest of Jesus." The adverb "thus" (Greek houtōs) is the same adverb discussed in 4.6. Here
also it seems to have the meaning of "just as he was," and is rendered
"from his position" in Anchor, but most translations leave its meaning

implicit. NAB translates the whole clause as "He leaned back against Jesus' chest," and JB has "so leaning back on Jesus' breast." What is indicated is that the disciple, from this position, was able to throw his head back and so speak to Jesus privately. That is, he was able to speak to Jesus without changing his position. It is not necessary to indicate specifically that the disciple moved closer to Jesus' side. One can simply say "that disciple moved closer to Jesus" or even "moved his head closer to Jesus" or "bent over toward Jesus."

And asked is literally "says," but once again the Greek verb "to say" is used to cover a large spectrum of meaning. A number of translations do retain the meaning "said," but the context obviously indicates a question, which in English is better represented by the verb "to ask."

13.26   Jesus answered, "I will dip some bread in
               the sauce and give it to him; he is the man."
               So he took a piece of bread, dipped it, and
               gave it to Judas, the son of Simon Iscariot.

The words translated he is the man appear in an emphatic position in the Greek sentence, as in TEV, though the position in TEV is different from that in the Greek sentence. In the UBS Greek text there are three verbs in this sentence. They appear in the order "dipped...took...gave" in NEB, NAB, Gdsp, Zür, and Luther Revised, and as took...dipped...gave in TEV, Phps, and Mft. It is possible that took was not an original part of the Greek text, and so the UBS Greek text has this verb in brackets. It may have been added by scribes, to recall Jesus' action at the last supper in taking bread (see Matt 26.26; Mark 14.22; Luke 22.19; 1 Cor 11.23). However, it is possible that it was omitted in some manuscripts as unnecessary, since in the Greek sentence order it comes after the verb dipped. It is omitted in JB and RSV, without a note, and in Segond, with a note. As indicated, TEV includes this verb, though placing it first in the sentence to achieve a more logical order.

The Greek word that TEV renders a piece of bread (psōmion) is so rendered in several other translations. RSV translates "the morsel," while NAB translates "the bit of food" in its first use and "a morsel" in its second use in the sentence. The Greek word literally means "a (small) piece of bread."

Although the Greek text simply reads "I will dip the bread," TEV supplies the words in the sauce, and some other translations supply the words "in the dish." It is not possible to say of what sauce consisted. Some have suggested that it was a kind of gravy, others insist that it was wine, and still others believe that it consisted of various herbs mixed with olive oil. The action itself is an expression of hospitality (see Ruth 2.14).

There is some textual support for the reading "Judas Iscariot, son of Simon," but the manuscript evidence is heavily in favor of Judas, the son of Simon Iscariot, and this reading is followed by most modern translators.

13.27   As soon as Judas took the bread, Satan entered
         into him. Jesus said to him, "Hurry and do what
         you must!"

As soon as Judas took the bread (so GeCL; NEB "As soon as Judas had
received it"; JB "At that instant, after Judas had taken the bread") is
literally "after the bread." TEV and these other translations make explicit what is clearly implied in the briefer Greek structure.
     Only here in John's Gospel does the name Satan occur; the word
"devil" is used in 6.70; 8.44; 13.2. Went into is used of evil spirits
in Mark 5.12 and Luke 8.30; Luke 22.3 uses this same verb in reference
to Satan's entering Judas. Satan entered into him may be expressed more
clearly in some languages as "Satan took control of him" or "Satan started
to command him."
     It is important to indicate that Jesus' statement was made to Judas
and not to Satan. Because of the confusion of antecedents for the pronoun him, it may be necessary in some languages to say "Jesus said to
Judas."
     Hurry and do what you must is literally "That which you are doing
do quickly." NAB translates "Be quick about what you are to do"; JB
"What you are going to do, do quickly"; and NEB "Do quickly what you have
to do."

13.28   None of the others at the table understood why
         Jesus said this to him.

None of the others at the table is literally "none of those reclining," the same verb used in verses 23 and 12.2.
     Here also TEV makes explicit the mention of Jesus, which is simply
"he" in the Greek text.

13.29   Since Judas was in charge of the money bag, some
         of the disciples thought that Jesus had told him
         to go and buy what they needed for the festival,
         or to give something to the poor.

Since Judas was in charge of the money bag, some of the disciples
thought is literally "But some thought, that since Judas was in charge
of the money bag." TEV simply inverts the order of the two clauses and
makes explicit the disciples, represented in the Greek text by "some."
     Money bag is the same word used in 12.6. It is not necessary to
introduce in translation such a phrase as money bag, since "to be in
charge of the money bag" was simply a way of indicating that Judas
handled the joint funds of the group. A literal translation of "in
charge of the money bag" may suggest that the disciples were rich.
     In the Greek sentence structure to go and...for the festival is
in direct discourse, while to give...to the poor is in indirect discourse. It is more natural in English to use the same type of discourse
for both. Accordingly, TEV and several other translations change the
Greek direct discourse to indirect.

The last part of verse 29 is difficult to translate, since there are several layers of embedding; that is, one clause is included within another. The principal subject-predicate construction is some of the disciples thought, and all that follows is the object of that verb of thinking, that is, what the disciples thought. On the next level there is the subject-predicate expression Jesus had told him, and what follows is the content of what Jesus said. In some languages it may be necessary to place both expressions in the form of direct discourse, for example, "Some of the disciples thought, Jesus has told him, You must go and buy what we need for the Festival..." It may, however, be possible to combine indirect and direct discourse, for example, "Some of the disciples thought that Jesus had told him, Go and buy what we need for the Festival..."

13.30   Judas accepted the bread and went out
               at once. It was night.

In Greek Judas is literally "he," and accepted is a participle which TEV makes into a finite verb.
It may be necessary to translate the bread as "the small piece of bread," to avoid the impression that Judas received a loaf of bread.
John's statement it was night has more than a temporal connotation; it is theological as well.

                TEV   (13.31-35)   RSV

        THE NEW COMMANDMENT

31 After Judas had left, Jesus said, "Now the Son of Man's glory is revealed; now God's glory is revealed through him. 32 And if God's glory is revealed through him, then God will reveal the glory of the Son of Man in himself, and he will do so at once. 33 My children, I shall not be with you very much longer. You will look for me; but I tell you now what I told the Jewish authorities, 'You cannot go where I am going.' 34 And now I give you a new commandment: love one another. As I have loved you, so you must love one another. 35 If you have love for one another, then everyone will know that you are my disciples."

31 When he had gone out, Jesus said, "Now is the Son of man glorified, and in him God is glorified; 32 if God is glorified in him, God will also glorify him in himself, and glorify him at once. 33 Little children, yet a little while I am with you. You will seek me; and as I said to the Jews so now I say to you, 'Where I am going you cannot come.' 34 A new commandment I give to you, that you love one another; even as I have loved you, that you also love one another. 35 By this all men will know that you are my disciples, if you have love for one another."

Some commentators take 13.31-38 as a transition to the last discourses (Chapters 14-17); others take this section to be an introduction to the

last discourses. Whether it is introductory or transitional, this section anticipates the themes of the last discourses, that is, Jesus' departure and of his command to love.

The present paragraph, The New Commandment, easily falls into three
subdivisions. Verses 31-32 deal with the glorification of the Son of Man;
verse 33 is concerned with the theme of Jesus' departure; verses 34-35
record the command to love one another.

13.31   After Judas had left, Jesus said, "Now
the Son of Man's glory is revealed; now God's
glory is revealed through him.

The time perspective in the last discourses is difficult, for there
are frequent shifts from past to present to future. Already in verses
31-32 the shift in time perspective is seen. Verse 31 speaks of now, and
at the same time speaks of the Son of Man's glory as something that is
already revealed. (Is revealed in this verse and in verse 32 translates
an aorist tense, which relates to past time.) Verse 32 speaks in the
future tense (God will reveal the glory of the Son of Man in himself).
The reason for this complexity of time sequence is John's perspective.
He writes not only from the time perspective of the actual historical
setting, but also from that of the actual time of his writing, toward
the end of the first century. That is, John narrates the historical situation, but at the same time he makes it relevant to his readers by introducing them into the time perspective.

Though Judas is not explicitly mentioned in the Greek text, TEV does
so because of the new section. NAB does likewise.

On the meaning of the Son of Man, see comments at 1.51.

Now the Son of Man's glory is revealed is "Now the Son of Man is
glorified" in most translations. JB ("Now has the Son of Man been glorified") and Gdsp ("Now the Son of Man has been honored") use the perfect
tense.

There are at least two problems in the translation of this clause.
The first relates to the choice of verb tense, whether present or past.
Sometimes John speaks from the point of view of Jesus' day, and sometimes from the perspective of the time of his writing. Most translators
prefer to maintain the present tense ("is glorified"), but others use
the past tense.

The second problem involves the meaning of the verb phrase rendered
"is glorified" in most translations. "Is glorified" or "has been glorified" is meaningless. Gdsp translates "Now the Son of Man has been honored, and God has been honored, through him"; TEV relates this phrase
to the revelation of the Son of Man's glory (see also GeCL "Now the
glory of the Son of Man has been revealed and through it God's own
glory"). A strong argument can be made for the meaning of "bring honor
to" in the second use of this term in verse 31 ("and in him God is glorified," that is, "and in him God is honored"). It can be argued that the
Son's obedience to the Father, which is a revelation of the Son's true
glory, is a means by which honor is brought to the Father. But this interpretation is made unlikely by the observation that the phrase "is
glorified," when applied to the Son of Man in the first part of this

verse, is difficult to interpret in that light. To translate "Now is the
Son of Man honored" assumes the situation at the time the Gospel was
written, when the Christian community honored the Son of Man because of
his sacrificial death. All in all, it is best to take the phrase "is
glorified" in the sense that TEV takes it in both places in this verse,
since this meaning is that of the phrase throughout Chapter 12. Through
his death the Son of Man reveals his true glory, and at the same time
his death becomes the means by which God's glory is revealed.

This verse presents an additional problem of translation in some
languages, for such an expression as "has been revealed" would imply
that the glory of the Son of Man was revealed entirely by the signs
(miracles) he had performed. In reality, however, this special "glorification" is obviously a reference to Jesus' death and resurrection.
One of the added complications in the use of the tense form is in the
adverb now. A literal translation with the present tense may suggest
in some languages that it was Judas' leaving which showed clearly the
glory of the Son of Man. Despite the fact that the Greek text itself
has the aorist tense here, it seems necessary in view of the context
and the writer's particular historical viewpoint to employ an anticipatory
tense or something which will indicate an immediate future, for example,
"Now the Son of Man's glory is about to be revealed."

It may be necessary to change is revealed to an active form, for
example, "people will see the Son of Man's glory."

In languages in which glory must be translated by an expression
meaning "honor," the rendering may be "Now people are about to see how
the Son of Man will be honored" or "...will receive honor" or "...will
be shown to have honor." But in some languages the focus of glory is
essentially "wonderfulness" or "being wonderful." Therefore one may
translate "Now people will soon see how wonderful the Son of Man is."
The final clause of verse 31 may then be translated "Now people will
see through Jesus how wonderful God is."

The phrase through him indicates clearly that Jesus is the means
by which people see God's glory. Therefore Jesus may be made the causative agent of this revelation, for example, "Now Jesus will cause people to see how wonderful God is."

13.32   And if God's glory is revealed through him,
then God will reveal the glory of the Son of
Man in himself, and he will do so at once.

And if God's glory is revealed through him does not appear in some
of the best Greek manuscripts. Most modern translations include these
words, though NAB places them in square brackets, and JB and NEB add a
footnote indicating that they do not appear in some of the Greek manuscripts. Ordinarily, when the manuscript evidence favors a shorter as
opposed to a longer reading, the shorter is considered more likely to
be the original. However, it is possible that these words were unin-
tentionally left out by some scribe. But it is also possible that a
scribe intentionally omitted these words, because he felt that they were
redundant. The UBS Committee includes these words in brackets and rates
its choice "C," indicating a considerable degree of doubt as to whether

the text or the apparatus contains the better reading.

If the clause we have just discussed was indeed an original part of the Greek text, it makes a good transition to the next clause: then God will reveal the glory of the Son of Man in himself. In the Greek text the Son of Man is literally "him," but to translate literally could create a serious ambiguity (RSV "God will also glorify him in himself"). In himself is best taken as a reference to God, and not to the Son of Man. Parallel in meaning to this verse is 17.5: Give me glory in your presence now, the same glory I had with you before the world was made. In some languages a literal translation of in himself would be relatively meaningless, for it would not indicate that God himself makes possible the revelation of the glory of the Son of Man. However, in the preceding clause God is indicated as the one who reveals this glory, and therefore it is possible to understand in himself as emphasizing God's agency. Accordingly, one may translate "Then God himself will show people how wonderful the Son of Man is."

And he will do so at once is more literally "and he will glorify him at once." For stylistic reasons TEV omits a further reference to revealing Jesus' glory in this verse. JB translates "and will glorify him very soon," and NEB has "and he will glorify him now." Once again the time sequence is difficult, and the translator need not try to make consistent in translation the time sequences which are not consistent in the original.

13.33   My children, I shall not be with you very much longer. You will look for me; but I tell you now what I told the Jewish authorities, 'You cannot go where I am going.'

My children (so several other translations) is literally "children." This word appears seven times in 1 John (2.1,12,28; 3.7,18; 4.4; 5.21), as well as in Galatians 4.19. Technically the word is a diminutive form, meaning "little children" (so Anchor), but most translations render it simply "children," since it is doubtful that the diminutive form has any special force here. A literal translation of my children may, in fact, suggest that the disciples were small boys rather than grown men. It may even indicate that Jesus was talking to his own sons. An equivalent in some languages is "my dear companions" or even "my dear ones" or "you whom I love." The use of the term children is certainly an expression of endearment.

I shall not be with you very much longer is in Greek a positive statement, "I will be with you a little while longer." A similar expression is used in 7.33, when Jesus addresses the Jewish leaders. No definite period of time can be specified for this "little while." The first time we find Jesus using this phrase is approximately six months before his crucifixion, whereas in the present context his crucifixion is only a few hours away. In some languages it may be necessary to employ an expression of time which will indicate only a few hours, for example, "I shall be with you for only a few more hours." The second sentence of this verse is somewhat restructured in TEV, as well as in most other translations.

I tell you now what I told the Jewish authorities refers back to 7.33 and 8.21.

You cannot go where I am going refers to Jesus' death and departure to the Father. For the present the disciples are not able to follow Jesus in this way, as indicated by his prediction of Peter's denial in the following verses. The verb go is the same verb discussed in 7.33; it is used several times in John's Gospel of Jesus' departure from the world and to the Father. In this chapter it is used in verses 3 and 36, as well as in this verse.

13.34   And now I give you a new commandment: love
         one another. As I have loved you, so you
         must love one another.

I give you a new commandment must often be shifted into a verb form, for example, "I'm commanding you something new" or "I'm commanding you in a new way" or "I'm commanding you in a way I have not commanded you before."

Love one another is the way TEV and several other translations render the Greek phrase "that you love one another" (RSV). In the Greek construction the word "that" (hina) serves as a means of introducing the content of the commandment.

As I have loved you, so you must love one another (NEB "as I have loved you, so you are to love one another") may be taken with the meaning "I have loved you so that you would love one another." However, the context favors the interpretation of TEV, and this interpretation is apparently followed in most other translations as well. An equivalent expression in many languages is "In the same way that I have loved you, you must love one another."

13.35   If you have love for one another, then every-
         one will know that you are my disciples."

This verse is inverted in TEV. The Greek order is represented by RSV: "By this all men will know that you are my disciples, if you have love for one another." For English readers the restructuring found in TEV is more natural. Note also NEB: "If there is this love among you, then all will know that you are my disciples."

The love referred to in verse 35 is the same kind of love indicated in the previous verse. It is possible to translate verse 35 "If you love one another in this way, then everyone will know that you are my disciples."

| TEV | (13.36-38) | RSV |

JESUS PREDICTS PETER'S DENIAL

36 "Where are you going, Lord?"   36 Simon Peter said to him,
Simon Peter asked him.   "Lord, where are you going?" Jesus

[449]

"You cannot follow me now where I am going," answered Jesus; "but later you will follow me."

37 "Lord, why can't I follow you now?" asked Peter. "I am ready to die for you!"

38 Jesus answered, "Are you really ready to die for me? I am telling you the truth: before the rooster crows you will say three times that you do not know me.

answered, "Where I am going you cannot follow me now; but you shall follow afterward." 37 Peter said to him, "Lord, why cannot I follow you now? I will lay down my life for you." 38 Jesus answered, "Will you lay down your life for me? Truly, truly, I say to you, the cock will not crow, till you have denied me three times.

The prediction of Peter's denial is common to all four Gospels (Matt 26.31-35; Mark 14.27-31; Luke 22.31-34). Mark and Matthew indicate that it was made after Jesus and his disciples had left the house and were on their way to Gethsemane. According to Luke, it was made during a short discourse following the supper.

13.36   "Where are you going, Lord?" Simon Peter asked him.
       "You cannot follow me now where I am going," answered Jesus; "but later you will follow me."

"Where are you going, Lord?" Simon Peter asked him is inverted from the Greek order. Again RSV represents the Greek sentence order: "Simon Peter said to him, 'Lord where are you going?'" For English readers it is more effective to introduce the words of Peter before indicating that he was the one who spoke them. This is the basis for the restructuring of TEV. Note also NAB "'Lord,' Simon Peter said to him, 'where do you mean to go?'"

In the Greek text answered Jesus comes before the words You cannot follow me now where I am going. Where I am going is emphatic in the Greek sentence structure. The verb follow is often used in the New Testament in the sense of "to follow as a disciple" (see comments at 1.37).

13.37   "Lord, why can't I follow you now?" asked Peter. "I am ready to die for you!?

There is some manuscript evidence for the omission of Lord. Some scholars believe it was not an original part of the verse but was added because of the way Peter addressed Jesus in verse 36. The UBS Committee favors the retention of this word in the text, because of the widespread manuscript evidence in its support. They suggest that in some manuscripts it may have been deliberately omitted as redundant after verse 36. Their decision is a "C" choice, indicating a considerable degree of doubt regarding the choice of text. Most modern translations include the word.

The words asked Peter, literally "Peter says to him," appear as the first words in the Greek of verse 37. Here also, as in the two instances in verse 36, TEV inverts the word order.

I am ready to die for you is rendered in many translations "I will lay down my life for you." The word "life" is literally "soul," but in this context the meaning "life" is obvious (compare 10.15). In light of the context, it would seem that the meaning of Peter's words is ready to die rather than "will die." He is not making a prediction but is affirming his readiness to lay down his life for his Lord. Phps renders "I would lay down my life for you!" The phrase for you must be understood, not in the sense of "because of you," but "on your behalf." It is rendered literally in some languages "as a means of helping you" or "for your benefit."

13.38   Jesus answered, "Are you really ready to die for me? I am telling you the truth: before the rooster crows you will say three times that you do not know me."

Are you really ready to die for me? reflects both a sense of irony on the part of Jesus and his understanding of human weakness. Phps renders "Would you lay down your life for me?"; Mft "Lay down your life for me?"; NAB "You will lay down your life for me, will you?" The irony in Jesus' question may be expressed in some languages as "How is it that you say you are ready to die for me?" or "How can you say that you are ready to die for me?"

I am telling you the truth is the same expression discussed in 1.51.
Before the rooster crows you will say three times that you do not know me is more literally "the rooster will not crow until you say three times that you do not know me." In Mark, Jesus' words are different: "Before the rooster crows two times tonight, you will say three times that you do not know me." In most languages it is necessary to change the rooster to "a rooster," since no particular rooster has been identified in the context. It may also be necessary to suggest crowing in the morning, for example, "before a rooster crows tomorrow morning."

A literal translation of you will say three times may be understood as indicating a repetition of the same statement to a single person. In reality, it is a prediction of what Peter will say on three different occasions to different people. Therefore, it may be necessary to say "will say on three occasions" or "will say to different people on three different occasions."

CHAPTER 14

TEV   (14.1-8)   RSV

JESUS THE WAY TO THE FATHER

14 "Do not be worried and upset," Jesus told them. "Believe*a* in God and believe also in me. 2 There are many rooms in my Father's house, and I am going to prepare a place for you. I would not tell you this if it were not so.*b* 3 And after I go and prepare a place for you, I will come back and take you to myself, so that you will be where I am. 4 You know the way that leads to the place where I am going."

5 Thomas said to him, "Lord, we do not know where you are going; so how can we know the way to get there?"

6 Jesus answered him, "I am the way, the truth, and the life; no one goes to the Father except by me. 7 Now that you have known me," he said to them, "you will know*c* my Father also, and from now on you do know him and you have seen him."

8 Philip said to him, "Lord, show us the Father; that is all we need."

*a*Believe; *or* You believe.

*b*There are...were not so; *or* There are many rooms in my Father's house; if it were not so, would I tell you that I am going to prepare a place for you?

*c*Now that you have known me...you will know; *some manuscripts have* If you had known me...you would know.

14 "Let not your hearts be troubled; believe*e* in God, believe also in me. 2 In my Father's house are many rooms; if it were not so, would I have told you that I go to prepare a place for you? 3 And when I go and prepare a place for you, I will come again and will take you to myself, that where I am you may be also. 4 And you know the way where I am going."*f* 5 Thomas said to him, "Lord, we do not know where you are going; how can we know the way?" 6 Jesus said to him, "I am the way, and the truth, and the life; no one comes to the Father, but by me. 7 If you had known me, you would have known my Father also; henceforth you know him and have seen him."

8 Philip said to him, "Lord, show us the Father, and we shall be satisfied."

*e*Or *you believe*

*f*Other ancient authorities read *where I am going you know, and the way you know*

Chapter 14 begins Jesus' final discourse to his disciples, a discourse which continues through Chapter 17. A problem arises from the content of 14.30-31, which sounds as if they are the closing words of the discourse. On the basis of this and other observations, some commentators suggest various rearrangements of these chapters. Among the major translations, however, only Mft makes use of any of the displacement theories. His rearrangement (13.1-31a; 15.1-27; 16.1-33; 13.31b-38; 14.1-31; 17.1-26) follows a very widely accepted theory. To rearrange the material in this order seems to resolve the problem mentioned, as well as the problems raised by 13.36 and 16.5. But there is no textual evidence to support any of the theories of displacement, and one may question whether any of the suggested reorderings of the text make significant improvements.

Some commentators try to overcome the difficulty of 14.30-31 by spiritualizing the words "Come, let us go from this place." Rather than take these words in the literal and natural sense of rising from the supper table and leaving the house, they understand them as an appeal either to go to the Father or to go forward to death and resurrection. Both these interpretations are merely fanciful attempts to overcome the difficulty raised by the literal understanding of Jesus' words.

A more logical solution is that Chapter 14 and Chapters 15-17 contain alternative versions of Jesus' last discourse to his disciples, and that the author or final editor of the Gospel, not wanting to tamper with the ending of Chapter 14, included it along with the account of Chapters 15-17. It has long been recognized that the Gospel originally ended with 20.30-31, and that Chapter 21 was added to the original Gospel. So it is not impossible that we have something similar in this final discourse: namely, one account that ends at 14.31, and a second account to be found in Chapters 15-17. This is also the best way to explain the large number of parallels between Chapters 14 and 15-16.

Chapter 14 itself falls naturally into two major divisions. In TEV they are entitled Jesus the Way to the Father (verses 1-14) and The Promise of the Holy Spirit (verses 15-31). The first division may be subdivided as follows: Verses 1-4 deal with the theme of Jesus' departure to the Father and of his return to his disciples. Verse 5 serves as a transition, in which Thomas' misunderstanding serves as a means of furthering the discourse. On the basis of Thomas' question, Jesus affirms that he is the way to the Father (verses 6-7). Verse 8 serves as a further transition by means of Philip's question, which also presupposes a misunderstanding. Verses 9-11 carry further the implications that Jesus is the way to the Father. Finally, verses 12-14 are concerned with the theme of the power of belief in Jesus.

The section heading Jesus the Way to the Father may present a rather difficult apposition. Some translators would prefer such a section heading as "How to go to the Father." In several translations this section is identified by the phrase "The way, the truth, and the life" (taken directly from verse 6).

14.1   "Do not be worried and upset," Jesus told them. "Believe^a in God and believe also in me.

^{a}Believe; *or* You believe.

In 13.38 Jesus was addressing Peter; in 14.1 he is addressing all his disciples. The Greek of 14.1 clearly indicates this shift: "Do not let your (plural) heart be troubled." Most translators indicate the change

in audience simply by rendering "heart" as "hearts" (NAB "Do not let
your hearts be troubled"). TEV marks the change explicitly by including
the information Jesus told them, and GeCL by "Then Jesus said to them
all." JB calls attention to the transition in a footnote. However, this
kind of transition is better made explicit in the text, for otherwise
the persons who hear the passage read may not correctly identify the
persons addressed. Futhermore, many readers probably do not read the
footnotes. Then, too, since Chapter 14 is frequently read as a unit,
it is important to indicate the persons to whom Jesus is speaking at the
very outset of the chapter. It may be useful to indicate this fact quite
clearly by saying "Jesus told his disciples."

On the use of the phrase be worried and upset, see the comments
at 11.33.

In both of its occurrences the verb believe may be either imperative
or indicative, since the Greek forms are the same. TEV, together with
most translations, takes both of them as imperatives (Believe in God,
and believe also in me); TEV alternative reading translates the first
as indicative and the second as imperative ("You believe in God, believe
also in me"). A third possible combination would be to render them both
as indicatives: "You believe in God, and you also believe in me." In favor of the choice accepted by TEV is the observation that the first verb
in this verse (Do not be worried and upset) is a specifically imperative
form in Greek. In this context Believe in me must be understood in the
sense of "put your confidence in me" or "trust in me" or "trust yourself
to me."

14.2   There are many rooms in my Father's house,
        and I am going to prepare a place for you. I
        would not tell you this if it were not so.[b]

        [b]There are...were not so; *or* There are many
         rooms in my Father's house; if it were not
         so, would I tell you that I am going to
         prepare a place for you?

There are many rooms in my Father's house represents a more natural
reordering in English of the Greek text, which reads literally "In my
Father's house there are many rooms." The word translated rooms (Gdsp,
Phps, JB; "dwelling-places" NEB, NAB; "abodes" Mft) has occasioned some
difficulty. The King James "mansions" comes originally from Tyndales's
translation, at which time the word "mansion" merely signified a dwelling, and not necessarily a large and luxurious one, as in contemporary
English. Some commentators take the Greek word used here (monē) to mean
"stopping place" or "resting place." This theory suggests that heaven is
a place of progression, with many resting places or stopping places along
the way. It seems better, however, to seek the meaning of this word in
another direction, interpreting it in light of the Greek verb (menō),
meaning "to remain," and so suggesting a permanent dwelling place. The
verb "to remain" plays a significant role in John's Gospel, and it is
natural to see a connection between the noun monē and the verb menō,
since both words come from the same stem. Moreover, the presupposition

that it means a permanent dwelling place is supported by the indications
in Jewish literature of a belief that heaven has many dwelling places.
Finally, this same noun is used in verse 23 in the clause translated
"My Father and I will come to him and live with him," which more literally reads "We will come to him and make our home (monē) with him" (RSV).
Hence, the word is best taken in a generic sense, meaning "a place of
dwelling"; since this dwelling is obviously one place within the whole
(house), the most natural English equivalent is "room."

My Father's house is best taken as a phrase descriptive of heaven
as a place having many rooms (that is, room enough for all).

I am going to prepare a place for you should be translated in a
rather general manner. If it is related specifically to rooms, it will
be possible to say "I'm going to prepare rooms for you" or "...get
rooms ready for you" or "...fix up rooms for you." At the same time,
one would not wish to use a term which would suggest that the rooms
were in need of repair and that Jesus had to fix them up to make them
habitable.

In Greek if it were not so immediately precedes the clause translated I would not have told you by TEV. Since Greek manuscripts have no
punctuation, it is possible to take this clause either as a declaration
(TEV I would not have told you) or as a question (RSV "would I have told
you...?"), expecting the answer "No." This of TEV represents "that I go
to prepare a place for you" (RSV), which in Greek follows I would not
have told you.

The clause I am going to prepare a place for you is immediately
preceded by a conjunction in Greek (hoti) which may signal either direct
discourse ("that") or a causual relation "since." In the Greek structure
this preposition may be omitted as superfluous, if it is understood to
mean "that," and so it is not found in some manuscripts. If one follows
the manuscripts which omit the conjunction, it is possible to translate
as JB: "if there were not, I should have told you. I am going now to
prepare a place for you."

The UBS Committee on the Greek text decided in favor of the manuscripts that include "that" or "because" (hoti), assuming that its
omission in some manuscripts may be explained as some scribe's attempt
to simplify the text by omitting a word which he considered unnecessary.
The choice between the meaning of "that" or "because" is more difficult.
Most translations obviously prefer to take the word in the sense of "that"
(RSV, for example). But the difficulty with this rendering is that, so
far in the discourse, Jesus has not told his disciples that he is going
to prepare a place for them. If the solution of TEV and GeCL is followed,
this problem is overcome. By taking "that" as a means of introducing the
content of what follows, and by referring the clause if it were not so
both forward and backward, a meaning is arrived at that makes good sense,
and is possible on the basis of the Greek text.

Many languages require an inversion of the conditional sentence to
read "If this were not so, I would not have told you this." However,
there are special difficulties in some languages with a condition contrary to fact in the present time; in these languages it may be necessary
to translate, for example, "If this was not the case (but it is), I would
not tell you this (but I am telling you this)."

14.3   And after I go and prepare a place for you,
          I will come back and take you to myself, so
          that you will be where I am.

     And after appears as "and if" in most translations. However, in
such a context the Greek particle (ean) translated "if" actually carries
the meaning "when," and TEV expresses this by translating and after. In
some languages the idea may be expressed more satisfactorily as cause
or reason in some languages, for example, "Since I am going and preparing
a place for you, I will come back..."
     In Greek the verb will come is a present tense which carries a
future force. John has chosen the present (literally "I am coming") to
emphasize the certainty of Jesus' return for his disciples.
     Take you to myself (NEB "receive you to myself"; NAB "take you with
me"; Mft "take you to be with me") is expressed in various ways, but
with essentially the same meaning in all translations. Take you to myself
may be expressed in some languages by means of a causative, for example,
"I will cause you to remain with me." This rendering fits well with the
clause that follows.
     In the statement so that you will be where I am, the pronouns you
and I are emphatic. In some languages a general term of "being," cannot
be used. One must choose an expression which more specifically indicates
existence, for example, "so that you will exist where I exist." This
meaning is often expressed in a more concrete form, for example, "so
that you will live where I will live" or even "so that you will sit
where I sit." (In some languages the verb "sit" is a general designation
for existence in a place.)

14.4   You know the way that leads to the place where
          I am going."

     You know the way that leads to the place where I am going is more
literally "and where I am going you know the way." Since the phrase that
John uses is difficult in Greek, and since Thomas in verse 5 distinguishes
between where Jesus is going and the way to get there, some ancient scribes
expanded the Greek text to read "You know where I am going and you know
the way" (NEB alternative reading). However, this reading is obviously an
attempt to make the text read more smoothly, and it is not followed by
most modern translations.

14.5   Thomas said to him, "Lord, we do not know
          where you are going; so how can we know the
          way to get there?"

     In 11.16 and 20.24 Thomas is further qualified as "the one called
the twin."
     The way to get there (GeCL "the way there") is literally "the way";
Phps translates "what road you're going to take." In some languages the
way to get there is expressed as "the road that leads there" or "the
path by which one goes in order to arrive there" or "the road which one
must follow in order to go there."

14.6   Jesus answered him, "I am the way, the
truth, and the life; no one goes to the Father
except by me.

I am the way, the truth, and the life (so most translations) is a
fairly literal translation of the Greek text. Of the major modern language translations, only GeCL has a dynamic equivalent: "I am the way,
and I am also the goal, since in me you have the truth and the life."
Even this restructuring is rather ambiguous for the average reader. What
is the relation between the words way, truth, and life? In the present
context Jesus as "the way" is the primary focus, and "truth" and "life"
are somehow related to Jesus as "the way." Thus there are two possible
interpretations: (1) The emphasis may be on the goal to which the way
leads (note GeCL). If this exegesis is followed, one may translate "I
am the way that leads to the truth and to life"; or, expressed more
fully, "I am the way that leads to the truth (about God) and to the life
(that God gives)." (2) However, the emphasis may be on the way itself.
If this exegesis is followed, "truth" and "life" must be taken as qualifiers of "way," which is primary in the context. One may then render
"I am the true way, the way that gives people life." Or, more fully, "I
am the way that reveals the truth (about God) and gives life (to people)."
In effect, the two possible interpretations are close in meaning, and it
is difficult to argue for one against the other. However, the context
would seem to favor the second.

For a discussion of truth, see 1.14; for life, see 1.4; and for as
I am, see 4.26.

That the way is in primary focus in this passage is indicated by
the words of Jesus in the second half of this verse: no one goes to the
Father except by me. That is, the way is in focus, and the Father is
the goal to which it leads. God is the source of all truth and life, and
Jesus leads people to him.

In most languages it is quite possible to speak of Jesus as "a way"
or "a road," in the sense of a means by which a person may arrive at a
particular destination. However, in some languages "way" or "road" does
not have this metaphorical possibility, and one must use a term which
more closely identifies the concept of "means," that is, "I am the means
by which people know the truth about God..." In such cases Jesus' statement could be rendered "I am the one by whom people know the truth about
God and receive the life that God gives" or "...become truly alive" or
even "...have true life."

Rather than employ a negative such as no one followed by an exception such as except by me, it may be better in some languages to make
the entire expression positive and include the concept of totality, for
example, "All people must go to the Father by me" or "I alone am the
one by whom people go to the Father." This relation of Jesus to the
Father as being a "way" or "road" may be rendered in some languages as
"I am the only road that leads to the Father" or "...that leads to my
Father."

14.7   Now that you have known me," he said to them,
"you will know^C my Father also, and from now on
you do know him and you have seen him."

^{C}Now that you have known me...you will know;
some manuscripts have If you had known me...
you would know.

In verse 1 Jesus began by addressing all the disciples, and in
verse 6 he replied to Thomas's question. Now he resumes his address to
the disciples, and TEV marks this fact by the words he said to them
(Anchor "If you men..."), thus removing the ambiguity of the word "you,"
which in English may be either singular or plural.

Now that you have known me,...you will know my Father also follows
the reading chosen by the UBS Committee, which takes the words of Jesus
as a promise. However, if one follows the alternative reading of the UBS
Greek text, the following translation results: "If you really knew me,
you would also know my Father." In this case the text reads as Jesus'
reproach of the disciples because they have not really come to know him.
The UBS Committee believes that the alternative reading developed either
because scribes recalled Jesus' reproach against the unbelieving Jews of
8.19 or because Philip's question and Jesus' answer (verses 8-9) intimated
that the disciples knew neither Jesus nor the Father. The second half of
the verse could also be taken to support the reading of the UBS Greek
text, but it seems doubtful that a positive statement regarding the disciples' faith would have been changed by a scribe to a negative statement; on the contrary, pious scribes generally had a tendency to change
texts in the other direction. The UBS text choice here is rated by the
Committee as "C," indicating considerable doubt.

Now that you have known me may be rendered best in some languages
as a reason followed by a result, for example, "He said to them, 'Since
you have known me, you will know my Father also.'" In this type of context, it is important to select a term for know which will be more meaningful than merely "get acquainted with." In some languages the most appropriate would be "since you have come to know who I really am, you will
therefore know who my Father really is."

From now on refers not to the moment when Jesus is speaking but to
the hour of his passion (see 13.31 and 16.5).

For thoughts similar to those expressed in this verse, see 12.44-45.
It is a recurrent theme of the Fourth Gospel that whoever knows Jesus
knows the Father, and whoever has seen Jesus has seen the Father.

14.8   Philip said to him, "Lord, show us the Father;
that is all we need."

Philip is first mentioned in 1.43. His request (Lord, show us the
Father) shows a misunderstanding, which enables Jesus to give further
and deeper teaching to the disciples. Philip seems to be requesting a
revelation of the Father which can be seen by human eyes, and Jesus, on
the basis of this misunderstanding, is able to develop his teaching further. Show us the Father may be rendered in some languages as "cause us

to see your Father" or "make us to see your Father with our own eyes."

That is all we need is rendered with the meaning "we shall be satisfied" in several translations (RSV; see also JB, Gdsp, Phps). NAB has "that will be enough for us"; NEB "and we ask no more"; and GeCL "we need nothing more."

TEV	(14.9-14)	RSV

9 Jesus answered, "For a long time I have been with you all; yet you do not know me, Philip? Whoever has seen me has seen the Father. Why, then, do you say, 'Show us the Father'? 10 Do you not believe, Philip, that I am in the Father and the Father is in me? The words that I have spoken to you," Jesus said to his disciples, "do not come from me. The Father, who remains in me, does his own work. 11 Believe me when I say that I am in the Father and the Father is in me. If not, believe because of the things I do. 12 I am telling you the truth: whoever believes in me will do what I do--yes, he will do even greater things, because I am going to the Father. 13 And I will do whatever you ask for in my name, so that the Father's glory will be shown through the Son. 14 If you ask me^d for anything in my name, I will do it.

9 Jesus said to him, "Have I been with you so long, and yet you do not know me, Philip? He who has seen me has seen the Father; how can you say, 'Show us the Father'? 10 Do you not believe that I am in the Father and the Father in me? The words that I say to you I do not speak on my own authority; but the Father who dwells in me does his works. 11 Believe me that I am in the Father and the Father in me; or else believe me for the sake of the works themselves.

12 "Truly, truly, I say to you, he who believes in me will also do the works that I do; and greater works than these will he do, because I go to the Father. 13 Whatever you ask in my name, I will do it, that the Father may be glorified in the Son; 14 if you ask^g anything in my name, I will do it.

^{g}Other ancient authorities add me

^{d}*Some manuscripts do not have* me.

14.9   Jesus answered, "For a long time I have been with you all; yet you do not know me, Philip? Whoever has seen me has seen the Father. Why, then, do you say, 'Show us the Father'?

With you all is rendered "with you" by most translators. In Greek the you in this phrase is plural, but in English there is no way to mark the difference between the plural (with you) and the singular (yet you do not know me) apart from the addition of all to the plural, as in TEV. It may be useful in some languages to indicate the distinction by rendering "I have been with all of you for a long time. How is it then, Philip, that you do not know me?" or "...really know who I am."

Whoever has seen me is literally "the one who has seen me," a construction similar to whoever believes in me of 12.44, where a Greek participle is used as the equivalent of an indefinite relative pronoun in English. The indefinite relative clause Whoever has seen me may be interpreted as a conditional, "if anyone has seen me," and the second part of this sentence may then be rendered "he has seen my Father."

Philip has obviously misunderstood both the person of Jesus and his mission in coming into the world. Jesus' answer (Whoever has seen me has seen the Father) at once affirms that he is the supreme revelation of God.

Why, then, do you say...? is more literally "how are you saying...?" ("how do you say...?" of most translations). Either expresses accurately the meaning of the Greek.

14.10 Do you not believe, Philip, that I am in the Father and the Father is in me? The words that I have spoken to you," Jesus said to his disciples, "do not come from me. The Father, who remains in me, does his own work.

To indicate that the first you of this verse is singular in the Greek text, TEV introduces the noun of address, Philip.

For a discussion of I am in the Father and the Father is in me see 10.38. The meaning may be expressed by translating "I am one with the Father, and the Father is one with me." In 10.38 GeCL has "I live in the Father, and the Father lives in me," while here it has "that you meet the Father in me." GeCL's rendering is very good in 10.38, but in the present passage it lacks the idea of the reciprocal relationship and focuses attention on another aspect which is not primary. In some languages the relationship between the Father and Jesus may be expressed as "my Father is united with me, and I am united with my Father" or "my Father and I are just as though we were one."

You in I have spoken to you is plural, and TEV indicates this by adding Jesus said to his disciples. Here again it is necessary to mark explicitly the change from singular to plural, since in English you may be either. Anchor translates you as "you men."

Do not come from me is literally "not from myself" (see 7.17) and is emphatic in the Greek sentence structure. It may be difficult in some languages to speak of words coming from a person, but the idea may be expressed as "The words that I have spoken to you, these are not what I myself have just thought" or "...they do not just come from my mind" or "these are not just my thoughts."

The Father, who remains in me, does his own work is a fairly literal rendering of the Greek text. These words indicate that Jesus' miracles were not accomplished by his own power or initiative (see 8.28); rather, they reveal his union with the Father. A number of translators attempt a dynamic translation: NEB has "it is the Father who dwells in me doing his own work"; NAB "it is the Father who lives in me accomplishing his works"; Mft "it is the Father who remains ever in me, who is performing his own deeds"; Gdsp "but the Father who is united with me is doing these things himself."

However, it may be difficult to speak of the Father "doing his own work." The reference is obviously very broad, for it includes both miracles and sayings. Sometimes one can employ such an expression as "my Father who remains in me causes these happenings." But in other instances a more satisfactory rendering may be "...does what he decides to do." Such a rendering indicates clearly that the agency and the initiative rest with God.

<u>14.11</u>   Believe me when I say that I am in the
      Father and the Father is in me. If not,
      believe because of the things I do.

<u>Believe me</u> does not mean "put your faith in me," but "believe what I am going to say to you" (Note NEB "Believe me when I say that..."; and JB "You must believe me when I say...").

The rendering of <u>I am in the Father and the Father is in me</u> should reflect the rendering of this same expression in verse 10.

<u>Believe because of the things I do</u> is literally "believe because of the works themselves." Some Greek manuscripts supply "me" after <u>believe</u>, as in the first part of this verse. The Greek manuscript evidence is against the inclusion of "me" here, but it may be required translationally. Several translations (for example, RSV, Phps, GeCL) do include "me," but probably on translational grounds. Note, for example, GeCL "Believe me: the Father and I are one. If you will not believe because of my word, then believe me because of these deeds." JB includes the pronoun "it" as the object of "believe," accomplishing essentially the same purpose: "believe it on the evidence of this work, if for no other reason."("It" refers to the statement "that I am in the Father and the Father is in me.") NEB supplies an object for "believe" by rendering "or else accept the evidence of the deeds themselves." Either meaning, "believe me when I say" or "believe what I say," is faithful to the context. The point is that the verse should not be so translated as to indicate that "believe" here refers to belief in Jesus in the ordinary sense of the word. The appeal is to believe the truth of what he says, best expressed in many languages by "believe me when I say."

The ellipsis in the condition <u>If not</u> must often be filled out, for example, "If you do not believe what I say" or "If you do not believe just because of what I say." This second rendering fits well with the following clause, "believe because of what I have done" or even "...what my Father has done through me."

<u>14.12</u>   I am telling you the truth: whoever believes
      in me will do what I do--yes, he will do even
      greater things, because I am going to the
      Father.

<u>I am telling you the truth</u> is the same formula first used in 1.51.
<u>Whoever believes</u> translates a Greek participial phrase (literally "the one believing"), similar in structure to <u>whoever has seen me</u> of verse 9. Here <u>believes in me</u> does refer to belief in Jesus.

<u>What things I do</u> refers to Jesus' miracles, and therefore one can

translate "will perform the kinds of miracles that I have performed."
It may be necessary to introduce such an expression as "kinds of" in
order to indicate clearly that the followers of Jesus are not expected
to duplicate the precise miracles performed by Jesus. Note, however,
that in using such a term as "miracles," it is important to avoid the
implication that they are merely spectacular instances of healing or the
like. It may be more satisfactory to use such an expression as "wonderful
things" or "surprising accomplishments."

Yes, he will do even greater things is literally "and greater than
these he will do." TEV introduces yes to stress the intended contrast;
JB accomplishes it by the inclusion of "even" ("he will perform even
greater works"). The reference to "greater works" does not mean that
the disciples will perform more outstanding miracles than Jesus did.
Their works will be greater because they will not have the geographical
and temporal limitations that have been imposed upon the historical Jesus.
Jesus' deeds were limited to the particular place where he has been at a
given time; but when he goes to the Father, his help will be available to
the disciples in all parts of the world and at all times. In that sense
their works will be "greater" than those that the historical Jesus was
able to perform during his earthly life. Specifically, the greater things
probably refers to the gathering in of converts from all the world. In
any case the reference is not limited to miracles, and the translator
must be careful that his translation does not carry this implication.

Because I am going to the Father gives the reason why the disciples
will be able to do even greater works than Jesus himself. Here as elsewhere, it may be necessary to say "my Father" rather than "the Father."
Furthermore, for the verb going it may be essential to employ a somewhat
expanded phrase to indicate that Jesus expected to remain with the Father,
for example, "I am going to remain with my Father." Otherwise, a reader
might assume from a literal translation that Jesus was only going to see
his Father for a brief period and would then return.

14.13   And I will do whatever you ask for in my
     name, so that the Father's glory will be
     shown through the Son.

This verse does not indicate to whom the prayer is to be addressed,
whether to the Father or to the Son, though in 15.16 and 16.23 the prayer
is directed to the Father. It is important to translate in my name in
such a manner as to avoid the possibility of interpreting the phrase as
a magical formula to be attached to the end of a prayer.

In my name is always difficult to translate, and so it will be helpful to discuss this phrase in more detail. As was indicated in 1.12, in
biblical thought the "name" of a person represents in some sense the person himself, and that is the basic clue to understanding the phrase in my
name. In this Gospel the phrase occurs in several connections:

(1) Ask for in my name (14.13,14; 15.16; 16.23,24,26) This phrase,
always related to a prayer context, is generally translated literally,
perhaps due to the influence of Christian prayer practice. Gdsp, one of
the few to attempt a dynamic equivalent, uses "as my followers," which
suits the context in each instance. It is based upon the argument that

in my name is equivalent to "because of your relation to me" or "because you are mine." The meaning "on my authority" would also be satisfactory in each of these contexts.

(2) Give you in my name (16.23). In the discussion of 16.23 it will be shown that the phrase in my name can be taken either with the verb "ask" or with the verb "give." Gdsp's "as my followers" is suitable for either interpretation, and that is why this verse is included under the previous heading.

(3) Keep them safe by the power of your name (17.11) is literally "Keep them (safe) by (Greek en) your name." (See also 17.12.) Most translations are similar to TEV (see comments at 17.11). A suggested translation may be "Keep them safe by your own power."

(4) That through your faith in him you may have life (20.31, literally "that believing you may have life in his name") is translated "and through believing you may have life as his followers" by Gdsp. GeCL is similar to TEV: "If you believe in him, you have life through him." See also the related passages at 1.12; 2.23; 3.18.

(5) With/by my Father's authority (5.43; 10.25) is literally "in the name of my Father" (see also 12.13 in the name of the Lord). In each of these three passages the name of the Father/Lord represents his authority, and TEV makes this meaning explicit in the two earlier passages. Most translations render 12.13 literally (but see GeCL "Praise God! Long live the one who comes in his behalf!" and Living Bible "Hail to God's Ambassador!"). In 12.13 the meaning would also seem to be "the one who comes with the Lord's authority" or "the one whom the Lord has sent."

(6) Because you are mine is the meaning of the related phrase "because of my name" in 15.21. Gdsp translates "on my account"; GeCL "because you acknowledge me"; and Living Bible "because you belong to me."

(7) Send in my name (14.26). Here the phrase may be taken in any of several ways, all of which suit the context: (a) "because you belong to me"; (b) "because I ask him"; (c) "with my authority"; or (d) "in my place" (Gdsp, Barclay). It is almost impossible to decide which alternative is most preferable.

That Jesus is not referring to irresponsible prayer in the expression whatever you ask is indicated by the goal of the prayer: so that the Father's glory will be shown through the Son. The glory of the father is the one purpose which Jesus has in responding to the requests of those who pray. Most translators render this purpose clause "so that the Father will be glorified in the Son." However, here as elsewhere "to be glorified" refers to a visible manifestation of the divine presence, and TEV makes this explicit in its rendering. GeCL renders "so shall the glory of the Father be revealed through the Son."

In some languages the passive expression so that the Father's glory will be shown through the Son must be made active. This means that the Son becomes the agent who shows the Father's glory. It may be necessary in some languages to render the Father's glory "how glorious the Father is" or "how wonderful the Father is," for example, "so that the Son may cause people to see how wonderful the Father is." However, in some instances it may be necessary for Jesus to identify himself in the first person and to indicate clearly his relationship to the Father, for example, "so that I may cause people to see how wonderful my Father is." Since the relationship of Jesus to the Father is clearly indicated by the possessive pronoun "my," it is not necessary to introduce a literal equivalent of "Son."

14.14   If you ask me^d for anything in my name, I will
         do it."

         ^{d}*Some manuscripts do not have* me.

This verse is entirely omitted by some Greek manuscripts, though the evidence favors its inclusion. The reason for its omission may have been accidental, or it may have been deliberately omitted by some scribe to avoid contradiction with 16.23. More probably it was omitted because it seemed redundant after verse 13.

Some manuscripts do not have me in the phrase If you ask me. However, this information should be included for translational reasons. The Father could be assumed as the one to whom the prayer is directed; but since it is Jesus who will answer the prayer, it is better understood as directed to him.

The translation of in my name can be handled here in the way suggested for verse 13, for example, "if you ask me for anything because you are my followers" or "...because you belong to me."

TEV   (14.15-17)   RSV

THE PROMISE OF THE HOLY SPIRIT

15 "If you love me, you will o-   15 "If you love me, you will
bey my commandments. 16 I will ask   keep my commandments. 16 And I
the Father, and he will give you   will pray the Father, and he will
another Helper, who will stay with   give you another Counselor, to be
you forever. 17 He is the Spirit,   with you for ever, 17 even the
who reveals the truth about God.   Spirit of truth, whom the world
The world cannot receive him, be-   cannot receive, because it neither
cause it cannot see him or know him.   sees him nor knows him; you know
But you know him, because he remains   him, for he dwells with you, and
with you and is^e in you.   will be in you.

^{e}is; *some manuscripts have* will be.

Even though TEV entitles 14.15-31 The Promise of the Holy Spirit, it is the theme of love and obedience that binds together verses 15-24. It opens with If you love me, you will obey my commandments and closes with Whoever does not love me does not obey my words (verse 24). To the disciples who love Jesus and are obedient to him he promises another Helper...who reveals the truth about God (verses 16-17). Jesus also promises to return and be with his disciples if they are obedient to him (verses 18-21).

Verse 22 is best taken as transitional, serving to further Jesus' teaching by means of a question raised on the basis of a misunderstanding (see verses 5 and 8). The question raised by Judas is not answered

[464]

directly, but it leads to the affirmation that Jesus will come with the Father to those who love him and are obedient to him (verses 23-24). It is the third promise that Jesus makes in this passage. Here also the demands of love and obedience are prerequisite for the coming of the Father, as they were for the coming of the Spirit. To those disciples who respond in love and obedience is given the promise that God the Father will live in them, just as they were promised that the Spirit and Jesus would live in them. Verse 24 emphasizes a recurring theme of the Gospel: the message of Jesus is in reality the message of God, and the reason why the world cannot see God is that it refuses to love Jesus and to obey his message.

Verses 25-27 form the conclusion to this part of the discourse. Although Jesus himself will no longer be physically present with the disciples, the Helper...the Holy Spirit whom the Father will send in his name, will teach them everything they need to know (verses 25-26). Moreover, Jesus leaves his peace with them. This peace will keep them from being worried and upset or afraid in their conflict with the world (verse 27). They should be happy that Jesus is returning to the Father, because this return will lead to Jesus' exaltation, to the revelation that the ruler of this world has no power over him, and to the recognition that his love for the Father is absolute (verses 28-31).

In place of The Promise of the Holy Spirit (which may be rendered "Jesus promises the Holy Spirit"), one may employ as a section heading "Love and obey" or "Loving Jesus and obeying his commandments" or "... what he has commanded."

14.15   "If you love me, you will obey my command-
          ments.

TEV and most other modern translations follow the Greek manuscripts which have the future tense: You will obey my commandments. There is also manuscript evidence in support of an imperative ("obey my commandments"), as well as a subjunctive (NAB "If you love me and obey the command I give you, I will ask the Father..."). The UBS Committee prefers the future tense, though judging its choice a "C" decision, indicating considerable doubt whether the superior reading is to be found in the text or in the apparatus.

The word translated obey in TEV technically means "to keep," but in this context the meaning "to obey" is obvious. This same expression appears twice in 15.10 (If you obey my commands), as well as in 1 John 2.3, 4; 3.22,24; 5.3. It is also the phrase used of obedience to the Ten Commandments in Matthew 19.17. In verses 15 and 21 the reference is to obeying commandments, while in verses 23 and 24 (so also 8.51 and 15.20) it refers to obeying Jesus' teaching (literally "word" or "words"). In verse 24 both the singular "word" and the plural "words" occur, without any apparent distinction in meaning. So there is no real difference between "commandments," "word," and "words." The equation of "word" and "commandment" comes from the Old Testament, where the Ten Commandments are referred to as "the words" of God (see, for example, Deut 5.5). In the present context, the "commandments" of Jesus, the "words" of Jesus, and the "word" of Jesus are all references to the command of love.

[465]

14.15

In some languages my commandments is rendered simply "what I have commanded you to do" or "what I have told you you should do." Thus the clause you will obey my commandments may be rendered "you will do what I have told you to do." Some languages make a clear distinction between two ways of rendering obey. One verb is used in connection with actions, and another is used in connection with persons. Therefore, obey my commandments may be rendered "do what I told you to do" while "obey me" would be rendered by a term indicating more specifically the attitude of obedience to a person with superior authority.

14.16   I will ask the Father, and he will give you
         another Helper, who will stay with you forever.

In translating the verb ask, it is important to distinguish clearly between requests for information and requests for benefits. The latter is clearly the meaning in this particular context; Jesus promises "to ask for something" rather than "to inquire of" or "to ask a question about."

One result of the disciples' love for Jesus will be their obedience to his commandments, and the other will be his sending them another Helper. It should be noticed that John speaks of the coming of the Helper in several different ways, though there is no real distinction to be made between them. Here the Helper is "given" by the Father at the request of the Son, while in verse 26 the Father will "send" him "in the name" of the Son. In 15.26 (see also 16.7) the Helper is "sent" from the Father by the Son.

The rendering another Helper is the form accepted by most translations. However, it is possible to punctuate this sequence by putting a comma after another, with the resultant meaning "another person to be a Helper." Evidently John considers Jesus a "Helper" whose work will be continued by the one who will be sent.

TEV's rendering Helper translates the Greek work paraklētos; Mft and Gdsp also use this terminology. It also seems to be essentially the meaning of Zür ("Beistand"). "Comforter" is the rendering of the King James Bible (see also Luther Revised "Truster"; and Segond "Consolateur"). However, the Spirit's role is never described as that of "consoling" or "comforting" the disciples, whereas there is support for the meaning of Helper in its every occurrence.

NEB and JB render paraklētos as "Advocate," and this meaning is perhaps also intended by Phps ("someone else to stand by you") and GeCL ("Stellvertreter" = "representative"). These interpretations take the Greek word etymologically, either in the generic sense of "one called alongside to help" or in the technical sense of "defense attorney." Although Matthew 10.20 and Acts 6.10 suggest that the Holy Spirit stands as a defender of the disciples when they are placed on trial, this is not the picture given in the Gospel of John. According to John, the Holy Spirit convicts the world of sin, but there is no intimation that he comes to defend the disciples. In Jewish court procedure no one really played the role of defense attorney. The judge made the interrogation, and those who supported the defense were primarily witnesses. So it is difficult to see how the technical sense of "advocate" or "defense attorney" can be supported for this use in the Gospel of John.

NAB recognizes the difficulty of translating paraklētos, and so settles for a transliteration ("Paraclete"). In their footnote the translators point out that none of the terms generally used (such as "defense attorney," "spokesman," or "intercessor") precisely fits the use in John. According to this Gospel, the Spirit is a teacher, a witness to Jesus, and a prosecutor of the world. Since these elements cannot all be gathered into any one term, the translators settle for a transliteration, which amounts to a zero term for most readers. The translator will probably not be fully satisfied with any term he chooses to render the Greek word. However, on the whole, it seems best to use a generic term such as Helper, rather than a specific term defining any one of the particular functions. But if one chooses to translate Helper more specifically the various contexts will assist in defining in what ways the Holy Spirit "helps."

In some languages the concept of Helper may be expressed quite idiomatically. For example, in one language in Central Africa a helper is "one who falls down beside another." This is a figurative expression, relating to circumstances in which one person finds another collapsed from exhaustion along the pathway. The individual who "falls down beside him" is one who stoops down, picks ups the exhausted individual, and helps him reach his destination.

Who will stay with you forever is literally "in order that he might be with you into the age." "Age" (Greek aiōn) is an expression for endless future time, and so "into the age" means "to eternity" or "eternally." In some languages who will stay with you forever may be expressed as "who will remain with you always." In other languages it is more natural to employ a negative, for example, "in order that he will never leave you."

14.17   He is the Spirit, who reveals the truth about
         God. The world cannot receive him, because it
         cannot see him or know him. But you know him,
         because he remains with you and is[e] in you.

[e]is; *some manuscripts have* will be.

He is the Spirit who reveals the truth about God is literally "the Spirit of truth." See Appendix II. In some languages the expression must be rendered "the Spirit that shows people what is true about God." However in other languages it is better to say simply "...what God is really like" or "...who God really is."

The world (see 1.10) in this context must be understood as "the people of the world," essentially equivalent to "unbelievers." The term is based upon a contrast between people who are related only to the system of the world and those whose faith and confidence is in God, who is in heaven.

In this particular context the translation of cannot receive him presents a problem. It may be necessary to employ a term which is not applicable to the reception of things, because receiving the Spirit would mean not only welcoming the Spirit into one's own life, but submitting to the Spirit's control over one. An equivalent in many languages is "cannot receive him into their hearts" or "cannot accept him as their helper."

In this verse the pronouns referring to the Spirit are actually neuter in Greek. This is because the Greek term for Spirit (pneuma) is neuter, although masculine pronouns are used elsewhere in reference to the Spirit (note 15.26; 16.7,8,13,14). If there is a choice in the receptor language between impersonal (neuter) and personal pronouns, it is better to choose personal pronouns, since in John's Gospel the Spirit has a very personal role. In 4.22 the pronouns which TEV renders whom are actually neuter in Greek, but the reference is obviously to a personal deity. In 1 John 1.1 the pronouns are also neuter, but since the reference is to Jesus Christ, they are better rendered as personal rather than impersonal pronouns.

In the phrase you know him, the pronoun you is emphatic.

There is some question regarding the tense of the verb rendered is in TEV. Some translations follow Greek manuscripts which have the present tense (TEV, Anchor, JB, Gdsp, NEB). Others follow those manuscripts which have the future tense "will be" or "will live" (NAB, GeCL, Phps, RSV, Mft). As is easily seen in this sampling of translations, there is a considerable difference of opinion regarding the original text here. JB and NEB each have footnotes indicating the possibility of the future tense, even though the translators prefer the present tense for their rendering. The UBS Committee favors the future tense, though rating its choice a "D" decision, indicating a very high degree of doubt regarding the original text. For some languages it seems almost essential to employ a future tense since, at least in the formal sense, the Holy Spirit had not as yet been given. He had simply been promised to his disciples. Accordingly, in some languages, a future form may be required by the context.

TEV	(14.18-24)	RSV

18 "When I go, you will not be left all alone; I will come back to you. 19 In a little while the world will see me no more, but you will see me; and because I live, you also will live. 20 When that day comes, you will know that I am in my Father and that you are in me, just as I am in you.

21 "Whoever accepts my commandments and obeys them is the one who loves me. My Father will love whoever loves me; I too will love him and reveal myself to him."

22 Judas (not Judas Iscariot) said, "Lord, how can it be that you will reveal yourself to us and not to the world?"

23 Jesus answered him, "Whoever

18 "I will not leave you desolate; I will come to you. 19 Yet a little while, and the world will see me no more, but you will see me; because I live, you will live also. 20 In that day you will know that I am in my Father, and you in me, and I in you. 21 He who has my commandments and keeps them, he it is who loves me; and he who loves me will be loved by my Father, and I will love him and manifest myself to him." 22 Judas (not Iscariot) said to him, "Lord, how is it that you will manifest yourself to us, and not to the world?" 23 Jesus answered him, "If a man loves me, he will keep my word, and my Father will love him, and we will come to him

loves me will obey my teaching. My Father will love him, and my Father and I will come to him and live with him. 24 Whoever does not love me does not obey my teaching. And the teaching you have heard is not mine, but comes from the Father, who sent me.

and make our home with him. 24 He who does not love me does not keep my words; and the word which you hear is not mine but the Father's who sent me.

14.18   "When I go, you will not be left all alone;
          I will come back to you.

     Alone is literally "orphans" (JB), but the more general meaning of "one left without anyone to care for him" is perhaps better in the context. The disciples of Socrates were said to have been left "orphans" at his death, and this term was also used in reference to disciples whose rabbi had died. Most translators choose a generic meaning, rather than the specific meaning of "orphan." Phps renders "alone in the world"; NEB "bereft"; Mft "forlorn"; Gdsp "friendless." One might also translate "helpless" or "without anyone to help you."
     I will come back to you (NEB "I am coming back to you") is literally "I am coming to you." In 14.3 the same verb is used, but with the addition of the adverb "again" (= back). The time reference may be either the resurrection appearances or Jesus' return in the person of the Holy Spirit, and both find support from the context. John has quite likely intentionally chosen vague language, and the translator should, if possible, avoid making the time reference explicit. However, in some languages one is forced to indicate a specific temporal reference by the selection of the verb tense. Under such circumstances it is probably best to use a tense applicable to the resurrection, since this would at least be the first fulfillment of Jesus' promise.

14.19   In a little while the world will see me no
          more, but you will see me; and because I
          live, you also will live.

     TEV's In a little while is also the rendering of NEB and Gdsp. NAB translates "a little while now," and Mft "a little while longer." Will see (both occurrences) is actually in the present tense in Greek ("sees"), but the time reference is obviously future, and most translators render it so. The event referred to is, of course, Jesus' death, which was destined to take place within a day's time. Accordingly, in some translations the rendering of the first clause in verse 19 is essentially equivalent to "within a day the world will see me no more" or "...people in the world..." In some languages no more must be rendered "again," for example, "within a day people of the world will not see me again." This rendering provides an excellent basis for the contrast to be found in the following clause: "but you will see me again." It is so important to render this second clause so as to indicate clearly that the disciples were not to continue to see Jesus during the entire time of his death, but rather that they would see him again at the time of his resurrection.

The pronouns you...I...and you are all emphatic.

Because I live, you also will live affirms that Jesus is the source of life for the believers, just as the Father is the source of life for him (see 6.57; because of him I live also). It is possible to punctuate this verse differently and so connect the clause because I live with what precedes (JB "but you will see me, because I live and you will live"; see NAB). Both interpretations are thoroughly Johannine and well suited to the context. JB sees the because clause as a continuation of the thoughts already presented, while TEV takes it as introducing a new idea.

A literal translation of because I live, you also will live might be understood to mean simply "because I have lived, you also will live" or "because I am now alive, you also will live." What seems clear in this context is that it is the continuing life of Jesus which forms a basis for the life of the disciples, that is, the fact that Jesus will himself rise from death. Therefore, one may translate "because I will continue to live, you also will live." However, a literal translation of "continue to live" might be an actual denial of his death, and readers might assume that Jesus only "pretended to die" or "seemed to die." It may, therefore, be necessary to indicate clearly "because I will live again, you also will live."

14.20   When that day comes, you will know that I am in my
        Father and that you are in me, just as I am in you.

When that day comes (literally "on that day") is used three times in John's Gospel (here and 16.23,26). Although in traditional biblical language the term refers to "the last day," the day of God's final intervention, in the present verse it refers to verse 18. Verses 18 and 20 both refer primarily to the time of Jesus' resurrection, but the thought is obviously extended to the permanent presence of the risen Lord with his people everywhere.

It is essential that the time referred to by that day be understood as the time when the disciples would see Jesus again (verse 19) or when Jesus would live again (implied in verse 19). In some languages an equivalent of When that day comes may be "When that happens." It may be made even more specific in some languages as "when I come back to life."

Once again the pronouns you and I are emphatic.

I am in my Father is almost identical with I am in the Father (10.38). Note also 14.10-11 and 17.21-23. GeCL expresses this idea of oneness as "I am inseparably one with the Father. Even so shall you be one with me and I with you." Here, as in the other passages listed, it may be difficult to express the idea of one person being in another person. It may be best expressed as "lives in" or "is united with" or even "is one with." As in many similar contexts, expressions involving one person being in another may be expressed as "just like one"; for example, "I and my Father are just like one person, and you and I are just like one person."

14.21   "Whoever accepts my commandments and obeys them is
        the one who loves me. My Father will love whoever loves
        me; I too will love him and reveal myself to him."

Whoever accepts is actually a participial phrase in Greek (literally "the one having"). On this construction see 12.44. The indefinite relative clause may be treated as a conditional clause, for example, "if anyone accepts my commandments."

Accepts is literally "has." Some commentators understand obeys (literally "keeps") as a step beyond accepting, but this interpretation is doubtful. It is better to take the two verbs as a kind of parallelism, as in NAB "He who obeys the commandments he has from me is the man who loves me." NEB renders "The man who has received my commands and obeys them..." It is very difficult in some languages to make a distinction between "accepting" and "obeying" commandments. Some translators try to render accepts my commandments as equivalent to "acknowledges my commandments" or "recognizes my commandments," as if there were two stages involved in a person's relation to the commandments of Jesus. This interpretation, however, does not carry the meaning of this passage; therefore it may be better to translate "whoever obeys my commandments" or "whoever does what I have commanded him to do."

My Father will love whoever loves me is literally "the one who loves me will be loved by my Father." TEV inverts the order of the Greek, changing the passive into an active construction, and making my Father, the agent of the passive verb, into the subject of the active verb. Just as the first clause of verse 21 may be treated as conditional, whoever loves me may also be treated as conditional, for example, "if anyone loves me, my Father will love him."

The verb translated reveal is used in John's Gospel only here and in the following verse. As in the Septuagint of Exodus 33.13 it is used of a special divine manifestation. I...will...reveal myself to him is more than merely "showing him who I am." An equivalent in some languages is "I will come to him" or "...come to him personally."

14.22   Judas (Not Judas Iscariot) said, "Lord, how can it be that you will reveal yourself to us and not to the world?"

This is the fourth time one of the disciples interrupts this final discourse of Jesus (see 13.37; 14.5,8). Again John uses the misunderstanding of one of Jesus' hearers as a means of furthering the discourse. Only Luke (6.16) and Acts (1.13) mention this apostle with the name Judas. The evidence for identifying him with Thaddaeus of Mark 3.18 and Matthew 10.3 is inconclusive.

Here Judas picks up the word reveal used by Jesus in verse 21. In this question the phrase to us appears first and so is to be stressed. It stands in contrast with to the world, which appears last in the Greek sentence order. The verb "to reveal" suggests a visible manifestation of Jesus in his final glory, and Judas does not understand how this manifestation can take place without being seen by the whole world. In reply Jesus indicates that the revelation of himself to his disciples is an internal, spiritual experience, which is dependent upon their obedience and love for him (see verse 23).

In some languages the question of Judas may be rendered "How can it be that you will cause us to see you, but you will not cause people in the world to see you?" However, to use a verb meaning "to cause to see" may not be adequate to render what is implied in the Greek term translated will reveal. The reference here is certainly to the glory which Jesus possesses, and therefore it may be appropriate to render this question "How is it that you will show to us how wonderful you are, but you will not show the same to the people of the world?"

14.23   Jesus answered him, "Whoever loves me will
               obey my teaching. My Father will love him, and
               my Father and I will come to him and live with
               him.

Jesus answered him is literally "Jesus answered and said to him," once again reflecting John's Semitic style, in which "said" is equivalent to quotation marks in English.
Whoever loves me is literally "If anyone loves me," but the Greek construction is equivalent to an indefinite relative pronoun in English.
Obey my teaching is literally "keep my word." The Greek "word" has a wide area of meaning. In the present context the specific reference is to the command of love (see comments at verse 15). Obey my teaching may be rendered "do what I have told him to do."
My Father and I will come to him is literally "we will come to him." It may not be necessary in the present context to mark explicitly the reference of the pronoun "we," but TEV does so.
And live with him is literally "and will make a dwelling (Greek monē) with him." The word "dwelling" is the same word translated rooms by TEV in 14.2. TEV renders in this way in the present context, because it is much more natural in English to say "live with" than "make a dwelling with."

14.24   Whoever does not love me does not obey my
               teaching. And the teaching you have heard
               is not mine, but comes from the Father, who
               sent me.

The first sentence of this verse expresses the other side of the truth stated in verse 23 (Whoever loves me will obey my teaching).
And the teaching you have heard is not mine identifies Jesus' message with God's word. This clause may be rendered "the words that you have heard from me are not just my own thoughts."
Comes from the Father is literally "is of the Father" and may be taken either as a genitive of possession ("is the Father's") or as a genitive of source ("is from the Father"). Ultimately, the meaning is the same. TEV takes it as a genitive of source, and so supplies comes from. In some languages it is difficult to speak of a "message coming from a person." One can usually say "a person sent a message by someone" and it is normally possible to say "a person spoke a message," but often one cannot say "a message comes." The only equivalent may be "my Father told me to say this message" or "...to deliver this message."

TEV　　　　(14.25-31)　　　　RSV

25 "I have told you this while I am still with you. 26 The Helper, the Holy Spirit, whom the Father will send in my name, will teach you everything and make you remember all that I have told you.

27 "Peace is what I leave with you; it is my own peace that I give you. I do not give it as the world does. Do not be worried and upset; do not be afraid. 28 You heard me say to you, 'I am leaving, but I will come back to you.' If you loved me, you would be glad that I am going to the Father; for he is greater than I. 29 I have told you this now before it all happens, so that when it does happen, you will believe. 30 I cannot talk with you much longer, because the ruler of this world is coming. He has no power over me, 31 but the world must know that I love the Father; that is why I do everything as he commands me.

"Come, let us go from this place.

25 "These things I have spoken to you, while I am still with you. 26 But the Counselor, the Holy Spirit, whom the Father will send in my name, he will teach you all things, and bring to your remembrance all that I have said to you. 27 Peace I leave with you; my peace I give to you; not as the world gives do I give to you. Let not your hearts be troubled, neither let them be afraid. 28 You heard me say to you, 'I go away, and I will come to you.' If you loved me, you would have rejoiced, because I go to the Father; for the Father is greater than I. 29 And now I have told you before it takes place, so that when it does take place, you may believe. 30 I will no longer talk much with you, for the ruler of this world is coming. He has no power over me; 31 but I do as the Father has commanded me, so that the world may know that I love the Father. Rise, let us go hence.

14.25　　　　"I have told you this while I am still with you.

I have told you this (literally "these things") will occur six more times in Chapters 15-16 (15.11; 16.1,4,6,25,33). It may be expressed in some languages as "I have spoken to you in this way" or "I have said these words to you."

While I am still with you is literally "remaining with you." John uses the verb "to remain" interchangeably with the verb "to be."

14.26　　　　The Helper, the Holy Spirit, whom the Father will send in my name, will teach you everything and make you remember all that I have told you.

The Helper, here identified as the Holy Spirit, was first mentioned in verse 16 (see there). GeCL avoids the difficult phrase Holy Spirit, and so renders "the Father shall send you his Spirit in my name." For in my name see comments at 14.13.

Everything stands in contrast to this (literally "these things")

[473]

of verse 25, and is best understood in light of 16.13. That is, the Helper will enable the disciples to understand the full implications of Jesus' words. Everything (in the context of will teach you everything) may seem too inclusive. The implication is simply "teach you everything you need to know about what I have said."

Make...remember is also used in Luke 22.61 where Peter recalls Jesus' words. It is best to take these two phrases (teach you everything and make you remember all that I have told you) as synonymous, the one reinforcing the other. The method by which the Spirit teaches the disciples everything is by "making them remember" all that Jesus has taught them, and by bringing out the implications of his teaching.

14.27   "Peace is what I leave with you; it is my
                   own peace that I give you. I do not give it
                   as the world does. Do not be worried and upset;
                   do not be afraid.

The word peace is used also in 16.33 in a similar context; it appears as a greeting in 20.19,21,26. Although the word represents the conventional Jewish greeting (Hebrew shalom), in Old Testament thought it had already developed a broader meaning, which is no doubt intended in the present passage. For example, in Psalm 29.11 (The Lord...blesses them with peace) and in Isaiah 57.19 (I offer peace to all) it has the special meaning of a gift from the Lord. In John's Gospel it is to be taken as equivalent to terms such as "light," "life," "joy," and "truth," all figurative terms descriptive of various aspects of salvation that God brings to men through Jesus Christ. It is not a negative term, referring to the absence of warfare or emotional tension, but rather a comprehensive term, including the benefits and blessings of the salvation that God brings to his people. In Romans 1.7; 5.1; 14.17 the term also has this broader meaning.

In some languages it is difficult to speak of "leaving peace with a person." The closest equivalent may be "I cause you to have a quiet heart" or "...joy within" or "...joy in the heart." One may then translate the first two clauses of verse 27 "I cause you to have joy within your hearts; the kind of joy that I have within my heart is what I am causing you to have."

The second sentence of verse 27 is perhaps more difficult than the first, since it may be assumed that what is being compared here is the peace, rather than the manner in which the peace is given. The meaning here is "I do not cause you to have this peace in the same way that the world causes people to have peace."

Do not be worried and upset translates the same expression used in 14.1. Here the exhortation do not be afraid is added. Literally the verb used here means "to be a coward," and a noun made from this same stem (TEV cowards) is used in Revelation 21.8. In a number of languages it is necessary to stipulate a grammatical goal of worried and upset. It must relate, as far as this context is concerned, to what the disciples are going to experience, namely, Jesus' leaving them. Therefore one can say "Do not be worried and upset about what is going to happen; do not fear what is going to happen."

[474]

14.28   You heard me say to you, 'I am leaving,
but I will come back to you.' If you
loved me, you would be glad that I am
going to the Father; for he is greater
than I.

I am leaving (Greek hupagō) is a term frequently used in John's
Gospel of Jesus' departure to the Father (note 13.33 and 14.4). It
should not be so translated as to suggest that Jesus was abandoning
his disciples. A frequent equivalent of I am leaving is simply "I am
going away."

I will come back to you is the same expression used in verse 18.

If you loved me may be translated "if you really love me" (NAB "If
you truly loved me") because it is an unfulfilled condition, that is, a
condition contrary to fact. Jesus is saying that the disciples do not
really love him at this point. This may be emphasized by translating
"If you loved me (but evidently you do not), you would be glad (but obviously you are not), that..."

That I am going to the Father is related to glad as a type of
cause and must be expressed in some languages by a causative formation,
for example, "the fact that I am going to the Father would make you
glad." Gladness may be expressed idiomatically in some languages as
"dancing of the heart," "coolness of the liver," or "sweetness of the
abdomen."

There have been many theological discussions concerning the statement because he is greater than I. In many passages in the Fourth Gospel,
Jesus is spoken of as the one whom the Father has sent, or the one who
has come from the Father, and it is in this light that the verse is to
be understood. The Father is greater than Jesus in the sense that the
one who sends a messenger is greater than the messenger he sends. Note
especially 13.16. Here the specific reference is probably to the coming
of Jesus into the world, by which he accepts the limitations of humanity, including physical death. But after Jesus' death God will raise
him to the position that he had before he came into the world. Note
17.4-5, which indicates that after Jesus had finished the work on earth
that the Father had given him to do, the Father restored him to the position that he had before the world was created. In some languages
greater is understood in the sense of "importance" rather than "strength"
or "power." This meaning reflects well the distinction between the one
who sends and the one who is sent.

14.29   I have told you this now before it all
happens, so that when it does happen,
you will believe.

This verse is similar to 13.19. The adverb now is emphatic in the
Greek sentence structure.

Believe may be understood in an absolute sense (NEB "may have
faith"), but in the present context it seems better to take it with the
meaning "believe me" (GeCL), that is, "believe that what I said is true."

14.30   I cannot talk with you much longer, because
             the ruler of this world is coming. He has no
             power over me,

I cannot talk with you much longer is more literally "I will no
longer talk much with you" (RSV). Most translations likewise render this
statement literally in the future tense. The temporal modifier much
longer must be understood in the sense of a few hours at most, since it
was later that same night that Jesus was betrayed and arrested.
     The ruler of this world was first mentioned in 12.31 (see there).
     He has no power over me is literally "and in me he has nothing."
This TEV rendering is also that of Gdsp, RSV, and JB. Most other translations have "He has no hold on me" or something similar. (See Mft,
Phps, NAB.) NEB renders "He has no rights over me," which is not entirely clear. It is probably based on the equivalent Hebrew, which means
"to have no claim upon someone." The context supports the meaning given
by TEV and most other translations. He has no power over me may be rendered as "he is not able to control me" or "...to command me."

14.31   but the world must know that I love the
             Father; that is why I do everything as
             he commands me.
                  "Come, let us go from this place."

     In Greek this verse reads literally "but in order that the world
may know that I love the Father, and just as the Father commanded me,
thus I am doing." TEV and most other translations restructure this verse
slightly; some do so rather radically. Note, for example, RSV "but I do
as the Father has commanded me, so that the world may know that I love
the Father."
     As in many other instances, the world must often be translated "the
people of the world." Similarly, I love the Father must often be translated "I love my Father." It is possible that in some languages the use
of the possessive pronoun my with Father may be misunderstood as referring to Jesus' earthly father. However, in view of the many other contexts in which it has been used, it seems unlikely that it will cause
any serious misunderstanding.
     That is why I do everything as he commands me may be rendered "that
is why I do everything in just the way he tells me to do it."
     Come, let us go from this place is very close to Mark 14.42 (Get up,
let us go), words spoken in Gethsemane immediately before the arrest of
Jesus. From this place may be best translated in some languages "from
this room" or "from this building." As observed in the introduction to
this section, these words should be taken literally, not spiritually.

TEV   (15.1-4)   RSV

JESUS THE REAL VINE

15 "I am the real vine, and my Father is the gardener. 2 He breaks off every branch in me that does not bear fruit, and he prunes every branch that does bear fruit, so that it will be clean and bear more fruit. 3 You have been made clean already by the teaching I have given you. 4 Remain united to me, and I will remain united to you. A branch cannot bear fruit by itself; it can do so only if it remains in the vine. In the same way you cannot bear fruit unless you remain in me.

15 "I am the true vine, and my Father is the vinedresser. 2 Every branch of mine that bears no fruit, he takes away, and every branch that does bear fruit he prunes, that it may bear more fruit. 3 You are already made clean by the word which I have spoken to you. 4 Abide in me, and I in you. As the branch cannot bear fruit by itself, unless it abides in the vine, neither can you, unless you abide in me.

These verses are generally considered to be a unit; the imagery of the vine in this chapter is last mentioned in verse 16, and there is a definite change of subject between verses 17 and 18. Although the unity of verses 1-17 is recognized by New Testament scholars, there are differences of opinion as to where the divisions within this section take place. Some make the major break after verse 10, while others make it after verse 8, and still others after verse 6. Wherever the break is made, it is recognized that the first part of the section deals with the parable of the vine, and the second part with the application of the parable. For the purpose of analysis, we shall divide this section into two major parts (1-6, 7-17), although in doing so we depart somewhat from TEV's presentation of the text. TEV divides this section into three paragraphs (verses 1-4, 5-10, and 11-17).

In verse 1 Jesus introduces himself as the real vine (an intimation that Israel is the "false vine"?) and his Father as the gardener. Verse 2 depicts the two activities of the gardener: cutting away the branches that cannot bear fruit, and pruning every branch that does bear fruit. The second half of verse 2 mentions the reason for the gardener's actions: so that it (the branch) will be clean and bear more fruit. Verse 3 interrupts the parable, assuring the disciples that they are already clean and so need not fear being "cut away." Verse 4 is an exhortation for them to remain in union with Christ, from whom they receive their life. Verse 5 reproduces the thought of verse 4, stating positively the thought that verse 4 states negatively. Verse 6 concludes the parable of the vine, indicating the fate of the useless branches.

Verses 5-6 present the alternatives of remaining or not remaining in Jesus, while verses 7-17 develop only the positive side of remaining. In this section it is explicit that Jesus is speaking to his disciples (verse 8). Verses 7 and 8 go closely together, in that verse 8 is the

[477]

fulfillment of what is asked for in verse 7. The theme of love, developed in verses 9-17, explains the imagery of fruit bearing (verse 8). In verse 9 Jesus affirms that the love he has for the disciples is the same that his Father has for him. In verse 10 he affirms that the disciples will remain in his love, if they obey his commands, just as he remains in the Father's love, because he obeys his Father's commands.

I have told you (verse 11) marks a transition between 7-10 and 12-17. Verse 12 repeats the command to love one another, and verses 13-15 make explicit some results of mutual love. Verse 16 indicates that Jesus' choice of his disciples was based on his love for them, while verse 17 repeats again the command to love, thus tying together the second division (verses 12-17) of this section.

The section heading, Jesus the Real Vine, poses two problems of translation and interpretation. First, it is an appositional expression, in which the Real Vine is in apposition to Jesus. Second, the Real Vine is an unusual metaphor and in some languages may require identification as a figurative expression by some means of marking the semantic relation. For example, one can make this metaphor into a simile by saying "Jesus is like the real vine" or "Jesus as the real vine." It is also possible to use the expression "The real vine" or "The true vine" as a section heading.

15.1   "I am the real vine, and my Father is the
              gardener.

On the use of I am in the Gospel of John, see comments at 4.26; for the first use of I am with a predicate, see 6.35.

The adjective real first appears in 1.9 in the phrase "real light" (see comments there).

In the Old Testament Israel is sometimes spoken of as a vine, and sometimes as a vineyard, and that is perhaps the background of the imagery used in this verse. In these Old Testament passages two emphases are made: (1) Israel's pure and favored origin, and (2) Israel's degenerate nature. See, for example, such passages as Psalm 80.8-16; Isaiah 5.1-7; Jeremiah 2.21; Ezekiel 15.1-8; 19.10-14; Hosea 10.1. Similar uses of the vine imagery are found in Jewish rabbinical literature, as well as in the New Testament (Matt 21.33-46). The portrayal of Jesus as the real vine is made in order to contrast him with Israel, which God planted like "a real vine" (the Septuagint of Jer 2.21 speaks of Israel as the real vine, the same words used here), but which became degenerate and worthless. In this way John again focuses attention on Jesus as the fulfillment of the Jewish faith. Although in the papyri the word here rendered vine is sometimes used with the meaning of "vineyard," in this passage the meaning vine is clear.

There are several serious complications in translating vine. Some translators make the mistake of selecting a term which indicates merely a vining plant; for example, in one language the term selected identified a sweet potato vine, and in another the term identified a kind of rattan vine which grows in the jungle but does not produce edible fruit. In yet another language the term for vine simply meant a squash vine. Obviously what is necessary is an expression which will identify a plant which

produces fruit and continues year after year. The only equivalent in
some languages is "a tree that produces good fruit." In others there is
a borrowed term for "grapes," when grapes are known but not the vine
which produces them. This term may be the best choice, and if it is
used, a descriptive term may be added, for example, "grape tree," where
"tree" identifies any woody plant.

Another translational problem involves finding an adequate term
for real. The meaning here is not that the vine actually exists, but
that it is the genuine vine, in contrast with a false one. This concept
of genuineness may be expressed in some languages by terms related to
the meaning of "trustworthy"; that is, the real vine is literally "the
vine that can be trusted," in the sense that it can be trusted to produce good fruit, rather than bad fruit or no fruit at all.

This is the only "I am" passage in the Gospel of John where the
equation is extended to include another; here Jesus is the real vine,
and his Father is the gardener. The translations vary in the choice of
gardener or "vinedresser" (NAB "vinegrower"). Elsewhere in the New Testament the word is used in 2 Timothy 2.6; James 5.7; and in the parable of
the tenants in the vineyard (Matt 21.33-36; Mark 12.1-12; Luke 20.9-19).
In the passages in 2 Timothy and James, TEV renders it by "farmer," while
in the parable of the tenants in the vineyard it is translated "tenant."
In some languages the equivalent of gardener is simply "one who takes
care of the vine," or, in some cases, "one who takes care of the ground
around the vine," since in many languages the focus is upon care of the
ground, not upon care of the plant itself.

15.2   He breaks off every branch in me that does
         not bear fruit, and he prunes every branch
         that does bear fruit, so that it will be
         clean and bear more fruit.

The two phrases every branch... and every branch... are emphatic
in the Greek sentence structure. The word rendered branch in this verse
does not appear elsewhere in the New Testament. It is specifically used
of vine branches, though it may also be used of other branches as well.

Some scholars contend that the Greek term translated vine really
means "vine stalk," and that the vine stalk must be clearly distinguished
from the branches. However, most exegetes understand this term to include both stalk and branches, since the branches can be regarded as
part of the vine, in the same way that believers may be regarded as
part of Christ; that is, they are in him even as he is in them.

Every branch in me must be rendered in some languages "every branch
that is a part of me" or "every branch that is attached to me." However,
if it is necessary to explain the relation of in me by a separate clause,
the structure may become relatively complex, for example, "He breaks off
every branch that is a part of me that does not bear fruit." This type
of structure is often impossible in translation. In some languages therefore it may be better to employ a conditional construction, for example,
"If a branch that is a part of me does not bear fruit, he breaks it off."

The verb translated breaks off literally means "to take away,"
while the verb rendered prunes...so that it will be clean literally means

"to cleanse," and occurs only here in the New Testament. In the present context the meaning is obviously "to make clean by pruning," which is the basis for the TEV rendering. Some translators render "to clean" (see NEB, Mft), while others have "to prune" (JB, RSV). NAB ("prunes away...trims clean") is essentially the same as TEV. To render as TEV and NAB do has two advantages: (1) It identifies the cleansing specifically as pruning, which is the meaning here; and (2) it brings out the idea of "to make clean," which is important in the present verse, since there is an obvious play on the verb "to make clean" of this verse and the adjective "clean" of verse 3. The entire phrase prunes...so that it will be clean and bear more fruit is literally "cleans...in order that it may bear more fruit."

The figurative meaning in the term prunes is difficult for many people to understand, for pruning is not a common practice in many parts of the world. Where it is practiced, it may be of quite a different type from that employed in the Middle East. The pruning to which this verse refers consists of cutting back individual branches so that the tree will produce better fruit. However, in many parts of the tropics, pruning is employed to reduce the number of branches, and thus give the remaining branches an opportunity to produce better fruit, as, for example, in pruning coffee trees. There are also difficulties in finding a term for "pruning." It may be necessary to use a descriptive phrase, for example, "to cut the branch short," "to cut the branch back," or "to cut off part of the branch."

There are also difficulties in relating pruning to a cleansing process, for pruning seems to have nothing to do with making something clean. A close approximation to this meaning may be obtained in some languages by rendering "so that it will be better and thus bear more fruit." This type of translation may be necessary in languages in which there is no relation between physical cleanliness and spiritual holiness. However, a serious difficulty may result from eliminating such a term as "clean," since the meaning of verse 2 must be preparatory for verse 3, in which the application must be made to persons rather than the branches of a vine. In some languages, therefore, instead of using "clean," translators employ a more general expression, for example, "prepared" or "properly prepared." This expression may be satisfactory in both verse 2 and verse 3.

15.3   You have been made clean already by the teaching
            I have given you.

The adverb already is in the emphatic position in the Greek sentence structure of this verse.

You have been made clean...by the teaching is literally "you (emphatic) are clean through the word." NEB rendered "you have already been cleaned by the word." Both TEV and NEB express the agency of the Greek sentence ("through the word") by the use of causative verbs (TEV have been made clean; NEB "have...been cleansed").

The passive expression in verse 3 may be transformed into an active one by rendering "What I have said to you has caused you to become clean already" or "My message to you has already caused you to become clean."

15.4   Remain united to me, and I will remain united to
you. A branch cannot bear fruit by itself; it can
do so only if it remains in the vine. In the same
way you cannot bear fruit unless you remain in me.

And I will remain united in you may also be understood as a comparison "as I remain united with you," since the Greek conjunction kai may mean either "and" or "as." If the clause is interpreted as a comparison, then the first clause is most appropriately understood as an imperative, for example, "continue to be a part of me even as I am a part of you" or "continue to be joined to me even as I will remain joined to you." However, if the second clause is not to be considered a type of comparison, in most languages a conditional relation would be more appropriate, for example, "If you remain joined to me, I will remain joined to you."

Most translations are literal, maintaining the imagery either of "living in" or "abiding in." The meaning is essentially that of 6.56 ("to live in fellowship/union with"). Since the spatial concept of one person living in another person may be difficult, it is better to follow TEV and translate "remain united with me."

By itself is the same expression translated on his own in the Son can do nothing on his own of 5.19 (see also 7.18; 16.13). In the same way that the Son can do nothing on his own, so the disciples can do nothing on their own; they must remain united with the Son, as the Son remains united with the Father.

It may not be easy in some languages to translate literally by itself. One equivalent may be "a branch alone cannot bear fruits," or it may be necessary to indicate clearly what the relation is of the branch to the trunk, for example, "if a branch is not attached to the trunk of a tree, it cannot bear fruit." This same truth is also expressed in the second part of this second sentence, which may be rendered "a branch can only bear fruit if it remains a part of the vine." These two parts of the sentence simply reinforce one another.

What may be difficult is the parallel stated in the third sentence of verse 4, since in some languages one cannot speak of a person's bearing fruit. Such a figure is simply meaningless. One can, however, translate this sentence "In the same way you can't do anything unless you remain a part of me..."

TEV   (15.5-10)   RSV

5 "I am the vine, and you are the branches. Whoever remains in me, and I in him, will bear much fruit; for you can do nothing without me. 6 Whoever does not remain in me is thrown out like a branch and dries up; such branches are gathered up and thrown into the fire, where they are burned. 7 If you remain in me and my words

5 I am the vine, you are the branches. He who abides in me, and I in him, he it is that bears much fruit, for apart from me you can do nothing. 6 If a man does not abide in me, he is cast forth as a branch and withers; and the branches are gathered, thrown into the fire and burned. 7 If you abide in me, and my words abide

remain in you, then you will ask for anything you wish, and you shall have it. 8 My Father's glory is shown by your bearing much fruit; and in this way you become my disciples. 9 I love you just as the Father loves me; remain in my love. 10 If you obey my commands, you will remain in my love, just as I have obeyed my Father's commands and remain in his love.	in you, ask whatever you will, and it shall be done for you. 8 By this my Father is glorified, that you bear much fruit, and so prove to be my disciples. 9 As the Father has loved me, so have I loved you; abide in my love. 10 If you keep my commandments, you will abide in my love, just as I have kept my Father's commandments and abide in his love.

15.5   "I am the vine, and you are the branches.
      Whoever remains in me, and I in him, will
      bear much fruit; for you can do nothing
      without me.

As noted in the discussion of verse 1, it may be possible to render vine as "vine stalk," but it seems better to translate it as meaning the entire plant and the branches as part of it.

In some languages it may be necessary to change the metaphor I am the vine to a simile, for example, "I am like the vine." This change would be similar to that required in verse 1. Likewise, you are the branches may be rendered as "you are like the branches."

Whoever remains is a participial construction in Greek (literally "the one remaining"), but it is equivalent in English to an indefinite relative clause (see 12.44). The indefinite relative clause Whoever remains in me, and I in him may be regarded as a conditional, for example, "If a person remains a part of me and I a part of him, then he will bear much fruit" or "...he will be able to accomplish much."

Will bear is in the present tense in Greek (most translations have "bear"), but the Greek present tense can be used to indicate the future, especially when the certainty of the action is to be emphasized. Moreover, if these words are viewed from the time perspective of Jesus' day, to translate as a future tense seems more natural.

The phrase without me is emphatic in the Greek sentence structure. Without me may be rendered in some languages "only with my help," for example, "you cannot do anything except with my help" or "you can do something only with my help" or "...only with me helping you."

15.6   Whoever does not remain in me is thrown out like
      a branch and dries up; such branches are gathered
      up and thrown into the fire, where they are burned.

This verse states negatively what was stated positively in verse 5. Whoever in Greek is literally "if someone," but it also has the force of an indefinite relative pronoun in English (see 12.26).

The verbs translated is thrown out and dries up are in the aorist indicative tense in Greek. The aorist indicative (normally indicating completed action in past time) is used here for one of two reasons: (1)

to indicate the certainty of the action, by speaking of a future action
as though it were already accomplished; or (2) to indicate habitual or
customary action. The context seems to suggest the first of these possibilities.

Like a branch must apply not only to being thrown out, but also to
drying up. It may be necessary to say, therefore, "Whoever does not remain in me is thrown out and dries up, just as a branch would be thrown
out and dry up."

Are gathered up and thrown is literally "they gather them and throw
(them)." But this Semitic use of the third person plural is the equivalent of a passive construction, and so a number of translations render
in essentially the same way as TEV. If a passive cannot be used, one
may translate "people gather them up and throw them into the fire." Since
the fire has not been previously identified, and cannot be directly related to any specific aspect of judgment, it is better in some languages
to translate "thrown into a fire."

15.7   If you remain in me and my words remain in
         you, then you will ask for anything you wish,
         and you shall have it.

Verse 7 again picks up the imagery of the disciples' remaining in
Jesus, and the metaphor of the vine is dropped.

There is no distinction between Jesus' remaining in his disciples
and his words' remaining in them; both Jesus and his words are the absolute revelation from God.

The specific content of the disciples' prayer you will ask for anything you wish is not indicated, though it is assumed that it is in keeping with God's will. You will ask (NAB, JB "you may ask") may also be
taken with the force of the imperative "ask" (so Mft, Gdsp, NEB, RSV).

If you remain in me and my words remain in you should be translated
in a manner parallel to that employed in previous verses which speak of
continuing the relationship of the believer to Jesus and of Jesus to the
believer. A most common way of expressing the relationship implied by
remain in is "remaining a part of" or "continue to be a part of." In
some instances the expression "be joined to" is very useful.

And you shall have it is a pseudo-passive construction in which
God is the "hidden subject." You will ask for anything you wish, and
you shall have it may then be translated, "you will ask the Father for
anything you wish, and he will give it to you."

15.8   My Father's glory is shown by your bearing
         much fruit; and in this way you become my
         disciples.

The Greek text begins with a phrase, "in this," which relates to
what follows, rather than to what precedes in verse 7. TEV indicates
this relation by restructuring: My Father's glory is shown by... (Note
also NEB "My Father has been glorified in your bearing much fruit and
becoming my disciples.) Gdsp translates "When you are very fruitful

and show yourselves to be disciples of mine, my Father is honored." JB
renders "It is to the glory of my Father that you should bear much
fruit, and then you will be my disciples; while GeCL reads "When you
bear much fruit, you will prove yourselves to be my disciples, and so
the glory of my Father will be shown."

In some languages the relation between the clauses in verse 8 must
be made clearer than is indicated by the order employed in TEV. In general, the order must be arranged to make by your bearing much fruit the
first part, followed by and in this way you become my disciples. These
two expressions state essentially the means by which the Father's glory
is shown. In some languages it is necessary to restructure the relations
between the various components of the first clause. If so, verse 8 may
have to be restructured to read, for example, "When you are accomplishing
much and in this way show that you are my disciples, you are showing people how wonderful my Father is."

My Father's glory is shown is more literally "My Father was glorified," rendered by RSV "My Father is glorified." It is perhaps best to
take the aorist "was glorified" to indicate something timeless, that is,
"is always glorified." This force of the verb is indicated in the translations quoted above, though they do not translate literally either "is
glorified" or "was glorified." "To glorify" means to reveal the Father's
true glory.

There is a textual problem in the last part of this verse, and it
relates to the verb translated become. If it is taken as a subjunctive
(as in the UBS Greek text), become my disciples is grammatically coordinate with bearing much fruit. NAB has "My Father has been glorified
in your bearing much fruit and becoming my disciples." This also seems
to be the meaning of Mft "As you bear rich fruit and prove yourselves my
disciples, my Father is glorified." So also NEB "This is my Father's
glory, that you may bear fruit in plenty and so be my disciples." However, TEV, JB ("It is to the glory of my Father that you should bear
much fruit, and then you will be my disciples"), and NEB footnote
("...that you may bear fruit in plenty. Thus you will be my disciples")
follow the reading in the apparatus of the UBS Greek text, which has
the verb in the future. The choice is difficult, and the UBS Committee
rates its decision a "D" choice, indicating a very high degree of doubt
as to the original text. To be a disciple means that one "remains in
Jesus" and simultaneously "bears much fruit."

15.9   I love you just as the Father loves me;
          remain in my love.

To achieve naturalness in English style, TEV inverts the order of
the first two Greek clauses, introducing the clause of comparison just
as the Father loves me after the main clause I love you.

Although the tense of the verb remain is aorist, and could have
the force of "begin to remain" or "start remaining," the context clearly
indicates that the disciples are already "in Jesus' love." The aorist
imperative was perhaps chosen to make the command more emphatic.

My love is best taken in the sense of "my love for you," rather
than "your love for me." What it means to remain in Christ's love is
shown in the following verse.

In some languages it may not be easy to say "remain in my love for you." Perhaps for this reason some translators take the easy way out by rendering "continue to love me." This, however, certainly does not seem to be the meaning, especially as indicated by verse 10. However, if one is to express the meaning of "my love for you," it may be necessary to say "remain joined to me so that I may love you." It may even be possible to anticipate the implications of verse 10 by translating "continue obeying me so that I may love you."

15.10   If you obey my commands, you will remain in
        my love, just as I have obeyed my Father's
        commands and remain in his love.

Obedience to the commands of Christ is the means whereby the disciples remain in his love. If you obey my commands was used in 14.15,21, 23-24. As indicated in 14.15, there is no distinction between the singular "command" and the plural "commands," and the reference is to the command to love.

The conditional statement If you obey my commands, you will remain in my love may be rendered in some languages "if you do what I say, I will continue to love you." This rendering provides the basis for a parallel construction in the second part of verse 10, for example, "in the same way I have done what my Father has told me to do, and he continues to love me."

The use of the perfect tense I have obeyed, if it has a special force in the context, may focus on the absolute quality of Christ's love and obedience, or it may reflect the time viewpoint of the author. The first possibility is the more probable.

The Father's commands are spoken of in the plural here. Note 1 John 3.22-23, where the text alternates between the plural and the singular.

The idea of "remaining in" someone's love may be difficult to translate, and so a possible restructuring of 9b-10 is here suggested: "(9)... Do not turn away from my love. (10) If you obey my commands, I will continue to love you, just as I have obeyed my Father's commands, and so he continues to love me."

TEV   (15.11-17)   RSV

11"I have told you this so that my joy may be in you and that your joy may be complete. 12 My commandment is this: love one another, just as I love you. 13 The greatest love a person can have for his friends is to give his life for them. 14 And you are my friends if you do what I command you. 15 I do not call you servants any longer, because a servant does not know what his master is doing.

11 These things I have spoken to you, that my joy may be in you, and that your joy may be full. 12 "This is my commandment, that you love one another as I have loved you. 13 Greater love has no man than this, that a man lay down his life for his friends. 14 You are my friends if you do what I command you. 15 No longer do I call you servants,[h] for the servant[i] does not know what his master is

[485]

Instead, I call you friends, because I have told you everything
I heard from my Father. 16 You did
not choose me; I chose you and appointed you to go and bear much
fruit, the kind of fruit that endures. And so the Father will give
you whatever you ask of him in my
name. 17 This, then, is what I command you: love one another.

doing; but I have called you
friends, for all that I have
heard from my Father I have made
known to you. 16 You did not
choose me, but I chose you and appointed you that you should go and
bear fruit and that your fruit
should abide; so that whatever you
ask the Father in my name, he may
give it to you. 17 This I command you,
to love one another.

^hOr *slaves*

ⁱOr *slave*

15.11   "I have told you this so that my joy may be
in you and that your joy may be complete.

I have told you this is literally "I have told you these things"
(see 14.25). It is difficult to define precisely what is referred to
by this, though it certainly includes more than what is said in verse
10. It includes at least verse 9 and perhaps all of verses 7-8 as well.
I have told you this may be rendered "I have told you all this" in order
to indicate that the reference is not limited to the immediately preceding words.
My joy (used of Jesus) refers to the joy that grows out of absolute
obedience to the Father and the perfect unity of love they share with
each other. So that my joy may be in you may be rendered in some languages "so that you will have the same kind of joy that I have." Joy
may be expressed idiomatically in some languages as "dance within the
heart" or "to have a happy heart."
Joy may be complete is a favorite Johannine expression (note John
3.29; 1 John 1.4; 2 John 12). The completeness of joy may be expressed
in some languages as "and so that you may be completely joyful" or
"...completely happy." In some languages, however, completeness is es-
pressed as a negative of lacking, for example, "so that there may be
nothing lacking in your joy" or "so that your joy may have nothing
missing."

15.12   My commandment is this: love one another,
just as I love you.

My commandment is this is literally "this is my commandment that..."
The structure is similar to that discussed in verse 8; here "that" of the
Greek text is used to introduce the content of the commandment. In some
languages such a statement as My commandment is this normally occurs
after the content of the command, rather than before it, for example,
"love one another just as I love you. This is what I command you." However, in some languages one may render "I command you the following

words: love one another just as I love you."

Love one another is in the present imperative, focusing on the need for a continuous love.

Just as I love you is more literally "just as I loved you." Here again the problem of tense sequences arises. This verb may be understood from the time perspective of the author of the Gospel, with specific reference to Jesus' act of love on the cross. However, it is better to take it in a timeless sense, as TEV does.

15.13   The greatest love a person can have for his
        friends is to give his life for them.

This verse literally begins "greater love than this no one has that..."; and so the construction is similar to the first part of verse 12 and to verse 8. TEV renders this part of the verse The greatest love a person can have for his friends is. The superlative degree of love may be expressed in some languages as a negative with a comparative, for example, "A man cannot love his friends any more than..."

To give his life is more literally "to lay down his soul." Here the verb "lay down" is used in the sense of "to give up," while "soul" is used with the meaning of "life" (see 10.11). This verse interprets and makes explicit the implication in verse 12. That is, it explains the way in which Jesus loves his disciples. To give his life for them is to manifest the greatest possible type of love. Therefore in some languages one may translate verse 13 "If a man dies for his friends, that shows that he has the greatest love that anyone could have" or "When a man dies for his friends, that shows that he could not have any greater love" or "...could not possibly love any more.

15.14   And you are my friends if you do what I com-
        mand you.

The immediate implication of this verse is that if the disciples obey Jesus' commands, they prove that they are his friends, and so he will give his life for them. In this respect, the verse is very close in meaning to verse 10. Throughout the Gospel, no distinction is made between remaining in Christ's love and being his friend. John uses two verbs for love (agapaō and philcō) and he uses them synonymously. It is significant that the noun friends (Greek philos) is made from the stem of one of these verbs. According to John's Gospel, Jesus' "friends" are those "whom he loves." Note that Lazarus is the "friend" of Jesus (11.11), and he is so because Jesus "loves" him (11.3,5). In the same way that Christ remains in the Father's love by obeying his commands, so the disciples must obey Jesus' commands in order to remain in his love.

In some languages the order of clauses in a conditional sentence must be inverted, for example, "If you do what I tell you to do, then you are my friends."

15.15   I do not call you servants any longer, because
          a servant does not know what his master is
          doing. Instead, I call you friends, because
          I have told you everything I heard from my
          Father.

    Servants (so most translations) may also be rendered "slaves" (NAB,
Gdsp, RSV footnote). In the present context the meaning of "servant" is
better than "slave," since the connotations of "slave" are derogatory.
Furthermore, the relationship of the disciples to Jesus was never that
of slaves to an owner.
    Does not know what his master is doing is difficult, for it is
almost impossible to imagine a household where the servants would not
know what their masters were doing. NEB and NAB try to overcome this
difficulty by rendering "does not know what his master is about," while
Phps renders "does not share his master's confidence" (JB "does not
know his master's business"). One may also render "does not know what
his master's intentions are" or "does not know the implications of what
his master is doing."
    In the last sentence of this verse you and everything are emphatic.
    Have told you is literally "made known to you" (NAB). However, since
Jesus is speaking of making known everything he has "heard," it is legitimate in the present context to render the Greek verb by the more
specific term "to tell." Everything I heard from my Father may be rendered "everything which my Father told me." Accordingly, the final part
of verse 15 may be translated "because I have told you everything my
Father told me."

15.16   You did not choose me; I chose you and appointed
          you to go and bear much fruit, the kind of fruit
          that endures. And so the Father will give you
          whatever you ask of him in my name.

    The pronouns you...I are emphatic. This verse emphasizes the fact
that discipleship is ultimately due to the divine choice, not to the
decision of the individual alone. The disciples are Jesus' friends,"
not because they took the initiative in choosing him, but because he
chose them.
    Appointed is the rendering of most translations; JB has "commis-
sioned." The verb is literally "to place" or "to lay down" (the same
verb used in verse 13 in the phrase "to lay down one's life"). NAB apparently takes it to be redundant ("...it was I who chose you to go
forth and bear fruit"), but in the present context it probably has the
meaning "to appoint" or "to set aside for a special task." The verb
appears to be used in a technical sense in such passages as Acts 20.28;
1 Corinthians 12.28; and 2 Timothy 1.11. In some languages appointed
may be best rendered "gave a work to do" or "assigned to a task."
    Bear much fruit is literally "bear fruit." As in similar contexts,
bear much fruit must be rendered "accomplish much," since the figurative
meaning of fruit, as related to accomplishment of a task or producing
results, is impossible in some languages.

The kind of fruit that endures is literally "and (that) your fruit may remain." Mft translates "fruit that lasts"; NEB "fruit that shall last"; Gdsp "fruit that shall be lasting." This reference to bearing fruit looks back to the metaphor of the vine with which the chapter began.

It is possible to take the last sentence in this verse (And so the Father will give you whatever you ask of him in my name) either as co-ordinate with the clause to go and bear much fruit or as dependent upon it. Most translators understand And so...my name to be dependent upon to go...much fruit. That is, if the disciples go out and bear much fruit, the kind of fruit that endures, then the Father will give them whatever they ask in Jesus' name. This last sentence is somewhat res-tructured in TEV; it literally reads "in order that whatever you ask the Father in my name he will give to you." TEV inverts the order of the Greek clauses, introducing the Father as the subject at the beginning, and using the pronoun him as a reference to the Father in the second half of the sentence.

Since the final sentence of verse 16 is also in a sense a condition, it may be proper to render it "If you do that, then the Father will give you whatever you ask for in my name" or "...because you are my followers."

Again the phrase in my name causes translational difficulty (see comments at 14.13). The meaning here is perhaps best taken as "because you are my followers."

15.17   This, then, is what I command you: love one
               another."

This verse literally begins "these things I am commanding you that ..." For this kind of structure see verses 8,12, and 13.

This verse repeats the theme of love, and so rounds off this sec-tion, which began in verse 12 with that theme. In a sense, verse 17 is transitional to the theme of the following section (15.18-16.4): the reason that the world hates the disciples is that they love one another and belong to Jesus.

Some of the complications involved in the reference of this may be avoided by translating verse 17 "Love one another is what I command you to do" or "What I command you is to love one another" or "My command to you is, Love one another."

TEV   (15.18-25)   RSV

THE WORLD'S HATRED

18 "If the world hates you, just   18 "If the world hates you,
remember that it has hated me first.   know that it has hated me before
19 If you belonged to the world,   it hated you. 19 If you were of
then the world would love you as   the world, the world would love
its own. But I chose you from this   its own; but because you are not
world, and you do not belong to it;   of the world, but I chose you out
that is why the world hates you.   of the world, therefore the world

20 Remember what I told you: 'No
slave is greater than his master.'
If they persecuted me, they will
persecute you too; if they obeyed
my teaching, they will obey yours
too. 21 But they will do all this
to you because you are mine; for
they do not know the one who sent
me. 22 They would not have been
guilty of sin if I had not come
and spoken to them; as it is, they
no longer have any excuse for their
sin. 23 Whoever hates me hates my
Father also. 24 They would not have
been guilty of sin if I had not
done among them the things that no
one else ever did; as it is, they
have seen what I did, and they hate
both me and my Father. 25 This, however, was bound to happen so that
what is written in their Law may
come true: 'They hated me for no
reason at all.'

hates you. 20 Remember the word
that I said to you, 'A servant[i] is
not greater than his master.' If
they persecuted me, they will persecute you; if they kept my word,
they will keep yours also. 21 But
all this they will do to you on
my account, because they do not
know him who sent me. 22 If I had
not come and spoken to them, they
would not have sin; but now they
have no excuse for their sin. 23 He
who hates me hates my Father also.
24 If I had not done among them
the works which no one else did,
they would not have sin; but now
they have seen and hated both me
and my Father. 25 It is to fulfil
the word that is written in their
law, 'They hated me without a
cause.'

[i]Or *slave*

Although there is general agreement that a new section begins with
15.18, opinions differ as to where this section ends. Some would make
a major break at the end of verse 25, since in verse 26 the Helper is
introduced again. However, the theme of the Helper is closely related
to that of persecution by the world, and links what precedes (verses
18-25) with what follows (verses 16.1-4a). So even though verses 26-27
introduce a new subdivision within the whole, it is difficult to see a
new section introduced with verse 26. On the other hand, some see a
major break at the end of Chapter 15, and this view is reflected in
Phps' translation. But the introductory words of 16.1 (I have told
you this) indicate a relation with what precedes, and 16.1-4a picks up
again the persecution theme that was the content of 18.25. Some scholars
see the major break as occurring after 16.11, while others see the major
break coming after verse 15. Most modern translations make the major
break either after 16.4a (TEV, JB, NAB, Segond, RSV, GeCL) or after
verse 4 (Luther Revised, Zür); 16.4a is also the point at which the UBS
Greek text makes a subdivision, and so the analysis of this section will
include 15.18--16.4a.

Although the entire section (verses 18-25) can be said to deal with
the world's hatred for the disciples, verse 22 introduces a new focus,
which is carried through verse 25. That is, verses 18-21 explain that
the world hates the disciples for the same reason that it hated Jesus.
In this section verse 21 summarizes the theme of persecution and indicates its cause: they will do all this to you because you are mine; for
they do not know him who sent me. Verses 22-25 introduce the theme of
the world's guilt, which grows out of its persecution of Jesus and his
disciples. Had Jesus not come into the world to tell them God's message,
they would not be guilty of sin; but as it is, they have seen what Jesus

did and have heard his teaching, and so they are guilty, because they hate both him and the Father who sent him.

As indicated, verses 26-27 reveal the source of strength for the disciples during their time of persecution. The Helper, the Spirit of truth, who comes from the Father, will enable them to endure.

Verses 1-4a of Chapter 16 renew the theme of persecution and describe some of the persecutions the disciples will have to face because of Jesus (verse 2). Jesus has told them these things in advance, so that when the persecutions come upon them, they will not fall away from their faith (16.1,4). Again the cause of persecution is reiterated: People will do these things to you because they have not known either the Father or me (verse 3).

The section heading, The World's Hatred, may need modification, especially in languages which require that the goal of hatred be expressed, for example, "The world will hate you" or "The world hates you." Furthermore, it may be necessary to indicate that this is not "the world" as such, but "the people of the world," for example, "The people of the world hate you." Since, however, the passage really deals with the reasons for hatred by the world, one may say "Why people of the world hate you."

15.18   "If the world hates you, just remember that
          it has hated me first.

If the world hates you states a real condition, not simply a conjecture, that is, the world does hate the disciples. In this present passage the world should be equated with the people who are aligned with the power of evil in opposition to God (see 1.10). Since If the world hates you states an actual fact, it may be necessary in some languages to say "If the world hates you, and it does." In other languages the condition may be better interpreted as cause or reason, for example, "Since the world hates you, you must remember." On the other hand, there is a sense of contrast, and therefore one may translate as "The world hates you, but you must remember that it hated me first."

For the theme of the world's hatred of Jesus see 7.7.

Just remember (Mft, Gdsp, JB "remember") is literally "know" (RSV, NAB). However, in the present context "remember" or "bear in mind" (NEB footnote) is apparently the meaning. It is possible to take this verb in the indicative (Phps "you know that it hated me first"; NEB "as you know well"), but most translators, whether translating "remember" or "know," understand it to be an imperative. In the ancient versions also it was translated as an imperative. In this type of context remember should not be understood in the sense of remembering something previously forgotten. The meaning here is "constantly bear in mind."

Has hated is in the perfect tense in Greek; it indicates the enduring hatred of the world.

In this context first must be understood in the sense of "prior to," for example, "The people of the world have hated me prior to their hating you" or "...before they hated you."

15.19   If you belonged to the world, then the world
would love you as its own. But I chose you
from this world, and you do not belong to it;
that is why the world hates you.

The "if" clause in verse 18 introduces a condition true to fact, but here the "if" clause introduces a condition contrary to fact ("If you belonged to the world, and you do not..."). Belonged to the world is a relatively difficult concept to translate in some languages. One may say in certain instances "to be a part of the world." In others it may be better to say "to be one with the people of the world" or "to be the same as the people of the world."

Then the world would love you as its own is more literally "then the world would love its own." But to translate literally would possibly convey a wrong impression. The purpose of this statement is to contrast the world's hatred of Jesus' disciples with the world's love for its own people. TEV makes this contrast explicit, as does also NAB. GeCL renders "The world would love you as its children, if you belonged to it."

Its own is a neuter construction in Greek, but here it is used in a collective sense to refer to persons (see the comments at 6.37 and 39). Would love you as its own may be rendered in some languages "would love you as people who belong to them" or "...who are the same as they are."

But I chose you emphasizes again Jesus' initiative in choosing his disciples (see verse 16).

From this world (several translations "out of the world"; JB "my choice withdrew you from the world") is intended to indicate the separation of the disciples from the world and its ways. John describes in absolute categories the contrast between the world and Jesus' disciples. See especially 17.14,16, which also indicate that the disciples do not belong to this world. Throughout this sentence the pronouns I and you are emphatic. TEV reverses the Greek sentence order, which has "you do not belong to the world" first and "I chose you from the world" second. TEV makes this rearrangement because both temporally and logically, the matter of choosing the disciples comes before their separation from the world.

The phrase from this world may be understood as an aspect of the purpose involved in Jesus' choosing the disciples, for example, "I chose you so that you wouldn't be a part of this world" or "...so that you wouldn't be the same as the people in the world."

And you do not belong to it may be rendered "and as a result you are not a part of the world."

That is why refers to both the preceding clauses of this sentence. To make this connection clear, it may be necessary to reorder the entire sentence and translate "The reason the world hates you is that I chose you from this world, and you do not belong to it." Note, for example, NAB "...the reason it hates you is that you do not belong to the world. But I chose you out of the world."

15.20   Remember what I told you: 'No slave is greater
than his master.' If they persecuted me, they
will persecute you too; if they obeyed my
teaching, they will obey yours too.

Remember what I told you (so also NAB) is literally "remember the
word that I said to you" (RSV). The reference is to the words of Jesus
that follow (No slave is greater than his master), and so NEB translates
"Remember what I said," while JB renders "Remember the words I said to
you." No slave is greater than his master refers back to 13.16. The emphasis in Chapter 13 is on imitating the humility of Jesus, while here
it relates to the necessity of sharing his fate.

Remember does not necessarily imply here that the disciples had
forgotten what Jesus had said. An appropriate equivalent may be "Think
about what I told you."

In this context greatness may be interpreted as a matter of importance, for example, "A slave is not more important than his master" or
"No slave surpasses his master in importance." In some languages the
relation may be inverted by saying "A master is always more important
than his slave."

If they persecuted me is a condition true to fact, as was the "if"
clause in verse 18. The meaning is that they did persecute Jesus, and so
they will also persecute his disciples. Though the clause If they persecuted me is formally a condition, it states a fact, and in combination with the following clause must be somewhat altered in some languages, for example, "They persecuted me, and they will persecute you
too" or "they caused me to suffer, and accordingly, they will cause you
to suffer also."

If they obeyed my teaching is literally "if they kept my word."
But the use of the verb "to keep" in this context has the meaning of
"to obey"; and "the word" of Jesus is a summary term for his teaching.

Throughout verses 18-20 the description of the world's attitude
has been completely negative, but here Jesus suddenly seems to change;
there are some who obey his teaching, and so there will also be some
who will obey the teaching of his followers. That is, Jesus is indicating that the attitude of the world toward his disciples will not be
completely negative, just as it was not completely negative toward him.
Some did respond to his teaching (for example, the disciples themselves),
and so some will also respond to the teaching of his followers. Some
commentators assume a negative implication behind Jesus' words here, for
example, NEB "they will follow your teaching as little as they have followed mine." This interpretation is apparently the basis for GeCL: "as
little as they have believed my word, so shall they believe yours." However, even though one might like to read this meaning into the present
passage, especially in view of the negative implications in verse 21,
it is difficult to arrive at this meaning on the basis of the Greek
sentence structure, and so it is probably better not to translate with
negative implications. Jesus' words should be taken to mean that if
there are some who persecuted him, there were also some who listened
to him; and accordingly, if there are some who persecute the disciples,
there will also be some who will respond to their message. One may,
therefore, translate the second part of verse 20 "Some persecuted me,

15.20

and they will persecute you also, but others obeyed what I said, and
they will obey also what you say."

15.21 But they will do all this to you because you
are mine; for they do not know the one who
sent me.

Because you are mine is literally "because of my name." JB renders
"on my account," but this translation leaves unclear the exact meaning
of the phrase. A footnote in NAB states "For John, association with
Jesus' name implies union with Jesus." This observation is true, and
it is the basis for the TEV rendering. Because of the disciples' union
with Jesus (that is, because they belong to him), they are persecuted
(see comments on "in my name" at 14.13). GeCL renders "because you
acknowledge me."
They will do all this to you refers to persecution, and this reference may be made explicit, for example, "They will persecute you because you are mine" or "because you follow me."
Note, however, the presence of a rather complex double causation.
Those who reject the disciples, and therefore persecute them, do it for
two reasons: first, because the disciples belonged to Jesus, and secondly, because they do not know the one who sent Jesus. It may be necessary to repeat in the second part of verse 21 what these persons actually do, for example, "But they will persecute you because you belong
to me; they will do this because they do not know the one who sent me."
The one who sent me is a reference to God the Father.

15.22 They would not have been guilty of sin if I had
not come and spoken to them; as it is, they no
longer have any excuse for their sin.

TEV inverts the first two clauses of this sentence, which literally
reads "If I had not come and spoken to them, they would not have sin."
But it is more natural in English to reorder as TEV does, and the phrase
"to have sin" (note RSV) means "to be guilty of sin," as most modern
translations make explicit. Again, as in verse 18, the condition of the
"if" clause is contrary to fact. If I had not come and spoken to them
means "I did come, and I did speak to them." The verbs come and spoken
are in the aorist tense, and point to the specific event of Jesus'
coming into the world and speaking his message.
Though in English it may be more appropriate in this type of context to place the condition after the main clause, in some languages
it is almost obligatory to place a condition first, for example, "If I
had not come and spoken to them, then they would not be guilty of sin."
It is particularly important to introduce the concept of "guilt," as
well as that of "sin," since the omission of a reference to guilt would
imply that the people had not sinned. What is important is that the
people's rejection of the message of Jesus made them guilty, since in
this way they had rejected his proclamation of the truth.
It may not be easy in some languages to speak of being guilty of

[494]

sin. Often the meaning is conveyed by figurative language, for example, "to carry the burden of one's sin" or "to have one's sin marked up against one" or "to bear the remembrance of sin" or "to have one's sins cling to one." The phrase guilty of sin suggests the impending punishment which comes as the result of having sinned. It is not a reference to the act of sin itself.

As it is (Mft, JB, Gdsp "but as it is") is literally "but now" (RSV), but the Greek expression used here (nun de) does not have true temporal significance. The meaning may be best expressed by rendering "but now in fact."

They no longer have is literally "they do not have." But the intimation is that they could have claimed an excuse had Jesus not come into the world. Since he did come, they no longer have any excuse.

The Greek word translated excuse (prophasis) is used only here in John; elsewhere in the New Testament it occurs in Mark 12.40; Luke 20.47; Acts 27.30; Philippians 1.18; and 1 Thessalonians 2.5. In the present context most translations render it with the meaning excuse, though it may also mean "motive" or "reason."

They no longer have any excuse for their sin may be rendered in some languages "they now cannot say, 'We did not know that what we did was sin'" or "...'we did not know our deeds were bad.'"

15.23   Whoever hates me hates my Father also.

Whoever hates is once again a participial construction in Greek (literally "the one hating"), which is the equivalent of an indefinite relative clause (see 12.44). This verse is similar to 5.23.

15.24   They would not have been guilty of sin if I had
               not done among them the things that no one else
               ever did; as it is, they have seen what I did,
               and they hate both me and my Father.

TEV inverts the sentence order in the first part of this verse. In Greek it literally reads "If I had not done the works among them that no one else did, they would not have sin." Here again the inversion of the sentence order is simply for the sake of attaining a more natural English style. As in verse 22, the phrase "to have sin" is taken by most commentators and translators with the meaning "to be guilty of sin." For the translational difficulties in the first part of verse 24, see comments on verse 22, which is essentially parallel.

As it is translates the same two particles mentioned in verse 22.

In Greek the verb seen has no object expressed. TEV supplies what I did, referring to the things earlier in the sentence. JB ("they have seen all this"), Zür, Luther Revised, GeCL, and the alternative reading of NEB all follow this exegesis. However, some translations (Mft, Gdsp, NEB, Phps, RSV, and Segond) take both "Jesus" and "my Father" as the objects of the verbs seen and hated. For example, NEB has "they have both seen and hated both me and my Father."

[495]

This, however, was bound to happen so that
                what is written in their Law may come true:
                'They hated me for no reason at all.'

The first part of this verse is more literally "But in order that
the word written in their Law might be fulfilled." Here again "to be
fulfilled" must be understood in the sense of "come true" (see 12.38).
NEB renders "However, this text in their Law had to come true." That is,
it renders "the word" of the Greek sentence by "the text," but TEV uses
a more generic term what is written. NAB also translates "the word" as
"the text," while some translations render simply "the word." It is obvious that the singular term "the word" will not do for most translations.
In this context Law refers to the entire Jewish Bible, and not merely to
that section of the Old Testament known as "the Law" (see also 10.34 and
12.34). The Greek is rather elliptical, and for this reason TEV supplies
This must be at the opening of the verse. It is possible to take the
Greek structure as the equivalent of an imperative (see the alternative
rendering of NEB "let this text in their Law come true"), but no translation suggests this interpretation. The scripture reference in this
verse is either to Psalm 35.19 or 69.5, since the expression those who
hate me without reason occurs in each of these Psalms.
        This...was bound to happen may be rendered "This had to happen" or
"It had to happen that they would hate me" or "Their hating me happened
so that."
        The purpose clause so that what is written in their Law may come
true may be rendered in some languages "so that what is written in their
Law might happen" or "...might take place" or "...might really occur."
        As noted in other contexts, in some languages Law may be expressed
more satisfactorily as plural, namely, "laws."
        For no reason at all indicates a type of contrast, and therefore
it may be combined with the preceding verb as "They hated me, but they
didn't have a reason for hating me" or "They hated me, but I had not
done anything to cause them to hate me."

                    TEV   (15.26-27)   RSV

    26 "The Helper will come--the   26 But when the Counselor comes,
Spirit, who reveals the truth   whom I shall send to you from the
about God and who comes from   Father, even the Spirit of truth,
Father. I will send him to you   who proceeds from the Father, he
from the Father, and he will speak   will bear witness to me; 27 and
about me. 27 And you, too, will   you also are witnesses, because
speak about me, because you have   you have been with me from the
been with me from the very begin-   beginning.
ning.

15.26   "The Helper will come--the Spirit, who
                reveals the truth about God and who comes
                from the Father. I will send him to you
                from the Father, and he will speak about me.

In Greek this verse reads literally "When the Helper comes whom I will send to you from the Father, the Spirit of truth, which comes from the Father, that one will testify concerning me." The Helper was first introduced in 14.16 (see there). TEV translates "the Spirit of truth" as the Spirit who reveals the truth about God (see 14.17). Because of the complicated clause relationships, TEV restructures the Greek by making the temporal clause of Greek ("when the Helper comes") into an independent clause. Then the main clause of the Greek sentence ("he will testify concerning me") is combined with the relative clause ("whom I will send to you from the Father") into a separate sentence: I will send him to you from the Father... NEB follows essentially the same restructuring.

Who comes from the Father does not refer to the inner life of the Trinity (which became a great theological topic during the fourth century), but rather to the source from which the Helper comes to the disciples.

The Helper is described not only as coming from the Father, but also as the one whom Jesus will send to his disciples. In 14.26 the Father is spoken of as the one who sends the Spirit, but it is doubtful if any theological distinction is to be made between these two verses. Whereas in 14.26 the pronoun referring to the Spirit is neuter, here a masculine pronoun is used, indicating that the Spirit is thought of in personal terms.

Since Helper is used as a title for the Holy Spirit, it may be essential in this type of context to indicate that the term is a title, for example, "the one who is called the Helper will come."

The locational relations in the clause I will send him to you from the Father are rather complex; and since the role of Jesus as the agent is primarily causative, it may be necessary to translate this clause "I will cause him to go from the Father and to come to you."

The verb rendered speak about is the verb normally rendered "to testify" or "to witness" by most translators. On this verb and the related noun, see the discussion at 1.7. In some languages it may be necessary to indicate to whom the Spirit speaks. One could say either "he will speak to you about me" or "he will speak to people about me." However, since the role of the Spirit was primarily in relation to the believer, and since the previous clause states specifically that Jesus is to send the Spirit to the believers, it seems preferable to render the final clause of verse 26 "and he will speak to you about me."

In verse 27, however, the grammatical goal of speaking would be other persons, for example, "and you will speak to others about me." It need not be assumed that too in verse 27 means that the two instances of the verb speak must have the same grammatical goal.

15.27   And you, too, will speak about me, because you
               have been with me from the very beginning.

The pronoun you is emphatic.

Will speak about is the same verb referred to in the previous verse.

From the very beginning translates a Greek phrase which occurs also

in 8.44. Whereas in 8.44 it means "from the beginning of the world"
or "from the beginning of his existence," here it means "from the beginning of Jesus' ministry." In this context from the very beginning
may therefore be translated "from the time that I began to teach."

CHAPTER 16

TEV (16.1-4a) RSV

16 "I have told you this, so that you will not give up your faith. 2 You will be expelled from the synagogues, and the time will come when anyone who kills you will think that by doing this he is serving God. 3 People will do these things to you because they have not known either the Father or me. 4 But I have told you this, so that when the time comes for them to do these things, you will remember what I told you.

16 "I have said all this to you to keep you from falling away. 3 They will put you out of the synagogues; indeed, the hour is coming when whoever kills you will think he is offering service to God. 3 And they will do this because they have not known the Father, nor me. 4 But I have said these things to you, that when their hour comes you may remember that I told you of them.

Although a new chapter begins here, the UBS Greek text and TEV both understand 16.1-4a of this chapter to be a continuation of 15.18-27. See the comments on Chapter 15.18-25.

16.1 "I have told you this, so that you will not give up your faith.

I have told you this is the same expression used in 15.11 and 14.25 (see there). The immediate reference is to 15.18-27.

Give up your faith translates the same verb used in 6.61 (see there); it occurs in John's Gospel only in these two verses, and in both it is a very strong term. So that you will not give up your faith is translated by JB "so that your faith may not be shaken" (NAB "to keep your faith from being shaken"), and by NEB "to guard you against the breakdown of your faith." The focus of TEV and NEB is closer to the meaning of the Greek text; the reference is to giving up or falling away from one's faith. It is not merely a matter of having one's faith shaken. In a number of languages "giving up faith" is essentially equivalent to "ceasing to believe," "stop trusting," or "cease putting one's confidence in."

16.2 You will be expelled from the synagogues, and the time will come when anyone who kills you will think that by doing this he is serving God.

For the expression be expelled from the synagogues, see 9.22 and 12.42. This meaning may be expressed in some languages as "They will no longer count you as members of their worship houses" or "They will exclude you from worship in the synagogues."

And the time will come is more literally "but an hour is coming." The conjunction that TEV translates and (Greek alla) literally means "but"; however, in the present context it is used to introduce an additional point ("not only that, but..."). Mft and NEB translate the

whole phrase as "indeed the time is coming," and Gdsp translates "the
time is coming." NAB uses a semicolon to express the force of the Greek
particle. For English readers the Greek word "hour" is best taken in
the present context with the more generic sense of "time." In some languages the equivalent of the time will come is simply "it will happen
that."

He is serving God is more literally "he is offering service to God"
(RSV). But this expression is redundant, for in Greek the verb "to offer"
and the noun "service" both refer primarily to worship offered to God.
JB translates "doing a holy duty for God," while NEB has "performing a
religious duty." Mft translates "will imagine that he is doing God a
service," and Gdsp "will think he is doing religious service to God."
In some languages he is serving God may be expressed as "he is helping
God." In others the concept of serving God may be expressed specifically
as "he is worshiping God by this means" or "he is honoring God by doing
what he does."

16.3   People will do these things to you because they
          have not known either the Father or me.

People will do these things to you may be expressed in some languages as "people will make you suffer in this way." It must be clear,
of course, that the reference is to what is described in verse 2.

The phrase to you (found in some Greek manuscripts) was perhaps
added by some scribe on the basis of 15.21. However, whether or not
these words are considered an original part of the Greek text, they are
essential in translation, and so it is legitimate to include them.

Some translations render have...known as TEV does, while others
have "knew" and still others "know." The verb is in the aorist tense,
which is best taken here as expressing a constant truth, that is, "they
have (never) known." As in many similar contexts, it is important to
use a verb for know which indicates intimate acquaintance with, or
knowledge based upon close association. The verb must convey something
more than the mere possession of information about someone.

16.4a   But I have told you this, so that when the time
          comes for them to do these things, you will re-
          member what I told you.

But I have told you this is the same expression used in 16.1, except for the addition of the conjunction "but."

When the time comes for them to do these things is literally "when
their hour comes" (see 16.2). NEB translates "when the time comes for
it to happen"; JB has "when the time for it comes."

Remember what I told you is more literally "remember that I told
you of them" (RSV). NEB translates "remember my warning" and JB "remember that I told you." As in many similar contexts, remember must be
understood in the sense of "pay attention to" or "think about." It does
not suggest that the disciples will, in the meantime, forget all that
Jesus has said.

TEV   (16.4b-11)   RSV

THE WORK OF THE HOLY SPIRIT

"I did not tell you these things at the beginning, for I was with you. 5 But now I am going to him who sent me, yet none of you asks me where I am going. 6 And now that I have told you, your hearts are full of sadness. 7 But I am telling you the truth: it is better for you that I go away, because if I do not go, the Helper will not come to you. But if I do go away, then I will send him to you. 8 And when he comes, he will prove to the people of the world that they are wrong about sin and about what is right and about God's judgment. 9 They are wrong about sin, because they do not believe in me; 10 they are wrong about what is right, because I am going to the Father and you will not see me any more; 11 and they are wrong about judgment, because the ruler of this world has already been judged.

"I did not say these things to you from the beginning, because I was with you. 5 But now I am going to him who sent me; yet none of you asks me, 'Where are you going?' 6 But because I have said these things to you, sorrow has filled your hearts. 7 Nevertheless I tell you the truth: it is to your advantage that I go away, for if I do not go away, the Counselor will not come to you; but if I go, I will send him to you. 8 And when he comes, he will convince^x the world concerning sin and righteousness and judgment: 9 concerning sin, because they do not believe in me; 10 concerning righteousness, because I go to the Father, and you will see me no more; 11 concerning judgment, because the ruler of this world is judged.

^{x}Or *convict*

Verses 4b-7 are concerned with Jesus' departure and the disciples' sadness. They serve as a background for the discussion of the work of the Holy Spirit in verses 8-15. In verses 8-11--a passage offering great difficulty to the exegete--Jesus speaks of the activity of the Holy Spirit in conflict with the world. Then, in verses 12-15, he turns to speak of the work of the Holy Spirit in relation to his followers.

It is often misleading to translate literally the section heading, The Work of the Holy Spirit, since it might seem to imply some kind of physical activity. Also, in some languages it is necessary to translate Work by a verb. If so, one must say "What the Holy Spirit does" or "What the Holy Spirit will do," since in this paragraph the reference is specifically to the future action of the Holy Spirit.

16.4b   "I did not tell you these things at the be-
            ginning, for I was with you.

These things is emphatic in the Greek sentence structure. It refers to the inevitability of persecution discussed in 15.18--16.4a.

At the beginning, though not the precise phrase used in 15.27, has the same meaning as the earlier phrase; that is, it refers to the beginning of Jesus' ministry. Jesus did not tell his disciples about future persecution at the beginning of his ministry, because he was then present to protect them, and because at that time the persecution was directed against him rather than against them. In some languages at the beginning may be rendered "when you began to follow me" or "when you first became my disciples" or "when I first began to teach you."

16.5   But now I am going to him who sent me, yet none of you asks me where I am going.

But now of this verse contrasts with at the beginning in 4b.

I am going to him who sent me (as always, a reference to the Father) repeats the words of 7.33. The same theme is repeated again in 16.10,17,28 (see also 14.12). In some languages there is a subtle obscurity involved in rendering to him who sent me. This phrase might appear to be a kind of indefinite reference, and thus not the equivalent of "to my Father who sent me." If a close correspondence to the Greek text is likely to lead to misunderstanding, it may be necessary to render this expression "to my Father who sent me."

Although the Greek text has direct discourse ("Where are you going?"), it is often better to translate by indirect discourse, as in TEV (note also GeCL "And none of you asked me where I am going"). Of course, here and in other such contexts, the translator should follow what is most natural in the receptor language.

16.6   And now that I have told you, your hearts are full of sadness.

And now that I have told you is literally "Because I have told you these things." Mft translates "No, your heart is full of sorrow at what I have told you." Although TEV brings in something of the temporal aspect (now that), it does retain the causative force as primary.

Hearts in the Greek text is literally "heart," but most translators find it natural to use the plural in English. GeCL merely translates "you are sad," while NAB renders "you are overcome with grief." Although normally in Hebrew thought the "heart" relates primarily to the intellect, here it is obviously connected with the emotions. In some languages such emotions as sadness are expressed in idiomatic ways, for example, "to weep within" or "to have tears within one's heart" or "to mourn within one's abdomen" or "to grieve within the spleen."

16.7   But I am telling you the truth: it is better for you that I go away, because if I do not go, the Helper will not come to you. But if I do go away, then I will send him to you.

Jesus indicates in this verse that the coming of the Holy Spirit as the disciples' Helper is dependent upon his going away to the Father; when he goes to the Father he will send the Helper, the Holy Spirit, to them.

But I am telling you the truth is a literal rendering of the Greek

text and is almost the same form as But I tell you the truth of 8.45.
It is not a dynamic rendering of "Amen, amen, I say to you" (see 1.51).
In some languages it may be best to translate I am telling you the truth
"What I am going to say to you is most certainly true."

It is better for you is the same expression used in 11.50 (compare
it was better of 18.14). It is better for you that I go away must be
restructured rather radically in some languages, for example, "my going
away is better for you" or "if I go away, you will be better off" or "my
going away will make you surpass in benefit" or even "...will help you
more."

The Helper was discussed at 14.16.

Here (see also 15.26) Jesus sends the Helper; in 14.26 it was the
Father who sends him.

It may be very awkward in some languages to juxtapose two such conjunctions as because if. Actually, the relation between it is better for
you that I go away and if I do not go, the Helper will not come to you
is quite clear. The second statement gives the reason for the first.
Therefore in some languages it is possible to omit the causal conjunction
because. Accordingly, one may translate "If I go away, it is better for
you; if I do not go, the Helper will not come to you." But one should
not render "If I go away" in a way which suggests that Jesus might not
go away. It may be better to employ a direct statement of what is to
happen, for example, "my going away will benefit you; if I do not go
away, the Helper will not come to you. That is why it will be better
for you."

16.8   And when he comes, he will prove to the people
          of the world that they are wrong about sin
          and about what is right and about God's judgment.

The exegesis of this verse is extremely difficult, and consequently
it is difficult to translate. The difficulties are basically two. (1)
The first major problem relates to the meaning of the Greek verb rendered
prove...wrong in TEV. It is the same verb translated prove...guilty in
8.46, and some commentators think it has the same meaning in the present
context. This meaning does suit the first noun (sin), for "prove guilty
of sin" makes good sense. However, it cannot be used satisfactorily with
"righteousness" (TEV what is right) and "judgment" (TEV God's judgment),
the two other nouns that follow. Barclay attempts to resolve the difficulty by translating the verb in two different ways ("he will convict
the world of its own sin, and he will convince the world of my righteousness and of the certainty of judgment"). However, there is no good reason for giving two different meanings to one verb within the same context. Accordingly, most modern translations use a single meaning which
is satisfactory for all three objects: "prove...wrong" (NEB); "show...how
wrong it was" (JB); "bring conviction" (Gdsp); "convince...of the meaning"
(Phps). Mft has "he will convict the world, convincing men of sin, of
righteousness, and of judgment"; GeCL translates "he will show that the
men on earth have wrong ideas about sin, about God's righteousness,
and his judgment."

(2) The second major problem of interpretation relates to the terms

[503]

rendered "sin" (TEV sin), "righteousness" (TEV what is right), and
"judgment" (TEV God's judgment). Actually, there is no basic problem
connected with the first of these terms, and all translations (except
NEB, which has "wrong") render it by the word "sin." Barclay qualifies
"sin" as "its own sin."

"Righteousness," the second of the three terms, is the most difficult. Translations generally take "righteousness" in the broadest
sense possible: "righteousness" (RSV, Mft), "justice" (NAB), "right"
(NEB), "uprightness" (Gdsp), "true goodness" (Phps), and what is right
(TEV). On the other hand, JB ("who was in the right") and Barclay ("my
righteousness") refer this term specifically to Jesus himself. And, although GeCL translates "God's righteousness" in this verse, in verse 10
it relates the term specifically to God's activity of showing that Jesus
was in the right. Verse 10, where the key to understanding the meaning
of "righteousness" must be sought, allows for either of these interpretations. That is, the reference may be either to God's righteousness
(justice) in showing that Jesus was in the right, or the focus may be
on Jesus' innocence. Arguments can be made for either viewpoint, and it
is extremely difficult to decide which is more in focus in the context.
In reality, the two ideas are closely intertwined, and it would be difficult to separate them either in meaning or in translation. If one sees
the focus on Jesus as the one who is innocent, one may translate "will
prove to the world that they were wrong about me, because God will show
that I was innocent (in the right)." But if one sees God's righteousness
in focus here, one may translate "will prove to the world that they were
wrong about God's justice, because he will show that I was innocent (in
the right)."

"Judgment," the last of these terms, is not so difficult. TEV and
GeCL make it explicitly a reference to God's judgment, while NAB affirms
that it is in fact "condemnation." Most other translations render simply
"judgment" (RSV, NEB, JB, Mft, Gdsp, Phps), while Barclay translates
"certainty of judgment," which seems to imply condemnation. The noun is
best taken to mean that God will judge (condemn) the world because of its
sin.

Note that TEV renders "the world" by the people of the world.

In certain respects, the translational difficulties in this verse
match the complications in exegesis. It may be necessary to render he
will prove as "he will show clearly" or "he will make it very plain" or
"he will speak so well that no one can answer."

They are wrong about may be rendered in some languages "they think
wrongly about" or "they do not have right ideas about" or "they do not
think correctly about."

About sin must sometimes be expanded to "about what sin is" or
"about what is involved when people do wrong" or "about what it really
means when one sins."

It may be very difficult in some languages to express the concept
"about righteousness," for any such abstract quality as "righteousness"
or "right" must be related to some kind of event or to a person who
engages in right acts. One can in some languages translate "about who
is right" or even "about who is innocent" or "...has done right."

Similarly, it may be necessary to restructure judgment as a verb,
for example, "how God will judge" or "...will certainly judge" or even
"...will condemn."

[504]

In some languages it may be necessary to restructure some of the syntactic and semantic relations in terms of specific direct discourse. For example, "They are wrong when they say, We know about sin and we know what is right and we know about God's judgment."

16.9   They are wrong about sin, because they do not
              believe in me;

They are wrong about sin is literally "concerning sin." Here, as elsewhere in the Gospel of John, the cardinal sin of the world is the refusal to believe in Jesus. Although the Greek simply has "do not believe," it is legitimate to make the idea of "refusal" specific, as NEB, JB, and NAB do. This verse may, therefore, be rendered in some languages "They are wrong about what sin is, because they refuse to put their trust in me."

16.10   they are wrong about what is right, because I
              am going to the Father and you will not see me
              any more;

What is right translates the noun ("righteousness") discussed in verse 8. It may be necessary in translating to repeat the expression "they are wrong," at the beginning of verses 10 and 11, for example, "they are wrong about what is right because..."
    Both Jesus' innocence and God's righteousness are shown in the fact that Jesus is going to the Father. Although Jesus was put to death by a human court, he was proved to be righteous and innocent by his exaltation and acceptance by God. As elsewhere, it may be necessary to translate "I am going to my Father."
    You will not see me any more does not stand in contradiction with 14.19 (in a little while...you will see me). The former passage refers specifically to the post-resurrection experiences, while the present passage refers to the presence of Jesus in his disciples through the Holy Spirit. Unless care is taken in rendering you will not see me any more, the reader may receive the impression that there is a definite contradiction with the content of verse 14.19. In some languages the problem may be avoided by rendering "you will not continue to see me any more." Such a rendering would make possible the post-resurrection appearances of Jesus, while at the same time indicating that he would not continue to remain with his disciples.

16.11   and they are wrong about judgment, because the
              ruler of this world has already been judged.

The ruler of this world is a Johannine term for the devil (see 12.31; 14.30). Jesus interprets his death, not as defeat, but rather as a triumph over the ruler of this world. Whereas 12.31 speaks of his judgment and defeat as a future event, the present verse speaks of it as a fact already accomplished.

The passive expression <u>has already been judged</u> must be made active in some languages. If so, it may be necessary to introduce God as the agent, for example, "because God has already condemned the ruler of this world." In this context, certainly, <u>judged</u> is to be understood in the sense of "judged against" or "condemned."

TEV	(16.12-15)	RSV

TEV	RSV
12 "I have much more to tell you, but now it would be too much for you to bear. 13 When, however, the Spirit comes, who reveals the truth about God, he will lead you into all the truth. He will not speak on his own authority, but he will speak of what he hears and will tell you of things to come. 14 He will give me glory, because he will take what I say and tell it to you. 15 All that my Father has is mine; that is why I said that the Spirit will take what I give him and tell it to you.	12 "I have yet many things to say to you, but you cannot bear them now. 13 When the Spirit of truth comes, he will guide you into all the truth; for he will not speak on his own authority, but whatever he hears he will speak, and he will declare to you the things that are to come. 14 He will glorify me, for he will take what is mine and declare it to you. 15 All that the Father has is mine; therefore I said that he will take what is mine and de- clare it to you.

16.12   "I have much more to tell you, but now it
        would be too much for you to bear.

<u>It would be too much for you to bear</u> (NEB "but the burden would be too great for you now") is more literally "but you are not able to bear (it) now." <u>Too much for you to bear</u> may also be rendered "your ears can- not hear it" or "it will be too much for your thoughts" or "my words would have no place in your minds."

16.13   When, however, the Spirit comes, who reveals
        the truth about God, he will lead you into all
        the truth. He will not speak on his own authority,
        but he will speak of what he hears and will tell
        you of things to come.

<u>The Spirit...who reveals the truth about God</u> is repeated from 14.17 and 15.26. This expression may have several different forms, for example, "the Spirit who shows what is true about God" or "the Spirit who speaks the true words about God" or "the Spirit who will reveal what God truly is."

The verb translated <u>lead</u> appears frequently in the Greek translation of the Psalms (for example, 5.8; 27.11; 106.9; 119.35). In Revelation 7.17 it is used of the Lamb, who will guide God's people to the springs of life-giving water. <u>Will lead you into all the truth</u> may be expressed as a causative, for example, "will cause you to know all the truth." In this context all the truth refers to what the Spirit will reveal, namely, what he hears from God. Therefore all the truth may be rendered "all the truth that comes from God."

The second half of verse 13 further describes the Spirit's role: he will speak of what he hears and will tell you of things to come. Like the Son (12.49; 14.10), the Spirit does not speak on his own authority but only what he hears. The present tense (he hears) has the support of some Greek manuscripts. The UBS Committee prefers the future tense ("he will hear"), but Anchor considers that he hears should be preferred as the more difficult reading, since all the verbs in the immediate context are future. Apart from the textual question, the present tense may be preferred on translational grounds. Although this verse does not indicate the source of what the Spirit hears, it is clearly the Father, just as Jesus himself tells the world only what he has heard from the Father (8.26).

The verb translated he...will tell is repeated in the following two verses. It is also used by the Samaritan woman in 4.25, where, as in 16.13,14,15, the object is divine revelation: when he (the Messiah) comes, he will tell us everything.

Things to come does not refer to events of the immediate future, such as Jesus' crucifixion and resurrection, since the Spirit will not be given until Jesus has been raised to glory (7.39). In the Old Testament to tell...of things to come is reserved to God alone (compare Isa 44.7).

16.14   He will give me glory, because he will take
         what I say and tell it to you.

He will give me glory is usually translated "he will glorify me" (RSV). Gdsp renders "He will do honor to me" and Phps has "He will bring glory to me." Although the Spirit will "bring glory to Jesus," by revealing his true glory, and here it is this aspect that is in focus. Note the GeCL: "in this way he will show you my glory." This revelation of Jesus' glory may be expressed as "he will show you how glorious I really am" or "...how wonderful I am."

He will take what I say and tell it to you is more literally "he will receive from what is mine and tell it to you." The revelation which comes to the Christian community through the Holy Spirit is the same divine revelation spoken to the disciples through Jesus Christ. This verse is similar in meaning to 14.26 (see there). In some languages it is necessary to be specific about the content of what I say. Note, for example, how GeCL restructures this verse and so connects it more closely with the previous verse: "(13)...but he shall tell you what he hears. He shall speak of what is coming. (14) He hears it from me and repeats it to you. In this way he will reveal my glory."

16.15   All that my Father has is mine; that is why I
         said that the Spirit will take what I give him
         and tell it to you.

All that my Father has is mine is related closely to the thought of 3.35 and 5.20 (see there). This same claim is repeated at 17.10. The specific reference here is to the truth which Christ communicates, and this fact is made clear in the second half of the verse.

The clause introduced by that is why I said that qualifies the content of what is referred to by all that the Father has is mine. The Spirit will take the full truth that Christ gives him and tell it to the disciples.

The Spirit will take what I give him is literally "...he receives from what is mine." TEV makes the pronominal reference "he" explicit as a reference to the Spirit; it also takes the Greek present tense ("receives") as the equivalent of the future in the previous verse, since the change of tense apparently carries no significance. Finally, it restructures the words "he receives from what is mine" to read will take what I give him. What is taken and received is, of course, the revelation. Accordingly, one may translate in some languages "the Spirit will listen to what I tell him and then he will tell it to you."

TEV	(16.16-24)	RSV

SADNESS AND GLADNESS

16 "In a little while you will not see me any more, and then a little while later you will see me."

17 Some of his disciples asked among themselves, "What does this mean? He tells us that in a little while we will not see him, and then a little while later we will see him; and he also says, 'It is because I am going to the Father.' 18 What does this 'a little while' mean? We don't know what he is talking about!"

19 Jesus knew that they wanted to question him, so he said to them, "I said, 'In a little while you will not see me, and then a little while later you will see me.' Is this what you are asking about among yourselves? 20 I am telling you the truth: you will cry and weep, but the world will be glad; you will be sad, but your sadness will turn into gladness. 21 When a woman is about to give birth, she is sad because her hour of suffering has come; but when the baby is born, she forgets her

16 "A little while, and you will see me no more; again a little while, and you will see me." 17 Some of his disciples said to one another, "What is this that he says to us, 'A little while, and you will not see me, and again a little while, and you will see me'; and, 'because I go to the Father'?" 18 They said, "What does he mean by 'a little while'? We do not know what he means." 19 Jesus knew that they wanted to ask him; so he said to them, "Is this what you are asking yourselves, what I meant by saying, 'A little while, and you will not see me, and again a little while, and you will see me'? 20 Truly, truly, I say to you, you will weep and lament, but the world will rejoice; you will be sorrowful, but your sorrow will turn into joy. 21 When a woman is in travail she has sorrow, because her hour has come; but when she is delivered of the child, she no longer remembers the anguish, for joy that

suffering, because she is happy
that a baby has been born into the
world. 22 That is how it is with
you: now you are sad, but I will
see you again, and your hearts will
be filled with gladness, the kind
of gladness that no one can take
away from you.

23 "When that day comes, you
will not ask me for anything. I
am telling you the truth: the Father will give you whatever you
ask of him in my name.ᶠ 24 Until
now you have not asked for anything in my name; ask and you will
receive, so that your happiness
may be complete.

ᶠThe Father will give you whatever
you ask of him in my name; *some
manuscripts have* if you ask the
Father for anything, he will give
it to you in my name.

a childʲ is born into the world.
22 So you have sorrow now, but I
will see you again and your hearts
will rejoice, and no one will take
your joy from you. 23 In that day
you will ask nothing of me. Truly,
truly, I say to you, if you ask
anything of the Father, he will
give it to you in my name. 24
Hitherto you have asked nothing
in my name; ask, and you will receive, that your joy may be full.

ʲGreek *a human being*

Even though verses 4b-15 and 16-33 are an overall unity (note, for
example, that because I am going to the Father in verse 17 refers back
to Jesus' words in verse 10), stylistically there is a difference: 16-33
are in the form of a dialogue between Jesus and his disciples, while
4b-15 contain a monologue. While agreement is lacking regarding the
manner in which 16-33 should be subdivided, the divisions made in the
UBS Greek text and followed by TEV (16-24 and 25-33) represent the conclusion of a number of scholars.

Verses 25-33 may logically be viewed as a self-contained unit,
since verse 25 opens with I have told you these things and verse 33
with I have told you this, suggesting that between these verses there
is an inclusion. On the other hand, though the formal structure of the
section may suggest a self-contained unit, the subject matter of 23b-24
is similar to that of 26-27; so it is difficult to be fully satisfied
with this subdivision. The problem in part arises from the very nature
of the Johannine discourse material. John introduces a theme, drops it
to pick up another, and then returns to the previous theme, sometimes
intertwining the two.

In a little while you will not see me anymore of verse 16 is an
obvious reference to Jesus' approaching death. However, it is not so
clear what is meant by the following statement (then a little while
later you will see me), and it is significant that the disciples themselves did not understand Jesus' meaning (verse 17). Some scholars
maintain that the little while refers to the time between Jesus' death
and the end of time, and so believe that the reference to the disciples'
seeing him again means his final return. Other scholars hold that, in
the original setting, Jesus thought of his resurrection and his final
return as one and the same event. So the distinction between seeing

Jesus during his post-resurrection appearances and at his final revelation may have developed out of the actual historical circumstances, in
that the resurrection of Jesus did not bring about his final appearance.
The problem of what is intended here is made more difficult by the fact
that the reader is never completely certain whether Jesus' words are to
be understood from the viewpoint of his own day, or from that of the
time of the writing of the Gospel. If they are to be understood from
the time perspective of the author of the Gospel, then "seeing Jesus"
would refer to the abiding presence of Jesus with his disciples through
the Holy Spirit.

In verses 17 and 18 the disciples ask among themselves what Jesus
means by these words; and verse 19 again reflects Jesus' knowledge of
what goes on in the minds of men. He lets his disciples know that he is
conscious of the question they are discussing among themselves. He does
not answer the question directly, but he instead tells a parable illustrating sadness and joy. Like a woman who is about to give birth to a
child, the disciples will experience sadness while Jesus is away, but
when he returns again, they will be filled with gladness, the kind of
gladness that no one can take away from them (verses 20-22). He follows
these words with the promise that, when that day comes, they may ask
anything from the Father and he will give it to them (verse 23). Anything in this verse must be taken to refer to anything in keeping with
their life as disciples.

Verse 24 concludes with Jesus' declaration that the disciples have
not yet asked anything in his name. But the implication is that after
his death they will receive the Spirit, so that they can ask in his
name. They will receive what they ask for, and their happiness will be
complete.

The section heading, Sadness and Gladness, must be somewhat expanded
in some languages, for example, "You will be sad, and then you will be
glad" or "Soon you will be sad, but later you will be glad" or even
"First sadness and then gladness."

16.16   "In a little while you will not see me any
                 more, and then a little while later you will
                 see me."

For the phrase In a little while, see 13.33 and 14.19. Note also
7.33 and 12.35.

Two different Greek verbs for see are used in this verse, one from
the stem theoreō, and the other from the stem horaō. Some commentators
believe that the latter refers to a deeper spiritual insight, but the
present consensus of New Testament scholarship is that the two verbs
are synonymous.

Then a little while later is more literally "and again a little
while," which NAB translates "but soon after that (you shall see me)
again." As indicated in the introduction to this section, Jesus was
most probably referring to his return to the disciples after death, not
distinguishing in this instance between the post-resurrection appearances
and his final appearance. In some languages it is impossible to be as
ambiguous as the phrase a little while is in Greek. It is probably best,

in this context, to assume that <u>in a little while</u> refers primarily to Jesus' immediate reappearance after his resurrection. Therefore one may translate <u>in a little while</u> as essentially equivalent to "in a few days."

16.17   Some of his disciples asked among them-
          selves, "What does this mean? He tells us
          that in a little while we will not see him,
          and then a little while later we will see him;
          and he also says, 'It is because I am going to
          the Father.'

<u>What does this mean? He tells us</u> is literally "What is this that he is saying to us?" NAB translates "What can he mean...?" NEB "What does he mean by this...?"; and JB "What does he mean...?" It may also be rendered as "What is he trying to say to us?" or "...to tell us?" This expression may be combined with what follows by saying "What is he trying to say to us when he tells us that...?"
<u>And he also says, 'It is because I am going to the Father'</u> is lit-erally "and because I am going to the Father." NEB renders "and by this: 'Because I am going to my Father'?" "My Father" is legitimate on trans-lational grounds, because Jesus is obviously referring to God as his Father.
In some languages it is essential to make a clear distinction be-tween two different possibilities of relating <u>It is because I am going to the Father</u> to the preceding question <u>What does this mean?</u> In some languages it may be best to render the final part of verse 17 "What does this mean when he says, It is because I am going to the Father?" It is also possible to interpret "It is" as referring directly to the temporal expression "in a little while" and the related idea that the disciples will no longer see Jesus. One may therefore translate "And he also says we will not see him because he is going to the Father."

16.18   What does this 'a little while' mean? We
          don't know what he is talking about!"

In Greek verse 18 begins with two words which may be rendered "so they were saying," which are omitted on translational grounds by TEV.
After the question <u>What does...mean?</u>, the UBS Greek text includes in brackets words that NEB renders "that he speaks of." TEV omits these words, not on textual grounds, but because they are redundant for the English reader.
It may be difficult in some languages to include a direct statement within a direct statement, and therefore the question asked by the dis-ciples may have to be restructured as "What does Jesus mean when he says the words, a little while?" or "What is Jesus trying to tell us when he speaks the words, a little while?"
<u>We don't know what he is talking about</u> (NAB "We do not know what he is talking about") is rendered "We do not know what he means" by RSV and NEB.

[511]

16.19   Jesus knew that they wanted to question him,
          so he said to them, "I said, 'In a little while
          you will not see me, and then a little while
          later you will see me.' Is this what you are
          asking about among yourselves?

In Greek, Jesus' reply to his disciples is a single sentence. Is
that what you are asking among yourselves? contains the first element
in the Greek sentence order. Compare, for example, the fairly literal
rendering of RSV: "Is this what you are asking yourselves, what I meant
by saying, 'A little while, and you will not see me, and again a little
while, and you will see me'?" JB translates Jesus' reply in a statement,
"You are asking one another what I meant by saying: In a short time you
will no longer see me again." NAB is similar to JB in its restructuring.

16.20   I am telling you the truth: you will cry and
          weep, but the world will be glad; you will be
          sad, but your sadness will turn into gladness.

I am telling you the truth translates the same formula first discussed at 1.51.
        The second occurrence of the pronoun you is emphatic in the Greek
sentence structure, and it is placed in immediate and direct contrast
to the world.
        The verbs cry and weep reflect the loud weeping and wailing that
was (and still is) customary on the occasion of a death in the Near
East. The first of these verbs appears in 11.31; 20.11; and Mark 16.10.
The other verb is used of the women who mourn for Jesus on the way to
the cross (Luke 23.27). Both verbs occur in the Septuagint of Jeremiah
22.10.
        In this context, as in many others, the world may be rendered "the
people of the world." (See discussion at 1.10.)
        The last occurrence of the pronoun you is also emphatic.
        Jesus' prediction your sadness will turn into gladness is fulfilled
in 20.20. It may be difficult to render this clause literally, because
in many languages there is no abstract term for either sadness or gladness. However, one can say "First you will be sad but then you will be
glad" or "...become glad."

16.21   When a woman is about to give birth, she is
          sad because her hour of suffering has come;
          but when the baby is born, she forgets her
          suffering, because she is happy that a baby
          has been born into the world.

This verse is a parable, illustrating what Jesus meant by his remarks in verse 20. The Greek literally has "when the woman," but the
definite article "the" is simply a reflection of Semitic parabolic style.
For example, in 12.24 a grain of wheat is literally "the grain of
wheat." In English, however, it is more natural to translate with the
indefinite article "a."

She is sad is literally "she has sadness."

In some languages there is a problem in choosing a word for sad, since the emotion characteristic of a woman about to give birth would not be described as the same sort of sadness the disciples would presumably experience in contemplating the departure of Jesus. It is important, however, that the same term be used in both contexts; otherwise, the explanation in verse 21 will not seem relevant to what is said in verse 20. The aspect of sadness emphasized here is anxiety about the future, and a woman often experiences this kind of anxiety before giving birth to a child. In some languages the more usual term for sadness focuses upon what has already happened, but in this context it is important to employ a term or phrase which will emphasize anxiety about the future.

The Greek text has "her hour," which TEV qualifies as her hour of suffering. NEB renders "her time" (so also NAB and JB). Jesus uses the ordinary experience of human birth to illustrate what he means, but his language reflects the language of the Old Testament, which speaks of the suffering of the faithful before the day of the Lord in terms of birth pangs. See, for example, Isaiah 26.17; 66.7; and Micah 4.9. Her hour of suffering may be expressed in many languages as "the time when she will suffer" or "the time when she will have great pain."

She forgets is expressed negatively in Greek as "she no longer remembers." An appropriate equivalent for she forgets may be "she no longer thinks about" or "thoughts about her suffering no longer come into her mind."

Since suffering is stated explicitly in the Greek text, it offers a basis for making explicit the meaning of "her hour" in the earlier part of the verse.

Baby renders the Greek word which normally means "man" or "human being"; but in English baby is more appropriate to the context.

16.22   That is how it is with you: now you are sad,
          but I will see you again, and your hearts
          will be filled with gladness, the kind of
          gladness that no one can take away from you.

That is how it is with you (JB, NEB "So it is with you"; NAB "In the same way") translates the Greek word kai, which means "and" or "also." Here it is used to draw a parallel between the parable and the experiences of the disciples. That is how it is with you may be rendered "that is what you are experiencing now" or "that is what is happening to you right now."

The pronoun you (you are sad) is emphatic in the Greek sentence structure.

You are sad translates the UBS Greek text, which has the verb in the present tense (literally "you have sadness"). However, in some manuscripts the Greek verb used here is in the future tense. Most translators evidently prefer the present tense; and the future tense was probably used in some manuscripts because of you will be sad in verse 20.

Your hearts will be filled with gladness is more literally "your (plural) heart will be glad." But in English it is natural to say your

hearts when speaking of more than one person. The translation will be
filled with gladness is simply an idiomatic way of saying "will be
glad." Gladness is often expressed in other idiomatic ways, for example,
"your heart will dance," "you will feel sweetness," or "happiness will
grab you."

Can take away appears in some manuscripts in the future tense (note
are sad above), but most translations prefer the present tense. Moreover, the Greek text is literally "no one takes it away from you," but
can (can take) is implicit, and many translations make it explicit as
TEV.

In some languages "taking away gladness" can be expressed as "causing someone not to feel gladness any longer." Thus the final clause of
verse 22 may be translated "You will be glad in such a way that no one
can cause you to cease being glad" or "...stop you from being glad" or
"...stop your hearts from dancing."

16.23   "When that day comes, you will not ask me for
           anything. I am telling you the truth: the Father
           will give you whatever you ask of him in my name.^{f}

^{f}the Father will give you whatever you ask of him
in my name; *some manuscripts have* if you ask the
Father for anything, he will give it to you in my
name.

When that day comes is literally "and in that day." The same phrase
appears again in verse 26 (see also 14.20).
There is a question regarding the interpretation of the verb rendered ask...for in TEV. RSV, NEB, and Barclay take it with the same
meaning that TEV does; but others GeCL, NAB, JB, Mft, Gdsp, Phps, Segond,
Zür, Luther Revised) take it to mean "ask a question." The problem of
interpretation is made more complex by the fact that two different verbs
meaning "to ask" are used in this verse. The one under discussion (Greek
erōtaō) originally meant "to ask a question," while the second (Greek
aiteō) originally meant "to ask for something." But the verb erōtaō is
also sometimes used in Greek literature with the meaning "to ask for
something," and John himself elsewhere uses it with that meaning (see
4.31,40,47; 14.16; 16.26b; 17.20). The question here is: does John use
both verbs with the meaning "to ask for something," or does he use the
first verb with the meaning "to ask a question"? The answer depends
upon whether verse 23a goes with what precedes or with what follows. If
it goes with what precedes, the meaning of the first verb will be "to
ask questions"; but if it goes with what follows (23b-24), the meaning
will be "to ask for something." Although John does use this verb elsewhere in the sense of "to ask for something," in the context of Chapter
16 it is definitely used three times with the meaning "to ask a question" (see 16.5,19,30). Then, too, in the present context the disciples
have not asked Jesus for anything, and he is apparently drawing a contrast between "now" (the time of his ministry) and "that day." On the
basis of this observation, the meaning seems to be that after Jesus
leaves, the disciples will no longer have to ask him any questions,

because the Holy Spirit will be able to guide them into full truth. Moreover, the solemn words I tell you the truth signal a change in subject matter between 23a and 23b, and so support this interpretation. If these conclusions are correct, the verb here means "to ask questions," and relates to what precedes (16-22). Then verses 23b-24 pick up a new subject, that of asking the Father for something in Jesus' name.

TEV inverts the last clause in verse 23, which literally reads "whatever you ask the Father in my name he will give you." As the TEV alternative rendering in the footnote points out, the placing of the phrase in my name poses a problem. In some Greek manuscripts it goes easily with the verb ask (TEV, NEB, GeCL, Barclay), while in others it goes only with the verb give (NAB, Mft, JB, Phps, Gdsp, RSV, Zür, Luther Revised). There is stronger textual support for placing the phrase with the verb ask. Also, the context is one of prayer, which the Gospel writer elsewhere connects with the name of Jesus (14.13,14; 16.16,24,26). On the basis of these observations, the UBS Committee on the Greek text favors placing the phrase in connection with the verb ask. However, it rates its choice a "C" decision, indicating considerable doubt whether the text or the apparatus contains the better reading.

In favor of the reading which places in my name with the verb give is the fact that this reading is the more difficult one. It is not likely that a scribe would move this phrase from a position where it goes easily with the verb ask to a position where it might be taken with the verb give, since nowhere else in John or in the New Testament is anything "given" in Jesus' name.

For a discussion of the phrase in my name, see 14.13. GeCL, which connects the phrase with the verb ask, renders "the Father will give you all that you ask if you will call on me." However, Gdsp, who connects it with the verb give, translates "whatever you ask the Father for, he will give you as my followers.

16.24   Until now you have not asked for anything
in my name; ask and you will receive, so
that your happiness may be complete.

Asked for translates the Greek verb aiteō (see verse 23). In this context in my name may be rendered either "by calling on me" or "because you are my disciples" or "...my followers."

The verb ask is in the present imperative, suggesting that the request should be persistent and continuous.

In some languages it may be necessary to indicate the agent with such an expression as you will receive. It may be rendered in an active form by "God will give it to you" or "you will receive it from God."

May be complete is more literally "may be full." So that your happiness may be complete may be rendered in some languages "so that you may be completely happy" or "so that there may be nothing lacking in your being happy."

So that translates a Greek conjunction (hina), which normally denotes purpose, but in the present context it appears to indicate result. However, in Jewish thought the ideas of purpose and result are not easily distinguished in declarations of God's will.

VICTORY OVER THE WORLD

25 "I have used figures of speech to tell you these things. But the time will come when I will not use figures of speech, but will speak to you plainly about the Father. 26 When that day comes, you will ask him in my name; and I do not say that I will ask him on your behalf, 27 for the Father himself loves you. He loves you because you love me and have believed that I came from God. 28 I did come from the Father, and I came into the world; and now I am leaving the world and going to the Father."

25 "I have said this to you in figures; the hour is coming when I shall no longer speak to you in figures but tell you plainly of the Father. 26 In that day you will ask in my name; and I do not say to you that I shall pray the Father for you; 27 for the Father himself loves you, because you have loved me and have believed that I came from the Father. 28 I came from the Father and have come into the world; again, I am leaving the world and going to the Father."

Verse 25 suggests that Jesus' words to his disciples are coming to an end. In these last few verses are united the themes of parables and plain speech, of Jesus' desertion by his disciples, and of the promise of ultimate victory. Jesus begins by telling his disciples that the time is coming when he will no longer speak to them in parables, but will tell them in plain words about the Father (verse 25). This seems to be a reference to the work of the Holy Spirit. Then the theme of speaking plainly to the disciples about the Father is united with that of asking and receiving from the Father (verses 26-27). Finally, Jesus affirms again his own origin and destination (verse 28). The disciples then respond, affirming that they do believe in Jesus' divine origin (verses 29-30). To this Jesus replies that their faith is not strong enough now (verse 31), for the time is coming when he will be left alone (verse 32). But his final remarks are words of encouragement: he has overcome the world, and his disciples must be brave in the confidence that they will ultimately share this victory (verse 33).

The section heading, Victory over the World, may require some expansion, for example, "Jesus will have victory over the world." It may even be possible to employ the last sentence of this section, "I have defeated the world," as a section heading. Or the immediately preceding admonition, "Be brave," may be used.

16.25   "I have used figures of speech to tell you these things. But the time will come when I will not use figures of speech, but will speak to you plainly about the Father.

These things is emphatic in the Greek sentence structure; and the word translated figures of speech is the same word translated parable in 10.6 (see there). The reference to Jesus' use of figures of speech in teaching must not be limited to the analogy of the woman in childbirth. It may include as well the symbolism involved in washing the disciples' feet (13.8-11) and the parable of the vine and the branches (15.1-17); and it may even be enlarged to include such discourses as that of the shepherd (10.1-18). In fact, the reference may be to everything that Jesus has thus far taught his disciples, including this last discourse, but not limited to it.

In many languages, figures of speech is rendered "likeness words" or "words which show likenesses." In some, one may even use such a phrase as "picture words." In others, such a descriptive phrase may be employed as "calling something by another name" or "using other words to speak of the same thing." In general, however, the equivalent of "parables" is "stories" or "stories which teach." A variety of expressions may be used in interpreting figurative language. Fortunately, figurative language is a universal phenomenon of speech, and its existence in any and all languages is readily recognized, though it may be described or spoken of in different ways.

The Greek word translated plainly (so also NEB, JB) is used in 7.4 in the phrase to be well known (see there). This word (Greek parrēsia) may mean "openly," "in boldness," or "plainly." NAB translates "in plain speech," while the whole phrase is translated "let you know plainly" by Mft; "tell you plainly" by Gdsp and Phps, and "tell you...absolutely clearly" by Barclay. In some languages a qualifier, such as plainly, must refer to the manner in which people comprehend, not the way a person speaks. Hence, one may render the last part of verse 25 "I will speak to you about the Father in such a way that you will clearly understand."

16.26   When that day comes, you will ask him in
       my name; and I do not say that I will ask
       him on your behalf.

When that day comes (literally "in that day") refers to the time mentioned in verse 25.

Him (a reference to the Father) is not explicit in the Greek text, though TEV and GeCL make it so.

For a discussion of in my name see comments at 14.13. Most translators apparently prefer to render the phrase literally, but Gdsp has "you will ask as my followers" and GeCL "then you will ask by appealing to me."

Two different verbs for ask are used in this verse: aiteō (you will ask him) and erōtaō (I will ask him). See the discussion of them in verse 23. In the context the petition specifically relates to deeper understanding. The implication is that the prayer will be granted and this fact is stated explicitly in 14.13: I will do whatever you ask for in my name.

And I do not say that I will ask him on your behalf (Phps "for I need make no promise to plead to the Father for you") indicates that Jesus will not have to call the Father's attention to the needs of the disciples, for they can pray to the Father directly through the help of the Spirit.

In some languages there are complications in the placement of the

[517]

negative not in the sentence I do not say that I will ask him on your behalf. This might mean in some languages "I say that I will not ask him on your behalf." Compare, for example, the English sentence "I don't think he will go," which is really equivalent to "I think he will not go." It may therefore be necessary to translate this last part of verse 26 "I will not need to ask him on your behalf" or "...ask him to help you."

16.27 for the Father himself loves you. He loves you because you love me and have believed that I came from God.

The Father loves the disciples. Therefore Jesus will not have to petition him in their behalf. The Greek verb used here for love is phileō. In 14.21,23 the verb is agapaō, but the two verbs are used synonymously (see comments at 3.35).

He loves you because is literally "because." Since TEV breaks the sentence here, it reintroduces the verb loves, with the Father as the subject. In 14.21,23 the disciples are required to love Jesus and to obey his commands if they are to be loved by the Father. Here they are to love Jesus and to believe in him if they are to experience the Father's love. These statements indicate that for John the concepts of love, obedience, and faith are simply different ways of expressing one's relation to the Son. The verbs you love and have believed are in the perfect tense in Greek, indicating a continuous attitude of life. In the clause because you love me and have believed that I came from God, the pronouns you, me, and I are emphatic.

In place of the reading from God, there is strong textual support for the reading "from the Father," but Gdsp is apparently the only modern translation which follows this reading. The UBS Committee on the Greek text assumes that the phrase "from the Father" was brought into this verse on the basis of its presence in the following verse.

Since the Father has already been identified in the first part of verse 27 and is referred to by the definite pronoun He in the second clause, some confusion may arise from translating literally have believed that I came from God. This translation might give the impression that there is some distinction between the Father and God. In fact, in some languages it is obligatory to translate "and have believed that I came from him." As elsewhere, it may be necessary to change the Father to "my Father." Similarly, one may wish to change the Father in verse 28 to "my Father."

16.28 I did come from the Father, and I came into the world; and now I am leaving the world and going to the Father."

This verse is a summary of John's teaching regarding the Son: he came from the Father into the world, and he leaves the world to return to the Father. I did come from the Father is omitted from some Greek manuscripts, but the UBS Committee considers this omission accidental.

All translations include this clause, though NAB places it in brackets, indicating some doubt regarding its authenticity.

In Greek the verb did come is in the aorist tense, pointing back to the particular moment of the Son's coming into the world, while came is in the perfect tense, emphasizing the lasting effect of his coming. GeCL translates the two verbs as one: "I have come from the Father into the world." Most other translations maintain two distinct verbs.

And now (so also JB; "now" of many translations) is literally "again" (so RSV, Mft), a particle used to indicate what is next in sequence.

TEV	(16.29-33)	RSV

29 Then his disciples said to him, "Now you are speaking plainly, without using figures of speech. 30 We know now that you know everything; you do not need to have someone ask you questions. This makes us believe that you came from God."

31 Jesus answered them, "Do you believe now? 32 The time is coming, and is already here, when all of you will be scattered, each one to his own home, and I will be left all alone. But I am not really alone, because the Father is with me. 33 I have told you this so that you will have peace by being united to me. The world will make you suffer. But be brave! I have defeated the world!"

29 His disciples said, "Ah, now you are speaking plainly, not in any figure! 30 Now we know that you know all things, and need none to question you; by this we believe that you came from God." 31 Jesus answered them, "Do you now believe? 32 The hour is coming, indeed it has come, when you will be scattered, every man to his home, and will leave me alone; yet I am not alone, for the Father is with me. 33 I have said this to you, that in me you may have peace. In the world you have tribulation; but be of good cheer, I have overcome the world."

16.29   Then his disciples said to him, "Now you are
             speaking plainly, without using figures of speech.

Then his disciples said to him is more literally "his disciples are saying" (RSV "His disciples said"). TEV includes the particle then to indicate the transition. To emphasize the disciples' words, NAB reorders the elements somewhat: "'At last you are talking plainly,' his disciples exclaimed, 'without talking in veiled language!'"

Now is emphatic in the Greek sentence structure; NAB renders by "at last."

Plainly and figures of speech translate the same words used in verse 25. Without using figures of speech may be rendered "you are not using words which show comparisons" or "you are not using similarities."

16.30   We know now that you know everything; you do
             not need to have someone ask you questions.
             This makes us believe that you came from God.

Now is in the emphatic position in the Greek sentence structure.
You know everything must be taken as a reference to verse 19,
where Jesus answered the disciples' question before they asked it, indicating that he knew what was in peoples' minds (see 2.24-25). It is
in this light also that their statement you do not need someone to ask
you questions must be understood. The verb rendered ask...questions
(so also NAB) is erōtaō (see verses 23 and 26), and relates to requests
for information. On the basis of the observation that Jesus knows what
is in their minds, and is able to answer their questions even before
they ask him, the disciples respond by saying This makes us believe
that you came from God. This makes us believe (so also Mft, Gdsp) is
literally "by this we believe" (RSV), and is rendered "because of this
we believe" in JB and NEB.
     In some languages it may be necessary to distinguish between two
meanings of the verb know. In one meaning We know may be equivalent to
"we are certain" or "we are sure." The other meaning of know indicates
complete comprehension. Hence, the first clause in verse 30 may be
translated "we are certain that you comprehend everything."
     You do not need to have someone ask you questions is a semantically
condensed expression. It really means that "in order to know what questions people have in their minds, it is not necessary for you to ask
them what they are thinking." It may be necessary to employ such a rendering to express the meaning of the second clause of verse 30.
     This makes us believe involves a complex causative relation in
some languages. This relation may be expressed as "because of this we
believe" or "because you know what people are thinking, we believe."

16.31   Jesus answered them, "Do you believe now?

     Do you believe now? is rendered as a question in most modern trans-
lations. However, GeCL ("now you believe; (32) but...") and the NEB margin ("At the moment you believe; but look...") punctuate it as a statement. The similar situation in 13.38 supports a question here, though
no absolute decision can be made. Either way, whether a question or a
statement, the impact of Jesus' words is to cast doubt on the strength
of the disciples' faith. To indicate clearly the inadequacy of the disciples' faith, it may be useful to render the question "Do you really
believe now?" or "Do you have complete confidence in me now?"

16.32   The time is coming, and is already here, when
             all of you will be scattered, each one to his
             own home, and I will be left all alone. But I
             am not really alone, because the Father is with
             me.

This verse begins in Greek with a particle (idou) used to signify emphasis. It is related to the particle used in verse 29.

The time is coming, and is already here refers to the events of Jesus' arrest and crucifixion, which are almost upon Jesus and his disciples. As noted in several other instances, it is impossible in some languages to speak of "time coming." An equivalent of this introductory temporal expression may be found in "It will soon happen--very, very soon" or "in just a little while--in fact, in a very short while." Such temporal expressions may be combined with the following clause: "soon, in fact very soon, all of you will be scattered."

When (so most translations) translates a particle in Greek which often indicates either purpose or result, but most translators see it as having a temporal significance here. If taken as a particle of purpose, it indicates that these things happened in order to fulfill the prophecy of Zechariah 13.7, referred to in this verse. As a parallel to this verse see Matthew 26.31,56 and Mark 14.26,49.

It is difficult in some languages to render satisfactorily will be scattered, because if this passive expression is changed into an active one, an agent must be specified. But to do so would involve introducing an explanation of just how the soldiers and others who went out to arrest Jesus caused the disciples to be scattered. It may, therefore, be better in this instance to translate "all of you will run away."

To his own home is also used in 19.27, where it is translated in TEV as to live in his home. Most other translations have the same meaning, though JB ("each going his own way") and NAB ("each will go his way") render in a more generic fashion. The use of this same phrase in 19.27 indicates that the meaning to his own home is preferable. But the question remains whether John has in mind the homes of the disciples in Galilee or the places where they were staying in Jerusalem during the festival. The former seems more likely.

I will be left all alone may be changed from a passive to an active expression by rendering the clause "no one will remain with me" thus providing an excellent basis for the contrast in the following clause. However, for some languages it may be difficult to contrast a future state of not being alone with a presumed present state of never being alone. Therefore it may be necessary to render But I am not really alone "but I am never really alone," which focuses upon the continuous presence of Jesus' Father with him. To translate the first part of the last sentence of verse 31 in this way makes it necessary to render because the Father is with me "because my Father is always with me."

But I am not really alone is more literally "and I am not alone" (RSV "yet I am not alone"). TEV includes the adverb really to indicate that even though Jesus is apparently alone, he is not really alone, because the Father is with him. Anchor expresses the contrast by translating "yet I am never alone."

16.33   I have told you this so that you will have
           peace by being united to me. The world will
           make you suffer. But be brave! I have defeated
           the world!"

I have told you this appears first in 14.25. The reference may be to the previous verse, but it more likely refers to the entire discourse, at least as far back as 16.1.

So that you will have peace by being united to me is more literally "so that in me you may have peace." For the meaning of peace, see comments on 14.27. Barclay translates "that in me you may have all that makes for true happiness." The meaning of "in me" is either "in union with me" or "in fellowship with me."

The phrase by being united to me expresses means. It may be rendered in some languages as causative, for example, "so that your being united to me will cause you to be truly happy." In some languages means may be expressed by a clause introduced by "because," for example, "so that you will have true happiness because you are united to me" or "...because you are one with me" or "...joined to me."

The world will make you suffer is literally "in the world you have suffering." Structurally "in the world" is in contrast with "in me." Since the world refers to the world of evil in its opposition to God (see 1.10), TEV restructures to indicate that the world is the source of the suffering brought on the disciples. The word used here for "suffering" (thlipsis) is the same one used in verse 21. Elsewhere in the New Testament it is used to refer to the sufferings believers must endure (see Mark 4.17; 13.19,24; Acts 11.19; Eph 3.13; and Rev 7.14).

But be brave is a word of encouragement (NAB "But take courage!"; NEB "But courage!"). An admonition to be brave may be expressed in some languages in an idiomatic form, for example, "stand up to the danger" or "do not run away." In some languages an expression for bravery may seem almost contradictory to our own ways of thinking; for example, for a person to be brave is in some languages "to have a hard heart" or even "to have a heart like stone."

The verb defeated is used only here in the Gospel of John, but note its use in 1 John 2.13-14; 4.4; 5.4-5. Both Paul (1 Cor 15.57) and the author of Revelation (5.5; 6.2; and 17.14) speak of Jesus as the one who defeats the world and so gives victory to his followers. In some languages have defeated would be rendered "have won the battle against" or "have been successful in fighting against." This figure of speech is probably acceptable, provided one does not use as an object of the verb such a rendering as "the people of the world." Though in many contexts the world may be rendered "the people of the world," in this particular instance John is emphasizing not Jesus' victory over people, but over the world force, or the system of the world. The only equivalent in some languages would be "the power of this world." However, in order to speak of "defeating the power of this world," it may be necessary to say "I have destroyed the power of this world."

C H A P T E R 17

TEV (17.1-5) RSV

JESUS PRAYS FOR HIS DISCIPLES

<u>17</u> After Jesus finished saying this, he looked up to heaven and said, "Father, the hour has come. Give glory to your Son, so that the Son may give glory to you. 2 For you gave him authority over all mankind, so that he might give eternal life to all those you gave him. 3 And eternal life means to know you, the only true God, and to know Jesus Christ, whom you sent. 4 I have shown your glory on earth; I have finished the work you gave me to do. 5 Father! Give me glory in your presence now, the same glory I had with you before the world was made.

<u>17</u> When Jesus had spoken these words, he lifted up his eyes to heaven and said, "Father, the hour has come; glorify thy Son that the Son may glorify thee, 2 since thou hast given him power over all flesh, to give eternal life to all whom thou hast given him. 3 And this is eternal life, that they know thee the only true God, and Jesus Christ whom thou hast sent. 4 I glorified thee on earth, having accomplished the work which thou gavest me to do; 5 and now, Father, glorify thou me in thy own presence with the glory which I had with thee before the world was made.

Chapter 17, traditionally known as "the high-priestly prayer," is acknowledged to be a unity, although there is no agreement as to where the divisions within the chapter should be made. The UBS Greek text has three paragraph (verses 1-5, 6-19, and 20-26); TEV has five paragraphs (verses 1-5, 6-8, 9-19, 20-23, and 24-26). Other ways of dividing the chapter are to make four sections (verses 1-5, 6-19, 20-23, and 24-26) or three (1-8, 9-19, and 20-26). These ways of dividing the chapter have some things in common. In particular, all have a major break after verse 19. The major question, it seems, is where to place verses 6-8. Do they fall more naturally with verses 1-5 or with verses 9-19? If they are taken with verses 9-19, then they introduce the disciples, in whose behalf the prayer in verses 9-19 is offered. This results in the division made in the UBS Greek New Testament: Jesus' prayer in behalf of himself (verses 1-5); Jesus' prayer for his present disciples (verses 6-19); Jesus' prayer for all who will come to believe in him through the testimony of his disciples (20-26). This division corresponds to Leviticus 16.17, according to which Aaron <u>performed the ritual for himself, his family, and the whole community</u>.

The theme of glory dominates verses 1-5. Verses 1-2 indicate that the Son should be glorified because to do so will bring glory to God and give life to Jesus' disciples. Verse 3 grows out of the mention of eternal life in verse 2, and expands this theme. Verses 4-5 indicate a further reason why the Son should be glorified: he has completed the work that the Father sent him to do.

The theme of verses 6-8 is revelation and response. Jesus had revealed the name of the Father to the men whom the Father had given him,

[523]

and they had responded by obedience (verse 6). Verses 7-8 deal with the implications of this revelation. The disciples recognize that everything Jesus has comes from the Father (verse 7), especially the message which he proclaims (verse 8a), and so they recognize that it is the Father who has sent Jesus (verse 8b).

Verses 9-16 have as their theme the relationship between the disciples and the world. Jesus prays for them because they belong to the Father (verse 9), and because through them Jesus' own true glory is revealed (verse 10). Since Jesus is leaving the world, he prays that the Father will keep them safe by the power of his name (verse 11). During the time that Jesus was with them, he was able to keep them safe by the power of God's name, so that not one of them was lost, except the man who was bound to be lost (verse 12). But Jesus is now going to the Father, and he wants his disciples to have hearts full of joy (verse 13), since the world will hate them because they do not belong to the world (verse 14). Although they do not belong to the world (verse 16), they must remain in the world, and Jesus prays for the Father to keep them safe from the Evil One (verse 15).

Verses 17-19 are concerned with the dedication of the disciples to the Father. Jesus prays that they may be dedicated to the Father in the same way that he himself was dedicated (verse 17), because he is sending them into the world in the same way that the Father sent him into the world (verse 18). Jesus dedicated himself absolutely to the Father so that his disciples might belong to the Father (verse 19).

In the remainder of his prayer (verses 20-26), Jesus prays for future disciples who will believe in him because of the message of his present disciples (verse 20). He prays that they may all be one, in the same way that he and the Father are one (verse 21a). He wants them to be one so that the world may believe that the Father sent him (verse 21b). For the sake of this unity Jesus gave his disciples the same glory the Father gave him (verse 22). Verse 23 repeats the nature of this unity and its purpose. Jesus prays that the disciples may be with him and see his glory (verse 24). They know the Father (verse 25) because Jesus has made him known to them and will continue to do so, that they may enjoy God's love and Jesus' presence (verse 26).

In rendering the section heading, Jesus Prays for His Disciples, it is important to use a term for disciples which will not restrict the meaning to the immediate company of twelve. A better wording may be "Jesus prays for his followers." In some languages it may be necessary to indicate to whom Jesus prays, and therefore one may say "Jesus prays to God for his followers" or "Jesus speaks to God on behalf of his followers."

17.1   After Jesus finished saying this, he looked up
            to heaven and said, "Father, the hour has come.
            Give glory to your Son, so that the Son may give
            glory to you.

After Jesus finished saying this (JB "After saying this"; NEB "After these words"; NAB "After he had spoken these words") is more literally "Jesus said these things." In Greek the first two clauses are coordinate ("Jesus said these things and lifting his eyes to heaven said..."), but TEV and most other modern translations make the first a subordinate clause (After Jesus finished saying this) and the second an independent clause (he looked up to heaven and said). Although some translations maintain the literalism "he lifted up his eyes to heaven," TEV, NEB, and NAB all translate he looked up to heaven. A similar expression is used in 11.41 (literally "he lifted his eyes up"). This of TEV ("these things" of the Greek) refers to the discourses of Chapters 13-16.

In some languages After Jesus finished saying this may be rendered "After Jesus finished saying these words" or "After Jesus finished talking to his disciples."

In rendering he looked up to heaven, it is important to avoid the impression that Jesus looked into heaven in a literal sense. In some languages, one must use such an expression as "he looked up toward heaven." Heaven, in this context, may be rendered "where God dwells" or "God's abode."

In 11.41 and 12.27, both of which introduce prayers, Jesus also addresses God as Father. It is important in rendering Father to employ a term applicable to an individual addressing his own father. In some instances the expression is simply "my Father," but in others special forms of direct address are used when an individual speaks to his own father.

The hour has come is used in 12.23 (see 13.1). Jesus' "hour" is first referred to in 2.4 (TEV my time). The reference is to the hour in which the Son of Man will reveal his true glory, and this glory will be accomplished by means of his death on the cross. In some languages the hour has come may be rendered "the time has come," but more often an equivalent expression is "this is the occasion" or "now is the time."

Where most translations have "glorify," TEV has give glory to (so also NAB; Gdsp "Do honor to"). However, the focus of "to glorify" is, not on giving honor to the Son and the Father, but on revealing their true glory. Note GeCL: "show the glory of your Son in order that the Son can show your glory." In place of the Son, some Greek manuscripts read "your Son." The UBS Committee on the Greek text had a difficult time deciding between the two readings. Some scribe may have omitted "your" because he thought it was superfluous in light of your Son earlier in the verse, or it may have been inserted for the sake of adding solemnity to the style. The weight of the manuscript evidence is in favor of omitting "your," and so the UBS Committee decided in favor of the reading the Son. However, a number of translations render it as "your Son," which may be necessary on translational grounds. Phps translates "he," referring to "your Son" in the earlier part of the verse.

In some languages it is difficult to translate such an expression as Give glory to your Son or the Son may give glory to you. How can the Son actually give glory to God who already possesses an absolute degree of glory? It may therefore be essential to translate give glory to your Son as "reveal your Son's glory," "show to people how glorious your Son is," or "...how wonderful your Son is." It may also be necessary to introduce a first person reference, since in many languages one cannot use a third person pronoun in speaking of oneself. Therefore it may be necessary to translate "reveal to people how glorious I, your Son, am."

After a first person reference to your Son, it may be necessary to employ a first person singular pronoun as the subject of the final clause, for example, "so that I may show people how wonderful you are."

There is a problem in choosing words for "glory," "glorious," or "wonderful," because in this type of context such terms may be understood as egotistical. That is, readers may assume that Jesus is requesting God to "show him off." The possibility of such a misinterpretation is greatly reduced by the purpose expressed, namely, that Jesus himself may reveal to people how wonderful God is. Nevertheless, the terms must be selected carefully to minimize the possibility of misunderstanding.

17.2   For you gave him authority over all mankind,
          so that he might give eternal life to all
          those you gave him.

The verb gave is in the aorist indicative tense, and points to a specific act in past time, most likely the giving of authority to the Son as a special prerogative of his earthly ministry.

Authority is the same noun translated the right in 1.12. Some translations render by "power," but the meaning of authority seems closer (see the comments at 1.12).

All mankind (so also JB, NEB, Gdsp, Barclay, NAB) is literally "all flesh" (RSV, Mft) and is rendered "all men" by Phps.

If a first person reference is introduced in verse 1, it must be continued in verse 2: "for you gave me authority over all mankind." The first person reference would then continue in the following clause, "so that I might give eternal life to all those you gave to me."

In some languages it is difficult to speak about "giving authority," but one may often say "assigned me to command," "allowed me to give orders to," "placed me in front of all men," or "...above all men."

As in many other contexts, give eternal life may be rendered as a causative, for example, "cause to live without ceasing" or "cause to live always." For a fuller discussion of eternal life, see comments at 1.4 and 3.15.

TEV reorders the last clause of this verse to make it sound natural in English. The Greek literally reads "so that everything which you gave to him he might give to them eternal life." Although the pronoun "everything which" is neuter singular in Greek, it is used in a collective sense for the masculine plural and so may be followed by the pronoun "to them," which is masculine in Greek. TEV combines the pronouns ("all which...to them") and translates to all those (RSV "to all whom"). The neuter is also used in 6.37,39, and it appears again in verses 7 and 24. That the reference is to "men" (= "people") is made clear both by the use of the masculine plural pronoun ("to them") of this verse and by the phrase "to the men you gave me" of verse 6.

It may be difficult to speak in some languages of "persons being given to someone," but one can speak of "those whom you put in my charge" or "those whom you sent to me" or "those whom you caused to be my followers."

17.3   And eternal life means to know you, the only true
God, and to know Jesus Christ, whom you sent.

This verse, which defines eternal life, is a kind of parenthetical
explanation, and so NAB places it in parentheses.

To know you is more literally "that they may know you." The belief
that knowledge is essential to salvation is common to both Jewish and
Greek thought. In particular, the Gnostic religions emphasized that
knowledge (that is, an intuitive understanding of the nature of God)
was essential to salvation. The Old Testament also indicates that the
knowledge of God is essential to salvation, but with a different focus.
In Judaism the knowledge of God is primarily the revelation of God contained in his Law, and obedience to this Law means life. That is, true
knowledge of God was tied to a particular historical revelation, and
this knowledge demanded faith and obedience. The same belief is reflected in the Gospel of John. The knowledge of God referred to here
is the knowledge which comes through the specific revelation in Jesus
Christ, and it demands a response of love and obedience on the part of
those who follow. Knowledge, then, for both Old Testament and New Testament writers is not a beatific vision or an intuitive feeling about God;
rather it is based on an objective revelation and demands a positive
response in obedience and love.

In 5.44 God is spoken of as "the only God," while 1 John 5.20 refers
to him as "the true (God)." These two attributes are the basic affirma-
tions of monotheism. They distinguish the God of the Old Testament (and
of the New Testament) from the many false gods of polytheism.

The only true God may be rendered in some languages "the only one
who is really God." This appositional definition of God must be closely
combined in some languages with the preceding pronoun you, for example,
"to know you, you are the only God that really exists" or "...you are
the only God there is."

The only other place where the title Jesus Christ occurs in the
Fourth Gospel is in 1.17. It is rather surprising to find it in this
particular context, where one would normally expect "the Son." However,
since one of the strong emphases here is on the historical revelation,
it may be that the historical name Jesus Christ was chosen specifically
for this purpose.

The thought that God sent Jesus is frequent in the Fourth Gospel
(note 3.17). The same thought occurs in verses 8, 18, 21, 23, and 25.

The principal difficulty for a translator in rendering verse 3 is
to know precisely the relation between the initial statement this is
eternal life and what follows. One could interpret the relation as one
of purpose, for example, "this is the purpose of eternal life, namely,
for people to know the only true God and Jesus Christ." Another possibility is that of means or cause; that is, through knowing the only
true God and Jesus Christ, one acquires eternal life, or, knowing the
only true God and Jesus Christ causes one to live eternally. In view of
the manner in which John emphasizes the importance of knowing God as
a means of eternal life, it may be possible in some languages to restructure verse 3 to read as follows: "By knowing you, the only true
God, and Jesus Christ whom you sent, people are caused to live forever";
or even, "If people know you, the only true God, and if they know me,

the one whom you sent, then they will live without ceasing." Note that
in the second restructuring the first person pronoun is used to refer
to "Jesus Christ," and that under these circumstances, the name "Jesus
Christ" would normally be omitted. It is possible to indicate in a footnote that, in the Greek text, a third person reference is employed and
the full name "Jesus Christ" occurs. It would be awkward in almost any
language to have an apposition with a first person pronoun, for example,
"to know me, Jesus Christ." The relation of means may be expressed somewhat differently, for example, "This is how people live forever; they
know you, the only true God, and they know Jesus Christ, whom you have
sent."

17.4   I have shown your glory on earth; I have
             finished the work you gave me to do.

     I have shown your glory (so GeCL) is rendered "I glorified you"
by most translators; Gdsp and NAB make a different emphasis (Gdsp "I
have done honor to you"; and NAB "I have given you glory"). Once more
the choice is between the meaning "give glory to" and "reveal the glory
of." In light of the whole context of this prayer (note especially verse
6 I have made you known), the meaning "to reveal the glory of" is more
appropriate.
     The second clause, I have finished the work you gave me to do, is
more closely tied to the first clause, I showed your glory on earth,
than may be indicated in TEV. These are not two separate actions. Rather
the second clause indicates the means by which God's glory was revealed,
that is, "by finishing the work you gave me to do." Note NEB "I have
glorified thee on earth by completing the work which thou gavest me to
do" and NAB "I have given you glory on earth by finishing the work you
gave me to do." GeCL translates "I have made known your glory on earth;
for I have accomplished the task which you gave me."
     The verbs have shown and have finished are in the aorist tense in
Greek, and so point to Jesus' work as already accomplished. The use of
the aorist may reflect either Jesus' own certainty that his end was at
hand or the temporal perspective of the Gospel writer.
     Certain complications are involved in translating I have finished
the work you gave me to do. Work might conceivably refer only to physical
activity, and in some languages one cannot speak of "giving work." Therefore one may need to restructure the second part of verse 4 to read "I
finished doing what you told me to do" or "I completed what you told me
to do."

17.5   Father! Give me glory in your presence now,
             the same glory I had with you before the
             world was made.

     Father was the word by which Jesus addressed God at the beginning
of this prayer (verse 1). In Greek, this entire verse reads literally
"and now glorify me, Father, in your presence with the glory which I
had with you before the world was created." The phrase "and now" (TEV

now) is used to strengthen the request made in verse 1. This conclusion is supported by the observation that the pronouns you and me are emphatic in the Greek sentence structure ("You" is not expressed explicitly in TEV, though it is implicit in the verb Give). Here again Gdsp makes explicit the idea of doing honor ("Now, Father, do such honor to me in your presence as I had done me there before the world existed"). Barclay reads "And now, Father, give me in your own presence the glory which I had with you, before the world came into existence" and NAB has "Do you now, Father, give me glory at your side, a glory I had with you before the world began." GeCL telescopes by not repeating the word glory and by seeing essentially the same meaning in the verse: ("Father, give me now again the glory which I had with you before the world was created."

In this context it is not possible to treat Give me glory in the same way as in contexts where the focus is upon the revelation of Christ's glory to people in the world. The emphasis here is upon the glorious state which Christ had before the incarnation, and thus quite a different type of rendering must normally be employed. Moreover, a literal rendering of "giving glory" is usually impossible. The more common type of expression would be causative, for example, "cause me to be glorious" or "cause me to be honored" or "show honor to me" or even "honor me."

In your presence may be rendered "where you are" or "there where you are."

Since, in some languages, glory cannot be used as a noun, the explanatory clause, the same glory I had with you before the world was made, may be restructured to read "honor me in the same way you did before the world was made" or "...before you made the world."

TEV	(17.6-8)	RSV
6 "I have made you known to those you gave me out of the world. They belonged to you, and you gave them to me. They have obeyed your word, 7 and now they know that everything you gave me comes from you. 8 I gave them the message that you gave me, and they received it; they know that it is true that I came from you, and they believe that you sent me.		6 "I have manifested thy name to the men whom thou gavest me out of the world; thine they were, and thou gavest them to me, and they have kept thy word. 7 Now they know that everything that thou hast given me is from thee; 8 for I have given them the words which thou gavest me, and they have received them and know in truth that I came from thee; and they have believed that thou didst send me.

17.6   "I have made you known to those you gave me out of the world. They belonged to you, and you gave them to me. They have obeyed your word,

I have made you known means the same as I showed your glory in

[529]

verse 4. The verb have made you known is in the aorist tense, and it sums up the total revelation of God in Jesus' ministry.

You is literally "your name." To refer to the "name" of God is another way to refer to God himself. This is the basis for rendering you in TEV and GeCL. See also the comments at 2.23; 3.18; and the detailed discussion at 14.13.

The verb make known was first used in 1.31. I have made you known must normally be treated as a causative, but this may result in complications in the clause structure. I have made you known may be rendered "I have caused men to know you." However, a difficulty results from the dependent clause you gave me out of the world. In some languages it may be related to the preceding clause as "Those you gave me out of the world, these I have caused to know you."

The phrase out of the world is the same rendered from this world in 15.19. In rendering those you gave me out of the world, it is important to avoid an expression implying that God had taken the people out of the world and given them to Jesus. The reference is, rather, to the disciples who remained in the world, but who were not in a sense "of the world." For the thought that the disciples were given to Jesus by the Father see 6.37; this thought is a frequently recurring theme throughout the priestly prayer (17.2,9,12,24).

They belonged to you, and you gave them to me simply expands the thought of the previous statement, those you gave me out of the world.

They have obeyed your word translates the same expression used in 8.51 (obeys my message), except for a different pronoun and the use here of the Greek perfect tense. The perfect tense suggests that this aspect of the prayer relates to the time the book was written. It suggests that the disciples had kept and were continuing to keep Jesus' word.

They have obeyed your word may be rendered in some languages "they have done what you told them to do." A complication here is that your word refers to the message God had relayed to the disciples through Jesus, but this fact can also be understood from the context.

17.7   and now they know that everything you gave
              me comes from you.

TEV does not have a full stop at the end of verse 6, as some translations do, but there is no shift in focus.

In Greek the adverb now is emphatic. The meaning is "now, at the end of my ministry."

The verb know is in the perfect tense in Greek, as is have obeyed in verse 6.

Everything you gave me comes from you sounds redundant to the English reader, but the Greek structure emphasizes the Son's dependence upon the Father. To avoid some of the redundancy of this expression, it may be possible to translate "everything you gave me comes really from you."

17.8   I gave them the message that you gave me, and
they received it; they know that it is true
that I came from you, and they believe that
you sent me.

In Greek this verse is introduced with a particle (hoti) that indicates a causal relation with the preceding verse. This particle appears as "for" or "because" in most translations; in TEV the causal
connection is left implicit.

The message (emphatic in the Greek sentence structure) is literally
"the words" (Greek rēmata). In verses 6 and 14 the singular of another
Greek term for "word" (logos) is used, but there is no real difference
in meaning (see the comments at 14.23). Both words refer to the revelation that comes through Jesus Christ.

Though in English the verb gave fits well with such a noun as the
message, this combination cannot be used in some languages. The first
part of verse 8 may be rendered "I told them what you told me" or "I
told them what you told me to tell them."

In the phrase and they received it the pronoun it of TEV also
translates "the words" (TEV the message), which in Greek serves as the
object of both I gave and they received.

In some languages one cannot speak of "receiving a message"; instead an idiomatic expression may be employed, for example, "they listened to it with open ears" or "they let the words go into their hearts."
In other languages the only appropriate equivalent is "they believed it."

They know that it is true that I came from you is more literally
"and they know truly that I came from you." TEV transforms the adverb
"truly" into a noun clause, that it is true. Barclay does something
similar ("and they have accepted it as true that you sent me"), but
most English translations retain the adverb. In some languages one may
translate "they know that I really came from you."

That Jesus comes from the Father who sent him is a constant theme
of this prayer (see 17.18,21,23,25), and of the Gospel (8.42; 16.28).

The verbs know and believe are parallel. The knowledge that Jesus
came from the Father is no different from the belief that the Father
sent Jesus. The point of reference in the verbs came and sent is the
earthly ministry of Jesus.

TEV   (17.9-19)   RSV

9 "I pray for them. I do not
pray for the world but for those
you gave me, for they belong to
you. 10 All I have is yours, and
all you have is mine; and my glory
is shown through them. 11 And now
I am coming to you; I am no longer
in the world, but they are in the
world. Holy Father! Keep them safe
by the power of your name, the name
you gave me,ᵍ so that they may be

9 I am praying for them; I am not
praying for the world but for
those whom thou hast given me,
for they are thine; 10 all mine
are thine, and thine are mine, and
I am glorified in them. 11 And now
I am no more in the world, but
they are in the world, and I am
coming to thee. Holy Father, keep
them in thy name, which thou hast
given me, that they may be one,

one just as you and I are one. 12
While I was with them, I kept them
safe by the power of your name,
the name you gave me.[h] I protected
them, and not one of them was lost,
except the man who was bound to be
lost--so that the scripture might
come true. 13 And now I am coming
to you, and I say these things in
the world so that they might have
my joy in their hearts in all its
fullness. 14 I gave them your message, and the world hated them, because they do not belong to the
world, just as I do not belong to
the world. 15 I do not ask you to
take them out of the world, but I
do ask you to keep them safe from
the Evil One. 16 Just as I do not
belong to the world, they do not
belong to the world. 17 Dedicate
them to yourself by means of the
truth; your word is truth. 18 I
sent them into the world, just as
you sent me into the world. 19 And
for their sake I dedicate myself
to you, in order that they, too,
may be truly dedicated to you.

even as we are one. 12 While I was
with them, I kept them in thy name,
which thou hast given me; I have
guarded them, and none of them is
lost but the son of perdition, that
the scripture might be fulfilled.
13 But now I am coming to thee;
and these things I speak in the
world, that they may have my joy
fulfilled in themselves. 14 I have
given them thy word; and the world
has hated them because they are
not of the world, even as I am not
of the world. 15 I do not pray that
thou shouldst take them out of the
world, but that thou shouldst keep
them from the evil one.[k] 16 They
are not of the world, even as I
am not of the world. 17 Sanctify
them in the truth; thy word is
truth. 18 As thou didst send me
into the world, so I have sent
them into the world. 19 And for
their sake I consecrate myself,
that they also may be consecrated
in truth.

[k]Or *from evil*

[g]Keep them safe by the power of
your name, the name you gave me;
some manuscripts have By the power
of your name keep safe those you
have given me.

[h]I kept them safe by the power of
your name, the name you gave me;
some manuscripts have By the power
of your name I kept safe those you
have given me.

17.9   "I pray for them, I do not pray for the world
              but for those you gave me, for they belong to you.

In this verse Jesus prays to the Father (verses 1,5) for the disciples.
    Them...those you gave me refers to Jesus' immediate disciples. In
verse 20 Jesus will pray for future believers.
    The world is used here again of those who oppose God (see comments
at 1.10). The fact that Jesus is not praying for the world is emphatic
in the Greek sentence structure.

The contrast between the positive I pray for them and the negative
I do not pray...but for those... presents some complications in translation. The contrast is particularly difficult because them in the
first sentence refers to those you gave me, who are specified in the
second sentence. As a result, it may be necessary to restructure the
relationships, for example, "I pray for the men you gave me because
they belong to you; I do not pray for the people of the world." It is
also possible to restructure this sentence in the following way; "I do
not pray for the people in the world; rather, I pray for the people you
gave me, because they belong to you."

Because they belong to you explains why Jesus prays for the disciples. How is it possible to reconcile the fact that Jesus does not
pray for "the world" and the fact that God loved "the world" and gave
his Son (3.16)? According to Johannine theology, the coming of the Son
into "the world" is not only the means whereby "the world" is saved,
but also the means by which it is judged. So "the world" consists of
those people who refuse Jesus and align themselves with the power of
Satan. From the viewpoint of Johannine theology, there is no hope of
salvation for "the world"; the only hope is that "the world" will be
proved wrong and defeated. However, even though "the world" is hostile
to Jesus and his followers, the precise reason for the disciples' existence in "the world" is that they may proclaim the message of salvation to "the world." In the same way that the presence of Jesus brought
either salvation or judgment, so will the word of the disciples. Those
who believe will also become Jesus' disciples, while those who will not
believe remain as part of "the world" in opposition to God. The last
part of this verse is similar to part of verse 6 (they belonged to you,
and you gave them to me).

Relating the clause because they belong to you to what precedes
presents a problem. A literal rendering of verse 9 may suggest that God
gave these people to Jesus, because they already belonged to God, but
that is not the meaning in this passage. Because they belong to you
must be directly related to the prayer. It may be necessary to say, for
example, "I pray for them because they belong to you."

<u>17.10</u>   All I have is yours, and all you have is
                mine; and my glory is shown through them.

All I have, though neuter in Greek, refers to those you gave me of
verse 9 (note also the use of the neuter in verse 2). The phrase all
you have is also neuter. To make clear that all refers to people (as
clearly shown by the pronoun them at the end of verse 10), it may be
necessary to expand the first part of verse 10, for example, "All those
people who belong to me, belong to you, and all who belong to you belong to me."

And my glory is shown through them is more literally "and I have
been glorified in them." The meaning of "to glorify" is not "to bring
honor to" (Gdsp "and they have done me honor"), but "to reveal the
glory of" (GeCL "through them is my glory seen"). The Greek is in the
perfect tense ("I have been glorified"), used to indicate the continuing
revelation of Jesus' glory through his disciples. The perfect tense

[533]

suggests that the time perspective is that of the writing of the Gospel rather than that of Jesus' own day; its force is probably best expressed by the present tense in English.

The passive expression, my glory is shown through them, must be made active and causative in some languages, for example, "they show how glorious I am" or "...what my glory really is."

17.11   And now I am coming to you; I am no longer
         in the world, but they are in the world.
         Holy Father! Keep them safe by the power
         of your name, the name you gave me,^{g} so
         that they may be one just as you and I are
         one.

         ^{g}Keep them safe by the power of your name,
         the name you gave me; *some manuscripts
         have* By the power of your name keep safe
         those you have given me.

TEV rearranges the order of the first three clauses in Greek. And now I am coming to you, which occurs first in TEV, is in third place in the Greek text after the two clauses I am no longer in the world, but they are in the world. This rearrangement does not alter the focus of the Greek, and it has the advantage of a more logical thought sequence. Elsewhere in the Gospel Jesus speaks of "going" to the Father, while here he speaks of "coming." The shift of verbs is natural, both in English and in Greek. When Jesus speaks of "going" to the Father he is addressing others; when he speaks of "coming" he is addressing the Father.

There are two essential problems involved in translating the statement now I am coming to you. The first is the space perspective (coming or going), and the second is the temporal relation. If the spatial perspective shifts from where Jesus is to the location of the Father, then it is possible to say "I am coming to you." However, in some languages this shift of perspective is impossible, and therefore one may have to translate "I am going to you."

Since Jesus was not at that moment going from the world to heaven, it may be necessary in some languages to translate "I will soon be coming (or going) to you." However, one may usually employ an expression which would suggest "I am already on my way to you."

In verse 13 Jesus affirms that he is still in the world, but here he states I am no longer in the world. In both verses Jesus says I am coming to you. In a sense, Jesus speaks paradoxically when he says I am no longer in the world, for he is at this moment still on earth. The paradox may be marked in some languages by saying "I am, as it were, no longer in the world"; but in other languages it may be necessary to say "very shortly I will no longer be in the world." The statement about the disciples may then be rendered "but they will continue to be in the world."

In verses 1 and 5 Jesus addressed God as Father, and here he addresses him as Holy Father (note Righteous Father of verse 25). In the

Old Testament and in Jewish prayers, God is frequently spoken of as "the Holy One," meaning that he is unique and distinct from all others. In the present context to address God as Holy is particularly appropriate, since the verb "to dedicate" (hagiazō) in verses 17 and 19 is made from the same stem in Greek.

Several problems are involved in translating the phrase Holy Father. First, the term Father must often be rendered "my father," or with a form of "father" never used with the attributive "holy." In some languages, for example, one could never say "my holy Father," for it would immediately suggest that the individual had another father who was not holy. In terms of the syntactic structure, it may be necessary to say "my Father, you who are holy." There is a further complication in selecting an appropriate term for holy. It may be difficult to use a word which, in other contexts, is satisfactory to translate holy, since the essential meaning of those terms in phrases such as "holy writings" or "holy mountain" focuses upon the meaning of positive taboo; that is, something so imbued with supernatural power that it must be avoided, or treated with particular respect. For Holy Father, it may be necessary to introduce the concept of "worship" or "reverence" as a way of indicating the underlying concept of "holiness," for example, "my Father, you who deserve worship" or "...you who should be greatly reverenced." Some translators use for holy a term which means essentially "separated," but this type of expression involves difficulties, for it may suggest a separation made by someone else, namely, an agent, as is implied by the use of a passive form. Moreover, a word meaning "separated" could imply that God is not interested in the world, and so wishes to be dissociated from mankind.

As the TEV footnote indicates, the reading keep them safe by the power of your name, the name you gave me appears in some manuscripts with the meaning "by the power of your name keep safe those you have given me." In the Greek text the difference is only in a single pronoun, the object of the verb gave (or "have given"). In some manuscripts it is a dative singular, referring to the name, while in others it is an accusative plural, referring to the disciples. Almost all modern translations (NEB is an exception) take it as a reference to the name, as the UBS Greek text recommends. This reading has stronger textual support than the other.

Keep...safe (so also GeCL; NEB, NAB "protect") is translated "keep" in several translations. The verb used here (tēreo) is used elsewhere in the New Testament of keeping persons safe (see verses 12, 15; Acts 16.23; 24.23; 25.4,21; and Jude 1). In 8.51 it is used with the sense "to obey."

TEV (so also Mft and NEB) makes "in your name" explicit by rendering it by the power of your name. Gdsp and Phps simply render "by your power." Barclay renders the entire phrase "protect them with your personal protection." There would seem to be no basis for rendering "keep in your name" with the meaning "keep...true to your name" (JB). See comments at 14.13.

The name is the means by which the Son is identified with the Father. Since the Son bears the divine name (see comments on "I am" at 4.26), it can be said that whoever has seen the Son has seen the Father (14.9). In Greek, the verb translated you gave is in the perfect tense, indicating that Jesus possessed, and continues to possess, the divine name. One may say that by possessing the divine name Jesus possesses the divine character and authority. But what particular aspect is in focus in this context, and how is it best expressed? The power of the divine name is what seems to be in focus, and a number of translations make this explicit, as noted in the translations cited above. Barclay (see above) understands the phrase "keep by your name" to mean "protect them with your personal protection," and interprets "which you gave me" to mean "as you did me" ("protect them with your personal protection, as you did me"). However, no other translations go in this direction, and this exegesis has little support in the commentaries. Gdsp, which omits mention of "the name," seems to have the best solution as far as the modern reader is concerned ("keep them by your power which you gave me"). To make this meaning more emphatic, a translator may build in a little redundancy and render "keep them safe by your power, the power you gave me."

Though it is relatively easy to say in English "Keep them safe by your power" or "protect them by your power," it may be difficult to produce a close equivalent in other languages, since some have no abstract noun for "power." The closest equivalent may be "by showing how powerful you are, keep them safe," or even "by your being powerful, keep them safe." It may be difficult to relate the first part of this statement to what follows, namely, the fact that this same kind of power (or name) has been given to Jesus. However, it may be possible to say "protect them by showing how powerful you are; in the same way you have caused me to be powerful." With this rendering it is important that the final clause, so they may be one just as you and I are one, express a purpose directly related to the initial request, Keep them safe. One may translate in some languages "Keep them safe, so that they may be one just as you and I are one. Do this by showing how powerful you are--powerful in the same way that you have caused me to be powerful."

The purpose of Jesus' prayer for the protection of the disciples is that they may be one, just as he and the Father are one. So that they may be one just as you and I are one is omitted in one important Greek manuscript and in several ancient translations. NAB therefore places this clause in brackets. Since the theme of unity is more natural in the last part of the prayer (verses 21-23), it may have been omitted by a scribe as redundant and out of place here. All other modern translations evidently include it as an integral part of the text.

17.12   While I was with them, I kept them safe by the
         power of your name, the name you gave me.[h] I
         protected them, and not one of them was lost,
         except the man who was bound to be lost--so that
         the scripture might come true.

         [h]I kept them safe by the power of your name, the
         name you gave me; *some manuscripts have* By the
         power of your name I kept safe those you have
         given me.

As indicated in the footnote of TEV, this verse presents the same textual problem as verse 11.

Except for the change of the imperative (keep them safe) to the indicative (I kept them safe), the first sentence of this verse repeats the thoughts of verse 11. I kept them safe by the power of your name, the name you gave me may be rendered "I kept them safe by your power, the power you gave me."

The verb protected is the same one rendered keep in 12.25 and obey in 12.47, the only other two occurrences of the verb in John's Gospel. Ordinarily protected would be considered a stronger term than keep... safe, but in the present context the two verbs are used synonymously, one reinforcing the other. The use of synonyms is characteristic of the Johannine style.

Was lost is the same verb rendered die in 3.16 and 10.28; in 12.25 it is used with the same meaning it has here. Because of the continuing relationship of Judas Iscariot to the developments described in Chapter 18, it may be necessary in some languages to use the perfect tense here, for example, "not one of them has been lost."

The man who was bound to be lost (NAB "him who was destined to be lost"; NEB "the man who must be lost"; JB "the one who chose to be lost"; Gdsp "the one who was destined to be lost") has been traditionally rendered "the son of perdition." The word rendered "perdition" in many translations is a noun made from the same stem as the verb translated was lost in TEV and most other translations. This word is frequently used in the New Testament of the final fate of those who are without God (see Matt 7.13; Acts 8.20; Rom 9.22; Phil 1.28; 3.19; 1 Tim 6.9; Heb 10.39; 2 Peter 2.1; 3.7; Rev 17.8,11). The phrase "son of (literally "man of") perdition" means "one who is going to be lost (eternally)." The same expression appears in 2 Thessalonians 2.3 and is rendered the...One...who is destined to hell in TEV.

In English the form lost fits very well into this type of context, but in other languages a literal rendering may be misleading, since it might suggest that in some way or other Jesus had lost sight of Judas. A more appropriate equivalent in some languages is "has gone astray" or "has suffered ruin." Accordingly, the phrase the man who was bound to be lost may be rendered "the man who would certainly go astray" or "the man for whom there was nothing else but to suffer ruin."

That the scripture might come true is best taken as a reference to Psalm 41.10, referred to in 13.18. To show the relation of the clause that the scripture might come true to what has preceded, it may be necessary to add such a phrase as "all this had to happen so that the scripture might come true" or "...so that what is written in the scripture would prove to be true" or "...would tell it as it really turned out to be."

17.13   And now I am coming to you, and I say these things in the world so that they might have my joy in their hearts in all its fullness.

And now I am coming to you is repeated from verse 11.

The phrase these things is best limited to the contents of Jesus' prayer so far, and not extended to include the entire discourse of Chapters 14-17.

In the world means "while I am still in the world," a reference to the time left before Jesus' departure to the Father.

They refers to Jesus' disciples.

Might have my joy in their hearts, in all its fullness (compare 15.11 and 16.24) is more literally "that they may have my joy fulfilled in themselves" (RSV). NAB translates "that they may share my joy completely" and NEB "so that they may have my joy within them in full measure." Gdsp renders "in order that they may have the happiness that I feel fully realized in their own hearts." In the context my joy means "the joy which I experience." In some languages one cannot speak of having another person's joy in his own heart. To communicate this concept, it is necessary to indicate the possibility of similar experience, for example, "that they may be completely happy in their hearts in the same way that I am completely happy."

17.14   I gave them your message, and the world hated them, because they do not belong to the world, just as I do not belong to the world.

The pronoun I is emphatic. I gave them your message is similar to I gave them the message that you gave me of verse 8, except that in 17.8 the Greek word for "message" is "words" (rēmata), while here it is "word" (Greek logos). The two terms are used synonymously.

There is a connection between I gave them your message and the world hated them, for the statement the world hated them is essentially the result of what Jesus has done in giving God's message to his disciples. To make this connection obvious, it may be necessary to translate "I told them what you told me, and as a result, the people of the world hated them."

The theme of the world's hatred is repeated from 15.18--16.4a. In that section also Jesus indicates that the disciples do not belong to the world (15.19). The final part of verse 14 tells why the world hates the followers of Jesus. It may be difficult to translate literally they do not belong to the world, for this might imply that they are not really human beings. The meaning of this statement may be expressed in some languages as "they are not one with the people of the world" or "they do not think as people of the world think."

17.15   I do not ask you to take them out of the world, but I do ask you to keep them safe from the Evil One.

Although the disciples are not a part of the world, they are in it (17.11), and it is their calling to remain in the world. So Jesus does not ask the Father to remove the disciples from the world, but to keep them safe from the Evil One. It is possible to translate the Evil One as an abstract noun meaning "evil." However, most translations see here a personal reference. The Evil One is to be identified with the devil, who, in Johannine theology, is "the ruler of this world." The Evil One is referred to again in 1 John 2.13-14; 3.12; and 5.18,19. To indicate clearly that the Evil One is a title, it may be necessary to say "keep them safe from the one who is known as the Evil One" or "...the one who is called the Evil One" or "...whose name is the Evil One." In some languages, one may use such an expression as "keep them safe from the one who is truly evil" or "...really evil." The identification of the Evil One with the devil may be made specific by means of a marginal note.

17.16   Just as I do not belong to the world, they
               do not belong to the world.

Compare this verse with they do not belong to the world, just as I do not belong to the world of verse 14.

17.17   Dedicate them to yourself by means of the
               truth; your word is truth.

Dedicate is rendered "consecrate" in several translations (Mft, Gdsp, NEB, NAB, JB). The Greek verb used here is the same as in 10.36 (TEV chose). The dedication is obviously to God, and TEV (Dedicate...to yourself) and Barclay ("consecrate...to yourself") make this explicit. GeCL has "make them your own."
The clause Dedicate them to yourself represents a Greek expression traditionally translated "sanctify them" or, literally, "make them holy." The biblical concept of sanctification always involves the dedication of something to the exclusive service of God. If God himself is involved in the act of sanctification, it would clearly be a matter of dedicating persons to himself, that is, to his own service or to be his own possession. In some languages there is no special term for "dedicate." The only equivalent is "give." One may say "give them to yourself," but it may be more appropriate to use such an expression as "receive them to yourself" or "take them to yourself" or "make them yours." The meaning of this final phrase fits well with certain renderings of a related Greek term traditionally translated "saints," but more frequently rendered in modern translations "the people of God."
By means of the truth (so also NAB) is rendered "by the truth" in a number of translations. Although it is possible to take this expression as purely adverbial (NEB alternative rendering "in truth"), it is doubtful that it has this meaning in the present context. In the Gospel of John Jesus himself is identified with the truth (14.6), and the truth has the power to act (note 8.32). The phrase by means of the truth poses two difficulties in some languages: (1) there may be no abstract noun meaning truth, and (2) it may be difficult to speak of truth as the means by which something is accomplished. The focus here is not essentially upon the abstract fact of truth, but upon the content of the message, which is true. But even in this context truth can perhaps best be understood as "the truth about God," himself, contained in the words God gave Jesus to communicate to his followers. The closest equivalent,

therefore, in some languages is "by means of your words, which are true."

Your word is truth is identical with the reading of one of the Septuagint manuscripts of Psalm 119.142. Elsewhere in the Gospel, Jesus himself is spoken of as the Word (1.14) and the truth (14.6).

17.18   I sent them into the world, just as you
                  sent me into the world.

TEV inverts the order of the two clauses in this verse. The Greek literally reads "just as you sent me into the world, so I sent them into the world." This inversion produces a more natural English style. GeCL has the same restructuring. Five times it is said in this chapter that the Father sent Jesus into the world, and in this verse Jesus speaks of sending the disciples into the world in the same way that the Father sent him into the world. The time perspective of this verse is best understood as the time of the writing of the Gospel, rather than that of Jesus' prayer. In fact, not until 20.21 (where the present tense is used) does Jesus actually send the disciples into the world.

If the past tense form of sent is retained in translation, the reference of this verse may be limited to such occasions as the one when Jesus sent his disciples out two by two to proclaim the kingdom in the villages and towns. The wider implications of this statement would then be lost. Therefore it may be preferable in some languages to use a perfect tense, and so avoid the resulting misunderstanding, for example, "I have sent them into the world."

17.19   And for their sake I dedicate myself to
                  you, in order that they, too, may be truly
                  dedicated to you.

I dedicate...to you is the same verb translated dedicate...to yourself in verse 17. Jesus dedicates himself to the Father so that his disciples might also be dedicated to the Father. I dedicate myself to you may be expressed in some languages as "I give myself to you." However, in others it may be appropriate to use an expanded phrase, for example, "I give myself to serve you." The purpose clause may then be expressed as "in order that they also may give themselves to serve you."

The Greek phrase rendered truly here is literally "in truth," while by means of the truth in verse 17 is literally "in the truth." If the phrase "in truth" appeared in isolation, it would be natural to translate it as an adverb (truly). However, in the present context it seems best to understand this phrase as equivalent to the former phrase and so to translate it "by means of the truth." Modern translations differ here, but some of them do render these two phrases exactly as suggested above. If truly is to be understood adverbially, it may be rendered in some languages "as they ought to," for example, "that they may give themselves to you as they ought to." It may also be possible to understand truly in the sense of "completely," for example, "so that they also may give themselves to you completely." But if one assumes that the appropriate meaning of truly is "by means of the truth," the closest equivalent may be "in order that they also may give themselves to you by means of your words, which are true" or "...by means of your true message."

| TEV (17.20-23) RSV |

20 "I pray not only for them, but also for those who believe in me because of their message. 21 I pray that they may all be one. Father! May they be in us, just as you are in me and I am in you. May they be one, so that the world will believe that you sent me. 22 I gave them the same glory you gave me, so that they may be one, just as you and I are one: 23 I in them and you in me, so that they may be completely one, in order that the world may know that you sent me and that you love them as you love me.

20 "I do not pray for these only, but also for those who believe in me through their word, 21 that they may all be one; even as thou, Father, art in me, and I in thee, that they also may be in us, so that the world may believe that thou hast sent me. 22 The glory which thou hast given me I have given to them, that they may be one even as we are one, 23 I in them and thou in me, that they may become perfectly one, so that the world may know that thou hast sent me and hast loved them even as thou hast loved me.

17.20   "I pray not only for them, but also for those who believe in me because of their message.

This verse extends Jesus' prayer from concern for his immediate disciples to concern for those who will believe because of their message. The verb (Greek erōtao; TEV pray) used here was also used in verse 9.
In some languages the contrast expressed in English by not only... but also is rendered by an expression of "also," for example, "I pray for them, and I also pray for those others who believe in me because of what my followers have said."
Believe, as TEV indicates, translates a verb (participle) in the present tense in Greek. If the time perspective is that of the Last Supper, then the force of the verb here is future (JB, NAB, Phps "will believe"; Gdsp "come to believe"). The use of a present tense with a future force is not unnatural, and it may convey emphasis. On the other hand, it may be that the present tense reflects the time of writing, when there were others who did believe because of the disciples' witness.
Because of their message is literally "through their word" (Greek logos). Gdsp and Phps translate "through their message"; Mft "by their spoken word"; NAB "through their word"; NEB and JB "through their words."
The order of the Greek permits the phrase in me to be connected

with because of their message; that is, "who believe because of their
message about me," but this possibility is not followed in any modern
translation. In any case, it may be necessary in some languages to translate fully, "who believe in me because of their message about me" or
"...because of what they will say about me."

17.21   I pray that they may all be one. Father! May
        they be in us, just as you are in me and I am
        in you. May they be one, so that the world will
        believe that you sent me.

In Greek, this verse is a continuation of the sentence begun in
verse 20 and consists of four separate clauses introduced in the following way: (1) that (Greek hina), (2) just as (Greek kathōs), (3) that
(Greek hina), (4) that (Greek hina). Since TEV has a full stop at the
end of verse 20 and begins a new sentence with verse 21, it reintroduces
the words I pray from verse 20. The first Greek clause is then represented by I pray that they may all be one; and because it is more natural in English to introduce the positive statement before the comparison, TEV reorders the second and third clauses. It places a full stop
at the end of the second clause also, making it necessary to introduce
this clause with such a formula as "I pray" or "may." For stylistic
reasons, the verb may is used, indicating that this is a continuation
of Jesus' prayer of request to the Father. The last clause in Greek is
literally "that the world may believe that you sent me," which TEV explicitly connects with the earlier petition, May they be one.
    The purpose expressed in the clause that they may all be one may
require modification, especially in languages in which a numeral such
as one must show agreement with a subject. For example, in such languages, a plural affix added to a numeral such as one would be meaningless. However, one may sometimes introduce an expression which will
result in a simile, for example, "I pray that they all may be just like
one." It may be possible, or even necessary, to be more specific in
terms of action or behavior, for example, "I pray that they may act
together just as though they were one person."
    Just as you are in me and I am in you develops the theme of unity
between Father and Son mentioned in verse 11 (Just as you and I are one).
The concept of one person in another is difficult, and it may be better
to translate "May they be united with us, just as you are united with
me and I am united with you" or "May they be united with us, just as
you and I are united to each other."
    TEV understands the clause at the end of verse 21 as expressing
the purpose of the unity of future believers among themselves (May they
be one, so that the world will believe that you sent me). GeCL has "Just
as you are in me and I am in you, Father, so must they also become one
through us! Then shall the world believe that you have sent me." This
translation is similar to TEV. However, it includes the word "one" contained in the variant reading discussed below ("so must they also become one through us") and translates the Greek preposition en "through"
rather than in. Other translations make the last clause express the
purpose of unity that future believers will have with the Father and

the Son. NEB has "so also may they be in us, that the world may believe
that thou didst send me"; Gdsp translates "let them be in union with us,
so that the world may believe that you sent me." The Greek text permits
either exegesis, although in the Greek sentence order May they be in us
is closer to the purpose clause than that they all may be one. The difference in meaning is not great, since the unity of future believers
among themselves is the result of their unity with the Father and the
Son.

   Instead of may they be in us, some Greek manuscripts have "that
they be one in us." The word "one" is most probably a repetition of the
same word earlier in the verse. It is often impossible to begin a sentence with such a request as May they be in us. Such a petition must be
introduced by a specific term for prayer, for example, "I pray that
they may be in us," "that they may be united to us," or "...be joined
to us." It may also be necessary to introduce the final petition, May
they be one, by a verb, for example, "I pray that they may be one."

17.22   I gave them the same glory you gave me, so
            that they may be one, just as you and I are
            one:

   In the Greek text the pronoun I is emphatic.
   The verb gave is in the perfect tense in both occurrences, indicating that, just as Jesus continues to possess the glory which the Father
has given him, so the disciples continue to possess the glory that Jesus
has given them. In translating I gave them the same glory you gave me
a difficulty exists in that one does not know precisely how this glory
is to be understood. It would appear that it is related to the glory
mentioned in verse 5. But how this glorious quality of existence, associated with the preincarnate Christ, can be transmitted to his disciples, and in what way it manifests itself in their lives and behavior,
is difficult to understand. It is evidently a reference to the wonderful
quality of life the disciples experienced as the result of their association with Jesus, but it is difficult in some languages to find a term
or phrase which will adequately suggest such an experience. The closest
equivalent may be "I cause them to be wonderful in the same way that you
caused me to be wonderful," yet this may suggest a self-centered or
egoistic attitude toward the Christian experience. In some cases one
may have an expression roughly equivalent to "I caused them to experience
wonderfulness, even as you caused me to experience it." Often it is necessary to settle for a relatively obscure expression, for example, "I
caused them to become glorious, even as you caused me to be glorious."
   Just as you and I are one is literally "just as we (are) one." The
Greek has no verb, but the verb "are" obviously must be supplied in
English. TEV changes the Greek "we" to you and I, making the participants
more specific.

17.23   I in them and you in me, so that they may be
            completely one, in order that the world may
            know that you sent me and that you love them
            as you love me.

I in them and you in me explains the meaning of one in the last part of verse 22. Again the matter of someone being "in" another person causes difficulty, and it may be best to translate "just as I am united with them, and you are united with me." GeCL translates "I work in them and you work in me," and NAB "I living in them, you living in me." To show the relation of this statement to the preceding statement in verse 22, it may be useful to have an introductory expression such as "that means," for example, "To be one means that I am in them and you in me" or "...I am living in them and you are living in me."

So that they may be completely one indicates both the intended purpose and the goal of I in them and you in me. Completely one is rendered "perfectly one" by Mft, RSV, and NEB. JB has "completely one," and Gdsp translates "be perfectly unified." NAB reads "that their unity may be complete," and GeCL has "so may they come to a perfect unity."

That the world may know that you sent me and that you love them as you love me may refer to the reason Jesus had for giving his disciples the same glory that he possessed (verse 22); or it may refer to the unity of the disciples mentioned in the previous clause. The second of these choices is preferable--the absolute unity of Jesus' disciples is to challenge the world to acknowledge that the Father sent the Son, and that the Father loves the disciples in the same way that he loves the Son.

In verse 21 Jesus speaks of the world's "believing" and here of the world's "knowing." There is no essential difference in the meaning of these terms in the present context. (See comments at 17.3.)

Them, in the clause that you love them, is taken by at least one commentator as a reference to the world. Elsewhere in his Gospel John does speak of God's love for the world (3.16), but in the present context the focus is on the relationship between the Father and the Son and the believers. Thus it is better to take them as a reference to the disciples, rather than to the world. Here Jesus prays that the world may recognize not only that he comes from the Father, but that the Father loves the Christian believers in the same way that he loves the Son.

TEV   (17.24-26)

24 "Father! You have given them to me, and I want them to be with me where I am, so that they may see my glory, the glory you gave me; for you loved me before the world was made. 25 Righteous Father! The world does not know you, but I know you, and these know that you sent me. 26 I made you known to them, and I will continue to do so, in order that the love you have for me may be in them, and so that I also may be in them."

24 Father, I desire that they also, whom thou hast given me, may be with me where I am, to behold my glory which thou hast given me in thy love for me before the foundation of the world. 25 O righteous Father, the world has not known thee, but I have known thee; and these know that thou hast sent me. 26 I made known to them thy name, and I will make it known, that the love with which thou hast loved me may be in them, and I in them."

17.24   "Father! You have given them to me, and I
          want them to be with me where I am, so that
          they may see my glory, the glory you gave me;
          for you loved me before the world was made.

You have given them to me is emphatic in Greek; it translates "which
(neuter singular) you have given me" of the Greek text. Some Greek
manuscripts have "whom (masculine plural) you have given me," but this
is an obvious attempt to simplify a difficult reading. John uses the
neuter singular pronoun to emphasize the unity of the persons in the
group.

If them in the last clause of verse 23 does refer to the disciples,
as suggested above, the same is true of them in this clause. It may be
helpful to make this explicit by translating them as "my disciples."

I want them to be with me where I am is more literally "I want
that where I am they may be with me." By placing the accent mark differently on the Greek verb I am, it is possible to translate "where I
am going," but no translator does so. The desire of Jesus that his disciples be with him is not a selfish wish; it is in keeping with the intention of the Father. Jesus' will is always identical with that of the
Father (see 4.34; 5.30; and 6.38). Moreover, Jesus' prayer does not relate to the present time, nor can it be fulfilled in this world. Jesus
is thinking of the final consummation, when the disciples will see his
true glory.

There may be complications in the use of the present tense in the
clause where I am, for it may suggest that Jesus desires that his followers remain where he is at the time of his prayer. Accordingly, it
may be necessary in some languages to translate "I want them to be with
me where I will be" or "...remain with me where I will be." As already
noted, in some instances there is a shift of time viewpoint between the
time of Jesus' speaking and the temporal perspective of the author as
he writes.

TEV changes the Greek noun phrase, "before the creation of the
world," into a verb phrase, before the world was made. In some languages
it may be necessary to translate "before you created the world."

It may be necessary to break up the rather involved structure of
verse 24 and to conclude a sentence after the glory you gave me. The
final expression of cause may then be introduced as a separate sentence
by saying "You gave it to me because you loved me before the world was
made."

17.25   Righteous Father! The world does not know you,
          but I know you, and these know that you sent me.

In verse 11 Jesus addressed God as Holy Father, while in this verse
he addresses him as Righteous Father. Both the Old Testament (Jer 12.1;
Psa 119.137) and the New Testament (Rom 3.26) speak of God as "righteous." He is righteous because he does what is right; and this is seen
primarily in the punishment of evil men and the saving of the innocent.
The term righteous is probably chosen for the present context because
the idea of judgment is implicit in the statement that the world does

[545]

not know the Father. However, Jesus knows the Father and Jesus' disciples know that the Father sent Jesus. In Greek, the verbs does not know...know...know are in the aorist indicative tense, and so they are rendered in the past tense in several translations (NAB, for example, "has known...have known...have known"). But the verbs may be used to summarize the total outcome of Jesus' ministry, and so the present, indicating timelessness, is a valid rendering. However, one may choose to render "The world has never known you, but I have always known you, and these have come to know that you sent me."

The phrase Righteous Father involves the same problems encountered in the expression Holy Father (verse 11). It may be necessary to use for Father an expression which cannot have such an attributive as righteous. Thus one may need to say "my Father, you who are righteous" or "...who are just." In some languages it is difficult to employ an adjective with the meaning "righteous." It is usually possible, however, to qualify an action, for example, "you who always do what is right" or "you who act fairly." It may even be necessary in some languages to say "you who judge fairly," since to judge fairly is an important aspect of God's relationship to people and is linked closely with any expression of God's righteousness.

17.26   I made you known to them, and I will continue
                 to do so, in order that the love you have for
                 me may be in them, and so that I also may be in
                 them."

I made you known to them is literally "I made your name known to them." Here God's name refers to what he is, and so it may legitimately be translated by the pronoun you. GeCL translates "I have shown them who you are."

And I will continue to do so is literally "and I will make (it) known." For stylistic reasons TEV translates continue to do so, instead of "continue to make you known to them."

In Greek the last clause of this verse reads "in order that the love with which you loved me may be in them and I in them." TEV renders "the love with which you loved me" as the love you have for me, and it supplies the verb may be in the clause "and I in them." To avoid the idea of one person being in another person, GeCL translates "the love which you have for me must also fill them, and I will work in them."

In some languages it may be difficult to speak of the love which one person has for another as being in someone else. A literal rendering of in order that the love you have for me may be in them is liable to be interpreted as "that you will love them in the same way you love me." What is intended here is that the disciples should love others in the same way that God has loved Jesus. Therefore, it may be best to translate the purpose clause in this verse as "in order that they may love others in the same way that you have loved me." The final purpose may then be expressed as "and in order that I may live in them" or "in order that I may be joined to them." The particular way of expressing this relationship depends upon what is semantically possible within the receptor language.

It is not within the scope of this commentary to present a detailed analysis of the relation between the Johannine account of the arrest and crucifixion of Jesus and the accounts in the Synoptic Gospels. However, relevant observations regarding certain specific details will be made in the exegesis to follow. Chapters 18-20 continue "The Book of Glory" that began with the account of the Last Supper in Chapter 13. These chapters fall nicely into two major divisions: the glory of Jesus revealed through his suffering and death (Chapters 18-19) and the glory of Jesus revealed in his resurrection (Chapter 20). Most scholars agree that the Gospel originally ended with the words of 20.31, to which Chapter 21 (a further resurrection appearance) was added later.

Although it is possible to divide each of these three chapters in several different ways, the division of the UBS Greek text (followed by TEV) will form the basis for our analysis and discussion. Chapter 18.1-11 tells of Jesus' arrest. Verses 1-3 provide the setting for the scene in the garden (verses 4-10). Between the two episodes of Jesus' encounter with those who had come out to arrest him (verses 4-8) and of Peter's attack on the High Priest's slave (verses 10-11) is found an explanatory addition of the Gospel writer (verse 9), which calls attention to the fulfillment of Jesus' saying in 17.12.

TEV   (18.1-11)   RSV

THE ARREST OF JESUS

18 After Jesus had said this prayer, he left with his disciples and went across Kidron Brook. There was a garden in that place, and Jesus and his disciples went in. 2 Judas, the traitor, knew where it was, because many times Jesus had met there with his disciples. 3 So Judas went to the garden, taking with him a group of Roman soldiers, and some temple guards sent by the chief priests and the Pharisees; they were armed and carried lanterns and torches. 4 Jesus knew everything that was going to happen to him, so he stepped forward and asked them, "Who is it you are looking for?"

5 "Jesus of Nazareth," they answered.

"I am he," he said.

Judas, the traitor, was standing there with them. 6 When Jesus

18 When Jesus had spoken these words, he went forth with his disciples across the Kidron valley, where there was a garden, which he and his disciples entered. 2 Now Judas, who betrayed him, also knew the place; for Jesus often met there with his disciples. 3 So Judas, procuring a band of soldiers and some officers from the chief priests and the Pharisees, went there with lanterns and torches and weapons. 4 Then Jesus, knowing all that was to befall him, came forward and said to them, "Whom do you seek?' 5 They answered him, "Jesus of Nazareth." Jesus said to them, "I am he." Judas, who betrayed him, was standing with them. 6 When he said to them, "I am he," they drew back and fell to the ground. 7 Again he asked them, "Whom do you

[547]

said to them, "I am he," they
moved back and fell to the ground.
7 Again Jesus asked them, "Who is
it you are looking for?"

"Jesus of Nazareth," they said.

8 "I have already told you that
I am he," Jesus said. "If, then,
you are looking for me, let these
others go." (9 He said this so
that what he had said might come
true: "Father, I have not lost
even one of those you gave me.")

10 Simon Peter, who had a
sword, drew it and struck the High
Priest's slave, cutting off his
right ear. The name of the slave
was Malchus. 11 Jesus said to
Peter, "Put your sword back in
its place! Do you think that I
will not drink the cup of suffering which my Father has given me?"

seek?" And they said, "Jesus of
Nazareth." 8 Jesus answered, "I
told you that I am he; so, if you
seek me, let these men go." 9 This
was to fulfil the word which he
had spoken, "Of those whom thou
gavest me I lost not one." 10 Then
Simon Peter, having a sword, drew
it and struck the high priest's
slave and cut off his right ear.
The slave's name was Malchus. 11
Jesus said to Peter, "Put your
sword into its sheath; shall I
not drink the cup which the Father
has given me?"

The passive nominal expression, The Arrest of Jesus, must be
changed in some languages into an active verbal expression, for example,
"Soldiers and guards arrest Jesus" or "The Jewish authorities arrest
Jesus" or "...send soldiers to arrest Jesus."

18.1   After Jesus had said this prayer, he left
         with his disciples and went across Kidron
         Brook. There was a garden in that place, and
         Jesus and his disciples went in.

After Jesus had said this prayer (so also GeCL) is more literally
"Jesus having said these things." NAB translates "After this discourse,"
while most other translations have either "these things" or "these
words." These introductory words are intended to form a close link between the discourse and prayer at the Last Supper and the events that
follow.

Instead of using such a noun expression as this prayer in the
clause After Jesus had said this prayer, it may be more appropriate in
some languages to use a verb meaning "to pray," for example, "After
Jesus had prayed to his Father in this way" or "After Jesus had prayed
this way."

Although TEV uses two verbs (left...went across), the Greek text
has only one verb, followed by a preposition (Note, for example, NAB
"went out...across"). However, several translations have two verbs
(JB "left...crossed"; NAB "went out...crossed"). Here again the basic
rule for the translator is to render in a way that sounds natural in
the receptor language.

Instead of he left with his disciples some languages require a
double subject, for example, "he and his disciples left together."

This would mean that both "he and his disciples" are the subjects of
the verb left as well as went across.

Brook is rendered "valley" in most translations. Mft and NEB translate "ravine" and Barclay "gulley." The Greek word (cheimarros) is actually an adjective, meaning "winter-flowing." When used as a noun it
can refer either to the stream itself (brook) or to the place where
the stream flows ("valley"). The Kidron Brook contains water only in
the rainy (winter) season. In Greek the word Kidron is preceded by the
singular article (tou) and has the accent on the final syllable. Some
Greek manuscripts have the accent on the first syllable of this word
and a plural article (tōn), so that the meaning is "of the Cedars" (see
Gdsp). This reading is not widely accepted, and the reading of the UBS
Greek text is generally preferred. It is certainly not necessary to
suggest that Jesus and his disciples "forded" the Kidron Brook, that is
to say, walked across through the water. The brook is relatively small,
and they probably crossed it by a bridge.

In Greek There was a garden in that place is actually a subordinate
clause, "where there was a garden." The word translated garden refers
to a place where flowers or vegetables are planted, and sometimes trees
also. Both Mark (14.32) and Matthew (26.36) use a more generic word
(Greek chōrion, meaning "a piece of land," "a place"), which they qualify
by the name Gethsemane. On the other hand, Luke states that Jesus and
his disciples went to the Mount of Olives (22.39). The word Gethsemane
means either "oil valley" or "oil press." Thus if one takes all the
Gospel information together, the place suggested is an olive grove on
the lower slopes of the Mount of Olives, directly across the Kidron
Brook from Jerusalem.

Jesus and his disciples went in is more literally "he went in and
his disciples," a construction in Greek similar to that discussed in
2.2.

18.2   Judas, the traitor, knew where it was, because
              many times Jesus had met there with his disciples.

Here and in verse 5 Judas is introduced as the traitor. This epi-
thet (literally "the man betraying him") is similar to the designation
of Judas in 6.64 (which one would betray him) and 6.71 (Judas...was
going to betray him). Although Judas was spoken of as the betrayer three
times in Chapter 13 (verses 2,11, and 21), the information is not redundant at the beginning of Chapter 18, since the passion narratives
were probably the first part of the Gospel to circulate independently.

An equivalent of the term traitor may suggest a conspirator against
the state or one who betrays state secrets, rather than one who betrays
a friend. It may therefore be more appropriate to use such a descriptive
expression as "the one who turned Jesus over to his enemies" or "the one
who betrayed Jesus." Judas was, in a sense, cooperating with the civil
authorities, and hence a more or less literal translation of traitor
could be misleading.

Knew where it was is literally "knew the place" (JB "knew the place
well").

Instead of the statement Jesus had met there with his disciples, it is appropriate in some languages to say "Jesus and his disciples had met there." A literal translation might suggest that the disciples had gathered in the garden, and that Jesus surreptitiously joined them.

18.3   So Judas went to the garden, taking with him
        a group of Roman soldiers, and some temple
        guards sent by the chief priests and the
        Pharisees; they were armed and carried lan-
        terns and torches.

TEV restructures the first part of this verse. In Greek went to the garden is literally "comes there" and is preceded by the long clause, taking with him a group of Roman soldiers, and some temple guards sent by the chief priests and the Pharisees. Moreover, they were armed, and carried lanterns and torches is literally "with lanterns and torches and weapons." In the Greek text this entire clause follows the verb "comes there." Most modern English translations restructure this complex sentence. However, RSV, attempting to follow the word order of the Greek, sounds as if Judas were the one who brought the lanterns and torches and weapons ("So Judas, procuring a band of soldiers and some officers from the chief priests and the Pharisees, went there with lanterns and torches and weapons.") Lanterns and torches are mentioned only in John's account.

A literal translation of the first part of verse 3 may be misleading, for it may imply that Judas first went to the garden and later took along a group of Roman soldiers. The situation is further complicated by the fact that the temple guards are described as having been sent by the chief priests and Pharisees, and their assignment to this task must have taken place before Judas led them to the garden. The fact that the syntactic order and the temporal order of events do not match may require some readjustment in structure, for example, "The chief priests and Pharisees sent some temple guards to accompany Judas. There was also a group of Roman soldiers, and Judas led them to the garden." It is unlikely that Judas himself was armed, and therefore one may translate "The soldiers and guards were armed and carried lanterns and torches." In translating were armed, one may say "they had their swords" or "they carried their weapons."

John is the only one of the four Gospels to mention Roman soldiers in connection with the arrest of Jesus. The Greek word translated a group of Roman soldiers (NEB "a detachment of soldiers"; GeCL and Barclay "Roman soldiers") is a technical military term (translated "cohort" by many), referring to the tenth part of a legion. Even though the full complement of a cohort was six hundred men, the actual number varied considerably; sometimes there were as few as two hundred. For that reason, it is better to use a generic term, such as "group" or "detachment," rather than the technical term "cohort." Out of this larger group apparently only a smaller detachment of soldiers was sent along with an officer in command (see verse 12).

The word translated temple guards is the same word translated "guards" in 7.32 (see there). The temple guards were no doubt Jewish, but the Roman soldiers were Gentiles.

18.4   Jesus knew everything that was going to
        happen to him, so he stepped forward and
        asked them, "Who is it you are looking for?"

In Greek knew is actually a participle (RSV "knowing") dependent
on the two main verbs stepped forward and asked. John is always careful
to indicate that Jesus knows what is going to happen to him (see 13.1)
and so is master of his own fate. Here Jesus takes the initiative in
stepping out and speaking to the people who come to arrest him.
    Rather than the generic expression everything that was going to
happen to him, it may be necessary in some languages to use a more
specific description of the impending events, for example, "all that
they were going to do to him" or "how they were going to treat him."

18.5   "Jesus of Nazareth," they answered.
            "I am he," he said.
            Judas, the traitor, was standing there with
        them.

Jesus of Nazareth is the rendering of most translations, though
some have "Jesus the Nazarene" (Mft, JB). NAB has "Jesus the Nazorean,"
with a note indicating that this is the form used in Matthew, in distinction from the form "Nazarene" in Mark. The Greek form used here is
unusual, but according to Matthew 2.23, it was interpreted as meaning
"from Nazareth." In any case, to translate as "Nazorean" produces a
zero term. It is best to go along with most translators and render of
Nazareth. However, in order to designate a town from which a person
comes, some languages use a descriptive phrase, "Jesus whose hometown
is Nazareth" or "Jesus who comes from Nazareth" or "Jesus known as from
Nazareth." In other languages the name of the hometown is made a type
of adjectival attributive, for example, "the Nazareth Jesus."
    In the Greek text they answered and he said come before the words
they introduce. For stylistic reasons TEV reverses this arrangement.
He said is literally "he said to them."
    I am he (so most translations) appears as "I am Jesus" in one im-
portant Greek manuscript. Though it is possible that "Jesus" was omitted accidentally by some ancient scribe, the weight of textual evidence
is strongly in support of the reading I am he, and it is followed by
nearly all modern translations. However, it may be necessary to translate "I am Jesus" in some languages.
    John states simply that Judas, the traitor, was standing there
with them, without indicating that Judas identified Jesus by a kiss
(contrast Mark 14.44-45). In John's Gospel Jesus identifies himself
and takes the initiative in giving himself up. In some languages it
may be necessary to indicate clearly the reference of the pronoun them;
for example, one may say "was standing there with the soldiers and
guards."

18.6-7   When Jesus said to them, "I am he," they moved
            back and fell to the ground. 7 Again Jesus asked
            them, "Who is it you are looking for?"
            "Jesus of Nazareth," they said.

When Jesus said to them is literally "when therefore (Greek oun) he said to them." But it is nesessary to identify Jesus by name rather than by pronominal reference, since the last person referred to in verse 5 is Judas.

They moved back and fell to the ground (so also JB) is fairly close to most other translations (note RSV and NEB "they drew back and fell to the ground"). This statement emphasizes Jesus' absolute authority in the situation; even those who have come to arrest him fall to the ground when he speaks. In some languages it is essential to indicate in which direction the soldiers and guards fell, whether forward or backward. To have them fall forward would seem strange, since they were moving backward. Therefore it seems more plausible to translate "and they fell backward to the ground." This rendering would also seem to emphasize more the power of Jesus' statement upon the crowd. Furthermore, if one uses an expression such as "fall forward," there is the possibility of interpreting it as a kind of obeisance or expression of reverence.

18.8   "I have already told you that I am he,"
         Jesus said. "If, then, you are looking for me,
         let these others go."

"I have already told you that I am he," Jesus said is literally "Jesus answered, 'I said to you that I am he.'"

In the clause If, then, you are looking for me, the pronoun me is emphatic.

These others is literally "these" (a masculine plural pronoun), which several other translations render as TEV does; RSV has "these men." However, since the disciples have been specifically mentioned only in verse 1, it may be necessary to render these others as "these followers of mine" or perhaps as "my followers here."

18.9   (He said this so that what he had said might
         come true: "Father, I have not lost even one
         of those you gave me.")

Since this verse is a kind of parenthetical statement, NEB and NAB also place it in parentheses. He said this so that is literally "so that" (Greek hina). No verb is included in the Greek text, but in translation it is necessary to supply one. Several translations are similar to NEB ("This was to make good his words"), while GeCL has "so what Jesus had said earlier came true." The verb rendered might come true is frequently used in the New Testament in relation to the fulfillment of prophecy, but only in John is it used of the fulfillment of Jesus' words (note also 18.32). Nowhere in the Gospel has Jesus said the exact words quoted here; but the reference is most probably to 17.12. In the Greek text the word Father is not explicit, though it is clear from the context that Jesus is speaking to the Father. TEV makes this information explicit.

Might come true may be rendered in some languages "might happen" or "might occur."

As noted several times in Chapter 17, it may be necessary to render Father as "my Father." Similarly, I have not lost even one of those you gave me may be rendered "I have not lost even one of those you committed to my care" or "...even one of those you told me to care for."

18.10   Simon Peter, who had a sword, drew it and struck the High Priest's slave, cutting off his right ear. The name of the slave was Malchus.

In Greek the verb translated had is a participle dependent on the verb drew, while cutting off is a finite verb. TEV restructures (as do most other modern translations) in a way that is more natural in English. In fact, if one translated the Greek text literally into English, it would suggest two separate actions on Peter's part ("striking" and "cutting off"). Obviously striking of the High Priest's slave and cutting off his right ear are one and the same action, and TEV makes this clear. The word translated sword (so most translations) literally means "knife" or "dagger," suggesting a small weapon that could easily be concealed. All four Gospels mention this incident, but only John gives the names of the persons involved, Simon Peter and Malchus. The various Gospels use three different Greek words for ear, and it may be that in John and in Mark the reference is only to the "earlobe." However, most translations render ear. Only John and Luke specify that it was the right ear.
    A literal translation of the TEV rendering, struck the High Priest's slave, cutting off his right ear, could be misunderstood, especially if the choice of a verb for struck suggests repeated blows. It is important here to use a term which indicates only one movement of the sword. In some languages it would be appropriate to say "Peter pulled out his sword and swung it at the High Priest's slave. In so doing, he cut off the slave's right ear." In other languages it might be better to say "Peter pulled out his sword and cut off the right ear of the High Priest's slave."

18.11   Jesus said to Peter, "Put your sword back in its place! Do you think that I will not drink the cup of suffering which my Father has given me?"

TEV uses the generic expression in its place to avoid the more difficult technical terms "scabbard" (JB) or "sheath" (NAB). "Sheathe your sword" (Mft and NEB) is rather high level. One may simply say "Put your sword back where it was."
    Do you think that I will not drink the cup of suffering which my Father has given me? is literally "The cup which the Father has given me, will I not drink it?" In Greek this is a rhetorical question that expects an affirmative answer. Most commentators point out that the cup refers to Jesus' cup of suffering, and so TEV makes this information explicit. "The Father" of the Greek text has the force of my Father in the present context.

[553]

In some languages it is almost impossible to preserve the metaphor of the cup, for "drinking" and "suffering" cannot be spoken of in the same context, nor can one "drink the cup." One can only drink the contents of a cup, and to speak of "drinking suffering" would be meaningless. Hence, the metaphor must be dropped, and such an expression may be used as "Do you think that I am not willing to suffer in the way in which my Father has ordained that I should suffer?" or "...that my Father has arranged that I should suffer?"

| TEV | (18.12-14) | RSV |

JESUS BEFORE ANNAS

12 Then the Roman soldiers with their commanding officer and the Jewish guards arrested Jesus, tied him up, 13 and took him first to Annas. He was the father-in-law of Caiaphas, who was High Priest that year. 14 It was Caiaphas who had advised the Jewish authorities that it was better that one man should die for all the people.	12 So the band of soldiers and their captain and the officers of the Jews seized Jesus and bound him. 13 First they led him to Annas; for he was the father-in-law of Caiaphas, who was high priest that year. 14 It was Caiaphas who had given counsel to the Jews that it was expedient that one man should die for the people.

Jesus before Annas may not be sufficiently meaningful as a section heading. It is, of course, possible to say "Jesus is led before Annas" or "They lead Jesus to Annas."

18.12   Then the Roman soldiers with their commanding
      officer and the Jewish guards arrested Jesus,
      tied him up,

The Roman soldiers is the same term discussed at verse 3. Commanding officer (JB "captain"; NEB "commander") literally means "commander of a thousand." It was a technical term in the Roman army for the commander of a cohort (see comments on verse 3). A more generic term, such as commanding officer, "commander," or "officer in charge" seems preferable to a specific term, such as "captain." In some languages the commanding officer must be mentioned before the soldiers, for example, "the commanding officer together with the Roman soldiers." One may, however, introduce the commanding officer in parentheses, for example, "the Roman soldiers (this included their commanding officer) and the Jewish guards."

Jewish guards is the same term translated temple guards in verse 3 (see also 7.32).

In some languages it is important in rendering tied him up to indicate specifically what happened. It would be wrong to suggest that Jesus was tied both hand and foot and therefore had to be carried, or that he was tied to some object such as a tree or post. What is indicated here is that his hands were tied, probably behind his back.

[554]

18.13   and took him first to Annas. He was the father-
         in-law of Caiaphas, who was High Priest that
         year.

According to Matthew 26.57, Jesus was tried before Caiaphas; Mark
(14.53) and Luke (22.57) simply mention the High Priest. But John clearly indicates that Jesus was taken first before Annas (verse 13), and
later before Caiaphas (verse 24). John does not indicate what happened
in the trial before Caiaphas. To resolve these difficulties one ancient
manuscript puts verse 24 in the middle of verse 13, thus indicating
that it was before Caiaphas that Jesus was tried (18.19-23). It is obvious that this reordering is simply an attempt to make the text conform to the Synoptic accounts. Mft is the only translation that reorders the verses. His reordering (13, 14, 19-24, 15-18, 25-27) is
rather radical and wholly without textual support.
    Annas is mentioned only here and in verse 24 in John's Gospel.
Elsewhere in the New Testament he is mentioned in Luke 3.2 and Acts
4.6. According to Josephus, the Jewish historian, Annas was appointed
High Priest in A.D. 6 but was deposed in A.D. 15. However, he remained
a very powerful man, and eventually each of his five sons became High
Priest. Only John's Gospel indicates that Annas was the father-in-law
of Caiaphas. Most languages have a term for father-in-law, but if such
a term does not exist, one can say "Annas was the father of the woman
Caiaphas married."
    For the statement who was High Priest that year, see the comments
at 11.49.

18.14   It was Caiaphas who had advised the Jewish
         authorities that it was better that one man
         should die for all the people.

This verse refers back to 11.50. It may be necessary to introduce
a temporal adverb to indicate that Caiaphas' advice to the other Jewish
authorities had been given at an earlier time, for example, "It was
Caiaphas who some time before had said to the Jewish authorities, 'It
is better that one man die...'" Obviously, the form of Caiaphas' statement should be as close as possible to the rendering of 11.50.

              TEV   (18.15-18)   RSV

          PETER DENIES JESUS

   15 Simon Peter and another dis-   15 Simon Peter followed Jesus,
ciple followed Jesus. That other   and so did another disciple. As
disciple was well known to the High this disciple was known to the
Priest, so he went with Jesus into   high priest, he entered the court
the courtyard of the High Priest's   of the high priest along with Je-
house, 16 while Peter stayed out-   sus, 16 while Peter stood outside
side by the gate. Then the other   at the door. So the other disciple,
disciple went back out, spoke to the who was known to the high priest,

girl at the gate, and brought Peter inside. 17 The girl at the
gate said to Peter, "Aren't you
also one of the disciples of that
man?"

    "No, I am not," answered Peter.

    18 It was cold, so the servants
and guards had built a charcoal
fire and were standing around it,
warming themselves. So Peter went
over and stood with them, warming
himself.

went out and spoke to the maid who
kept the door, and brought Peter
in. 17 The maid who kept the door
said to Peter, "Are not you also
one of this man's disciples?" He
said, "I am not." 18 Now the servants*l* and officers had made a
charcoal fire, because it was cold,
and they were standing and warming
themselves; Peter also was with
them, standing and warming himself.

*l*Or *slaves*

    The section heading, Peter Denies Jesus, may require expansion
because of the complex meaning involved in the word denies. One may
say, for example, "Peter tells people he doesn't know Jesus" or "Peter
says he has never known Jesus" or "Peter says he doesn't know who Jesus
is."

18.15   Simon Peter and another disciple followed
                    Jesus. That other disciple was well known to
                    the High Priest, so he went with Jesus into
                    the courtyard of the High Priest's house,

    The identity of another disciple is disputed. Some have identified
him with the other disciple (20.3), whom others further identify with
the disciple whom Jesus loved (13.23). However, there is no firm basis
for this identification, and it should not be used in translation. Some
languages have two distinct terms for disciple, one of which is used in
speaking of the twelve and another which designates a larger group of followers. Because another disciple is not identified as a member of the
twelve, some translators prefer to use the second of these terms. However, only someone who had been present with Jesus in the garden would
be likely to have followed him to the High Priest's house after his
arrest.

    The Greek word gnōstos, rendered well known (Phps "known personally
to"; Mft, Gdsp "an acquaintance of"; NEB "who was acquainted with"; JB,
NAB "who was known to"), is used in the Septuagint (note Psa 55.13, for
example) to mean a close friend." If this disciple was a "close friend"
of the High Priest, it is hard to identify him with the disciple whom
Jesus loved (13.23; see the comment in the previous paragraph).

    The Greek word aulē, rendered courtyard of the...house, also ap-
pears in the Synoptic accounts of Peter's denial. There the word is used
of the place where Peter was warming himself by the fire (Mark 14.54;
Luke 22.55), which suggests a large enclosed space open to the sky. In
John's account, however, aulē occurs only in verse 15. The fact that the
other disciple was admitted to the aulē because he was well known to the
High Priest and that Peter was admitted only after the other disciple...
spoke to the girl at the gate (verse 16) suggests that John may understand aulē to mean a building rather than an open courtyard, which would

not normally be so restricted. This explains the translation "palace" in JB, Luther Revised, and the note of NAB. However, most translations agree with the rendering of TEV.

18.16   while Peter stayed outside by the gate.
               Then the other disciple went back out,
               spoke to the girl at the gate, and brought
               Peter inside.

In the Greek text, the expression translated in TEV as the other disciple is literally "the other disciple who was well known to the High Priest." Since, however, this same expression occurs in verse 15, it seems better from the standpoint of English style to say "the other disciple." The Greek text repeats the expression who was well known to the High Priest for emphasis.

The girl at the gate is one word in Greek. The word may be either masculine or feminine; however, since it is used with the feminine article, it is definitely feminine in this context.

18.17   The girl at the gate said to Peter, "Aren't
               you also one of the disciples of that man?"
                    "No, I am not," answered Peter.

The girl at the gate renders the same Greek word that was translated in this way in verse 16. However, in verse 17 this person is further described as "a servant girl" (paidiskē). RSV has "the maid who kept the door" in both verses. Some translations give the impression that two different persons were involved. NEB has "the woman at the door...the maid on duty at the door," and NAB translates "the woman at the gate...This servant girl kept the gate." The translator should either use the same phrase in verses 16 and 17 or introduce in verse 16 the information that the girl was a servant and then render "the girl" in verse 17: "(16) ...spoke to the servant girl at the gate and led Peter inside. (17) The girl said to Peter..."

In Greek the question Aren't you also one of the disciples of that man is introduced by a particle (mē) which normally expects the answer "no." The same particle is used in the second question that Peter is asked (verse 25). However, since the third question (verse 26) definitely expects a positive answer, it may be best to translate the first two questions as expecting positive answers also, especially since the particle mē may have lost its original force in John.

Also probably does not mean "in addition to the other disciple," since if the other disciple had been known to be Jesus' disciple, he would not have been admitted (verse 15). More likely it means "like the others who were with Jesus when he was arrested." Almost all translations (RSV, NEB, GeCL, JB, Gdsp, Phps, Barclay, Segond, Zür, Luther Revised) have "also" or an equivalent. NEB translates "Are you another of this man's disciples?"

In Greek that man is literally "this man" (so most translations), but TEV's rendering is more natural for English readers, since Jesus is

not present. In some languages it may be necessary to translate <u>one of
the disciples of that man</u> as "one of the disciples of that man Jesus."
Otherwise, the reader might misunderstand the phrase to mean "a disciple of 'the other disciple.'"

<u>"No, I am not," answered Peter</u> is literally "That man says, 'I am
not.'" <u>I am not</u> may be rendered in some languages "I am not one of his
disciples" or "No, indeed!"

18.18   It was cold, so the servants and guards
                had built a charcoal fire and were standing
                around it, warming themselves. So Peter went
                over and stood with them, warming himself.

TEV radically restructures the first sentence in verse 18. It reads
literally "But the servants and the guards were standing, having made a
charcoal fire because it was cold, and they were warming themselves."
TEV (also JB) introduces first in the sentence the information that it
was cold, since this fact explains the actions which follow. JB reads
"Now it was cold, and the servants and guards had lit a charcoal fire
and were standing there warming themselves." <u>The servants and guards</u>
refers to the personal servants of the High Priest and the temple
guards (verse 3 and 10). The Greek word translated <u>charcoal fire</u> appears in the New Testament only here and in 21.9.

Since charcoal is known in almost all parts of the world, there
should be no difficulty in translating <u>a charcoal fire</u>. In some instances it may be necessary to say "a fire of coals" or "a fire of burning embers" to distinguish it from a wood fire, which would give off a
lot of smoke and not be suitable in a courtyard.

<u>Peter went over and stood with them, warming himself</u> also repre-
sents some restructuring. The Greek literally reads "But Peter was with
them standing and warming himself."

TEV   (18.19-24)   RSV

THE HIGH PRIEST QUESTIONS JESUS

19 The High Priest questioned
Jesus about his disciples and
about his teaching. 20 Jesus answered, "I have always spoken publicly to everyone; all my teaching
was done in the synagogues and in
the Temple, where all the people
come together. I have never said
anything in secret. 21 Why, then,
do you question me? Question the
people who heard me. Ask them what
I told them--they know what I said."

22 When Jesus said this, one of
the guards there slapped him and

19 The high priest then questioned Jesus about his disciples
and his teaching. 20 Jesus answered him, "I have spoken openly
to the world; I have always taught
in synagogues and in the temple,
where all Jews come together; I
have said nothing secretly. 21 Why
do you ask me? Ask those who have
heard me, what I said to them;
they know what I said." 22 When he
had said this, one of the officers
standing by struck Jesus with his
hand, saying, "Is that how you

said, "How dare you talk like that to the High Priest!"

23 Jesus answered him, "If I have said anything wrong, tell everyone here what it was. But if I am right in what I have said, why do you hit me?"

24 Then Annas sent him, still tied up, to Caiaphas the High Priest.

answer the high priest?" 23 Jesus answered him, "If I have spoken wrongly, bear witness to the wrong; but if I have spoken rightly, why do you strike me?" 24 Annas then sent him bound to Caiaphas the high priest.

18.19 The High Priest questioned Jesus about his disciples and about his teaching.

Although John has said that Caiaphas...was High Priest that year (verse 13), the statement at the end of the trial scene that Annas sent him (Jesus) to Caiaphas (verse 24) makes clear that the High Priest in verse 19 must be Annas and not Caiaphas. Annas could loosely be referred to as the High Priest, since he had previously held that office, was father-in-law to Caiaphas, and was a highly influential man. But it is better for the translator to render merely the High Priest, without indicating the man referred to.

John states that the High Priest questioned Jesus about his disciples and his teaching; no reference is made to questions regarding Jesus' messiahship and the accusation of blasphemy, which are the two main points of the trial in the Synoptic accounts.

After the verb questioned it may be necessary in some languages to introduce direct discourse, for example, "The High Priest asked Jesus, 'Who are your disciples and what do you teach?'"

18.20 Jesus answered, "I have always spoken publicly to everyone; all my teaching was done in the synagogues and in the Temple, where all the people come together. I have never said anything in secret.

Jesus answered is more literally "Jesus answered him."

I have always spoken publicly to everyone is more literally "I have spoken publicly to the world." TEV includes the adverb always, which carries through the force of Jesus' words. Publicly translates the Greek word first used in 7.4 (see also 7.13,26; 10.24; 11.14,54; 16.25,29). Have always spoken publicly may be rendered in some languages "have always spoken so that everyone could hear." The converse of this statement is given negatively in the last sentence of this verse, I have never said anything in secret.

In this context "the world" refers to everyone that Jesus had come in contact with; NAB reads "to any who would listen."

All my teaching was done in is literally "I have always taught in..."

The word for Temple is the same word used in 2.14 (see there). It refers to the entire Temple area. This same word is also used in 7.14,28; 8.20; and 10.23. In the synagogues (Mft, Gdsp, RSV, "in synagogues") is literally "in synagogue" (NEB). Since Jesus taught in more than one synagogue, it is more natural in English to use either the plural or an implied plural (note, for example, NAB "I always taught in a synagogue or in the temple area").

Many commentators believe that the clause where all the people come together is a comment of the Gospel writer, since it would be an unusual thing for Jesus to be saying to the High Priest. However, in translation, it may have to be presented as a word of Jesus. Come together would be more appropriately rendered "meet" or "meet together."

I have never said anything in secret is more literally "...and in secret I said nothing." This same contrast between "in the open" and "in secret" occurs in 7.4, which TEV renders No one hides what he is doing if he wants to be well known.

18.21   Why, then, do you question me? Question the
               people who heard me. Ask them what I told
               them--they know what I said."

There is no Greek equivalent for then in Jesus' question Why, then, do you question me? However, it is natural to include it in English, since Jesus' question is based on what he has said in verse 20.

Question the people who heard me. Ask them what I told them is one sentence in Greek: "Ask the people who heard what I said to them."

In Greek they know what I said begins with the interjection ide, which was discussed at 16.29. It is used for emphasis, and most translators omit it.

Jesus' argument in verses 20-21 must be understood in the light of contemporary court procedures. According to a later Jewish law, which may have been in force in Jesus' day, it was improper for an accused person to be asked to testify against himself. Jesus is demanding that the trial be conducted in legal fashion, with proper witnesses.

18.22   When Jesus said this, one of the guards there
               slapped him and said, "How dare you talk like that
               to the High Priest!"

This is actually a plural in Greek ("these things"), but the singular pronoun is more natural in English. The Greek does not introduce Jesus' name until later on in the verse (RSV "When he had said this, one of the officers standing by struck Jesus with his hand"). However, in English it is customary to mention a person by name (When Jesus said this) and then use a pronominal reference (one of the guards there slapped him).

Slapped him is literally "gave Jesus a slap (rapisma)." The primary meaning of the Greek noun is a blow with a club, rod, or whip, but it also can be used of a blow with the hand. In this instance, a blow with the open hand was the more likely. In some languages it is necessary to stipulate where such a blow is given, and it is best in this instance to say "he slapped Jesus on the face."

Guards is the same word used in verse 3 (see there); the reference is to the Jewish Temple guards.

How dare you talk like that to the High Priest! is actually a question in Greek (RSV "Is that how you answer the high priest?"), for which a number of translations attempt a dynamic equivalent. Note, for example, Barclay "How dare you answer the High Priest like that?" It was expected that the people show proper regard for God and for the leaders whom he had appointed (note Exo 22.28 and Acts 23.4-5). However, in the present context Jesus is simply asking for a fair trial. How dare you talk like this...? may be rendered in some languages "How do you judge yourself big enough to talk like this...?" or "How can you try to talk like this...?" or even "Who told you that you could talk like this...?"

18.23   Jesus answered him, "If I have said any-
         thing wrong, tell everyone here what it was.
         But if I am right in what I have said, why
         do you hit me?"

If I have said anything wrong (NAB "If I said anything wrong"; JB "If there is something wrong in what I said"; Mft "If I have said anything wrong") is more literally "If I have spoken wrongly" (RSV). Jesus' words are an implicit denial that he has violated the law of Exodus 22.28. Since Jesus knows he has said nothing wrong, he challenges the High Priest to produce the evidence that would prove him guilty: tell everyone here what it was (literally "testify concerning the evil"). Mft renders "prove it" and JB "point it out"; NEB ("state it in evidence") and NAB ("produce the evidence") make the reference to court evidence explicit. It seems clear that Jesus' response is not to the man who slapped him, but to the High Priest. The guard would presumably not have been the person to give evidence of Jesus' presumed wrongdoing, and it is unlikely that the guard would have acted unless prompted to do so by the High Priest. Thus the final clause why do you hit me? may be rendered "why do you cause me to be hit?" or "why did you cause the guard to slap me?"

But if I am right in what I have said is more literally "If I have spoken rightly" (so RSV). Mft translates "if I said what was true," and NAB has "but if I spoke the truth."

The verb hit is literally "beat" and is used in the Lukan account (Luke 22.63; TEV beat). In 2 Corinthians 11.20 TEV renders it slaps. Here the verb must be rendered as to convey the fact that Jesus has just been slapped.

18.24   Then Annas sent him, still tied up, to
         Caiaphas the High Priest.

As earlier indicated, this verse implies that the questioning in verses 19-23 was done by Annas.

As noted in the discussion of verse 13, some commentators favor placing verse 24 in the middle of verse 13, to make Caiaphas the interrogator of verse 19. However, there is no textual basis for such a shift.

Nor are there grammatical grounds for assuming that the verb sent of this verse has the force of a pluperfect ("had sent"), suggesting that Annas had sent Jesus to Caiaphas, the High Priest, before the questioning of verse 19. The text must be translated as it stands, and the difficulty allowed to remain.

Then Annas sent him must be treated in some languages as a causative, for example, "So Annas caused him to be led to Caiaphas the High Priest." A literal translation of sent might imply that Jesus went by himself. Obviously, since he was under arrest, he was escorted from Annas to Caiaphas.

There is a question whether the Greek participle used here has the force of still tied up or merely "tied up." It may carry either force, and the answer really depends on whether Jesus was untied during his interrogation by the High Priest, since verse 12 explicitly states that he was tied up at his arrest. Since the text does not indicate that he was untied in the interim, it is logical to assume that he remained tied during the interrogation. If this conclusion is valid, the perfect participle should be translated still tied up. In some languages still tied up must be rendered as a separate sentence, for example, "He was still tied up" or "His hands were still tied" or "The guards kept his hands tied."

TEV   (18.25-27)   RSV

PETER DENIES JESUS AGAIN

25 Peter was still standing there keeping himself warm. So the others said to him, "Aren't you also one of the disciples of that man?"

But Peter denied it. "No, I am not," he said.

26 One of the High Priest's slaves, a relative of the man whose ear Peter had cut off, spoke up. "Didn't I see you with him in the garden?" he asked.

27 Again Peter said "No"--and at once a rooster crowed.

25 Now Simon Peter was standing and warming himself. They said to him, "Are not you also one of his disciples?" He denied it and said, "I am not." 26 One of the servants[l] of the high priest, a kinsman of the man whose ear Peter had cut off, asked, "Did I not see you in the garden with him?" 27 Peter again denied it; and at once the cock crowed.

[l]Or slaves

In rendering the section heading, Peter Denies Jesus Again, it is important to employ a form parallel to the one preceding verse 15 (Peter Denies Jesus).

18.25   Peter was still standing there keeping himself warm. So the others said to him, "Aren't you also one of the disciples of that man?"
But Peter denied it. "No, I am not," he said.

This verse resumes the scene described in verse 18 after the interruption of verses 19-24. According to verse 18, Peter was standing by the fire warming himself, and so TEV and other translations (for example, Gdsp, Phps, GeCL) include the adverb <u>still</u> to maintain the continuity between the two accounts. Since John is apparently narrating what happened while Jesus was being interrogated, some translations render the Greek particle <u>de</u> (literally "but") rather freely: "all through this" (NAB); "in the meantime" (Anchor); "Meanwhile" (NEB); "As Simon Peter stood there warming himself" (JB).

The Greek text has "Peter" in verse 18 and "Simon Peter" in verse 25, but no theological importance attaches to the use of the full name. Therefore TEV, GeCL, and Barclay have <u>Peter</u> in both verses.

<u>So the others said to him</u> is literally "so (Greek <u>oun</u>) they said to him." The plural verb ("they said") contrasts with the singular noun (<u>the girl</u>) in verse 17, which explains TEV's rendering (compare NEB "The others asked"). JB's use of a singular ("someone said to him") has no basis in the text. <u>So the others said to him</u> may be expanded in translation, for example, "So some of the others who were standing there said to him."

Both the question and Peter's answer are almost identically the same as the question and answer in verse 17. In verse 25 the Greek has "his disciples," but TEV renders the same way as in verse 17 (<u>the disciples of that man</u>). Peter's second denial is emphasized by the introductory words <u>But Peter denied it</u> (Greek "that man denied"), whereas the first denial had simply <u>answered Peter</u> (Greek "that man says"). <u>Denied</u> can be rendered "said it was not so" or "said, 'No.'"

<u>18.26</u>   One of the High Priest's slaves, a relative of
             the man whose ear Peter had cut off, spoke up.
             "Didn't I see you with him in the garden?" he asked.

The word <u>slaves</u> is the same word rendered <u>servants</u> in verse 18. Since the same category of persons is referred to it is better to translate the same in each instance.

<u>Spoke up</u> is literally "says"; NEB and NAB translate "insisted."

The first part of this verse is rather complicated, for the phrase <u>a relative of the man whose ear Peter had cut off</u> is in apposition with <u>one of the High Priest's slaves</u>. However, the appositional phrase involves a complex relative clause <u>whose ear Peter had cut off</u>. It may be necessary to restructure as follows: "One of the High Priest's slaves was there. He was related to the man whose ear Peter had cut off. This man spoke up. He asked Peter..."

The third question (<u>Didn't I see you with him in the garden?</u>) expects an affirmative answer. One may employ such a form as "I saw you in the garden with Jesus, didn't I?" It may be necessary to use the name "Jesus," rather than the pronoun "him," in order to avoid a possible misinterpretation of the antecedent of the pronoun, for in some languages the pronoun could refer to the man whose ear Peter had cut off.

18.27   Again Peter said "No"--and at once a rooster
             crowed.

Again Peter said "No" is literally "Again therefore (Greek oun) Peter denied." The restructuring of TEV into direct discourse is a stylistic device to achieve dramatic effect.

For the prediction that Peter would deny Jesus, see 13.38. Some commentators maintain that the phrase translated a rooster crowed actually refers to the blowing of the trumpet at the close of the third watch during the night, the watch called "rooster's crow." This would mean that the interrogation of Jesus went on until three o'clock in the morning, since the third watch of the night extended from twelve midnight until three in the morning. However, it is more natural to take the phrase literally, as most translators do. It is reported that in Jerusalem the time that roosters crow is between three and five in the morning.

<table>
<tr><td>TEV</td><td>(18.28-32)</td><td>RSV</td></tr>
</table>

JESUS BEFORE PILATE

28 Early in the morning Jesus was taken from Caiaphas' house to the governor's palace. The Jewish authorities did not go inside the palace, for they wanted to keep themselves ritually clean, in order to be able to eat the Passover meal. 29 So Pilate went outside to them and asked, "What do you accuse this man of?"

30 Their answer was, "We would not have brought him to you if he had not committed a crime."

31 Pilate said to them, "Then you yourselves take him and try him according to your own law."

They replied, "We are not allowed to put anyone to death." (32 This happened in order to make come true what Jesus had said when he indicated the kind of death he would die.)

28 Then they led Jesus from the house of Caiaphas to the praetorium. It was early. They themselves did not enter the praetorium, so that they might not be defiled, but might eat the passover. 29 So Pilate went out to them and said, "What accusation do you bring against this man?" 30 They answered him, "If this man were not an evildoer, we would not have handed him over." 31 Pilate said to them, "Take him yourselves and judge him by your own law." The Jews said to him, "It is not lawful for us to put any man to death." 32 This was to fulfil the word which Jesus had spoken to show by what death he was to die.

Jesus' trial before Pilate includes the section from 18.28 to 19.16a. TEV divides this section into two parts (18.28-38a and 18.38b--19.16a). It is possible to divide the passage into even shorter units, indicating which events took place outside the palace, where the Jewish authorities and the crowd were gathered, and which events took place inside the palace, where Jesus was. If this arrangement is followed, a balance is achieved between the first three scenes and the last three; the only scene in which Pilate does not figure prominently is the central one, in which the soldiers mock Jesus (19.1-3). The first scene (18.28-32) and the seventh (19.12-16a) both take place outside the palace. In the first scene the Jewish authorities demand the death penalty for Jesus, while in the last their goal is achieved, and Jesus is condemned to death by Pilate. There is also a balance between the second

(18.33-38a) and the sixth scenes (19.8-11), both of which take place
inside the palace between Jesus and Pilate. In the second scene Pilate
asks Jesus if he is the king of the Jews, which leads Jesus to a statement concerning the nature of his kingdom. In the sixth scene the matter
of authority is also discussed. Finally, the third (18.38b-40) and the
fifth scenes (19.4-8) are in balance, for both take place outside the
palace. In each of these two scenes Pilate declares Jesus innocent. The
result is a rather carefully worked out arrangement of the material,
which contrasts with the simple outline of the Synoptic Gospels.

The section heading, Jesus before Pilate, may be meaningless, or
even misleading, if translated literally. One may, however, employ such
a title as "The Jewish authorities accuse Jesus before Pilate" or "Pilate judges Jesus" or "Jesus is tried before Pilate."

18.28   Early in the morning Jesus was taken from
           Caiaphas' house to the governor's palace. The
           Jewish authorities did not go inside the palace,
           for they wanted to keep themselves ritually clean,
           in order to be able to eat the Passover meal.

Early in the morning (RSV "early"; JB "morning"; Mft, NEB "early
morning"; NAB "at daybreak") translates one word in Greek (prōi). This
is a technical term, referring to the last Roman division (or "watch")
of the night, from three to six in the morning. If the questioning before the High Priest (18.19-23) lasted until three and Jesus was then
several hours with Caiaphas (18.24), he may have been taken to Pilate
around six in the morning.

Jesus was taken translates "They take Jesus" of the Greek text.
The second sentence in this verse (they wanted to keep themselves ritually clean, in order to be able to eat the Passover meal) makes clear
that Jews are meant. Some Roman soldiers may have been included in the
escort.

In many languages a passive or impersonal construction is impossible, and the pronoun "they" would be misleading, since it could refer
to those who had been questioning Peter. It may be best to say "The Jewish authorities took Jesus" or "The Jewish authorities ordered Jesus
taken." In some languages, however, the verb "take" is too general in
this context, and it is necessary to use a more specific term, for example, "the guards led Jesus from Caiaphas' house to the governor's
palace."

From Caiaphas' house (so also Barclay) is literally "from Caiaphas." Mft, RSV, and JB render "from the house of Caiaphas."

The governor's palace (NEB "the Governor's headquarters"; Gdsp
"the governor's house"; GeCL "the palace of the Roman Governor") translates a Greek word transliterated praetorium in several translations
(RSV, JB, NAB, Mft). In New Testament times the word was used of the
official residence of a Roman governor. Normally, the governor of Judea
lived in Caesarea (note Acts 23.33-35), but on the occasion of important
feasts he would go to Jerusalem to keep down disturbances or popular
uprisings. There is no unanimous agreement as to the precise building
referred to. It may have been the palace of Herod in the western part of

the city, but some recent scholars argue that it was the fortress of
Antonia, north of the Temple area. In some languages there is no special
term such as palace for the dwelling of an important ruler. However, one
can say "the governor's large house" or "the large house where the governor stayed."

The Jewish authorities translates "they" of the Greek text. As indicated above, the references to being ritually clean and to the Passover
meal make clear that Jews are meant. GeCL, NEB, Barclay translate "the
Jews."

The word palace translates the same word rendered governor's palace above.

Because they wanted to keep themselves ritually clean (Barclay
"They did not want to risk being ceremonially defiled"; NAB "for they
had to avoid ritual impurity") is more literally "so that they might
not be defiled" (RSV). The reference is specifically to ritual impurity,
and some translators make this information explicit. "To keep oneself
ritually clean" is expressed in some languages in an idiomatic form,
for example, "to keep dirt away from oneself" or "to prevent spots from
coming upon a person." However, in general, a desire to be preserved
ritually pure or uncontaminated is expressed in a negative attitude toward defilement--literally, "they didn't want to be defiled," for example, "they didn't want to be thought of as sinners" or "they didn't
want to be contaminated" or, as expressed in one language, "they didn't
want to smell like Gentiles."

To eat the Passover meal is literally "to eat the passover." It
was important for a Jew not to become ritually unclean, because he would
then have to postpone celebration of the Passover for a month (see Num
9.9-11). To eat the Passover meal may be expressed in some languages as
"to have a share in the Passover festival" or "to be a part of the Passover festival."

18.29   So Pilate went outside to them and asked,
             "What do you accuse this man of?"

This is the first mention of Pilate in the Gospel of John. The
author presumes that Pilate is known to his readers, so he does not
identify him further. He was governor of Judea A.D. 26-36; a good deal
is known about him from Jewish sources, most of which is unfavorable.
In translation it may be necessary to identify him specifically as the
governor the first time he is mentioned. Accordingly one may translate
the first part of this verse "so Governor Pilate went outside to them"
or "so Pilate, who was the governor, went outside to them."

Only John mentions that Pilate went outside to the Jews. The constant movement of Pilate in and out of the building is a feature of the
Johannine account.

And asked is literally "and says," but a question is involved,
and so TEV uses a more specific verb.

The term accused may be translated in some languages only by making
specific what is involved, for example, "What bad thing do you say this
man did?" or "What wrong do you say this man did?" or "Do you say, This
man did something bad?"

18.30   Their answer was, "We would not have brought
him to you if he had not committed a crime.

Their answer was is literally "they answered and said to him,"
a Semitic way of introducing direct discourse.
TEV inverts the order of the Jews' reply from the way it appears
in the Greek text, which reads, "If this man were not an evildoer, we
would not have handed him over" (RSV). But in most languages, the order
of the Greek text must be preserved. Note, furthermore, that the condition is contrary to fact, for example, "If he had not done something
that was a crime, we would not have brought him to you." In some languages, an equivalent may be "Only if he had done something that is a
crime would we bring him to you."
The verb translated brought is more literally "handed...over"
(RSV). This same verb also means "to betray," and it has already been
used in this Gospel eight times in relation to Judas (6.64,71; 12.4;
13.2,11,21; 18.2,5).

18.31   Pilate said to them, "Then you yourselves take
him and try him according to your own law."
They replied, "We are not allowed to put anyone
to death."

In Greek the pronoun you is emphatic, and so TEV translates You
yourselves (note Mft and JB "Take him yourselves").
The Greek expression "the Jews" is rendered they since they were
mentioned only three verses earlier as the Jewish authorities in TEV.
Try him according to your own law may be rendered "judge him according to your own laws" or "judge what should be done to him using
your own laws to decide."
In Matthew and Mark no clear indication is given why the Jews
brought Jesus to Pilate, instead of putting him to death themselves
for blasphemy, a religious crime which carried the death penalty. John
tells us they brought Jesus to Pilate because they themselves did not
have the authority to put a person to death. There is much controversy
among biblical scholars as to whether the Jews at that time did in fact
have the authority to inflict the death penalty, even on religious
charges. But, even if the Roman government had given the Jews this authority, each case probably required the approval of the Roman government. The overall evidence suggests probably the Roman authorities
guarded rather closely the matter of capital punishment, since the Jews
might otherwise have put to death persons favorable to the Roman government.
The passive expression We are not allowed must be changed into
an active form in some languages. An equivalent might be "The Roman
government will not allow us," but it is also possible to make this
statement more specific by identifying Pilate as a representative of
the Roman power, for example, "You Romans will not allow us" or "You
Romans will not say to us, 'You can put someone to death'" or "...You
can try someone and put him to death."

(This happened in order to make come true what
             Jesus had said when he indicated the kind of
             death he would die.)

     This verse, which in Greek is introduced in the same way as 18.9
(Greek "so that"; TEV He said this so that) is a comment of the Gospel
writer. In Greek the conjunction hina introduces a subordinate clause
of purpose (Mft "that the word of Jesus might be fulfilled"), but most
modern English translations restructure this verse as a complete sentence: "by saying this they made it certain that..." (Barclay); "Thus
they ensured the fulfillment of the words..." (NEB); "This was to fulfill what Jesus had said" (NAB). The reference is to 12.32 (see also
12.33). In some languages This happened in order to make come true may
be rendered "Their words caused it to happen that" or "What they said
showed that what Jesus had said was coming true" or "...would happen."
     The kind of death he would die is a reference to crucifixion. Since
the Jews did not have the power to put Jesus to death, he would suffer
the Roman form of execution. The kind of death he would die may be rendered simply "how he would die."

                    TEV   (18.33-38a)   RSV

     33 Pilate went back into the
palace and called Jesus. "Are you
the king of the Jews?" he asked
him.
     34 Jesus answered, "Does this
question come from you or have others told you about me?"
     35 Pilate replied, "Do you think
I am a Jew? It was your own people
and the chief priests who handed
you over to me. What have you
done?"
     36 Jesus said, "My kingdom does
not belong to this world; if my
kingdom belonged to this world, my
followers would fight to keep me
from being handed over to the Jewish authorities. No, my kingdom
does not belong here!"
     37 So Pilate asked him, "Are you
a king, then?"
     Jesus answered, "You say that I
am a king. I was born and came into the world for this one purpose,
to speak about the truth. Whoever
belongs to the truth listens to
me."
     38 "And what is truth?" Pilate
asked.

     33 Pilate entered the praetor-
ium again and called Jesus, and
said to him, "Are you the King of
the Jews?" 34 Jesus answered, "Do
you say this of your own accord, or
did others say it to you about
me?" 35 Pilate answered, "Am I a
Jew? Your own nation and the chief
priests have handed you over to me;
what have you done?" 36 Jesus answered, "My kingship is not of this
world; if my kingship were of this
world, my servants would fight,
that I might not be handed over to
the Jews; but my kingship is not
from the world." 37 Pilate said to
him, "So you are a king?" Jesus
answered, "You say that I am a
king. For this I was born, and for
this I have come into the world, to
bear witness to the truth. Every
one who is of the truth hears my
voice." 38 Pilate said to him,
"What is truth?"

18.33   Pilate went back into the palace and called
          Jesus. "Are you the king of the Jews?" he asked
          him.

Called Jesus is literally "called Jesus and said to him," which
reflects the Semitic redundancy used to introduce direct discourse.
     Even though the Greek text literally says called Jesus (many trans-
lations "summoned Jesus"), the meaning is perhaps best expressed as
"had Jesus brought to him." Called Jesus must be rendered in the sense
of "summoned Jesus before him" or "commanded Jesus to be brought before
him" or "commanded soldiers to lead Jesus in front of him."
     According to all the Gospel accounts, the first thing Pilate said
to Jesus was Are you the king of the Jews? This is the first time in
John's Gospel that Jesus is referred to as "the king of the Jews" (but
see 1.49, where he is designated the King of Israel. This designation
will play an important part in what follows (note 18.33-37,39; 19.3,12,
15,19-22). In Pilate's question the pronoun you is emphatic and may be
used scornfully.
     In languages which have no special term for king it is always pos-
sible to use a verb meaning "ordering" or "ruling," for example, "Are
you the one who rules over the Jews?" or "Are you the one who commands
the Jews?"

18.34   Jesus answered, "Does this question come
          from you or have others told you about me?"

Does this question come from you...? is literally "from yourself
are you saying this...?" NEB translates "Is that your own idea...?";
NAB renders "Are you saying this on your own...?" The force of the question is to ascertain whether Pilate has any reason of his own, apart
from the accusation of the Jewish leaders, to believe that Jesus claims
to be the king of the Jews. Does this question come from you...? may
often be rendered "Are you the one who thought of this question?" or
"Did you yourself have reason to ask this question?"

18.35   Pilate replied, "Do you think I am a Jew?
          It was your own people and the chief priests
          who handed you over to me. What have you done?"

Pilate's reply to Jesus, Do you think I am a Jew?, is more literally "Am I a Jew?" (RSV). The Greek is in the form of a question that
expects a negative answer. NAB makes this an exclamation "I am no Jew!";
NEB translates "What! am I a Jew?" It may be that Pilate's response expresses contempt for the Jews. However, the more obvious meaning is that
Pilate is disclaiming any real knowledge of Jesus, other than the information given him by the Jewish authorities. This is made clear by
the following sentence (It was your own people...). Some readers may not
see clearly the connection between Jesus' question and Pilate's reply.
To some extent the relation may be indicated by rendering Pilate's reply
"Why would such a question come from me? I'm not a Jew." However, this

expansion is probably unnecessary, since the following statement indicates clearly that the accusation came from the Jewish authorities.

18.36   Jesus said, "My kingdom does not belong to this
             world; if my kingdom belonged to this world, my fol-
             lowers would fight to keep me from being handed over
             to the Jewish authorities. No, my kingdom does not
             belong here!"

    Jesus does not give a direct answer to Pilate's question, What
have you done? Rather, he describes the nature of his kingdom; though
he is a king, his kingdom does not belong to this world (so also NEB,
NAB, Barclay; Mft "My realm does not belong to this world"). Jesus'
statement is literally "my kingdom is not of this world" (see JB "Mine
is not a kingdom of this world"). Gdsp translates "My kingdom is not a
kingdom of this world"; the Living Bible has "I am not an earthly king."
Jesus is not denying that his kingdom exercises authority in this world;
rather, he is affirming that the origin and nature of his kingly authority are not the same as those of the kings of this world. His authority
is not of human origin, and the nature of his rule is different from
that exercised by the rulers of this world. One may translate the whole
of Jesus' response: "My kingly authority does not have its origin in
this world. If it did, my followers would fight to keep me from being
handed over to the Jews. No, my authority is not like that of earthly
kings" (or "...No, my kingly authority does not have its origin in this
world"). One may also translate: "I am not an earthly king. If I were,
my followers would fight to keep me from being handed over to the Jews.
No, my kingly authority does not have its origin in this world." On the
other hand, it may be very difficult to speak of "kingly authority" or
of "having its origin in this world." The closest equivalent in some
languages may be "I am not like kings who rule here in this world." The
rest of Jesus' statement may then be rendered "If I were like kings who
rule in this world, then my followers would fight in order not to have
me handed over to the Jewish authorities." Jesus' final statement, No,
my kingdom does not belong here!, may then be rendered "No, I am not
like those kings who rule here on earth."
    No translates "but now" of the Greek text, the same expression
used in 8.40; 9.41; 15.22. Its force is to contrast the real situation
with that presupposed by Pilate.

18.37   So Pilate asked him, "Are you a king, then?"
             Jesus answered, "You say that I am a king. I was
             born and came into the world for this one purpose,
             to speak about the truth. Whoever belongs to the
             truth listens to me."

    So Pilate asked him is literally "therefore (oun) Pilate said to
him." Here again the verb "to say" is used to introduce a question
(compare verse 33).

Then translates a Greek particle (oukoun), which occurs only here in the New Testament. This particle brings the conversation back to Pilate's initial question in verse 33 (Are you the king of the Jews?), since Jesus has not answered the charge expressed in that verse. Here an affirmative answer is expected. NAB translates "So, then, you are a king?" To bring out the emphatic force of the pronoun you, Mft translates "'So you are a king?' said Pilate. 'You!'" Pilate's question may be posed as "But are you a ruler then?"

In Jesus' answer, You say that I am a king, the pronoun you is emphatic. Jesus' reply is generally taken as an affirmative answer to Pilate's question (note, for example, Mft "'Certainly,' said Jesus, 'I am a king...'"). Some translations, however, render otherwise (NEB "'King' is your word..."; NAB "It is you who say that I am a king"). The footnote of NAB is interesting: "It is a reluctant affirmative, equaling 'Yes, but the terminology is yours!" Since there is no consensus of scholarly opinion, it is best to render this reply of Jesus in the most general way possible, implying neither agreement nor disagreement with Pilate's statement. However, in some languages, it is impossible to employ a completely ambiguous answer. It may therefore be better to employ one interpretation in the text, while indicating in a footnote the possibility of another meaning.

I was born and came into the world are parallel expressions. Came into the world affirms the otherworldly origin of Jesus, who, like his kingdom, does not originate in this world. If one preserves both expressions, was born and came into the world, it may be necessary to reverse the order to approximate more nearly what would appear to be the chronological sequence of events, namely, "I came into the world and was born."

To speak about the truth is the one purpose for which Jesus has come.

Truth is one of the key words of John's Gospel (see 1.14). Though John the Baptist spoke on behalf of the truth (5.33), Jesus is the truth (14.6), since he is one with the Father (10.30). Although in many contexts the truth may be interpreted as "the truth about God," it is probably better here to understand the truth in the sense of "true words" or "what is true" or "what really is." For Pilate's question in the following verse (what is truth?) indicates that he understands the truth (verse 37) in the broadest possible sense.

Whoever belongs to the truth is a participial construction in Greek ("everyone being of the truth"). An indefinite relative clause, introduced by Whoever, is the natural way of rendering this construction in English. For the use of "to be of" with the sense of "to belong to" see verse 36 (My kingdom does not belong to this world). Mft and Gdsp are similar to TEV.

Listens to me is more literally "hears my voice." But the focus is not merely on "hearing," but on listening to and responding to with understanding and obedience. In this context listens to me may be understood as "pays attention to what I say" or "heeds what I say."

18.38a   "And what is truth?" Pilate asked.

This statement is literally "Pilate says to him, 'what is truth?'"
TEV inverts the order of the Greek for dramatic effect. The way of translating And what is truth? will depend primarily upon the way in which
verse 37 is rendered. If, for example, one has translated to speak about
the truth as "to speak true words," then the question by Pilate will
probably be "And what are true words?"

TEV   (18.38b-40)   RSV

JESUS SENTENCED TO DEATH

Then Pilate went back outside to the people and said to them, "I cannot find any reason to condemn him. 39 But according to the custom you have, I always set free a prisoner for you during the Passover. Do you want me to set free for you the king of the Jews?" 40 They answered him with a shout, "No, not him! We want Barabbas!" (Barabbas was a bandit.)

After he had said this, he went out to the Jews again, and told them, "I find no crime in him. 39 But you have a custom that I should release one man for you at the Passover; will you have me release for you the King of the Jews?" 40 They cried out again, "Not this man, but Barabbas!" Now Barabbas was a robber.

Instead of the passive form of the section heading, Jesus Sentenced to Death, it may be preferable to use an active form, such as
"Pilate sentences Jesus to death" or "...condemns Jesus to death" or
"...judges that Jesus must die." However, in view of Pilate's statement
in 18.38 (I cannot find any reason to condemn him), it may be more satisfactory to draw the section heading from 19.16, for example, "Pilate
hands Jesus over to be crucified." It is also possible to focus on
19.6-7,15: "The crowd insists that Jesus must die" or "The crowd shouts,
'Kill Jesus.'"

18.38b   Then Pilate went back outside to the people and said to them, "I cannot find any reason to condemn him.

Then is literally "And having said this." Several translations
render "with these words"; JB has "and with that." All these translations convey the transitional force of the Greek phrase. However, it
is also possible to omit it altogether (GeCL "Pilate went out again to
the Jews").
    Pilate is not explicitly mentioned in the Greek text. However,
since a new section begins here, it is helpful to the reader that he be
named.
    I cannot find any reason to condemn him is literally "I find in
him no ground for complaint." NEB renders "I find no case against him";
Barclay translates "There is nothing of which I can find this man
guilty." In some languages one may say "This man has done nothing which
would cause me to say, 'He must die'" or "There is no reason why I must

[572]

condemn him" or "I cannot discover how I can condemn him."

18.39   But according to the custom you have, I always
              set free a prisoner for you during the Passover.
              Do you want me to set free for you the king of
              the Jews?"

There is no extrabiblical evidence for the custom to which Pilate
refers. According to Matthew 27.15, At every Passover Festival the Roman
governor was in the habit of setting free any one prisoner the crowd
asked for (compare Mark 15.6). According to Luke 23.17, which is textually uncertain, At every Passover Festival Pilate had to set free one
prisoner for them.
    Set free a prisoner is literally "set free someone." NEB and JB
translate "one prisoner."
    It may be misleading to translate literally according to the cus-
tom you have. It would imply in some languages that the Jews themselves
had a custom of freeing a prisoner. A more appropriate translation may
be "It is customary for me to set free a prisoner for you during the
Passover" or even "Customarily I set free a prisoner for you during the
Passover" or "...at the time of each Passover." In some languages it may
be necessary to indicate that this was a yearly event, for example, "...
each year at the time of the Passover Festival."
    For Jesus as the king of the Jews see verse 33. It is uncertain
why Pilate continues to refer to Jesus by this title after he has declared him innocent (verse 38).
    To render satisfactorily the phrase for you, it may be necessary
to translate "Do you want me to do you a favor by setting free the King
of the Jews?" This statement is awkward to translate since Pilate addresses the Jews themselves as "you" and then speaks of Jesus as "the
King of the Jews." In some languages one may say "Do you want me to do
you the favor of setting free your king?" Otherwise, readers might assume that Pilate was either addressing non-Jews, or that he was telling
Jews about someone who ruled over some other group of Jews.

18.40   They answered him with a shout, "No, not
              him! We want Barabbas!" (Barabbas was a
              bandit.)

They answered him with a shout is literally "therefore (Greek oun)
they shouted again saying," which reflects Semitic Greek style.
    No, not him! We want Barabbas! is literally "Not this one, but
Barabbas." Nothing is known of Barabbas other than what is said of him
in this episode. The Greek noun translated bandit was translated "robber" in 10.1,8. This noun may have been used of guerrilla fighters engaged in subversive activity against the Romans. Such bandits would
have been popular among the common people.

TEV   (19.1-3)   RSV

19 Then Pilate took Jesus and had
him whipped. 2 The soldiers made
a crown out of thorny branches and
put it on his head; then they put
a purple robe on him 3 and came to
him and said, "Long live the King
of the Jews!" And they went up and
slapped him.

19 Then Pilate took Jesus and
scourged him. 2 And the soldiers
plaited a crown of thorns, and put
it on his head, and arrayed him in
a purple robe; 3 they came up to
him, saying, "Hail, King of the
Jews!" and struck him with their
hands.

Chapter 19.1-16a continues the section begun at 18.28. For an
analysis of this section, see the comments there.

19.1   Then Pilate took Jesus and had him whipped.

Then Pilate took Jesus and had him whipped is literally "Then,
therefore (Greek oun), Pilate took Jesus and whipped him." The context
makes clear that "whipped" is causative in meaning, that is, Pilate
ordered the soldiers to whip Jesus (compare verse 2). This explains the
rendering of TEV (had him whipped), NEB ("had him flogged"), and NAB
("have him scourged"). It is less certain whether the Greek verb "took"
is also to be understood in a causative sense, that is, "caused Jesus
to be taken." Such an interpretation is the basis for JB's rendering
("Pilate then had Jesus taken away and scourged"), which is similar to
GeCL. A variation of this translation would be "Pilate ordered the soldiers, 'Take Jesus away and whip him.'" If the Greek verb "took" is not
understood in a causative sense, it is really redundant and can be omitted in translation: "Then Pilate had Jesus whipped."

19.2   The soldiers made a crown out of thorny branches
                   and put it on his head; then they put a purple
                   robe on him

Even though the verb made is literally "plaited" (NEB, RSV) or
"wove" (NAB), it is doubtful that John intends so careful an action as
these translations imply. For this reason JB and Phps render "twisted."
A crown out of thorny branches is literally "a crown of thorns."
However, the thorns must have been on small branches; thus the basis
for TEV. A crown is generally representative of kingship, but the crown
of thorny branches in the present context may be in specific contrast to
the crown of laurel leaves worn by the Emperor. In some languages there
is no specific term for crown, nor is such an object as a crown associated with power or reign. Thus the best one can do is to describe a
crown of thorny branches as "thorny branches woven into a circle" or
"...twisted into a circle." The fact that this crown was a mocking symbol of the crown worn by the Emperor can be stated in a marginal note.

The word translated robe is a generic term for "clothing" (Greek
himation). Matthew 27.28 specifically mentions a "robe" or "cloak,"
such as Roman soldiers wore (Greek chlamus). However, most translations
render by "robe" or "cloak" in both contexts. According to John, the
color of the garment was purple (the imperial color); according to
Matthew, it was scarlet. Though in some languages there is no specific
color term for purple, it may be described as "dark red" or even "bluish
red." In some languages certain colors are described in terms of a flow-
er or a bird which has such a color.

19.3   and came to him and said, "Long live the King
          of the Jews!" And they went up and slapped him.

Came translates the imperfect tense in Greek, which focuses on
the repetition of the action. For this reason NAB has "Repeatedly they
came" and JB "They kept coming up." NEB translates "Then time after
time they came."
Long live (many translations "hail") translates a greeting of
well wishing used in addressing the Emperor. Here again Jesus is referred to as the King of the Jews. But it would be a mistake to attempt
a literal translation of Long live the King of the Jews! It is a highly
specific idiom, well known in English, but not easily adapted to other
languages. The closest equivalent may be "May you, the King of the Jews,
be prosperous!" or "May you, as the King of the Jews, rule forever!" or,
in some languages, "May you, the King of the Jews, conquer all your enemies!" or "King of the Jews, may your right arm always be strong!" All
such expressions are simply idiomatic ways of acclaiming a ruler.
And they went up and slapped him is more literally "and they were
slapping him." The verb slapped, like the verb came, is in the imperfect
tense in Greek and indicates repetitive action. Although TEV begins a
new sentence with these words, it is possible to take all of verse 3 as
one sentence: "And they kept coming up to him, slapping him, and saying
'Long live the King of the Jews!'" As noted in connection with 18.22, it
may be necessary to indicate where the soldiers slapped Jesus. Presumably it was on the face.

TEV   (19.4-7)   RSV

4 Pilate went back out once
more and said to the crowd, "Look,
I will bring him out here to you
to let you see that I cannot find
any reason to condemn him." 5 So
Jesus came out, wearing the crown
of thorns and the purple robe. Pilate said to them, "Look! Here is
the man!"
6 When the chief priests and the
temple guards saw him, they shouted,
"Crucify him! Crucify him!"

4 Pilate went out again, and said
to them, "See, I am bringing him
out to you, that you may know that
I find no crime in him." 5 So Jesus came out, wearing the crown of
thorns, and the purple robe. Pilate said to them, "Behold the
man!" 6 When the chief priests and
the officers saw him, they cried
out, "Crucify him, crucify him!"
Pilate said to them, "Take him
yourselves and crucify him, for I

Pilate said to them, "You take him, then, and crucify him. I find no reason to condemn him."

7 The crowd answered back, "We have a law that says he ought to die, because he claimed to be the Son of God."

find no crime in him." 7 The Jews answered him, "We have a law, and by that law he ought to die, because he has made himself the Son of God."

19.4   Pilate went back out once more and said to the crowd, "Look, I will bring him out here to you to let you see that I cannot find any reason to condemn him."

Once more is literally "again" (so many translations).

To the crowd is literally "to them." NAB renders this sentence "Pilate went out a second time and said to the crowd." Instead of to the crowd or "to them" NEB has "to the Jews" (so also GeCL). In 18.38 the text says that Pilate went out, but there is no indication that he went back in again; obviously, however, we are to assume that he did so while the soldiers were whipping Jesus.

Look (Greek ide) is a particle that first appeared in 1.29 (see there); it is also used in 18.21. Since its function is to attract attention, it may be better here to render it "Listen" rather than Look.

I will bring him out here to you must be rendered in some languages as a causative, since Pilate himself did not bring Jesus out, for example, "I will cause him to be brought out here to you."

To let you see is an expression of purpose and may be rendered, for example, "in order that you can see that..."

I cannot find any reason to condemn him is essentially the same expression used in 18.38.

19.5   So Jesus came out, wearing the crown of thorns and the purple robe. Pilate said to them, "Look! Here is the man!"

The crown of thorns is a slightly different Greek expression from that used in verse 2, though no distinction should be made in translation.

Pilate said is literally "he says." It is necessary to mention Pilate by name, so that the reader will not suppose that the subject of the verb is Jesus, mentioned earlier in the verse.

Look (Greek idou) renders a particle used to draw attention; it occurs elsewhere in the Gospel at 4.35; 12.15; 16.32.

Here is the man is interpreted variously by the commentators. Some assume that Pilate was attempting to elicit pity; others maintain that he was expressing contempt. It seems best to interpret Pilate's words as an attempt to make the Jews see how absurd it was to crucify this person, who obviously was no political threat. Pilate, then, was actually arguing for Jesus' release.

19.6   When the chief priests and the temple guards
        saw him, they shouted, "Crucify him! Crucify him!"
        Pilate said to them, "You take him, then, and
        crucify him. I find no reason to condemn him.

Temple guards was used in 18.3.

They shouted is literally "they shouted saying," reflecting a Semitic way of introducing direct discourse.

In the present context no object is expressed for the verb crucify (note NEB "Crucify! crucify!"), but Jesus is the understood object, and so most translators render it as Crucify him! "Him" is expressed in the Greek text of verse 15. The repetition of Crucify him! indicates the intensity with which the people were demanding that Pilate put Jesus to death. In Pilate's answer, You take him, then, and crucify him. I find no reason to condemn him, the pronouns you and I are stressed. The Jews could not, of course, take Jesus and crucify him (see 18.31), so Pilate's words are best taken as an attempt to fix responsibility for the death of Jesus on the Jews. For I find no reason to condemn him see 18.38 and 19.4.

In languages which have no special term for "crucify," an equivalent phrase must be employed, for example, "Execute him on a cross" or "Kill him by nailing him to a cross" or "Kill him on a cross." Some languages do not even have a term for "cross," in the sense of the type of cross on which Jesus was crucified. It is always possible, however, to speak of the design of a cross, to which may be added "wooden cross" or "cross of beams."

19.7   The crowd answered back, "We have a law that
        says he ought to die, because he claimed to be
        the Son of God."

We have a law that says he ought to die is literally "We have a law, and according to the law he must die." Here the pronoun we is emphatic. The law referred to is Leviticus 24.16, which demands the death penalty for blasphemy. In some languages it is not possible to say "a law says," for a law cannot speak. However, the statement may be translated "We have a law, and according to that law he ought to die" or "...ought to be killed."

For John, the real reason that the Jews wanted Jesus put to death was because he claimed to be the Son of God (literally "he made himself God's Son"). The Greek text does not have the definite article "the" before the phrase Son of God, and so NEB renders "he has claimed to be Son of God." However, John's statement that Jesus had said that God was his own Father and in this way had made himself equal with God (5.18) makes clear that Jesus' claim was unique. Therefore it is better to render the Son of God, as most translations do. The crowd's charge that Jesus claims to be the Son of God parallels the High Priest's question in the Synoptic tradition: Are you...the Son of the Blessed God? (Mark 14.61). The clause because he claimed to be the Son of God must be expressed as direct discourse in some languages, for example, "because he said, 'I am the Son of God.'"

[577]

8 When Pilate heard this, he was even more afraid. 9 He went back into the palace and asked Jesus, "Where do you come from?"

But Jesus did not answer. 10 Pilate said to him, "You will not speak to me? Remember, I have the authority to set you free and also to have you crucified."

11 Jesus answered, "You have authority over me only because it was given to you by God. So the man who handed me over to you is guilty of a worse sin."

12 When Pilate heard this, he tried to find a way to set Jesus free. But the crowd shouted back, "If you set him free, that means that you are not the Emperor's friend! Anyone who claims to be a king is a rebel against the Emperor!"

13 When Pilate heard these words, he took Jesus outside and sat down on the judge's seat in the place called "The Stone Pavement." (In Hebrew the name is "Gabbatha.")

8 When Pilate heard these words, he was the more afraid; 9 he entered the praetorium again and said to Jesus, "Where are you from?" But Jesus gave no answer. 10 Pilate therefore said to him, "You will not speak to me? Do you not know that I have power to release you, and power to crucify you?" 11 Jesus answered him, "You would have no power over me unless it had been given you from above; therefore he who delivered me to you has the greater sin."

12 Upon this Pilate sought to release him, but the Jews cried out, "If you release this man, you are not Caesar's friend; every one who makes himself a king sets himself against Caesar." 13 When Pilate heard these words, he brought Jesus out and sat down on the judgment seat at a place called The Pavement, and in Hebrew, Gabbatha.

19.8   When Pilate heard this, he was even more afraid.

Heard this (JB "heard them say this") is literally "heard this word"; Mft and NEB render "heard that." One may also translate "When Pilate heard what they said."

He was even more afraid (NAB "he was more afraid than ever"), though it carries a comparative force in Greek, may have the meaning "he became very frightened." However, it is more natural to see the comparative force here (so most translations).The fact that the text does not make an explicit reference to Pilate's fears earlier in the scene presents no problem, since his reluctance to condemn Jesus (18.38; 19.4,6) may well have been motivated by fear. In some languages it will be obligatory to indicate what Pilate was afraid of. One can, of course, say "he was all the more afraid to condemn Jesus" or "...to pass judgment on Jesus."

19.9   He went back into the palace and asked Jesus,
          "Where do you come from?"
               But Jesus did not answer.

     In Greek this verse is a continuation of the sentence begun in
verse 8. It begins with "and," reflecting Semitic Greek style.
     Asked is literally "says to"; but here again the verb "to say"
is used to introduce a question.
     There is no mention that Pilate sent Jesus back to the palace,
but this verse implies that he had done so, since Pilate now goes back
into the palace to speak to him.
     Although Pilate's question Where do you come from? refers to the
part of Palestine from which Jesus originates, John intends for his
readers to see here the larger question of whether Jesus came from heav-
en or from earth. In asking this question, Pilate is probably seeking
a loophole, so that he can shift the responsibility for deciding Jesus' case to someone else (compare Luke 23.6).
     Jesus' refusal to answer calls to mind the Suffering Servant, who
never said a word (Isa 53.7). However, in John's Gospel Jesus does speak
again (verse 11), whereas in the Synoptic tradition he is silent throughout his trial, with the exception of his answer to Pilate, So you say
(Mark 15.2 and parallels).

19.10   Pilate said to him, "You will not speak to me?
          Remember, I have the authority to set you free
          and also to have you crucified."

     Pilate's question You will not speak to me? may be expressed in
some languages as "How is it that you will not speak to me?" or "Why
will you not speak to me?" Pilate was evidently surprised that Jesus
was unwilling to defend himself.
     The word translated authority is the same word translated "right"
by TEV in 1.12. Although the word occurs twice in the Greek text, TEV
leaves its meaning implicit in its second occurrence: I have the authority to set you free and also (the authority) to have you crucified. In
languages in which it is difficult to speak succinctly of authority, a
paraphrase, such as "the government has made me able to set you free,"
may be employed or "the Emperor has caused me to be able to set you
free." However, the simplest and most satisfactory equivalent in many
languages is "I am able to set you free." To have you crucified may be
expressed as "to cause you to be crucified" or "to cause soldiers to
crucify you."

19.11   Jesus answered, "You have authority over me
          only because it was given to you by God. So the
          man who handed me over to you is guilty of a worse
          sin."

     In the Greek text Jesus' answer is a contrary-to-fact condition
(see, for example, RSV "You would have no power over me unless it had

[579]

been given you from above"). "From above" (TEV by God) is the same expression used in 3.3 (TEV again); here the reference is to God, as TEV indicates (so also GeCL).

The translation of authority in this verse is even more complex than in verse 10. In fact, it may be necessary here to indicate precisely what the authority involved, for example, "You are able to have me crucified only because God has made you able." However, it may be preferable to express authority in more general terms, for example, "You are able to command men to do things to me only because God has caused you to be able."

Although handed over translates the same Greek verb rendered betray in 6.64,71 with reference to Judas, it is doubtful that Judas is meant here by the man who handed me over to you. TEV's rendering (the man) suggests an individual, probably Caiaphas. However, the Greek participle ("the one handing over") can be understood as a generalizing reference to the Jews. That Caiaphas (or the Jews) is guilty of a worse sin than Pilate may be explained as meaning that the sin of Caiaphas is willful and deliberate, whereas Pilate is simply trying to carry out his duties as a representative of the Emperor.

Is guilty of a worse sin may be expressed as "has sinned worse" or "has surpassed you in sinning" or "has sinned even more than you are sinning."

19.12   When Pilate heard this, he tried to find a way to set Jesus free. But the crowd shouted back, "If you set him free, that means that you are not the Emperor's friend! Anyone who claims to be a king is a rebel against the Emperor!"

The Greek phrase translated When Pilate heard this is taken by most translators in a temporal sense, though it may be causal ("because of this").

He tried to find a way to set Jesus free is more literally "he was trying to set him free." NEB translates "Pilate tried hard to release him," and JB translates "Pilate was anxious to set him free." Mft takes When Pilate heard this as indicating a cause, and so translates "This made Pilate anxious to release him."

But the crowd shouted back is literally "but the Jews shouted saying."

The Emperor's friend is literally "a friend of Caesar." This was an honorific title, bestowed in recognition of special service to the Emperor. Originally "Caesar" was a proper name, but by New Testament times it had become a title equivalent to Emperor, and so the basis for the TEV rendering. Most translators prefer to retain "Caesar," though Gdsp also translates "Emperor."

Anyone who claims to be a king must be rendered as direct discourse in some languages, for example, "anyone who says, 'I am a king'" or "... 'I am a ruler.'"

Is a rebel against the Emperor may often be rendered as "is rebelling against the Emperor" or "...against the great ruler." In some

[580]

languages *Emperor* may be expressed as "the ruler of all the countries." The role of an Emperor is that of one who rules many countries, while individual kings or governors are described as ruling over single countries.

19.13   When Pilate heard these words, he took Jesus outside and sat down on the judge's seat in the place called "The Stone Pavement." (In Hebrew the name is "Gabbatha.")

The verb translated <u>sat down</u> may be either intransitive, meaning "to sit down," or transitive, meaning "to cause (someone) to sit down." Most translators prefer to take the verb intransitively. However, Mft ("Pilate brought Jesus out and seated him on the tribunal") and Gdsp ("he brought Jesus out and had him sit in the judge's seat") take it transitively. The verb is used transitively in 1 Corinthians 6.14 and Ephesians 1.20. However, it is most unlikely that a Roman governor, at the point of pronouncing the death sentence, would mock in such a manner the person he was about to condemn.

The exact site of the place called <u>the Stone Pavement</u> (most translations "the Pavement") is unknown. The Greek word itself (lithostrotos) may refer either to a mosaic of small stones or to a pavement of large stones. In the Septuagint of 2 Chronicles 7.3, the word is used of the pavement of Solomon's temple, and so most scholars understand the word here to refer to a pavement of large stones. A large court, paved with stones more than a yard square and a foot thick, has been excavated on the lower levels of the fortress Antonia. This may well be the place referred to by John; but, as indicated in comments on 18.28, not all agree that the fortress Antonia was the governor's palace. In the absence of definite evidence, it seems best merely to indicate an area paved with large stones.

<u>In Hebrew</u> is the same expression used in 5.2 (see also 19.17,20; 20.16); the form of the word <u>Gabbatha</u> indicates that Aramaic is meant. Gabbatha is not the Aramaic equivalent of the Greek word meaning "stone pavement." The derivation of the word is disputed, and so it is best merely to transliterate the term, as most translators do. <u>In Hebrew the name is "Gabbatha"</u> may be rendered in several different ways, for example, "When Hebrews speak, they say 'Gabbatha'" or "The name of this in the Hebrew language is Gabbatha" or "Gabbatha is the Hebrew name for this same place."

	TEV	(19.14-16a)	RSV

14 It was then almost noon of the day before the Passover. Pilate said to the people, "Here is your king!"

15 They shouted back, "Kill him! Kill him! Crucify him!"

Pilate asked them, "Do you want

14 Now it was the day of Preparation of the Passover; it was about the sixth hour. He said to the Jews, "Behold your King!" 15 They cried out, "Away with him, away with him, crucify him! Pilate said to them, "Shall I

me to crucify your king?"

The chief priests answered, "The only king we have is the Emperor!"

16 Then Pilate handed Jesus over to them to be crucified.

crucify your King?" The chief priests answered, "We have no king but Caesar." 16 Then he handed him over to them to be crucified.

19.14   It was then almost noon of the day before the Passover. Pilate said to the people, "Here is your king!"

The first sentence of this verse is literally "Now it was the day of Preparation of the Passover; it was about the sixth hour" (RSV). TEV inverts the order of the Greek sentence, placing the time (noon) before the day (the day before the Passover). It was then almost noon translates the same expression rendered It was about noon in 4.6 (see the comments there). The Greek word paraskeuē, translated the day before, means literally "preparation." In the Synoptic Gospels (Matt 27.62; Mark 15.42; Luke 23.54) the word refers to the day before the Sabbath. Since no work could be done on the Sabbath, all the preparations had to be made the day before. In John also Jesus died on the day before the Sabbath (19.31,42). However, for him this particular Sabbath was also the Passover, and therefore in 19.14 paraskeuē is used in the phrase "Day of Preparation for Passover."

In Greek Pilate said is simply "he says." Since Jesus (verse 13) was the last proper name mentioned, TEV makes the reference to Pilate explicit, in order to avoid confusion on the part of the reader.

Here is your king! (so most translations; Mft and Gdsp have "there is your king") is translated "Look at your king!" by NAB, and "Look, here's your king!" by Phps. In Greek this sentence has no verb; it begins with the particle ide (see 19.4 and 18.21), which has the force of drawing attention to the subject that follows.

19.15   They shouted back, "Kill him! Kill him! Crucify him!"

Pilate asked them, "Do you want me to crucify your king?"

The chief priests answered, "The only king we have is the Emperor!"

Kill him! Kill him! (so also Gdsp) is rendered "Away with him! Away with him!" in most translations; JB renders "Take him away, take him away!" (so also Phps). The root meaning of the Greek verb is "lift up" (compare 8.59); here it has the extended meaning of "kill" (by "lifing up" or "taking away").

Crucify him is the same verb used in verse 6, but here the object him is explicitly expressed in Greek.

The only king we have is the Emperor is more literally 'We do not have a king except Caesar." TEV states positively what the Greek text states negatively; "Caesar" is a title for the Roman Emperor (see verse 12). This response of the chief priests may be expressed in various ways, for example, "The Emperor is our only ruler" or "Only the Emperor rules over us" or "The Emperor is the only one we acknowledge as our ruler" or "...as our king."

19.16a   Then Pilate handed Jesus over to them to
                be crucified.

Pilate handed Jesus over to them is literally "he handed him over to them." TEV makes the first two pronominal references explicit. GeCL makes the third pronominal reference explicit also and transforms the passive verb be crucified into an active verb: "then Pilate handed him over to the soldiers for them to crucify him." In the Greek text the nearest antecedent for them is the chief priests. However, Pilate could not have handed Jesus over to the priests for crucifixion, since crucifixion was a Roman type of punishment, which had to be carried out by Roman soldiers. In Matthew and Mark the statement that Pilate/he... handed him over to be crucified (Matt 27.26; Mark 15.15) is immediately followed by a reference to Pilate's/The soldiers (Matt 27.27; Mark 15.16), who take Jesus off to mock him and beat him. Consequently, it is evident that Pilate handed Jesus over to the Roman soldiers. In Luke (23.25) and John (19.16) Pilate's action in handing Jesus over is not followed by the mocking of Jesus by the Roman soldiers, and therefore it is unclear to whom the pronoun them refers in these two Gospels. Although the soldiers are mentioned later on in the crucifixion scene (Luke 23.36; John 19.23), it may be that both Luke and John have intentionally left it unclear to whom Jesus was handed over, in order to suggest that the crowd (Luke 23.20) or The chief priests (John 19.16) were responsible for Jesus' crucifixion. NEB translates "Then at last, to satisfy them, he handed Jesus over to be crucified." NAB renders "In the end, Pilate handed Jesus over to be crucified," but adds this note: "...according to the sequence this would seem to mean 'handed him over to the chief priests'..."

| TEV | (19.16b-22) | RSV |

JESUS IS CRUCIFIED

So they took charge of Jesus. 17 He went out, carrying his cross, and came to "The Place of the Skull," as it is called. (In Hebrew it is called "Golgotha.") 18 There they crucified him; and they also crucified two other men, one on each side, with Jesus between them. 19 Pilate wrote a notice and had it put on the cross. "Jesus of Nazareth, the King of the Jews," is what he wrote. 20 Many people read it, because the place	17 So they took Jesus, and he went out, bearing his own cross, to the place called the place of a skull, which is called in Hebrew Golgotha. 18 There they crucified him, and with him two others, one on either side, and Jesus between them. 19 Pilate also wrote a title and put it on the cross; it read, "Jesus of Nazareth, the King of the Jews." 20 Many of the Jews read this title, for the place where Jesus

where Jesus was crucified was not far from the city. The notice was written in Hebrew, Latin, and Greek. 21 The chief priests said to Pilate, "Do not write 'The King of the Jews,' but rather, 'This man said, I am the King of the Jews.'"

22 Pilate answered, "What I have written stays written."

was crucified was near the city; and it was written in Hebrew, in Latin, and in Greek. 21 The chief priests of the Jews then said to Pilate, "Do not write, 'The King of the Jews,' but, 'This man said, I am King of the Jews.'" 22 Pilate answered, "What I have written I have written."

Chapter 19.16b-30 is John's account of the crucifixion. Jesus, under guard (verse 16b), carries his own cross to the place of execution (verse 17). There he is crucified along with two others (verse 18). The chief priests protest against the inscription over the cross, but Pilate abides by what he has written (verses 19-22). The soldiers divide Jesus' clothes and cast lots for his robe (verses 23-24).

The three women by the cross are mentioned (verse 25), and Jesus entrusts his mother to the beloved disciple (verses 26-27). Jesus asks for something to drink (verse 28) and is given some wine in a sponge (verse 29). With a cry of triumph Jesus bows his head and dies (verse 30).

The section heading, Jesus Is Crucified, must be changed to an active form in some languages, for example, "The soldiers crucify Jesus."

19.16b   So they took charge of Jesus.

GeCL takes the unexpressed subject of the Greek verb "they took charge" to be the Roman soldiers: "the soldiers took charge of Jesus." A literal translation of they took charge of Jesus could be misunderstood to mean "they took care of Jesus." In some languages the most satisfactory equivalent is "they led Jesus off" or "the soldiers led Jesus away."

19.17   He went out, carrying his cross, and came to "The Place of the Skull," as it is called. (In Hebrew it is called "Golgotha.")

He went out is translated "he went out of the city" by JB (GeCL has "he left the city"). This meaning is indicated by verse 20 (the place...was not far from the city).

Carrying his cross is translated "carrying his own cross" by several translators and "carrying the cross by himself" by others. "By himself" is a pronoun in Greek. The picture of Jesus carrying his own cross contrasts with the Synoptic accounts (Mark 15.21 and parallels), according to which Simon of Cyrene is forced to carry Jesus' cross. John's version emphasizes that Jesus is master of his destiny.

It was customary for the condemned man to carry the crossbeam--not the entire cross--on his shoulder (GeCL "with his own cross on his shoulder, he left the city"). To indicate that Jesus carried his cross all the

way to the place of execution, it may be best to translate "he carried
his own cross, and thus went out of the city and came to The Place of
the Skull."

The exact location of The Place of the Skull is not known. However, it is generally assumed that the name came from the topology of
the place, that is, that it was a hill that somehow resembled a skull.
The equivalent of came to "The Place of the Skull" may be expressed in
some languages as "came to a place called Skull Hill."

In Hebrew (see verse 13) means "in Aramaic"; NEB translates "in
the Jews' language." The Aramaic word Golgotha means "skull" or "head."
For a discussion of different ways in which transliterated names may be
introduced, see verse 13.

19.18   There they crucified him; and they also
      crucified two other men, one on each side,
      with Jesus between them.

In Greek this verse is a continuation of the sentence begun with
verse 17, but most translations, like TEV, have a full stop at the end
of verse 17 and begin a new sentence here.

It was customary for a condemned man to be either nailed or tied
to the crossbeam with his hands spread out. Then the crossbeam was lifted
into place on the vertical post. The man's body rested on a peg attached
to the vertical post, and the feet were either nailed or tied.

The persons crucified on either side of Jesus are not identified
by John, but Matthew and Mark speak of them as "bandits" (Matt 27.38;
Mark 15.27) and Luke as "criminals" (Luke 23.33). They are usually
thought to be men who were arrested in the same revolutionary attempt
in which Barabbas was taken prisoner.

19.19   Pilate wrote a notice and had it put on the
      cross. "Jesus of Nazareth, the King of the
      Jews," is what he wrote.

Pilate wrote a notice and had it put on the cross is literally
"Pilate wrote a notice and placed it on the cross." However, it is evident that others did these things at Pilate's command. NAB translates
"Pilate had an inscription placed on the cross," while Barclay translates "Pilate had an inscription written and fixed to the cross." It is
appropriate in most languages to treat the actions by Pilate as causa-
tives, for example, "Pilate caused a notice to be written, and caused
it to be put on the cross" or "...attached to the cross." It may be
expressed in some languages as a command with direct discourse, for
example, "Pilate commanded, 'Write a notice and attach it to the cross.'"

The Greek word translated notice in TEV is the technical name for
the board bearing the name of the condemned man, or his crime, or both.
The Greek term used by Mark (15.26) and Luke (23.38) is a different
word.

For Jesus of Nazareth see the discussion at 18.5. The only other
Gospel besides John which includes Jesus' name in the notice is Matthew

(27.37): "This is Jesus, the King of the Jews." Mark (15.26) has the shortest version: "The King of the Jews." Luke (23.38) has "This is the King of the Jews."

19.20   Many people read it, because the place where
             Jesus was crucified was not far from the city.
             The notice was written in Hebrew, Latin, and
             Greek.

Many people is literally "Many Jews." The Romans customarily crucified condemned persons in places where they would be seen by many people. This was to serve as a warning against committing similar crimes.

In some languages it is necessary to translate not far (Greek "near") as a spatial expression, for example, "a few hundred yards away."

The notice was written in Hebrew, Latin, and Greek is more literally "and it was written...," reflecting Semitic style. John is the only one of the Gospels to mention the languages in which the notice was written. A literal rendering of The notice was written in Hebrew, Latin, and Greek could imply a mixture of languages. It may be better to say "The notice was written three times; first in Hebrew, then in Latin, and then in Greek."

19.21   The chief priests said to Pilate, "Do not write
             'The King of the Jews,' but rather, "This man said,
             I am the King of the Jews.'"

In the Greek text The chief priests is literally "the chief priests of the Jews," but "of the Jews" is redundant in this context.

Said to Pilate (so most translations) is translated by NEB "tried to tell Pilate," to indicate that their attempt effected no result.

This man (literally "that one") may be used in a derogatory sense.

19.22   Pilate answered, "What I have written stays
             written."

What I have written stays written is literally "what I have written I have written" (so most translations). The notice was the equivalent of a legal decision, and it could not be altered. What I have written stays written may be rendered "what I have written will remain just that way" or "...will remain just as I have written it." However, if wrote in verse 19 has been translated as a causative, a causative expression must be employed at this point, for example, "What I have caused to be written will remain just in that form" or "The notice which I ordered written must not be changed."

TEV (19.23-24) RSV

23 After the soldiers had crucified Jesus, they took his clothes
and divided them into four parts,
one part for each soldier. They
also took the robe, which was made
of one piece of woven cloth without any seams in it. 24 The soldiers said to one another, "Let's
not tear it; let's throw dice to
see who will get it." This happened in order to make the scripture
come true:
"They divided my clothes
    among themselves
  and gambled for my robe."
And this is what the soldiers did.

23 When the soldiers had crucified Jesus they took his garments and made four parts, one for
each soldier; also his tunic. But
the tunic was without seam, woven
from top to bottom; 24 so they
said to one another, "Let us not
tear it, but cast lots for it to
see whose it shall be." This was
to fulfil the scripture,
"They parted my garments among
    them,
  and for my clothing they cast
    lots."

19.23   After the soldiers had crucified Jesus,
            they took his clothes and divided them into
            four parts, one part for each soldier. They
            also took the robe, which was made of one
            piece of woven cloth without any seams in it.

It was customary to remove the clothing from a condemned man before he was crucified, and according to Roman law his clothes became
the property of the executioners. The word translated clothes is the
same word used in 13.4 (TEV outer garment). Here the reference is
clearly to all the clothes that Jesus was wearing.
    Although we cannot be sure that the four parts consisted of four
individual items of clothing, it may be necessary in some languages to
translate as though this were the case, for example, "they took his
clothes and divided them, each soldier taking one piece of clothing."
    The four soldiers probably formed a military unit; note Acts
12.4, which speaks of four groups of four soldiers each.
    In Greek the clause they also took the robe is literally "also
the robe," and is part of the first sentence. Most translators render
these words as a separate sentence or connect them with the following
sentence, as TEV does. The robe (many translations "tunic") was a long
garment worn next to the skin. That it was made of one piece of woven
cloth, without any seams in it precluded the possibility that it was
made of more than one material (note the law of Deut 22.11). This type
of garment could be made by an ordinary weaver, so it need not have
been expensive. To translate "tunic" as robe may give the impression
that it was an outer garment. On the other hand, to use such an expression as "inner garment" may give the impression that it was underwear.

[587]

<u>19.24</u>   The soldiers said to one another, "Let's
not tear it; let's throw dice to see who
will get it." This happened in order to
make the scripture come true:
   "They divided my clothes
     among themselves
      and gambled for my robe."
And this is what the soldiers did.

The soldiers is literally "they," but TEV makes the pronominal
reference explicit.

Throw dice (so also JB and NAB) translates a Greek verb which
means to get something either by casting or by drawing lots (so RSV,
Mft, Gdsp, Phps). However, for contemporary readers the idea of throwing dice or tossing a coin (NEB "let us toss for it") may be the nearest cultural equivalent. In some languages a generic expression may be
employed, for example, "let us gamble for it." However, in some parts
of the world where there is no cultural equivalent of gambling, a parallel type of behavior can be described, for example, "let us play a
game to see who wins and therefore gets the robe."

This happened in order to make the scripture come true is literally "so that the scripture may be fulfilled." That is, in Greek this
sentence is introduced by a conjunction (hina) which means "so that"
(the same construction found in 18.9). This happened to make the scripture come true may be rendered in some languages as "This happened so
as to cause to become true what was written in the holy writings." The
scripture referred to is Psalm 22.18, and the Septuagint is quoted exactly.

Gambled for is literally "cast a lot for," but TEV uses a more
generic expression, avoiding the less familiar expression "to cast
lots."

	TEV	(19.25-27)	RSV

25 Standing close to Jesus'
cross were his mother, his mother's
sister, Mary the wife of Clopas,
and Mary Magdalene. 26 Jesus saw
his mother and the disciple he
loved standing there; so he said
to his mother, "He is your son."

  27 Then he said to the disciple,
"She is your mother." From that
time the disciple took her to live
in his home.

25 So the soldiers did this.
But standing by the cross of Jesus were his mother, and his mother's sister, Mary the wife of
Clopas, and Mary Magdalene. 26
When Jesus saw his mother, and the
disciple whom he loved standing
near, he said to his mother, "Woman, behold, your son!" 27 Then he
said to the disciple, "Behold,
your mother!" And from that hour
the disciple took her to his own
home.

<u>19.25</u>   Standing close to Jesus' cross were his
mother, his mother's sister, Mary the wife of
Clopas, and Mary Magdalene.

There is a problem related to the number of women mentioned by
John. Are there two, three, or four? It is grammatically possible to
assume that only two women are mentioned, if one understands Mary the
wife of Clopas to be in apposition with his mother and Mary Magdalene
to be in apposition with his mother's sister. But it is not likely that
John would have identified the mother of Jesus as "Mary the wife of
Clopas," and it seems improbable, though not impossible, that two sisters would both be named Mary. It is also possible to understand the
list as consisting of three women: (1) Jesus' mother, (2) his mother's
sister, Mary the wife of Clopas, and (3) Mary Magdalene. However, one
is still faced with the problem of having two sisters named Mary. Most
translators take the list to include four women, and this interpretation
accords most naturally with the Greek structure. Nothing else is known
of Mary, the wife of Clopas, though it is possible that this Clopas
should be identified with the one mentioned in Luke 24.18. Mary Magdalene has not been mentioned previously in John's Gospel, but she will
appear again as the first witness to the empty tomb and the resurrected
Lord (20.1-2, 11-18). She is mentioned also in Matthew 27.56,61; 28.1;
Mark 15.40,47; 16.1; and Luke 8.2; 24.10.

In most languages it is natural to introduce the four women in a
typical subject position. In English this would be "his mother, his
mother's sister, Mary the wife of Clopas, and Mary Magdalene were standing close to Jesus' cross" or "...to the cross on which Jesus was crucified." It may be essential to avoid a possessive construction in
speaking of the cross. Obviously Jesus did not possess the cross; it
was simply the instrument used for his execution.

In some languages it is necessary to translate his mother's sister
with a specific term, such as "his aunt," for which there are often two
distinct words, one indicating a mother's sister and the other a father's
sister. A literal translation of his mother's sister might suggest that
Jesus was estranged from his aunt.

Mary Magdalene may be rendered "Mary from Magdala," since Magdalene indicates a place of origin or residence.

19.26   Jesus saw his mother and the disciple he loved
           standing there; so he said to his mother, "He
           is your son."

In Greek Jesus saw is literally "So (oun) Jesus, having seen..."
RSV translates with a subordinate clause: "When Jesus saw..." TEV uses
an independent clause for the sake of a more natural English style.

The disciple he loved is first mentioned in 13.23 (see the comments there). Since there are two attributives to the disciple, namely,
he loved and standing there, it may be necessary to restructure: "The
disciple whom Jesus loved was also standing there, next to Jesus' mother. When Jesus saw them both, he said..."

In Greek Jesus addresses his mother as "Woman." TEV has dropped
this form of address (compare 2.4, where TEV also omits it, and 4.21,
where TEV has kept it), in order to avoid the impression that Jesus was
being impolite to his mother.

Since the beloved disciple was not actually the son of Jesus' mother, He is your son may have to be translated "Consider him as your son," in order to avoid suggesting a kinship relationship which is not explained. Similarly in verse 27 She is your mother may be rendered "Consider her as your mother."

19.27   Then he said to the disciple, "She is your
                mother." From that time the disciple took her
                to live in his home.

She is translates the same particle (literally "behold") used in verse 26. From that time is generally rendered "from that hour," but the generic "time" is more natural in English than "hour." NEB and JB translate "from that moment." To live in his home translates a phrase first used in 1.11 (TEV to his own country); it was also used in 16.32 (TEV to his own home). Took her to live in his home can be rendered in some languages "made her a member of his household" or "considered her a member of his family" or "treated her as a member of his own household."

TEV   (19.28-30)   RSV

THE DEATH OF JESUS

28 Jesus knew that by now everything had been completed; and in order to make the scripture come true, he said, "I am thirsty."
29 A bowl was there, full of cheap wine; so a sponge was soaked in the wine, put on a stalk of hyssop, and lifted up to his lips.
30 Jesus drank the wine and said, "It is finished!"
Then he bowed his head and gave up his spirit.

28 After this Jesus, knowing that all was now finished, said (to fulfil the scripture), "I thirst." 29 A bowl full of vinegar stood there; so they put a sponge full of the vinegar on hyssop and held it to his mouth. 30 When Jesus had received the vinegar, he said, "It is finished"; and he bowed his head and gave up his spirit.

The section heading, The Death of Jesus, may be rendered in some languages "How Jesus dies" or "This is the way Jesus dies" or simply "Jesus dies."

19.28   Jesus knew that by now everything had been
                completed; and in order to make the scripture
                come true, he said, "I am thirsty."

In Greek this verse begins with "after this" (see the discussion at 2.12). Both TEV and GeCL omit the phrase in translation.
In Greek Jesus knew is the same participial construction used in 13.1. There John affirmed Jesus' knowledge of what was about to happen to him. Now he affirms Jesus' awareness of a prophecy which was to be fulfilled.

In some languages by now must be rendered "by that time" or "by then" or "at that time," since the reference is to past, not present, time.

Had been completed is also the translation of JB (Phps "was now completed"; NEB "had...come to its appointed end"). In the context the meaning is that Jesus had completed everything that God had sent him into the world to do. The translator must be sure that his rendering carries this positive force and does not suggest that the "end" of Jesus' work in death was a failure. Had been completed is from the verb teleō; make...come true is from the related verb teleioō. This second verb is also used in 17.4 (I have finished the work you gave me to do). This is not the verb John normally uses of the fulfillment of scripture (pleroō), and its use in 19.28 after teleō may be significant: it is through Jesus' completion (teleō) of the work God gave him to do that the scripture is fulfilled (teleioō).

In some languages the passive expression Everything had been completed must be changed to an active form, for example, "Jesus had done everything that he should have done" or "everything had happened that should have happened."

It is possible to take the clause in order to make the scripture come true as depending either on what precedes ("everything had been completed in order to make the scripture come true") or on what follows (in order to make the scripture come true, he said). Most translations agree with TEV in seeing Jesus' words (I am thirsty) as the fulfillment of scripture. If John is thinking of a specific Old Testament text, the most likely reference is to Psalm 69.22: when I was thirsty, they offered me vinegar. Therefore GeCL translates "in order to make the prophecy in the Pslams come true." To make clear that the purpose clause depends on he said, it may be necessary to change the order in the second part of the verse: Jesus said, 'I am thirsty.' He said this in order to make the scripture come true."

19.29   A bowl was there, full of cheap wine; so a
sponge was soaked in the wine, put on a stalk
of hyssop, and lifted up to his lips.

Cheap wine (NAB "common wine") appears as "sour wine" in Gdsp, Phps, and NEB; Barclay has "bitter wine"; Mft, JB, and GeCL render "vinegar." The Greek word refers to a diluted, vinegary wine. Since it was cheaper than regular wine, it was a favorite drink of laborers, soldiers, and other persons in moderate circumstances. The translations "sour wine," "bitter wine," and "vinegar" suggest that offering this drink to Jesus was an act of cruelty, whereas in fact it had the humanitarian purpose of relieving his thirst.

So a sponge was soaked in the wine, put on a stalk of hyssop is literally "so putting on hyssop a sponge full of wine." NEB translates "they soaked a sponge with the wine, fixed it on a javelin." TEV prefers a passive construction. In some languages it may be necessary to paraphrase the verb "soak," for example, "they caused a sponge to drink up the wine" or "they caused a sponge to become wet with the wine."

The noun hyssop causes a difficulty, since the Palestinian variety of this small, bushy plant does not have a stalk large enough to support a wet sponge. In the parallel passages in Matthew (27.48) and Mark (15.36) the sponge is put on the end of a stick, in TEV's translation. One Greek manuscript reads "javelin" (Greek hussos) in place of hyssop (Greek hussopos), and this is the basis for the rendering of Gdsp ("pike"), Mft, NEB, and Phps. However, this reading is almost certainly an attempt to solve the difficulty mentioned above, and it is better for the translator to follow either TEV or JB ("a hyssop stick"), leaving open the precise identification of the plant.

If the term used to render stalk clearly designates the stalk of a plant, then hyssop is sufficiently identified. Otherwise, it may be necessary to say "on a branch of a plant called hyssop."

To his lips (so a number of translations) is literally "to his mouth."

19.30   Jesus drank the wine and said, "It is finished!"
         Then he bowed his head and died.

In Greek this verse begins with a temporal clause (RSV "When Jesus had received the vinegar"). TEV, along with several other translations, uses an independent clause.

If a literal rendering of Jesus took the wine would imply "Jesus received the wine in his hands," it may be necessary to say "Jesus sucked the wine and swallowed it," since Jesus' hands were fixed to the cross.

It is finished is the same verb rendered had been completed in verse 28.

Then he bowed his head and died is literally "and bowing the head, he handed over the spirit." TEV starts a new sentence, beginning with Then. TEV translates "he handed over the spirit" in the same way it translates the verb used in the parallel verses in Mark (15.37) and Luke (23.46), that is, simply he...died. Some commentators understand "the spirit" in 19.30 to be the Holy Spirit and see in the phrase "he handed over the spirit" a fulfillment of what John referred to in 7.39: Jesus said this about the Spirit, which those who believed in him were going to receive. But this interpretation is highly improbable and should not be introduced in translation.

            TEV   (19.31-37)   RSV

JESUS' SIDE IS PIERCED

31 Then the Jewish authorities asked Pilate to allow them to break the legs of the men who had been crucified, and to take the bodies down from the crosses. They requested this because it was Friday, and they did not want the bodies to stay on the crosses on the Sabbath,

31 Since it was the day of Preparation, in order to prevent the bodies from remaining on the cross on the sabbath (for that sabbath was a high day), the Jews asked Pilate that their legs might be broken, and that they might be taken away. 32 So the

since the coming Sabbath was especially holy. 32 So the soldiers
went and broke the legs of the
first man and then of the other man
who had been crucified with Jesus.
33 But when they came to Jesus,
they saw that he was already dead,
so they did not break his legs. 34
One of the soldiers, however,
plunged his spear into Jesus' side,
and at once blood and water poured
out. (35 The one who saw this happen has spoken of it, so that you
also may believe.[h] What he said is
true, and he knows that he speaks
the truth.) 36 This was done to
make the scripture come true: "Not
one of his bones will be broken."
37 And there is another scripture
that says, "People will look at him
whom they pierced."

soldiers came and broke the legs
of the first, and of the other who
had been crucified with him; 33 but
when they came to Jesus and saw
that he was already dead, they did
not break his legs. 34 But one of
the soldiers pierced his side with
a spear, and at once there came
out blood and water. 35 He who
saw it has borne witness--his
testimony is true, and he knows
that he tells the truth--that you
also may believe. 36 For these
things took place that the scripture might be fulfilled, "Not a
bone of him shall be broken." 37
And again another scripture says,
"They shall look on him whom they
have pierced."

[h]believe; *some manuscripts have*
continue to believe.

This section contains the final episode of the crucifixion scene.
The usual Roman custom was to leave the body of a crucified person on
the cross. However, the Jews requested that the bodies of Jesus and the
two other men be removed, since the next day was a holy day (verse 31).
To hasten the death of the men who were being crucified on each side of
Jesus (verse 32), their legs were broken. However, when the soldiers
came to Jesus they saw that he was already dead, and so they did not
break his legs (verse 33). Instead one of them plunged his spear into
Jesus' side (verse 34). Both the fact that Jesus' legs were not broken
and the fact that his side was pierced are understood to be the fulfillment of scripture (verses 36-37); and the validity of these events
is said to rest on the testimony of an eyewitness (verse 35).

Instead of the passive construction Jesus' Side Is Pierced, it
may be preferable in some languages to use an active form, for example,
"The soldiers pierced Jesus' side" or "A soldier thrusts a spear into
Jesus' side."

19.31   Then the Jewish authorities asked Pilate to
allow them to break the legs of the men who had
been crucified, and to take the bodies down from
the crosses. They requested this because it was
Friday, and they did not want the bodies to stay
on the crosses on the Sabbath, since the coming
Sabbath was especially holy.

TEV rather radically restructures this verse. For a literal rendering see RSV.

The Jewish authorities is best understood as a reference to the chief priests of verse 21.

The request of the Jewish authorities must be put in the form of direct address in some languages, for example, "Then the Jewish authorities asked Pilate, 'Allow us to break the legs of the men who have been put to death and then to take down their bodies from the crosses.'" Note that in speaking of the removal of the men from their crosses, it may be necessary in some languages to speak of "taking down their bodies from the crosses." There may even be a technical term for the body of a dead person, for example, "their corpses."

The legs of the men who had been crucified is literally "their legs," but a literal translation could sound as if the Jews were asking Pilate to break their own legs (note RSV "the Jews asked Pilate that their legs might be broken"). Other translations avoid this ambiguity by changing the possessive pronoun "their" to "the" before "legs " (for example, Mft "in order to prevent the bodies remaining on the cross during the sabbath...the Jews asked Pilate to have the legs broken..."). Breaking the legs of criminals with a heavy mallet was originally also a form of capital punishment. Generally only the legs were broken, but sometimes other limbs were broken as well. Although this was in itself a cruel form of capital punishment, when done to a person who was being crucified, it was looked upon as a merciful act, since it ended more quickly the agony of a lingering death on the cross.

And take their bodies down from the crosses is more literally "and that they be taken away." According to Greek syntax, the subject of the verb "be taken away" is "their legs," though it is obvious that John is referring to the bodies of the men. (Compare Mft "the legs broken and the bodies removed"; compare NEB, JB.)

They did this because it was Friday is literally "since it was (the day of) preparation." The noun "preparation" is the same one used in verse 14 in the phrase the day before the Passover (literally "the preparation of the Passover"). When used without a qualifier, this word always refers to the day of preparation before the Jewish Sabbath, that is, to the period from 6 P.M. on Thursday to 6 P.M. on Friday, when the Sabbath day begins. It is possible to translate: "It was Friday, the day of preparation for the Sabbath day, and the Jews did not want the bodies to stay on the crosses on the Sabbath day."

Since the coming Sabbath was especially holy is more literally "for the day of that Sabbath was great." According to John, in the year of the crucifixion the Passover fell on a Sabbath day, which made the day especially holy. JB translates "since that sabbath was the day of special solemnity"; Gdsp "for that Sabbath was an especially important one"; Phps "for that was a particularly important Sabbath"; and Brc "for that Sabbath was a specially great day."

Following the wording of TEV, with the two changes suggested above, one may reorder the sentence to read "It was Friday, the day of preparation for the Sabbath, and the Jews did not want the bodies to stay on the crosses on the Sabbath day, since the coming Sabbath was especially holy. So they asked Pilate to allow them to break the legs of the men who had been put to death and to take their bodies down from the crosses."

19.32   So the soldiers went and broke the legs of the
         first man and then of the other man who had been
         crucified with Jesus.

No indication is given why the soldiers first broke the legs of
the men on either side of Jesus before going to Jesus himself. It may
be that Jesus already appeared to be dead, and the soldiers wanted to
put to death the men who were obviously alive.

In some languages one cannot translate the word broke without indicating how the legs were broken. As already suggested, it was accomplished by a severe blow with a heavy instrument, probably with a large
mallet, a sledge hammer, or a club.

Who had been put to death with Jesus is more literally "who had
been crucified with him."

19.33   But when they came to Jesus, they saw that he was
         already dead, so they did not break his legs.

According to Mark 15.44, Pilate was surprised that Jesus had died
so quickly, because it was not unusual for a person who had been crucified to linger for two or three days. John is careful to make note of
the fact that they did not break Jesus' legs, seeing in their failure
to do so the fulfillment of the scriptural passage cited.

19.34   One of the soldiers, however, plunged his spear
         into Jesus' side, and at once blood and water
         poured out.

The word translated plunged (NEB "stabbed"; JB "pierced") translates a verb which can express a superficial injury (Mft "pricked") or
even the action used to arouse a sleeping person. But the word may also
be used of deeper wounds intended to kill someone, and the context certainly suggests a deeper wound in the present case.

In translating water there is a question whether what John describes is a natural or supernatural occurrence. If taken to be the former, water must be understood to refer to the lymph fluid, for which,
in most languages, a technical term will have to be used. However, the
fact that John calls attention to the presence of an eyewitness (verse
35) suggests that what he narrates in verse 34 is not a natural occurrence. It is probably better, therefore, to translate water literally,
with a note indicating that blood and water may also be intended to
convey a theological significance.

19.35   (The one who saw this happen has spoken of it,
         so that you also may believe.[h] What he said is
         true, and he knows that he speaks the truth.)

[h]believe; *some manuscripts have* continue to believe.

The one who saw this happen has spoken of it is best interpreted
in the light of 21.24: He is the disciple who spoke of these things.
The question which disciple is meant seems answered by the fact that,
apart from Jesus' mother, only the disciple he loved (19.36) is said
to have been present at the crucifixion. As far as translation is concerned, a third person reference should be maintained. There is no exegetical basis for the Living Bible's "I saw all this myself and have
given an accurate report so that you also can believe."

Has spoken of it is literally "has testified" or "has witnessed."
What he said translates the noun "testimony" or "witness." (See comments at 1.7.)

TEV's restructuring makes clear that so that you also may believe
expresses the purpose of the eyewitness's testimony (The one who saw
this happen has spoken of it) and not simply of his telling the truth.
In the Greek sentence structure he speaks the truth immediately precedes the purpose clause.

It is better not to supply an object for believe, as GeCL does
("therefore you also may believe it"), since here the verb means not
simply accepting the truth of what the eyewitness has said but coming
to faith in a theological sense. Compare Gdsp "to lead you also to believe."

There is a textual problem connected with you...may believe. Some
manuscripts have the Greek verb in the present tense, implying the meaning "that you may keep on believing." Other manuscripts have the aorist
tense, which, strictly interpreted, means "that you may come to believe."
If the present tense is accepted, the intimation is that the Gospel was
written to believers, to strengthen their faith. The aorist tense would
imply that it was written for non-Christians, to call them to believe.
No final decision is possible, and the UBS Committee on the Greek text
has left the choice open. (See at 21.3, where the same problem exists.)

He knows that he speaks the truth may be rendered "he knows that
what he has said is true" or "he knows that what he has said actually
happened."

19.36   This was done to make the scripture come true:
               "Not one of his bones will be broken."

This was done refers to verse 33 (they did not break his legs).
Not one of his bones will be broken may be an allusion to the Passover
lamb (Exo 12.46; Num 9.12) or to the "good man" whom the Lord watches
over (Psa 34.20). In the context of John's Gospel, it is best to take
the reference as primarily to the Passover lamb. It would be misleading
to introduce an agent for the passive expression Not one of his bones
will be broken unless the agent can be made indefinite, for example,
"they will not break one of his bones." Sometimes a pseudopassive may
be used, for example, "He will not experience the breaking of any of his
bones."

19.37   And there is another scripture that says,
               "People will look at him whom they pierced."

For languages in which one cannot speak of the scripture as "saying" anything, it may be possible to translate "there is another scripture in which one can read."

The scripture passage referred to in this verse is Zechariah 12.10. John does not follow exactly either the Hebrew text or the most commonly accepted Septuagint reading. People will look at is literally "they will look at." The term pierced must often be made more explicit, for example, "pierced with a spear" or "stuck into with a spear."

TEV   (19.38-42)   RSV

THE BURIAL OF JESUS

38 After this, Joseph, who was from the town of Arimathea, asked Pilate if he could take Jesus' body. (Joseph was a follower of Jesus, but in secret, because he was afraid of the Jewish authorities.) Pilate told him he could have the body, so Joseph went and took it away. 39 Nicodemus, who at first had gone to see Jesus at night, went with Joseph, taking with him about one hundred pounds of spices, a mixture of myrrh and aloes. 40 The two men took Jesus' body and wrapped it in linen cloths with the spices according to the Jewish custom of preparing a body for burial. 41 There was a garden in the place where Jesus had been put to death, and in it there was a new tomb where no one had ever been buried. 42 Since it was the day before the Sabbath and because the tomb was close by, they placed Jesus' body there.

38 After this Joseph of Arimathea, who was a disciple of Jesus, but secretly, for fear of the Jews, asked Pilate that he might take away the body of Jesus, and Pilate gave him leave. So he came and took away his body. 39 Nicodemus also, who had at first come to him by night, came bringing a mixture of myrrh and aloes, about a hundred pounds' weight. 40 They took the body of Jesus, and bound it in linen cloths with the spices, as is the burial custom of the Jews. 41 Now in the place where he was crucified there was a garden, and in the garden a new tomb where no one had ever been laid. 42 So because of the Jewish day of Preparation, as the tomb was close at hand, they laid Jesus there.

This section concludes John's Passion Narrative. Joseph of Arimathea receives permission from Pilate for Jesus' body (verse 38). Together with Nicodemus, another secret disciple, Joseph prepares the body for burial (verses 39-40) and lays it to rest in a new tomb in a garden close by (verses 41-42).

In some languages The Burial of Jesus must be changed into a verbal expression, such as "They bury Jesus" or "Joseph of Arimathea and Nicodemus bury Jesus." In languages in which a proper name by itself always designates a living person, one must say "They bury the body of Jesus" or "They put the body of Jesus in a tomb."

As in translating 11.38, so here too it may be essential to speak of "putting the body of Jesus in a tomb" or "...a cave," in order not to imply that Jesus was put in a grave and covered with earth. It is essential that all expressions relating to the burial be consistent with the description of the tomb in Chapter 20.

19.38   After this, Joseph, who was from the town of
            Arimathea, asked Pilate if he could take Jesus'
            body. (Joseph was a follower of Jesus, but in
            secret, because he was afraid of the Jewish
            authorities.)

After this is literally "but after these things," a generalizing temporal marker often used by John to introduce new sections in his narrative.

Joseph, who was from the town of Arimathea is literally "Joseph from Arimathea." Since the name Arimathea is not widely known, it is important to identify it as a town. Joseph from Arimathea is mentioned in all four Gospels in connection with Jesus' burial, but nowhere else in the New Testament. The location of the town of Arimathea is not definitely known, but none of the suggestions for its location place it in Galilee. Joseph was evidently from Judea.

Rather than saying, take Jesus' body, it may be necessary to say "take the body of Jesus to bury it" or "...to place it in a tomb." Otherwise, such an expression as "take a body" could suggest some evil intention.

Follower translates the Greek word mathētēs, which elsewhere in John's Gospel is rendered disciple. TEV uses follower here to avoid confusing the reader with the notion of a "secret disciple."

According to 12.42, many Jewish authorities believed in Jesus; but because of the Pharisees they did not talk about it openly. In 12.43 John is critical of such persons: They loved the approval of men rather than the approval of God. In 19.38, however, no such harsh judgment is expressed. Perhaps John considers Joseph to be no longer a secret follower of Jesus, now that he has openly requested Jesus' body for burial. But in secret may be rendered "but he had not let other people know about it" or "but he hadn't told anyone about it."

Jewish authorities is literally "Jews." (See Appendix I.)

Pilate told him he could have the body is literally "and Pilate permitted (it)." The clause so Joseph went and took it away is literally "so he came and took away his body." Since TEV mentions the body in the first part of this sentence, it may be referred to in the second part by the pronoun it. In order to avoid pronominal ambiguities, TEV identifies Joseph explicitly in this verse.

In some languages it is necessary to say specifically what took it away implies. That is, one must indicate that Joseph of Arimathea either personally carried the body of Jesus or had it carried. Furthermore, many languages require terms which indicate how a corpse would be carried. The likelihood is that Jesus' body was carried on a kind of stretcher or bier, such as were often used in ancient times to transport a body to a tomb or grave.

19.39   Nicodemus, who at first had gone to see Jesus
         at night, went with Joseph, taking with him
         about one hundred pounds of spices, a mixture
         of myrrh and aloes.

For Nicodemus, see 3.1-2 and 7.50.

To see Jesus is a pronominal phrase in Greek (literally "to him"), which TEV changes to an infinitive of purpose, making the pronominal reference "him" explicit as Jesus.

Taking with him must refer to Nicodemus. In some languages the manner in which Nicodemus took this quantity of spices must be specifically indicated, not only whether he personally carried the spices, but also the manner in which they were carried. It is altogether likely, in view of Nicodemus' position in society, that a servant or servants carried the spices for him.

About one hundred pounds of spices, a mixture of myrrh and aloes is more literally "a mixture of myrrh and aloes, about a hundred pounds." The "pound" referred to (Greek litra) is the Roman pound, equal to about eleven and a half ounces or thirty-one grams.

Instead of the word for mixture (migma) some Greek manuscripts have a word meaning "roll" or "package" (heligma). Although this alternative reading is more difficult (and a more difficult reading is usually considered to be the original one), the reading followed in TEV has stronger textual support, and so the UBS Committee on the Greek text decided in its favor. Among modern translations, only Gdsp ("a roll") follows the alternative reading.

One must be careful in rendering spices, a mixture of myrrh and aloes. Spices are often used for seasoning food, but neither myrrh nor aloes have this function. To make clear that spices in this context have a preservative function, it may be best to translate "substances used for embalming." The terms "myrrh" and "aloes" would then be transliterated and placed in apposition to the expression "substances used in embalming." In certain languages substances used in embalming would be classed as "medicines"--frequently a particular kind of medicines, namely, those derived from herbs.

Myrrh (elsewhere in the New Testament only in Matt 2.11) was a fragrant resin used for embalming the dead. Aloes (only here in the New Testament) are not known to have been used at burial. They are a powdered aromatic sandlewood, spoken of as providing perfume for the bed or clothes (Prov 7.17; Psa 45.8).

19.40   The two men took Jesus' body and wrapped it in
         linen cloths with the spices according to the
         Jewish custom of preparing a body for burial.

The Greek word translated linen cloths (so also JB and GeCL) occurs in 20.5,6,7 but nowhere else with certitude in the New Testament. (Luke 24.12 is textually uncertain.) Since the word may be diminutive in form, NEB translates "strips of linen cloth." However, there is no solid basis for this rendering, and it is better to understand the word generically to mean the linen cloths used in burying the dead.

Wrapped it in linen cloths may be rendered in some languages "wrapped linen cloths around and around it."

The word translated spices (elsewhere in the New Testament only in Mark 16.1; Luke 23.56; 24.1) may also have the meaning "aromatic oil." Most modern English translations, with the exception of NEB ("perfumed oils"), render with the meaning "spices," as TEV does. If the word means "aromatic oil," it was a mixture made by blending myrrh and aloes into a vegetable oil base, and so creating a fragrant oil. If the word means "spices," the picture of the preparation for burial is that of wrapping the body with the linen cloths and sprinkling the spices between the folds.

According to the Jewish custom of preparing a body for burial is more literally "as is the burial custom of the Jews" (RSV). One may say in some languages "That is how the Jews habitually prepared a body in order to put it in a tomb" or "...before putting it in a tomb."

19.41   There was a garden in the place where Jesus had
         been put to death, and in it there was a new
         tomb where no one had ever been buried.

John is the only Gospel to mention a garden in connection with Jesus' burial. There was a garden in the place where Jesus had been put to death need not be pressed to mean that Jesus was crucified in a garden. The tomb was in the garden, and, as the following verse makes clear, the tomb was close to the place of crucifixion.

Where Jesus had been put to death is literally "where he was crucified."

A new tomb where no one had ever been buried is in keeping with the elaborate burial preparations mentioned in verse 39. Buried translates the same Greek verb rendered placed in verse 42. Where no one had ever been buried may be rendered "where no body had ever been placed" or "where no corpse had previously been put."

19.42   Since it was the day before the Sabbath and
         because the tomb was close by, they placed
         Jesus' body there.

Since it was the day before the Sabbath is literally "because of the (day of) preparation of the Jews." The noun translated day before the Sabbath is the same word used in verse 31 (see also verse 14).

In Greek the adverb there appears first in the sentence, but in restructuring TEV places it last.

CHAPTER 20

THE EMPTY TOMB

20 Early on Sunday morning, while it was still dark, Mary Magdalene went to the tomb and saw that the stone had been taken away from the entrance. 2 She went running to Simon Peter and the other disciple, whom Jesus loved, and told them, "They have taken the Lord from the tomb, and we don't know where they have put him!"

3 Then Peter and the other disciple went to the tomb. 4 The two of them were running, but the other disciple ran faster than Peter and reached the tomb first. 5 He bent over and saw the linen cloths, but he did not go in. 6 Behind him came Simon Peter, and he went straight into the tomb. He saw the linen cloths lying there 7 and the cloth which had been around Jesus' head. It was not lying with the linen cloths but was rolled up by itself. 8 Then the other disciple, who had reached the tomb first, also went in; he saw and believed. (9 They still did not understand the scripture which said that he must rise from death.) 10 Then the disciples went back home.

20 Now on the first day of the week Mary Magdalene came to the tomb early, while it was still dark, and saw that the stone had been taken away from the tomb. 2 So she ran, and went to Simon Peter and the other disciple, the one whom Jesus loved, and said to them, "They have taken the Lord out of the tomb, and we do not know where they have laid him." 3 Peter than came out with the other disciple, and they went toward the tomb. 4 They both ran, but the other disciple outran Peter and reached the tomb first; 5 and stooping to look in, he saw the linen cloths lying there, but he did not go in. 6 Then Simon Peter came, following him, and went into the tomb; he saw the linen cloths lying, 7 and the napkin, which had been on his head, not lying with the linen cloths but rolled up in a place by itself. 8 Then the other disciple, who reached the tomb first, also went in, and he saw and believed; 9 for as yet they did not know the scripture, that he must rise from the dead. 10 Then the disciples went back to their homes.

John's Gospel originally ended with Chapter 20 (see verses 30-31). This chapter comprises the third part of the "Book of Glory." The first part centered around the events of the Last Supper (Chapters 13-17), and the second part concerned the trial and crucifixion of Jesus (Chapters 8-19). This last part deals with the accounts of his resurrection. In the Synoptic Gospels, the resurrection accounts center on the witness of the empty tomb or on the appearance of Jesus to his disciples. John skillfully weaves these two aspects together, presenting them in two balanced scenes (verses 1-18 and 19-29).

The first scene, which takes place at the tomb, may be further divided into two parts: visits to the empty tomb (verses 1-10) and the appearance of Jesus to Mary Magdalene (verses 11-18). The second scene, which takes place where the disciples are gathered behind locked doors, may likewise be divided into two scenes: Jesus appears to his disciples

without Thomas (verses 19-23) and Jesus appears to the disciples with
Thomas present (verses 24-29). It may be further observed that in each
case the second part of the scene is concerned with Jesus' appearance
to an individual: in the first scene to Mary Magdalene (verses 14-18)
and in the second to Thomas (verses 26-29). While the first part of
each scene is introduced by a temporal and place setting (verses 1-2
and 19), the second part of each scene contains several verses of transition (verses 11-13 and 24-25). The major events of each scene are found
in verses 3-10, 14-18, 19b-23, 26-29).

Though the section heading The Empty Tomb is effective in some
languages, in others it may be more meaningful to use such a section
heading as "Jesus arises from the dead" or "Jesus comes back to life."

20.1   Early on Sunday morning, while it was still
              dark, Mary Magdalene went to the tomb and saw
              that the stone had been taken away from the
              entrance.

Early...morning translates the same Greek adverb rendered early in
the morning at 18.28. On Sunday (so also Barclay; NEB "on the Sunday")
is literally "on the first day of the week" (so most translations); GeCL
has "on the day after the Sabbath." "The first day of the week" is Sunday,
and TEV, NEB, and Barclay make this information explicit. The entire
phrase Early on Sunday morning could include all or part of the period
from around three A.M. to around six A.M. (see note at 18.28). John further qualifies the time as while it was still dark. Mark has "very early
on Sunday morning, at sunrise" (16.2), and Luke has "very early on Sunday morning" (24.1), a term which implies daylight. Matthew also indicates that it was daylight, "after the Sabbath, as Sunday morning was
dawning" (28.1).

Although the Greek word sabbatōn occurs in this verse, its plural
form has the meaning "week" and not "sabbath." GeCL's "after the Sabbath" has the difficulty that for many Christians "the sabbath" is
erroneously identified with Sunday, rather than with Saturday. A literal
translation of the Greek phrase, "the first day of the week," could be
misleading, since for many people Monday is the first day of the week,
and Sunday is part of the "weekend." Therefore, it is usually better to
identify the particular day of the week, rather than to use a possibly
ambiguous expression.

Mary Magdalene was first mentioned in 19.25 (see comments there).
The number and names of the women who go to the tomb differ in the various Gospel accounts. Matthew names two women, and Mark three. Luke mentions three women by name and includes in addition "the other women."
In each case Mary Magdalene is mentioned first.

John does not suggest why the women went to the tomb, but Mark
and Luke indicate that they were going to anoint Jesus' body, while
Matthew states that they went to see the tomb.

Although Mark (15.46) and Matthew (27.60) indicate that a large
stone was rolled against the entrance to the tomb after the burial of
Jesus, 20.1 is the first mention of the stone in John's Gospel. John
does not indicate how the stone had been taken away, but the implication

is that it was done by supernatural means.

Since the stone has not been mentioned earlier in John's Gospel, there may be some difficulty in translating the phrase literally. The final clause of this verse may therefore be modified to read "that a stone which had been at the entrance to the tomb had been taken away" or "...had been moved." In some languages the passive expression "had been moved" may cause difficulty because it may be necessary to indicate an agent, and no agent is mentioned in the text. Therefore it may be best to say simply that the stone "was no longer there."

From the entrance (so also NEB) is literally "from the tomb" (so most translations). The results of archaeological studies indicate that the entrance to burial tombs of this type was on ground level through a small entryway, usually no more than three feet (or one meter) high. Hence, to enter the tomb, an adult would have to bend over and crawl in (note verse 5: He bent over). The entrance may be expressed in some languages as "the hole that led into the tomb" or "the hole by which a person could go into the tomb." The use of such a term as "hole" may be necessary to indicate that the tomb was entered by a small opening, rather than an ordinary door.

Several different types of tombs were in use in Palestine in Jesus' day. Verse 12 (two angels...sitting where the body of Jesus had been, one at the head and the other at the feet) suggests that Jesus' body had lain in a niche carved in one of the sides of the cave. Under no circumstances was the body laid on the floor.

20.2   She went running to Simon Peter and the other
         disciple, whom Jesus loved, and told them, "They
         have taken the Lord from the tomb, and we don't
         know where they have put him!"

In this section (verses 1-10) John uses his favorite particle oun six times, with its first occurrence in this verse. It occurs more frequently in the accounts of Jesus' death and resurrection than in the other sections of the Gospel and contributes to the dramatic tension.

Both Simon Peter and the other disciple, whom Jesus loved were mentioned during the passion narrative; now they appear together in the empty tomb story. The disciple, who Jesus loved (13.23; 19.26) is now identified with the other disciple (compare 18.15: another disciple). The two disciples obviously set off for the tomb from the same place (verse 3), and this may imply that they were staying together (compare verse 19). It may therefore be appropriate to translate "She went running to Simon Peter and the other disciple, whom Jesus loved, where they were" or "...to where Simon Peter and the other disciple, whom Jesus loved, were staying." In some languages it may be useful to start a new sentence at this point, for example, "She told them..."

The pronoun they (in the phrase they have taken) is the equivalent of a passive ("the Lord has been taken"). GeCL translates "(some) one has taken the Lord from the tomb." One may also say "some people have taken the Lord from the tomb." However, in many languages it is necessary to specify that it was the body of the Lord which was taken, rather than the Lord himself. Otherwise the implication would be that Jesus had not died.

Mary uses the plural we in this verse (we don't know where they have put him) but the singular in verse 13 (I do not know where they have put him). Some suggest that the first person plural reflects Galilean Aramaic, while others see in verse 2 a reflection of the Synoptic tradition, according to which two or more women went to Jesus' tomb. Whatever the explanation, the plural should be retained in translating verse 2.

In the context They have taken is the most natural rendering of the Greek aorist verb which is used here. In some languages this verb must be rendered "they have carried away," and it may be necessary to make explicit that this was done surreptitiously.

They have put renders the same Greek verb translated they placed in 19.42. In some languages it may be necessary to provide an object, for example, "the body" or "the Lord's body."

In all such references to the Lord it may be necessary to use a possessive form in some languages, for example, "our Lord" or "the one who rules over us."

20.3   Then Peter and the other disciple went to
            the tomb.

Peter and the other disciple went is literally "Peter left (a singular verb) and the other disciple, and they went." The verb structure is similar to that discussed in 2.2 (see there). Though the verb form is singular, it is obvious that both Peter and the other disciple are included in the action.

20.4   The two of them were running, but the other
            disciple ran faster than Peter and reached
            the tomb first.

In the Greek text rendered The two of them were running there is an adverb (homou) rendered "side by side" by NEB and NAB. TEV and several other translations omit it as superfluous. This same adverb is rendered all together in 21.2 and together in 4.36.

Ran faster than ("outran" in many translations) translates a rather redundant Greek expression. Most translations do not express the redundancy, but some do, for example, Anchor Bible ("being faster, outran"), Barclay ("ran on ahead, faster than"), and Mft ("ran ahead, faster than").

Reached the tomb first is literally "came first to the tomb." The preposition rendered "to" in the literal translation usually has the meaning of "into," but since Peter and the other disciple do not enter the tomb until verses 6 and 8, respectively, this preposition must mean "to" in verses 3 and 4.

20.5   He bent over and saw the linen cloths, but he
            did not go in.

In Greek this verse continues the sentence begun in verse 4 (literally "and bending over..."). Care must be exercised in the translation of bent over, since it might be taken to mean "looked down at his feet" with the implication that the linen cloths were left in a pile outside the tomb. It may be necessary in some languages to translate "he stooped down and looked in and saw the linen cloths" or "he bent over to look in and saw the linen cloths."

We are not told why the other disciple did not go in, and speculation is useless. This verse implies that there was now at least some daylight, otherwise the other disciple would not have been able to see the linen cloths (the same word discussed in 19.40) when he looked into the tomb.

20.6　　　Behind him came Simon Peter, and he went
　　　　　straight into the tomb. He saw the linen
　　　　　cloths lying there

Behind him came Simon Peter is literally "So Simon Peter also comes following him." JB translates "Simon Peter who was following now came up," while NEB renders "Simon Peter came up, following him."

He went straight into the tomb is more literally "he went into the tomb." The implication is that Simon Peter went immediately into the tomb (note JB "went right into the tomb").

In some languages verbs for movement express quite clearly not only the direction but also the gradient (or slope) of the movement. In this instance it would be best to translate "went" as "went on a level," since "went down" might suggest going down into a grave. Some tombs in ancient times had steps leading down to the vault, but here the floor of the tomb was on the level of the ground outside (see comments at verse 1).

The Greek does not indicate where the linen cloths were lying, but TEV includes the adverb there, as do several other translations. JB includes "on the ground," but the context suggests that an idefinite adverb of place is better than a term indicating a specific location.

The sentence He saw the linen cloths lying there must be rendered in some languages as two paratactically combined sentences, for example, "He saw the linen cloths. They were lying there." However, it is also possible to say "He saw the linen cloths there." The first part of verse 7 may then be rendered "and he also saw the cloth which had been around Jesus' head" or "...which had been wound around Jesus' head."

20.7　　　and the cloth which had been around Jesus'
　　　　　head. It was not lying with the linen cloths
　　　　　but was rolled up by itself.

The cloth is the same word used in 11.44 (see there); around is more literally "on" (so most translations). Probably this cloth was used to prevent the dead man's mouth from falling open, by being passed under the chin and tied above the head. Jesus is not explicitly mentioned in the Greek text of the phrase around Jesus' head, but TEV does so, since so far in this passage he has not been referred to by name (in verse 2 he is referred to as the Lord).

In Greek, all of verse 7 is a continuation of the sentence begun in verse 4. TEV breaks the sentence at this point, introducing a new sentence with it was.

Not lying with the linen cloths but was rolled up by itself indicates that the cloth which had been around Jesus' head was in a position separate from the linen cloths with which his body had been wrapped, and that it was rolled up. The verb "to roll up" is not found in the Septuagint, and elsewhere in the New Testament it appears only in Matthew 27.59 and Luke 23.53, where it is used of wrapping Jesus' body for burial. In the present context it is possible to take the verb to mean "neatly rolled up," in contrast to the grave cloths, which may have been left lying about in some disorder. But more probably the verb should be taken to indicate that the cloth with which the head had been wrapped was left in the shape that it had (that is, an oval loop) when it was wrapped around the head of Jesus. If so, the grave cloths are pictured as lying flat in the place where the torso had been, while the cloth with which the head was wrapped retained its oval shape and was lying in the place where the head had been.

20.8 Then the other disciple, who had reached the tomb first, also went in; he saw and believed.

The content of what the other disciple believed is not indicated. Moreover, the affirmation that he believed causes difficulty in light of what is said in verse 9: They...did not understand the scripture which said that he must rise from death. But the most natural solution is that the other disciple believed that Jesus had been raised from the dead. This belief was based on his own observation of the empty tomb, rather than on the testimony of the scripture, which was another witness to the resurrection.

In some languages one cannot use such a verb as believed without indicating what was believed, for example, "he saw and believed that Jesus had risen from the dead" or "he saw the cloths lying there and therefore believed that..."

20.9 (They still did not understand the scripture which said that he must rise from death.)

They still did not understand the scripture may be translated "but even then they did not understand what the scripture meant when it said that..." or "...did not really understand what the words of the scripture meant which said that..." or "...did not know how to understand the words of the scripture, He must rise from death."

Which said that he must rise from death is more literally "that he must rise from (the) dead." John does not indicate what scripture he has in mind. Although the word scripture commonly refers to a single passage of the Old Testament (note 19.36-37), in the present passage the term is better taken as a reference to the Old Testament as a whole.

The word <u>must</u> indicates a necessity based on the divine will and purpose.

<u>20.10</u>   Then the disciples went back home.

Home must mean the place where the disciples were staying in Jerusalem, rather than their homes in Galilee. The purpose of this verse is to remove the disciples from the scene, in order to prepare the way for the appearance of Jesus to Mary Magdalene. If a literal translation of <u>went back home</u> would mean that the disciples returned to their home <u>town</u>, <u>one must</u> translate "went back to where they were staying."

| TEV | (20.11-18) | RSV |

JESUS APPEARS TO MARY MAGDALENE

11 Mary stood crying outside the tomb. While she was still crying, she bent over and looked in the tomb 12 and saw two angels there dressed in white, sitting where the body of Jesus had been, one at the head and the other at the feet. 13 "Woman, why are you crying?" they asked her.

She answered, "They have taken my Lord away, and I do not know where they have put him!"

14 Then she turned around and saw Jesus standing there; but she did not know that it was Jesus. 15 "Woman, why are you crying?" Jesus asked her. "Who is it that you are looking for?"

She thought he was the gardener, so she said to him, "If you took him away, sir, tell me where you have put him, and I will go and get him."

16 Jesus said to her, "Mary!"

She turned toward him and said in Hebrew, "Rabboni!" (This means "Teacher.")

17 "Do not hold on to me," Jesus told her, "because I have not yet gone back up to the Father. But go to my brothers and tell them that I am returning to him who is my Father and their Father, my God and their God."

18 So Mary Magdalene went and

11 But Mary stood weeping outside the tomb, and as she wept she stooped to look into the tomb; 12 and she saw two angels in white, sitting where the body of Jesus had lain, one at the head and one at the feet. 13 They said to her, "Woman, why are you weeping?" She said to them, "Because they have taken away my Lord, and I do not know where they have laid him." 14 Saying this, she turned round and saw Jesus standing, but she did not know that it was Jesus. 15 Jesus said to her, "Woman, why are you weeping? Whom do you seek?" Supposing him to be the gardener, she said to him, "Sir, if you have carried him away, tell me where you have laid him, and I will take him away." 16 Jesus said to her, "Mary." She turned and said to him in Hebrew, "Rabboni!" (which means Teacher). 17 Jesus said to her, "Do not hold me, for I have not yet ascended to the Father; but go to my brethren and say to them, I am ascending to my Father and your Father, to my God and your God." 18 Mary Magdalene went and said to the disciples, "I have seen the Lord"; and she told them that he had said these things to her.

told the disciples that she had
seen the Lord and related to them
what he had told her.

A section heading is particularly necessary before verse 11, since
there has been no indication that Mary Magdalene has returned to the
tomb. In some languages it may be more natural to employ such a section
heading as "Mary Magdalene sees and speaks with Jesus" rather than
Jesus Appears to Mary Magdalene. "Mary Magdalene recognizes Jesus" or
"Jesus speaks with Mary Magdalene" may also be used.

20.11   Mary stood crying outside the tomb. While she
               was still crying, she bent over and looked in the
               tomb

In some languages such an expression as Mary stood crying must be
expressed by paratactically combined verbs, for example, "Mary stood
there; she was crying." The phrase outside the tomb must be combined
with standing rather than with crying. Accordingly one may translate
"Mary was standing there just outside the tomb; she was crying."
    Outside the tomb is more literally "at/by/near the tomb outside,"
which JB renders "outside near the tomb; NEB "at the tomb outside; and
Gdsp and Phps "just outside the tomb." Barclay has "beside the tomb,
outside it." The Greek preposition indicates proximity. This force is
implicit in TEV, RSV, Mft, and others by the rendering "outside." NAB
has "beside the tomb."
    She bent over and looked in the tomb is more literally "she bent
over into the tomb." The verb "to look" is definitely implied, and a
number of other translations make this information explicit (RSV "she
stooped to look into the tomb"; JB "she stooped to look inside").

20.12   and saw two angels there dressed in white, sitting
               where the body of Jesus had been, one at the head
               and the other at the feet.

The Greek verb translated saw is in the present tense, used to
make more vivid the narration of a past event.
    In the Synoptic accounts of the Empty Tomb story, where John speaks
of two angels, Mark has "a young man" (16.5) and Luke has "two men"
(24.4); in the Emmaus story (Luke 24.23) the disciples refer to a vision
of angels. According to Matthew 28.2, "an angel of the Lord came down
from heaven, rolled the stone away, and sat on it." The mention of white
(Matt 28.3; Mark 16.5; John 20.12) or "bright shining clothes" (Luke
24.4) is an indication of heavenly origin.
    For a discussion of the arrangement of the interior of the tomb,
see comments at verse 1.
    In some languages angels are spoken of as "messengers from God"
or sometimes as "heavenly messengers."
    The phrases which qualify the dress and position of the angels
must often be expressed as separate sentences. Accordingly, verse 12

may be translated "and saw two angels there. They were dressed in white garments. They were sitting where the body of Jesus had been. One was sitting where his head had been, and the other was where his feet had been." Instead of "dressed in white garments," one may say in some languages "their clothes were white."

20.13   "Woman, why are you crying?" they asked her.
             She answered, "They have taken my Lord
             away, and I do not know where they have put
             him!"

"Woman, why are you crying?" they asked her is literally "and they say to her, 'Woman, why are you crying?'" The conjunction "and" at the beginning of a sentence suggests Semitic Greek. "They say" is rendered they asked by TEV and most other translations, since a question follows. They asked her is placed after the angels' words, in order to achieve a more dramatic effect.

Woman is the same noun of address used in 2.4 and 19.26. As indicated previously, it is a term of respect. In languages in which there is no appropriate polite form of address which would be suitable in this context, it may be better simply to omit entirely a noun of address. The question why are you crying? should be sufficient.

She answered is literally "she says to them."

The last part of verse 13 repeats essentially the words of the last part of verse 2. The differences are my Lord instead of the Lord, I do not know instead of we don't know, and the omission of from the tomb (verse 2).

20.14   Then she turned around and saw Jesus standing
             there; but she did not know that it was Jesus.

The Greek adverbial expression rendered around is the same one translated back in 18.6.

And saw Jesus standing there is literally "and saw Jesus standing" (so RSV). To translate without the adverb there in English would focus the reader's attention on standing as opposed to sitting, rather than on the fact that Jesus was at that particular place, which is the point in focus here. JB, NEB, NAB, and others include the adverb there for the same reason. In some languages the statement she...saw Jesus standing there seems inconsistent with what follows, namely, she sid not know that it was Jesus. Since a literal translation of she...saw Jesus standing there might imply that she recognized who he was, it may be better to render the second part of this verse "she saw a man standing there; it was Jesus, but she did not know that it was Jesus" or "...did not recognize him as Jesus."

But she did not know that it was Jesus (so RSV; NEB "but did not recognize him"; NAB "But she did not know him"; JB "though she did not recognize him") represents a literal rendering of the Greek text. John does not suggest why Mary did not recognize Jesus.

<u>20.15</u>   "Woman, why are you crying?" Jesus asked her.
"Who is it that you are looking for?"
     She thought he was the gardener, so she said
to him, "If you took him away, sir, tell me where
you have put him, and I will go and get him."

     A literal rendering of <u>woman</u> in an expression of direct discourse
may be misleading in some languages, since this term is often used for
"wife." Unless some other expression of polite address can be employed,
it may be best to omit the word (compare verse 13).
     In Greek this verse begins with the words <u>Jesus asked her</u> (liter-
ally "Jesus says to her"). TEV divides Jesus' question into two parts,
placing the words <u>Jesus asked her</u> in the middle. This stylistic device
adds dramatic effect to the narrative in English. Jesus' first question,
<u>why are you crying?</u> is the same one the angels asked Mary in verse 13.
     <u>She</u> is a demonstrative pronoun in Greek (literally "that woman"),
while the verb rendered <u>thought</u> in TEV is a participle (RSV "supposing").
     The Greek word for <u>gardener</u> (kēpouros) appears only here in the
New Testament, though this word is often found in the nonbiblical papyri.
The mention of the <u>gardener</u> is in keeping with John's information that
the tomb was in a garden (19.41). <u>Gardener</u> may be rendered "one who
worked in the garden" or "one who took care of the plants in the garden."
     In Mary's words to the angel, <u>sir</u> comes first in the Greek sentence
structure. This same word can also mean "Lord," but not in this context,
in which Mary does not recognize who Jesus is (verse 14). The rendering
<u>sir</u> is also used in 4.11 (see there).
     <u>If you took him away</u> must be rendered in some languages "if you
carried away the body (of Jesus)." Similarly, the two other occurrences
of the pronoun <u>him</u> later in this same verse must be so rendered as to
make clear that Jesus' corpse is meant.
     <u>I will go and get him</u> is more literally "I will take him away"
(RSV, NEB, NAB). The action of "going," though not expressed explicitly
in the Greek, is implicit in the context, and so TEV (note also JB and
GeCL) includes this information. Mary intends to <u>go and get</u> the body
of Jesus from the place to which it has been taken and return it to the
tomb.

<u>20.16</u>   Jesus said to her, "Mary!"
     She turned toward him and said in Hebrew,
"Rabboni!" (This means "Teacher.")

     <u>Jesus said to her</u> must be stated more fully in some languages, for
example, "Jesus called her by name" or "Jesus spoke her name in addressing her."
     Mary did not recognize who Jesus was until he spoke to her by name,
then <u>she turned toward him</u>. In Greek <u>she turned toward him and said in
Hebrew</u> is literally "turning she said to him in Hebrew." The expression
<u>in Hebrew</u> (5.2; 19.13,17,20) means "in Aramaic." According to John the
meaning of this word is <u>Teacher</u> (so also RSV, Mft, NAB, Barclay). Some
ancient scribes evidently felt that the use of <u>Teacher</u> to address the
risen Lord was too weak, and so they changed their manuscripts to read

either "Lord, Teacher" or "Teacher, Lord," but the textual support for this reading is very weak. Other scribes felt that the transition between verses 16 and 17 needed improving, and so they added, after the word Teacher, "and she ran forward to touch him." That Mary would address Jesus as Teacher is perfectly natural in this situation, since this was obviously the title by which she had known him. She...said in Hebrew, "Rabboni!" may be rendered "She spoke to him in the Hebrew language saying, Rabboni" or "she spoke a Hebrew word, 'Rabboni.'" However, it may be more satisfactory to say "she...said 'Rabboni' (this is a word in the Hebrew language which means 'Teacher')."

20.17   "Do not hold on to me," Jesus told her, "because
          I have not yet gone back up to the Father. But go
          to my brothers and tell them that I am returning
          to him who is my Father and their Father, my God
          and their God."

In Greek this verse begins with the words rendered Jesus told her in TEV (literally "Jesus says to her"). For stylistic reasons TEV introduces the words of Jesus first and then breaks into them by indicating the speaker (Jesus told her).

Do not hold on to me (RSV "Do not hold me") translates a present imperative in Greek which suggests the meaning "stop holding on to me" or "stop trying to hold on to me." NEB, JB, and NAB all render "Do not cling to me." NAB indicates in a note that this means literally "Don't keep touching me," while NEB gives an alternative translation, "Touch me no more." Mft brings out this same force in "Cease clinging to me." As seen from this sampling of translations, the problems are at least two. (1) What is the meaning of the Greek verb itself? Does it mean "to touch" or "to take hold of"? (2) What is the force of the present tense? Does it mean "stop holding on to me" or "stop trying to hold on to me"? Translations such as TEV and RSV are ambiguous, while "Do not cling to me" (NEB, JB, NAB) suggests that Mary is already holding on to Jesus. In the parallel scene in Matthew 28.9, the women take hold of Jesus' feet and worship him, and something similar may be intimated in the present verse.

It is difficult to interpret the words because I have not yet gone back up to the Father. They seem to imply the possibility of touching Jesus after the ascension, though not before; and that is precisely the opposite of what one might expect. Fortunately for the translator, this problem need not be resolved in order to give an accurate rendering. Commentators give a variety of interpretations, but the best solutions see here a reflection of the Johannine concept of the relation between the resurrection and the exaltation of Jesus. Time and space, which characterized the Lord's earthly existence, no longer apply to him after the resurrection. The resurrected Lord has already been exalted to his rightful place beside the Father, and any appearances that he makes to his disciples are appearances "from heaven." So the solution to this difficulty lies somewhere within the theological perspective of the author.

Some Greek manuscripts read "my Father" instead of the Father.

[611]

Both "my Father" and the Father are Johannine, but it is more likely
that a scribe would have changed the Father to read "my Father" than
the reverse. In any case, "my Father" is a legitimate translation of
the Greek "the Father."

In Greek, the words which follow the command but go to my brothers
and tell them are given in direct discourse, but it is possible to render them as indirect discourse, as in TEV (see also NEB "but go to my
brothers, and tell them that I am now ascending to my Father..."). The
brothers referred to are, of course, Jesus' disciples, and not the
"brothers" of 7.5. In some languages it is essential to translate "my
disciples" or "my followers." In The Acts of the Apostles brothers or
brethren may be rendered "fellow Christians" or "fellow believers," but
that would not be appropriate in this passage. However, such an expression as "those who believe in me" may be used.

That I am going back up to him who is my Father and their Father,
my God and their God is literally "I am going up to my Father and your
Father and my God and your God." The present tense of the verb translated going back up in TEV is significant. It indicates that Jesus is
in the process of ascending to the Father, but has not yet arrived at
his destination. In the Gospel of John Jesus' return to the Father is a
frequent theme (see 7.33; 14.12,28; 16.5,10,28).

In some languages a literal translation of my Father and their
Father, my God and their God would be interpreted to mean four different
persons. Accordingly, it may be necessary to restructure the grammatical
relations, for example, "my Father who is also their Father; this same
person is my God, and he is also their God." In a number of languages,
however, one cannot say "my God" or "their God," since God cannot be
grammatically possessed. One can, however, say "the God whom I worship"
and "the God whom they worship."

20.18   So Mary Magdalene went and told the disciples
               that she had seen the Lord and related to them
               what he had told her.

The verb told is actually a participle in Greek. TEV renders it as
a finite verb, as do many other translations. Note, for example, RSV
"went and said."

The Greek text of Mary's words presents a strange combination of
direct and indirect discourse, which TEV renders entirely as indirect
discourse. Among other translations, NEB retains the form of the Greek:
"'I have seen the Lord!' she said, and gave them his message." As far
as most languages are concerned, it is more natural to follow through
with either direct or indirect discourse, and not try to combine the
two. It is also possible to preserve the direct discourse in the first
part of this verse by saying, "told the disciples, I have seen the Lord;
she also related to them what Jesus had told her."

JESUS APPEARS TO HIS DISCIPLES

19 It was late that Sunday evening, and the disciples were gathered together behind locked doors, because they were afraid of the Jewish authorities. Then Jesus came and stood among them. "Peace be with you," he said. 20 After saying this, he showed them his hands and his side. The disciples were filled with joy at seeing the Lord. 21 Jesus said to them again, "Peace be with you. As the Father sent me, so I send you." 22 Then he breathed on them and said, "Receive the Holy Spirit. 23 If you forgive people's sins, they are forgiven; if you do not forgive them, they are not forgiven."

19 On the evening of that day, the first day of the week, the doors being shut where the disciples were, for fear of the Jews, Jesus came and stood among them and said to them, "Peace be with you." 20 When he had said this, he showed them his hands and his side. Then the disciples were glad when they saw the Lord. 21 Jesus said to them again, "Peace be with you. As the Father has sent me, even so I send you." 22 And when he had said this, he breathed on them, and said to them, "Receive the Holy Spirit. 23 If you forgive the sins of any, they are forgiven; if you retain the sins of any, they are retained."

The section heading, Jesus Appears to His Disciples, must be treated in some languages as a causative, for example, "Jesus causes his disciples to see him." One may also use such an expression as "Jesus meets with his disciples" or "...with his followers."

20.19   It was late that Sunday evening, and the disciples were gathered together behind locked doors, because they were afraid of the Jewish authorities. Then Jesus came and stood among them. "Peace be with you," he said.

In Greek, verse 19 is one sentence, which TEV breaks into three.
That Sunday evening (so also NEB, GeCL) is more literally "that day, the first day of the week" (RSV). A literal translation produces an awkward expression of time in English, and so Barclay translates "on the evening of the same day, the Sunday."
TEV also restructures somewhat the rest of this verse. And the disciples were gathered together behind locked doors, because they were afraid of the Jewish authorities is more literally "and the doors had been locked where the disciples were because of the fear of the Jews." It is possible, of course, to restructure in other ways. For example, NAB has "even though the disciples had locked the doors of the place where they were for fear of the Jews"; and Phps "the disciples had met together with the doors locked for fear of the Jews." As in most other places, TEV understands "the Jews" to be the Jewish authorities.
Although John explicitly states that it was their fearfulness which caused the disciples to be gathered behind locked doors, he

obviously has another reason for indicating that the doors were locked. It is to emphasize the miraculous nature of Jesus' sudden appearance among the disciples. In some languages it may be more satisfactory to introduce a new clause in speaking about locked doors, for example, "the disciples gathered together; they locked the doors because they were afraid of the Jewish authorities."

Jesus' greeting to his disciples was "Peace be with you," repeated in verses 21 and 26. On the meaning of the word peace see 14.27 (note also 16.33). In some languages the closest equivalent of Peace be with you is "I wish you well" or "I pray that all may be well with you." Since this type of peace was in dramatic contrast with the fear the disciples had, it is sometimes possible to use an idiomatic expression such as "I pray that you may sit down in your hearts" (with the meaning "being relieved of anxiety").

20.20   After saying this, he showed them his hands and
         his side. The disciples were filled with joy at
         seeing the Lord.

After greeting the disciples, he showed them his hands and his his side. According to Luke 24.40, Jesus showed the disciples his hands and his feet. However, John is more interested in the wound in Jesus' side than in the wounds in his feet, as indicated by the specific mention of the piercing of Jesus' side in his account of the crucifixion (see 19.34). In some cases it may be necessary to stipulate specifically what Jesus showed in connection with his hands and his side, for example, "he showed them the wounds in his hands and in his side."

Were filled with joy (so also NEB and JB) is translated in various ways, but the meaning in all translations is the same. For example, Mft and NAB have "rejoiced," while Phps translates "were overjoyed." In some languages the equivalent of were filled with joy is simply "were very, very happy."

Here John begins to use the Lord of the resurrected Jesus. The phrase at seeing the Lord indicates the cause for the disciples' joy. Therefore, it may be expressed most effectively in some languages "because the disciples saw the Lord, they were filled with joy" or "...they were very happy."

20.21   Jesus said to them again, "Peace be with you.
         As the Father sent me, so I send you."

Peace be with you is the same greeting used in verse 19. It is repeated in verse 26.

Though in the Greek of this verse two different verbs for sent are used, commentators agree that they are used synonymously. The sending of the Son by the Father is a frequent theme of the Gospel; several passages in John's Gospel also speak of Jesus sending his disciples (note, for example, 4.38; 13.16,20; and 17.18).

In some languages it is essential to indicate the place to which a person is sent; otherwise, the implication of the verb may be

[614]

"banishment" or "rejection." Accordingly, one may need to translate the second sentence of this verse "in the same way that my Father sent me into the world, so I am sending you out into the world."

20.22   Then he breathed on them and said, "Receive the
              Holy Spirit.

He breathed on them and said is literally "he breathed on and said to them." It is possible for "them" to be at the same time the object of "breathed on" and the indirect object of "said." Therefore, in restructuring into English, it is necessary either to express "them" twice (RSV "he breathed on them, and said to them"), or to introduce "them" as the object of "breathed on" and leave it implicit after "said," as in TEV.
     The verb translated breathed on (emphusao) appears only here in the New Testament. In the Septuagint it is used in Genesis 2.7 of God's breathing the breath of life into man; it is also used in Ezekiel 37.9. John expects his readers to see a parallel between God's creative breath in Genesis 2.7 and Jesus' act of breathing here. In a number of languages breathed on must be rendered "blew upon." A term literally meaning "breathe" may refer only to normal inhaling and exhaling of the breath, while anything as striking as this action of Jesus would be expressed as "blowing upon."
     In Greek the definite article "the" does not appear in the phrase the Holy Spirit. However, it is also missing in other passages that clearly refer to the Holy Spirit (note Acts 2.4). Most modern translators render as the Holy Spirit (GeCL "God's Holy Spirit"); but Phps translates "receive holy spirit," with a footnote indicating that "Historically the Holy Spirit was not given until Pentecost." However, it is impossible to fit John and Acts together in a chronological arrangement. This is John's interpretation of the giving of the Holy Spirit to the Christian community, as Pentecost is Luke's interpretation of the same experience.
     It may be difficult to find the most appropriate expression to translate the verb receive as it is used here. A literal rendering would sometimes imply "taking in one's hands," which is obviously not meant. A fuller expression may be required in some languages, for example, "accept the Holy Spirit in your lives," "welcome the Holy Spirit in your hearts," or "make room for the Holy Spirit within you."

20.23   If you forgive people's sins, they are forgiven;
              if you do not forgive them, they are not forgiven."

They are forgiven translates a verb in the perfect tense in Greek. Some Greek manuscripts have the present tense here and others the future tense, but virtually all scholars accept the perfect tense as the original reading. In general it may be said that the perfect tense expresses a past action which results in a present state, and on that basis it has been argued that God's action of forgiveness (they are forgiven) is therefore said to have taken place prior to the offering of forgiveness through Jesus' disciples (If you forgive people's sins). But in a conditional sentence the perfect tense is used with essentially the same meaning as the present and the future, except that it emphasizes the continuous character of the action (note, for example, NEB "they stand forgiven"). So the first part of verse 23 may be rendered "If you forgive people's sins, God also forgives them, and they remain forgiven."

If you do not forgive them, they are not forgiven is more literally "if you hold (the sins) of any people, they are held." "To hold" is used here with the meaning of "not to forgive"; the two halves of this verse are simply a kind of parallelism. NEB renders "if you pronounce them unforgiven, unforgiven they remain." Phps translates "and if you hold them unforgiven, they are unforgiven."

There are several ways in which the forgiveness of sins is described, for example, "to erase one's sins," "to wipe out one's sins," "to throw a person's sins away," "to forget about a person's sins," or even "to give a person's sins back to him." In some languages highly idiomatic expressions are used. For example, in Shilluk forgiveness of sins is spoken of as "spitting on the ground in front of," a reference to a ritual which is performed after a case has been tried, punishment meted out, and all accusations terminated.

| | TEV | (20.24-29) | RSV |

JESUS AND THOMAS

24 One of the twelve disciples, Thomas (called the Twin), was not with them when Jesus came. 25 So the other disciples told him, "We have seen the Lord!"

Thomas said to them, "Unless I see the scars of the nails in his hands and put my finger on those scars and my hand in his side, I will not believe."

26 A week later the disciples were together again indoors, and Thomas was with them. The doors were locked, but Jesus came and stood among them and said, "Peace be with you." 27 Then he said to Thomas, "Put your finger here, and look at my hands; then reach out your hand and put it in my side. Stop your doubting, and believe!"

28 Thomas answered him, "My Lord and my God!"

29 Jesus said to him, "Do you believe because you see me? How happy are those who believe without seeing me!"

24 Now Thomas, one of the twelve, called the Twin, was not with them when Jesus came. 25 So the other disciples told him, "We have seen the Lord." But he said to them, "Unless I see in his hands the print of the nails, and place my finger in the mark of the nails, and place my hand in his side, I will not believe."

26 Eight days later, his disciples were again in the house, and Thomas was with them. The doors were shut, but Jesus came and stood among them, and said, "Peace be with you." 27 Then he said to Thomas, "Put your finger here, and see my hands; and put out your hand, and place it in my side; do not be faithless, but believing." 28 Thomas answered him, "My Lord and my God!" 29 Jesus said to him, "Have you believed because you have seen me? Blessed are those who have not seen and yet believe."

The section heading, Jesus and Thomas, may be misleading in some
languages, since it may suggest that Jesus and Thomas were engaged in
some common activity. It may be better to use such a section heading
as "Jesus appears to Thomas," "Jesus speaks with Thomas," or "Thomas
acknowledges Jesus as Lord and God."

20.24   One of the twelve disciples, Thomas (called
           the Twin), was not with them when Jesus came.

Verse 19 does not make explicit the size of the group of disciples
gathered behind locked doors. However, verse 24 intimates that it was
the eleven (more precisely ten, since Thomas was missing) rather than
the larger group of Jesus' followers. The first resurrection scene was
concluded with the appearance of Jesus to Mary, and this second scene
reaches its climax in the revelation of Jesus to Thomas. For Thomas,
see 11.16; 14.5; and 21.2.

Called the Twin may be rendered "his other name was the Twin" or
"his nickname was Twin." In some languages it is necessary to indicate
whether a twin was the first or the second to be born. Unfortunately,
there is no biblical information to guide the translator in the present
case.

When Jesus came refers to Jesus' appearance to the disciples after
his resurrection. It may therefore be necessary to use such an expression
as "when Jesus appeared to them" or "when Jesus showed himself to them."
Thus there will be no ambiguity or misunderstanding.

20.25   So the other disciples told him, "We have seen the
           Lord!"
              Thomas said to them, "Unless I see the scars of
           the nails in his hands and put my finger on those
           scars and my hand in his side, I will not believe."

In Greek the verb translated told is in the imperfect tense, which
may imply repeated action (Phps "kept on telling"; NAB "kept telling").

Thomas said to them is literally "but he said to them."

Scars of the TEV text translates a noun that is singular in Greek
("mark" of many translations), but in English a plural such as "nail
prints" is more natural (NAB "nailmarks"; Gdsp "marks"; JB "holes"). The
phrase on those scars translates the same Greek phrase rendered the scars
of the nails by TEV. NEB translates the first phrase "the mark of the
nails" and the second "the place where the nails were." Phps translates
the first phrase "the mark of the nails" and the second "where the nails
were." These changes are simply for stylistic reasons.

And my hand in his side is literally "and throw my hand into his
side," but in the restructuring of TEV it is not necessary to repeat the
verb.

I will not believe is a very strong expression in Greek. NAB renders "I will never believe it," while JB translates "I refuse to believe."

The expression I will not believe may require some grammatical
object, for example, "I will not believe that he arose from the dead,"

20.25

"I will not believe that he is really alive," or even "I will not believe that you really saw him."

20.26   A week later the disciples were together again indoors, and Thomas was with them. The doors were locked, but Jesus came and stood among them and said, "Peace be with you."

A week later (so also NEB, NAB, Gdsp, Barclay) is translated "Just over a week later" by Phps. The phrase is more literally "eight days later" (so RSV). John means the Sunday following the first resurrection appearances.

The disciples (so also NAB, GeCL, JB) is literally "his disciples." However it is more natural in English to speak of the disciples in such a context rather than "his disciples."

The adverbial expression indoors must be rendered as a complete clause in some languages, for example, "the disciples were together again; they were inside a house."

The doors were locked, but Jesus came represents an inversion of the Greek sentence order, which reads "Jesus comes, even though the doors were locked." John emphasizes the fact that the doors were locked. In this instance John does not mention that the doors were locked because the disciples were afraid of the Jews, as in verse 19. He probably intends to emphasize the miraculous aspect of Jesus' sudden appearance among his disciples even though the doors are closed. The passive expression the doors were locked may also be rendered as active, for example, "they had locked the doors" or "they had shut the doors with locks."

Peace be with you is the same greeting as in verses 19 and 21.

20.27   Then he said to Thomas, "Put your finger here, and look at my hands; then reach out your hand and put it in my side. Stop your doubting, and believe!"

In Greek, the words of Jesus to Thomas are in one sentence, which TEV divides into two. The first sentence is rendered fairly literally in TEV, and its structure is similar to that of most other English translations. However, Stop your doubting and believe is more literally "and do not be unbelieving but believing." The TEV rendering achieves two goals: (1) A more natural English style by using verbs rather than nouns or adjectives (note, for example, JB "Doubt no longer but believe"). (2) The proper focus of Jesus' words, since he is commanding Thomas to stop one activity and begin another. NEB achieves the same effect by translating "be unbelieving no longer, but believe"; NAB translates "do not persist in your unbelief, but believe"; Mft has "be no more unbelieving but believe." By whatever means is natural in the receptor language, the translation should indicate that Jesus is calling on Thomas to give up his unbelief and to start believing.

It may be necessary to designate a more specific location than merely employing an adverb such as here, for example, "put your finger here on the scar in my hand" or "put your finger on my hand."

20.28   Thomas answered him, "My Lord and my
             God!"

Thomas answered him is more literally "Thomas answered and said to him," once again reflecting a Semitic formula for introducing direct discourse.

Thomas' response My Lord and my God is the rendering in almost all translations. In order to indicate clearly that Thomas addressed Jesus as both Lord and God, it may be necessary to introduce his statement by "Thomas spoke to Jesus as," "Thomas addressed Jesus as," or "in speaking to Jesus, Thomas said." In some languages it may be more appropriate to translate "Thomas answered him, You are my Lord and my God." In languages in which the use of the conjunction and would imply two individuals, it may be necessary to translate "you are my Lord, even my God." In certain languages one cannot possess such terms as "Lord" or "God." If so, it may be necessary to translate "you are the one who rules over me, and you are God whom I worship."

20.29   Jesus said to him, "Do you believe because
             you see me? How happy are those who believe
             without seeing me!"

The use of a question in rendering Jesus' words (Do you believe because you see me?) is also done in several other translations (RSV, Mft, Gdsp, Phps, GeCL, Barclay); others prefer a statement (Zür, Luther Revised, Segond, JB, NEB, and NAB). The earliest Greek manuscripts have no punctuation, and so it is impossible to determine whether a question or a statement was intended. If a question is used, the form should indicate that the expected answer is "yes."

How happy translates the same word discussed in 13.17.

Those who believe without seeing me may also be rendered "those who have believed even though they have not seen." That is, the Greek verbs which are in the aorist tense may be taken as representing either timeless action (so TEV) or action that is past from the viewpoint of Jesus or the author of the Gospel (NAB "Blest are they who have not seen and have believed"). The pronoun me is not explicit in the Greek text.

                TEV   (20.30-31)   RSV

        THE PURPOSE OF THIS BOOK

    30 In his disciples' presence Je-   30 Now Jesus did many other signs
sus performed many other miracles   in the presence of the disciples,
which are not written down in this   which are not written in this book;
book. 31 But these have been writ-   31 but these are written that you
ten in order that you may believe^j   may believe that Jesus is the Christ,

                        [619]

that Jesus is the Messiah, the Son   the Son of God, and that believing
of God, and that through your faith you may have life in his name.
in him you may have life.

*j*believe; *some manuscripts have*
continue to believe.

It is the consensus of New Testament scholars that these two verses
form the original conclusion to the Gospel.
The section heading, The Purpose of This Book, may be rendered as
"Why this book was written" or "Why the words of this book say what they
do" or "What is the reason for this book."

20.30   In his disciples' presence Jesus performed
             many other miracles which are not written down
             in this book.

Miracles is literally "signs" (see comments at 2.11).
Some Greek manuscripts do not have his before disciples', but the
meaning is clearly implicit, and his may be included on translational
grounds. One Latin translation reads after in his disciples' presence,
"after his resurrection from the dead," but it is obviously a later
scribal addition. In his disciples' presence may be rendered "when his
disciples were with him" or even "while his disciples were watching."
The clause which are not written down in this book suggests a contrast.
The first sentence of this verse may therefore be translated: "Jesus
performed many other miracles when his disciples were with him; these
are not written down in this book."

20.31   But these have been written in order that you
             may believe*j* that Jesus is the Messiah, the
             Son of God, and that through your faith in him
             you may have life.

             *j*believe; *some manuscripts have* continue to
             believe.

These may refer either to the miracles of verse 30 or, more generally, to everything included in the Gospel ("these things").
That you may believe translates an aorist subjunctive in Greek,
but some manuscripts have a present subjunctive; hence TEV alternative
rendering "continue to believe." The use of the aorist tense here suggests that John's Gospel was written to non-Christians with the hope
that they might come to believe that Jesus is the Messiah, the Son of
God. The present tense suggests that the author's intention was to
strengthen the faith of those who were already believers. The choice
between the Greek readings is difficult, but the UBS Committee on the
Greek text favors the aorist, though rating its choice a "C" decision,
indicating a considerable degree of doubt as to whether this or the
alternative reading is to be preferred.

The word Messiah is literally "Christ." On the meaning of this term see comments at 1.20.

The passive expression these have been written may in this context be made active: "I have written these." The use of the first person singular does not in any way presume to identify the author of the book.

The first reference to Jesus as the Son of God is in 1.34 (compare 1.18). In this context one may translate that Jesus is the Messiah, the Son of God as "that Jesus is the one whom God has specially chosen, the one who is his Son" or "that Jesus is God's Son, the one whom God has specially chosen."

Through your faith in him you may have life is literally "that believing you may have life in his name." TEV has transformed the participle "believing" into a prepositional phrase (through your faith) and understood the "name" to stand for the person: "in his name" = in him. On the translation of "in his name" see 14.13.

TEV   (21.1-14)   RSV

JESUS APPEARS TO SEVEN DISCIPLES

21 After this, Jesus appeared once more to his disciples at Lake Tiberias. This is how it happened. 2 Simon Peter, Thomas (called the Twin), Nathanael (the one from Cana in Galilee), the sons of Zebedee, and two other disciples of Jesus were all together. 3 Simon Peter said to the others, "I am going fishing."

"We will come with you," they told him. So they went out in a boat, but all that night they did not catch a thing. 4 As the sun was rising, Jesus stood at the water's edge, but the disciples did not know that it was Jesus. 5 Then he asked them, "Young men, haven't you caught anything?"

"Not a thing," they answered.

6 He said to them, "Throw your net out on the right side of the boat, and you will catch some." So they threw the net out and could not pull it back in, because they had caught so many fish.

7 The disciple whom Jesus loved said to Peter, "It is the Lord!" When Peter heard that it was the Lord, he wrapped his outer garment around him (for he had taken his clothes off) and jumped into the water. 8 The other disciples came to shore in the boat, pulling the net full of fish. They were not very far from land, about a hundred yards away. 9 When they stepped ashore, they saw a charcoal fire there with fish on it and some bread. 10 Then Jesus said to them, "Bring some of the fish you have just caught."

11 Simon Peter went aboard and dragged the net ashore full of big fish, a hundred and fifty-three in

21 After this Jesus revealed himself again to the disciples by the Sea of Tiberias; and he revealed himself in this way. 2 Simon Peter, Thomas called the Twin, Nathanael of Cana in Galilee, the sons of Zebedee, and two others of his disciples were together. 3 Simon Peter said to them, "I am going fishing." They said to him, "We will go with you." They went out and got into the boat; but that night they caught nothing.

4 Just as day was breaking, Jesus stood on the beach; yet the disciples did not know that it was Jesus. 5 Jesus said to them, "Children, have you any fish?" They answered him, "No." 6 He said to them, "Cast the net on the right side of the boat, and you will find some." So they cast it, and now they were not able to haul it in, for the quantity of fish. 7 That disciple whom Jesus loved said to Peter, "It is the Lord!" When Simon Peter heard that it was the Lord, he put on his clothes, for he was stripped for work, and sprang into the sea. 8 But the other disciples came in the boat, dragging the net full of fish, for they were not far from the land, but about a hundred yards^{m} off.

9 When they got out on land, they saw a charcoal fire there, with fish lying on it, and bread. 10 Jesus said to them, "Bring some of the fish that you have just caught." 11 So Simon Peter went aboard and hauled the net ashore, full of large fish, a hundred and fifty-three of them; and although there were so many, the net was not torn. 12 Jesus said to them,

all; even though there were so many, still the net did not tear. 12 Jesus said to them, "Come and eat." None of the disciples dared ask him, "Who are you?" because they knew it was the Lord. 13 So Jesus went over, took the bread, and gave it to them; he did the same with the fish.

14 This, then, was the third time Jesus appeared to the disciples after he was raised from death.

"Come and have breakfast." Now none of the disciples dared ask him, "Who are you?" They knew it was the Lord. 13 Jesus came and took the bread and gave it to them, and so with the fish. 14 This was now the third time that Jesus was revealed to the disciples after he was raised from the dead.

^{m}Greek *two hundred cubits*

John originally intended his Gospel to end with 20.30-31. However, on the basis of the available manuscript evidence, it is clear that the Gospel was never circulated independently of Chapter 21. Scholars have developed various theories regarding the authorship of Chapter 21, some arguing that it was written by the same person who wrote the first twenty chapters, and others maintaining that it was written by someone else. In any case it was written by someone within the Johannine circle. This chapter is best considered an epilogue to the Gospel, that is, a section added at the end to supplement the body of the text. In this way it balances with the prologue at the beginning of the Gospel.

Scholarly opinion also differs regarding the purpose of this epilogue. At least two factors seem to be involved: (1) The author desired to include some important material which might otherwise be lost; and (2) he hoped to clear up a misunderstanding (verses 20-24). The chapter falls into three parts: verses 1-14; 15-19; and 20-24, to which a conclusion is added (verse 25). The first part of the chapter records a Galilean appearance of the resurrected Lord (the appearances of the previous chapter all took place in or around Jerusalem). The second part, loosely attached to the first, relates a dialogue between Jesus and Peter. The last part concerns the fate of the disciple, whom Jesus loved (verse 20). It is followed by a brief conclusion.

Instead of Jesus Appears to Seven Disciples, it is possible to employ as a section heading "Jesus appears to his disciples in Galilee," "Jesus appears in Galilee," or "Jesus appears to his disciples beside the lake."

21.1   After this, Jesus appeared once more to his disciples at Lake Tiberias. This is how it happened.

After this is the same transitional formula used in 3.22. If a receptor language requires a more definite indication of time, one may say "a few days later."

The verb translated appeared (NAB, Gdsp, Phps, NEB, JB "showed himself") is frequently used in John's Gospel (1.31; 2.11; 3.21; 7.4; 9.3; 17.6), but it is used of a resurrection appearance only in this verse (twice) and in verse 14.

The adverbial phrase once more should not be so rendered as to suggest that this was the final appearance of Jesus to his disciples.

Instead of once more, one may translate "again."

His disciples (so also NEB) is literally "the disciples" (so most translations). In the following verse seven disciples are mentioned.

In this verse Lake Galilee is referred to as Lake Tiberias. In 6.1 it is referred to as "Lake Galilee," followed by a parenthetical explanation that it was also known as "Lake Tiberias."

This is how it happened is literally "but he showed (himself) in this way." Mft translates "it was in this way," while Gdsp renders "and he did so in this way."

21.2   Simon Peter, Thomas (called the Twin), Na-
        thanael (the one from Cana in Galilee), the
        sons of Zebedee, and two other disciples of
        Jesus were all together.

The words were all together (literally "were together") occur at the beginning of the Greek sentence, with the names following, but most English translators restructure in a way similar to TEV to meet the demands of English style. The use of the full name Simon Peter is typically Johannine.

Thomas was first mentioned in 11.16. Nathanael is mentioned in the episode in 1.43-51; otherwise he appears in John's Gospel only in this verse. In the earlier account no mention is made of his coming from Cana in Galilee. The sons of Zebedee are James and John. They are not mentioned by name anywhere in the Gospel and only here as the sons of Zebedee. In this Gospel the name "John" always refers to John the Baptist, unless specifically marked otherwise, as at 21.15, Simon son of John.

Along with this group of five disciples mentioned by name are two other disciples of Jesus whose identity is not given.

In some languages, rather than beginning with a list of names, followed by a statement that all these persons were together, it is necessary to say "The disciples who were together included Simon Peter, Thomas..." or "The following disciples were all together: Simon Peter, Thomas..."

21.3   Simon Peter said to the others, "I am going
        fishing."
            "We will come with you," they told him.
        So they went out in a boat, but all that
        night they did not catch a thing.

Said to the others is literally "says to them" (most translations have "said to them"). JB and NEB have simply "said."

I am going fishing is literally "I am going to fish." The verb "to fish" is used only here in the New Testament; it appears in Jeremiah 16.16 of the Septuagint, but nowhere else in the Greek Bible. Some argue that the present tense of the verb "to go" suggests that Peter is going back to fishing as a trade. This could have been the meaning of I am going fishing if 21.1-14 circulated independently as a story of Jesus' first appearance to his disciples. But in this episode's present context, following Jesus' two appearances to the disciples in Jerusalem (Chapter 20), such an intention on Peter's part is excluded. The words I am going fishing serve rather to get the disciples from Jerusalem to Lake Tiberias. In some languages it is necessary to use a more specific verb which indicates the manner of fishing (with spears, hook and line, or nets). Here a term for fishing with nets should be used (see verse 6).

In the statement we will come with you the pronoun we is emphatic. The decision of the other disciples to accompany Peter meant that they would help him fish, not that they were just going along for the ride. In some languages this must be rendered "we will go along to help you fish."

As in Chapter 6, two different Greek nouns are used for boat: ploion (verses 3 and 6) and ploiarion (verse 8). The second noun is a diminutive in form, but since it refers to the same boat, no shift in meaning can have been intended. In translation it is essential to employ a term which means a boat large enough to hold seven men with their nets.

All that night is literally "in that night." RSV has "that night" (so most translations), but NAB renders "All through the night."

As with fishing, so too with catch it may be necessary to use a specific term, for example, "they caught no fish in their nets" or "they netted no fish."

21.4   As the sun was rising, Jesus stood at the water's
         edge, but the disciples did not know that it was
         Jesus.

As the sun was rising is more literally "But when dawn was already coming." Only here in John's Gospel is the word "dawn" (Greek prōia) used. NAB translates "just after daybreak"; Gdsp renders "but just as day was breaking"; NEB has "morning came"; and JB translates "it was light by now."

At the water's edge is more literally "on the beach" (so RSV and many other translations). NAB translates "on the shore." It may be important in some languages to state specifically "on the shore of the lake."

It is difficult to understand why the disciples did not know that it was Jesus, if they had already seen him twice after the resurrection. Possibly this account was originally a first resurrection appearance of the Lord to his disciples. Some assume that the disciples did not recognize Jesus because of the distance between the boat and the shore or because of the early morning mist. However, the failure to recognize Jesus was also mentioned in the appearance to Mary Magdalene (20.14), where these two factors played no role.

21.5   Then he asked them, "Young men, haven't you
         caught anything?"
              "Not a thing," they answered.

Then he asked them is literally "therefore (oun) Jesus says to them." The English discourse structure does not demand the inclusion of the proper name "Jesus," since he was mentioned by name in verse 4.

The Greek term _paidia_, rendered here _young men_, is used elsewhere in John's Gospel only twice. In 4.49 it is translated _child_ by TEV, and in 16.21 it is rendered _baby_. The form is perhaps best taken as a colloquialism such as might be used in addressing a group of fishermen. Mft, Phps, and Barclay translate "lads," while JB and NEB render "friends." "Children" (RSV, NAB, Gdsp) is pushing the literal meaning too far and does not suit the present context.

Haven't you caught anything? is translated "Have you caught anything?" by Phps, NEB, and JB (Barclay "have you caught any fish?"). Though the Greek form of the question expects a negative answer, this force should not be emphasized here (but note Anchor "you haven't caught anything to eat, have you?"). The verb translated _caught_ by TEV and others is literally "have" (Mft "have you got anything?"; RSV "have you any fish?").

The Greek word rendered _anything_, "anything to eat" (so also NAB), and "fish" is _prosphagion_. It does not occur elsewhere in the New Testament or in the Septuagint, and it is rare in other Greek literature. Although the etymology of the word suggests the meaning "something to eat," it is disputed just how it was used. Some maintain that it had the specific meaning "fish." In the present context this meaning seems required, since the disciples were fishing for a living and not just for their breakfast. The meaning "fish" is implicit in TEV's _caught anything_.

Not a thing is literally "No," which GeCL renders "Not one fish." The translation should reflect colloquial usage. A literal translation of _Not a thing_ could suggest that the net was completely empty, which is not very likely. It would be possible to say "We haven't caught a fish" or "...a single fish."

They answered is more literally "they answered him," but in the context "him" is clearly implied and need not be expressed explicitly.

21.6   He said to them, "Throw your net out on the
          right side of the boat, and you will catch some."
          So they threw the net out and could not pull it
          back in, because they had caught so many fish.

He said to them (so most translations) is literally "but he said to them."

Throw your net out on the right side of the boat is similar to most translations. NEB has Jesus using the technical language of an English seaman: "Shoot the net to starboard."

The Greek word translated _boat_ in this verse is the same one used in verse 3. It is different from the one used in verse 8, but the two words should be considered as synonymous.

In Greek the verb _you will catch_ does not have an expressed object, but one must be supplied translationally. TEV reflects most other translations, but Phps has "you'll have a catch," and NEB "you will make a catch." In some languages the equivalent expression would be "you will net some fish" or "you will catch some fish in your net."

So they threw the net out is literally "therefore (_oun_) they

threw," but English requires an object, though the Greek obviously does
not require it. The Greek term translated net is a very general one,
applicable to various kinds of nets. In this context the net was probably a circular net with small weights around the edge. Such nets are
still used in many parts of the world.

They...could not pull it back in must be rendered in some languages as "they could not pull the net and fish back into the boat"
or "...up into the boat."

Because they had caught so many fish translates a noun phrase in
Greek (literally "from the number of the fish"). Since the fish were
still in the water, it may be necessary to say in some languages "because they had netted so many fish" or "because there were so many fish
in the net."

21.7   The disciple whom Jesus loved said to Peter,
          "It is the Lord!" When Peter heard that it was
          the Lord, he wrapped his outer garment around
          him (for he had taken his clothes off) and
          jumped into the water.

The Greek verb translated loved in the phrase the disciple whom
Jesus loved, is agapaō. This same verb is used in verse 20, as it is
in 13.23 and 19.26. In 20.2 (the other disciple, whom Jesus loved) the
Greek verb for loved is phileō. John uses these two verbs synonymously,
which is important for the exegesis of verses 15-19. The Living Bible
has gone far beyond the bounds of legitimate translation by rendering
the disciple whom Jesus loved as "I." This version maintains the first
person pronoun in the earlier part of the chapter, but in verse 20 it
introduces the third person ("the disciple Jesus loved"). The use of
"I" presupposes a particular view of the authorship of this chapter, a
view not substantiated by the evidence. Moreover, the shift from the
first person ("I") to the third person ("the disciple Jesus loved") is
bad English style. The third person reference should be maintained
wherever this particular phrase occurs.

It may be necessary in some languages to make specific the antecedent of it in the sentence It is the Lord! A literal translation
could be confusing. Accordingly, one may translate "The person on the
shore is the Lord" or "The one who spoke to us is the Lord."

Similarly, in translating the clause When Peter heard that it was
the Lord, it may be necessary to say "When Simon Peter heard that the
person on the shore was the Lord" or "...that the person who had spoken
to them was the Lord." The expression in the second sentence of this
verse must be made consistent with that used in the first sentence.

He wrapped his outer garment around him (for he had taken his
clothes off) is translated in various ways. RSV has "he put on his
clothes, for he was stripped for work"; NEB "he wrapped his coat about
him (for he had stripped)"; JB "...who had practically nothing on,
wrapped his cloak round him"; Mft "Simon Peter threw on his blouse (he
was stripped for work)"; Gdsp "he put on his clothes, for he had taken
them off"; Phps "slipped on his clothes, for he had been naked"; GeCL
has simply "he put on his outer garment." Anchor renders "tucked in his

outer garment (for he was otherwise naked)."

For he had taken his clothes off is literally "for he was gumnos."
The Greek adjective gumnos usually means "naked," but it can also mean
"lightly clothed." This second meaning is indicated here, since a Jew
would never disrobe completely while fishing. Most commentators and
translators suppose that Peter was fishing with only a loincloth on;
before leaping into the water he put on his outer garment. However,
this interpretation has been challenged on three counts: (1) The Greek
verb diazōnnumai means properly not "put on" but "tuck in" or "tie up."
It occurs twice in 13.4-5: he...tied a towel around his waist...and began to wash the disciples' feet and dry them with the towel around his
waist. The purpose of the action in 21.7 is to give Peter greater freedom of movement. (2) Outer garment (Greek ependutēs) designates a garment worn over the underclothing. In this context it refers to the
fisherman's smock that Peter was wearing to ward off the chill of the
morning air. Peter in his fisherman's smock is described as "lightly
clad." (3) Peter would not have put on an additional garment before
jumping into the water, since this would have made swimming more difficult. Rather he tucked in the garment that he already had on.

21.8   The other disciples came to shore in the boat,
        pulling the net full of fish. They were not very
        far from land, about a hundred yards away.

The other disciples came to shore in the boat is literally "the
other disciples came with the boat." TEV makes explicit the information
that they came to the shore. In Greek, all of verse 8 is one sentence,
in which pulling the net full of fish (literally "pulling the net of
fish") comes last. English structure requires that this information be
given in the first part of the verse.

In some languages it is necessary to specify the means by which a
boat is made to move through the water. In this instance it would no
doubt have been "by means of oars." Therefore one may translate the first
clause of this verse "the other disciples rowed to shore in the boat."

Pulling the net full of fish may be translated as a separate
clause, for example, "while pulling behind them the net full of fish,
the other disciples rowed to shore in the boat.

About a hundred yards (so most modern translations) is literally
"about two hundred cubits." A cubit is about 18 inches (45 centimeters).
In English it is more natural to speak of yards than of cubits. Some
translations (GeCL, for example) give the measurement in terms of meters
("about a hundred meters"), an increasingly favored way of measuring
distance. In some languages a natural way of incorporating the measurement into the preceding statement would be to translate "they were only
about a hundred yards from land."

21.9   When they stepped ashore, they saw a charcoal
        fire there with fish on it and some bread.

Charcoal fire is the same word used in 18.18; it occurs nowhere
else in the New Testament.

The word used for fish is the same word used in 6.9,11. Although
in Chapter 6 the word seems to have the meaning "dried fish" or "pickled
fish," in this and the following verse the reference is evidently to the
fresh fish which had just been caught. The English word fish may be
either singular or plural when applied to food, but the Greek text uses
the singular here (NAB "a fish"). It is possible to understand the Greek
text to mean that both the fish and bread were on the fire, but most
translations indicate that only the fish were being cooked.

21.10   Then Jesus said to them, "Bring some of the
               fish you have just caught."

Then does not appear in the Greek text. TEV introduces it here because the English demands a transitional marker.

21.11   Simon Peter went aboard and dragged the
               net ashore full of big fish, a hundred and
               fifty-three in all; even though there were
               so many, still the net did not tear.

The verb translated went aboard (so most translations) literally
means "went up." Some commentators take this to mean that Peter was
just now coming up on the shore. However, John seems to imply that by
jumping into the water and swimming Peter reached shore first. Other
commentators take this verb to mean that Peter climbed up on the bank
to help pull the net in. But the most satisfactory interpretation is
that Peter got into the boat to help the other disciples pull in the
load of fish. In Matthew 14.32 and Mark 6.51 the verb is used with the
meaning "to go aboard," and is accompanied by the phrase "into the
boat." Since the net full of fish was dragged behind the boat as the
men rowed to shore, Peter would have to get into the stern of the boat
to help drag the net onto the shore.
          Symbolic interpretations of the number a hundred and fifty-three
have been suggested, but fortunately the translator is concerned only
with the literal meaning.
          The description of the net and the fish may require several para-
tactically combined sentences, for example, "Simon Peter went back
aboard the boat and helped drag the net ashore; the net was full of big
fish; altogether there were 153 fish."
          The net did not tear may be rendered as "no holes were made in
the net" or "no part of the net broke."

21.12   Jesus said to them, "Come and eat." None of
               the disciples dared ask him, "Who are you?"
               because they knew it was the Lord.

In classical Greek the verb translated eat here and had eaten in
verse 15 means "to eat breakfast." The only other instance of this verb
in the New Testament is in Luke 11.37, where the reference is to the

main meal of the day. The related noun is used in Matthew 22.4; Luke 11.38; 14.12. In all three verses the word designates the main meal of the day, rather than breakfast. However, it is possible to translate the verb here with the original meaning "to eat breakfast," because of the contextual setting. NEB has "Come and have breakfast."

The Greek verb translated dared may also be rendered "was brave enough" or "...bold enough." The reason given (because they knew it was the Lord) seems illogical, since it suggests that the disciples did not need to ask Jesus who he was. Nevertheless, even though they knew it was Jesus, they may have wanted some confirmation from him.

As in verse 7 (It is the Lord), so in this verse the title Lord is used of the resurrected Jesus.

21.13   So Jesus went over, took the bread, and gave
             it to them; he did the same with the fish.

In Greek this verse has no translational marker, but TEV supplies so for the English reader. Compare JB ("Jesus then stepped forward") and NEB ("Jesus now came up").

The verb went over (NAB "came over"; NEB "came up") need not imply that Jesus was standing at a distance from the fire. It seems better to take it with the verb took which follows (Gdsp "Jesus went and got the bread"; Barclay "Jesus went and took the loaf").

He did the same with the fish translates a noun phrase in Greek (RSV "and so with the fish").

21.14   This, then, was the third time Jesus
                 appeared to the disciples after he was
                 raised from death.

This verse ties Chapter 21 to Chapter 20, making this resurrection appearance to the disciples sequential to the two in Chapter 20.

Appeared translates a passive form in Greek (RSV "was revealed"), but its meaning is equivalent to the active form used with an object in verse 1. Barclay translates "this was the third time that Jesus appeared to his disciples," and NAB has "this marked the third time that Jesus appeared to the disciples."

It may be necessary to translate after he was raised from death by an active form, such as "after God raised him from death."

| TEV | (21.15-19) | RSV |

JESUS AND PETER

15 After they had eaten, Jesus said to Simon Peter, "Simon son of John, do you love me more than these others do?"	15 When they had finished breakfast, Jesus said to Simon Peter, "Simon, son of John, do you love me more than these?" He said to
"Yes, Lord," he answered, "you	him, "Yes, Lord; you know that I

know that I love you."
Jesus said to him, "Take care of my lambs." 16 A second time Jesus said to him, "Simon son of John, do you love me?"
"Yes, Lord," he answered, "you know that I love you."
Jesus said to him, "Take care of my sheep." 17 A third time Jesus said, "Simon son of John, do you love me?"
Peter became sad because Jesus asked him the third time, "Do you love me?" and so he said to him, "Lord, you know everything; you know that I love you!"
Jesus said to him, "Take care of my sheep. 18 I am telling you the truth: when you were young, you used to get ready and go anywhere you wanted to; but when you are old, you will stretch out your hands and someone else will tie you up and take you where you don't want to go." 19 (In saying this, Jesus was indicating the way in which Peter would die and bring glory to God.) Then Jesus said to him, "Follow me!"

love you." He said to him, "Feed my lambs." 16 A second time he said to him, "Simon, son of John, do you love me?" He said to him, "Yes, Lord; you know that I love you." He said to him, "Tend my sheep." 17 He said to him the third time, "Simon, son of John, do you love me?" Peter was grieved because he said to him the third time, "Do you love me?" And he said to him, "Lord, you know everything; you know that I love you." Jesus said to him, "Feed my sheep. 18 Truly, truly, I say to you, when you were young, you girded yourself and walked where you would; but when you are old, you will stretch out your hands, and another will gird you and carry you where you do not wish to go." 19 (This he said to show by what death he was to glorify God.) And after this he said to him, "Follow me."

The purpose of this section is to restore Peter to his discipleship. Three times he had denied Jesus (18.17,25,27); now he will affirm his love for Jesus three times (21.15,16,17). The question do you love me? is put to Peter three times, not because Jesus doubts Peter's love for him, but rather to indicate how earnest that love is. Even though Peter had denied Jesus three times, his love for him is genuine, and so Peter appeals to Jesus' own knowledge (you know that I love you) as evidence of this.

Rather than Jesus and Peter, it may be better to employ as a section heading such an expression as "Jesus talks with Peter" or "Jesus asks Peter some questions" or "Jesus questions Peter about his love."

21.15   After they had eaten, Jesus said to Simon Peter, "Simon son of John, do you love me more than these others do?"
"Yes, Lord," he answered, "you know that I love you."
Jesus said to him, "Take care of my lambs."

After they had eaten serves as a transition to the following episode. Although seven disciples are mentioned at the beginning of this account (21.2), this particular section is concerned solely with a dialogue between Jesus and Simon Peter.

To facilitate the discussion of the remainder of this verse and of verses 16 and 17, the following chart is provided.

Jesus' Question	Peter's Answer	Jesus' Response
verse 15: love (agapaō)	know (oida)...love (phileō)	take care of (boskō)... lambs (arnion)
verse 16: love (agapaō)	know (oida)...love (phileō)	take care of (poimainō)... sheep (probaton)
verse 17: love (phileō)	know (oida) everything... know (ginōskō)... love (phileō)	take care of (boskō)... sheep (probaton)

As can be seen from the chart, John uses two words for "love," agapaō and phileō. At one time it was fashionable to see a distinction in meaning between the two words, but most scholars now agree that the words are used synonymously. This conclusion is reflected in most modern translations, since they render both verbs in the same manner (RSV, NEB, NAB, Mft, JB, Barclay, Luther Revised, Zür Bible, GeCL, Français Courant). A few translations do, however, make a distinction in meaning. For example, Phps and the Living Bible translate phileō with the meaning "to be one's friend" (note also Segond and the NEB alternative rendering), while Gdsp translates agapaō as "to be devoted to." In a footnote on the two verbs, Barclay remarks: "It is almost certain that there is no difference in meaning between them." However, he does give the alternative possibility of "to be dear to" for phileō. It is suggested that the translator select as generic a term as possible for "to love," and use that term throughout the passage.

In reply Peter uses two verbs meaning "to know." Here again the consensus of New Testament scholarship is that the verbs are used synonymously.

Finally, in his command to Peter, Jesus uses two different verbs, both of which are translated take care of in TEV. The verb used in verses 15 and 17 (boskō) is used of herdsmen who "feed" or "tend" their herds. For example, it is used in Luke 15.15, where the prodigal son is sent to the fields to take care of the pigs; it is used of pig herders in Matthew 8.33; Mark 5.14; and Luke 8.34. In each of these occurrences the verb is used of people who are taking care of (not merely feeding) animals. So in John 21.15,17 Take care of is better than the more limited meaning "feed" found in most translations. The verb used in verse 16 (poimainō) originally meant "to be a shepherd" (see Mft and Barclay "be a shepherd to my sheep"), but it is also widely used in the figurative sense "to lead," "to guide," or "to rule." Although most translations distinguish in meaning between these two verbs, they seem to be used synonymously in the present context.

The object of these verbs is lambs (arnion) in verse 15 and sheep (probaton) in verses 16 and 17. Translators sometimes make a distinction, but these nouns are probably used synonymously in the present context. Variation in the choice of nouns and verbs is a stylistic feature of the Johannine writer, and no real distinction in meaning should be looked for either in this passage. That different verbs and different nouns are used here to describe the same event and object is no more significant than the use of three different words for "fish" in verses 5-13. In verse 17 there is some manuscript support for the reading probation, technically meaning "little sheep" (Living Bible). However, the rendering "little sheep" does not appear in any of the major translations.

More than these others do (Mft; see also GeCL, Phps, Barclay, NEB alternative rendering) is to be preferred to the meaning "more than all else" (NEB).

Since Jesus posed a question to Simon Peter, it may be best to translate "Jesus asked Simon Peter," rather than merely Jesus said to Simon Peter.

The ellipsis involved in the clause than these others do may need to be made explicit, for example, "than these others love me." If it is assumed that these refers to objects (as in NEB), then the question must be rendered "do you love me more than you love all these things?" "These things" would refer to the boats, the net, and, by implication, Peter's previous occupation as a fisherman. This interpretation, however, seems far less satisfactory.

In his answer Simon Peter does not attempt to qualify his own love in contrast with the love which others might have. This may be interpreted as a recognition of his own failure to acknowledge his love for Jesus during the trial. In some languages it may be best to translate you know that I love you as "you know how much I love you."

Since take care of my lambs must be understood figuratively, it may be wise to treat this expression as a simile, for example, "Take care, as it were, of my lambs" or "Take care of my followers, just as though they were lambs."

21.16-17 A second time Jesus said to him, "Simon son of John, do you love me?"

"Yes, Lord," he answered, "you know that I love you."

Jesus said to him, "Take care of my sheep." 17 A third time Jesus said, "Simon son of John, do you love me?"

Peter became sad because Jesus asked him the third time, "Do you love me?" and so he said to him, "Lord, you know everything; you know that I love you!"

Jesus said to him, "Take care of my sheep.

On these verses, see comments at verse 15. It should be noted further that the four occurrences of Jesus in the TEV rendering of verses
16 and 17 represent "he" of the Greek text, though some manuscripts
have "Jesus" before the command in verse 17. For stylistic reasons, TEV
makes the references explicit.

The pronoun you in Peter's response is emphatic in both instances
(you know everything; you know).

21.18   I am telling you the truth: when you were
         young, you used to get ready and go anywhere
         you wanted to; but when you are old, you will
         stretch out your hands and someone else will
         tie you up and take you where you don't want
         to go."

I am telling you the truth is the same formula that was first used
in 1.51 (see there), except that you is singular in 21.18.

The verbs rendered you used to get ready and go are in the imperfect tense in Greek, expressing customary action in the past. NAB renders "as a young man you fastened your belt and went about as you
pleased," and NAB has "when you were young you fastened your belt about
you and walked where you chose." The Greek verb rendered "fastened your
belt" expresses the action of putting a girdle around one's loose,
flowing robes before going out into the street or embarking on a journey. Since this practice is unknown to the English reader, TEV renders
you used to get ready.

The second part of this verse is more difficult. On the basis of
verse 19 it is clear that the reference is to Peter's death as a Christian martyr. Since the earliest tradition is that Peter was crucified,
a number of commentators take you will stretch out your hands as an
explicit reference to his crucifixion. Someone else will tie you up
would then refer to the binding of a prisoner to lead him off to
crucifixion. If this interpretation is valid, the fact that the stretch-
ing out of the hands is mentioned first, even though the tying up would
be first in chronological order, is explained by the fact that the reference to crucifixion was the central point of the saying. NAB says in
a note that this verse is "A figurative reference to the crucifixion
of Peter."

Some have argued that verse 18b cannot refer to Peter's martyrdom,
since the verb rendered tie...up (the same verb translated get ready
in the first half of the verse) is never used in Greek of tying up a
prisoner. If verse 18b cannot refer to Peter's martyrdom, then, it is
suggested, the contrast in the verse is between the alertness of Peter's
youth and the helplessness of his old age; as a young man he was able
to get himself ready to go wherever he wished, but when he grows old,
he will have to stretch out his hands for someone else to help him
dress, and he will be taken where he does not want to go. This interpretation, however, cannot be reconciled with the Gospel writer's explanation in the following verse: In saying this, Jesus was indicating
the way in which Peter would die and bring glory to God.

An intermediate position would be to admit on the basis of verse 19 that verse 18b refers to Peter's martyrdom but to leave open the question whether an explicit reference to crucifixion is intended by <u>you will stretch out your hands</u>. In an interpretation of verse 18b as a reference to martyrdom the use of zōnnumi ("fasten one's belt") to refer to tying up a prisoner would be an extension of its original meaning, allowable for the sake of the parallelism with verse 18a.

A number of translators (RSV, GeCL, Mft, Gdsp, Segond, Luther Revised, Zür, Phps) keep the literal sense of "gird" or "dress" in verse 18b. However, others translate on the basis of the context: NAB "tie... fast"; NEB "bind...fast"; Barclay "bind."

In some manuscripts the plural "others" is used instead of the singular (someone else). This change may have been made so that the prediction of Peter's arrest corresponds with the arrest of Jesus, where the plural is used (18.12). A plural may be preferable in 21.18 on translational grounds, but it may be better in some languages to use a passive construction: "you will be taken where you don't want to go." One may also say "people will lead you off where you do not want to go" or "...will cause you to go where you do not want to go."

<u>21.19</u>   (In saying this, Jesus was indicating the
          way in which Peter would die and bring glory
          to God.) Then Jesus said to him, "Follow me!"

TEV, together with Mft, RSV, and NAB, includes the first part of this verse in parentheses, indicating that it is a comment by the Gospel writer. Such explanatory comments are characteristic of Johannine style.

Neither <u>Jesus</u> nor <u>Peter</u> is mentioned by name in the Greek text. Most translations make only the mention of Peter explicit.

<u>The way in which Peter would die and bring glory to God</u> is more literally "by what kind of death he would glorify God." TEV avoids the archaism "glorify" by translating <u>bring glory to</u> (Gdsp, GeCL "honor"). One may also translate "Jesus was showing how Peter was going to die and in this way honor God" or "...show how glorious God is."

<u>Then Jesus said to him</u> is literally "And having said this, he says to him." TEV renders the force of "having said this" by <u>then</u> and makes the reference to Jesus explicit.

In the context <u>follow</u> means not only "follow as a disciple" but also "follow in death." However, this extended meaning should not be made explicit in translation. One may say "adhere to me as a follower." Terms meaning "track down" or "come up behind" should be avoided, since they do not express the point of the metaphor.

| TEV | (21.20-24) | RSV |

JESUS AND THE OTHER DISCIPLE

20 Peter turned around and saw behind him that other disciple, whom Jesus loved--the one who had

20 Peter turned and saw following them the disciple whom Jesus loved, who had lain close to

leaned close to Jesus at the meal and had asked, "Lord, who is going to betray you?" 21 When Peter saw him, he asked Jesus, "Lord, what about this man?"

22 Jesus answered him, "If I want him to live until I come, what is that to you? Follow me!"

23 So a report spread among the followers of Jesus that this disciple would not die. But Jesus did not say he would not die; he said, "If I want him to live until I come, what is that to you?"

24 He is the disciple who spoke of these things, the one who also wrote them down; and we know that what he said is true.

his breast at the supper and had said, "Lord, who is it that is going to betray you?" 21 When Peter saw him, he said to Jesus, "Lord, what about this man?" 22 Jesus said to him, "If it is my will that he remain until I come, what is that to you? Follow me!" 23 The saying spread abroad among the brethren that this disciple was not to die; yet Jesus did not say to him that he was not to die, but, "If it is my will that he remain until I come, what is that to you?"

24 This is the disciple who is bearing witness to these things, and who has written these things; and we know that his testimony is true.

In place of Jesus and the Other Disciple, it is possible to employ as a section heading such a phrase as "Jesus speaks about the other disciple" or "Jesus speaks about the disciple whom he loves."

21.20   Peter turned around and saw behind him
             that other disciple, whom Jesus loved--the
             one who had leaned close to Jesus at the
             meal and had asked, "Lord, who is going to
             betray you?"

Saw behind him that other disciple, whom Jesus loved is more literally "sees the disciple whom Jesus loved following." Although the verb "to follow" usually has the sense "to follow as a disciple," the focus here seems to be on its literal meaning, "coming up behind." Peter and Jesus are walking together, with the disciple whom Jesus loved following behind them.

The second half of this verse, another explanatory comment, alludes to the question asked at the Last Supper by the disciple whom Jesus loved (13.25). In the Greek text Jesus is not explicitly mentioned. Had leaned close to Jesus is literally "had reclined on his breast." In Greek the disciple's words are in direct discourse, and this form is followed by most modern language translations. However, it is possible to restructure the passage as indirect discourse, for example, "the one who had leaned close to Jesus at the meal and had asked him who was going to betray him." Since "the meal" was the last meal Jesus ate with his disciples, GeCL translates "he was the same one who had eaten next to Jesus during the last meal."

Instead of using a dash as a mark of punctuation, it may be better to begin a new sentence in the middle of verse 20: "That other disciple was the one who leaned close to Jesus..." It may also be necessary to indicate clearly to whom the other disciple directed his question, for example, "and asked Jesus, 'Lord, who is going to betray you?'" or '"... turn you over to your enemies?'"

<u>21.21</u>   When Peter saw him, he asked Jesus, "Lord, what about this man?"

Since verse 20 already contains a reference to Peter's seeing the other disciple, it may be necessary to mark this fact at the beginning of verse 21 by some transitional device, for example, "and so when Peter saw him."

<u>What about this man?</u> (so also RSV) is literally "but this man what?" Several translations render "what about him?" (Mft, Phps, JB, NAB), while NEB has "what will happen to him?" One may also render this question "what will this man experience?" or "what is he going to undergo?" or "how are people going to treat him?"

<u>21.22</u>   Jesus answered him, "If I want him to live until I come, what is that to you? Follow me!"

The verb rendered <u>to live</u> by TEV literally means "to remain," but the meaning in the context is "to remain alive." This is clearly marked in the following verse where the writer distinguishes between <u>would not die</u> and "remain" (TEV <u>live</u>). One may translate <u>to live</u> as "to keep on living" or "to continue living" or "to stay alive." Mft translates "If I choose that he should survive till I come back..." NAB renders "Suppose I want him to stay until I come"; NEB translates "If it should be my will that he wait until I come"; JB has "If I want him to stay behind till I come." Since Jesus will go away and then return, it is necessary in some languages to translate "until I come back" or "until I return."

<u>What is that to you?</u> may be rendered "why are you worried about that?" or "why are you concerned about that?" or "why is that your concern?" In some languages one may translate "why are you thinking about that?" or "why does this matter enter your heart?"

For the expression <u>Follow me!</u> see discussion under verse 19.

<u>21.23</u>   So a report spread among the followers of Jesus that this disciple would not die. But Jesus did not say he would not die; he said, "If I want him to live until I come, what is that to you?"

This verse was written to correct a misinterpretation of Jesus' statement to Peter. It is intended to explain that Jesus' words were a hypothetical statement and not a prophecy of what would actually take place.

In some languages one cannot say "a report spread," but one can say "more and more people were hearing" or "more and more people thought." In this particular context one may translate the first part of the verse: "As a result more and more of the followers of Jesus thought that this disciple would not die" or "...was not going to die."

The following sentence may employ direct discourse in both parts, for example, "But Jesus did not say, He will not die; rather he said, 'If I want him to stay alive until I come back, why should that concern you?'"

21.24   He is the disciple who spoke of these things,
the one who also wrote them down; and we know
that what he said is true.

A witness was referred to in 19.35, though he was not explicitly identified. This verse also mentions a witness, who is responsible for writing at least part of the Gospel and is identified as "the disciple whom Jesus loved" (verse 20). At least four problems are involved in the interpretation and translation of this verse:

(1) Who spoke of these things is in the present tense in Greek (RSV "who is bearing witness to these things"; Gdsp "who testifies to these things"), in contrast to the past (aorist) tense of wrote them down. What is the significance of the present tense here? Some commentators believe that the use of the present indicates that the witness on whose testimony the Gospel depends (or the part of the Gospel referred to in these things) was still alive at the time this verse was written; and this interpretation seems to be the one followed by most translations. However, the present tense may simply signal that the disciple's testimony was considered to be present in the Gospel which he wrote.

(2) What is the precise reference of these things? Does it refer to what immediately precedes (verses 20-23), to all of Chapter 21, to Chapters 1-20, or to the entire Gospel? Since no answer to this question is agreed on by all, the translator should render these things with a term which can refer to any of the possibilities mentioned.

(3) What is the meaning of wrote them down (so also Mft, NAB; JB "has written them down")? Did the disciple write down these things himself or did he cause them to be written down? In 19.19 wrote was used causatively: Pilate did not personally write the inscription on the cross. If wrote is understood causatively in 21.24, does it mean that the disciple dictated the Gospel, that he supervised the writing, or merely that his testimony was the source for the material used (compare 19.35)? If wrote is understood as referring to the testimony behind the Gospel, then it tells us nothing about the authorship of the work. Commentators are sharply divided on the meaning of wrote, and the translator should not favor a particular interpretation in rendering the text.

(4) Who does we refer to (we know that what he said is true)? Some have maintained that the reference is to the disciple who spoke of these things. However, there is no parallel for the third person (he) and the first person (we) being used within the same sentence to designate the same individual. Therefore, it is best to take we as referring to a group which includes the writer of verse 24 but does not include the disciple, whom Jesus loved (verse 20). In languages which distinguish between an inclusive and an exclusive first person plural, the exclusive form should be used here.

TEV   (21.25)   RSV

CONCLUSION

25 Now, there are many other things that Jesus did. If they were all written down one by one, I suppose that the whole world could not hold the books that would be written.

25 But there are also many other things which Jesus did; were every one of them to be written, I suppose that the world itself could not contain the books that would be written.

Instead of Conclusion it may be preferable to use a brief sentence as a section heading, for example, "Jesus did so many other things" or "Jesus did so much."

21.25   Now, there are many other things that Jesus did. If they were all written down one by one, I suppose that the whole world could not hold the books that would be written.

In Greek verse 25 is a single sentence, which TEV divides into two. This verse forms a second conclusion to the Gospel, and in this sense it parallels 20.30-31. Who is referred to by the first person pronoun in I suppose? Is it someone distinct from the author of verse 24, or is the same person referred to by the plural (we) and singular (I) pronouns?

TEV takes the negative not as going with the verb hold (could not hold), as do many other translations (RSV, Phps, NEB, JB, GeCL). Others take it with the verb suppose and render "I do not suppose" (Mft, Gdsp; Barclay "I do not think"; NAB " I doubt"). Essentially the same meaning is arrived at by either rendering. Many languages have "negative movement," that is, the expression of negation is moved from what is actually negated to a verb of thinking, saying, seeing, etc. In this instance the negative (not) would be moved from the verb hold to the verb suppose. However, what is actually negated is the content of the supposition, and in most languages one must therefore translate I suppose that the whole world could not hold the books.

The whole world (RSV "the world itself") is literally "the world." In contrast to the more usual Johannine use of world (see the comments at 1.10), the word here means the universe. Instead of the whole world could not hold the books it may be better to say "in the whole world there would not be enough room for the books."

The books that would be written may be rendered by an active expression, such as "the books that people could write."

[639]

APPENDIX I

"THE JEWS" IN THE GOSPEL OF JOHN

Robert G. Bratcher

(Reprinted from Practical Papers for the Bible Translator 26, October 1975, pages 401-409.)

Readers and translators of the Gospel of John will be struck not only by the number of times the expression "the Jews" occurs, but also by the strange way in which it is used. In 9.22, for example, it is said that the parents of the man whom Jesus had cured of his blindness were afraid of the Jews. But the man himself, and his parents, were Jews. And in 3.25 we read, "Some of John's disciples began arguing with a Jew about the matter of religious washing." But John's disciples were Jews themselves, were they not?

The word ioudaios "Jew" is an adjective, formed from iouda "Judah." In the Gospel of John it occurs only once as an adjective, in 3.22, modifying "land." Other than that it is used as a noun, three times in the singular (3.25; 4.9; 18.35). The frequency of the plural hoi Ioudaioi, "the Jews," compared with its occurrence in the other Gospels, is striking. In the other Gospels it appears mostly in the phrase "the king of the Jews," applied to Jesus. Elsewhere it is used only four more times, each time in its natural sense, of "people of Judah."

"The world" in the Gospel of John

In order to better understand the meaning of "the Jews" in the Gospel of John, we must first look at the use and meaning of "the world" in this Gospel. The author sees everything in terms of opposite forces: light and darkness, truth and error, life and death, God and the Devil. And he makes a sharp distinction between the world and Jesus and his followers, especially in the last half of the Gospel. Of course the world is the object of God's love and of Christ's saving mission (3.16-17; 12.47; 17.21,23), but it is not the object of the love of the followers of Jesus: they are not commanded to love the world. The disciples of Jesus are in the world (13.1), but they do not belong to it (15.19). The world hates Jesus and his disciples, because they do not belong to it (15.18-19; 17.14-16). The world loves only those who belong to it (15.19). It does not know Jesus (1.10), or the Father (17.25), and cannot receive the Spirit of truth (14.17). The world's ruler is to be overthrown (12.31; 14.30; 16.11). When Jesus is parted from his disciples, they will be sad, but the world will be glad (16.20). Jesus has overcome the world (16.33); his kingdom is not of this world (18.36). In the Gospel of John "the world" stands in opposition to Jesus and his disciples.

"The Jews" and "the world"

"The Jews" belong to "the world," as compared with Jesus and his

followers. The Jews, like the world, do not know the Father. They have
never heard his voice or seen his face, nor do they believe in the one
whom he sent (5.37-38). Jesus says to the Jews, "You come from this
world, but I do not come from this world" (8.23). Bultmann says, "For
John 'the Jews' are representatives of 'the world' in general which refuses to respond to Jesus with faith " (Theology of the New Testament,
part 2, page 5). C. J. Wright comments, "To him 'the Jews' symbolised
the Darkness which hated the Light, the 'sons of the devil' who hated
the Son of the Father " (The Mission and Message of Jesus by Major,
Manson and Wright, page 664).

The author clearly places himself, and those whom he represents,
as separate from the Jews. He speaks of "the Passover of the Jews"
(2.13; 6.4; 11.55), the religious rules of the Jews about purification
(2.6), a religious festival of the Jews (5.1), the Festival of Shelters
of the Jews (7.2), the Day of Preparation of the Jews (19.42), and the
way in which Jews prepare a body for burial (19.40).

And quite as clearly he regards Jesus as not "a Jew." In talking
to the Jews, Jesus speaks of "your Law" (7.19; 8.17; 10.34) and "your
circumcision" (7.22). Abraham is "your father" (8.56). When the Jews
say to him, "Our ancestors ate manna in the desert" (6.31), Jesus replies,
"What Moses gave you was not the bread from heaven" (6.32), and later
on says, "Your ancestors ate the manna in the desert" (6.49).

It is true that twice Jesus is called a Jew: by the Samaritan woman (4.9) and by Pilate (18.35). But in both instances the term is used in
its sense of "person of Judah," contrasted with the Samaritan and the
Roman. The same applies in 4.22, where Jesus says to the Samaritan woman, "You (Samaritans) do not really know whom you worship; we (Jews)
know whom we worship, for salvation comes from the Jews.

Apart from those two instances, it is only in 1.11 that Jesus is
identified as a Jew, in the statement that he came to "his own country,"
but "his own people" did not receive him. This passage, however, does
not go against the Gospel as a whole, in which Jesus is shown as not
being a part of "the Jews." As Bultmann says, "Jesus already appears as
no longer a member of the Jewish people or its religion but speaks to
the Jews...as if he were a non-Jew " (Theology of the New Testament,
part 2, page 5).

What accounts for this? It seems clear that the deep differences
shown between Jesus and "the Jews" of his time reflect the hostility
between Church and Synagogue at the time the author wrote his Gospel.
He has moved back the disputes and arguments of his own time into the
time of Jesus, and they are represented as taking place between Jesus
and the people of his time.

The prominent part played by the Pharisees in the opposition to
Jesus is worthy of note here. The High Priest and the chief priests are
mentioned often, especially in chapters 18-19, as we would expect. They
were, after all, the religious authorities responsible for arresting
Jesus and turning him over to Pilate. What is surprising is that the
Pharisees appear so often in the Gospel (see 1.24; 4.1; 7.32,47,48;
8.13; 9.13,15,16,40; 11.46; 12.19,42), and are at times identified as
"the Jews," that is, the authorities. Their part in relation to Jesus in
the Gospel of John is different from the part they play in the other
Gospels. In John it is their refusal to believe in Jesus and his claims

that brings them into conflict with him. They are not, as in the other
Gospels, condemned by Jesus because of their hypocrisy or their understanding of the Law. Raymond Brown points out that the Pharisees are so
prominent because "they are precisely that Jewish sect which survived
the calamity of A.D. 70. The Judaism of the time in which the Gospel was
written was Pharisaic Judaism " (The Gospel According to John, volume 1,
page lxxii). The argument between Church and Synagogue when the Gospel
was written was over the question of whether or not Jesus was the Mes-
siah--and this argument is of the greatest importance in the Gospel.

The right approach for the translator

The translator is bound to represent faithfully the way in which
the author describes the ministry of Jesus. But the way in which he will
translate the Greek hoi Ioudaioi every time it appears in the Gospel is
not an easy matter to decide. (1) Should he not, always and everywhere,
translate it by "the Jews"? This certainly may be argued, since the author does not use the expression in a precise national or racial sense of
the people of Israel in the years A.D. 30-33, but of the opponents of his
own time who denied the claims the Church makes about Jesus the Messiah.
If the translator did this, however, he would almost be forced to use
quotation marks--"the Jews"--to show the strangeness of the phrase. (2)
But since the author has placed these disputes in the time of Jesus, it
is at this level that the translation must take place, so that "the Jews"
must be identified in terms of the people of Jesus' own time. But as a
matter of fact Jesus was a Jew, and to translate a passage, for example,
"Jesus, in Jerusalem, said to the Jews," is as unnatural as to say, "The
President, in Washington, said to the Americans," or, "The Queen, in
London, said to the British."
In translating on this "historical" level, however, does not the
translator somehow distort the meaning of the text? The answer depends
on whether we believe that the author intended his readers to understand
his Gospel as reporting historical events which took place in Judea,
Samaria, and Galilee in the early part of the first century. Assuming
that he did, it seems to me that the translator does not have much of a
choice, unless he says something like "the enemies of Jesus," or "the
unbelievers" every time "the Jews" is used of the opponents of Jesus.
Consequently, in following the course which I think is the
only right one to take, the translator must carefully observe the different senses in which "the Jews" is used in the Gospel of John--and this
is what will be done in this study, with an examination of every occurrence of the phrase and its meaning in the "historical" setting of the
Gospel.

The use and meaning of "of the Jews"

We may first consider the passages in which the phrase "of the
Jews" occurs. The phrase serves virtually as an adjective, modifying
Jewish festivals, classes, and customs: (1) an unnamed festival (5.1);
the Passover Festival (2.13; 6.4; 11.55); the Festival of Shelters (7.2);
and the Day of Preparation, that is, the day before the Sabbath (19.42);
(2) a leader (3.1); the temple guards (18.12); and the chief priests

(19.11); (3) a ritual cleansing (2.6). We should add here, also, a similar phrase in 19.40 "as is the custom for the Jews to bury (people)." In these passages the adjective "Jewish" (and not the awkward "of the Jews") is a natural rendering, in English, at least. But even more natural would be the omission of the adjective, since its presence implies a misleading contrast. To say "the Jewish Passover Feast" is to imply the existence of non-Jewish Passovers; the same holds true for the other festivals, the Day of Preparation, and the chief priests. In 3.1 Nicodemus could be styled "a leading Pharisee" (combining "from the Pharisees" with "leader of the Jews"), or even "a Pharisee who was a famous teacher" (see verse 10). But in the other passages the adjective, or its equivalent, is required. The guards in 18.12 need to be distinguished from the Roman soldiers, either as Jewish guards or else identified as temple guards (which is what the Greek word means; see verse 3). In 2.6 and 19.40 the use of the adjective in English is natural and not misleading, since Jewish customs are referred to.

The meaning of "the Jews" in each occurrence

We will now examine all the other occurrences of "a Jew" and "the Jews" in the Gospel of John (not including the 6 times the phrase "the king of the Jews" occurs, which offers no difficulty). A summary is provided at the end of the discussion showing the way the expression should be translated in each place, in my opinion.

The Deputation to John the Baptist (1.19-28). "The Jews" who send priests and Levites from Jerusalem to John are clearly the authorities; they are identified in verse 24 as the Pharisees. W. F. Howard, however, says that in this passage the Sadducean group of the Sanhedrin is meant, since the Pharisees would hardly send priests and Levites (Interpreter's Bible, volume 7, page 481). It may be questioned whether the writer really had such a distinction in mind. The deputation in verse 24 seems clearly to be the same as in verse 19. But this is irrelevant to the translator; "the Jews" in verse 19 are the authorities in Jerusalem.

Jesus in the Temple (2.13-21). Again, "the Jews" who challenge Jesus when he drives the animals from the Temple area (probably the Court of the Gentiles) are the authorities.

The Argument between John's Disciples and a Jew (3.25). The reference could be to a religious leader, but in light of the statement in 5.35 about the attitude of "the Jews" toward John it seems unlikely that there was any dispute between John's group and the authorities. The context supplies no help, but it seems more natural that simply an unnamed individual is meant. To say, however, in translation, that some of John's disciples started arguing with a Jew is to identify them as non-Jews. (Of course, from the author's point of view, John's disciples were not "Jews.") But to say "with another Jew" seems too emphatic; the simpler "man" or "individual" seems preferable.

Jesus and the Samaritan Woman (4.1-40). In this section "Jew" and "Jews" are used in their natural sense, contrasted with "Samaritan" and "Samaritans" as a separate group, and so must be represented in translation. (In verse 22, in English, which does not easily distinguish between the second person singular and plural, "You Samaritans...we Jews" seems a good way to put it clearly.)

The Healing at the Pool (5.1-18). In Jerusalem, Jesus heals a sick man on the Sabbath. "The Jews" immediately told the man that it was wrong to carry his mat on the Sabbath. The man later reports to them that it was Jesus who had healed him and so they begin to persecute Jesus. Stung by Jesus' claim to a special relationship with God, they become the more determined to kill him. There is no doubt that these are the authorities.

In the passage that follows (5.19-47) Jesus continues speaking to them, expanding on the theme of his relation with the Father. In verse 33 he says to them, "You sent messengers to John," a reference back to 1.19,24, which may allow the translator to identify "the Jews" in that section as the Pharisees. But it seems better to say simply "the authorities."

Jesus in Capernaum (6.22-59). After feeding a large crowd on the east side of Lake Galilee (6.1-15), Jesus joins his disciples on the lake and the crowd crosses to the west side (6.16-22). The following day the crowd that had stayed on the east side crosses the lake, goes to Capernaum, and finds Jesus. In the discussion that follows in the synagogue they are friendly, until Jesus states that he is the heavenly bread that gives life to men. At this "the Jews" begin to grumble, and when Jesus says that the bread is his flesh, they get into an angry argument. It is reasonable to suppose that "the Jews" here are the same as "the crowd," and that it is when they begin to contest Jesus' claims that they are called "the Jews." Of course they could be the authorities, as some commentators believe, but if so they are brought in without any previous notice. And this incident takes place in Galilee, not in Judea.

Jesus in Jerusalem at the Festival of Shelters (7.1-52). This episode begins with the statement that Jesus stayed in Galilee and did not want to travel around in Judea because "the Jews" wanted to kill him. This could be the people in general, or those living in Judea in particular, but in light of 5.18 it seems quite clear that the authorities in Jerusalem are meant. When Jesus eventually goes to Jerusalem "the Jews" were looking for him. They are the authorities, distinguished from "the crowd" who are divided in their opinion about him, but who do not talk openly because they are afraid of "the Jews," that is, the authorities. Jesus goes to the Temple and begins teaching; "the Jews" (authorities) are surprised at his teaching, and a discussion follows. When he asks them, "Why do you want to kill me?" the crowd reacts in surprise. The "you" in verse 19 must be the authorities; there is no evidence that the people want to kill Jesus, and verses 16-19 are addressed to the authorities. The crowd reacts in surprise because they do not know that the authorities want to do away with Jesus. The reply of Jesus is directed mostly at the authorities (verse 23, "Why are you angry with me because I made a man completely well on the Sabbath?"--a reference back to 5.16-18).

In verses 25-26, "some of the people of Jerusalem" ask, "Isn't this the one they want to kill?" "They" are the authorities, as verse 26 shows.

In verse 30, "They tried to arrest him" may refer to the authorities, but this is not clear from the text. Brown thinks this refers to the people, "for this attempt seems to be distinct from that of the authorities in verse 32." (The Gospel According to John, volume 1, page 313). The plural "they were trying" may be impersonal: "an attempt was made to arrest him...." A similar statement is made in verse 44, in which some of the crowd try to arrest Jesus. If we identify the subject here in verse 30 as the people, it seems better, then, to translate the verb by "seize," and not "arrest," which has an official feel about it.

In the section verses 32-36 the Pharisees and chief priests send temple guards to arrest Jesus. Jesus says to them and, presumably, to "the crowd" that is there, that he will soon go away to a place where they will not be able to go. This causes "the Jews" to ask among themselves, "Where is he going?" Are these the authorities? They are hardly the Pharisees and chief priests, but it may be that "the Jews" are the guards who represent the authorities. To whom does Jesus say, "You will look for me, but you will not find me"? To the crowd in general, or to the guards? Although Brown thinks that here the people of Jerusalem are meant, I think that perhaps these are the temple guards, acting as representatives of the authorities, who are hostile to Jesus. (Notice that, still in this same section, "the crowd" is still present: in verses 40-44 they are divided in their opinion about Jesus, and "some wanted to seize him, but no one laid a hand on him." It must be admitted, however, that the phrase in 7.35 is one of the hardest to decide about.

Another Argument (8.12-59). In verses 12-20 Jesus is criticized by the Pharisees and answers their criticism. The narrative continues, "Jesus said to them again, 'I will go away; you will look for me, but you will die in your sins. You cannot go where I am going.'" To whom is he speaking? The words refer back to what he said in 7.34. Here in 8.22, again it is "the Jews" who answer, exactly as in 7.35. Here again, I think, the authorities must be meant. In particular, Jesus' words "When you lift up the Son of Man" can hardly have been directed to the people as a whole. This section concludes with the statement that "many believed in him." These are many of the listeners, people in the crowd, not the authorities. The narrative continues immediately, "So Jesus said to the Jews who believed in him," that is, to these same people. But in the narrative that follows, as the argument between Jesus and these believers develops, the tone becomes increasingly bitter. In verse 37 Jesus accuses them of trying to kill him. The charge is repeated in verse 40, and Jesus continues by calling them sons of the Devil, not sons of God, as they claimed. They reply, "Were we not right in saying that you are a Samaritan and have a demon in you?" (This is what "the crowd" at the Temple said in 7.20.) They repeat their charge, and finally, made angry by Jesus' claim, attempt to stone him, but he hides himself and leaves the Temple. So ends this strange section, in which "the Jews who believed in him" become his opponents who at the end try to kill him. Barrett comments, "Either John is writing very carelessly or he means that the faith of these Jews was very deficient " (The Gospel According to St. John, page 287). Brown supposes that verse 30 ("many believed in him") is put in by a later editor to break up the passage, and this required the addition of a phrase in verse 31, identifying the participants in the angry discussion that follows. This simply shifts the blame from the author to the editor, however, and brings the translator no nearer to a satisfactory solution. But the translator must translate the text before him, and throughout this section "the Jews" are people in Jerusalem, not the authorities.

Jesus Heals a Man Born Blind (9.1-34). In this section "the Jews" in verses 18, 22 are clearly the authorities in Jerusalem, who are practically identified as the Pharisees. They call in the parents of the man and question them. The parents refuse a direct answer because they are afraid of the authorities, who had agreed to put out of the synagogue anyone who professed Jesus as Messiah. An argument arises between the authorities and the man, and finally they expel him from the synagogue.

The Good Shepherd (10.1-21). This speech and the argument that follows are not given any setting. Jesus, using the picture of a shepherd and flock, claims to be the shepherd of Israel. A new argument breaks out among "the Jews." Some repeat the accusation that he is mad (see also 7.20 where "the crowd" says this, and 8.48 where "the Jews" say it). Again this seems to be the reaction of the people, not that of the authorities.

Jesus at the Festival of Dedication (10.22-39). Jesus is in Jerusalem for the festival, and his opponents, "the Jews," appear to be the people in general, not the authorities. Their question, their hostile reaction in wanting to stone him, and finally their attempt to seize him, seem to be those of the people, not of the authorities.

Jesus leaves Judea and goes to Perea (10.40-42).

Jesus in Bethany (11.1-12.11). In chapters 11-12 "the Jews" seem always to be Judeans, that is, people who live in the province of Judea. They are not the Jerusalem authorities or only Jesus' opponents, but both those who oppose him and those who accept him.

When Jesus decides to go back to Judea, his disciples protest that just recently "the Jews" were trying to stone him (a reference to 10.31; see also 8.59). Jesus arrives in Bethany, which is a bit less than 2 miles from Jerusalem. This explains why many "Jews," that is, people living in or near Jerusalem, had gone to Bethany to comfort Martha and Mary over the death of their brother. They are further identified as "the Jews" in verses 31, 33, 36. They are sympathetic with the sisters' sorrow, and when Lazarus is raised many of them believe in Jesus, but some of them return to Jerusalem and report to the Pharisees what Jesus had done.

Aware of the Jewish Council's decision to put him to death, Jesus no longer travels openly "among the Jews." This is clearly a reference to the people who live in Judea, and particularly those who live in and near Jerusalem. Jesus leaves there (Bethany, which is practically a suburb of Jerusalem), and goes off to the town of Ephraim, a place near the wilderness. We cannot be sure where this place was, but it would seem that it is not in Judea, but in the province east of the Jordan, Perea.

In 11.55 it is said that "the Passover Feast of the Jews was near, and many went up to Jerusalem from the region..." This region may be the province of Judea, or, in a broader sense, the country generally. These pilgrims are identified in chapter 12 as "the crowd."

Jesus returns to Bethany, and a "large crowd of the Jews" goes there, not only because of him but also to see Lazarus who had been raised from death. The chief priests make plans to put Lazarus to death also, because on his account "many Jews" were abandoning their religion and believing in Jesus. These are people from Judea, particularly from Jerusalem and Bethany.

At the close of this part of the Gospel, the author says that many of the authorities believed in Jesus, but did not openly confess it because of the threat of the Pharisees to put out of the synagogue those who did.

The Last Meal. Jesus tells his disciples what he had told "the Jews," "You cannot go where I am going" (13.33). This refers back to 8.21, or to 7.34. In both those instances, it seems to me, the authorities are meant, and here the same meaning must be given to the expression.

Jesus' Arrest (18.1-18). Jesus is arrested in the garden by an armed group made up of a detachment of Roman soldiers, and some Jewish temple guards supplied by the chief priests and Pharisees. He is taken to Caiaphas, the one who had advised "the Jews" that it was better that one man die for all the people. This is a reference back to 11.49-51, and "the Jews" are clearly the authorities, here the members of the council (Sanhedrin).

Jesus Questioned by the High Priest (18.19-24). In answer to the High Priest's questioning, Jesus refers to his public teaching in the synagogues and the Temple, "where all the Jews come together." The word here means simply people. It is interesting to notice how the author brings together here "the world," to which Jesus had spoken openly, and "the synagogues and the Temple," where he taught. It is as though, in the author's mind, the synagogues and the Temple define "the world."

Jesus Tried by Pilate (18.28-19.16). The authorities hand over Jesus to Pilate. He tells them to try Jesus, but they reply that they do not have the authority to put anyone to death. Here they are identified as "the Jews."

Pilate questions Jesus again, and he replies that his kingdom is not of this world: if it were of this world, his followers would have fought to keep him from being handed over to "the Jews." Here, if there is any distinction, the authorities are meant. Then Pilate goes out and addresses "the Jews." It seems probable that here, and for the rest of the section, the expression is not restricted to the authorities, but includes the hostile crowd as well. (Notice that in 18.35 Pilate tells Jesus, "Your own people and the chief priests handed you over to me.") The chief priests and the temple guards are referred to in 19.6, and the chief priests in 19.16. After the trial Pilate turns Jesus over to the authorities (the chief priests, 19.15) to be crucified.

The Crucifixion of Jesus (19.16-37). In verse 20 it is said that "many Jews" read the notice on the cross, "because the place where Jesus was crucified was near the city (of Jerusalem)." These are clearly Judeans, people who live in and near Jerusalem (as in chapters 11-12).

In verse 31 "the Jews" request Pilate that the bodies be removed from the crosses (breaking the legs would hasten the death of the condemned). They are most likely the authorities, not a group of common people.

In 19.38 and 20.19 the phrase "on account of fear of the Jews" is used with reference to Joseph of Arimathea and to the disciples. In both instances the authorities are meant, as in 7.13.

Summary

According to this review, "the Jews" in the Gospel of John may have four different meanings:

(1) its natural sense, meaning simply Jewish people: 2.6,13; 3.1,25; 4.9,22; 5.1; 6.4; 7.2; 8.31; 11.55; 18.12,35; 19.21,40,42;

(2) Judeans, people who live in and near Jerusalem: 11.8,19, 31,33,36,45,54; 12.9,11; 19.20;

(3) people hostile to Jesus: 6.41,52; 8.48,52,57; 10.19,24, 31,33; 18.20,38; 19.7,12,14;

(4) the authorities in Jerusalem: 1.19; 2.18,20; 5.10,15,16, 18; 7.1,11,13,15,35; 8.22; 9.18,22; 13.33; 18.14,31,36; 19.31,38; 20.19.

TRANSLATING "IN SPIRIT AND TRUTH" AND "THE SPIRIT OF TRUTH"
IN THE GOSPEL OF JOHN

Barclay M. Newman

(Reprinted from Understanding and Translating the Bible: Papers in
Honor of Eugene A. Nida, New York: American Bible Society, 1974, pages
122-139.)

Translators have found particularly difficult the Johannine expressions "in spirit and truth" (4.23-24) and "the spirit of truth"
(14.17; 15.26; 16.13). Consequently, most all modern language translations have done nothing more than reproduce verbal equivalents of
the Greek in these few passages. The purpose of this present study
will be to investigate the passages where these phrases occur in the
Gospel of John and to suggest an exegetically sound restructuring
into English. But first it will be necessary to examine those passages
in the Gospel where the words "spirit" (pneuma) and "truth" (alētheia)
appear apart from these combinations.
    I. "Spirit" in the Gospel of John (1.32,33; 3.5,6,8,34; 4.23-24;
6.63; 7.39; 11.33; 13.21; 14.17,26; 15.26; 16.13; 19.30; 20.22).[1]
    "The spirit" that comes down like a dove from heaven (1.32) is
specifically identified as the Holy Spirit (1.33b);[2] and so one may
legitimately translate John the Baptist's words as, "I saw God's
Spirit come down like a dove from heaven" (Die Gute Nachricht).[3]
    But the use of "spirit" in the dialogue between Jesus and Nico-
demus (3.5-8) is more difficult. In its first occurrence in this
passage (3.5) "spirit" is used without the definite article, and so
Goodspeed and the New English Bible have translated "water and spirit"
(see also Phillips "from water and from spirit"). The New American
Bible has also rendered the phrase without the article, though making
it an obvious reference to God's Spirit ("water and Spirit"), while
a number of other English translations go so far as to supply the
definite article before Spirit (note Revised Standard Version, Jerusalem Bible, Today's English Version, Barclay, and Moffatt). The German translations, by retaining the anarthrous form ("Wasser und Geist,"
so GN, Zürich Bible, Luther Revised), have remained beautifully ambiguous, since "Geist" may or may not be taken as a reference to God's
Spirit. Segond Revised also retains the anarthrous form, though
indicating that the reference is to the Spirit ("d'eau et d'Esprit");
while Bonnes Nouvelles Aujourd'hui includes the article before Spirit
("d'eau et de l'Esprit").[4]
    In 7.39b "spirit" is also used without the definite article, but
most all translations supply the definite article and translate "the
Spirit."[5] In fact, the Zürich Bible's "(den heiligen) Geist" is even
more emphatic. Of course, it can be argued that the reference in
7.39b is clearly to God's Spirit, because in 7.39a the definite article is used before Spirit. But the same argument may be used in defense

of including the article at 3.5, since the article is used in 3.6, 8b, and the context makes it obvious that the same Spirit is referred to in each instance. Moreover, in 20.22 the phrase "holy spirit" is anarthrous, but the context makes it evident that "the Holy Spirit" is referred to, and apparently all translations and commentators support this interpretation. One may argue that the presence of the adjective "holy" is the basis on which the article is included in 20.22; but this is not the case, for even if the adjective were absent, it would still be plain that God's Spirit is meant.[6]

It has been noted that the anarthrous use of "spirit" in 3.5 appears in a context where the article does elsewhere appear with the noun "spirit" (3.6, 8b). But there is an even more convincing argument in favor of the translation "the Spirit" (or, better, "God's Spirit"), and that is the over-all context of the Gospel itself in which the power to give life is an important function of the Spirit. In fact, that is the primary focus in the verse under consideration. The birth which comes from above (3.3), by which one is able to see and to enter the Kingdom of God (3.5), is made possible through the activity of God's Spirit. So, then, to translate "be born of water and spirit" misses the basic intention of the verse. Indeed, one wonders what is really meant by the literal translation "born of water and spirit" (lower case "s"). If this strange-sounding juxtaposition of words has any meaning, then one takes it to be expressing a contrast between the lower, earthly realm (a strange meaning for "water"!) and the heavenly world, which may be spoken of as "spirit." One readily admits that the Johannine writer elsewhere sees a contrast between these two spheres of existence, and that this contrast is explicitly made in verse 6, but it is not present in verse 5. Here the focus is on the new life that the Spirit gives, not on a contrast between the two realms of existence.[7]

Verse 6 (literally "that which is born of the flesh is flesh and that which is born of the spirit is spirit") does speak of two contrasting orders of existence and of the means by which one enters each of these two realms. Here "the flesh" is best taken as a reference to human parents who make physical life possible (TEV "a man is born physically of human parents"; Barclay "physical birth can only beget a physical creature"; Goodspeed "whatever owes its birth to the physical is physical"), and "the spirit" as a reference to God's Spirit who brings about spiritual birth (TEV "but he is born spiritually of the Spirit"; Barclay "but spiritual birth begets a spiritual creature"; Goodspeed "and whatever owes its birth to the Spirit is spiritual"). In fact, this entire verse is a kind of parable by which Jesus makes an analogy between a familiar experience in this world and that which happens in the realm where God's Spirit operates: Human parents give life to their children, but only God's Spirit can give the birth by which one becomes a child of God.[8]

There is a play on words in verse 8a, one which comes through nicely in Greek or Hebrew, but which is difficult, if not impossible, to bring out in English translation without the help of a footnote. In Greek, as in Hebrew, the same word may mean either "wind" or "spirit." In this context most translations take "wind" to be the basic comparison, and so have translated in this way; and some have been provided a footnote, indicating the play on words (RSV, JB, NEB, NAB, ZB). Here also, as in verse 6, Jesus is drawing an analogy between something that happens in this world (the freedom of the wind to blow where it will) and what happens in the realm where God's Spirit is operative (the freedom of the Spirit to give spiritual life to whomever he will).

There is one further mention of "the spirit" in this third chapter of the Gospel, and there the reference is plainly to God's Spirit: "He whom God sent speaks God's words, for he does not give the Spirit by measure" (3.34). In this first clause "he" is the Son; and so this first half of the verse states the basis for the Son's authority: he is the one whom God has sent. The second half of the verse occasions more difficulty, though it also attests to the Son's authority, no matter in what direction the exegesis is pursued. The problem is that in Greek the subject of the verb "does...give" is ambiguous, and no indirect object (the one to whom the Spirit is given) is indicated. Some scholars hold that the Son is the subject of the verb "does... give," which would mean that the intended indirect object would be "those who believe in the Son." In support of this view is the argument that 6.63 forms a good parallel to this verse; since there it is Jesus who speaks the words that bring God's life-giving Spirit. On the other hand, God is elsewhere spoken of as the one who sends the Spirit (14.26), and several ancient scribes have added either "God" or "the Father" or "God the Father" as the subject of "does...give" in 3.34. On the basis of the following verse it appears that this is the correct conclusion, and several modern translations have made this explicit (Goodspeed, NEB, JB, TEV, GN). It is God who gives the Spirit, and in the context he gives it to the one whom he has sent, that is, to the Son.9 This makes better sense of the passage and adds strength to the argument regarding the source of the Son's authority. The GN translates the entire verse as "The one whom God sent speaks God's words, since God fills him completely with his Spirit."

In 6.63 "spirit" is mentioned twice, once with the article ("the spirit gives life") and once without the article ("the words I have spoken to you are spirit and life"). In its first occurrence in the verse "the spirit" is obviously a reference to God's Spirit (TEV "What gives life is God's Spirit"; GN "The Spirit of God gives life"), and it is indeed strange that some translations should use a lower case "s" for "Spirit" (RSV, NEB, JB, NAB). That God's Spirit is a life-giving Spirit is a concept frequently met in the Old Testament (Gen. 2.7; 6.3,17; 7.15; Job 34.14-15; Ps. 104.29-30; Ezekiel 37.5-6,9) as in the New Testament. And in particular it is an emphasis found in John's Gospel; for example, it is the Spirit which brings about the new birth (3.5,8), and in 7.38,39 the Spirit is the source of life-giving water. On the other hand, "flesh" ("the flesh is of no use") is used here with a meaning that it also frequently has in the Old Testament; it refers to mortal man, who stands in contrast to God who is life-giving Spirit. The TEV ("man's power is of no use at all"), as the GN ("Alles Menschliche ist dazu unbrauchbar"), has made this meaning explicit, though most all other translations have retained the literal Greek ("the flesh is useless"), which is a zero meaning, to say the least.

"The words I have spoken to you are Spirit and life" is essentially the way that the last half of this verse appears in most translations, though some translations spell "Spirit" with a lower case "s." Phillips departs from the traditional translation and renders "Spirit" as "spiritual." However, it is almost impossible to see any reasoning behind what he has done, as it is difficult to see any meaning in "are spirit and life."[10] The exegesis of those who render "are Spirit (= God's Spirit) and life" must be accepted. But one must still ask what is the intended relation between the nouns "Spirit" and "life." That is, are these nouns really in a paratactic relation as the conjunction "and" suggests, or is there another clue to understanding them? In the Old Testament one frequently finds words linked by "and" which are not really in a coordinate and balanced relation as the conjunction might suggest. Harry M. Orlinsky describes the phenomenon in the following terms: "A figure of speech in biblical Hebrew that is well known to scholars but rarely recognized in the traditional translations is hendiadys (Greek for 'one through two'), where essentially one thought is expressed by means of two words connected by 'and.'" (1969:36). If "Spirit and life" is here taken as a hendiadys,[11] then it is possible to take the phrase to mean "Spirit who gives life." Such an exegesis is in keeping with John's theology, in which he refers to the Spirit as life-giving, and it is also in keeping with his Semitic Greek style. This interpretation also fits the over-all context of the discourse on the bread of life, in which there is an implicit contrast between Jesus and Moses; and one is reminded of 2 Corinthians 3.6 ("The written law brings death, but the Spirit gives life"). If this exegesis is followed, then the following translation results: "The words I have spoken to you are/bring God's life-giving Spirit."

In 11.33 and 13.21 "spirit" is not used of the Spirit of God, as in the passages so far discussed. The reference in each of these two verses is to Jesus' own "inner being," and this is clearly indicated in the context. There is a problem of interpretation connected with 11.33, but this relates to the meaning of the Greek verb (whether embrimaomai means "to be troubled" or "to be angry"[12]), rather than to the interpretation of the phrase. And in 19.30 "spirit" is used with a related meaning. There the clause "he gave up the spirit" (see also Matthew 27.50 for a similar expression) means simply "he died"; there is no further, theological implication to be found here, as some commentators have attempted to impose on the text.

So then, in all passages so far considered "spirit" or "the spirit" must be taken as a specific reference to God's Spirit, unless the context clearly indicates otherwise, as in 11.33; 13.21; and 19.30. This conclusion will be important in the exegesis of the phrases "in spirit and truth" (4.23-24) and "spirit of truth" (14.17,[26]; 15.26; 16.13).

II. "Truth" in the Gospel of John (1.14,17; 3.21; 4.23-24; 5.33; 8.32,40,44,45,46; 14.6,17; 15.26; 16.7,13; 17.17,19; 18.37,38).[13]

Following the example of Pilate we ask, "What is truth?" (18.38); and we begin our search for an answer in the passage 8.31-47, where "truth" is used some five times. Jesus is in dialogue with the Jews who have believed in him and he tells them, "If you obey my teaching you are really my disciples; you will know the truth and the truth will make you free" (31b-32). It is obvious that for Jesus "truth" is not used here simply in the sense of that which is opposed to what is false; it is used of Ultimate Reality, of God who is real, and the meaning of verse 32 is "you will know (the true) God, and he will make you free," or even, "you will know God himself, and he will set you free."[14]

This meaning can also be seen in verse 44, where Jesus says of the Devil, "He has never been on the side of truth, because there is no truth in him. When he tells a lie he is only doing what is natural to him, because he is a liar and the father of all lies" (TEV). In the Greek text of this verse "a lie" is literally "the lie," and this is significant for the exegesis. Jesus is speaking in absolute categories, as he often does in the Fourth Gospel; and he is contrasting God with the Devil, the Truth with the Lie. God and the Truth are one, as the Devil and the Lie are one; and so there can be nothing in common between God and the Devil or between the Truth and the Lie.

In 8.46, 16.7, and 18.37a Jesus claims that he "tells the truth," and in 5.33 he says that John the Baptist "spoke on behalf of the truth." But here again the meaning is not merely "telling the truth" as opposed to "telling a lie." If God is truth, then "to tell the truth" means "to reveal God." Thus the idea of truth is extended to include not only God himself, but the revelation of God. So 8.40 may be rendered, "I have always spoken to you the truth about God, the truth which I received from God himself"; while 8.45 may be translated, "I tell the truth about God, and that is why you do not believe me." This same meaning is found in 17.17, where truth is equated with Jesus (note verses 6, 14) and with the word of revelation that he speaks: "Dedicate them to yourself, by means of the truth; your word is truth" (TEV).

This is probably also the significance of the phrase "in/by the truth" of 17.19. It is possible, on the basis of Greek usage, to take this phrase adverbially with the meaning of "truly" or "really"; but in light of the over-all context of the Gospel the meaning is better taken to be "by means of the truth," that is, by means of the true revelation of God that has come through Jesus.[15] This meaning also offers the best solution to the difficult "grace and truth" that appears in 1.14,17. A number of modern commentators understand "grace" to be the equivalent of the Hebrew hesed, the term used of God's covenant love; while "truth" is the Greek counterpart of the Hebrew emeth ("faithfulness"), referring to God's faithfulness in keeping the covenant.[16] But while it must be agreed that the form of the phrase is Hebraic, the meaning of the phrase is another matter. As C. H. Dodd indicates, this sense can hardly be expected to come through to Greek readers; and one must conclude: "Thus, while the mould of the expression is determined by Hebrew usage, the actual sense of the words must be determined by Greek usage. It is 'truth,' i.e. knowledge of reality, that comes through Jesus Christ" (1954:176). On the basis of this observation 1.14 may be translated, "We saw his glory, the glory which he had as the Father's only Son. Through him God has completely revealed himself and his love for us"; and 1.17 may be translated, "God gave the Law through Moses; but through Jesus Christ he has completely revealed himself and his love for us."

It is in this light that the words of Jesus in 14.6 must be understood. "I am the way, the truth, and the life" is a fairly literal translation, and it represents what most all major modern language translations have done. In the context Jesus as "the way" is the primary focus, and somehow "truth" and "life" are related to Jesus as the way.[17] The result is that there are two possibilities of interpretation. (1) The emphasis may be on the goal to which the way leads (note the GN "I am the way and I am also the goal, since in me you have the truth and the life"). If this exegesis is followed, then one may translate "I am the way that leads to truth and life." Or, expressed more fully, "I am the way that leads to the truth (about God) and to the life (that God gives)." (2) The emphasis may be on the way itself, in which case "truth" and "life" must be taken as predications of "way." One may then render, "I am the true way, the way that gives men life." Or, more fully, "I am the way that reveals the truth (about God) and gives life (to men)." The resultant meaning of these two possibilities is very close, and it is difficult to argue in favor of one as against the other, though the context would seem to support the second somewhat more than the first.[18]

Finally, "truth" in the Gospel of John is used of persons who have responded to God's revelation of himself. This is definitely the meaning of "whoever belongs to the truth" in 18.37b; and this is also the most logical understanding of "whoever does the truth" of 3.21. "To do the truth" (see also 1 John 1.6) is a Hebraic idiom meaning "to keep faith" or "to practice faithfulness"; but in the Johannine context it has the specialized sense of obedience to the truth of God's self-revelation.[19]

III. The "Spirit-Truth" Combination in the Gospel of John (4.23-24; and 14.17; 15.26; 16.13).

The two major conclusions reached in this paper have been: (1) Wherever "spirit" appears unmarked in John's Gospel the reference is to God's Spirit; and (2) "truth" in this Gospel refers primarily to God himself, though it may be extended to include the revelation of God or a description of persons who respond to that revelation. If one accepts these two conclusions, then the interpretation and translation of "the Spirit of truth" (14.17; 15.26; 16.13) is not difficult. The genitive expression may be taken to mean either "the Spirit who is truth (i.e. God himself)" or "the Spirit who reveals the truth (about God)." Either of these solutions is acceptable on the basis of Johannine theology, but the primary role of the Spirit in John's Gospel is that of revealing and testifying to the truth (see 16.13), and so it is best to take this phrase in the second sense.[20]

Among the major language translations only the GN has seriously attempted a dynamic equivalent restructuring of 4.23-24.[21] In the GN the restructuring has been accomplished by placing the two verses together: "23/24But a time will come, and it has already begun, when the Spirit who reveals God's truth, will enable men to worship the Father in every place. God is Spirit, and those who would worship him must be born anew by the Spirit of Truth. By such men the Father will be worshiped." The translators of the GN have taken the Greek phrase "spirit and truth" with the meaning "God's Spirit who reveals God's truth"; and at the same time they have made explicit the life-giving power of God's Spirit, which is an important emphasis in this

Gospel. Moreover, they have made explicit the implied contrast between worshiping God at a given locality (whether the Jewish temple
or the Samaritan temple) and the gift of worshiping God in any place
by including the information "will enable men to worship the Father in
every place."

The translators of the GN must be commended for the step forward
that they have taken in the translation of this verse. However, there
remains one serious problem, and that is the part that reads "God is
Spirit." Recently the present author was in Indonesian New Guinea for
a translators' institute and had occasion to get responses to this
statement. It is obvious that for many peoples with animistic backgrounds the translation will be understood to mean either "an animistic
spirit" or "a spirit of a departed ancestor." One might argue that
it is only natural for these primitive people to misunderstand the
words, and that their understanding will have to be guided by missionaries. But a more serious problem exists, and that is the implication
conveyed to the intelligent English reader. At the same translators'
institute several of the non-biblical staff (men with Ph.D.'s or near
Ph.D.'s in linguistics and/or anthropology) were asked how they understood the words as native speakers of the language, and in each instance they indicated that the words meant to them that God was "spirit"
as opposed to matter. Doubtless this reflects the understanding of
the majority of English readers who have occasion to read these words,
but this is evidently not the way that the Johannine author intended
for them to be taken. Barrett is certainly correct in pointing out
that for John the emphasis is on the "creative and life-giving power
of God's Spirit"; and that he is not combating "unspiritual" views
about God.[22]

If the above observations and judgments are correct, then some
serious thought needs to be given to clarifying the meaning of this
verse for English and other readers. The recently completed Common
Malay New Testament attempted to come to grips with this problem, and
so translated 4.23-24 in the following way: "[23] The time is coming,
and is already here, when God's Spirit will enable men to worship God
as he really is. These are the worshipers the Father wants to worship
him. [24] God is the source of life, and men can only worship him as he
really is when his Spirit enables them to do so by giving them new
life." This exegesis follows essentially that of the GN, except that
the translator has attempted to make explicit his understanding of "God
is Spirit"; while he has left implicit the contrast between worshiping
God at any place and worshiping him at a specified sanctuary.

NOTES

1. Dodd offers a valuable background study of "Spirit" as well
as an exegesis of the word in its various occurrences in John's Gospel
(1954:213-227). Barrett also presents a helpful discussion of the
role of the Holy Spirit in Johannine thought (1955:74-8).

2. In 1.33b the Greek text does not have the definite article

in the phrase "with (the) Holy Spirit," but almost every translation includes the article. This is true even of the New American Standard and of the King James II, both of which interestingly enough include the article without placing it in italics, contrary to their principle of indicating with italics words that are in the translation though not in the original languages; and the same is true at 7.39b. A noteworthy exception to the inclusion of the article is Brown (1966:55), who translates "a holy Spirit"; but in his comments on the verse he makes no mention of the significance of the absence of the article. Moffatt, though including the article, is apparently unwilling to let John the Baptist speak in the full Christian sense of the Holy Spirit, and so he translates "the holy Spirit." Even though the mention of the Holy Spirit may be technically anachronistic on the lips of John the Baptist, it is not contrary to the theology of the Fourth Gospel to have him speak in these terms. Moreover, the difinite article is sometimes omitted in prepositional phrases (Blass-Debrunner-Funk 1962:133-4). The baptism with the Holy Spirit is, of course, a beneficial action as opposed to the destructive force of the baptism by fire (included in the Matthaean and Lukan accounts).

3. In the recently completed Common Malay, for which the author served as translation consultant, 1.32-34 has been restructured in the following way: "32-34 John said, 'I did not know who this one would be, but God, who sent me to baptize with water, said to me, "You will see God's Spirit come down and stay on a man; he is the one who baptizes with the Spirit." I have seen it,' said John; 'I saw the Spirit come down from heaven and stay on him, and I tell you that he is the Son of God.' "

4. Attention should be called to the fact that even though the translator may render "Spirit" with an initial capital, this does not take into consideration the needs of the person who hears the Scripture read; he needs more than an initial capital to understand that the reference is to God's Spirit. Note Nida's comment, "Capitalization is not sufficient to correct the meaning of otherwise ambiguous or misleading translations" (1969:29).

5. The NAB ("There was, of course, no Spirit as yet") does not supply the definite article; however, it does render "Spirit" with an initial capital and includes a footnote indicating that the reference is definitely to God's Spirit: "...in relation to the Christian the sending of the Spirit was not to take place until Jesus' death, resurrection, and ascension; cf. John 20.22."

6. Acts 2.4 is similar, where the definite article is also lacking before "Holy Spirit," though "the Spirit" occurs in the second half of the verse. But the over-all context of Acts, and especially the immediate context of Acts 2, makes it evident that "the Holy Spirit" is meant; and one wonders at the advantage of translating "all were filled with Holy Spirit" (Lake and Cadbury 1965:18).

7. Bultmann questions the originality of the words "water and" (1971:138, fn. 3), but there is no textual evidence for their omission. The Living Bible takes "born of water" to mean "the normal process observed during every human birth"; however, this is certainly not the contrast intended by the author of the Gospel, and this interpretation is far from the mainstream of exegesis. It is possible to take "born

[657]

of water" as a reference to the baptism of John the Baptist, which accords well with the polemical aspect of the Gospel. But many inter- preters see here a reference to Christian baptism: "The immediate background of the close association of spirit and water is provided by the relation between Jesus and John the Baptist (1.26,31-34) and by the relation also between Jesus and Jewish practices of purification by water (2.6; 3.25). For the Evangelist and his readers the words are, however, even more directly applicable to Christian baptism (4.2) .... The Evangelist is, therefore, not introducing the language of genera- tion in order to accommodate Christianity to the soil of Hellenism, where immortality was supposed to be conferred by sacramental regenera- tion...; he is rather confronting the visible Christian practice and experience of baptism with that invisible and spiritual baptism which is the miracle of God" (Hoskyns and Davey 1961:214). For a full discussion see Brown's note "The Baptismal Interpretation of vs. 5" (1966:141-144).

8. Bultmann's existential interpretation, however valid for the theologian or expositor, offers little help to the translator: "The statement assumes a general understanding of sarx and pneuma; i.e. that sarx refers to this-worldly, human mode of being, and pneuma to the other-worldly, divine mode. Yet neither sarx nor pneuma refers here to a material substance, however much this may have been the case in some cosmological theories. Rather sarx refers to the nothingness of man's whole existence; to the fact that man is ultimately a stranger to his fate and to his own acts; that, as he now is, he does not enjoy authentic existence, whether he makes himself aware of the fact or whether he conceals it from himself. Correspondingly, pneuma refers to the miracle of a mode of being in which man enjoys authentic exis- tence, in which he understands himself and knows that he is no longer threatened by nothingness" (1971:141).

9. Bernard (1962:125), Barrett (1955:189-90), and Bultmann (1971: 164) are among the commentators who support this exegesis. Brown (1966:161-2) presents both viewpoints and then concludes, "One wonders if it is crucial to decide whether John means that the Father or Jesus gives the Spirit; the two ideas are found in John (14.26; 15.26). In the present context, the Spirit that begets and the Spirit that is com- municated in Baptism comes from above or from the Father, but only through Jesus."

10. Note also the Living Bible, which again goes beyond the limits of sound exegesis, "But now I have told you how to get this true spiri- tual life."

11. Dodd (1954:224) refers to this phrase as a "virtual hendiadys." See also pp. 342-43: "Meanwhile, however, the words which Christ spoke are charged with pneuma kai zōē (once again a virtual hendiadys, meaning the life which is generated ek pneumatos) ..."

12. The RSV has "deeply moved in Spirit"; the NEB "he sighed heavily"; the NAB "he was troubled in spirit"; JB "said in great dis- tress"; Goodspeed "repressing a groan"; Moffatt "chafed in spirit"; Phillips "deeply moved"; and the TEV "his heart was touched." Ety- mologically, the word means "to snort like a horse," and in the Septua- gint of Daniel 11.30 it means "to be enraged" or "to be greatly angry." The verb appears again in verse 38; and elsewhere it is used of Jesus

in addressing the leper whom he had cleansed (Mark 1.43), and in addressing the blind man whose sight he had restored (Matthew 9.30). In
both of these instances the TEV has rendered with the meaning "to speak
harshly to." In Mark 14.5 the word is used of the anger of the guests
in the house of Simon the leper toward the woman who poured the expensive perfume on Jesus' head (TEV "and they criticized her harshly").
The GN, the ZB, and the LR all maintain in 11.33 the idea of "to become
angry," while the NAB gives a footnote, "He was troubled in spirit ...
deepest emotions: probably signifies that Jesus was angry, perhaps at
the lack of faith or at the presence of evil (death)." It is impossible
to conclude that anything less than anger is intended in 11.33 and 38.
The use of the verb and its cognates, both outside the New Testament and
within the New Testament itself, clearly imply anger. Evidently, the
translations which attempt to move the theme of anger from these verses
do so on theological, rather than on linguistic or exegetical grounds.
The basis for Jesus' anger is not explicitly indicated though the context of this verse, and of verse 37, would imply that it is due to the
immature faith of the Jews present.

13. Dodd has an important study of "truth" (1954:170-8), and much
of the following discussion has its basis in his observations. See also
Brown (1966:499-501).

14. Other than Dodd's discussion, note the comments of Strathmann
(1971:143): "'Wahrheit' ist dabei für Johannes nicht ein weltanschau-
lich-philosophischer oder auch ein erkenntnistheoretischer, sondern
ein religiöser Begriff. Er meint die gnadenvolle Wirklichkeit Gottes,
wie sie in der Gestalt Jesu sichtbar geworden ist (vgl. 1, 14.17)."

15. The translations are divided on the interpretation of this
phrase. For example, the RSV, NAB, JB, and the TEV all have the meaning
of "truly" or "in truth"; while "by the truth" is the rendering of
the NEB (with a fn. "in truth"), Moffatt, Barclay, Goodspeed, and
Phillips.

16. The GN, "In him God has shown his entire goodness and faithfulness," apparently accepts this exegesis.

17. "Die beiden Begriffe 'Wahrheit' und 'Leben' sind also dem
Begriff 'Weg' zwar formal, nicht aber sachlich koordiniert, sondern
wollen ihn erläutern und die Behauptung zugleich sachlich rechtferti-
gen" (Strathmann 1971:199). See Brown (1970:620-21) for a brief
summary of the history of interpretation.

18. In the Common Malay this verse is translated "I am the one
who leads men to God and who reveals who and what God is; and I am the
one who gives life to men."

19. In the Common Malay 5.33 is translated, "... and he spoke
concerning the truth, that is, concerning me," which is in keeping
with the context where Jesus is specifically identified as the one
concerning whom John spoke. In 17.17 there is no real problem, since
there the word of revelation is equated with the truth. At 3.21 the
Malay has, "...whoever obeys the truth, that is God himself, comes
to the light ..."; and 16.13a appears as, "...he will lead you into
the full truth about God" (GN "die ganze Wahrheit"). Similarly, in
18.37 Jesus affirms, "...I came into the world to reveal the truth
about God, and whoever obeys God listens to me."

20. See Brown (1970:639), "In Johannine thought the genitive is

objective: the Spirit communicates truth (see 16.13), although there might also be an element of the appositive genitive (1 John 5.6 [7] 'the Spirit is truth')"; and Barrett (1955:386) "John means 'the Spirit who communicates truth.'"

21. With one exception -- the Living Bible, which places verses 21-24 together: "Jesus replied, 'The time is coming, ma'am, when we will no longer be concerned about whether to worship the Father here or in Jerusalem. For it's not where we worship that counts, but how we worship -- is our worship spiritual and real? Do we have the Holy Spirit's help? For God is Spirit, and we must have his help to worship as we should. The Father wants this kind of worship from us. But you Samaritans know so little about him, worshiping blindly, while we Jews know all about him, for salvation comes to the world through the Jews.'"

22. "Spirit in the Old Testament is regularly not an order of being over against matter, but life-giving, creative activity, and it is in this sense that John commonly uses the word pneuma (see especially 3.5-8; 6.63; 7.38f; 14.17-19). It is natural to suppose that it is so used here, and that John is not so much combating 'unspiritual' views of God as asserting his creative and life-giving power. On any other interpretation it is difficult to understand the combination in this passage of the two sets of ideas -- true and false water, true and false worship. They are bound together by the facts that the living water Christ gives is the Spirit (7.38f), and that God who is worshiped is himself Spirit .... en pneumati draws attention to the supernatural life that Christians enjoy, and en alētheia to the single basis of this supernatural life in Christ through whom God's will is faithfully fulfilled" (1955:199-200).

REFERENCES

Barrett, C. K. 1955. The Gospel According to St. John. London: S.P.C.K.

Bernard, J. H. 1962. A Critical and Exegetical Commentary on the Gospel According to St. John. Volume I. Edinburgh: T. and T. Clark.

Bernard, J. H. 1963. A Critical and Exegetical Commentary on the Gospel According to St. John. Volume II. Edinburgh: T. and T. Clark.

Blass, F. and A. Debrunner. 1962. A Greek Grammar of the New Testament and Other Early Christian Literature. A Translation and Revision of the ninth-tenth German edition incorporating supplementary notes of A. Debrunner by Robert W. Funk, Chicago: The University of Chicago Press.

Brown, Raymond E. 1966. The Gospel According to John. The Anchor Bible. Volume 29. Garden City, New York: Doubleday and Company, Inc.

Brown, Raymond E. 1970. The Gospel According to John. The Anchor Bible. Volume 29A. Garden City, New York: Doubleday and Company, Inc.

Bultmann, Rudolf. 1971. The Gospel of John. A Commentary. Translated by G. R. Beasley-Murray, General Editor, R. W. N. Hoare and

J. K. Riches. Philadelphia: The Westminster Press.

Dodd, C. H. 1954. The Interpretation of the Fourth Gospel. Cambridge: The University Press.

Hoskyns, Edwyn Clement and Francis Noel Davey. 1961. The Fourth Gospel. London: Faber and Faber Limited.

Lake, Kirsopp and Henry J. Cadbury. 1965. The Beginnings of Christianity. Part I. The Acts of the Apostles. Edited by F. J. Foakes-Jackson and Kirsopp Lake. Grand Rapids, Michigan: Baker Book House.

Nida, Eugene A. and Charles R. Taber. 1969. The Theory and Practice of Translation. Leiden: E. J. Brill.

Orlinsky, Harry M. 1969. Notes on the New Translation of the Torah. Philadelphia: The Jewish Publication Society of America.

Strathmann, Hermann, and Gustav Stählin. 1971. Das Evangelium nach Johannes Die Apostelgeschichte. Das Neue Testament Deutsch. Zweiter Band. Göttingen: Banderhoeck und Ruprecht.

Westcott, B. F. 1950. The Gospel According to St. John. Grand Rapids, Michigan: William B. Eerdmans Publishing Company.

BIBLIOGRAPHY

BIBLE TEXTS AND VERSIONS CITED

Bibel. 1956 (NT), 1964 (OT). Stuttgart: Württembergische Bibelanstalt. (Luther Revised)

Bible: A New Translation. 1922. James Moffatt. New York: Harper and Row. (Mft)

Good News for Modern Man: The New Testament in Today's English Version. Fourth edition 1975. New York: American Bible Society. (TEV)

Gute Nachricht. Das Neue Testament in heutigem Deutsch. 1971. Stuttgart: Württembergische Bibelanstalt. (GeCL)

Holy Bible: A Translation from the Latin Vulgate in Light of the Hebrew and Greek Originals. 1950. John Knox. New York: Sheed and Ward, Inc. (Knox)

Jerusalem Bible. 1966. Garden City: Doubleday and Company, Inc. (JB)

King James Version. 1611. (KJV)

Living Bible. The Bible in Everyday Language for Everyone. 1971. Kenneth Taylor. London: Houghton and Stoughton and Coverdale House Publishers.

New American Bible. 1970. Washington: Confraternity of Christian Doctrine. (NAB)

New English Bible. 1970. London: Oxford University Press and Cambridge University Press. (NEB)

New Testament: A New Translation. 1968. William Barclay. New York: Collins. (Brc)

New Testament: An American Translation. 1923. Edgar J. Goodspeed. Chicago: University of Chicago Press. (Gpd)

New Testament in Modern English. 1962. J. B. Phillips. New York: The Macmillan Company. (Phps)

Revised Standard Version. 1952. New York: Nelson and Sons. (RSV)

Segond Revisé, Nouveau Testament. 1964. Paris: French Bible Society. (Seg)

Synodale Version, La Sainte Bible. 1956. Paris: Alliance Biblique. (Syn)

Bibliography

Twentieth Century New Testament. 1904. Chicago: Moody Press.

Zürcher Bibel. 1931. Zürich: Zwingli-Bibel. (Zür)

GENERAL BIBLIOGRAPHY

Barrett, C. K. 1953. The Gospel According to St. John. An Introduction
    with Commentary and Notes on the Greek Text. London: S.P.C.K.

------. 1972. John. In Matthew Black and H. H. Rowley, eds., Peake's
    Commentary on the Bible. London: Thomas Nelson and Sons.

Bernard, J. H. 1962. A Critical and Exegetical Commentary on the Gospel
    According to St. John. Volume I. The International Critical Com-
    mentary. Edinburgh: T. and T. Clark.

------. 1963. A Critical and Exegetical Commentary on the Gospel According
    to St. John. Volume II. The International Critical Commentary.
    Edinburgh: T. and T. Clark.

Brown, Raymond E. 1966. The Gospel According to John. (I-XII). The Anchor
    Bible. Garden City: Doubleday and Company, Inc.

------. 1970. The Gospel According to John (XIII-XXI). The Anchor Bible.
    Garden City: Doubleday and Company, Inc.

Bruce, F. F. 1968. The Gospel According to John. In Raymond E. Brown,
    Joseph A. Fitzmyer, and Roland E. Murphy, eds., The Jerome
    Biblical Commentary. Englewood Cliffs, N.J.: Prentice-Hall.

Bultmann, Rudof. 1971. The Gospel of John. A Commentary. Translated by
    G. R. Beasley-Murray, R. W. N. Hoare, and J. K. Riches. Philadelphia:
    The Westminster Press.

Dodd, C. H. 1954. The Interpretation of the Fourth Gospel. Cambridge:
    Cambridge University Press.

------. 1965. Historical Tradition in the Fourth Gospel. Cambridge:
    Cambridge University Press.

Dodds, Marcus. n.d. The Gospel of St. John. The Expositor's Greek Testa-
    ment. Grand Rapids: Eerdmans.

Hoskyns, Edwyn Clement, and Francis Noel Davey. 1961. The Fourth Gospel.
    London: Faber and Faber.

MacGreggor, G. H. C. 1949. The Gospel of John. The Moffatt New Testament Commentary. London: Hodder and Stoughton.

Metzger, Bruce M. 1971. A Textual Commentary on the Greek New Testament. London: United Bible Societies.

Nicol, W. 1972. The Sēmeia in the Fourth Gospel. Leiden: E. J. Brill.

Shepherd, Massey H., Jr. 1971. John. In Charles M. Laymon, ed., The Interpreter's One-volume Commentary on the Bible. New York and Nashville: Abingdon Press.

Smith, Dwight Moody, Jr. 1965. The Composition and Order of the Fourth Gospel. New Haven and London: Yale University Press.

Smith, T. C. 1959. Jesus in the Gospel of John. Nashville: Broadman Press.

Strathmann, Hermann. 1971. Das Evangelium nach Johannes. Das Neue Testament Deutsch. Göttingen: Vandenhoeck und Ruprecht.

Teeple, Howard M. 1974. The Literary Origin of the Gospel of John. Evanston: Religion and Ethics Institute.

Westcott, B. F. 1950. The Gospel According to St. John. The Authorized Version with Introduction and Notes. Grand Rapids: Eerdmans.

This glossary contains terms which are technical from an exegetical or a linguistic viewpoint. Other terms not defined here may be referred to in a Bible dictionary.

abstract refers to terms which designate the qualities and quantities (that is, the features) of objects and events but which are not objects or events themselves. For example, "red" is a quality of a number of objects but is not a thing in and of itself. Typical abstracts include "goodness," "beauty," "length," "breadth," and "time."

active voice is the grammatical form of a verb which indicates that the subject of the verb performs the action. "John hit the man" is an active expression, while "the man was hit" is called a passive expression.

adjective is a word which limits, describes, or qualifies a noun. In English, "red," "tall," "beautiful," "important," etc. are adjectives.

adverb is a word which limits, describes, or qualifies a verb, an adjective, or another adverb. In English, "quickly," "soon," "primarily," "very," etc. are adverbs.

adversative expresses something opposed to or in contrast to something already stated. "But" and "however" are adversative conjunctions.

affix is a part of a word which cannot stand alone and which is added to a root or stem, for example, "im- (in impossible)," "-ly (in friendly)," "-est (in largest)."

agency, agent. In a sentence or clause, the agent is that which accomplishes the action, regardless of whether the grammatical construction is active or passive. In "John struck Bill" (active) and "Bill was struck by John" (passive), the agent in either case is "John."

ambiguity is the quality of being ambiguous in meaning.

ambiguous describes a word or phrase which in a specific context may have two or more different meanings. For example, "Bill did not leave because John came" could mean either (1) "The coming of John prevented Bill from leaving" or (2) "The coming of John was not the cause of Bill's leaving." It is often the case that what is ambiguous in written form is not ambiguous when actually spoken, since features of intonation and slight pauses usually specify which of two or more meanings is intended. Furthermore, even in written discourse, the entire context normally serves to indicate which meaning is intended by the author.

anachronism is an expression which is incorrectly used through being historically or chronologically misplaced. For example, to refer to Jonah buying a ticket for his sea voyage would be an anachronism because it introduces a modern custom into an ancient setting.

analogy is a comparison between two items that have some features which are similar.

antecedent is the word, phrase, or clause to which a pronoun refers.

anticlimax is any part of a story or speech, etc., which follows the climax but is less important than the climax. See climax.

aorist refers to a set of forms in Greek verbs which denote an action completed without the implication of continuance or duration. Usually, but not always, the action is considered as completed in past time.

apposition is the placing of two expressions together so that they both identify the same object or event, for example, "my friend, Mr. Smith." The one expression is said to be the appositive of the other.

Aramaic is a language whose use became widespread in Southwest Asia before the time of Christ. It became the common language of the Jewish people in place of Hebrew, to which it is related.

attributive. An attributive is a term which limits or describes another term. In "the big man ran slowly," the adjective "big" is an attributive of "man," and the adverb "slowly" is an attributive of "ran." Attribution, therefore, is the act of assigning a certain quality or character to an object or an event. See adjective, adverb.

auxiliary is a word having no complete meaning in itself, and is used in combination with or reference to another word which has a meaning of its own (prepositions, conjunctions, auxiliary verbs such as "may," "shall").

benefactive refers to goals for whom or which something is done. The pronoun "him" is the benefactive goal in each of the following constructions: "they showed him kindness," "they did the work for him," and "they found him an apartment."

borrowed term refers to a foreign word that is used in another language.

case is the syntactical relation of a noun, pronoun, or adjective to other words in a sentence.

causative (also causal relation, etc.) relates to events and indicates that someone caused something to happen, rather than that he did it himself. In "John ran the horse," the verb "ran" is a causative, since it was not John who ran, but rather it was John who caused the horse to run.

chiastic arrangement (chiasmus) is a reversal of the order of words or phrases in an otherwise parallel construction. Example: "I (1)/was shapen (2)/in iniquity (3)//in sin (3)/did my mother conceive (2)/me (1)."

classifier is a term used with another term (often a proper noun) to indicate to what category the latter belongs. "Town" may serve as a classifier in the phrase "town of Bethlehem" and "river" as a classifier in "river Jordan."

clause is a grammatical construction normally consisting of a subject and a predicate. An independent clause may stand alone as a sentence, but a dependent clause (functioning as a noun, adjective, or adverb) does not form a complete sentence.

climactic element is that part of a story or speech, etc., which serves as the climax. See climax.

climax is the point in a story or speech, etc., which is the most important or the turning point or the point of decision.

cognates are words which are allied because of their derivation from a common source. The English words "love," "loving," "lovable," "lovely," and "lovingly" are cognates.

collective refers to a number of things (or persons) considered as a whole. In English, a collective noun is considered to be singular or plural, more or less on the basis of traditional usage, for example, "The crowd is (the people are) becoming angry."

components are the parts or elements which go together to form the whole of an object; for example, the components of bread are flour, salt, shortening, yeast, and water. The components of the meaning (semantic components) of a term are the elements of meaning which it contains; for example, some of the components of the term "boy" are "human," "male," and "immature."

concessive means expressing a concession, that is, the allowance or admission of something which is at variance with the principal thing stated. Concession is usually expressed in English by "though" ("even though," "although"). Example: "Though the current was swift, James was able to cross the stream."

conditional refers to a clause or phrase which expresses or implies a condition, in English usually introduced by "if."

conjunctions are words which serve as connectors between words, phrases, clauses, and sentences, "And," "but," "if," "because," etc., are typical conjunctions in English.

connective is a word or phrase which connects other words, phrases, clauses, etc.

connotation involves the emotional attitude of a speaker (or writer) to an expression he uses and the emotional response of the hearers (or readers). Connotations may be good or bad, strong or weak, and they are often described in such terms as "colloquial," "taboo," "vulgar," "old-fashioned," and "intimate."

construction. See structure.

context is that which precedes and/or follows any part of a discourse. For example, the context of a word or phrase in Scripture would be the other words and phrases associated with it in the sentence, paragraph, section, and even the entire book in which it occurs. The context of a term often affects its meaning, so that it does not mean exactly the same thing in one context that it does in another.

converse means reversed in order, relation, or action.

coordinate structure is a phrase or clause joined to another phrase or clause, but not dependent on it. Coordinate structures are joined by such conjunctions as "and" or "but," or they are paratactically related. See subordinate structure, paratactic.

dative in Greek and certain other languages is the case which indicates the indirect or more remote object of the action or influence expressed by a verb. This is generally indicated in English by "to" or "for."

deliberative refers to forms of speech that indicate the speakers are carefully weighing and considering a matter before coming to a conclusion.

diminutive is a word form indicating primarily smallness of size, but also familiarity, endearment, or (in some cases) contempt.

direct discourse. See discourse.

discourse is the connected and continuous communication of thought by means of language, whether spoken or written. The way in which the elements of a discourse are arranged is called discourse structure. Direct discourse is the reproduction of the actual words of one person embedded in the discourse of another person, for example, "He declared, 'I will have nothing to do with this man.'" Indirect discourse is the reporting of the words of one person embedded in the discourse of another person in an altered grammatical form, for example, "He said he would have nothing to do with that man."

displacement refers to the theory that certain portions of an original text, when copied, were placed in a different position from the original one, either by accident or on purpose.

distributive refers not to the group as a whole, but to the members of the group.

dynamic equivalence is a type of translation in which the message of the original text is so conveyed in the receptor language that the response of the receptors is (or, can be) essentially like that of the original receptors, or that the receptors can in large measure comprehend the response of the original receptors, if, as in certain instances, the differences between the two cultures are extremely great.

ellipsis (plural ellipses) or elliptical expression refers to words or phrases normally omitted in a discourse when the sense is perfectly clear without them. In the following sentence, the words within brackets are elliptical: "If (it is) necessary (for me to do so), I will wait up all night."

embedded subject-predicate expression is a dependent clause inserted within the structure of another clause. See parenthetical statement.

equational statement indicates that one object or event is the same as or equivalent to another.

eschatological refers to the end of the world and the events connected with it. In this connection, the term "world" is understood in various ways by various persons.

etymology is the study of the derivation or history of words. While this can be a helpful study in many ways, it is much more important to know how a word is understood by its users in the actual context of the source language.

euphemism is a mild or indirect term used in the place of another term which is felt to be impolite, distasteful, or vulgar; for example, "to pass away" is a euphemism for "to die."

event is a semantic category of meanings referring to actions, processes, etc., in which objects can participate. In English, most events are grammatically classified as verbs ("run," "grow," "think," etc.), but many nouns also may refer to events, as, for example, "baptism," "song," "game," and "prayer."

exclusive first person plural excludes the person(s) addressed. That is, a speaker may use "we" to refer to himself and his companions, while specifically excluding the person(s) to whom he is speaking. See inclusive first person plural.

exegesis is the process of determining the meaning of a text (or the result of this process), normally in terms of "who said what to whom under what circumstances and with what intent." A correct exegesis is indispensable before a passage can be translated correctly. Exegetical refers to exegesis.

exhortation is the verbal act of encouraging, attempting, urging, or making someone change a course of action or a matter of belief.

expletive is a word or phrase which appears in the place of the subject
or object in the normal word order, anticipating a subsequent word or
phrase which will complete the meaning. For example, in the statement
"It is difficult to sing the high notes," the word "it" is an expletive
which anticipates the real subject, "to sing the high notes."

explicit refers to information which is expressed in the words of a discourse. This is in contrast to implicit information. See implicit.

figure of speech or figurative expression is the use of words in other
than their literal or ordinary sense, in order to suggest a picture or
image, or for some other special effect. Metaphors and similes are
figures of speech.

finite verb is any verb form which distinguishes person, number, tense,
mode, or aspect. It is usually referred to in contrast to an infinitive verb form, which indicates the action or state without specifying
such things as agent or time.

generic has reference to all the members of a particular class or kind of
objects; it is the contrary of specific. For example, the term "animal"
is generic, while "dog" is specific. However, "dog" is generic in relation to "poodle."

genitive case is a grammatical set of forms occurring in many languages,
used primarily to indicate that a noun is the modifier of another noun.
The genitive often indicates possession, but it may also indicate measure, origin, characteristic, separation, source, etc.

gnostic refers to the teachings of the Gnostics, teachers who mixed Greek
and Oriental philosophy with Christian doctrines. They claimed possession of superior spiritual knowledge but were denounced as heretical by
most Christians.

goal is the object which receives or undergoes the action of a verb. Grammatically, the goal may be the subject of a passive construction ("John
was hit," in which "John" is the goal of "hit"), or of certain intransi-
tives ("the door shur"), or it may be the direct object of a transitive
verb ("[something] hit John").

Hebraism. See Semitic, Semitism.

honorific is a form used to express respect or deference. In many languages such forms are obligatory in talking about royalty and persons of
social distinction.

hortatory refers to forms of speech in which an exhortation occurs. See
exhortation.

idiom or idiomatic expression is a combination of terms whose meanings cannot be derived by adding up the meanings of the parts. "To hang one's

head," "to have a green thumb," and "behind the eightball" are English idioms. Idioms almost always lose their meaning completely when translated from one language to another.

imperative refers to forms of a verb which indicate commands or requests. In "go and do likewise," the verbs "go" and "do" are imperatives. In most languages, imperatives are confined to the grammatical second person; but some languages have corresponding forms for the first and third persons. These are usually expressed in English by the use of "may" or "let," for example, "May we not have to beg!" "Let them eat cake!"

imperfect tense is a set of verb forms designating an uncompleted or continuing kind of action, especially in the past.

implicit refers to information that is not formally represented in a discourse, since it is assumed that it is already known to the receptor. This is in contrast to explicit information, which is expressed in the words of a discourse.

inclusive first person plural includes both the speaker and the one(s) to whom he is speaking. See exclusive first person plural.

indicative refers to a group of modal forms of verbs in which an act or condition is stated or questioned as an actual fact rather than a potentiality or unrealized condition.

indirect discourse. See discourse.

intensive is a word which has the effect of making stronger the action expressed in another word, for example, "very" in "very active," or "highly" in "highly competitive."

interrogative pertains to asking a question.

intransitive refers to a verb which does not have or need a direct object to complete its meaning, for example, "he lives." See transitive.

ironical is having the quality of irony. See irony.

irony is a sarcastic or humorous manner of discourse in which what is said is intended to express its opposite; for example, "That was a wise thing to do!" intended to convey the meaning, "That was a stupid thing to do!"

lexical refers to individual words, apart from the way in which they are used in the structure of a particular sentence.

locative refers to a grammatical form or term which indicates a place in or at which an event occurs or an object or person is located.

markers are features of words or of a discourse which signal some special meaning or some particular structure. For example, words for speaking

[673]

may mark the onset of direct discourse, a phrase such as "once upon a time" may mark the beginning of a fairy story, and certain features of parallelism are the dominant markers of poetry. The word "body" may require a marker to clarify whether a person, a group, or a corpse is meant.

metaphor is likening one object to another by speaking of it as if it were the other, for example, "flowers dancing in the breeze." Metaphors are the most commonly used figures of speech and are often so subtle that a speaker or writer is not conscious of the fact that he is using figurative language. See simile.

neuter is one of the Greek genders. A "gender" is any of the three subclasses of Greek nouns and pronouns (called "masculine," "feminine," and "neuter"), which determine agreement with and selection of other words or grammatical forms.

nominal refers to nouns or noun-like words. See noun.

nominative case in Greek and certain other languages is the case which indicates the subject of a finite verb.

noun is a word that is the name of a subject of discourse, as a person, place, thing, idea, etc.

orthography refers to a system of writing and is often used in speaking of a similarity or difference in spelling.

parabolic style refers to those features of style that are typical of parables.

paratactic expression or relationship (parataxis) refers to two or more clauses of equal rank which stand together without being joined by a connective, for example, "I came, I saw, I conquered."

parenthetical statement is a digression from the main theme of a discourse which interrupts that discourse. It is usually set off by marks of parenthesis ( ).

participial indicates that the phrase, clause, construction, or other expression described is governed by a participle.

participle is a verbal adjective, that is, a word which retains some of the characteristics of a verb while functioning as an adjective. In "singing waters" and "painted desert," "singing" and "painted" are participles.

particle is a small word whose grammatical form does not change. In English the most common particles are prepositions and conjunctions.

partitive genitive is a construction in which one constituent identifies a part of the other; for example, in the phrase "the hand of the man," the noun "hand" identifies a part of "the man." See also genitive.

passive voice is a grammatical construction in which the subject is the goal of the action; for example, in "the man was hit," the grammatical subject "man" is the goal of the action "hit." (See active, agent, goal.)

Pentateuch is the term which is used to refer to the first five books of the Bible, sometimes called "the Torah," "the Law," or "the Books of Moses."

perfect tense is a set of forms which indicate an action already completed when another occurs. The perfect tense in Greek also indicates that the action continues into the present.

person, as a grammatical term, refers to the speaker, the person spoken to, or the person or thing spoken about. First person is the person(s) or thing(s) speaking ("I," "me," "my," "mine," "we," "us," "our," "ours"). Second person is the person(s) or thing(s) spoken to ("thou," "thee," "thy," "thine," "ye," "you," "your," "yours"). Third person is the person(s) or thing(s) spoken about ("he," "she," "it," "his," "her," "them," "their," etc.). The examples here given are all pronouns, but in many languages the verb forms distinguish between the persons and also indicate whether they are singular or plural.

phrase is a grammatical construction of two or more words, but less than a complete clause or a sentence. A phrase may have the same function as the head word of the phrase. For example, "the old man" has essentially the same functions as "man" would have, or it may have a function which is different from the function of either set of constituents, for example, "to town," "for John."

pluperfect means, literally, "more than perfect" (see perfect tense) and refers to a verb form which indicates an action already completed when another action occurred. For example, in "the meeting had already ended when the speaker arrived," the verb "had...ended" is a pluperfect.

plural refers to the form of a word which indicates more than one. See singular.

polemic is a strong argument or disputation, often used in relation to refuting errors of doctrine.

possessive pronouns are pronouns such as "my," "our," "your," "his," etc. which indicate possession.

predicate is the part of a clause which contrasts with or supplements the subject. The subject is the topic of the clause, and the predicate is what is said about the subject.

[675]

progressive is an aspect of an event referring to its continuation. Progressive is often used more or less synonymously with continuative and durative.

pronominal refers to pronouns.

pronouns are words which are used in place of nouns, such as "he," "him," "his," "she," "we," "them," "who," "which," "this," "these," etc.

qualifier is a term which limits the meaning of another term. See attributive.

reading. See textual.

receptor is the person(s) receiving a message. The receptor language is the language into which a translation is made. The receptor culture is the culture of the people for whom a translation is made, especially when it differs radically from the culture of the people for whom the original message was written.

redundancy is the expression of the same information more than once. Anything which is completely redundant is entirely predictable from the context.

referent is the thing(s) or person(s) referred to by a pronoun, phrase, or clause.

relative clause is a dependent clause which qualifies the object to which it refers. In "the man whom you saw," the clause "whom you saw" is relative because it relates to and qualifies "man."

restructure is to reconstruct or rearrange. See structure.

rhetorical refers to special forms of speech which are used for emphasis or to create an effect on the receptor. A rhetorical question, for example, is not designed to elicit an answer but to make an emphatic statement.

Semitic refers to a family of languages which includes Hebrew. Greek belongs to quite another language family, with a distinct cultural background. In view of the Jewish ancestry and training of the writers, it is not surprising that some Semitic idioms and thought patterns (called Semitisms or Hebraisms) appear in the Greek writings of the New Testament.

Semitism. See Semitic.

Septuagint is a translation of the Old Testament into Greek, made some two hundred years before Christ. It is often abbreviated as LXX.

[676]

simile (pronounced SIM-i-lee) is a figure of speech which describes one
    event or object by comparing it to another, as "she runs like a deer,"
    "he is as straight as an arrow." Similes are less subtle than meta-
    phors in that they use "like," "as," or some other word to mark or sig-
    nal the comparison. See metaphor.

singular refers to the form of a word which indicates one thing or person,
    in contrast to plural, which indicates more than one.

source language is the language in which the original message was produced.
    For the Gospel of John, this is the form of the Greek language widely
    spoken at the time the New Testament was being written (called Koine
    Greek).

staccato style is a manner of speech in which individual utterances are
    detached from those immediately preceding and those following, inter-
    rupting the continuity of the utterances.

structure is the systematic arrangement of the form of language, includ-
    ing the ways in which words combine into phrases, phrases into clauses,
    and clauses into sentences. Because this process may be compared to the
    building of a house or a bridge, such words as structure and construc-
    tion are used in reference to it. To separate and rearrange the various
    components of a sentence or other unit of discourse in the translation
    process is to restructure it.

subject. See predicate.

subjunctive refers to certain forms of verbs that are used to express an
    act or state as being contingent or possible (sometimes as wish or de-
    sire), rather than as actual fact.

subordinate structure designates a clause connected with and dependent on
    another clause. See coordinate structure, paratactic.

synonyms are words which are different in form but similar in meaning, as
    "boy" and "lad." Expressions which have essentially the same meaning
    are said to be synonymous.

Synoptic Gospels are Matthew, Mark, and Luke, which share many character-
    istics that are not found in John.

syntactic refers to syntax, which is the arrangement and interrelationships
    of words in phrases, clauses, and sentences.

Syriac is the name of a Semitic language, a part of the Aramaic family,
    used in Western Asia, into which the Bible was translated at a very
    early date.

temporal refers to time. Temporal relations are the relations of time
    between events. A temporal clause is a dependent clause which indicates

the time of the action in the main clause. Similarly, a temporal modifier indicates the time of the action of the word it modifies.

tense is usually a form of a verb which indicates time relative to a discourse or some event in a discourse. The most common forms of tense are
past, present, and future.

textual refers to the various Greek manuscripts of the New Testament. A
textual reading is the form in which words occur in a particular manuscript (or group of manuscripts), especially where it differs from others.
Textual evidence is the cumulative evidence for a particular reading.
Textual problems arise when it is difficult to reconcile or to account
for conflicting readings. Textual variants are readings of the same
passage that differ in one or more details.

transitional expressions are words or phrases which mark the connections
between related events. Some typical transitionals are "next," "then,"
"later," "after this," "when he arrived."

transitive is a predicate construction in which the verb has a direct object, for example, "hit the man." (See intransitive.)

translational refers to translation. A translator may seem to be following an inferior textual reading (see textual) when he is simply adjust-
ing the rendering to the requirements of the receptor language, that is,
for a translational reason.

transliterate is to approximate in the receptor language the sounds of
words occurring in the source language. Unfamiliar proper names are
usually transliterated in a translation.

variants, textual variants. See textual.

verbs are a grammatical class of words which express existence, action, or
occurrence, as "be," "become," "run," "think," etc.

zero is the lack or absence of a feature, considered as a positive feature
in the paradigm, for the sake of paradigmatic regularity.

Index